CISCO IOS

IN A NUTSHELL

Other networking resources from O'Reilly

CISCO IOS

IN A NUTSHELL

Second Edition

James Boney

Beijing • Cambridge • Farnham • Köln • Paris • Sebastopol • Taipei • Tokyo

Cisco IOS in a Nutshell, Second Edition
by James Boney

Copyright © 2005, 2002 O'Reilly Media, Inc. All rights reserved.
Printed in the United States of America.

Published by O'Reilly Media, Inc., 1005 Gravenstein Highway North, Sebastopol, CA 95472.

O'Reilly books may be purchased for educational, business, or sales promotional use. Online editions are also available for most titles (*safari.oreilly.com*). For more information, contact our corporate/institutional sales department: (800) 998-9938 or *corporate@oreilly.com*.

Editor:	Mike Loukides and Debra Cameron
Production Editor:	Jamie Peppard
Cover Designer:	Ellie Volckhausen
Interior Designer:	David Futato

Printing History:

January 2002:	First Edition.
August 2005:	Second Edition.

 This book uses RepKover,™ a durable and flexible lay-flat binding.

ISBN: 0-596-00869-4
ISBN13: 978-0-596-00869-7
[M]   [12/07]

Table of Contents

Preface

This is a book for everybody who has to deal with Cisco's routers.

As you well know, Cisco Systems has created an extremely diverse line of routers and other network products. One unifying thread runs through the product line: virtually all of Cisco's products run the Internetwork Operating System (IOS). This is both a great advantage and a great disadvantage. On the one hand, when you're familiar with one Cisco router, you're reasonably familiar with them all. Someone using a small DSL router in a home office could look at a configuration file for a high-end router at an ISP and not be lost. He might not understand how to configure the more esoteric routing protocols or high-speed network interfaces, but he'd be looking at a language that was recognizably the same.

On the other hand, this uniformity means that just about everything has been crammed into IOS at one time or another. IOS is massive—there's no other way to say it. And it has evolved over many years. The command-line interface isn't graceful, and is often non-uniform: many commands don't do what you think they should, and the same command verbs can mean completely different things in different contexts. This inconsistency is probably a natural result of evolution at an extremely large company with an extremely large number of developers, but it doesn't make life any easier.

So, where do you find out what commands you need to know? There's the almost mythical "green wall" of Cisco documentation, but it's difficult to find what you need in tens of thousands of pages. Of course, even getting to Cisco's online documentation may be impossible if your router doesn't work. And the volume of documentation is imposing. A search for `ip cef traffic-statistics`—not one of the more frequently used commands—yields 163 hits. How do you get to the right one? Beats me. That's why I wrote this book.

This book is primarily a quick reference to the commands that are most frequently needed to configure Cisco routers for standard IP routing tasks. There are plenty of weasel words in there, and they're needed. This is far from a complete quick ref to all of IOS—such a quick ref would probably be well over 2000 pages long, clearly too long to be useful. Therefore, I haven't attempted to cover protocols other than IP (although there is support for everything from AppleTalk to SNA), nor any of the more exotic creatures in the IP space. And even in areas I have covered thoroughly, I was still forced to exclude commands that are useful only in limited cases.

Above all, this is a network administrator's book: it represents practical experience with IP routing on Cisco routers and covers the commands that you're likely to need. No doubt some readers will disagree with the choices I've made—such disagreement is inevitable. But though you occasionally won't find information about a command you need to use, you will far more often find, at your fingertips, precisely what you need to know.

More than anything else, the goal of this book is to give you information quickly. It aspires not to give you in-depth knowledge of how IP routing works, but to help you remember what arguments you need to give to the snmp-server enable traps command, or to help you scan through the many commands that start with ip to jog your memory about which one configures the forwarding of broadcast packets to selected subnets. If I succeed in doing that, I'm happy.

Organization

This book consists primarily of two parts. The first could be considered a tutorial, but that doesn't quite capture its purpose. I try to teach the basic principles behind configuring the router, but there are many other sources for that information (for example, Scott Ballew's *Managing IP Networks with Cisco Routers*, or Kevin Dooley and Ian J. Brown's *Cisco Cookbook*, both from O'Reilly). This part of the book quickly breezes through as many examples of different configuration tasks as possible. I provide explanations, but the focus is on the examples. By studying them, you'll see how to accomplish many of the tasks involved in setting up a router.

The bulk of the book is the quick reference. There's nothing fancy here—it's organized alphabetically and shows the commands that I felt were most useful to someone using a Cisco router in an IP environment.

What's New in This Edition

In this edition, we updated the book with features that were integrated into Cisco's latest major IOS release, 12.3, along with highlights from minor release 12.4. Some of the new features you'll find are AutoSecure, AutoQoS, and the new IOS naming model. We've also expanded other sections to include IS-IS routing, MPLS, and some new hardware types. Previously neglected topics such as quality-of-service and multicast routing have been expanded (a new chapter, Chapter 11, covers quality-of-service; multicasting is discussed in Chapter 13). You'll also find a new appendix that covers IP subnetting, the OSI network model, and other useful nuggets.

We've broken from our previous mantra of "routing-only topics" to include VLANs and switching, adding a new chapter on these topics (Chapter 14). Since the book was first written, routing and switching have come quite a long way; switches are a pretty fundamental part of Cisco's product line. And now, you'll find IOS on most of their newer switches instead of CatOS.

This book has grown substantially since its first edition. And I hope you'll find that its usefulness has grown as well.

Conventions

The following conventions are used in this book:

Italic
> Used for filenames, URLs, and occasionally for emphasis or clarity

Constant width
> Used for commands, command keywords, and anything else that has to be typed literally

Constant width italic
> Used for parameters or arguments that must be substituted in commands

Constant width bold
> Used for user input

[Keywords and other stuff]
> Used for optional keywords and arguments

{choice-1 | choice-2}
> Used to signify either choice-1 or choice-2

 This icon signifies a tip relating to the nearby text.

 This icon indicates a warning relating to the nearby text.

One of the confusing things about working with a Cisco router is the notion of a *command context*. Most commands are legal only in limited situations; all of the quick-reference entries include a command context that indicates how the command is to be used. A context of "command" means that the command is for interactive use and is not entered into the router's configuration; you do not need to enter the configuration mode (configure terminal) to give the command, and you can't include it in a configuration file that you upload. A context of "global" indicates that a command doesn't require any specific context; you can give it as soon as you've entered the configuration mode. A context of "interface" indicates that you must be in the interface configuration submode to give the command; "line" means that you must be in the line configuration submode, and so on.

IOS has no concept of a continuation character for breaking up command lines that are too long. That may be okay for a router, but it's a problem for a book;

still, I've decided not to invent a continuation character for the purposes of this book. I've split long commands across lines as it seemed most convenient and clear; just remember that you have to type it all on one line.

Safari Enabled

 When you see a Safari® Enabled icon on the cover of your favorite technology book, that means the book is available online through the O'Reilly Network Safari Bookshelf.

Safari offers a solution that's better than e-books. It's a virtual library that lets you easily search thousands of top tech books, cut and paste code samples, download chapters, and find quick answers when you need the most accurate, current information. Try it free at *http://safari.oreilly.com*.

We'd Like to Hear from You

Please address comments and questions concerning this book to the publisher:

O'Reilly Media, Inc.
1005 Gravenstein Highway North
Sebastopol, CA 95472
(800) 998-9938 (in the United States or Canada)
(707) 829-0515 (international or local)
(707) 829-0104 (fax)

There is a web page for this book, which lists errata and any additional information. You can access this page at:

http://www.oreilly.com/catalog/cisiosnut2/

To comment or ask technical questions about this book, send email to:

bookquestions@oreilly.com

For more information about books, conferences, Resource Centers, and the O'Reilly Network, see the O'Reilly web site at:

http://www.oreilly.com

Acknowledgments

As I began to plan the second edition of this book, I proclaimed that this time the writing would be effortless. I reassured everyone that the book would be completed very quickly. Evidently, I had tossed away lessons learned from the previous writing experience.

As it turned out, this edition wasn't easy or quick. Looking back, this edition proved to be every bit as long a journey as the first one. Now that the journey is over, I'd like to thank the people who helped me along the way.

I wish to thank my editors for their heroic efforts. For the first edition, Mike Loukides performed a great deal of work and provided fantastic guidance.

Without him, this book would not exist today. For the second edition, I owe editor Deb Cameron a tremendous amount of gratitude. Besides being a terrific editor, she displayed a depth of patience when faced with my seemingly natural ability for procrastination. Without her help and hard work, this second edition would never have been completed.

I'd like to thank all the reviewers from the first edition: Terry Slattery, Scott Ballew, Kevin Kelleher, Kennedy Clark, Val Pavlichenko, and Duke Meesuk. For the second edition, new reviewers provided invaluable feedback and deserve my thanks: Trey McMahon, Kevin Dooley, Ian J. Brown, and Theodore Wallingford. You guys went above and beyond the call of duty.

I'd like to thank my wife Peggy. Once again, she provided moral support. And she had to listen to me say, countless times, "I have to go work on the *new* book," which she probably found significantly more irritating than before. Also, she had the added strenuous task of watching our beautiful little daughter while I wrote this edition.

Finally, I need to rectify a glaring omission from the acknowledgments in the first edition. I'd like to thank my parents, George and Gail Boney. Not only did they tolerate me for the last thirty-three years, but they provided an endless amount of support, which would be too much to quantify and impossible to repay.

1

Getting Started

In the first edition of this book, I may have dated myself a bit by starting this chapter off with the following paragraph:

> The modern world is networked in a way that could barely be imagined a few decades ago. Today, the Internet reaches into virtually every business and almost every home. Our children and even our grandparents speak of dot-coms, email, and web sites. The Internet is now part of our culture.

Almost four years have passed since then, which does not seem like much time at all. But in the networking and computer fields, that's a very long time indeed. Our children and grandparents now speak of dot-bombs, MP3s, broadband, voice over IP, instant messaging, and outsourcing. Even the once–killer app email has been surpassed by the gratification of instant messaging. Things have certainly changed, which leaves us to wonder what the next few years will bring.

No matter what happens, Cisco is likely to continue its dominance of the networking world. Even that little router sitting on your cable or DSL connection at home could very well be a Cisco device. Routers and switches are the glue that holds the Internet together. And Cisco is the most prominent router manufacturer, holding the largest share of the market. Their routers come in all shapes and sizes, from inexpensive units for homes and small offices to equipment that costs hundreds of thousands of dollars, used by very large ISPs and telcos. Almost all of their devices—from the smallest to the largest—run the Internetwork Operating System (IOS). Therefore, they share the same command set, the same user interface, and the same configuration techniques. While a small home network router doesn't have the features or the capacity of an ISP's router, you configure them pretty much the same way. Both routers use access lists, have similar security mechanisms, support the same set of protocols in the same way, and so on.

As Cisco continues developing its product line, it's clear that the Internetwork Operating System (IOS) is a key part of its strategy. As new products come out, they all have the familiar IOS interface.

IOS is an extremely powerful and complex operating system with an equally complex configuration language. There are many commands, with many options, and if you get something wrong you can easily take your company offline. That's why I've decided to provide a quick-reference guide to IOS. As large a book as this is, though, it's impossible to cover all of IOS. Therefore, I've limited the discussion to IOS configuration for the TCP/IP protocol family. I've included all the commands that you need to work with TCP/IP and the lower-level protocols on which it relies. In the last edition, I apologized for not including other protocols such as IPX due to the lack of space in a handy reference. Today, there is hardly a need for such an apology, as TCP/IP has become the standard networking protocol for all but the most legacy network environments.

This book is intended as a quick reference, not as a step-by-step exposition of routing protocols or as an IOS tutorial. I haven't focused on thorough explanation; instead, I've tried to give lots of examples of the things people most frequently need to do when configuring a Cisco router, with just enough explanation to get you by. I'll start with the user interface (Chapters 1, 2, and 3), then talk about configuring lines and interfaces (Chapters 4, 5, and 6), access lists (Chapter 7), and routing protocols (Chapters 8, 9, and 10). Chapter 11, new in this edition, addresses quality of service issues, while Chapter 12 describes dial-on-demand routing. Chapter 13 covers a variety of networking topics, including bridging, Network Address Translation (NAT), tunnels, and Multiprotocol Label Switching (MPLS). Chapter 14, also new to this edition, describes working with switches and VLANs. Chapters 15 and 16 cover IOS security and trouble-shooting, respectively. Chapter 17 is the quick reference. Chances are, by the time the next edition of this book appears, the quick-reference section will be pretty well thumbed and worn out.

At first, the Cisco user interface appears cryptic. After learning the interface's structure, you'll become much more comfortable with it. Once you have learned some special features, you'll be able to work with the router's configuration easily.

IOS User Modes

IOS has two primary modes of operation: user mode and privileged mode. When you first connect to the router, you are placed in *user mode*. The Cisco documentation refers to this as the *user exec mode*; I am going to omit "exec" throughout this book. The user mode is indicated by the prompt:

    Router>

 The word "Router" is replaced with your router's hostname if the hostname is already configured.

The show commands in user mode are limited to a few basic levels. You cannot edit or view configurations at this stage; you can only view the router status and other miscellaneous information. To obtain a basic listing of commands, type a question mark:

    Router>?

Editing the router's configuration requires you to be in the privileged exec mode, which I call "privileged mode." Use the enable command to enter this mode:

```
Router>enable
Password:
Router#          Privileged mode prompt
```

You can always tell whether you are in user mode or privileged mode by looking at the prompt. The user mode prompt has a > at the end; the privileged mode prompt always has a # at the end, regardless of the submode.

If you are familiar with Unix, you can equate privileged mode to "root" access. You could also equate it to the administrator level in Windows 2000 or the supervisor in NetWare. In this mode, you have permission to access everything inside the router, including configuration commands. However, you can't type configuration commands directly. Before you can change the router's actual configuration, you must enter a submode of the privileged mode by giving the command configure terminal (see "Command-Line Completion" later in this chapter for a shortcut). This command can be entered only when you are in privileged mode.

```
Router#configure terminal
Enter configuration commands, one per line. End with Ctrl-Z
Router(config)#       Configuration mode
```

To exit configuration mode, you can use the command exit or type Ctrl-z. To exit privileged mode, you can use the disable command. So to exit both configuration and enable mode, use the following sequence of commands:

```
Router(config)#exit
Router#disable
Router>
```

Privileged mode has several submodes in addition to configuration mode; each has its own prompt. To enter these submodes, you must first enter configuration mode by giving the configure terminal command. Here's a summary of the most common modes and prompts (there are many others):

Global configuration mode
Prompt: Router(config)#

This level allows you to enter commands directly into the router configuration. From this level, you can enter any of the other three levels listed here. Once you are done entering commands into the configuration, use Ctrl-z, exit, or the end command to return to the privileged prompt. The device's hostname is a good example of a configuration item you would find in the global configuration mode.

Interface configuration mode
Prompt: Router(config-if)#

At this level, you are entering interface-specific commands. To enter this mode from the configuration prompt, use the command interface followed by an interface name, such as ethernet0, serial0, or serial1. Interface commands are discussed in Chapter 5. Use the exit command to exit this prompt and return to the configuration prompt.

Line configuration mode
Prompt: Router(config-line)#

From this prompt, you can enter line-specific commands. To enter this mode from the configuration prompt, use the command line, followed by a line type—such as vty, console, tty, or async—and a line number. The line configuration commands are discussed in Chapter 4. Once again, use the exit command to exit this mode and return to the configuration prompt.

Router configuration mode
Prompt: Router(config-router)#

From this prompt, you can enter only routing commands. To enter this mode from the configuration prompt, use the router command, followed by a routing protocol, such as rip or igrp. These commands differ widely depending on the routing protocol being used. Routing configuration commands are discussed in Chapters 8 through 10. Use the exit command to exit this mode and return to the configuration prompt.

Figure 1-1 is a flowchart that illustrates the transitions between the most common command modes and submodes. (This list is not comprehensive.) The arrows are labeled with the commands that cause the transitions between the modes.

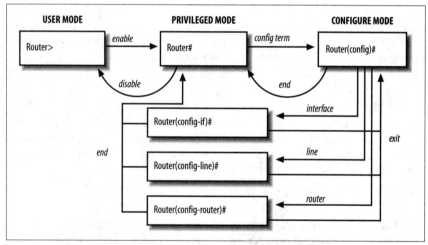

Figure 1-1. Transitions between IOS command modes

Configuration submodes provide a *context* in which certain commands are legal and others disallowed. It's one way that IOS tries to prevent you from making mistakes when configuring a router. In the quick-reference section, I list each command with the context (or mode) in which it can be given. Contexts are clearly important on the command line, where the prompt shows the submode you're in. They are equally important in configuration files, where there are no such hints; you just have to know.

Command-Line Completion

Command-line completion makes the IOS interface much more user-friendly. It saves you extra typing and helps out when you cannot remember a command's syntax. In a previous example, we used the command configure terminal:

    Router#**configure terminal**

But you could have saved wear and tear on your hands by typing:

    Router#**conf t**

IOS expands the command conf t to configure terminal, completing the command for you. It may seem like extra work to learn these short versions of the commands, but doing so really pays off, especially for the commands you use frequently. But if you haven't learned the shortcut, you can try pressing Tab. In this case, you could have pressed Tab after typing conf; the router fills in the best completion, which is configure. If you press Tab and the router doesn't fill in the rest of the command, type a few more letters and press Tab again.

Here is another example:

    Router#**show running-config**

This long command can be shortened to:

    Router#**sh ru**

The router knows that show is what you wanted, because show is the only command that begins with "sh"; likewise, the only subcommand of show that begins with "ru" is running-config.

If the router does not understand a command, it repeats the entire command line and places a caret (^) under the point at which it ran into trouble. For example:

    Router>**show itnerface e0**
    >show itnerface e0
                ^
    % Invalid input detected at '^' marker.

The caret symbol is pointing to the "t" in "itnerface", which is the command the router does not understand. We can quickly fix that by retyping the command:

    Router>**show interface e0**

We now get the correct output! Since we also know how to use shortcuts, we can type:

    Router>**sh int e0**

With this command we get the same result as with its lengthy counterpart. Command-line completion saves a lot of typing, and it helps you keep your sanity when you're working with long commands.

Get to Know the Question Mark

Previously, I said that you can get the available commands by typing ? at the prompt. You can also use this trick to find the subcommands of any command.

For example, if you know you want to use the copy command but cannot remember which subcommand you need, type:

```
Router#copy ?
  WORD            Copy from flash device - format <dev:>[partition:][filename]
  flash           Copy from system flash
  flh-log         Copy FLH log file to server
  mop             Copy from a MOP server
  rcp             Copy from an rcp server
  running-config  Copy from current system configuration
  startup-config  Copy from startup configuration
  tftp            Copy from a TFTP server
```

Another use of the question mark is to find all commands that match what you have typed so far. For example, if you know the first part of a command, type it, and then type a question mark. The router will return a list of all the matching commands. In the following example, we remember that the configure command begins with "co", but that's it. The router gives us the matching commands:

```
Router#co?
configure  connect  copy
```

Note the important difference between these two examples. In the first example, there was a space before the question mark, which gave us the next command that complements copy. Had there not been a space, the router would have tried to complete the word "copy" for us, not given us the next available commands. In the next example, we did not add the space, so the router tried to complete "co" with all the commands it could find that start with "co".

What if you don't see the command you're looking for? Bear in mind that the router returns only commands that are relevant to the mode you are currently in. For example, if you are in user mode, you are given only commands that apply to that mode.

Command-Line Editing Keys

IOS provides a number of keyboard shortcuts that let you edit the line you're typing. They should be familiar to any user of Unix or Emacs, though the details are a little different in some cases. Table 1-1 lists the command-line editing keys.

Table 1-1. Command-line editing keys

Keys	Commands
Ctrl-a	Returns the cursor to the beginning of the current line.
Ctrl-b	Moves the cursor back one character. (Equivalent to the left-arrow key.)
Ctrl-d	Deletes the character to the left of the cursor.
Ctrl-e	Moves the cursor to the end of the line.
Ctrl-f	Moves the cursor forward one character. (Equivalent to the right-arrow key.)
Ctrl-k	Deletes all the characters from the current cursor position to the end of the line.
Ctrl-n	Goes to the next command in the session history. (Equivalent to the down-arrow key.)
Ctrl-p	Goes to the previous command in the session history. (Equivalent to the up-arrow key.)
Ctrl-t	Switches the current character with the character to the left of the cursor.

Table 1-1. Command-line editing keys (continued)

Keys	Commands
Ctrl-r	Redraws or redisplays the current line.
Ctrl-u	Clears the line.
Ctrl-w	Deletes the word to the left of the cursor.
Ctrl-x	Deletes from the cursor position to the beginning of the line.
Ctrl-y	Pastes the most recently deleted characters at the current cursor position.
Ctrl-z	Exits the current configuration mode and returns at the previous configuration mode.
Tab	Tries to finish the current command. (Command completion.)
Up arrow	Moves back through the history of commands.
Down arrow	Moves forward through the history of commands.
Left arrow	Moves the cursor to the left.
Right arrow	Moves the cursor to the right.
Ctrl-^, then x	Aborts the sequence. Breaks out of any executing command.

Pausing Output

Using the `terminal` command, you can set an important feature of the user interface: the pausing of lengthy output. For example, if you run a command that has more than one page of output, the router will pause after 24 lines with a `--More--` prompt. The value 24 is the default terminal length. Depending on the size of your terminal window, this might not be adequate. You can change the length and width using the `terminal` command, like this:

```
Router>terminal length 10
Router>terminal width 80
```

These commands set the terminal length to 10 and the width to 80, which means the router will pause after 10 lines of output and that each of these lines will be 80 characters long. You can disable the pausing altogether by setting the terminal length to 0:

```
Router>terminal length 0
```

show Commands

As you work with IOS, you'll become intimately familiar with the `show` commands. They are among the most useful commands you will ever use; they allow you to view just about any settings within the router. Issuing the command `show ?` produces output like this:

```
Router>show ?
  clock     Display the system clock
  history   Display the session command history
  hosts     IP domain-name, lookup style, nameservers, and host table
  sessions  Information about Telnet connections
  snmp      snmp statistics
  terminal  Display terminal configuration parameters
  users     Display information about terminal lines
  version   System hardware and software status
```

The show command has many different subcommands. However, notice that we are in user mode. In privileged mode, the show command has a lot more subcommands, which would take up a few pages if we listed them here. The important thing to remember is that show commands often have more than one keyword. For example, the command show ip route works by itself, but many other options can be applied to it. For example:

```
router#show ip route ?
  Hostname or A.B.C.D  Network to display information about or hostname
  bgp                  Border Gateway Protocol (BGP)
  connected            Connected
  egp                  Exterior Gateway Protocol (EGP)
  eigrp                Enhanced Interior Gateway Routing Protocol (EIGRP)
  igrp                 Interior Gateway Routing Protocol (IGRP)
  isis                 ISO IS-IS
  odr                  On Demand stub Routes
  ospf                 Open Shortest Path First (OSPF)
  rip                  Routing Information Protocol (RIP)
  static               Static routes
  summary              Summary of all routes
  supernets-only       Show supernet entries only
  <cr>
```

I certainly haven't explained routing enough for you to understand the output of this command. However, you can see how to find show keywords with the question mark. The <cr> shown in the previous example indicates that you can hit Enter at this point and the command will work.* In other words, show ip route is a valid command. The other keywords are optional.

In each section of this book, I emphasize the appropriate show commands for the topic. For the topics covered in this chapter, the following show commands are extremely useful:

- show version
- show history
- show users

The show version command gives a lot more information than just the version of IOS that the router is currently running. You will see this command pop up a few more times later in this book. For now, you can see that it tells us the router type, the IOS image, the system uptime, the current IOS version, all the available interfaces, and the amount of memory on the router:

```
Router#show version
Cisco Internetwork Operating System Software
IOS (tm) C3550 Software (C3550-I9Q3L2-M), Version
12.1(22)EA1a, RELEASE SOFTWARE (fc1)
Copyright (c) 1986-2004 by cisco Systems, Inc.
```

---

* Just for the record, "cr" stands for carriage return. This hails from the days of the typewriter. When you type on a typewriter, the carriage moves to the right as you type. When you press Return (the key is called "Enter" on most PC keyboards), the typewriter's carriage would move back to the starting position—in other words, it returned.

Compiled Fri 20-Aug-04 00:30 by yenanh
Image text-base: 0x00003000, data-base: 0x006C5C6C

ROM: Bootstrap program is C3550 boot loader

3550 uptime is 3 weeks, 6 days, 13 hours, 11 minutes
System returned to ROM by power-on
System image file is
"flash:c3550-i9q3l2-mz.121-22.EA1a/c3550-i9q3l2-mz.121-22.EA1a.bin"

cisco WS-C3550-24 (PowerPC) processor (revision P0)
with 65526K/8192K bytes of memory.
Processor board ID CAT0849Z07W
Last reset from warm-reset
Running Layer2/3 Switching Image

Ethernet-controller 1 has 12 Fast Ethernet/IEEE 802.3
interfaces

Ethernet-controller 2 has 12 Fast Ethernet/IEEE 802.3
interfaces

Ethernet-controller 3 has 1 Gigabit Ethernet/IEEE
802.3 interface

Ethernet-controller 4 has 1 Gigabit Ethernet/IEEE
802.3 interface

24 FastEthernet/IEEE 802.3 interface(s)
2 Gigabit Ethernet/IEEE 802.3 interface(s)

The password-recovery mechanism is enabled.
384K bytes of flash-simulated non-volatile
configuration memory.
Base ethernet MAC Address: 00:12:D9:56:67:00
Motherboard assembly number: 73-5700-12
Power supply part number: 34-0966-04
Motherboard serial number: CAT08490BLH
Power supply serial number: LIT08410CCQ
Model revision number: P0
Motherboard revision number: A0
Model number: WS-C3550-24-SMI
System serial number: CAT0849Z07W
Configuration register is 0x10F

The show history command gives a log of the router commands you have used.
The length of this history log depends on the size set by the terminal history
command. The default is 10 lines.

Router#**show history**
    show history
    show terminal
    show users
    enable
    show version

The show users command gives a complete listing of all currently connected users:

```
Router#show users
    Line     User      Host(s)              Idle Location
  2 tty 2    steve1    idle
  5 tty 5    john2     Async interface         2
```

2

IOS Images and Configuration Files

Eventually you will want to upgrade your router's software. The IOS (Internetwork Operating System) is the software that resides inside the Cisco device. Upgrading IOS involves transferring a new IOS image to your router from some kind of server. As we'll see in this chapter, there are several methods for uploading a new IOS image: the most common include using Trivial File Transfer Protocol (TFTP), Remote Copy Protocol (RCP), or Secure Copy Protocol (SCP). Before we discuss how to transfer a new image, let's define exactly what is meant by an "image file" and how it differs from a configuration file.

IOS image files contain the system code that your router uses to function, that is, the image contains the IOS itself, plus various feature sets (optional features or router-specific features). However, the features are not configured in any way. The router's actual configuration—which features are enabled and how they are used in your particular network environment—is stored in a configuration file written in IOS's configuration language. The commands in this file describe everything from the router's name and the IP address of each interface to the protocols that you're using, address translation, security, and more. The router is useless without a concrete configuration—just like an operating system kernel is useless without the configuration files (such as the Windows registry or the files in /etc on a Unix system) that tell the kernel how you want it to operate in a particular situation.

IOS Image Filenames

IOS is the software that resides inside the Cisco device. You can think of IOS as the kernel or the actual operating code within your router. The IOS image has a name, which specifies the platform for which the image was built, the features it includes, and where the image is located in memory. To see the name of the image your router is running, give the command show version:

```
Router>show version
Cisco Internetwork Operating System Software IOS (tm)
  3600 Software (C3640-JS-M), Version 12.0(5)T1,  RELEASE SOFTWARE (fc1)
```

In this example, C3640-JS-M is the IOS image name. The name has three parts: platform identifier, feature set, and image execution location. In this example, C3640 is the platform identifier, JS is the feature set, and M is the image execution location.

Platform Identifier

The platform identifier indicates the hardware for which the image was built. Table 2-1 lists the most common platform identifiers. This list is quite extensive and grows as new products are released.

Table 2-1. Common platform identifiers

Identifier	Platforms
as	Access Server 5200 series
ca	Cisco Advantage
cpa	Cisco Pro
cs	Communication Server
c800, c1000, c1005, c1600	Cisco 800, 1003, 1004, 1005, 1600
c2500	Cisco 2500-2525 series routers
c2600	Cisco 2610-2613 series routers
c2800	Catalyst 2800
c2900	Cisco 2910, 2950
c29atm	Cisco 2900 ATM
c3620, c3640, c3800	Cisco 3620, 3640, 3800
c5200, c5300	Cisco AS5200, AS5300
c4000, c4500, c4700	Cisco 4000 series routers
c5fsfc	Catalyst 5000 series
c5rsm	Catalyst 5000 RSM
c5atm	Catalyst ATM
c6400s, c6400r	Cisco 6400 NSP, Cisco 6400 NRP
c6msm	Catalyst
c7000	Cisco 7000, 7010
c7200	Cisco 7200
Igs	IGS, 2500, 3000, and 5100 series routers
gs3	AGS and AGS+ gateway routers
gs7	7000 series gateway routers
Gsr	Gigabit Switch Router (12000)
ls1010	LightStream 1010
Mc3810	Multiservice Cisco 3810
Rpm	MGX 8850
RSP	Cisco 7500 series

Feature Set

The feature set describes the options that are included in the IOS image. Table 2-2 lists the most popular feature sets. Keep in mind that features are often tied to platforms—any given platform supports only some feature sets. Also, note that the feature set indicators may be combined. For example, the IOS image C3640-JS-M has the feature set JS, which combines the Enterprise Subset feature set (J) with the Source Route Switch feature set (S).

Table 2-2. Common feature sets

Feature set	Contents
A	APPN
A2	ATM
B	AppleTalk
BOOT	Boot image
C	Remote Access Server
D	Desktop subset (SNMP, IP, BRIDGING, WAN, Terminal Services, IPX, ATALK, ARAP)
D2	Desktop Plus
Dsv	Desktop/IBM
EBOOT	Ethernet boot image for MC3810
F	FRAD subset
G	ISDN subset
G2	Gatekeeper proxy, voice and video
G3	ISDN subset for c800 (IP, ISDN, Frame Relay)
I	IP subset
I2	IP subset for 3600
I3	Reduced IP subset with BGP/EGP/NHRP removed
Is	IP Plus
Is56i	IP IPSec 56
J	Enterprise subset (protocol translation)
Js40	Enterprise 40
Jsv56	Enterprise IPSec 56
Js	Enterprise Plus
Js40	Enterprise Plus 40
Js56i	Enterprise Plus IPSec 56
K	Kitchen sink
K1	Privacy key encryption (11.3 and above)
K3	Triple DES (11.3 and above)
K4	168-bit encryption with SSH
L	IpeXchange IPX, static routing, gateway
M	RMON
N	IPX
O	Firewall
O2	Firewall (3xx0)

Table 2-2. Common feature sets (continued)

Feature set	Contents
O3	Firewall with SSH (36x0, 26x0)
P	Service provider (IP RIP/IGRP/EIGRP/OSPF/BGP CLNS ISIS/IGRP)
R	RSRB (remote source route bridging); this option can be added to other feature sets
S	Source route switch (SNMP, IP, BRIDGING, SRB)
V	VIP and dual RSP support
V2	Voice V2D
V3	Voice feature card
X	X.25 (11.1 and earlier), and on 12.0T on c800 series
X	Frame Relay in 11.2
X	H.323 Gatekeeper/Proxy for 2500, 3620, 3640, MC3810
Y	Reduced IP (SNMP, IP RIP/IGRP/EIGRP, BRIDGING, ISDN, PPP), for low-end routers
Y2	IP variant (SNMP, IP RIP/IGRP/EIGRP, WAN -X.25, OSPF, PIM)
Y3	IP/X.31
Y4	Reduced IP variant (Cable, MIBs, DHCP, EZHTTP)
Y5	Reduced IP variant (Cable, MIBs, DHCP, EZIP) for home office
Y6	Reduced IP variant (c800)

Image Execution Location

The image execution location describes where the image is to be located in the router's memory. For example, given the image name C3640-JS-M, the M indicates that the image can be stored in RAM. Table 2-3 lists the most common execution locations. Keep in mind that some of these can be combined; for example, the location LZ indicates that the image is relocatable and has been compressed.

Table 2-3. Execution locations

Flag	Location
F	Flash
M	RAM
R	ROM
L	Relocatable
C	Flash card (PCMIA)
Z,X,W	Image is compressed

The New Cisco IOS Packaging Model

In release 12.3, Cisco changed the image package naming model. As you can see from the previous explanations, image selection had become overly complex and difficult to understand. In the new packaging model, the image selection has been reduced from 44 to 8 possible packages.

Some of the advantages of the new package model are:

- Easier to select the features you want
- Feature set reduced from 44 to 8 packages
- Consistent image names across platforms
- Consistent functionality across platforms

Figure 2-1 shows the eight major packages. This figure illustrates the concept of package inheritance. With package inheritance, any package automatically inherits all the features of the packages below it. For example, IP Base is the first package in the tree. Its features are inherited by all the packages above it.

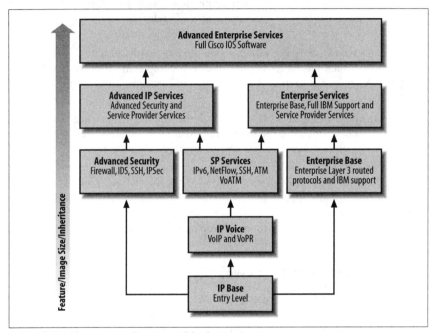

Figure 2-1. New image packaging model inheritance

As of this writing, the new feature packaging is available only on 800, 1700, 2600, 3600, 2700, and 7000 series routers. However, you can expect more devices to join this group in the future.

Example of New Image Name

Here's an example of the new image naming scheme:

```
c3745-entbase-mz.123-9a.bin
```

This name translates to a platform of 3745, a feature set of "Enterprise Base," and a release of 12.3.9a.

Status of the Release

As we have just seen, the filenames for a given release are packed with information. They do not, however, tell you the status of the release. Cisco has three codes for the status of the release:

GD

General Deployment indicates that the code is extremely stable for the most demanding production environments. Although this image is very stable, the number of new features is extremely limited.

LD

Limited Deployment means that some newer maturing features have been added, but the release is not as stable as a GD release.

ED

Early Deployment is the cutting-edge version, with the latest and greatest features, which means testing has not been completed. In other words, bugs probably still exist in this release, which makes it unsuitable for most production environments.

The release in our example is LD, so is for limited deployment. Since the status of the release is not included in the filename, how do you find out? You must look it up at Cisco's web site. For an easier way of doing this, see the next section, which explains the Cisco Feature Navigator.

This method of classifying releases replaces Cisco's old convention, in which releases were labeled with certain characters in their filenames. For example, "x" meant that an image had added features to support new hardware but wasn't very well tested. This labeling has been replaced with the GD, LD, and ED classifications.

Finding the Release on Cisco's Web Site

Recently, Cisco changed the way you find the IOS image you are looking for with the release of the Cisco Feature Navigator. You can find this web page at *http://tools.cisco.com/ITDIT/CFN/jsp/index.jsp* or by searching on Cisco's site for "Cisco Feature Navigator." However, to access this feature you need a CCO account. To create an account, click on the "Register Now" link at the top heading on the main web site at *http://www.cisco.com*.

While a basic CCO account will give you access to the Cisco Feature Navigator, you'll need a service contract tied to your CCO account in order to download the new images. The CCO registration page requests the required information when you sign up.

The Cisco Feature Navigator lets you quickly select the IOS release you want, based on the device model number and the desired feature set. You can search by feature, release, or platform. You can even compare different releases of IOS, a very handy tool that takes the burden out of selecting images.

Loading Image Files Through the Network

From time to time you will need to load a new system image, either to upgrade the image that was shipped with your router, to install bug fixes, or to add new feature sets that you've purchased. The most common way to upload an image is to copy it to the router from some other system on your network—after all, the router is a network device, and it's easiest to use the router's networking capabilities. You can also use the console port or an AUX port to upload an image using Xmodem. In this book, I'll focus on loading image files over the network. We'll cover TFTP first, then provide details on using RCP or SCP, which is often preferred today for its security features.

Using TFTP to Download Files

Say that you have just purchased a 2501 router and want to upgrade to the latest version of IOS. Assume that you have downloaded the new image from Cisco's web site or that you have it on a CD or some other medium. If you haven't already set up the router, you'll need a serial connection from a terminal (or a PC with a terminal-emulation program) to do some simple configuration before you can install the image: at a minimum: you need to set up an IP address. You'll also need a connection to the network so that the router can access your TFTP server. Once you've set things up, your primitive network will look like Figure 2-2.

Figure 2-2. Getting an IOS image from a TFTP server

Before you start the upgrade, you must configure the IP address for the router's Ethernet interface (in this case, ethernet0). Let's assume that the address 10.10.1.1

is available for the router and that the TFTP server is 10.10.1.2. Before you load the new image, enter the following commands:

```
Router>enable
Router#config terminal
Router(config)#interface ethernet0
Router(config-if)#ip address 10.10.1.1 255.255.255.0
Router(config-if)#no shutdown
Router(config-if)#exit
Router(config)#exit
Router#ping 10.10.1.2
```

The ping command is a simple sanity check: it proves that the router can actually communicate with the TFTP server. Once you've done this, you're ready to start retrieving the image file. In a sense, TFTP is a blind FTP. There are no user logins and there are no directory listing commands. You cannot ask the server to show you what files are available: the requesting system must know the exact name of the file it wants to download. Because TFTP is primitive and has no concept of authentication, it is a well-known security risk. We won't discuss how to set up a TFTP server here, but make sure your server is not accessible from the outside world. (See "Using SCP to Download Files" later in this chapter for a more secure alternative.)

The TFTP server can be another router that is "serving" image and configuration files. To configure a Cisco router as a TFTP server, use the command tftp-server flash:*ios_filename*.

Here is the sequence of steps for upgrading a router from an IOS file called *igs-j-l.110* to *igs-j-l.120*:

1. Ensure there is enough flash memory on your router to load the IOS image you want. Give the show flash command and compare the output with the size of the image file on the server.

   ```
   Router#show flash
   System flash directory:
   File  Length    Name/status
     1   6070088   igs-j-l.110
   [6070152 bytes used, 2318456 available, 8388608 total]
   8192K bytes of processor board System flash
   ```

   The router's flash memory has 8192K bytes total with 2318456 bytes available. A directory listing on our TFTP server shows that our new image is the same size as the current one. Therefore, as long as we replace the old image with the new one, we have enough memory for the upgrade.

2. Make a backup of the current IOS image to the network server. This is always a good idea. If the new image does not work or causes problems, you can always load your backup image.

   ```
   Router#copy flash tftp
   System flash directory:
   File  Length    Name/status
     1   6070088   igs-j-l.110
   [6070152 bytes used, 2318456 available, 8388608 total]
   ```

```
Address or name of remote host [255.255.255.255]? 10.10.1.2
Source file name? igs-j-l.110
Destination file name [igs-j-l.110]? igs-j-l.110.bak
Verifying checksum for 'igs-j-l.110' (file # 1)... OK
Copy 'igs-j-l.110' from Flash to server as 'igs-j-l.110.bak? [yes/no]yes
Writing...
Done...
```

3. Load the new IOS.

```
Router#config terminal
Router(config)#config-reg 0x2101
Router(config)#exit
Router#reload
```

Wait for the router to reboot, then reconnect. Once you're back online, re-enter the enable mode.

```
Router>enable
Router#copy tftp flash
Address or name of remote host [255.255.255.255]? 10.10.1.2
Source file name? igs-j-l.120
Destination file name [igs-j-l.120]? igs-j-l.120
Accessing file ' igs-j-l.120' on 172.16.101.101...
Loading igs-j-l.120 from 10.10.1.2 (via Ethernet0): ! [OK]
Erase flash device before writing? [confirm] y
Flash contains files. Are you sure you want to erase? [confirm] y
Copy ' igs-j-l.120' from server
 as 'igs-j-l.120' into Flash WITH erase? [yes/no] yes
Erasing device... eeeeeeeeeeeeeeeeeeeeeeeeeeeeeeeee...erased
Loading file1 from 10.10.1.2 (via Ethernet0): !
[OK - 6070088 bytes]
Verifying checksum... OK (0x14x4)
Flash copy took 0:00:31 [hh:mm:ss]
```

Now undo the configuration register.

```
Router#config terminal
Router(config)#config-reg 0x2102
Router(config)#exit
```

To abort TFTP, type Ctrl-Shift-^ and then type x.

4. Verify your newly loaded image. Even though there are checksums in the image, it is a good idea to verify on your own; you want to be absolutely sure that the new image is not corrupted.

```
Router#verify flash
```

If the verify fails, do *not* move on to Step 5 or reboot your router. Instead, retrieve your backup image with Step 3 by loading the backup copy of the IOS image, which we saved as *igs-j-l.110.bak* in Step 2.

5. Reboot.

```
Router#reload "IOS Upgrade"
```

What you type between the quotes does not matter to the router. It is an informational message to tell users and administrators that are currently logged in what caused the router to reboot.

The reload command reboots the router. There is no reboot command. See the entry for reload in Chapter 17 for options.

Using RCP to Download Files

RCP uses the Unix remote copy protocol to store and retrieve files. The server on which the file is stored is usually a Unix or Linux system, though some implementations of RCP are available for other platforms. To set up the server, you must create a user account for the router and an *.rhosts* file for that account that gives access to the router. See your Unix manuals for more details.

Why would we want to use RCP? On a slow network, TFTP may time out because it is UDP-based. RCP uses TCP for the network connection, which provides a more reliable connection in tough network conditions. Because RCP requires an account, you might be tempted to think that it is also more secure than TFTP. It probably is, but the additional security is so minimal that it can hardly be considered an advantage. As with TFTP, you'll want to take steps to ensure that outsiders can't access your RCP server.

To configure the router to use RCP, set the username to be used by the rcp command:

```
Router(config)#ip rcmd remote-username name
```

Replace *name* with the username you have assigned to the router on the RCP server. To upload a new image, use the same five-step process outlined in the previous section, but replace tftp with rcp in the copy commands. For example, in Step 2, use the command:

```
Router#copy flash rcp
```

Be aware that many sites consider the remote shell protocols a security problem and disable them.

You can also run RCP from your Unix workstation. And it's a lot easier to have your routers trust the Unix box than it is to list all your routers in one *.rhosts* file.

Using SCP to Download Files

Secure Shell (SSH) is now the more modern way to securely access remote nodes. With SSH, the network session is encrypted, which keeps your data secure. And unlike FTP and Telnet, SSH passwords are not sent in clear text across the network. SCP is the "secure copy" form of SSH. Most modern operating systems support SSH service.

As in the previous examples, we use a username of bob and the server 10.1.1.2:

```
Router#copy scp://bob@10.1.1.2/igs-j-1.120 flash:
Address or name of remote host [10.1.1.2]?
Destination username [bob]?
Destination filename [igs-j-1.120]?
Writing igs-j-1.120
Password:
```

The system prompts you for the SSH password for the user bob. Once you enter the password (the password is not echoed on the screen), the transfer continues as usual. Secure Shell support was introduced in IOS 12.2.

Using the IOS Filesystem for Images

The upgrade procedure described in the previous sections is for a Class B IOS filesystem. Class B filesystems are probably the most common, but they aren't universal—particularly on high-end routers. There are also Class A and Class C filesystems; the filesystem you have depends on the router you're using. Table 2-4 shows which filesystem a number of different routers use.

Table 2-4. Flash filesystem types

Filesystem type	Router
Class A	7000 series, C12000, and LightStream 1010
Class B	1003, 1004, 1005, 2500, 2600, 3600, 4000, AS5200, 800
Class C	3810, disk0 of SC3640

As far as a user is concerned, the filesystems differ primarily in the commands that they support. Table 2-5 lists the filesystem commands and what they do.

Table 2-5. Filesystem commands

Command	Filesystem	Description
cd	All	Changes the working directory.
delete	All	Deletes a file. On Class A filesystems, this command marks the file for deletion; the squeeze command purges deleted files from the filesystem. On Class B filesystems, the files disappear from directory listings (unless you use /all), but there is no way to reclaim the space, short of erasing the entire filesystem. On Class C filesystems, the file is deleted immediately.
dir	All	Displays the directory's contents. The /all option shows deleted and undeleted files.
erase	A, B	Erases the entire filesystem.
format	A, C	Formats the filesystem.
fsck	C	Verifies the filesystem's consistency.
mkdir	C	Makes a new subdirectory.
more	All	Displays a file's contents.
pwd	All	Displays the current directory.
rename	C	Renames a file.
rmdir	C	Deletes a directory.
show file descriptors	All	Shows open file descriptors.
show file information	All	Shows file size, location, etc.
show file system	All	Shows available filesystems on the device.
squeeze	A	Makes more room by moving files to the beginning of the flash memory, removing deleted files, and removing files with errors. Note that while this is a class A filesystem command, it is also IOS-dependent. Not all versions have this command.
tftp-server	All	Sets the device to act as a TFTP server.
undelete	A, B	Recovers any deleted files. Erased files cannot be undeleted.
verify	All	Verifies that a file's checksum is correct.

All filesystems use a notation similar to a URL to specify filenames and locations. File specifications look like this:

```
prefix:path/filename
prefix://server-name/path/filename
prefix://username:password@server-name/path/filename
```

The prefix indicates where the file is located; Table 2-6 lists the valid prefixes. The path indicates the directory where the file is found. If the prefix is ftp, rcp, or tftp, the URL refers to a file located on a server; you must supply a server name and, if necessary, a username and a password.

Table 2-6. Valid prefixes

Prefix	File location
bootflash	Boot flash memory.
flash	Flash memory.
ftp	FTP server.
null	Bit bucket; files copied to a null destination are discarded. The null prefix is useful for testing connectivity and determining file size.
nvram	Nonvolatile memory.
rcp	RCP server.
slot0	First PCMCIA flash memory card.
slot1	Second PCMCIA flash memory card.
system	Volatile system memory. Often used for access to the currently running system configuration.

You can view and copy files on remote servers using the TFTP, RCP, and FTP protocols, but you cannot delete files from them. For example, the following command uses TFTP to view the file config1 on the server myserver:

```
Router1# more tftp://myserver/config1
!
!
version 12.0
...
```

Upgrading Flash Memory Using the Filesystem Commands

The following example upgrades a 3640 router using flash, slot0 (PCMCIA flash card), and the IOS filesystem. The router is initially running IOS 11.2, which doesn't have the filesystem commands; we will upgrade to a version that does. The new IOS image was shipped to us on a flash card, which we have inserted into slot0 on the router. Now that the card is in, we can see the two images by using the show flash and show slot0 commands:

```
Router#show flash
System flash directory:
File  Length   Name/status
  1   5061960  c3640-ajs40-mz.112-23.P
[5062024 bytes used, 11715192 available, 16777216 total]
16384K bytes of processor board System flash (Read/Write)
```

```
Router#show slot0
PCMCIA Slot0 flash directory:
File  Length    Name/status
  1   8611616   c3640-js-mz_120-5_t1.bin
[8611680 bytes used, 8165536 available, 16777216 total]
16384K bytes of processor board PCMCIA Slot0 flash (Read/Write)
```

We have to use the show commands because IOS 11.2 doesn't have commands like dir. The first command shows the contents of the router's flash memory; the second shows the contents of the card we inserted into slot0.

Now we tell the router to load the image in slot0 instead of the image in the flash memory. We use the boot command to tell the router where the image is located; by default, the router loads the first image it finds in flash memory. The boot command modifies the router's running configuration; we copy the running configuration to the startup configuration, then reboot. Upon reboot, the router loads the image from the flash card in slot0:

```
Router#conf terminal
Router(config)#boot system flash slot0:c3640-js-mz_120-5_t1.bin
Router#copy run start
Router#reload
```

After the router reboots, the show version command shows we are running the new image:

```
Router>show version
Cisco Internetwork Operating System Software
IOS (tm) 3600 Software (C3640-JS-M), Version 12.0(5)T1,  RELEASE SOFTWARE
(fc1)
Copyright (c) 1986-1999 by cisco Systems, Inc.
Compiled Tue 17-Aug-99 22:32 by cmong
Image text-base: 0x600088F0, data-base: 0x60F24000

ROM: System Bootstrap, Version 11.1(20)AA2, EARLY DEPLOYMENT RELEASE
SOFTWARE (fc1)

Router uptime is 0 minutes
System returned to ROM by reload
System image file is "slot0:c3640-js-mz_120-5_t1.bin"
```

Now we can use the filesystem commands:

```
Router#dir flash:
Directory of flash:/
  1  -rw-    5061960               <no date>  c3640-ajs40-mz.112-23.P
16777216 bytes total (11715192 bytes free)
```

```
Router#dir slot0:
Directory of slot0:/
  1  -rw-    8611616               <no date>  c3640-js-mz_120-5_t1.bin
16777216 bytes total (8165536 bytes free)
```

Next, we want to copy the image from the PCMCIA card to the router's flash memory—it's not a good idea to rely on booting from the flash card. We can use the filesystem commands to perform this copy:

```
Router#copy slot0:c3640-js-mz_120-5_t1.bin flash:c3640-js-mz_120-5_t1.bin
Destination filename [c3640-js-mz_120-5_t1.bin]?
Erase flash: before copying?[confirm]n
CCCCCCCCCCCCCCCCCCCCCCCCCCCCCCCCCCCCCCCCCCCCCCCCCCCCCCCCCCCCCCCCCCCCCCCC
Verifying checksum...  OK (0xB648)
8611616 bytes copied in 38.440 secs (226621 bytes/sec)
```

Check the flash contents:

```
Router#dir flash:
Directory of flash:/
  1  -rw-     5061960                 <no date>  c3640-ajs40-mz.112-23.P
  2  -rw-     8611616                 <no date>  c3640-js-mz_120-5_t1.bin
16777216 bytes total (3103512 bytes free)
```

Now, we can either delete the old 11.2 image or tell the router which image to boot. If we don't use the boot command to specify an image, the router will load the first available image, which will be the old 11.2 image. (Note that this wouldn't have been an issue if we had told the router it could erase flash memory before copying. However, that would have left us without a backup image to boot if the new image failed.) So we issue two more boot commands: the first to tell the router not to boot the image in slot0, and the second to specify the image we want. We then copy the running configuration into the startup configuration. Finally, we reboot and remove the slot0 memory card.

```
Router#config terminal
Router(config)#no boot system flash slot0:c3640-js-mz_120-5_t1.bin
Router(config)#boot system flash c3640-js-mz_120-5_t1.bin
Router(config)#^Z
Router#copy run start
Router#reload
```

When it reboots, the router loads the right image from its flash memory:

```
Router>show version
Cisco Internetwork Operating System Software
IOS (tm) 3600 Software (C3640-JS-M), Version 12.0(5)T1,  RELEASE SOFTWARE
(fc1)
Copyright (c) 1986-1999 by cisco Systems, Inc.
Compiled Tue 17-Aug-99 22:32 by cmong
Image text-base: 0x600088F0, data-base: 0x60F24000

ROM: System Bootstrap, Version 11.1(20)AA2, EARLY DEPLOYMENT RELEASE
SOFTWARE (fc1)
ROM: 3600 Software (C3640-AJS40-M), Version 11.2(23)P,  RELEASE SOFTWARE
(fc1)

Router uptime is 0 minutes
System returned to ROM by power-on
System image file is "flash:c3640-js-mz_120-5_t1.bin"
```

Let's delete the old image anyway:

```
Router#delete c3640-ajs40-mz.112-23.P
Delete filename [c3640-ajs40-mz.112-23.P]?
Delete flash:c3640-ajs40-mz.112-23.P? [confirm]y
Router#dir /all flash:
Directory of flash:/

  1  -rw-    5061960       <no date>  [c3640-ajs40-mz.112-23.P]
  2  -rw-    8611616       <no date>  c3640-js-mz_120-5_t1.bin

16777216 bytes total (3103512 bytes free)
```

IOS Images

Notice that our deleted file is still there; it won't be deleted permanently until we give the erase command. On a Class A filesystem, we could use the squeeze command to erase the deleted file. With this filesystem, though, we are stuck with the deleted file until we give the erase command, which erases the entire filesystem. In this case, we would have to reload our new image. Since there's plenty of room in flash, there is no need to clean the filesystem out now. Next time we upgrade this router, though, we will probably answer "yes" to the "Erase flash before copying" question.

The Router's Configuration

Every router has two different configurations to consider:

Running configuration
> The router's active configuration, which is stored in the router's RAM. Every configuration command you give is stored in the running configuration. If you reboot your router, this configuration is lost. If you make changes that you want to save, you must copy the running configuration to a safe location, such as a network server, or save it as the router's startup configuration.

Startup configuration
> The configuration that is loaded when the router boots. This configuration is stored in the router's nonvolatile memory (NVRAM). You cannot edit a startup configuration directly. All commands you enter are stored in the running configuration, which can be copied into the startup configuration.

In other words, when you boot a router, the startup configuration becomes the initial running configuration. As you modify the configuration, the two diverge: the startup configuration remains the same, while the running configuration reflects the changes you have made. If you want to make your changes permanent, you must copy the running configuration to the startup configuration.

The following command copies the router's current running configuration into the startup configuration:

```
Router#copy running-config startup-config
Building configuration...
```

Similarly, to save the running configuration on a network server using TFTP, you would give the command:

```
Router#copy running-config tftp
```

You'll be prompted for additional information, such as the remote host and the name for the saved file.

The terms "running configuration" and "startup configuration" were added in recent versions of IOS. In earlier versions, you used the command write terminal to display the current router configuration and write memory to store the current configuration. This terminology is outdated; use the copy command.

Loading Configuration Files

Loading and saving configuration files is much simpler than loading a kernel image. This section summarizes the commands that load and save the configuration.

Loading the running-config

Once loaded, the running configuration is used by the router immediately. Use these commands to load it using either TFTP or RCP:

```
Router#copy tftp running-config          (for TFTP)
Router#copy rcp running-config           (for RCP)
Router#copy scp://user@ip:. running-config   (for SCP)
```

Loading the startup-config

The startup configuration is not used until the router is rebooted. Loading the startup configuration can be dangerous because the router doesn't parse the configuration file and won't give you any warning if the file has errors. The configuration is not parsed until the router is rebooted—and if the configuration is incorrect, the router may not boot properly. Therefore, use the following commands with care:

```
Router#copy tftp startup-config          (for TFTP)
Router#copy rcp startup-config           (for RCP)
Router#copy scp://user@ip:. startup-config   (for SCP)
```

Saving running-config to startup-config

The following command is the most important command of all, because if you don't save your running configuration, all your configuration changes will be lost during the next reboot of the device. Once you are satisfied that your current router configuration is correct, copy your configuration to the startup configuration with this command:

```
Router#copy running-config startup-config
```

Viewing a Configuration

The following commands display the startup or the running configuration:

```
Router#show startup-config
Router#show running-config
```

Options for the show config command

For the two show commands listed above, we can add some optional modifiers to change the output format. One option is to add line numbers to the output. You can do this with the linenum option:

```
Router1#show running-config linenum
Building configuration...

Current configuration : 868 bytes
    1 : !
    2 : version 12.3
    3 : service timestamps debug datetime msec
    4 : service timestamps log datetime msec
    5 : service password-encryption
    6 : service udp-small-servers
    7 : service tcp-small-servers
    8 : !
    9 : hostname Router
```

With the interface option, you can tell the router to just show you the configuration of a certain interface:

```
Router#show running-config interface ethernet 0
Building configuration...

Current configuration : 109 bytes
!
interface Ethernet0
 description local lan
 ip address 192.168.0.100 255.255.255.0
 no ip route-cache
end
```

If you want, you can have the output of the show command go directly to a URL for storage. In this example, we direct the output of the show command to be stored on a TFTP server.

```
Router# show running-config | redirect tftp://192.168.0.4/config1.txt
```

Finally, the output of the show command can be massaged with a regular expression. In this example, we are going to exclude any lines that have the "!" symbol. What we will see is a configuration without any comments or separators:

```
Router#show running-config | exclude !
Building configuration...

Current configuration : 868 bytes
version 12.3
service timestamps debug datetime msec
service timestamps log datetime msec
service password-encryption
service udp-small-servers
service tcp-small-servers
hostname Router
boot-start-marker
boot-end-marker
enable password 7 1445475BBE
```

Stopping the --More-- prompt

When you show running or starting configurations, you'll get a prompt when the router thinks it has filled your terminal screen. This prompt is --More--. And it means that the router wants you to hit a key before it displays more information. While this feature is extremely useful, sometimes you don't want this prompt to appear. For example, if you are writing a script to capture the configuration output, the --More-- prompt can be intrusive.

This feature is easy to disable. With the terminal length command, you can set the number of lines that your terminal can display. This number is what the router uses to calculate when to prompt. If you set this value to 0, the prompting is disabled for the entire session.

```
Router#terminal length 0
```

Erasing a Stored Configuration

The following command deletes the startup configuration. Obviously, this is not a very frequently used command. For example, you might delete the startup configuration if you were retiring your router.

```
Router#erase startup-config
```

Saving a Configuration to a Network Server

The following commands save the running configuration or the startup configuration to a server on the network, using TFTP, RCP, or SCP:

```
Router#copy running-config tftp            (for TFTP)
Router#copy running-config rcp             (for RCP)
Router#copy running-config scp://user@ip   (for SCP)
Router#copy startup-config tftp            (for TFTP)
Router#copy startup-config rcp             (for RCP)
Router#copy startup-config scp://user@ip   (for SCP)
```

3

Basic Router Configuration

Managing a handful of routers quickly becomes a large task, and managing thousands of routers is even worse. You can minimize your administrative burden by configuring your routers carefully, completely, and consistently. I strongly recommend that you use every helpful item possible—even if the configuration item is not required. Every moment spent doing configuration groundwork translates into many hours saved when you are troubleshooting or performing maintenance tasks. When you try to solve a network problem at 2 A.M., the importance of properly configured routers becomes painfully clear.

This chapter covers most of the configuration items that make routers more manageable and easier to tame.

Setting the Router Name

The examples in this book use "Router" as the router's name. That's fine for examples, but a bad idea in real life. Eventually, a router should be given a name. To set the router name to "Sphinx", use the hostname command:

```
Router(config)#hostname Sphinx
Sphinx(config)#
```

The router instantly responds by updating the prompt to reflect the new router name. The name can be up to 254 characters long, but don't use a name so long that you can't type it comfortably.

It's a good practice to follow a naming convention for your routers. With a logical, consistent naming scheme, it's easy to remember a router's name, or guess the name if you've forgotten it. For example, let's say that your router names all start with "rtr", followed by the city initials, followed by a number. Then, late one night when you're staring at a blank terminal screen trying to remember the name of the backbone router in New York, you can type *rtr-ny-01* and be reasonably confident that you've guessed correctly.

Don't use underscores (_) in router names. They are hard to type, often lead to confusion, and aren't legal in Domain Name System (DNS) names. Use a hyphen (-) instead. Similarly, avoid mixing upper- and lowercase. Instead of "routerOneNewYork," use "router-one-newyork." The router won't care, but your users will!

Setting the System Prompt

By default, the router uses its hostname as the prompt; the hostname is "Router" if you haven't defined it explicitly. It's often a good idea to put other useful information in the prompt by using the prompt command. For example:

```
Sphinx(config)#prompt %h:%n%p
Sphinx(config)#exit
Sphinx:5#
```

We've used three escape sequences to set the prompt to the hostname (%h), followed by the command number (%n), followed by the appropriate prompt character for the current command mode (%p). The escape sequences for the prompt command are listed in Table 3-1.

Table 3-1. Prompt variables

Escape sequence	Meaning
%%	Percent character
%h	Hostname of the router
%n	TTY number for this EXEC session
%p	Prompt character: either > for user level or # for privileged level
%s	Space character
%t	Tab character

The no prompt command returns the router to the default prompt.

Configuration Comments

It's a good idea to keep your routers' configuration files on a server somewhere. You can then modify the configuration files using a convenient text editor and upload the files to your routers as necessary. One advantage to this procedure is that you can include comments within your configuration files. A comment is any line beginning with an exclamation point. For example:

```
!
! This is a comment.
!
```

You can also type comments when you are configuring the router from the command line, but comments are never saved as part of the router's configuration. Therefore, when you try to view or save the router's configuration, the comments are gone.

The Enable Password

The enable password secures the privileged mode, which is required for all commands that change the router's configuration. Configuring the enable password therefore keeps people with general access to your router from changing the router's configuration. It takes only one person with enough knowledge to be dangerous to take down your whole network, so securing the privileged (enable) mode is always the right thing to do.

To set the password, use the enable password command:

```
Router(config)#enable password not2secure
```

The password is now set to not2secure. Once the password is set, the router prompts you for the password before it enters privileged mode.

By default, passwords are stored in clear text, which means that anybody who can find your router configuration file or watch you list the configuration on the console can see the enable password. The command service password-encryption (with no arguments) configures the router to store the password in an encrypted form.

Chapter 15 discusses better ways to manage passwords and authentication.

Mapping Hostnames to IP Addresses

Like all network equipment, routers work naturally with numeric IP addresses. However, using IP addresses isn't convenient for humans—including network administrators. It is much more convenient to work with hostnames. Like any other network host, routers implement DNS and can use DNS to look up IP addresses. But the use of DNS presents a problem in a routing environment. If the router can't access the Internet, it can't look up addresses; one reason that the router might not be able to access the Internet could be a routing problem; and if the router is configured to use DNS but can't access the Internet, you will have trouble using the commands needed to diagnose and fix the problem.

There is a good halfway point, however. Like other network hosts, the router can maintain a host table, and you can place any IP addresses that appear in your configuration in the host table. You can then use DNS to look up any hostnames that aren't actually involved in the router's configuration. This will make it easier to understand the output from show commands or to use commands such as ping to check your network connectivity.

IP Host Tables

The ip host command builds and maintains the router's host table. This command takes a hostname, followed by one or more IP addresses. You can have up to eight IP addresses per hostname.

```
ip host pyramid 10.10.1.3
ip host sphinx 10.10.1.2 10.10.1.4 10.10.1.5
```

Deleting a host requires you to type the entire hostname and IP address over again!

```
no ip host pyramid 10.10.1.3
no ip host sphinx 10.10.1.2 10.10.14 10.10.1.5
```

Enabling DNS

The Domain Name System (DNS) reduces the need for host entries—although, as I said before, you should have explicit host entries for any IP addresses that appear in your configuration. DNS is enabled by default; to enable it explicitly, use the command ip domain-lookup. To configure DNS, you must specify one or more name servers and the domain name to be used to complete unqualified names (typically, your own domain name). A typical configuration looks like this:

```
! Specify the DNS servers
ip name-server 10.10.9.1
ip name-server 10.10.9.2
!
! Set the name for unqualified hostnames
ip domain-name your-domain.com
```

To disable DNS lookups, use the no form of the command:

```
no ip domain-lookup
```

To re-enable DNS lookups, leave off the no keyword:

```
! Enable DNS lookups
ip domain-lookup
```

Use the show hosts command to view the cached hostnames and the DNS configuration:

```
Router>show hosts
Default domain is your-domain.com
Name/address lookup uses domain service
Name servers are 10.10.9.1 10.10.9.1

Host              Flags       Age Type  Address(es)
Foxtrot           (temp, OK)  18   IP    10.10.1.3
sphinx            (temp, OK)  18   IP    10.10.1.2
```

Setting the Router's Time

The router's internal clock is set with the clock set command. This command is not a configuration command (i.e., you must be in enable mode to give it, but you don't need to give the configure terminal command) and is not stored in the router's configuration. The time is in military (24-hour) time. For example:

```
Router#clock set 13:00:00 20 jun 1999
```

In addition to setting the time itself, you need to set the time zone using the clock timezone command. This command is part of the router's configuration. For example, a router on the east coast of the United States would have the line:

```
Router(config)#clock timezone EST -5
```

-5 is the UTC (Coordinated Universal Time) offset for the Eastern time zone.

Now that the time and time zone have been set, one final configuration item exists: in most places, you want to observe Daylight Savings Time. The following command tells the router to use Daylight Savings Time in the Eastern time zone:

```
Router(config)#clock summer-time EDT recurring
```

The Calendar Versus the Clock

High-end Cisco routers have a calendar that is separate from the system clock. The calendar runs continuously, even if the router is off. After the calendar has been set, the system clock automatically sets itself every time the router is booted. The following commands set the router's calendar and set the clock's time from the calendar time. The calendar set command simply sets the time and is not stored in the router's configuration.

```
Router#calendar set 12:10:00 5 September 2004
Router#clock read-calendar
```

Configuring NTP

The Network Time Protocol (NTP) is available in IOS Versions 9.21 and above. This protocol uses an NTP server to synchronize the router's time with other clocks on the network. Configuring NTP is as simple as setting the address of an NTP server. There are several NTP servers on the Internet for your use; your ISP may have its own NTP server.

```
clock timezone EST -5
ntp server 10.10.1.5
```

When you enable NTP, a new command called ntp clock-period appears in the router's configuration. (If you do a show running-config, you will see it in there even if you didn't enter it.) This command is set automatically by the NTP software and it is best to leave it alone.

 Did you allow an NTP server on the gateway router's access list? If NTP is not working after issuing these commands, check the gateway router's access list.

On a high-end router, we add a command to the configuration to tell the router to update its internal clock with the NTP time:

```
clock timezone EST -5
clock update-calendar
ntp server 10.10.1.2
```

A high-end router can also be the NTP server for the network. To use the router as an NTP server, add the following commands to the configuration. These commands tell the router to use the internal calendar for NTP time:

```
clock timezone EST -5
clock calendar-valid
ntp master
```

Never use the ntp master command on a router that is participating in NTP over the Internet. It will declare the router as a stratum 1 NTP server. Not only will the router no longer change its own time based on NTP information it learns, but it might disturb other NTP hosts on the Internet.

Enabling SNMP

It should be obvious that since you're trying to manage a network, you should be able to use the network to help manage your network equipment. That's the goal of the Simple Network Management Protocol (SNMP). This protocol enables network-management stations to gather information from network nodes. Network nodes can be almost anything, ranging from the simplest bridge to the largest router, and even including software running inside the servers. Virtually all modern network equipment includes an SNMP agent, which is the software that communicates with the management station. Network-management stations can run commercial management software, or they can use homegrown tools.

I will not try to give an introduction to SNMP, nor will I talk about management software.[*] In this section, I'll briefly describe how to configure the SNMP agent in a Cisco router. If you're not using SNMP, you can skip this section—though you should certainly investigate what SNMP can do for you.

By default, SNMP access is not enabled. To enable SNMP, use the command:

```
snmp-server community name mode access-list
```

The parameters are as follows:

name

> The community string the management station will use to ask for information. This string acts like a password. SNMPv1's implementation is insecure because the string travels across the network in clear text. Anyone snooping on your network will be able to see the community string pass back and forth. To improve security, use the access-list option.

mode

> Either RO for read-only access (unprivileged) or RW for read-write access (privileged). RO means that the management station can read information about the router but can't change anything; RW allows the management station to use SNMP to change the router's state. SNMP management stations typically use different community strings for read and write operations.

access-list

> The name or number of a standard access list to control SNMP access. The router responds only to SNMP requests from hosts that are on the access list. Note that you can apply different access lists to different modes. For example, your RW (read-write) access list might allow only a small number of hosts, while your RO (read-only) access list might allow many more hosts. See Chapter 7 for access list commands.

---

[*] For more information about SNMP, see *Essential SNMP* by Douglas Mauro and Kevin Schmidt (O'Reilly).

It's a good policy to set up different community strings for read-only and read-write access and to give the read-write community string only to a few trusted people. If you enable SNMP, make sure that you change the community strings from their default values, not only on your router but on any other hosts you are monitoring. Almost all vendors configure their SNMP devices to use public as the default community string, so it is the first thing an outsider trying to break into your network will try. You should also use access lists to restrict which hosts can use SNMP to interact with your router.

Here is a simple configuration that allows basic SNMP access:

```
! Set up public access with a community string of "not-public"
snmp-server community not-public RO
!
! Set up privileged access with a community string of "not-secure"
snmp-server community not-secure RW
```

Basic
Configuration

Now, we add some security. We allow public SNMP access only from the 10.10.1.0 network and allow privileged SNMP access only from host 10.10.1.35:

```
! Enable public access and apply access-list number 1
snmp-server community not-public RO 1
!
! Enable privileged access and apply access-list number 2
snmp-server community highly-secure RW 2
!
! Access-lists (See chapter 7 for syntax and usage)
access-list 1 permit 10.10.1.0 0.0.0.255
access-list 2 permit 10.10.1.35
```

There's one thing left to configure for basic SNMP capabilities. A trap is an asynchronous message generated by an SNMP agent and sent to an SNMP management station. SNMP defines a small number of standard traps, but traps can also carry vendor-specific (and even site-specific) information. To use traps, you must define the address of the management station that will receive them, plus a community string that will be sent with the traps; most SNMP management stations ignore traps that don't have an appropriate community string. Here's how to configure a Cisco router to send traps:

```
! Specify what SNMP management station will receive our traps
! Our community string is "little-secure"
snmp-server host 10.10.1.2 little-secure traps
```

The management station, if it is configured properly, will know what to do with the traps when they arrive.

There's a lot more you can do with SNMP configuration, but this is enough to get you started.

Cisco Discovery Protocol

The Cisco Discovery Protocol (CDP) is tremendously helpful when configuring a wide variety of Cisco equipment. It allows you to see what the adjacent routers or switches are, as well as their configured protocols and addresses.

CDP is enabled by default on most available interfaces. (There are a few exceptions, such as ATM interfaces.) This protocol automatically detects neighbor Cisco devices that are directly connected. The following command enables CDP globally:

    cdp run

To disable CDP, use the no form of the command:

    no cdp run

You can disable CDP on particular interfaces by using the no cdp enable command in interface configuration mode.

CDP can display useful information about other routers or switches that are directly connected:

```
Router>show cdp neighbors
Capability Codes: R - Router, T - Trans Bridge, B - Source Route Bridge
                  S - Switch, H - Host, I - IGMP

Device ID      Local Intrfce    Holdtme    Capability  Platform  Port ID
switch1          Eth 0          162          T S         1900     AUI
router2          Eth 0          176          R           4000     Eth 0
```

To learn even more about your neighbor device, use the command show cdp neighbors detail, which will give you much more information, such as the IP addresses of the interfaces.

Disable CDP on any router that is directly connected to the Internet or to another site that you don't trust (e.g., a customer site). CDP can be considered a security risk because it provides information to outside devices. It doesn't provide much information, but there's no reason to give any information to potential intruders.

System Banners

A router maintains a number of standard messages for communicating with users. These messages are typically associated with the process of logging into the router. For example, a user is typically shown a "message of the day," followed by a login banner, followed by the login prompt itself. After a successful login, the user is usually shown an "exec banner"; in the special case of a reverse telnet connection (see Chapter 4), the user is shown the "incoming banner" rather than the exec banner. In other words, for a typical console session, you would see:

```
This is the message of the day banner. (motd banner)
This is the login banner.               (login banner)
User access verification

Password:    (not echoed)
This is the exec banner. (exec banner)
Router>      (user mode prompt)
```

Each banner configuration statement has the same format: *banner-type # message #*. The pound character (#) represents the delimiting character of your choice and marks the beginning and end of your message. You cannot use the delimiting character inside the message body. For example, this command sets the message of the day:

```
Router(config)#banner motd #  Router will be rebooted today for maintenance.
#
```

Messages can contain blank lines and line breaks, as in the following example:

```
Router(config)#banner motd $
Enter TEXT message.  End with the character '$'.

Router will be down until tomorrow.

I guess we should have planned it better.
$
Router(config)#
```

Creating Banners

To create a banner of any type, use the banner command followed by the type of banner and the message:

```
Router(config)#banner motd # message #
Router(config)#banner login # message #
Router(config)#banner exec # message #
Router(config)#banner incoming # message #
```

Disabling Banners

Normally, once banners are defined, they are displayed. You can't disable a banner; you must delete it with the no form of the banner command:

```
Router(config)#no banner incoming
```

Unlike the other banners, the exec and message-of-the-day banners can be disabled on individual lines by using the no exec-banner and no motd-banner commands:

```
Router(config)#line 5
Router(config-line)#no exec-banner
Router(config-line)#no motd-banner
```

An unusual side effect is that disabling the exec banner also disables the message-of-the-day banner; disabling the message-of-the-day banner has no effect on the exec banner. To re-enable either of these banners, give the exec-banner or motd-banner command.

4

Line Commands

Cisco routers make a fairly basic distinction between the characteristics of a serial line (which you might want to think of as "physical" characteristics) and the characteristics of the protocols running over the line. The physical characteristics of a line are configured by the line command (and various commands that follow it) and include items such as parity and port speed. The high-level protocol characteristics are configured by the interface command (and the commands that follow it); these characteristics include IP addresses and other properties.

The line command can configure:

- The router's console port (CTY)
- The router's asynchronous ports (TTYs), used for dial-in and dial-out modem connections
- The router's auxiliary port (AUX), used for backup modem connections
- Telnet, SSH, and rlogin connections to the router ("virtual terminals" or VTYs)

The line Command

The line command specifies which line or group of lines you want to configure by entering the line configuration mode. It doesn't actually do the configuration; it is followed by other commands that set up the specific properties you want. Here's the syntax of the line command:

```
line [aux | console | tty | vty] starting-line-number ending-line-number
```

The possible line types are aux, console, tty, and vty. These line types are discussed individually in this chapter. The following example shows how to use the line command to configure some properties of the router's console interface:

```
Router>enable                      Enter the privileged command
                                   mode
Router#config terminal             Enter configuration mode
Router(config)#line console 0      Select the console line
```

```
Router(config-line)#exec-timeout 30     Set the timeout to 30 minutes
0
Router(config-line)#exit                Exit the line configuration
                                        mode
Router(config)#exit                     Exit the configuration mode
Router#
```

If you want to apply line commands to more than one line, you can specify the starting and ending numbers of a group of lines. For example, say you want to apply the command exec-timeout to TTY lines 5 through 10. Instead of typing this command five times, you can configure the entire group with one line command:

```
Router(config)#line tty 5 10
Router(config-line)#exec-timeout 30 0
```

Absolute and Relative Line Numbering

When you're typing the line command, you give it "relative" line numbers: the first TTY is tty0,* the first virtual terminal is vty0, and so on. This numbering scheme is intuitive and convenient. Internally, the router uses an absolute numbering scheme to keep track of the lines. It would be nice if you could ignore the router's internal bookkeeping, but a number of commands use absolute line numbers when reporting information about a line's status.

Absolute line numbers are calculated by their location on the router, in the order of CTY, TTY, AUX, and then VTY. The console port is first; its absolute line number is zero (0). The TTY ports are next, starting at absolute line number 1 and continuing for the number of TTY lines on the router. If you have eight TTY ports, absolute numbers 1 through 8 will be the TTYs on your router. Next is the AUX port, whose absolute line number is the last TTY number plus 1. Finally, the VTYs begin at the AUX port's number plus 1. Table 4-1 clarifies absolute and relative line numbering.

Table 4-1. Absolute and relative line numbers

Line type	Absolute number	Relative number
Console (CTY)	0	0
TTY1	1	1
TTY2	2	2
TTY3	3	3
...	...	...
TTYn	n	n
AUX	$n+1$	0
VTY0	$n+2$	0

* On some routers, like the 2600, TTY numbering depends on the placement of modules on the router's chassis. On a device such as this, TTY numbers don't necessarily start at 0; depending on how modules are installed, they might start at 32 or some other number. Likewise, the AUX port may be 65, depending on card placement.

Table 4-1. Absolute and relative line numbers (continued)

Line type	Absolute number	Relative number
VTY1	$n+3$	1
VTY2	$n+4$	2
VTY3	$n+5$	3

To view this table on the router, use the command show users all. The first column of the output shows the absolute line number, followed by the line type, followed by the line's relative number:

```
Router>show users all
       Line    User      Host(s)              Idle Location
     0 con 0                                  00:00:00
     1 tty 1             incoming          6 10.3.21.229
     2 tty 2             incoming          6 10.3.21.229
     3 tty 3             incoming          6 10.3.21.229
     4 tty 4                                  00:00:00
     5 tty 5                                  00:00:00
     6 tty 6                                  00:00:00
     7 tty 7             incoming          3d13h 10.208.8.103
     8 tty 8             incoming          3d13h 10.208.8.103
     9 tty 9             incoming          3d13h 10.208.8.103
    10 tty 10            incoming          3d08h 10.226.76.6
    11 tty 11            incoming          3d08h 10.226.76.6
    12 tty 12            incoming          3d08h 10.226.76.6
    13 tty 13                                 00:00:00
    14 tty 14                                 00:00:00
    15 tty 15                                 00:00:00
    16 tty 16                                 00:00:00
    17 aux 0                                  00:00:00
  * 18 vty 0             idle              0 10.10.187.204
    19 vty 1                                  00:00:00
    20 vty 2                                  00:00:00
    21 vty 3                                  00:00:00
```

The Console Port

Each router has one console port. This port always has line number 0. You make a connection to the console port by attaching a standard RS232 cable, as shown in Figure 4-1. This cable is often shipped with your router.

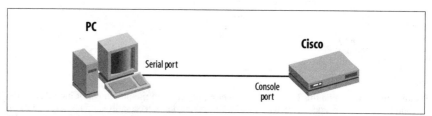

Figure 4-1. Console cable connection

You can use any VT100 terminal-emulation program to talk to the router; just select the correct PC serial interface (the one the console cable is plugged into) and then hit the Enter key a few times. The router responds by starting an EXEC session, which is the process within the router that provides the command-line interface. The default settings for the port are 9600 baud, 8 databits, no parity, and 1 stop bit. If you changed any of these defaults on the device, you will have to change the settings on your terminal program to match.

Using the line commands, we can define and control access to the console port. Here is a basic configuration:

```
Router#config terminal
Router(config)#service linenumber
Router(config)#line console 0
Router(config-line)#location Building-2A
Router(config-line)#exec-timeout 30 0
```

The location command identifies the router's location to the users. The command service linenumber displays the location information automatically to the user upon login. This information can be useful when you are administering your routers. Next, we add a basic security measure: a timeout. If the console port is idle for more than 30 minutes, the session automatically closes. You do not want the session active all the time in a real environment. If you forget to log out, someone might come in after you and modify the router's configuration!

A little more security can be achieved by adding a user login:

```
Router(config)#username bob password letmein
Router(config)#line console 0
Router(config-line)#login local
```

These commands provide only minimal security; for more effective security measures, see Chapter 15.

Virtual Terminals (VTYs)

VTYs are logical connections from the network to the router; these are typically telnet, SSH, or rlogin connections. When a user telnets to a router from the network, as in Figure 4-2, the router starts an EXEC process to handle this connection.

Figure 4-2. VTY connections

Although no physical link is associated with a virtual terminal, VTYs are configured just like normal TTY lines. VTYs are enabled once they are configured. If you do not configure any VTYs, then logical connections, such as telnet, cannot be made to your router from the network. Here is a VTY configuration example:

```
Router(config)#line vty 1
Router(config-line)#login              Must be enabled for login
access
Router(config-line)#exec-timeout 30 0  Set the timeout to 30 minutes
Router(config-line)#password letmeinhere  Set one password for telnet
access
Router(config-line)#transport input ssh  Allow only ssh access
Router(config-line)#access-class 10 in   Apply access list 10 to this
line
Router(config-line)#exit
Router(config)#access-list 10 permit host 10.10.1.2
```

This example shows a semi-secure configuration for a VTY terminal. We set a timeout for 30 minutes and apply only one password. We then use the transport input command to define the protocols that are allowed to use this line; in this case, we are allowing only ssh access. (If you want to be less secure, you can use telnet instead of ssh.) The access-class command applies an access list to this interface. We won't explain access lists here; in this example we use a simple access list to permit access from the host at address 10.10.1.2.

 You should configure all your VTYs in the same manner, because there is no way to predict which VTY a user is going to receive when he telnets into the device.

Asynchronous Ports (TTYs)

TTYs are asynchronous connections between the router's async interfaces and serial devices (modems). If you are connecting modems to your router or access server for dial-up or dial-out connections, you will need to configure the TTY ports.

The TTY ports correspond directly to async interfaces. Therefore, whenever you configure a TTY line, you will probably also configure the corresponding interface. If you plugged a modem into async port 1, you would use TTY1 to configure all the hardware aspects of the connection between the router and the modem, and the interface Async1 would configure the protocol. (The interface commands are defined in Chapter 5.) Figure 4-3 demonstrates the possible modem configuration on a router or terminal server.

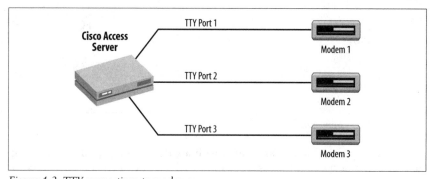

Figure 4-3. TTY connections to modems

Here is an example of a modem configuration on TTY port 3:

```
! Select line 3
line tty 3
  ! Tell the router to use its local username list
  login local
  ! This line is for dial-in access only
  modem dialin
  ! The speed of the serial connection is 115200 bps
  speed 115200
  ! Use hardware flow control
  flowcontrol hardware
  ! The type of modem is autoconfigured by the router
  modem autoconfigure discovery
```

The configuration isn't difficult to read. The router, which is some sort of terminal server, maintains its own list of usernames and passwords (login local); the modem is used only for dial-in; the serial connection between the modem and the router is set to 115200 baud; hardware flow control is used; and the modem is configured by the router.

The Auxiliary (AUX) Port

The router's auxiliary (AUX) port functions as a backup async port. It is most commonly used as a backup console port, but it can also be used as a dial-up port for remote router management and many other functions. It doesn't have the performance of an asynchronous line; its speed is often limited (particularly on older routers), and it does only per-character I/O, which creates a high CPU load if used continuously.

Figure 4-4 shows how you might use the AUX port as a backup for a T1 line. If the T1 connection goes down, Router 1 automatically dials Router 2 using the modem connected to the AUX port. Obviously, the speed of the backup link is not comparable to the T1 connection, but it does provide some level of backup support.

Figure 4-4. Using an AUX port as a backup connection

The following configuration examples show how to use the AUX port as backup connection. This example uses many commands that are well beyond the scope of this chapter; they are included here to make the configuration complete. The comments describe some of the more advanced commands; for more information about PPP and dial-on-demand routing, see Chapter 12.

```
! Configure the primary (T1) interface, with async 4 as a backup.
! See Chapter 5 for info on interface configuration.
```

```
!  See Chapter 12 for the dialing commands
interface serial0
  ip address 10.10.1.1 255.255.255.0
  backup interface async 4
  backup delay 10 1
!
! The AUX line translates to the async 4 interface.
interface async 4
  ip address 10.10.1.2 255.255.255.0
  dialer in-band
  dialer string 410-555-5555
  dialer-group 1
  async dynamic routing
!
! Build our dialer lists.
dialer-list 1 protocol ip permit
chat-script script1 " " "atdt 410-555-5555" timeout 60 "connected"
!
! Finally, configure the AUX port using the line commands.
line aux 0
  modem chat-script script1
  modem inout
```

show line

To display the status of a line, use the command show line. This is not a privileged command and can be executed by any user. On an eight-port terminal
server, show line gives output like this:

```
Router>show line
   TTY TYP     Tx/Rx       A Modem  Roty AccO AccI  Uses    Noise    Overruns
     0 CTY                 -    -      -    -    -     0        0       0/0
     1 TTY     9600/9600   -    -      -    -    -     3      542       0/0
*    2 TTY     9600/9600   -    -      -    -    -     1        0       0/0
     3 TTY   38400/38400   - RIisCD   -    -    -     1        0       0/0
I    4 TTY   38400/38400   - inout    -    -    -    25        0       0/0
I    5 TTY   38400/38400   - inout    -    -    -  3940        0       0/0
I    6 TTY   38400/38400   - inout    -    -    -  1483        0       0/0
I    7 TTY   38400/38400   - inout    -    -    -   364        0       0/0
I    8 TTY   38400/38400   - inout    -    -    -    12        0       0/0
```

Table 4-2 describes the fields in this report.

Table 4-2. Fields in a show line display

Column	Meaning
1st column	I = line is idle; * = line is active.
TTY	Actual line number.
TYP	Type of line: CTY (console), AUX, TTY, VTY, LPT.
TX/RX	Transmit and receive baud rates for this line.
A	Autobaud (automatic baud rate detection) is active.
Modem	Type of modem signal configured for this line (callin, callout, cts-req, dtr-act, inout, RIisCd).
Roty	Rotary group configured for this line.

Table 4-2. Fields in a show line display (continued)

Column	Meaning
AccO, AccI	Access lists for this line, both output and input (see access-class in Chapter 17).
Uses	Number of connections made to this line since the router was booted.
Noise	Number of times noise was detected on this line. Can be used to gauge line quality.
Overruns	Number of buffer overruns that have occurred on this line, in the format *hardware/software*. Hardware overruns occur when the hardware receives data from the software faster than it can process it. Software overruns occur when the software receives data from the hardware faster than it can process it. A bad cable could cause overruns.

You can retrieve more detailed information by selecting a single line:

```
Router>show line 5
  Tty Typ     Tx/Rx     A Modem  Roty AccO AccI  Uses   Noise   Overruns
A  5 TTY  38400/38400   - inout    -    -    -   3969     0      0/0

Line 5, Location: "", Type: ""
Length: 24 lines, Width: 80 columns
Baud rate (TX/RX) is 38400/38400, no parity, 1 stopbits, 8 databits
Status: Ready, Active, No Exit Banner, Async Interface Active
Capabilities: Hardware Flowcontrol In, Hardware Flowcontrol Out
  Modem Callout, Modem RI is CD, Line usable as async interface
Modem state: Ready
Special Chars: Escape  Hold  Stop  Start  Disconnect  Activation
               ^^x     none   -     -       none
Timeouts:     Idle EXEC    Idle Session    Modem Answer  Session  Dispatch
              0:00:30         never                       none    not set
Session limit is not set.
Time since activation: 2:08:08
Editing is enabled.
History is enabled, history size is 10.
Full user help is disabled
Allowed transports are lat telnet rlogin mop.  Preferred is lat.
No output characters are padded
No special data dispatching characters
Modem hardware state: CTS DSR  DTR RTS
Line is running PPP for address 192.101.187.165.
0 output packets queued, 1 input packets.
 Async Escape map is 000000000000000010100000000000000
Group codes:    0
  Interface Async5: (passive, compression on)
    Rcvd:    5711 total, 4516 compressed, 0 errors
             0 dropped, 0 buffer copies, 0 buffer failures
    Sent:    5085 total, 4032 compressed,
             138729 bytes saved, 3943290 bytes sent
             1.3 efficiency improvement factor
    Connect: 16 rx slots, 16 tx slots, 1275 long searches, 765 misses
             84% hit ratio, five minute miss rate 0 misses/sec, 1 max
```

The first part of this report has the same format given in Table 4-2. However, the rest of the report goes into great detail about the line's characteristics. Table 4-3 shows what these additional fields mean.

Table 4-3. Fields in a show line for a single port

Field	Meaning
Line	TTY line number.
Location	Value of the location keyword set for this line. See location in Chapter 17.
Type	Value specified by the line configuration.
Length	Terminal display length in characters.
Width	Terminal display width in characters.
Baud	Transmit (TX) and receive (RX) baud rates.
Status	State of the line (ready, connected/disconnected, active/inactive, exit banner).
Capabilities	How or for what this line can be used.
Modem state	Control state of the modem. If not Ready, suspect a modem problem.
Special chars	Settings of characters defined for this line.
Timeouts	Timeouts as specified by the configurations.
Session limit	Maximum number of sessions for this line. Controlled by the session-limit command.
Time since activation	Time elapsed since line activation (i.e., how long the line has been considered active).
Editing	Whether command-line editing is enabled.
History	Length of the command history buffer. Set by the user with the history command.
Full user help	Whether the full-help command has been activated for this line.
Transport methods	Transport mechanisms allowed on this line. See the transport command in Chapter 17 for more information.
Character padding	See the padding command in Chapter 17.
Data dispatching characters	Whether any data-dispatching characters are configured. See dispatch-character in Chapter 17 for more information.
Line protocol	The protocol and address specified for this line.
Output/input packets	Queued packet counts for this line.
Group codes	AT group codes for this line.

Reverse Telnet

When a user telnets to a router, she is "logged on" directly to the router. Cisco adds a special twist: if you telnet to a special port on the router, the router redirects the incoming telnet connection back out a selected asynchronous line, rather than internally accepting the incoming connection. This is called *reverse telnet*. Here are two telnet commands you might give on your Unix or Windows workstation:

```
% telnet router1          Telnet directly into router1
% telnet router1 2001     Telnet to port 2001 on router1
```

The first telnet command connects to the standard telnet port (TCP port 23; remember that we're now talking about TCP ports, not the router's physical ports) and initiates a virtual terminal session with the router. The second command is tricky. It connects to TCP port 2001; the router maps this port to one of its asynchronous lines. The router performs any login requirements, then connects the telnet session to the mapped line. The mapping is simple: just subtract 2000 from the port used for the telnet connection. So in this example, the user would be connected to asynchronous line 1 (tty1). Line 2 (tty2) would be 2002, and so on. If a modem is connected to tty1, the user would be talking directly to the modem.

The only catch to this mapping is the AUX port. The number of the AUX port is the last TTY port, plus 1. So, on a router with 18 TTY ports, the AUX port would be port 2019 (the last TTY, port 2018, plus 1). On a router with no TTY interfaces, the AUX port would be port 2001.

In addition to port 2000, ports 4000 and 6000 can be used. Port 4000 plus the tty1 gives you a raw TCP port, which is usually for sending data directly to a printer. On port 2000, each carriage return is translated into a carriage return plus a linefeed. Port 6000 is just like port 2000, except it turns off the carriage-return translation.

Reverse telnet requires that the TTY line be configured to allow outbound connections. Here's how you do this:

```
Router(config)#line tty2
Router(config-line)#modem inout
```

The modem inout command allows both incoming and outgoing connections. Another way to configure the line is:

```
Router(config)#line tty2
Router(config-line)#modem callout
```

The modem callout command allows only outgoing connections.

Another useful command for reverse telnet is ip alias. This command lets you assign an IP address to a reverse telnet connection. In other words, the router associates an IP address with a reverse telnet port. If you telnet to this address, the router will connect you directly to the specified port. For example, assume that a router has an Ethernet interface with an address of 10.1.1.1. The following commands configure it to route incoming telnet connections for the addresses 10.1.1.2, 10.1.1.3, and 10.1.1.4 to asynchronous ports 1 through 3:

```
interface ethernet0
 ip address 10.1.1.1 255.255.255.0
 no shutdown
!
! Now configure our reverse telnet IP address
ip alias 10.1.1.2 2001
ip alias 10.1.1.3 2002
ip alias 10.1.1.4 2003
```

Now, when you telnet to 10.1.1.2, you will be connected to the device that is connected to port 1.

Common Configuration Items

This section summarizes the configuration items you are likely to encounter when configuring a line on a router or a terminal server.

Communication Parameters

These useful commands set the low-level physical parameters of a line. To set the line speed (baud) you can use the speed, txspeed, or rxspeed commands. For databits, stop bits, and parity, use the commands databits, stopbits, and parity, respectively. For automatic baud rate detection, use the autobaud command.

For flow control, use the flowcontrol command, which takes as arguments none, software, or hardware. In a modern environment, hardware flow control is almost always appropriate.

Transport Type

The transport command defines which protocols can be used to connect to a line. The default protocol is none, which means that no incoming connections are allowed. The command transport input telnet specifies that telnet can be used as an incoming protocol, but no other protocols are allowed.

You can also specify the preferred protocol to use after a user has connected to a line. By default, the preferred protocol is telnet. Therefore, when users are connected to the router, they can type a hostname, and the router will assume they want to telnet to a device. To disable this behavior, use the command transport preferred none.

Session Limits and Timeouts

IOS provides two ways to limit the number of ongoing sessions. To limit the number of sessions allowed on a line, use the session-limit command. To limit a session's idle time, use the session-timeout command. If the session is idle longer than the specified time, the router automatically logs the user out. Note that these commands apply to the configuration of lines and not to the router as a whole.

Special Characters and Key Sequences

IOS allows you to specify a number of special characters that control the interaction between a user and the router. The activation character is the character that starts a terminal session when it is typed at a vacant terminal. The default activation character is Enter; you can set it to another value using the activation-character command. Other special characters are the disconnect character and the hold character, both of which have no defaults. The disconnect character disconnects (terminates) a session, while the hold character pauses a session until any other key is pressed. These characters are set using the disconnect-character and hold-character commands.

All three of these commands apply to lines; the argument for each command is the ASCII value for the character. For example, to set the disconnect character for line 2 to Ctrl-d (ASCII value 4), use the following commands:

```
Router(config)#line 2
Router(config-line)#disconnect-character 4
```

5

Interface Commands

Interface configuration is one of the most fundamental aspects of getting a router online. There are many kinds of interfaces, corresponding to different physical media and lower-level protocols; some of the interface types are listed in Table 5-1. For the most part, each media type has its own configuration commands, although a few commands are common to all interfaces. The interface is where much of IP configuration takes place: it's where you set addresses and netmasks and specify how the interface interacts with the routing protocol you have chosen.

Table 5-1. Interface types

Type	Description
async	Async lines are for modem dial-in and dial-out connections. The AUX port is an async line. Terminal servers have numerous async lines for modem connections.
atm	ATM (Asynchronous Transfer Mode) interfaces are used for connections to an ATM switch. This includes DSL connections.
serial	Serial ports are often connected to CSU/DSUs for point-to-point leased lines (56k, T1, etc.).
ethernet	Ethernet ports supporting 10 megabits/second.
fastethernet	Ethernet ports supporting 10 and 100 megabits/second.
gigabitethernet	Gigabit Ethernet ports supporting 10/100/1000 megabits/second.
bri	BRI (Basic Rate Interface) for ISDN (2B + D service).
tokenring	Token ring network interfaces.
fddi	Fiber Distributed Data Interconnect.
hub	A hub that is built into the router and treated as an interface.
hssi	High-Speed Serial Interface. Supports speeds up to 52 Mbps.
loopback	A virtual interface on the router.
null	Bit bucket interface. Anything sent to this interface is discarded. Used for simple route filtering.
pos	Packet over SONET interfaces.
vlan	Virtual LAN interfaces.

Naming and Numbering Interfaces

Interfaces are configured with the `interface` command, followed by an interface name, followed by a port number. The space between the interface name and the port number is optional. For example:

```
interface serial 0      Serial port 0
interface serial 1      Serial port 1
interface ethernet 0    Ethernet port 0
interface ethernet 1    Ethernet port 1
```

On high-end routers, the interface cards are in slots; each slot has a series of ports. To specify these interfaces, use the *slot/port* naming scheme. For example, the Ethernet interface on port 5 of the card in slot 4 would be called:

```
interface ethernet 4/5
```

The `interface` command is followed by other commands that perform the actual configuration. If you're entering commands at the console, the `interface` command changes the prompt to `Router(config-if)#`.

VIP2 (Versatile Interface Processor) cards have two Ethernet ports per card. To accommodate these cards, use the syntax *card/slot/port* to specify a particular Ethernet interface. For example, Fast Ethernet card 2 on slot 1 on port 0 would be called:

```
interface fastethernet 2/1/0
```

Subinterfaces

Subinterfaces provide a way to have multiple logical configurations for the same interface; they are most commonly used in Frame Relay, ATM, and Fast Ethernet in switched environments. To specify a subinterface, add a period and the subinterface number to the regular interface name. For example:

```
interface serial 1.1
interface serial 1.2
```

On a high-end router that uses the slot/port notation, append the subinterface number to the port number:

```
interface serial 1/2.1
interface serial 1/2.2
```

Subinterface zero (0) refers to the actual interface; i.e., `serial1` is equal to `serial1.0`.

Here's a simple example that shows how subinterfaces are typically used. Frame Relay permits subinterfaces in both point-to-point and multipoint modes. Each mode can have its own IP address and subnet mask. This multiple-IP address configuration can be accomplished only with the subinterface commands:

```
interface serial 1
    no shutdown
interface serial 1.1 point-to-point
    ip address 10.10.1.2 255.255.255.0
interface serial 1.2 point-to-multipoint
    ip address 10.10.2.2 255.255.255.0
```

In this example, we apply the no shutdown command to serial 1, which includes both subinterfaces. We then assign a different IP address to subinterface 1 and subinterface 2, each with a subnet mask of 255.255.255.0.

Most commands that apply to interfaces can also be applied to subinterfaces. However, a few commands can be applied only to an interface *or* to a subinterface.

Basic Interface Configuration Commands

The following basic commands apply to just about any type of interface.

shutdown

The shutdown command disables an interface. The interface does not transmit packets after it has been shut down; all routing protocols are informed that the interface is unavailable.

```
interface serial0
  shutdown
```

Use the no shutdown command to restart an interface that has been shut down:

```
Router#config terminal
Router(config)#interface serial 0
Router(config-if)#no shutdown
```

There can be side effects to an interface shutdown. The nature of these side effects depends on the interface type. Table 5-2 shows some of the possible side effects.

Table 5-2. Possible side effects of an interface shutdown

Interface	Side effect of a shutdown
Ethernet	Drops link-status indicator to the remote hub or switch.
Serial	Drops DTR signal.
FDDI	Activates optical bypass switch.
Token ring	Removes interface from the token ring.

The shutdown command can also be applied to a subinterface. In this case, it stops protocol processing on that subinterface without affecting the other subinterfaces or dropping the entire interface.

Interface Descriptions

An interface's description shows up in the router's configuration and in the output from the show interfaces command. This description is for informational purposes only; it helps you remember the configuration of the interface. For example:

```
interface serial0
  description T1 Connection to Baltimore (Good place to document the
  circuit id!)
```

Use the no form of this command to remove the description:

```
no description
```

Setting the IP Address and Subnet Mask

Setting the IP address on an interface is fairly simple: use the `ip address` command, followed by the address and the subnet mask. For example:

```
interface ethernet0
    ip address 10.10.1.65 255.255.255.224
```

This command sets the interface IP address to 10.10.1.65 and the subnet mask to 255.255.255.224.

Secondary IP address(es)

The secondary keyword allows an interface to have more than one IP address. You can have as many secondary addresses as you like, but keep in mind that each will take processing power and will have an effect on the router. If you are using more than one secondary address, chances are you are doing something wrong with your network configuration.

For example, suppose we had an Ethernet segment with a 255.255.255.224 subnet, which allows 30 hosts per subnet, as in Figure 5-1 (before). Everything is working fine. Then one day your boss comes in and tells you to add 30 more hosts on the segment. The bad news is that there are no more Ethernet ports on your router and you need to add the new machine's addresses today.

Figure 5-1. Using a secondary IP address

After a few minutes of panic, you weigh your options. One is to resubnet the network. You would then need to change the subnet masks on every machine, which is time-consuming. Even if you are using DHCP, a massive network reorganization is bound to be disruptive for your users.

The second, easier option is to add another subnet to the Ethernet segment by using the secondary command. In the old configuration, the original subnet was 10.10.1.64 with 30 hosts. In the new configuration, we add a second subnet, 10.10.1.96, to the segment:

```
interface ethernet0
  ip address 10.10.1.65 255.255.255.224
  ip address 10.10.1.97 255.255.255.224 secondary
```

Initially, the interface was assigned the address 10.10.1.65; we could assign .66 through .94 to hosts on the segment (.95 is reserved for broadcasts). After adding the .96 subnet, we can assign addresses 10.10.1.98 through 10.10.1.126 as well; .97 is assigned to the ethernet0 interface as its secondary address. We can go a step further and add yet another subnet, 10.10.1.128, by assigning 10.10.1.129 as an additional secondary address. This gives us a total of three subnets. We can add as many secondary addresses as we want.

```
interface ethernet 0
  ip address 10.10.1.65 255.255.255.224
  ip address 10.10.1.97 255.255.255.224 secondary
  ip address 10.10.1.129 255.255.255.224 secondary
```

Some pitfalls with secondary addresses are:

- Secondary IP addresses are not supported by OSPF.
- Routing updates are not sent out to secondary subnets due to split horizon. For a definition of split horizon and how it relates to routing, see Chapter 8. However, split horizon can be disabled.
- Too many secondary IP addresses often means you are doing something wrong with your network design.
- Host broadcasts may or may not be heard by hosts on other subnets, depending on the broadcast address used by the host and the hosts' implementations.

Other Common Interface Commands

You will encounter the following commands frequently as you work with interfaces on Cisco routers:

bandwidth

The bandwidth command does not have anything to do with configuring the speed of an interface. Rather, it defines the interface speed for calculating routing metrics and other purposes. You would use this command to tell the router the interface's actual speed if for some reason the default bandwidth was not correct (for example, for a fractional T1 line, the router will use the speed of a full T1 as the default bandwidth), or to "lie" about an interface's bandwidth to influence route metric calculations and steer traffic in a particular direction. Obviously, giving the router incorrect information about an interface's bandwidth is an iffy proposition, but there are times when that's the easiest way to achieve the result you want.

ip directed-broadcasts

A directed broadcast is a broadcast that is sent to a specific network or set of networks. They are frequently used in denial-of-service attacks, in which someone outside your network tries to overwhelm it with illegitimate traffic. To reduce your vulnerability to such attacks, Cisco routers drop directed broadcasts by default. To enable forwarding of directed broadcasts, use the ip directed-broadcasts command.

ip proxy-arp

Enabling proxy ARP on an interface allows the router to respond to ARP requests for hosts that it knows about, but that aren't directly reachable by the host making the ARP request. If the router receives an ARP request for a host and the router has a route to that host, the router sends an ARP response with its own data link address to the requestor. The requesting host then sends packets to the router, who in turn forwards them on to the correct destination host.

For example, a host connected via a PPP dial-up link won't be visible to hosts connected to the router via an Ethernet. If a host on an Ethernet sends an ARP request for a host connected via PPP, the router will respond to the ARP request on behalf of the PPP host, listing its own Ethernet address as the destination. The router then takes responsibility for forwarding the packets to the PPP host.

ip unreachables

This command enables the generation of ICMP protocol unreachable messages (the default). These messages are generated when the router receives a nonbroadcast message for a protocol it doesn't recognize. This command is usually used in its negative form (no ip unreachables) and is often used on the null interface.

Now let's look at some of the specific interface types you're likely to encounter.

The Loopback Interface

The loopback interface is a virtual interface that is always up and available after it has been configured. Note that the loopback interface is not tied to the address 127.0.0.1. It's an interface like any other, and can be assigned its own address. A loopback interface is often used as a termination address for some routing protocols, because it never goes down.

Another common use of a loopback address is to identify a router. For example, say you want to find out whether a particular router is up. You know that the router has an ethernet0 interface with an IP address of 10.10.1.1. You ping 10.10.1.1 and don't get a response. Does this mean your router is down? It's possible that the router is up and that the ping reached the router on another interface, but you didn't receive a response because ethernet0 is down. To find out unambiguously whether the router is alive, you have to ping another interface. But that interface might be down, causing the same scenario to occur. To avoid this problem, you can configure the router's loopback interface with a unique address. Then, when you want to telnet or ping your router, use the loopback interface's IP address. This method ensures that you will get a response no matter how your packets reach the router.

Here's how to assign an IP address to a loopback interface:

```
interface loopback 0
    ip address 10.10.1.2 255.255.255.255
```

Other ways to use the loopback interface include:

1. Using the unnumbered command on serial links mixed with the loopback interface to eliminate wasted IP addresses on serial links.

2. Various routing protocols, such as OSPF and BGP, make use of a router ID, which should be the address of a link that is always up. The loopback interface is great for this purpose. (OSPF and BGP are discussed in Chapters 9 and 10, respectively.)

3. Use the address of a loopback interface as the IP address for all management software. The management software will test whether the router is alive by pinging the loopback interface's IP address.

The Null Interface

The null interface is the "bit bucket" or "black hole" interface. All traffic sent to this interface is discarded. It is most useful for filtering unwanted traffic, because you can discard traffic simply by routing it to the null interface. You could achieve the same goal using access lists, but access lists require more CPU overhead. If you have fairly simple filtering requirements, it may be more effective to route the offending traffic to the null interface.

There can be only one null interface (null0), and it is always configured. This interface accepts only one configuration command, no ip unreachables. All other commands for this interface are ignored.

```
interface null 0
    no ip unreachables
```

In Figure 5-2, we have networks 10.10.1.0, 10.10.2.0, and 10.10.3.0 (networks 1, 2, and 3). To keep users on network 2 (10.10.2.0) from reaching network 3 (10.10.3.0), we can add a static route on Router 2 that sends all traffic destined for 10.10.3.0 to the null interface. With this route, any traffic destined for the 10.10.3.0 network from the 10.10.2.0 network is automatically discarded.

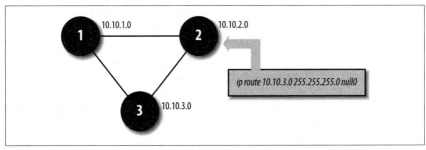

Figure 5-2. Filtering with a null interface

Here's the configuration command that creates the static route:

```
ip route 10.10.3.0 255.255.255.0 null0
```

The null0 interface is often used as part of a security strategy. Pointing unwanted routes to the null0 interface is a good way of stopping undesirable traffic. You can also use null0 to prevent routing loops when using summarized addresses.

Ethernet, Fast Ethernet, and Gigabit Ethernet Interfaces

Give an Ethernet, Fast Ethernet, or Gigabit Ethernet interface an IP address, and it's ready to go. It's a good idea to give the interface a description, but that's not required. Also, as with all interfaces, don't forget the no shutdown command. For Fast Ethernet interfaces, you can also specify the interface speed and whether it's operating at full or half duplex:

```
interface Ethernet0
   description Internal Office Network
   ip address 10.10.1.1 255.255.255.248
   no shutdown
!
interface FastEthernet1
   description Fast Network for fileservers
   ip address 10.10.1.17 255.255.255.248
   ! Set the speed to 100 (which is the default)
   speed 100
   ! Set the duplex to full
   duplex full
   no shutdown
!
interface gigabitethernet 0/0
   description our new gigabit ethernet network
   ip address 10.10.5.1 255.255.255.0
   duplex full
   no shutdown
```

Token Ring Interfaces

Defining a token ring interface is almost as simple as defining an Ethernet interface. In addition to setting the IP address, you must specify the correct token ring speed. All devices in a ring, including devices like sniffers, must be configured for the same speed or the whole ring will shut down. There is no way for a token ring device to autosense ring speed. To set the speed, use the ring-speed command. The allowable speeds are 16 Mbps and 4 Mbps.

The other common configuration command for a token ring network, early-token-release, tells the router to release the token as soon as it has sent its packet. The default behavior is to wait for acknowledgment after sending packets, then release the token. Here's a simple token ring configuration:

```
interface tokenring0
   ip address 10.10.14.1 255.255.255.0
   ring-speed 16
   early-token-release
```

ISDN Interfaces

ISDN is a standard for sending digital data over telephone lines. An ISDN link can carry two different kinds of information: the data itself, and control information for the ISDN circuit. Data channels are called B ("bearer") channels and carry either 56 or 64 kilobits/second; the control channels are called D ("data") channels.

ISDN is packaged in two different ways. BRI (Basic Rate Interface) is commonly used over residential phone lines. It provides two B channels plus a D channel, for a maximum B-channel capacity of 128 kbps. PRI (Primary Rate Interface) is more like a T1 connection—in fact, it's really just a repackaged T1 connection. PRI provides 23 B channels and 1 D channel, with a maximum rate of 1.544 Mbps in the U.S. In Europe, on E1 lines you get 30 B channels, for 2.048 Mbps.

BRI is a reasonably common technology for providing home or small-office connectivity. Although it's being displaced by technologies like ADSL and cable modems, there are many places where those technologies are unavailable. ISDN reaches almost anywhere. Let's look briefly at what you need to understand to configure a BRI connection:

- Because ISDN connections are dial-up connections, they rely on DDR (dial-on-demand routing). DDR is discussed in Chapter 12, but we'll look at a simple example in this section.

- It shouldn't be a surprise that PPP is almost always used as an encapsulation protocol for ISDN links. HDLC is also possible, but it's supported only by Cisco equipment. Using PPP guarantees compatibility with other vendors. We will use PPP in all our examples.

- An ISDN configuration requires you to know the type of switch in the telephone office at the other end of your phone line. Table 5-3 shows some basic switch types, but you should consult with your provider about which ISDN switch type it is using.

Table 5-3. Some possible ISDN switch types

Keyword	Switch type
basic-5ess	AT&T 5ess BRI
basic-dms-100	Nortel BRI
basic-ni	National BRI
primary-ni	AT&T National PRI
primary-5ess	AT&T 5ess PRI

 If you change the switch type, reboot the router to be sure that the new switch type is used.

- With most ISDN connections, you receive some number of Service Profile Identifiers (SPIDs), which are essentially phone numbers with a few extra digits. One SPID is assigned to each B channel. Therefore, you normally receive two SPIDs for a BRI line. There are some exceptions: for some AT&T point-to-point services you receive only one SPID, and with some 5ESS connections you don't always need a SPID (this is especially true for connections outside the U.S.). With PRI connections, you never receive a SPID.

- Finally, you can configure an ISDN connection to use one B channel, both B channels, or as many channels as are needed given the bandwidth requirements. The latter option is a good way to reduce the cost of your ISDN link, since most carriers charge on a per-minute basis. However, this type of configuration relies on more advanced methods of dial-on-demand routing. (See Chapter 12 for more information.) In this chapter, we'll stick with a single B channel. You can also configure the B channels to carry 56 kbps or 64 kbps.

A Simple ISDN Configuration

Following are configurations for two routers connected by a dial-up ISDN connection. The connection is activated only on demand; Router 1 dials Router 2 when it has traffic for Router 2's networks, and vice versa. The local network for Router 1 is 192.168.9.0; the local network for Router 2 is 192.168.10.0. The subnet 10.10.1.0 is used for the connection between the two routers. This example uses only one B channel for the ISDN connection, so only one SPID is used for each router.

The configuration for Router 1 looks like this:

```
hostname router1
!
! Define the switch type for the ISDN provider
isdn switch-type basic-dms100
!
! Set up the user for the CHAP authentication
! The username is the hostname of the remote system and MUST match exactly
! Passwords must also be the same on both ends of the connection
username router2 password letmein
!
! Configure the ISDN line (interface bri0)
interface BRI0
    ip address 10.10.1.10 255.255.255.0
    encapsulation ppp
    ! Configure the bandwidth for routing metric caluclations
    bandwidth 56
    ! Set the Dialer commands
    ! Define the map for the remote site
    dialer map ip 10.10.1.11 name router2 speed 56 broadcast 14105551234
    dialer hold-queue 5
    dialer load-threshold 100
    dialer-group 1
    dialer idle-timeout 300
    !
    ! SPID numbers are provided by your ISDN service provider
    isdn spid1 505555123401 5554321
    !
```

```
! PPP should authenticate with the CHAP protocol
ppp authentication chap
!
! Since we used a dialer group of 1 in the BRI configuration,
! we need to define the access list (see Chapter 7) to specify
! what traffic should cause our ISDN line to activate
dialer-list 1 list 101
!
! Our access list 101 is going to deny BROADC* TRAFFIC
! (Not actually deny, but makes broadcast traffic "uninteresting")
! Everything else is permitted
access-list 101 deny ip any 255.255.255.255 0.0.0.0
access-list 101 permit ip any any
!
! Important! Create a static route to the other side of the ISDN link.
ip route 192.168.10.0 255.255.255.0 10.10.1.11
```

Here is the configuration for Router 2. It's similar to Router 1, but without the comments.

```
hostname router2
!
isdn switch-type basic-dms100
!
username router1 password letmein
!
interface BRI0
  ip address 10.10.1.11 255.255.255.0
  encapsulation ppp
  bandwidth 56
  dialer map ip 10.10.1.10 name router1 speed 56 broadcast 15055551234
  dialer hold-queue 5
  dialer load-threshold 100
  dialer-group 1
  dialer idle-timeout 300
  !
  isdn spid1 410555123401 5551234
  !
  ppp authentication chap
  !
  dialer-list 1 list 101
!
access-list 101 deny ip any 255.255.255.255 0.0.0.0
access-list 101 permit ip any any
!
ip route 192.168.9.0 255.255.255.0 10.10.1.10
```

Serial Interfaces

Serial interfaces are interfaces that connect to a device like a CSU/DSU, which in turn connects to a leased line to complete a point-to-point connection.

Serial Encapsulation

The three primary encapsulation types for a serial interface are PPP, HDLC, and Frame Relay. Other encapsulation types include X.25, SMDS, and ATM DXI. To see which encapsulation is being used on a given interface, use the show interface command. Here are brief descriptions of the different encapsulation types:

PPP

Point-to-Point Protocol (PPP) encapsulation is specified in RFC 1331 and 1332 (and many others). Echo requests are used as keepalives; use no keepalives to disable this feature. PPP is popular and supported by all router vendors. If you are creating a serial link with two different types of routers, you will need to use PPP for the two routers to communicate.

HDLC

HDLC encapsulation provides synchronous frames and error detection without windowing or retransmission. HDLC is the default encapsulation method for a serial interface but is not supported by all vendors. If you build a serial link with a Cisco router at one end and another type of router at the other end, you might have to use PPP.

Frame Relay

In Frame Relay, your packets are handled by a switched network that provides virtual circuits between you and the sites with which you communicate. The switched network is largely invisible to you; it's managed by your Frame Relay provider. Note that Frame Relay really is an encapsulation type, not an interface type; there's no such thing as a "Frame Relay communications line." Frame Relay communication takes place over some other medium, typically a T1 line. See Chapter 6 for information on Frame Relay.

Serial T1 Connection

Here's a simple configuration for a T1 connection. PPP is used as the encapsulation method. The router at the other end of the connection would have the same configuration, differing only in its IP address.

```
interface Serial1
  description T1 to site xyz
  ip address 10.10.1.1 255.255.255.0
  encapsulation ppp
```

T1 Configuration on a 2524 with a CSU/DSU Card

Routers such as the 2524 allow CSU/DSU cards to be inserted into them. These cards eliminate the need for an external CSU/DSU. The service-module command is used for configuring these modules. In the following example, the service-module command specifies that we have purchased a full T1 from our provider and that we want to use all 24 of the T1's timeslots for this interface:

```
! configuration for a 2524 with a CSU/DSU card
interface Serial0
  description Alternet Link
  no ip address
```

```
    encapsulation frame-relay ietf
    bandwidth 1536
    service-module t1 timeslots 1-24
    frame-relay lmi-type ansi
    !
interface Serial0.1 point-to-point
    ip unnumbered Ethernet0
    ip access-group 127 in
    bandwidth 1536
    frame-relay interface-dlci 500 ietf
```

After configuring the service module, we specify Frame Relay encapsulation. We next configure a subinterface of serial0 for use as a Frame Relay connection. Chapter 6 covers Frame Relay configuration in more detail.

Channelized T1

Some routers have Multi-Channel Interface Processor (MIP) cards. These cards allow a single controller to handle more than one T1 connection by dividing the controller and a single T1 circuit into separate channels. Each of these channels supports a related serial interface. The next example shows a configuration in which a MIP card is in slot 2, port 1 of the router, which we divide into channel 1 and channel 2. We create the two channel groups by assigning some of the T1 connection's time slots to each group. (Note that not all of the time slots are used, which allows us to create more channel groups later if we want.) After that, we configure the serial interfaces for each of the channels at serial slot 2, port 1.

Notice the use of the colon after the serial command (serial 2/1:2). The number after the colon refers to the channel group number, not to be confused with a subinterface. (A subinterface is a period followed by a number, e.g., serial 1.1.)

```
! Configure Control Slot 2, Port 1
!
controller t1 2/1
    framing esf
    line code b8zs
    !
    ! Define the first channel group for this MIP card
    ! Use only 2 timeslots (1-2). Allow the speed to default to 56K
    channel-group 1 timeslots 1,2
    !
    ! Define the second channel group for this MIP card
    ! The default speed is 56K, but we want to set it to 64K
    channel-group 2 timeslots 5,7,12-15,20 speed 64
!
! Now configure the interface for channel group 1, which is serial 2/1:1
interface serial 2/1:1
    ip address 10.10.1.4 255.255.255.0
    encapsulation hdlc
!
! Now configure the interface for channel group 2, which is serial 2/1:2
interface serial 2/1:2
    ip address 10.10.2.4 255.255.255.0
    encapsulation hdlc
```

Asynchronous Interfaces

Asynchronous interfaces are almost always used to provide dial-in PPP access. The hardware configuration of the asynchronous line (parity, baud rate, etc.) is determined by the corresponding TTY line; for more information about configuring TTY lines, see Chapter 4. When you configure an async interface, you specify logical aspects of the connection. Here is a configuration for an async port with dial-in access. Each command is preceded by a comment describing the command's function.

```
interface Async1
 ! Assign IP address for the router's end of the link
 ! by assigning it the ethernet0 port
 ip unnumbered ethernet0
 ! Set the serial encapsulation to PPP
 encapsulation ppp
 ! Set the interface mode to dedicated since this is a dial-up connection
 async mode dedicated
 ! Assign the IP address for the remote connection
 peer default ip address 10.10.1.20
```

Notice that the asynchronous interface doesn't need its own IP address; it can borrow the IP address of the ethernet0 interface using the unnumbered command. However, we do need to assign an address to the PPP peer that connects through this port. That address is assigned by the peer default ip address command; in this configuration, the peer is given the address 10.10.1.20. It is also worth mentioning that the IP address of the ethernet0 interface should be on the same network as the 10.10.1.20 address.

Using the group-async Command

Here's a basic fact of life: async lines usually occur in large numbers. If you're configuring async interfaces, you're often working with a terminal server that supports many dial-in ports. Therefore, you don't want to configure each interface individually, as we did in the previous example; you want to deal with them in batches.

The group-async command allows you to configure many async interfaces without a lot of repetition. You can apply a list of configuration items to all the interfaces that belong to the group. For example, let's give async ports 1 through 5 the same configuration we set up in the previous example:

```
interface group-async 1
 ! Specify the async interfaces in this group
 group-range 1 5
 ! The configuration items to include in all interfaces
 ip unnumbered ethernet0
 encapsulation ppp
 async mode dedicated
 ! Each interface has a different IP address for the remote end
 member 1 peer default ip address 10.10.1.21
 member 2 peer default ip address 10.10.1.22
 member 3 peer default ip address 10.10.1.23
 member 4 peer default ip address 10.10.1.24
 member 5 peer default ip address 10.10.1.25
```

In this configuration, async ports 1 through 5 are configured identically. However, we need to assign IP addresses to the remote side of the interface, and these have to be unique. We use the member command to assign a different peer IP address to every interface: someone who dials in to async port 1 is assigned the IP address 10.10.1.21, and so on. We've reduced the amount of configuration work, but we still have some configuration left to do for the individual interfaces. We'll see how to go even further in the next example.

Specifying an IP Address Pool

There's an easy alternative to using the member command to assign an IP address to each async interface: we can create an *address pool*. A pool of IP addresses is a group of addresses that can be assigned dynamically to a group of interfaces, as needed. When an IP address is in use, another interface cannot use it.

To create a pool of IP addresses, use the ip local pool command. In this example, we create an address pool named ip-pool1 for the async group we defined earlier. Notice that the pool commands are not interface commands! We use a variation of the peer default ip address command to tell the router that it should assign addresses from the pool to PPP peers that connect to an interface in the async group.

```
! Create an address pool named ip-pool1 for
! addresses 10.10.1.21 through 10.10.1.25
ip address-pool local
ip local pool ip-pool1 10.10.1.21 10.10.1.25
! Now define our async group, this time using the pool
! instead of assigning a separate IP address for every interface
interface group-async 1
  ! Specify the async interfaces in this group
  group-range 1 5
  ! The configuration items to include in all interfaces
  ip unnumbered ethernet0
  encapsulation ppp
  async mode dedicated
  ! Assign the pool for this group to use
 peer default ip address pool ip-pool1
```

Using BOOTP Configuration Items for Dial-in Connections

Async interfaces can provide responses to BOOTP requests, making it much simpler for dial-in users to automate their configuration process. The async-bootp command is used to configure the responses the router will send in response to BOOTP requests. In this example, we define the BOOTP options for subnet-mask, default-gateway, dns-server, and lpr-server. They are defined even though some dial-in clients don't support them.

```
async-bootp subnet-mask 255.255.255.0
async-bootp gateway 10.10.18.196
async-bootp dns-server 10.10.18.204
async-bootp lpr-server 10.10.18.200
```

BOOTP can also provide many more aspects of the client's configuration; for more information, see the async-bootp command in Chapter 17. The show async bootp command displays the BOOTP attributes that are currently configured:

```
Router>show async bootp
The following extended data will be sent in BOOTP responses:

subnet-mask 255.255.255.0
gateway 10.10.18.196
dns-server 10.10.18.204
lpr-server 10.10.18.200
```

BOOTP does not accommodate IP pools or understand leases.

Using DHCP for IP Addresses and Dial-in Configuration Items

DHCP represents a significant advance over BOOTP in automating client configuration. It can also be used to assign addresses to PPP peers; when someone dials in, the router requests the peer address from the DHCP server. The client can then request additional configuration information from the router using DHCP, which acts as a proxy and relays the request to the actual DHCP server. The following configuration uses a DHCP server to provide the IP address and other configuration information.

```
! Configure our IP address pool to come from our DHCP server at 10.10.1.2
ip address-pool dhcp-proxy-client
ip dhcp-server  10.10.1.2
! Configure the required BOOTP information, nbns points to our WINS
! server, which in this case happens to be our DHCP and DNS server
async-bootp dns-server 10.10.1.2
async-bootp nbns-server 10.10.1.2
!
! Configure the async interface to use PPP and DHCP
interface Async1
   ip unnumbered ethernet0
   encapsulation ppp
   async mode dedicated
   peer default ip address dhcp
```

You can also use routers as standalone DHCP servers, eliminating the need for a separate server. The proxy configuration shown here is probably more common, however.

Interface show Commands

The router keeps track of lots of information about its interfaces: the number of packets sent, the number of errors, addresses, and so on. You can get most of this information by using one of the show commands.

Clearing the show Command Counters

Much of the information the router tracks is numeric, such as running counts of the number of packets that went out the interface. These counters aren't particularly

---

meaningful unless you know when the counter started counting. To clear the counters that are displayed in the `show interface` commands, use the `clear counters` command. This command does not clear the values that are retrieved from SNMP commands, but only the values reported by the `show` commands discussed in this section. Here are some typical `clear counters` commands:

```
Router#clear counters ethernet0
Router#clear counters serial0
Router#clear counters
```

The first two commands clear the counters for a specific interface; the last command clears the counters for all the interfaces.

 All counters are unsigned long integers, which means they can go up to about 4 billion before they roll over to 0 ($2^{32}-1$).

Listing All Interfaces

If you don't know what physical interfaces are available on your router, use the `show version` command. You'll find a list of interfaces at the end of its output. Here's what happens on a Cisco 2524:

```
Router>show version
...
cisco 2524 (68030) processor (revision J) with 6144K/2048K bytes of memory.
Processor board ID 08291960, with hardware revision 00000000
Bridging software.
X.25 software, Version 2.0, NET2, BFE and GOSIP compliant.
1 Ethernet/IEEE 802.3 interface(s)
2 Serial network interface(s)
FT1 CSU/DSU for Serial Interface 0
No module installed for Serial Interface 1
32K bytes of non-volatile configuration memory.
8192K bytes of processor board System flash (Read ONLY)
```

This router has one Ethernet port, two serial ports, and one built-in CSU/DSU installed on serial interface 0.

Using the show interface Commands

The `show interface` command displays protocol-specific statistics for the interface. All interfaces report both generic information and media-specific information. For example, here's what you get if you ask for information about an Ethernet segment:

```
Router>show interface ethernet0
Ethernet0 is up, line protocol is up
  Hardware is Lance, address is 0010.7b39.e28e (bia 0010.7b39.e28e)
  Description: Office Ethernet segment
  Internet address is 10.10.1.1/29
  MTU 1500 bytes, BW 10000 Kbit, DLY 1000 usec, rely 255/255, load 1/255
  Encapsulation ARPA, loopback not set, keepalive set (10 sec)
  ARP type: ARPA, ARP Timeout 04:00:00
```

```
Last input 00:00:00, output 00:00:00, output hang never
Last clearing of "show interface" counters never
Queueing strategy: fifo
Output queue 0/40, 0 drops; input queue 0/75, 0 drops
5 minute input rate 2000 bits/sec, 3 packets/sec
5 minute output rate 17000 bits/sec, 3 packets/sec
    11938498 packets input, 4102863937 bytes, 0 no buffer
    Received 60515 broadcasts, 0 runts, 0 giants, 0 throttles
    8 input errors, 0 CRC, 0 frame, 0 overrun, 8 ignored, 0 abort
    0 input packets with dribble condition detected
    12556989 packets output, 1981671402 bytes, 0 underruns
    0 output errors, 11702 collisions, 1 interface resets
    0 babbles, 0 late collision, 20150 deferred
    0 lost carrier, 0 no carrier
    0 output buffer failures, 0 output buffers swapped out
```

Table 5-4 shows how to interpret this information.

Table 5-4. Information from a show interface command

Field	Meaning
Up/down	Whether the interface is up and configured. If the interface is administratively down, the shutdown command has been applied to this interface. If the interface is down, it is not receiving any signal from the attached network cable.
Line protocol	Whether the encapsulation protocol is up or down for this interface. If your interface is up but the line protocol is down, check the encapsulation or see if the line has been unplugged.
Hardware	The type of interface (serial, Ethernet, etc.).
Internet address	The IP address and subnet mask for this interface.
MTU	The Maximum Transmission Unit for this interface (the maximum frame/packet size).
BW	The bit rate in kbps (default is 1544 for serial, 10000 for Ethernet). This value is actually the setting from the interface's bandwidth command, which is used in route metric calculations but has no other impact on the router. In particular, this value has nothing to do with the actual speed at which data is transferred.
DLY	The expected delay for a packet traversing this interface. Like the bandwidth, this parameter is used only for IGRP/EIGRP route metric calculations. Its value can be set with the delay interface command.
rely	The reliability of this link, as a number between 1 and 255. The value 255/255 indicates that the link is 100% reliable.
load	The traffic load on the segment, as a number between 1 and 255. The value 255/255 indicates that the link is at 100% of capacity. 1/255 is the lowest value.
Encapsulation	The encapsulation type for this link. For serial links, the encapsulation might be PPP or HDLC. For Ethernet, it might be ARPA.
loopback	Whether the interface is in the loopback state. If you cannot send packets across your link, you may have loopback set.
keepalive	Whether keepalives are active on this link.
ARP Type	Type of Address Resolution Protocol
Last input/last output	How long it has been since a packet was received or sent on this interface. This field is not an actual time value, but the number of hours, minutes, and seconds since the packet was received or sent. If the time exceeds 24 hours, the field overflows and asterisks are printed.
output hang	The time since this interface was last reset because of a transmission that took too long to complete. If the time exceeds 24 hours, the field overflows and asterisks are printed.

Table 5-4. Information from a show interface command (continued)

Field	Meaning
Last clearing of "show interface" counters	The time since a `clear counters` command has been run on this interface. (In other words, the time since counters were reset.)
Queueing strategy	The type of queuing that is enabled on this interface: First In First Out (FIFO), Weighted Fair Queuing (WFQ), Priority, Custom, and so on.
Output queue/input queue	The number of packets in both the input and output queues. The number is in the format "number in queue/max size of queue, number of drops."
5 minute	The five-minute average input and output rate. The rate is given in both bits per second and packets per second over the last five minutes.
packets input	Number of successful error-free packets this interface has received.
bytes input	Number of successful error-free bytes this interface has received.
broadcasts	Number of multicast or broadcast packets this interface has received.
runts	Number of packets this interface threw away because they were smaller than the minimum packet size.
giants	Number of packets this interface threw away because they were larger than the maximum packet size. Can be caused by a bad NIC card somewhere on the network.
throttles	Number of times the receiver on the port was disabled. This can occur because of buffer or processor overload.
input error	Total number of errors encountered by this interface. These errors can include runts, giants, CRC errors, overruns, ignored packets, aborts, buffer overflows, and frame errors.
CRC	The number of checksum failures encountered by this interface. A checksum failure occurs when the calculated checksum does not match the checksum sent by the sending device. Lots of CRC errors mixed with a low number of collisions on an Ethernet interface is an indicator of excessive noise, which points to cable issues.
frame	The number of frame errors encountered by this interface. These occur when a packet that is malformed or does not contain the correct number of bytes is delivered to the interface. Can be caused by cabling or duplex mismatch.
overrun	The number of overrun errors within this interface. This occurs when the low-level device driver fails to read a byte before the serialization hardware completes receiving the next byte.
ignored	The number of packets ignored by this interface. This occurs when the internal buffers are full and the interface ignores incoming packets because it has no place to store them. Can be caused by broadcast storms.
abort	The number of aborts on this interface. Occurs because of a timing problem between the router and serial device.
dribble condition detected	This counter increments every time a frame is too long. The frame is still accepted by the router.
packets output	The total number of packets this interface has transmitted.
bytes output	The total number of bytes this interface has transmitted.
underruns	The number of underrun errors on this interface. Occurs when the low-level device driver fails to provide the next byte to be serialized before the previous one has been completely transmitted. Can be caused by a device transmitting to the interface faster than it can handle.
output errors	The number of errors that occurred when this interface tried to transmit.
collisions	The number of times two hosts sent a packet at the same time; a small number is normal.
interface resets	The total number of times this interface reset due to errors.
babbles	The number of times that the Transmit Jabber Timer expired. A jabber is a frame that is longer than 1518 octets, but does not end with an even number of octets.

Table 5-4. Information from a show interface command (continued)

Field	Meaning
late collisions	The number of times a collision is detected late in the packet transmission process. This number should always be 0 on a properly configured network. If you see these, suspect a duplex setting or a hardware problem.
deferred	The number of frames that have been transmitted successfully after they had been waiting because the media was busy. Most often seen in half-duplex environments.
lost carrier	Number of times the interface lost carrier during a transmission. If you are seeing these on your interface, suspect a bad cable. (Check both sides of the connection.)
no carrier	Number of times no carrier was present on the interface. As in lost carrier, suspect a bad cable (on both sides) if you see these.
output buffer failures/ output buffers swapped out	The number of failed buffers and the number of buffers swapped out. These counters can be a normal sign of an overworked segment. It might mean that the buffers filled up and packets were dropped. If the segment isn't all that busy, look at the speed/duplex settings and see if they match the amount of traffic this interface is handling.

show interface accounting

Another interesting show command is show interface *interfacename* accounting. This command gives you a quick overview of the interfaces and their packet counts:

```
Firewall#show interface ethernet0 accounting
Ethernet0
           Protocol    Pkts In   Chars In   Pkts Out  Chars Out
                 IP   10659150   62307981   13906422 3947809402
                ARP     272756   17240212     126066    7563960
                CDP      76294   23585301     186904   57192624
```

This command displays the accounting statistics for the ethernet0 interface. It shows the packets received (Pkts In), characters received (Chars In), packets transmitted (Pkts Out), and characters transmitted (Chars Out) for each protocol. On this router, the protocols in use are IP, ARP (Address Resolution Protocol), and CDP (Cisco Discovery Protocol).

show ip interface

The show ip interface command gives you detailed information about an interface's IP configuration. The related command show ip interface brief provides a summary of the IP configuration for all the router's interfaces. Here's the result of show ip interface ethernet0:

```
Router#show ip interface ethernet0
Ethernet0 is up, line protocol is up
  Internet address is 10.200.212.1/24
  Broadcast address is 255.255.255.255
  Address determined by non-volatile memory
  MTU is 1500 bytes
  Helper address is not set
  Directed broadcast forwarding is disabled
  Multicast reserved groups joined: 224.0.0.10
  Outgoing access list is not set
  Inbound  access list is 145
```

```
Proxy ARP is enabled
Security level is default
Split horizon is enabled
ICMP redirects are always sent
ICMP unreachables are always sent
ICMP mask replies are never sent
IP fast switching is disabled
IP fast switching on the same interface is disabled
IP multicast fast switching is disabled
Router Discovery is disabled
IP output packet accounting is disabled
IP access violation accounting is disabled
TCP/IP header compression is disabled
Probe proxy name replies are disabled
Gateway Discovery is disabled
Policy routing is disabled
Network address translation is disabled
```

Table 5-5 explains each line in the output.

Table 5-5. Explanation of show ip interface output

Output	Explanation
Internet address is 10.200.212.1/24.	Gives the IP address and subnet mask that are currently set for the interface. For this interface, the network mask is /24, which is equivalent to 255.255.255.0.
Broadcast address is 255.255.255.255.	Gives the broadcast address for this interface. The default is 255.255.255.255; it can be modified with the ip broadcast-address command.
Address determined by non-volatile memory.	Specifies the source from which the IP address for the interface was retrieved.
MTU is 1500 bytes.	Specifies the Maximum Transmission Unit for this interface. This can be modified with the ip mtu command.
Helper address is not set.	The ip helper-address command sets a destination address for UDP broadcasts. In this example, it is not set. It is normally used to forward BOOTP or other UDP services to a server.
Directed broadcast forwarding is disabled.	Specifies whether directed broadcasts are enabled. Directed broadcasts are normally disabled, but can be enabled using the ip directed broadcasts command. See the description of directed broadcasts earlier in this chapter.
Multicast reserved groups joined.	Lists the multicast group joined by this interface.
Outgoing access list is not set.	Shows the outgoing access list for the interface. The ip access-group *number* out command sets the access list.
Inbound access list is 145.	Shows the incoming access list for the interface. The ip access-group *number* in command sets the access list.
Proxy ARP is enabled.	Gives the status of proxy ARP, either enabled or disabled. See the ip proxy-arp description earlier in this chapter.
Security level is default.	Gives the IPSO security level for this interface.
Split horizon is enabled.	Gives the status of split horizon on this interface, either enabled or disabled. Use the command ip split-horizon to enable it. This topic is covered in Chapter 8.
ICMP redirects are always sent.	Shows the status of ICMP redirects, either allowed or not. The ip redirects command enables them.

Table 5-5. Explanation of show ip interface output (continued)

Output	Explanation
ICMP unreachables are always sent.	Specifies whether ICMP unreachable messages are sent from this interface. The `ip unreachables` command enables this feature.
ICMP mask replies are never sent.	Specifies whether ICMP mask replies are sent. The `ip mask-reply` command enables this feature.
IP fast switching is disabled.	Specifies whether the fast-switching cache for outgoing packets is enabled. Use `ip route-cache` to enable it.
IP fast switching on the same interface is disabled.	Specifies whether the fast-switching cache for packets on the same interface is enabled. Use `ip route-cache` to enable it.
IP multicast fast switching is disabled.	Specifies whether the fast-switching cache for outgoing multicast packets is enabled. Use `ip mroute-cache same-interface` to enable it.
Router Discovery is disabled.	Specifies whether router discovery is enabled. Use the `ip irdp` command to enable it.
IP output packet accounting is disabled.	Specifies whether IP output packet accounting is enabled. If enabled, this line will also describe the accounting threshold. Use the `ip accounting` command to enable it.
IP access violation accounting is disabled.	Specifies whether access violation accounting is enabled. Use the `ip accounting access-violations` command to enable it.
TCP/IP header compression is disabled.	Specifies whether TCP header compression is enabled. Use the `ip tcp header-compression` command to enable it.
Probe proxy name replies are disabled.	Specifies whether the IP probe proxy is enabled. Use the `ip probe proxy` command to enable it.
Gateway Discovery is disabled.	Specifies whether gateway discovery is enabled. Use the `ip gdp` command to enable it.
Policy routing is disabled.	Specifies whether policy routing is enabled. The `ip policy` command enables it.
Network address translation is disabled.	Specifies whether NAT is enabled on this interface. The `ip nat` command enables address translation. However, it requires some extensive configuration. For more information, see Chapter 13.

Here's the output from show ip interface brief. The output is fairly straightforward, except for the meaning of the Method column. This column is the same as the Address determined by non-volatile memory field in Table 5-5.

```
Router#show ip interface brief
Interface    IP-Address     OK? Method Status                Protocol
Ethernet0    10.200.212.1   YES NVRAM  up                    up
Ethernet1    10.200.210.30  YES NVRAM  up                    up
Serial0      unassigned     YES unset  administratively down down
Serial1      unassigned     YES unset  administratively down down
```

6

Networking Technologies

In this chapter, we'll cover some networking technologies that you are likely to encounter, such as frame relay, ATM, cable, DSL, and VoIP. ISDN also fits into this grouping but is covered separately in Chapter 12.

Frame Relay

In the past decade, Frame Relay has become a popular wide-area network (WAN) switching method. Building a WAN by creating virtual circuits inside a provider's Frame Relay network has become a much more attractive option than ordering leased lines between the locations you want to connect. Instead of paying for all those leased lines, you just pay for access to the provider's network. Of course, there is still a leased line to the provider, but it is typically fairly short—much shorter than a leased line between your end locations. It's easy to order the bandwidth you need for each link; furthermore, Frame Relay allows you to reserve a guaranteed minimum bandwidth (called the "committed information rate" or CIR) but lets you use as much bandwidth as is available on the network. In fact, you don't need the same speed circuits at all your sites. For example, your corporate headquarters might use a DS-3 (45-Mbps line), while your regional offices all have T1 lines.

At the physical level, a Frame Relay connection looks just like a serial interface—because it is. A standard leased line (typically a T1 line) connects your site to the Frame Relay provider. Although it's more complex than a simple serial interface, the complexity comes mostly from mapping the IP addresses of the nodes on your network into Data Link Connection Identifiers (DLCIs), which are the Frame Relay equivalent of addresses.

Important Frame Relay Terminology

Before we look at some basic Frame Relay configurations, we need to go over a few important topics and terms. Figure 6-1 shows two routers that connect to each other through a Frame Relay network.

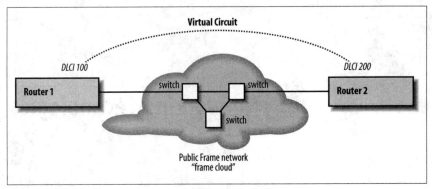

Figure 6-1. A virtual circuit on a Frame Relay network

Here are some terms you'll need to understand when working with Frame Relay:

Frame cloud

When connecting to a public frame network, you only know about your points of entry to the network; the interior of the network (the "cloud") is invisible to you. The network itself is often called a cloud, because you can't see what happens to your packets after they enter it.

Virtual circuit (VC)

A virtual circuit is a logical connection created by the frame provider from Point A to Point B across a frame cloud.

Data Link Connection Identifier (DLCI)

A DLCI is a value assigned by the frame provider to identify a virtual circuit. In other words, it's the Frame Relay equivalent of an address. DLCIs are unique only locally. That is, your router will have a unique DLCI for each virtual circuit it uses from one Frame Relay provider. However, as far as the Frame Relay provider is concerned, DLCIs are just numbers; the provider can reuse DLCIs throughout its network.

The router maps IP addresses to DLCIs so that it can communicate with a remote router by using the appropriate DLCI. There are two ways to map a DLCI to an IP address. First, you can allow the router to discover the DLCI by using inverse ARP, which is enabled by default. Second, you can explicitly map an IP address to a DLCI.

Local Management Interface (LMI)

The LMI is based on the type of Frame Relay switch you are connecting to. Your provider will give you this information. The LMI types are Cisco, Ansi, and q933a; Cisco is the default. Note that the routers at each end of the link may have different LMI settings, because they are connected to different types of switches.

Point-to-point

A point-to-point connection is a single virtual circuit that connects two points. In Figure 6-1, Router 1 connects to Router 2 with a frame network between them. On either side of the frame cloud is a router that knows that there is only one router at the other end. This kind of configuration is similar to connecting two routers directly over a serial line.

Multipoint

In a multipoint network, a single interface is connected to multiple virtual circuits with multiple DLCIs. Each virtual circuit is still point-to-point, but many logical point-to-point connections share the same physical interface. Subinterfaces should be used for each fully-meshed portion of the multipoint network. Remember that subinterfaces use the *X.Y* notation, where *X* is the interface and *Y* is the subinterface.

There are two types of multipoint networks: partially-meshed and fully-meshed. In a fully meshed network, all the routers have direct connections to each other. In contrast, in a partially meshed network, each router is connected to at least one other router, but may not have a direct connection to all the routers in the network. For example, you might have three routers, A, B, and C; Routers B and C are connected to Router A, but do not have a direct connection to each other.

Split horizon

Split horizon is a technique commonly used in routing protocols; it means that the router will not send information about a route out the same interface from which it learned the route. Split horizon is normally used to prevent routing loops. However, it can cause problems in a partially-meshed multipoint Frame Relay network. More than one router may be listening at the other end of any interface. Therefore, we don't want to suppress route announcements. For example, assume that we have three routers (i.e., three virtual circuits) connected to our multipoint interface. If a route comes to our interface from any of those points, we want to announce the route to the other two points. If split horizon is enabled, we can't send the route out our interface because that is where the route originated. However, split horizon should be enabled on a fully meshed multipoint Frame Relay network.

Frame Relay Configuration

Here is the most basic Frame Relay configuration. We don't give the serial interface an IP address; instead, we use the unnumbered command to tell it to "borrow" the address of the ethernet0 interface. To use this command, we must tell the router explicitly that serial2 is a point-to-point interface:

```
interface serial2
  no ip address
  encapsulation frame-relay ietf
  no shutdown
interface serial2.1 point-to-point
  ip unnumbered ethernet0
```

Okay, it will probably never be that easy. So, let's use the network pictured in Figure 6-1, where Router 1 has a DLCI of 100 and Router 2 has a DLCI of 200. Here's the configuration for Router 1:

```
interface serial1
  no ip address
  encapsulation frame-relay ietf
  frame-relay lmi-type ansi
  no shutdown
```

```
!
interface serial1.1 point-to-point
   description connection to baltimore
   ip unnumbered ethernet0
   ! Give the DLCI of the local end of the virtual circuit
   frame-relay interface-dlci 100
```

And here's the configuration for Router 2. The only thing that's different is the DLCI:

```
interface serial1
   no ip address
   encapsulation frame-relay ietf
   frame-relay lmi-type ansi
   no shutdown
!
interface serial1.1 point-to-point
   description connection to new-york
   ip unnumbered ethernet0
   ! Give the DLCI of the local end of the virtual circuit
   frame-relay interface-dlci 200
```

Some notes about this configuration:

- We were forced to break up the configuration into subinterfaces because IOS does not allow us to apply the point-to-point keyword to the main interface.

- There's no IP address for serial1's main interface, since we tie the IP address to the subinterface.

- We used ip unnumbered to establish an IP address for serial1.1. This means that the interface doesn't have its own IP address; it borrows an address from one of the router's other interfaces (in this case, ethernet0). For this to work, we had to specify that the interface is point-to-point and configure both routers appropriately.

- We explicitly defined the DLCIs on each link. We are relying on inverse ARP (enabled by default) to map the IP address of the remote end of the link to the DLCI. The next section discusses how to map addresses to DLCIs in more detail.

Mapping IP Addresses to DLCIs

A key part of Frame Relay configuration is mapping IP addresses to DLCIs. This mapping can take place either explicitly or implicitly. The previous example used an implicit mapping: we simply listed the DLCI for our connection and let the router use inverse ARP to map the DLCI to an IP address. With inverse ARP, the router automatically infers the IP address of the router at the other end of the DLCI. To do so, the router waits for a packet to arrive on the DLCI. The source IP address of the packet is then associated with the remote router's DLCI, allowing the router to build a map of DLCIs and IP addresses.

The primary advantage of an implicit mapping is that you don't have to reconfigure your router if the address of the remote end changes. As your network changes, the router notices the new addresses and adjusts its tables accordingly.

All you have to do is list the DLCIs you know about. To clear any maps created by inverse ARP, use the command clear frame-relay-inarp. Inverse ARP is enabled by default.

For an explicit mapping, we would build the map by hand using the frame-relay map ip command. While this method removes the possibility of an error being made by inverse ARP, it is difficult to manage, especially if you have a large network with many virtual circuits.

The next two sections go into more detail about creating an explicit mapping and using implicit mapping in a multipoint configuration.

Explicitly mapping DLCIs

Here's how to create an explicit mapping between IP addresses and DLCIs. In the next section, we will see how to use the multipoint connection with implicit listing of the DLCIs.

```
interface serial1
  encapsulation frame-relay ietf
  frame-relay map ip 192.168.2.1 100
  ! disable inverse mapping because we no longer need it
  no frame-relay inverse-arp
```

With this configuration, DLCI 100 is mapped to IP address 192.168.2.1. We would add additional frame-relay map ip statements for any other addresses we care about. We don't need inverse ARP with an explicit mapping, so we disabled it.

Configuring a multipoint connection

With a multipoint connection, we have one serial interface connected to a Frame Relay network. However, that interface can reach multiple destinations. For example, if we need to communicate with three destinations through the Frame Relay network, as in Figure 6-2, we can create three logical interfaces on a single physical serial interface and then treat each destination as if it has its own interface.

Figure 6-2. Multipoint configuration

There are a couple of ways to configure the router for this network. The simple, laborious way is to list every virtual circuit, giving each one a point-to-point subinterface. Here's the configuration for Router 0:

```
interface serial1
  encapsulation frame-relay ietf
  frame-relay lmi-type ansi
  no shutdown
!
interface serial1.1 point-to-point
  ip address 192.168.1.5 255.255.255.252
  description connection to New York
  frame-relay interface-dlci 100
!
interface serial1.2 point-to-point
  ip address 192.168.2.5 255.255.255.252
  description connection to Texas
  frame-relay interface-dlci 200
!
interface serial1.3 point-to-point
  ip address 192.168.3.5 255.255.255.252
  description connection to Pasadena
  frame-relay interface-dlci 300
```

Let's do it again, this time using the multipoint option so we don't have to configure each virtual circuit separately:

```
interface serial1
  no ip address
  encapsulation frame-relay ietf
  frame-relay lmi-type ansi
  ! disable split-horizon
  no ip split-horizon
  no shutdown
!
interface serial1.1 multipoint
  description connection to New York, Texas, and Pasadena
  ip address 192.168.1.1 255.255.255.0
  ! List all the DLCIs and let the router figure out the mapping
  frame-relay interface-dlci 100
  frame-relay interface-dlci 200
  frame-relay interface-dlci 300
```

Once again, we listed all the DLCIs that are available for this interface. However, we pushed them all into one multipoint subinterface. The router uses inverse ARP to figure out the IP addresses for the remote end of the connection. We could also have used the frame-relay map command to explicitly map each DLCI to an IP address, but that would be much more work in a large network.

Frame Relay Traffic Shaping

With traffic shaping, we control how fast packets are sent or received on our interface (this and many other topics are described in detail in Chapter 11). But the control that frame relay traffic shaping offers is more fine-grained than this. We can shape our traffic for each virtual circuit, not just by interface. In this way, we can ensure that busy virtual circuits do not hog all the bandwidth. We can also use the FECN and BECN signals to modify our traffic shaping.

Before we look at some examples of traffic shaping, let's review a few terms:

Committed Information Rate (CIR)
> The rate at which our network is allowed to transfer packets over a frame relay network. This rate (in bits per second) is a guaranteed by our provider. We might be able to go faster than this rate, but it's not guaranteed.

Burst size (Bc)
> The committed burst size or "sustainable" burst size. Under normal operating conditions, your service provider allows you to reach this traffic level.

Interval (Tc)
> This parameter cannot be configured. The router calculates this measurement using the following formula:
>
> Tc = Bc/CIR in seconds
>
> This value is the interval (in seconds) that you send the Bc bits in order to maintain the average rate of the CIR in seconds.

Excess burst size (Be)
> The excess burst size is well outside the CIR value. It's the burst size that you can send out on your network, but the traffic is not guaranteed for delivery. Traffic that reaches this burst rate is marked for discard eligibility within the frame-relay network. At least, this is true in theory. In practice, not all carriers mark traffic for discard eligibility (DE), making DE statistics difficult to trust.

Forward Explicit Congestion Notification (FECN)
> A bit that's set within a packet to notify the receiving device that there is congestion within the frame relay network. Although, the device is receiving the packet—hence the "forward notification"—the device can still use that information when it comes time to transmit its own packets.

Backward Explicit Congestion Notification (BECN)
> A bit that's set within a packet to notify the sending device that one of its frames encountered congestion. It doesn't apply to the packet that is marked with a BECN; it's an automatic action taken after setting an FECN. The next packet that goes back to the device (hence the term "backward") is marked with BECN to notify the device that it should probably slow down its transmissions.

Enabling traffic-shaping on a frame relay link

Before we start configuring traffic-shaping on a frame relay interface, we need to use the frame-relay traffic-shaping command. We can use this command on the main interface instead of the subinterface. In this configuration, we see the standard frame relay configuration on serial0 with two frame relay virtual circuits, 100 and 200. We enable traffic-shaping on the serial0 interface.

```
interface serial0
  no ip address
  encapsulation frame-relay
  frame-relay traffic-shaping
!
interface serial0.100
  ip address 10.1.1.1 255.255.255.252
  frame-relay interface-dlci 100
!
interface serial0.200
  ip address 10.1.1.5 255.255.255.252
  frame-relay interface-dlci 200
```

Now we can enable some traffic-shaping commands. First, we'll set some CIR values with the frame-relay traffic-rate command. For DLCI 100, we want the average to be 64,000 with a peak of 128,000. DLCI 200 runs a little slower, with an average of 4,800 and a peak of 9,600.

```
interface serial0
  no ip address
  encapsulation frame-relay
  frame-relay traffic-shaping
!
interface serial0.100
  ip address 10.1.1.1 255.255.255.252
  frame-relay interface-dlci 100
  class fast-class
!
interface serial0.200
  ip address 10.1.1.5 255.255.255.252
  frame-relay interface-dlci 200
  class slow-class
!
map-class frame-relay fast-class
  frame-relay traffic-rate 64000 128000
!
map-class frame-relay slow-class
  frame-relay traffic-rate 4800 9600
```

Although we used the frame-relay traffic-rate command, which allowed us to define all the values on one line, we could have used frame-relay cir, frame-relay mincir, frame-relay be out, and frame-relay bc out commands, which accomplish the same thing. In the previous example, we had 64,000 for our average CIR rate and 128,000 for our peak rate. In this example, we'll set the max burstable size to 128,000 and our minimum cir (guaranteed rate) to 64,000. For example:

```
map-class frame-relay fast-class
  ! Set the CIR to the average rate we WANT to send out
  frame-relay cir 128000
  ! Set the mincir to the guaranteed rate from our ISP
  frame-relay mincir 64000
```

```
! Set our burst rates
frame-relay bc 16000
frame-relay be 16000
```

Adaptive shaping

Adaptive shaping allows the router to adapt its transmit rate in response to BECNs received. If any BECNs are received from by the router during the current time interval, the transmit rate is decreased by 25 percent. The rates continue to drop with each BECN until the rate reaches the guaranteed CIR rate (mincir). There can be only one rate drop per interval. Once BECNs are no longer received, the router waits for 16 time intervals to pass with no more BECNS before it starts to increase the rate again. To enable this feature, use the frame-relay adaptive-shaping becn command:

```
map-class frame-relay slow-class
  !
frame-relay adaptive-shaping becn
```

Frame Relay show Commands

Table 6-1 lists the show commands that are useful for configuring and trouble-shooting frame relay connections.

Table 6-1. Useful show commands for frame relay

Command	Displays
show interface	DLCI and LMI settings
show frame-relay lmi	LMI statistics
show frame-relay pvc	Frame relay PVC statistics
show frame-relay map	Current frame relay map information
show frame-relay traffic	Traffic statistics and information
show frame-relay route	Configured static routes for frame relay
show frame-relay svc	Current SVCs

ATM

Asynchronous Transfer Mode (ATM) is a a cell-switched network technology used for building high-speed backbones. ATM breaks data into fixed-size cells of 53 octets. Five octets are used for the cell header; the remaining 48 are available for data. The fixed size allows an ATM switch to handle the cells quickly and efficiently. An ATM switch is allowed to drop cells as necessary if the switch's capacity is exceeded. There is a mechanism for distinguishing between cells that can be discarded and high-priority cells that should not be discarded (although even high-priority cells can be discarded if there is no alternative).[*]

---

[*] An exception to this rule is AAL1 (ATM Adaptation Layer 1). In the case of AAL1, no cells should be discarded. If the switch builds the AAL1 VC, it should pass all the cells. Since this is not a book about ATM, I don't have the time or space to discuss ATM adaptation layers in detail.

Sending IP packets over an ATM network presents some interesting problems. Each packet must be broken into multiple cells, since most IP packets won't fit into 48 octets. If any of the cells are dropped, the packet won't make it through the network undamaged. Therefore, the packet will probably be re-sent (it will certainly be re-sent if it's a TCP segment). In turn, this means dumping many additional cells into a switch that is already suffering from congestion. This problem is less serious if your ATM network is designed for minimal cell loss.

To run, ATM requires special (and sometimes expensive) hardware. Some of the common ATM hardware products provided by Cisco include:

- ATM Network Processor Module (4500/4700-series routers)
- ATM Interface Processor (7500-series routers)
- ATM Port Adapter (7500-series routers)

ATM-DXI allows ATM over a non-ATM interface, such as a serial interface (like HSSI). In this configuration, you typically have an ADSU (ATM CSU/DSU) connected to a high-speed serial port on your router.

ATM Terminology

ATM is a connection-oriented protocol. A separate connection must be established for every device with which a router wants to communicate within the ATM network. These connections are called virtual circuits (VCs). VCs can be either permanent (PVCs) or switched (SVCs). PVCs are typically used for WAN connections; SVCs are typically used for LAN connections. The main difference between PVCs and SVCs is that SVCs can be created and destroyed automatically by the software. This dynamic creation of circuits makes administration a bit easier. On the other hand, PVCs are—for a lack of a better word—permanent. It's hard to imagine a wide-area network in which you wouldn't want permanent circuits between your nodes. You can think of a PVC as a leased line, while an SVC is more like a dialed phone call.

A virtual circuit is defined by two numbers, assigned by your ATM provider: a Virtual Path Identifier (VPI) and a Virtual Channel Identifier (VCI). The VPI identifies a bundle of circuits, while the VCI identifies a circuit within a bundle. It is easier to think of the VPI/VCI pair as a single parameter, like a DLCI in a Frame Relay configuration.

Before we examine our first configuration, let's look at ATM encapsulation. Several types of encapsulation are used for ATM:

aal5snap
    All traffic is on one ATM circuit.

aal5mux
    A dedicated circuit is set up for each protocol (IP, IPX, etc.).

aal5nlpid
    Works with ATM-DXI and encapsulates over Frame Relay.

Another acronym you'll see when working with ATM is LANE, which stands for LAN Emulation. In this mode, the LANE device emulates a more traditional LAN technology, such as Ethernet. We'll discuss LANE after we learn to configure ATM.

Configuring Permanent Virtual Circuits

When configuring ATM for a WAN connection, you need to:

- Assign an IP address and VPI/VCI to a PVC.
- Define the encapsulation method.
- Map a remote IP address (the IP address of the router at the other end of the circuit) to the PVC.

The last step (mapping an IP address to the PVC) is required only for static mappings. Just as in Frame Relay, there are two ways to manage IP addressing: statically map the IP address of the remote router or let the router figure out the mapping itself with inverse ARP. I'll show examples of both configurations.

ATM commands tend to be hardware-specific, partly because ATM is present on products ranging from low-end DSL routers to high-end routers to ATM switches. I've tried to choose examples and commands that work in most environments, but it's important to check the documentation for your router.

Configuring an ATM interface with static IP mapping

Figure 6-3 shows our ATM connection. You will see that we are again using subinterfaces to implement ATM; in more advanced settings, using subinterfaces simplifies the configuration. Here is the configuration for Router 1:

Figure 6-3. An ATM configuration

```
interface atm0
  no shutdown
!
interface atm0.1
  ! assign our interface's IP address
  ip address 10.10.1.1 255.255.255.0
  ! Create PVC 20 with a VPI of 0 and a VCI of 60
  atm pvc 20 0 60 aal5snap
  map-group atm-map1
!
map-list atm-map1
ip 10.10.2.1 atm-vc 20 broadcast
```

This configuration is simple. We have all three steps that we mentioned earlier:

- We assigned a local IP address to our ATM interface.
- We created a PVC with the atm pvc command. This command creates PVC 20, which has a VPI of 0 and a VCI of 60, and uses the aal5snap encapsulation

method. The number we assign to the PVC (20) is used only for referring to the PVC in other parts of the router configuration; it has no other significance.

- We mapped a remote IP address to the PVC with the map-list command. The broadcast option within the map list is important because it allows routing-protocol updates to propagate to remote hosts. Most routing protocols rely on multicasts or broadcasts, for which ATM has no native support.

Configuring an ATM interface with dynamic IP mapping

Instead of statically mapping an IP address to the PVC, we can use inverse ARP and let the router figure out the mapping itself. Inverse ARP is not the default for ATM; we need to configure it explicitly. The following configuration is identical to the previous one, except that it uses inverse ARP instead of static mapping. As a result, the configuration is noticeably shorter, even on a simple network. For larger networks, the savings could be significant.

```
interface atm0
  no shutdown
interface atm0.1
  ip address 10.10.1.1 255.255.255.0 inarp 5
  atm pvc 20 0 60 aal5snap
```

The inarp 5 option tells the interface to use inverse ARP for mapping the IP address to the PVC and to set the time period for inverse ARP (the amount of time between inverse ARP requests) to five minutes. The default time period is 15 minutes. Now the system can respond to changes in remote addressing without a change to the ATM configuration; the router will notice any changes on the ATM network the next time it sends an ARP request. Therefore, at most five minutes will elapse before the router notices the change and adjusts its address mappings.

Configuring Switched Virtual Circuits

SVCs are created automatically by software. However, the software that creates and destroys SVCs requires two PVC channels for communication; these must be created explicitly, like any other PVC. One PVC channel uses VPI 0 and VCI 5 for signaling; this channel uses the encapsulation method qsaal. The other required PVC exchanges management information and uses VPI 0 and VCI 16, with ilmi encapsulation. Both of these channels are associated with the "main" ATM interface and not with any subinterfaces.

Another important piece of the SVC picture is the Network Service Access Point (NSAP) address. This address is something like a MAC address for ATM networks. That is, it's a higher-level concept than a physical address (essentially, the VPI/VCI pair) and is persistent: it doesn't change, even though the VPI/VCI to reach any destination will change as the circuit is created and destroyed. The process for creating an SVC operates like this:

1. A device is ready to communicate with another device, so it sends the NSAP address of the destination device to the network signaling channels.
2. The device waits for the circuit to be created.
3. The device can now use the newly created circuit.

NSAP addresses are unique 20-octet hex values.

For example, consider the network in Figure 6-3. If we were to add a router named Router 3 with an IP address of 10.10.3.1, an SVC configuration for Router 1 might look like this:

```
interface atm1
  ! Configure the two signaling channels that are required for SVC
  atm pvc 1 0 5 qsaal
  atm pvc 2 0 16 ilmi
!
interface atm1.1
  ! Our interface's IP address
  ip address 10.10.1.1 255.255.255.0
  atm nsap-address 22.0011.01.FF1111.00FF.0000.AAAA.1111.1111.1111.11
  atm map-group atm-map
!
map-list atm-map
ip 10.10.2.1 atm-nsap 22.0011.01.AAAAAAA.00FF.0000.AAAA.1111.1111.AAAA.11
broadcast
ip 10.10.3.1 atm-nsap 22.0011.01.BBBBBBB.00FF.0000.AAAA.1111.1111.BBBB.11
broadcast
```

With this configuration, circuits to 10.10.2.1 and 10.10.3.1 will be created on demand. There are only a few new concepts here: the signaling channels, the nsap-address for the interface, and the static mapping of the NSAP addresses for the end routers. The configuration for the signaling channels is simple and is the same on every ATM router that uses SVCs. Similarly, the NSAP addresses are fairly easy to understand if you can deal with the long hex numbers; your biggest problem will be typing them correctly. That's a big problem, particularly in a large network: we don't want to be typing dozens of 20-byte hex numbers, which may change as the network is reconfigured. What makes the problem even worse is that this map must be replicated on all the routers in your network. The only address excluded from the map is the NSAP address of the router itself. So for a network of 10 routers, you would have to type 90 of these 20-octet NSAP addresses.

It would be great if we didn't need to configure those long NSAP addresses for every IP address on our network. But since ATM isn't a broadcast protocol, there is no way for it to learn about the possible remote NSAP addresses. However, you can do dynamic mapping if your network has an ATM ARP server. This server knows about all the NSAP addresses for your network, which means a router can query the server for NSAP addresses. This is considered Classical IP. If we had an ATM ARP server on our network, our configuration could be reduced to this:

```
interface atm1
  ! Configure the two signaling channels that are required for SVC
  atm pvc 1 0 5 qsaal
  atm pvc 2 0 16 ilmi
interface atm1.1
  ! Our interface's IP address
  ip address 10.10.1.1 255.255.255.0
  atm nsap-address 22.0011.01.FF1111.00FF.0000.AAAA.1111.1111.1111.11
  !
  ! Now just supply the NSAP address of the ARP server
  atm arp-server nsap 22.0011.01.AAAAAAA.00FF.0000.AAAA.1111.1111.AAAA.11
```

Now we have an SVC configuration with dynamic addressing.

ATM ARP server

Since having an ATM ARP server on our network greatly simplified our configuration in the previous example, I'll show you how to configure one. Only one ATM ARP server should exist for each logical IP subnet of an IP network. The configuration of an ATM interface as an ARP server is as simple as this:

```
interface atm0
    ip address 10.10.1.2 255.255.255.0
    atm esi-address 3031.11ba.1181.20
    atm arp-server self
```

We could have used the atm nsap-address command instead of the atm esi-address command. However, the End System Identifier (ESI) is preferred because it allows the ILMI address registration to work better should a router move within the ATM network.

Configuring with DXI

Using the ATM-DXI mode basically means that you have an ADSU connected to a high-speed serial port on your router. The ADSU in turn connects to the ATM switch and acts like a CSU/DSU. Configuration is not as complicated as having the native ATM interface: we're dealing with a familiar serial interface, and almost all of the ATM-specific complexity is handled by the ADSU. In other words, since we are using outside hardware to communicate via ATM, there is only so much we can do. Consider the following configuration:

```
interface serial 1
    ip address 10.10.1.1 255.255.255.0
    encapsulation atm-dxi
    ! configure for VPI of 1 and VCI of 2
    dxi pvc 1 2 mux
    ! map the IP 10.10.1.2 to VPI 1 and VCI 2
    dxi map ip 10.10.1.2 1 2 broadcast
```

The line dxi pvc 1 2 mux gives us a permanent virtual circuit with a VPI of 1 and a VCI of 2. It also sets the mux option, which means that only one protocol is to be used over this PVC. That protocol is defined in the next line, which maps the remote IP address 10.10.1.2 (i.e., the address of the router at the other end of this circuit) to the VPI/VCI pair. The broadcast option allows routing-protocol updates to be sent over this PVC.

ATM show Commands

The show commands listed in Table 6-2 are useful for configuring and troubleshooting ATM.

Table 6-2. Useful show commands for ATM

Command	Displays
show atm map	All configured static ATM maps
show atm vc	Information about ATM virtual connections
show atm interface	ATM-specific information for an interface

LAN Emulation (LANE)

LAN Emulation (LANE) allows an ATM network to emulate legacy LAN types, specifically Ethernet and token ring. In other words, LANE provides the advantages of ATM's larger bandwidth, which allows you to scale your network while keeping already deployed LAN applications. LANE allows you to run any broadcast LAN protocol (IP, IPX, AppleTalk, etc.) across the ATM network without the applications knowing about it. Among other things, LANE provides a way to accommodate broadcast traffic (required for LANs) over ATM, which is not a broadcast technology.

LANE works by encapsulating the LAN packets inside the ATM frames, which results in a smaller MTU because the packets are restricted by the MTU size of the emulated protocol. LANE resolves LAN MAC addresses to ATM addresses through the use of an Emulated LAN (ELAN), which is similar to a virtual LAN (VLAN). Four components are part of every LANE configuration. They are:

LAN Emulation Client (LEC)
> The LEC is the ATM client that is participating in the ELAN. A device has one LEC for each ELAN in which it is participating. However, if a device participates in multiple ELANS, it can have multiple LECs (that's plural LEC, not LECS!). Devices that would use the LEC are ATM hosts, LAN switches, and routers. The LEC handles all the communications to the ELAN servers and establishes a mapping to and from LAN MAC addresses and the ATM NSAP addresses. Once the mappings are correct, the LEC opens a private virtual circuit directly to the remote device's LEC.

LAN Emulation Configuration Server (LECS)
> The LECS contains the database that lists each client (LEC) and the ELAN to which the client belongs. There is one LECS per ATM network. The clients (LECs) query this server to get the NSAP address (ATM address) of the LES (the server) for their assigned ELAN.

LAN Emulation Server (LES)
> The LES maps MAC addresses to NSAP addresses and maintains a database showing which clients are currently active in the ELAN. There is one LES for every ELAN.

Broadcast Unknown Server (BUS)
> The BUS forwards unknown, broadcast, and multicast data to the clients in the ELANs. There is one BUS for every ELAN. Because the LES and BUS are so closely related, they are configured as one entity within the router. From this point on, we will refer to the both of them as one object called the LES/BUS.

LANE configuration notes

The following notes will help you to understand LANE configuration:

- The LECS is configured on the major ATM interface.
- The LES and LEC of the same ELAN can be configured on the same subinterface.
- Clients of different ELANs cannot be configured on the same subinterface.

- Servers of different ELANs cannot be configured on the same subinterface.
- For one client on an ELAN to talk to a client on another ELAN, a router must be present to route between the two ELANs.
- Using automatic NSAP addresses is much easier than supplying a unique NSAP address for every ELAN client. The router will automatically generate a unique NSAP address by itself with the command lane auto-config-atm-address. We use this command throughout the following examples.

Configuring the LECS

Because the LECS needs to know where the LES for each ELAN is located, and because your network may have a large number of ELANs, the LECS configuration can be quite lengthy. All of these examples include the ATM signaling configuration—if ATM isn't working, you're not going to get anywhere with LANE.

In this configuration, we establish two ELANs in the LECS database. The database is called elandatabase1 and the ELANs are elan1 and elan2.

```
! Define the NSAP address of the LES for each and every ELAN
lane database elandatabase1
  name elan1 server-atm-address 47.00918100000000613E5D0301.00603E0DE841.01
  name elan2 server-atm-address 47.00918100000000613E5D0301.008876EF0356.08
  ! We set a default ELAN for LECs that don't know which ELAN they should
  ! join
  default-name elan1
!
! Set up the major ATM interface signaling
interface atm 0
  atm pvc 1 0 5 qsaal
  atm pvc 2 0 16 ilmi
  ! Attach the LANE database that we created to the interface
  lane config elandatabase1
  ! Tell the LECS to use automatic addressing
  lane auto-config-atm-address
```

Configuring the LES/BUS

We could configure the LES/BUS on the same server as the LECS. In this case, we configure it on a separate router. Once again, we are going to configure the signaling for ATM. Then we'll configure the LES/BUS with the lane server-bus command. Finally, we'll configure the interface as a client of the ELAN. If you don't make the LES/BUS a client of the ELAN, the router will function as the LES/BUS but will not be able to do any routing for the ELAN. Making it a client of the ELAN ensures that the router can be the LES/BUS for the ELAN and also route traffic for the ELAN.

```
! Set up the major ATM interface signaling
interface atm 0
  atm pvc 1 0 5 qsaal
  atm pvc 2 0 16 ilmi
  ! Set up LANE default addressing
  lane auth-config-atm-address
!
```

```
! Configure the LES/BUS on a separate subinterface
interface atm0.1
   ip address 10.1.1.1 255.255.255.0
   ! Configure this router as LES/BUS
   lane server-bus ethernet elan1
   ! Also make it a client of the ELAN
   lane client ethernet elan1
```

Configuring the LEC

The previous example used the `lane client` command to make the LES/BUS a client of the ELAN. This case is much simpler: we will make the router a LANE client and assume that the LES/BUS is on another device.

```
! Set up the major ATM interface signaling
interface atm 0
   atm pvc 1 0 5 qsaal
   atm pvc 2 0 16 ilmi
   ! Set up lane default addressing
   lane auth-config-atm-address
!
! Configure the LES/BUS on a separate subinterface
interface atm0.1
   ip address 10.2.1.1 255.255.255.0
   lane client ethernet elan2
```

LANE show commands

The commands in Table 6-3 are useful for configuring and troubleshooting LANE.

Table 6-3. Useful show commands for LANE

Command	Displays
show lane default-atm-addresses	The automatically assigned ATM address of each LANE component
show lane client	All LANE information for each LANE client configured on an interface

DSL

Digital Subscriber Line (DSL) has become one of the standard home and business broadband connection methods (the other method, cable, is described in the next section). To enable DSL you need to have a DSL connection to your home or office from an ISP that is servicing your area. This assumes, of course, that DSL is available in your area. Since DSL is distance restricted, if you are a certain distance—which varies by the type of DSL service and the provider—from the nearest telco switch, you can't get a DSL line. If you are outside the service area, check periodically with providers because the technology is improving and more areas are able to get DSL connections.

Most ISPs provide DSL modems as part of their service. If you happen to get a Cisco router, it's mostly likely going to have a built-in DSL modem such as an 800 series. Other options include the 1700, 2600, and 3600 series with an ADSL WIC card installed.

In our sample configurations, we use Network Address Translation (NAT) and Point-To-Point Protocol over Ethernet (PPPoE). Chapter 13 covers NAT configurations in great detail. I am including NAT here because it's such an important part of a DSL (or cable) Internet connection. Most DSL providers use PPPoE, which provides authentication, encryption, and compression. Running PPPoE on our router eliminates the need for running PPPoE on all our network clients. (For example, if you did not have a router and only had a PC and a DSL modem, you would have to run PPPoE software directly on the single PC.) By putting PPPoE on the router, the router handles all the authentication and networking to the ISP. Our local PCs require no extra software or network configuration, just basic networking configurations.

Configuring Our DSL Client Router

The configurations of a DSL connection differ depending on the router type and the way that your provider implements the connection. For example, some providers use bridging rather than a dialer method. In the example we are using, our provider has given us a PVC of 1/100. For more information on what a PVC is, see the ATM section earlier in this chapter.

To configure the router, we enable Virtual Private Dialup Network (VPDN) and configure the virtual dialer interface, and the ATM interface itself. VPDN configures the router so that PPPoE requires "dial-in" in order to connect. Why is PPPoE configured as dial-in? Because it's the same PPP protocol that's used for authentication in dial-up connections, in this case running *over Ethernet* (which is the "oE" in PPPoE). The virtual dialer interface handles the IP address of the connection, the PPP authentication, and outside NAT information. Configuring the ATM interface simply entails applying the PVC value given to you by your ISP.

```
!
hostname ournetworkrouter
!
! Enable VPDN
vpdn enable
no vpdn logging
!
! VPDN group pppoe requires "dialin". These commands configure
! a VPDN group called "pppoe" that is used to establish the PPPoE sesions
vpdn-group pppoe
   ! this command means that our router is the PPPoE client
   ! that is requesting to establish a PPPoE session
   request-dialin
   protocol pppoe
!
! Create a "virtual" interface that handles the "dialing" to the
! ISP's DSL line. This virtual interface is used on the ATM0 interface
interface Dialer1
   ip address negotiated
   ! if you have a static IP address, replace the negoatiated line above
   ! with the provided IP address.
   encapsulation ppp
   ! Adjust Mtu because 1492 + PPPoE headers = 1500
   ip mtu 1492
```

```
    ip nat outside
    dialer pool 1
    ppp authentication pap callin
    ! Our ISP gave us the username of bob1 and password of notsecure
    ppp pap sent-username bob1 password notsecure
!
interface FastEthernet0
    description Our local network interface
    ip address 10.10.1.1 255.255.255.0
    ip nat inside
!
! Our ISP gave us a PVC of 1/100. Depending on your ISP,
! you might get a different PVC
interface ATM0
    description our DSL interface
    no ip address
    no atm ilmi-keepalive
    dsl operating-mode auto
!
interface ATM0.1 point-to-point
  pvc 1/100
      protocol pppoe
      ! Tie this interface to the virtual Dialer Interface
      pppoe-client dial-pool-number 1
!
! Configure NAT to use access-list 1 as the "source" traffic
! to perform NAT on
ip nat inside source list 1 interface Dialer1 overload
!
! Our default route is the virtual dialer interface
ip route 0.0.0.0 0.0.0.0 dialer1
!
! Used in the ip nat command
access-list 1 permit 10.10.1.0 0.0.0.255
```

If your ISP says to use CHAP for authentication, replace the PPP PAP commands
with these:

```
    ppp authentication chap callin
    ppp chap hostname <username>
    ppp chap password <password>
```

Troubleshooting a DSL Connection

Troubleshooting DSL involves looking at several different things: the PPP layer
(layer 4), the Ethernet layer (layer 3), the ATM layer (layer 2), and finally, the DSL
physical layer (layer 1).

After checking your local Ethernet connections by pinging your local devices from
your router and vice versa, you can begin looking at your PPP layer with debug
vpdn pppoe-events.

If the PPPoE layer is being established, which you will be able to see from the debug output, try to look at the VPDN sessions with the show vpdn command:

```
# show vpdn session all

session id: 1
local MAC address: 0001.aacc.b57a, remote MAC address: 0001.bbed.abb0
virtual access interface: Vi1, outgoing interface: AT0, vc: 1/100
    16499 packets sent, 203455 received, 163424 bytes sent, 2032934 received
```

In this output, we can see the packets sent and received, which shows that we are making a connection to our DSL link.

After we've verified that information, we check our local network. For example, is our local routing working? Is our default route set to the correct address? Are our network devices set with the correct default route (our router local interface IP)? Is NAT working correctly?

Cable

Cable is becoming an increasingly popular broadband medium. Its main limitation is that you are effectively sharing the network (on the other side of your router) with everyone in your neighborhood, which is normally unnoticeable because most ISPs place bandwidth restrictions on your cable modem. These restrictions keep one person in the neighborhood from using up all the bandwidth. However, if you ever notice that cable speeds seem to decline at about three in the afternoon and then pick back up later in the evening, it's not your imagination.

In this example, we are going to provide the same sort of scenario as we did with the DSL sections, which is a standard connection using NAT. The router provides some of the cable modem settings automatically during power-up. These commands, like cable-modem channel and cable-modem mac-timer, used to be available for user configuration. However, since IOS 12.1(2)T, these commands are strictly for DOCSIS use.[*] In other words, they appear in the IOS configuration but you are unable to change them because they are automatic settings that the router learns from your provider.

We enabled routing on this cable modem by issuing the command no cable-modem compliant bridge, which allows us to use routing instead of the default bridging.

```
! Our local network interface
interface ethernet0
  ip address 10.10.1.1 255.255.255.0
  ip nat inside
!
! Our cable modem interface
interface cable-modem0
  ! Some older cable modems might report an actual IP address here
  ! instead of "negotiated"
  ip address negotiated
```

---

[*] The Data Over Cable Interface Specification is the standard for communication between routers and cable modems. It is designed to be self-configuring.

```
ip nat outside
! ISP Provided settings.
cable-modem downstream saved channel 555000000 42 1
cable-modem mac-timer t2 80000
! Put our cable-modem into routing mode instead of bridging mode
no cable-modem compliant bridge
!
! apply our nat access-list to the cable-modem0 interface
ip nat inside source list 1 interface cable-modem0 overload
!
ip routing
ip classless
!
! Default route
ip route 0.0.0.0 0.0.0.0 172.32.30.1
!
access-list 1 permit 10.10.1.0 0.0.0.255
```

VoIP

Voice over IP (VoIP) might seem out of place among the other topics in this chapter. However, VoIP is becoming a major networking application and it's appearing everywhere. VoIP is running over Ethernet, frame relay, ISDN, ATM, DSL, cable, and other high-speed connections. When thought about that way, this is a great place to discuss it.[*]

VoIP works by encoding analog voice signals into IP packets. These packets are sent across the network and reassembled and decoded at the other end back into analog sound. Since these packets take the same paths and share the same bandwidth with all other networking applications, it's important to configure quality of service (QoS) for voice traffic. Interruptions in voice conversations are extremely annoying (but thanks to cell phones, customers are far more tolerant than they used to be). With proper QoS settings, you can assure that voice traffic gets the highest priority. In other words, if you're sending a large file across your cable modem link, your VoIP phone will keep working without dropping bits of your sentences. Well, that's the hope anyway. For details on configuring QoS, see Chapter 11. If your setup is straightforward (that is, your only high-priority traffic is VoIP), take a look at AutoQoS, described at the end of that chapter.

VoIP Protocols

There are a few methods of VoIP configuration including H.323, Media Gateway Control Protocol (MGCP), and Session Initiation Protocol (SIP).

H.323

The H.323 standard was the first standard for call control on Cisco VoIP devices. H.323 defines a set of protocols and components that support VoIP as well as

---

[*] I cover VoIP briefly here, but if you are involved with setting up VoIP, you will doubtless want a book dedicated to that topic. I recommend *Switching to VoIP* by Theodore Wallingford (O'Reilly).

real-time video. Specifically, H.323 uses Q.931 for signaling, H.245 for negotiation, and Registration Admission and Status (RAS) for session control. Other components of a VoIP setup under H.323 are the gatekeeper, gateway, MCU, and terminal. Here's a primer.

Gatekeeper
A device that manages other nodes on the H.323 network. There can only be one gatekeeper per zone. The gatekeeper's jobs include call setup, call waiting, and related services.

Gateway
A device that allows users of conventional phone lines to communicate with VoIP users.

MCU
MCU stands for Multipoint Control Unit, a device that is sometimes integrated into the gateway or gatekeeper. An MCU is a multi-call conference mixer, which allows conference calls to take place.

Terminal
An end user device such as an IP phone or PC phone.

MGCP

The MGCP standard followed H.323. It defines a distributed system that appears to outside networks as a single VoIP gateway. In order to configure MGCP, we need to define a call agent, which handles the call routing and setup. With Cisco VoIP, the call agent is an application called CallManager. In the MGCP example later in this chapter, we will show the IOS commands for configuring access to the CallManager. However, the CallManager itself is a sophisticated application with its own GUI and configuration; covering it in detail is beyond the scope of this book.

SIP

Session Initiation Protocol is an open standard that is quickly gaining popularity not only because it's an open standard but because it combines voice and Internet traffic and can coexist and interoperate with already deployed H.323 networks. Another reason that it's popular is that it is an ASCII (text) based protocol, just like HTTP and SMTP. For addresses, SIP uses an address of the format *username@gateway*, where the *username* can be an actual username or an E.164 address, the type of address used by ATM networks.

SIP is a peer-to-peer protocol with two types of peers: User Agent Clients (UAC) and User Agent Servers (UAS). The UAC is a client application that initiates the SIP request. And the UAS is a server application that responds to a request and answers on behalf of the user. Most SIP endpoints are capable of performing both UAC and UAS functions. SIP uses these requests and responses to set up a connection between the two endpoints.

For a list of all Cisco devices that support SIP, see *http://www.cisco.com/warp/public/cc/techno/tyvdve/sip*.

VoIP Terminology

Before we go into our examples, there is some more terminology that we need to discuss. Some of these terms we have already used.

PSTN
> The Public Switched Telephone Network is the regular legacy phone system.

POTS
> Plain Old Telephone Service, also known as analog phone service.

PBX
> Private Branch Exchange. A private telephone network used inside an organization.

FXS
> Foreign Exchange Station. An interface for directly connecting individual devices such as phones, faxes, or a regular PBX telephone system to the router.

FXO
> Stands for Foreign Exchange Office. It is an interface that connects to the phone company. Basically, this connection is for trunk lines. For example, when you connect a PBX to the phone company, you plug the lines into the FXO ports on the PBX. The line is a trunk line, which handles many connections at once.

E&M interfaces
> Oddly enough, E&M can stand for "ear and mouth" signaling, "recEive and transMit", or "Earth and Magnet." E&M interfaces are analog trunk connections to different systems, such as a PBX to a Central Office (CO).

RTP
> RTP or Real-Time Transport Protocol is used for transmitting audio and video across IP networks. RTP is usually used for the actual call data in VoIP after all the signaling and call handling have been established. For example, SIP might be used to initiate the call between two endpoints, but RTP actually handles the voice transmission during the call.

Examples

Here are a few examples that cover some of the possibilities of VoIP on Cisco devices. The first example is an FXO gateway to the PSTN, which uses nothing more than the dial-peer connections to each office. A dial peer defines the connection type between the source and destination endpoints. Each connection that makes up a VoIP connection might have different "call legs" over the entire connection, and each leg of the connection might be a different dial-peer connection. For example, you might have source and destination POTS phones that are connected to routers over an IP network. The connection from the source POTS phone to the first router is a POTS dial peer. The connection from the source's router to the destination router over an IP network is a VoIP dial-peer. And finally, the connection from the destination router to the destination POTS connection is another POTS dial-peer.

FXO Gateway to PSTN

This example provides a way for our VoIP users in Office 1 to reach PSTN users at Office 2, which is outside their VoIP network (see Figure 6-4). Office 1 has a VoIP phone, which is assigned the number 1-410-555-0001. Office 2's router is directly connected to the PSTN via an FXO interface. The phone we want to be able to connect to at Office 2 has a phone number of 1-555-555-0001. With this configuration, the VoIP phone can call the POTS phones in Office 2 using the IP connection between the two routers, and vice versa.

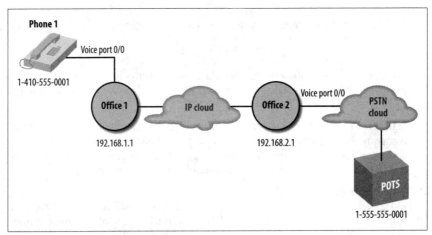

Figure 6-4. FXO to PSTN Example

Here's the configuration for Office1's router :

```
hostname Office1
!
! Configure voice port 0/0
dial-peer voice 1 pots
 destination-pattern 14105550001
 port 0/0
!
! Office2 phone number
dial-peer voice 2 voip
 ! office2's phone number
 destination-pattern 15555550001
 ! The target is office2's router
 session target ipv4:192.168.2.1
 ip precedence 5
!
! Our wan connection
interface serial1
 ip address 192.168.1.1 255.255.255.0
```

Here's the configuration for Office2's router :

```
hostname Office2
!
! Configure voiceport 0/0
dial-peer voice 1 pots
```

```
    destination-pattern 15555550001
    port 0/0
    !
    ! Configure office1 voip
    dial-peer voice 2 voip
     ! office 1's phone number
     destination-pattern 14105550001
     ! the target is office1's router
     session target ipv4:192.168.1.1
     ip precedence 5

    ! Configure serial interface 0
    interface serial0
     ip address 192.168.2.1 255.255.255.0
```

H.323 call routing

This example uses the same two-office setup as the previous example. However, in this case, each office is considered a zone and we configure call routing between the two zones. Each office has a gatekeeper machine and gateway machine. Office 1 will use 555-555-0002 and Office 2 will use 666-555-0002 as phone numbers. Each office has one phone plugged into port FXS 1/0 on each gateway device.

The gatekeeper's job is to group gateways into logical zones and perform call routing decisions between them. The gateway manages connections between the PTSN and our H.323 network.

Here's the configuration for Office1's gatekeeper:

```
hostname office1-gatekeeper
!
interface fastethernet 0/1
  ip address 192.168.1.2 255.255.255.0
  !
  gatekeeper
  ! Specify our local zone, which is controlled by our gatekeeper
  zone local office1zone xyzcorp.com
  ! Specify the remote zone (office2) and the remote keeper's IP address and
port
  zone remote office2zone xyzcorp.com 192.168.2.2 1719
  ! Assign a prefix for the zones. The  dots are wildcards
  zone prefix office1zone 555.......
  zone prefix office2zone 666.......
  ! Define the technology prefix, which is stripped before checking the zone
prefix
  gw-type-prefix 1#* default technology
```

Here's the configuration for Office 1's gateway:

```
hostname office1-gateway
!
interface fastethernet0/0
  ip address 192.168.1.1 255.255.255.0
  h323-gateway voip interface
  ! Define the gatekeeper to work with (192.168.1.2)
  h323-gateway voip id office1zone ip addr 192.168.1.2 1718
```

```
! Define an alias for this gateway
h323-gateway voip h323-id office1_gw
! again, specify the technology prefix
h323-gateway voip tech-prefix 1#
!
dial-peer voice 1 voip
 ! The pattern for office 2, the .'s are wildcards
 destination pattern 666.......
 session target ras
!
dial-peer voice 2 pots
 destination-pattern 5555550002
 port 0/0
```

Here's the configuration for Office 2's gatekeeper:

```
hostname office2-gatekeeper
!
interface fastethernet 0/1
 ip address 192.168.2.2 255.255.255.0
 !
 gatekeeper
 zone local office2zone xyzcorp.com
 zone remote office1zone xyzcorp.com 192.168.1.2 1719
 zone prefix office1zone 555.......
 zone prefix office2zone 666.......

 gw-type-prefix 1#* default technology
```

Here's the configuration for Office 2's gatekeeper:

```
hostname office2-gateway
!
interface fastethernet0/0
 ip address 192.168.2.1 255.255.255.0
 h323-gateway voip interface
 ! Define the gatekeeper to work with (192.168.2.2)
 h323-gateway voip id office1zone ip addr 192.168.2.2 1718
 ! Define an alias for this gateway
 h323-gateway voip h323-id office2_gw
 h323-gateway voip tech-prefix 1#
 h323-gateway voip bind srcaddr 192.168.2.1
!
dial-peer voice 1 voip
 ! The pattern for office 1, the .'s are wildcards
 destination pattern 555.......
 session target ras
!
dial-peer voice 2 pots
 destination-pattern 6665550002
 port 0/0
```

You can use the show commands in Table 6-4 to verify H.323 configurations.

Table 6-4. Useful show commands for H.323 configurations

Command	Displays
show gateway	The current status of the gateway
show gatekeeper endpoints	Status of all registered endpoints for a gatekeeper
show gatekeeper zone status	Status of all zones related to a gatekeeper
show dial-peer voice	The configuration for all VoIP and POTS dial peers

MGCP call routing

In MGCP, the gateway configuration and the managed VoIP phones are configured from the CallManager software. On the gateway, we only need to identify the CallManager and enable MGCP. In Figure 6-5, we have a possible MGCP VoIP configuration. We have three managed phones, a CallManager box, and an MGCP gateway router.

Figure 6-5. MGCP Network Example

In Figure 6-5, the phones, CallManager, and the MGCP gateway are all connected on the Ethernet segment. The following example configures our MGCP gateway to identify the CallManager:

```
Hostname gateway
!
! Enable MGCP
mgcp
!
! This next line is enabled by default for MGCP. It causes the gateway to
! validate that it is in the same domain as the call manager box
mgcp validate domain-name
!
! Identify the call manager (whose IP address is 192.168.1.54)
mgcp call-agent 192.168.1.54 mgcp 0.1
!
```

```
! Identify the codec type and the dual-tone multifrequency (DTMF)
! DTMF really means touch-tone
mgcp dtmf-relay voip code all mode cisco
!
! Enabled this gateway to support call manager
ccm-manager mgcp
!
interface fastethernet0/1
    ip address 192.168.1.1 255.255.255.0
```

To verify the configuration, you can use the show mgcp command.

For more information on configuring the CallManager software, see *http://www.cisco.com/en/US/products/sw/voicesw/ps556/index.html*.

SIP Configuration for VoIP

If we want to configure SIP on a Cisco router, we need to configure our SIP user agent and our dial peers.

In this example, our router is a terminating SIP gateway, so we need to configure it as SIP user agent in order to receive incoming calls, which we do with the sip-ua command. Next, we'll configure our VoIP dial peers to use the already specified SIP server.

```
Hostname Office1
!
! enter the SIP User Agent mode
sip-ua
    ! The transport command sets the router up for SIP signalling.
    ! The type can be udp or tcp. udp is default
    transport udp
    ! Set the address of the SIP server
    sip-server ipv4:192.168.2.1
!
! Now configure a VoIP dial peer
dial-peer voice 1 voip
    ! define phone number associated with this peer
    destination-pattern 15555550001
    ! set the SIP transport type for the SIP user agent
    transport udp
    ! specify the SIP procotol type
    session protocol sipv2
    ! Tell the voice peer to use the sip server
    session target sip-server
```

We can also revisit our earlier example with Office1 and Office2 and use SIP. In this example, we enabled SIP using the exact same configuration as before, except that we added two commands, application session and session protocol sipv2, which are shown in bold:

```
! Office2 phone number
dial-peer voice 2 voip
    ! Enable standard session application for this dial peer
    application session
    ! office2's phone number
```

```
destination-pattern 15555550001
! enable SIPv2 for this dial-peer
session protocol sipv2
! The target is office2's router
session target ipv4:192.168.2.1
ip precedence 5
```

7

Access Lists

In the most intuitive sense, an access list is a series of rules that instruct the router on how to select or match a route or packet. IOS uses access lists as an extremely general mechanism for controlling many kinds of router behavior, but the best way to understand how they work is to start with the simplest application: controlling the traffic that flows into or out of an interface.

Each rule in a standard access list contains three important parts:

- a number that identifies the list when you refer to it in other parts of the router's configuration
- a deny or permit instruction
- a packet identifier (such as an address)

As incoming or outgoing packets reach an interface that has an access list, the router compares the packets to each rule in the access list and decides whether the traffic should be blocked (denied) or permitted.

For IP traffic, there are two fundamental types of lists: standard and extended. Standard access lists filter based on source network addresses. A typical standard access list looks like this:

```
access-list 1 deny 10.10.1.0 0.0.0.255
access-list 1 deny 10.10.2.0 0.0.0.255
access-list 1 permit any
```

This list blocks any traffic from the 10.10.1.0 and 10.10.2.0 subnets, regardless of the packet's destination, and permits anything that makes it past the first two lines. In other words, all traffic is permitted except for the 10.10.1.0 and 10.10.2.0 subnets. Once you have the list, you can apply it to the packets going into or out of a particular interface. To apply this list to the traffic arriving at (i.e., coming into) a particular interface, we would use the ip access-group command:

```
interface ethernet0
  ip access-group 1 in
```

As I mentioned, there are many other contexts in which access lists can be used. You can use them to restrict who can access a particular TTY line, to specify what routes are sent in and out of various routing processes, and to perform many other functions. It's also worth noting that while applying access list 1 to the packets arriving at ethernet0 prevents traffic from subnets 10.10.1.0 and 10.10.2.0 from passing through the router, it doesn't affect traffic arriving at any other interface, nor does it have any effect on protocols other than IP. You have to watch each interface and protocol separately.

Standard access lists perform filtering on the basis of source IP addresses. Extended access lists allow you to build much more flexible filters that use source and destination addresses, in addition to higher layer protocol information. For example, you can build a filter based on ICMP type and code values. For TCP and UDP, you can filter on destination and source ports. Figure 7-1 shows a router with an extended access list applied to ethernet0. This access list blocks incoming TCP traffic for port 23, regardless of the traffic's source or destination address. Since port 23 is the telnet port, this list prevents any hosts on Network A from telnetting to hosts on Network B or to the router itself.

Figure 7-1. An extended access list to block telnet

Access lists can also be applied in the outbound direction. For example, we can create a list that denies traffic on port 80 and apply that list to outbound packets traveling through ethernet0. This will prevent hosts on Network B from accessing web servers on Network A:

```
! Deny traffic on port 80 (www traffic)
ip access-list 111 deny tcp any any eq 80
ip access-list 111 permit ip any any
!
interface ethernet0
  ! Apply access list 111 in the outbound direction
  ip access-group 111 out
```

The access lists we've seen so far have been very simple, but they can be much more complex.

How Packets Match a List Entry

A standard access list is composed of a series of rules. These rules are processed in order and describe which packets should be allowed or denied based on their source addresses. The syntax of an entry in a standard access list is:

```
access-list number action source
```

The parameters are:

number
    A number between 1 and 99, identifying the list for future reference

action
    The keyword permit or deny, indicating whether to allow or block the packet

source
    The packet's source address

Table 7-1 shows three ways to write the source and destination addresses. In most cases, you'll use address/mask pairs to specify blocks of addresses: if we had to write access lists based on individual IP addresses, they wouldn't be very interesting.

Table 7-1. Specifying addresses in access lists

Syntax	Example	Explanation
address mask	192.168.2.0 0.0.0.255	Describes a block of IP addresses. The mask is used as a wildcard; a one (1) in the mask indicates that we "don't care" about the corresponding bit in the address. A zero (0) in the mask means that the corresponding bit must match exactly. This example specifies addresses from 192.168.2.0 to 192.168.2.255. That is, the wildcard mask says that we ignore the last byte of the address when figuring out whether an address matches.
host *address*	host 192.168.2.1	The given address must be matched exactly.
any	any	Any IP address will match.

Address/Mask Pairs (Wildcards)

Nearly every user starting out with access lists has a problem understanding wildcard masks. The problem is that wildcard masks look like subnet masks, but they aren't; a wildcard is actually the complement of the corresponding subnet mask. For example, to permit any IP traffic to the 192.168.2.0/24 network (i.e., 192.168.2.0 with a subnet mask of 255.255.255.0), we write an access list entry like this:

```
access-list 10 permit 192.168.2.0 0.0.0.255
```

Now, let's say that a packet comes along with a destination address of 192.168.2.1. How do we tell if a match occurs? The wildcard mask is bitwise ORed with both the actual destination address and the address given in the access list rule. If the two results are equal, a match occurs and the packet is either permitted or denied. To see how this works, let's look at the bits. Table 7-2 shows the relevant addresses and masks in binary.

Table 7-2. Converting addresses to binary

	Decimal form	Binary
Wildcard mask	0.0.0.255	00000000.00000000.00000000.11111111
Access list address	192.168.2.0	11000000.10101000.00000010.00000000
Destination IP	192.168.2.1	11000000.10101000.00000010.00000001

Here is the computation:

```
WildCard Mask  = 00000000.00000000.00000000.11111111
Access List    = 11000000.10101000.00000010.00000000
Result One     = 11000000.10101000.00000010.11111111

WildCard Mask  = 00000000.00000000.00000000.11111111
Destination IP = 11000000.10101000.00000010.00000001
Result Two     = 11000000.10101000.00000010.11111111

Result One = Result Two
```

Because the two results match, the destination address 192.168.2.1 matches the access list. In short, the mask value of 0.0.0.255 means that the last byte of the incoming address can have any value; we don't care about its value. In this case, we match all IP addresses from 192.168.2.0 through 192.168.2.255. Furthermore, since the mask states that we will match any value in the last byte of the incoming address, the last byte of the address in the access list can have any value. That sounds confusing, but all it really means is that 192.168.2.0 0.0.0.255 is the same as 192.168.2.139 0.0.0.255; both address/mask pairs match the same group of addresses (192.168.2.0 through 192.168.2.255).

Computing a Wildcard for a Given Subnet Mask

Because the wildcard mask is the complement of the subnet mask, there's a simple formula for computing the correct wildcard mask for any subnet mask. For each byte of the subnet mask, calculate the corresponding byte of the wildcard mask using the formula:

```
Wildcard = 255 - Subnet
```

The wildcard mask that corresponds to a subnet mask of 255.255.255.224 (30 hosts per subnet) is 0.0.0.31 (255 – 224 = 31). Here are two access list entries using this wildcard mask:

```
! For a network of 192.168.2.64 255.255.255.224
access-list 10 permit 192.168.2.64 0.0.0.31
!
! For a network of 192.168.2.96 255.255.225.224
access-list 10 permit 192.168.2.96  0.0.0.31
```

Access List Processing

Most of the access lists we have seen so far have consisted of a single rule. But access lists frequently contain many rules. In this case, rules are processed sequentially. The source address of each packet is tested against each rule in the list, starting with the first and ending when a match occurs. Let's take the example in the beginning of this chapter, which permitted everything except traffic from two particular subnets. Here is what the list looked like:

```
access-list 1 deny 10.10.1.0 0.0.0.255
access-list 1 deny 10.10.2.0 0.0.0.255
access-list 1 permit any
```

The router processes each line in order until it finds a match. Therefore, if a packet arrives from 10.10.2.13, it matches the second rule in the list and so is denied. What happens if we change the list, placing the last line first?

```
access-list 1 permit any
access-list 1 deny 10.10.1.0 0.0.0.255
access-list 1 deny 10.10.2.0 0.0.0.255
```

Now all traffic would be permitted through this list. The first line permits all traffic because all incoming packets match it. The second and third lines are never used because processing stops when a match is found, and the first line matches all IP addresses. For this reason, access lists must be ordered carefully.

Implicit Deny

Every time you create an access list, the router adds a line to the end stating, "If nothing matched this list, deny it." If we could see it, this line would look like this:

```
access-list 1 deny any
```

All traffic that makes it to the end of an access list is blocked by the implicit deny. This helps us write more efficient access lists. It would be a pain to write access lists that listed every host (and, for extended lists, every port) you want to permit and every host (and port) you want to deny. Furthermore, the router overhead for processing such large lists would be prohibitive. However, you can take advantage of the implicit deny to write lists that itemize only the traffic you want to permit. Don't bother to list traffic you want to deny—it will be handled by the implicit deny. (But do be careful not to inadvertently permit traffic you want to deny.) A good rule of thumb for designing access lists is to use lots of permit rules and relatively few deny rules.

Access Lists Are Additive

Access lists cannot be freely edited once they have been entered in the router's configuration. If you want to change a single entry in the list, the entire list must be deleted and then re-entered. For example, consider this list:

```
access-list 1 deny host 10.10.1.5
access-list 1 deny host 10.10.1.7
```

After typing this list, you realize there is a mistake: in the first line, the IP address 10.10.1.5 should be 10.10.1.17. Your first attempt to fix the problem is to add another rule by typing:

```
access-list 1 deny host 10.10.1.17
```

This new rule is simply added to access list 1. The result is that you're now denying access by 10.10.1.17—but you are also denying access by 10.10.1.5, which wasn't your original intent. Can you fix this problem by adding a fourth rule that explicitly permits access from 10.10.1.5? No. Because rules are processed in order, the first line (denying access) will always be processed before the additional line permitting access. So, can you delete the first line? Trying to do so, you type:

```
no access-list 1 deny host 10.10.1.5
```

This doesn't work either, because instead of deleting just one line, the router sees no access-list 1 and removes the entire list. It is a common mistake to think that a single rule can be deleted from an access list. If you make a mistake in an access list, or want to change it for some reason, your best approach is to delete the entire list and build it again from scratch. Modifying an existing list usually isn't a good idea. In this case, to fix your list you would enter:

```
no access-list 1
access-list 1 deny host 10.10.1.17
access-list 1 deny host 10.10.1.7
```

The best way to edit access lists is to keep an editor open with the access list in it. After you have modified your list, simply paste it into the router. That way, if you make a mistake, you can easily change it within your editor and paste it again.

Outbound Access Lists Are More Efficient Than Inbound

It is much more efficient to filter outgoing packets than to filter incoming packets. This is counterintuitive; at first glance, it seems that filtering incoming packets would save the router from processing all the blocked packets and routing them through to an outbound port. The difference is that an outgoing packet has already been routed (i.e., an outbound interface has been selected for it) before the access list processes it. Incoming packets must be processed by the access list before they arrive, and that's where the problem lies. Processing the access list first means that the router can't use its fast-switching paths and must process-switch the packet. What does this mean? Normally, the router has a cache of routes, which allows it to look up a known route quickly. With an inbound access list, the router can't use this cache and is forced to select the route another way.

In addition, an outbound access list is often smaller than the corresponding incoming list. For example, if a packet is coming in one interface, you have to write an inbound access list that considers all the possible routes the packet might take. On an outbound list, you already have a lot of information about the packet's destination (e.g., which interface it's going through), which allows you to write shorter, more efficient access lists.

This isn't to say that inbound access lists shouldn't be used. There are plenty of times when you need to use an inbound access list; I'll cover some of these in the next few sections.

Types of Access Lists

There are many different kinds of access lists. The basic concepts I've introduced with standard access lists apply to all of them: for example, they are processed sequentially, new rules are added to old rules rather than overriding old rules, and they permit or deny certain actions (typically, processing of a packet) based on information in the packet's headers.

With a few exceptions, you can tell an access list's type by looking at its number. Each type of access list has been assigned a group of 100 numbers. Table 7-3 summarizes the access list types and their numeric ranges.

Table 7-3. Access list numbers

List type	Numeric range
Standard IP access lists	1–99
Extended IP access lists	100–199
Ethernet type code	200–299
DECnet	300–399
XNS	400–499
Extended XNS	500–599
AppleTalk	600–699
Ethernet address	700–799
Novell	800–899
Extended Novell	900–999
Novell SAP	1000–1099
Additional standard IP access lists[a]	1300–1999
Additional extended IP access lists[a]	2000–2699
Named access lists	None
Reflexive access lists	None
Dynamic access lists	None

[a] These additional ranges were added in recent releases of IOS (11.1(cc) and 12.0).

Extended Access Lists

Extended access lists are a relatively straightforward variation on standard access lists. Standard lists are limited to filtering based on the source and destination addresses of IP packets. Extended lists add the ability to filter based on the protocol and the port specified in the packet. Here's the syntax of an extended access list:

```
access-list number action protocol source s-port destination d-port
[optional-args]
```

The action and source address are the same as for standard access lists. The other fields are:

number
>A number identifying the list. For extended access lists, this number must be between 100 and 199.

protocol
>An indication of the protocol to which the rule applies. This must be either ip, tcp, udp, or icmp.

s-port
>For TCP or UDP packets, the packet's source port. There are a number of ways to specify ports. This field is optional. If the protocol is IP or ICMP, this field is omitted.

destination
>The packet's destination address, specified the same way as the source address. That is, you can have an IP address followed by a wildcard mask, the keyword host followed by the IP address of a specific host, or the keyword any.

d-port
>For TCP or UDP packets, the packet's destination port. There are a number of ways to specify ports. This field is optional. If the protocol is IP or ICMP, this field is omitted.

optional-args
>An optional keyword that is applicable only if the protocol is TCP. For example, the keyword established is optional.

Specifying ports

When writing extended access lists for TCP or UDP, you can specify source and destination ports along with the source and destination addresses. You can specify either individual ports or a range of ports. By specifying ports you can permit or deny access to specific services, such as SMTP or HTTP. Here are the different ways to specify ports:

lt *n*
>All port numbers less than *n*

gt *n*
>All port numbers greater than *n*

eq *n*
>Port *n*

neq *n*
>All ports except for *n*

range *n* *m*
>All ports from *n* through *m*, inclusive

For example, eq 80 refers to the well-known port for a web server; gt 1023 refers to all ports greater than 1023. For most well-known ports, you can use the standard name for the service rather than the actual port number. For example, eq www refers to the well-known HTTP port, which is 80. Likewise, you can use smtp to refer to port 25, and so on. Here are some examples.

The following two rules match (and permit) packets with any source address destined for the SMTP or HTTP ports on the host 10.10.1.5:

```
access-list 110 permit tcp any host 10.10.1.5 eq 25
access-list 110 permit tcp any host 10.10.1.5 eq 80
```

The next rule matches TCP packets with a destination port less than 1024, regardless of the source and destination addresses and denies access:

```
access-list 110 deny tcp any any lt 1024
```

This rule matches TCP packets with a destination port from 3000 to 3010, inclusive, and denies access:

```
access-list 110 deny tcp any any range 3000 3010
```

Finally, this rule matches UDP packets with a destination port of 3535, regardless of the source and destination addresses, and permits access:

```
access-list 110 permit udp any any eq 3535
```

Established connections

The established keyword can be added to access rules for TCP. Technically, this keyword matches packets that have the ACK or RST (Reset) bit set. If either the ACK or the RST bit is set, the router assumes that the packet is not the first packet of a session and that a session has already been established.

What does this mean in practice? It gives us a way to distinguish sessions originating inside our network from sessions originating elsewhere. For example, let's say that we want to allow our staff to initiate telnet connections with any site on the Internet but that we don't want people outside our site to be able to establish telnet connections to our systems. An easy way to enforce that policy is to block incoming packets that don't have the ACK or RST bits set by using the established keyword. This means that we allow return traffic for connections that are already established from the inside, and that we don't allow outsiders to establish connections with us. In short, the only people who can establish connections are the users inside our network. Here's how you might create and apply that list:

```
! Inbound access list
access-list 110 permit tcp any any established
access-list 110 deny ip any any
!
! Outbound access list
access-list 111 permit tcp any any eq telnet
access-list 111 deny ip any any
!
interface serial0
  access-group 110 in
  access-group 111 out
```

In practice, it would be a good idea to specify our network's address as the destination for the inbound list, rather than relying on any. The established keyword is almost always used on incoming packet filters, which allows connections to originate "behind" the router but prevents connections from the outside. (It could be used on outgoing access lists, but this would not be particularly useful.) This method of blocking unwanted traffic originating outside the network can be circumvented; it is possible to forge a packet with the appropriate bits set. Later in this chapter, "Reflexive Access Lists" covers another way to allow established connections.

ICMP protocol entries

ICMP packets are becoming increasingly important, as they have been used in many recent denial-of-service attacks. We can construct access list rules that permit or deny ICMP packets, allowing us to receive (or block) network error messages and ping packets. Here's a typical ICMP rule:

```
access-list 110 permit icmp any any echo-reply
```

ICMP is a surprisingly complicated protocol with lots of different packet types. It would be nice if you could either block ICMP entirely or allow it into your network without worrying about it. Unfortunately, neither approach is a good idea. You can't just block ICMP, because a number of important mechanisms for controlling traffic flow depend on it. (For example, Path MTU discovery relies on ICMP; if ICMP is blocked, you might find connections that start but die for no apparent reason.) And you can't allow ICMP in unquestioned, because it's the basis for a number of denial-of-service attacks.

Here's a set of access list rules that should be appropriate for most situations. They allow what you need and block packet types that you don't need or are dangerous:

```
! Allow pings into the network
access-list 110 permit icmp any any echo
! Allow ping responses
access-list 110 permit icmp any any echo-reply
! Allow ICMP source-quench (flow control)
access-list 110 permit icmp any any source-quench
! Allow Path MTU discovery
access-list 110 permit icmp any any packet-too-big
! Allow time-exceeded, which is useful for traceroute
access-list 110 permit icmp any any time-exceeded
! Deny all other ICMP packets
access-list 110 deny icmp any any
```

Applying an access list to an interface or line

We've already used the commands that apply access lists to interfaces fairly liberally, but it's worth looking at them in detail. To apply an access list to an interface, use the access-group command. Here are two examples:

```
interface ethernet0
  ip access-group 110 in
  ip access-group 112 out
```

This code applies access list 110 to inbound packets and access list 112 to outbound packets on the interface ethernet0. Again, packets arriving at an interface and packets leaving the interface are filtered separately. You can apply only one access list per direction to an interface.

To apply a standard access list to a line, use the access-class command. For example:

```
line vty0
  access-class 10 in
```

This means that access list 10 is used to control which hosts can access virtual terminal 0. In effect, this command limits telnet access to the router. You cannot apply an extended access list to a line.

There are many other contexts in which you can use access lists. Unfortunately, each has its own command for applying the list. The commands are more or less similar: you specify an access list number and usually specify whether the list applies to traffic leaving or entering the router.

Named Access Lists

So far, all the access lists we've seen have been identified by numbers. Numbers have some obvious problems: they're difficult to remember, and they're limited— you get only 100 access lists of each type. While this should be plenty, it's strange to have this kind of limitation built into such a critical mechanism. (The most recent versions of IOS have added some additional blocks of numbers for standard and extended IP access lists, but numbers are still awkward, and the more you use, the more inconvenient they are.)

IOS 11.2 and later allow you to dispense with numbers and give access lists logical names. To create a simple access list named simplelist, use the command:

```
ip access-list standard simplelist
```

To create an extended list named inboundfilter, use the command:

```
ip access-list extended inboundfilter
```

Follow the ip access-list command with the rules that make up the list, omitting everything up to and including the number. For example, here's a standard list named filter1:

```
ip access-list standard filter1
  permit 10.10.1.0 0.0.0.255
  deny 10.10.0.0 0.0.255.255
  permit any
```

If you're typing access lists at the command line, named access lists give you yet another prompt to worry about. Here's how we'd type the preceding list in a console session:

```
Router(config)#ip access-list standard filter1
Router(config-std-nacl)#permit 10.10.1.0 0.0.0.255
Router(config-std-nacl)#deny 10.10.0.0 0.0.255.255
Router(config-std-nacl)#permit any any
```

To apply a named access list to an interface, use the `access-group` command as shown in the previous section, but specify the list's name instead of its number:

```
interface serial 1
 ip access-group filter1 in
```

Besides being more descriptive, named access lists have another advantage: you can edit them much more conveniently. That is, you can delete a line from within the access list; you don't have to delete the entire access list and re-enter it, as you do with numbered access lists. The following commands modify the `filter1` list defined earlier:

```
Router(config)#ip access-list standard filter1
Router(config-std-nacl)#no permit 10.10.1.0 0.0.0.255
Router(config-std-nacl)#exit
Router#show access-list filter1
ip access-list standard filter1
 deny 10.10.0.0 0.0.255.255
 permit any any
```

As you can see, the no command didn't erase the entire access list. Instead, it removed only the line we didn't want. However, the editing capabilities aren't perfect. Access lists are still additive; any new rules you add to `filter1` will be added to the end. There's no way to modify a rule that's in the list. Therefore, you still must be careful when constructing your lists.

Most commands that require an access list as an argument will take either a numbered or a named list. Some won't. Cisco is gradually fixing this problem by converting all commands to accept either a name or a number.

Entering noncontiguous ports

As of IOS 12.4, you are allowed to enter noncontiguous ports on a single line within a named access list. Why is this a big deal? Before, you would write such an access list like this:

```
ip access-list extended acllist1
 permit tcp any host 192.168.1.1 eq telnet
 permit tcp any host 192.168.1.1 eq www
 permit tcp any host 192.168.1.1 eq smtp
 permit tcp any host 192.168.1.1 eq pop3
```

With noncontiguous port support, you can write it much more compactly, like this:

```
ip access-list extended acllist1
 permit tcp any host 192.168.1.1 eq telnet www smtp pop3
```

Reflexive Access Lists

Reflexive access lists are an important tool that was added in IOS 11.3. They allow you to create lists that dynamically change based on what services your users need. Basically, you create an inbound and an outbound access list. The outbound access list creates entries in a temporary access list. This temporary access list is "evaluated" by the inbound access list. To put it another way, packets going out the interface create temporary entries to allow packets of the same session back in. When an outbound session ends, the temporary entries are destroyed, which closes the hole in the inbound access list.

Reflexive lists are similar to extended TCP access lists with the established keyword in that you will usually use reflexive lists to allow communications that have been initiated by your users. As I explained earlier, established connections rely on two bits (ACK and RST) being set in the incoming packet. While the established keyword works, it presents two problems. First, someone attempting to crack your site can exploit the established assumption by illegitimately setting the ACK and RST bits in a packet that doesn't belong to an established session, tricking the router into thinking the packet is legitimate. Second, the system is always open for attacks, even if no outbound sessions are in progress. With reflexive lists, however, we open the entry in the inbound access list only for valid current sessions.

The outbound reflexive list doesn't actually do any filtering, but rather detects attempts to initiate a TCP session. When a new session is started, an entry is automatically entered in the corresponding inbound list, allowing only the traffic belonging to that session. If that session is idle for a certain amount of time (by default, 300 seconds), the automatically generated entry expires, and traffic from the session is no longer allowed.

Creating the outbound reflexive list

The outbound reflexive list doesn't do any filtering; it simply provides a mechanism for generating the corresponding inbound list. The key to the outbound list is the reflect command, which watches for attempts to initiate TCP sessions and adds those sessions to the temporary list. Here's a simple list named outlist; the temporary list we're building is called tmplist:

```
ip access-list extended outlist
  ! Allow everything and add it to the reflexive list called tmplist
  permit tcp any any reflect tmplist
```

All traffic automatically matches this list and is passed through the interface. All outbound traffic will create an entry in the temporary list called tmplist.

Creating the inbound reflexive list

Now we need to create an inbound list that evaluates tmplist. To do so, we create a list named inlist that uses those temporary entries, and we add it to our configuration. This list is processed in order, just like any other access list, which means you can use deny and permit rules as in any other inbound list. In this example, we allow incoming access to our web server, plus any traffic that has been added to tmplist. All other traffic is denied.

```
ip access-list extended inlist
  ! allow tcp to our web server
  permit tcp any host 192.168.1.1 eq www
  ! evaluate our temporary reflexive list
  evaluate tmplist
  ! deny everything else
  deny ip any any
```

An entry can be in the tmplist only if it corresponds to a session that was initiated from within our internal network.

Applying the inbound and outbound reflexive lists to an interface

To apply the reflexive list to an interface, we just apply the outbound list and the inbound list in the appropriate directions:

```
interface serial0
  description  Internet Gateway interface
  ip access-group inlist in
  ip access-group outlist out
```

Now we do a show access-list. The tmplist will appear with all the temporary entries that are currently in the list. If there are no temporary entries, the list will be blank.

```
Router1#show access-list
Extended IP access list inlist
    permit tcp any host 192.168.1.1 eq www
    evaluate tmplist
    deny ip any any
Extended IP access list outlist
    permit tcp any any reflect tmplist
Reflexive IP access list tmplist
```

Setting the reflexive timeout

By default, entries in the reflexive list time out after 300 seconds with no traffic; that is, if the session is idle for 300 seconds, the reflexive entry will be removed from the temporary list. If the session was not complete, it will need to be restarted. Five minutes is a long time for a connection to be idle, so let's reduce this to 200 seconds:

```
ip reflexive-list timeout 200
```

Reflexive list notes

Here are a few things you should keep in mind when you use reflexive lists:

- Reflexive lists are designed for use on gateway routers (routers that connect you to the Internet, to a shared backbone, or to another company or organization).
- The reflect keyword, which establishes a reflexive list, can be used only on permit statements.
- Entries in reflexive lists automatically expire after a certain idle period, even if the session is not complete.
- Entries are removed from the temporary list when the session is complete.
- The outgoing IP addresses/ports and incoming IP addresses/ports will be "swapped" in the temporary lists.
- Reflexive lists do not work on protocols such as FTP in which the incoming port does not match the outgoing port. To get FTP to work, perform the steps outlined later in "Permitting FTP through an access list."

Specific Topics

Here are a few ideas and tricks that will help you write access lists that are appropriate for your network.

Adding Comments to an Access List

You can add comments to access lists by using the remark keyword. Place any descriptive text you want after this keyword. Remarks work in named and numbered access lists.

```
access-list 110 remark Block traffic to 192.168.1.0. They cause trouble
access-list 110 deny ip 192.168.1.0 0.0.0.255 any
access-list 110 remark Worker bob surfs the internet all day, so stop him
access-list 110 deny tcp host 192.168.2.1 any eq www
```

Timed Access Lists

Sometimes, we want to control traffic based on the time of day. For example, we might want to prevent staff members from browsing the Web during work hours. So far, we don't have a way to do that aside from reconfiguring access lists every day at 8 A.M. and 5 P.M. IOS provides an easy solution to this problem. We can use the time-range command to establish a time range; then we can apply the time range to access list rules, establishing times when the rule is active.

For example, let's build a time range that includes working hours on weekdays:

```
! This is a global command
time-range block-http
    periodic weekdays 8:00 to 17:00
```

This time range has the name block-http and is periodic, which means that the time range repeats. (In contrast, an absolute time range has a single fixed starting and ending point.) Now, it is just a matter of adding the time range to a rule in an extended access list:

```
! Timed range works only in extended access lists
ip access-list extended list1
    ! block-http is the name of the time range we defined earlier
    deny tcp any any eq www time-range block-http
    permit any any
```

The first rule blocks all HTTP traffic whenever it is in effect; the time range block-http defines when the rule is active. The second rule allows all other traffic.

Building a Gateway Router

Figure 7-2 shows a common configuration in which a router serves as a gateway from a local network to the Internet. If a firewall is unavailable, adding an access list on this router can dramatically increase network security.

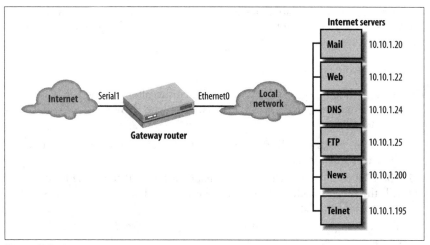

Figure 7-2. A gateway router

 This access list does not provide all the possible security for an Internet connection. Use it with caution!

Before we build the list, we need to review some topics the list will cover.

IP address spoofing

IP spoofing is the act of forging network packets that appear to come from an internal IP address. Because most sites trust their internal hosts more than they trust hosts on the Internet, spoofing allows crackers to evade security restrictions that would otherwise keep them out. For example, packets with a spoofed (internal) IP address might make it through an access list that was designed to prevent access from hosts on the Internet. Once inside your network, these packets may be able to access services that shouldn't be available to the outside world.

Preventing spoofing attacks is relatively easy. Packets originating from our network should never arrive from the Internet or any other external network. Hence, we can easily set up an access list that blocks all IP traffic with our network addresses as the source address, then apply this list to incoming packets on our Internet interface. For example, if our network address is 198.168.10.0/24, the access list for spoofing would be:

```
! List to block spoofing
access-list 111 deny ip 198.168.10.0 0.0.0.255 any
access-list 111 permit ip any any

! Internet interface; to block spoofing, apply 111 to incoming packets
interface serial0
  ip access-group 111 in
```

This access list blocks any traffic with a source address in the 198.168.10.0/24 network.

Another suggestion is to apply an outgoing list that denies packets with source addresses that don't belong to our network. Doing so will keep users from within our network from spoofing to the outside.

Permitting FTP through an access list

FTP has a number of quirks that make it difficult to allow through an access list. "Classic" (nonpassive) FTP is a particular problem. A nonpassive connection proceeds as follows:

1. The client requests an FTP session to the FTP server using port 21 (ftp), and the server authenticates.
2. The FTP client sends a PORT command to the FTP server. This command tells the server which port to use for the session. The FTP client waits on this new port for the data.
3. The server opens a new connection from port 20 (ftp-data) to the given port on the FTP client.
4. The client and server can now communicate with each other on the new port.

The problem lies in the acceptance of the new port for the FTP session: as it arrives, the access list blocks it because it looks like a new incoming session, not an established one. The new port number for the connection is never known. Therefore, we need to add a line to the access list that allows incoming connections from the ftp-data port to any host on the network:

```
access-list 110 permit tcp any eq ftp-data any gt 1024
```

This line allows incoming FTP connections with two restrictions: the source must be a packet from the ftp-data port on any host, and the destination must be a host on the network with a port greater than 1024.

If you don't add this line to your gateway router's access list, your users will probably complain that they can't FTP to the outside world.

Passive FTP

Passive FTP is an alternative to traditional FTP that is supported by most clients and servers today. However, it isn't the default; you may need to configure the client to use passive mode when it initiates a connection. With passive FTP, the client sends a PASV command to the server instead of a PORT command. PASV tells the FTP server to communicate with the FTP client on the same port it is using. Thus, the incoming packets look like they belong to an established connection on the FTP port. If you use the established keyword in your access list rule for FTP (or if you have a more general rule that permits all established connections), it will allow the packets from the server back into your network.

The FTP client software must support the passive option for this to work. If you decide to go this route, you must configure all your internal network hosts to use passive FTP, which may prove to be quite a chore.

The actual access list

List 110 implements a simple access policy for our Internet gateway router:

```
! Block spoofing of our IP addresses
access-list 110 deny    ip 10.10.1.0 0.0.0.255 any
!
! Permit any outgoing TCP connections to come back into our network
access-list 110 permit tcp any any established
!
! Allow email (SMTP port 25) to our SMTP server
access-list 110 permit tcp any host 10.10.1.20 eq smtp
!
! Allow web traffic (port 80) to our web server only
access-list 110 permit tcp any host 10.10.1.22 eq www
!
! Allow DNS traffic to our DNS server, both TCP and UDP
access-list 110 permit tcp any host 10.10.1.24 eq domain
access-list 110 permit udp any host 10.10.1.24 eq domain
!
! Allow Internal hosts to access the outside DNS server (192.168.1.100)
access-list 110 permit upd host 192.168.1.100 eq domain any gt 1023
!
! Allow FTP traffic to our FTP server
access-list 110 permit tcp any host 10.10.1.25 eq ftp
access-list 110 permit tcp any host 10.10.1.25 eq ftp-data
!
! Allow news only from legit NNTP servers to our internal NNTP client
access-list 110 permit tcp host 198.168.1.98 host 10.10.1.200 eq nntp
access-list 110 permit tcp host 192.168.1.99 host 10.10.1.200 eq nntp
!
! Allow telnet (port 23) to only one host!
access-list 110 permit tcp any host 10.10.1.195 eq telnet
!
! Some things we know we want to deny: Xwindows, NFS
access-list 110 deny tcp any any range 6000 6003
access-list 110 deny tcp any any range 2000 2003
access-list 110 deny tcp any any eq 2049
access-list 110 deny udp any any eq 2049
!
! Since we are doing nonpassive FTP on our FTP clients, we need the
! following line to allow their FTP sessions back in. If you have an
! FTP server, you have to create a separate entry for it.
access-list 110 permit tcp any eq ftp-data any gt 1024
!
! Allow ICMP into our network
! Warning! ICMP is more than just ping. If you decide to deny it, you
! should explictly deny specific ICMP types (echo, echo-reply, etc.).
! MTU path discovery and source quench rely on ICMP and are very
! important to some links.
! First disallow ICMP redirects broadcasts
access-list 110 deny icmp any any redirect
! Then allow everything else
access-list 110 permit icmp any any
!
```

```
! Allow NTP time messages to all our internal machines
access-list 110 permit udp any any eq ntp
!
! Implicit deny
! It is here by default, but we list it so that the show access-list
! command will show the number of packets blocked by the implicit deny.
access-list 110 deny ip any any
```

Apply the list to interface serial1 with the following commands:

```
interface serial1
  ip access-group 110 in
```

Optimizing Your Access Lists

You can list and view all access lists with the show access-list command. If you are interested in only one specific list, use the number of the list at the end of the show command:

```
Router#show access-list 124
Extended IP access list 124
    deny    ip 10.10.1.0 0.0.0.255 any (1855 matches)
    permit tcp any any established (6105063 matches)
    permit tcp any host 10.10.1.20 eq smtp (10246 matches)
    permit tcp any host 10.10.1.21 eq pop3 (11220 matches)
    permit tcp any host 10.10.1.22 eq www (72583 matches)
```

At the end of each line, the router lists the number of times that particular access list rule has been matched. Bear in mind that the numbers are from the last router reboot or counter reset. You must check the number of matches several times over a long period before you get numbers that reflect your actual network traffic. Traffic fluctuates for many reasons, so you're really interested in long-term averages.

The number of matches is useful information because access lists are processed in order, and processing terminates with the last match. Putting the lines with the most matches at the beginning of the list reduces the load on the router because most matches will occur earlier. In this case, we can move the line allowing WWW connections higher in the list. Note, however, that this line can't become the first line in the list; in order to work effectively, the rule that prevents spoofing attacks must be applied to all incoming packets and therefore must be first in the list. There's a moral here: don't get too excited about optimizing your access lists. Think through the consequences of your changes. Here's how our reordered list would look:

```
! We can't change the first line: it is looking for spoofing and must be
! the first entry.
access-list 124 deny ip 10.10.1.0 0.0.0.255 any
access-list 124 permit tcp any any established
access-list 124 permit tcp any host 10.10.1.22 eq www
access-list 124 permit tcp any host 10.10.1.21 eq pop3
access-list 124 permit tcp any host 10.10.1.20 eq smtp
```

Emulating a Packet Sniffer

You can use some clever access list commands to emulate a simple packet sniffer that logs all traffic arriving at an interface. First, build an access list that catches all IP traffic. Then add a debug statement for the list (debugging is discussed in Chapter 16):

```
access-list 110 permit ip any any
debug ip packet 110
```

Now apply the list to an interface in both directions:

```
interface ethernet0
  ip access-group 110 in
  ip access-group 110 out
```

All traffic traveling across this interface will now be logged by the debug command. This example can be taken a few steps further by redirecting the debugging output to a syslog server; the commands for doing so are also covered in Chapter 16. (This can be dangerous: if the route to the syslog server goes through the interface you're trying to debug, you'll create an infinite loop.) When you are done sniffing traffic, turn off logging:

```
no debug ip packet 110
```

We used an access list here on our debug ip packet statement, which kept the output to a minimum. If our access list was too generic or we didn't use one at all, the router would have started displaying every packet. This behavior can effectively render a busy router useless until you issue the undebug command. Be careful how and where you use the debug command.

Logging Access List Violations

You can log access list violations with IP accounting:

```
ip accounting access-violations
```

You can also use the extended access list keywords log and log-input to log information about packets that attempt to violate an access list. The log keyword causes entries that match that line to be logged:

```
access-list 110 deny tcp any host 10.10.1.22 eq www log
```

The log-input keyword not only logs the packet, but also supplies the packet's source interface.

If you configure the router with the command logging buffered, you will be able to use the show log command to view the stored log entries.

Securely Updating Access Lists

The most secure method for modifying access lists is to shut down the router's interfaces, make your modifications, and then bring the interfaces back up. This method is unpopular for an obvious reason: no traffic is being routed while the lists are being edited. This means that your users will have a broken network while you're doing your work, and that's often unacceptable.

Another way to provide the same security without shutting down the interface is to let the access-group command handle it. At any time, an interface can have only one "in" and one "out" access list. For example:

```
interface ethernet 0
    ip address 10.10.1.1 255.255.255.0
    ip access-group 110 in
    ip access-group 115 out
```

Let's say we want to modify access list 110. To do this, we might shut down the interface, delete list 110, write a new list, and bring the interface back up. Alternatively, we could create a new list, 112, that reflects the changes we want. We can then apply the list to the interface with a single command:

```
interface ethernet 0
    ip access-group 112 in
```

There is no need to do a no access-group 110 in, because the router automatically replaces list 110 with list 112. Since this happens in real time, the change is immediate and there is no need to shut down the interface. List 110 still exists, but it's inactive. You should probably delete it so it won't confuse you later. Happily, you can now delete it without inconveniencing your users.

The only drawback to this trick is that it can be confusing to network administrators, since your access list numbers change every time you edit the list. However, that's a small price to pay for satisfied users.

Getting the List to a Router with TFTP, RCP, or SCP

When you need to edit an access list, you can TFTP the router's configuration from the router to the TFTP server, edit the configuration on the server, and then TFTP the access list back to the router. This technique lets you use a familiar editor to modify your access lists, which is much more reliable than trying to type access lists directly into the router's configuration.

Here's an outline of the steps:

1. TFTP, RCP, or SCP the entire configuration to your server:
   ```
   Router#copy running-config tftp
   ```
2. Edit the configuration file, removing everything except the access lists.
3. Add a no access-list command before each access list in the file:
   ```
   no access-list 10
   access-list 10 deny 1.2.3.4 1.5.6.7
   ```
4. Edit the access lists and save the file so you do not have to repeat Steps 1-3 in the future.
5. Use TFTP, RCP, or SCP to copy the file back to your router. This file contains only the access lists, not the entire router configuration. It deletes each access list, then creates a new access list with the desired configuration.
   ```
   Router#copy tftp running-config
   ```
6. Once you are satisfied that the modified access lists work, save the running configuration:
   ```
   Router#copy running-config startup-config
   ```

8

IP Routing Topics

To do the job right, a router needs information about how to reach various parts of the network. It can get this information through static routing (i.e., including commands in the configuration that explicitly specify how to reach certain networks) or by exchanging routing information with other routers. To share this information, the router uses a routing protocol such as RIP, IGRP, EIGRP, OSPF, IS-IS, or BGP. In this chapter, we discuss a number of topics that are common to all (or most) of these protocols.

Autonomous System (AS) Numbers

An autonomous system is a collection of routers that is under the control of one organization (for example, one corporation's network). Within this organization, the routers share routing information only among themselves. At a macroscopic level, autonomous systems can be viewed as single entities. An exterior routing protocol, such as BGP, needs to worry only about autonomous systems and can ignore any structure within the autonomous system.

Properly speaking, AS numbers are assigned by ARIN (the American Registry for Internet Numbers) and are used only by BGP. A limited number are available, so they are assigned only to organizations that really need them.[*]

However, IGRP and EIGRP use a unique number to define boundaries between groups of routers that share information. This number can be considered a "locally significant AS" or "local-AS," which means the number is important only to your network. You can configure a router to run multiple routing processes using the same protocol, but they won't share routing information because their local-AS numbers differ.

---

[*] For more information on AS number assignment, see *http://www.arin.net/regserv/asnguide.htm*.

Consider the following configuration:

```
router igrp 100
  network 192.168.1.0
router igrp 200
  network 10.0.0.0
```

Here, we have two routing processes running IGRP. However, the two processes don't share information because they have different local-AS numbers (100 and 200). Using local-AS numbers in this way allows you to divide a network into separate domains. A local-AS number is more properly called a process number to distinguish it from a true AS number. But you'll see both terms used frequently, and I'll use both in this book.

OSPF uses a unique number called a process ID to identify the routing process on the router. These numbers do not partition the network the way a local-AS number does.

RIP does not use AS numbers because it shares routes with any neighboring RIP router that will listen. Therefore, the routing domains are defined by router boundaries. These boundaries can be border routers that are not running RIP, access lists that prohibit the RIP packets from traveling past a certain router, or any router more than 15 hops away, which RIP considers unreachable.

In Figure 8-1, Routers 1, 2, and 3 in Network 1 are running the RIP protocol. Similarly, in Network 2, Routers 4, 5, and 6 share routing information via RIP. Each network distributes routing information to all its routers because RIP communicates with all adjacent routers that are also running RIP. However, RIP routes are not distributed from one network into the other because we are not running RIP on the link between Router 3 and Router 5. Instead, we run EIGRP across the WAN connection with a local-AS number of 98. Since both Routers 3 and 5 use the same local-AS number, they can exchange routing information. However, by default, the EIGRP processes don't know anything about the RIP routes. To make this information available via EIGRP, we need to add route distribution, which is covered later in this chapter.

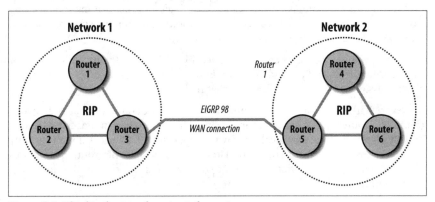

Figure 8-1. The distribution of routing information

When troubleshooting EIGRP and IGRP routing problems, you should always make sure that the local-AS numbers agree among routers that are running the same protocol. If they are different, the routers will not share routes.

Interior and Exterior Gateway Protocols

Functionally, routing protocols are divided into two types: interior gateway protocols (IGPs) and exterior gateway protocols (EGPs). Interior gateway protocols are used on routers within the same autonomous network, the same administrative domain, or the same intranet. Exterior gateway protocols are used to route traffic between routers in different autonomous systems; for example, between Internet service providers (ISPs) or between a single corporate net and two or more ISPs. You might also use an exterior protocol on a single large network that is so widely distributed that it can't be managed as a single unit (for example, a corporate network that spans several continents).

Put simply, internal protocols are intended for routing within an organization, and external protocols are intended for routing between unrelated organizations.

Interior gateway protocols, such as RIP, IGRP, EIGRP, and OSPF, are easier to configure and are designed to handle routing on a smaller scale than exterior gateway protocols. If you have a network with three routers and one connection to the Internet, RIP and a few static routes are all you need. Large networks, or networks with multihomed Internet connections (i.e., more than one ISP) might require a more sophisticated interior protocol, such as EIGRP or OSPF, and may force you to use an exterior protocol for routing to the Internet or between your own autonomous systems.

BGP is the only exterior gateway protocol that is widely used. EGPs are much more complicated than IGPs because they handle more routing information while performing better route summarization. BGP comes at a price in configuration, processing, and the size of the routing table. When configuring BGP for Internet use, you may need a router with sufficient memory to support a full Internet routing table, which contains over 70,000 routes.

Distance-Vector and Link-State Routing Protocols

Interior protocols are further divided into two classes, based on the way they make routing decisions and the kind of information they share. The two classes are distance-vector protocols and link-state protocols.

Distance-Vector Protocols

Distance-vector protocols provide two pieces of information for every route: a distance and a vector. These two pieces of information are distributed as part of a network map to all other routers. The distance is some measurement of the route's quality, based on parameters such as bandwidth, delay, or the number of intervening routers; the distance is never related to the actual physical distance between routers. To avoid confusion, I'll use the term "metric" instead of

IP Routing

distance. The vector is simply the IP address of the router to which the packet should be delivered in order to reach its final destination; this is frequently called the "next hop."

Each routing protocol has its own way to calculate the metric. For RIP, the metric is simply the number of hops (i.e., routers) between the current router and the destination. IGRP and EIGRP use a link's bandwidth and delay to calculate a metric value. The router "decides" which path is more cost-effective by using the metric value. A lower metric value means a better route. In RIP, two hops is better than three hops, even if the two hops are slow links and the three hops are fast links. Because IGRP and EIGRP use a more complex metric, they can take into account factors such as link speeds. We'll discuss metrics in more detail when we talk about specific protocols.

Link-State Routing Protocols

Link-state protocols build snapshots of the network topology on each router. This topology of the surrounding network is then distributed to all other routers, which allows all the routers to build a picture of the entire network. This picture allows each router to compute the best path to any destination at any time.

Once all routers have received the initial flood of network information, they broadcast only changes to the entire network. For example, if a link goes down, the router noticing the problem distributes only that change to the network; it doesn't distribute the entire network table. This link-state information saves network bandwidth by reducing the amount of routing traffic needed for routing updates.

Administrative Distance

The router can learn about routes from many sources: it already knows about any interfaces to which it is directly connected, it can be configured with static routes, and it can learn routes from any number of routing protocols that are running concurrently. The routing protocols, of course, have mechanisms for deciding which routes they prefer. But how does the router decide whether to use a route learned from BGP, a route learned from RIP, or a static default route?

That's where the concept of administrative distance comes in. Each route is assigned an administrative distance, based on how the route was learned. The administrative distance tells the router how trustworthy the route is; a lower administrative distance means that a route is more trustworthy and should be used in preference to routes with higher administrative distances. Think of the route's metric as the preference of a route, while the administrative distance is the preference of how the route was discovered. The maximum administrative distance is 255; a route with an administrative distance of 255 is considered to have an unknown source and is unusable. Table 8-1 lists the default administrative distances for all route sources.

Table 8-1. Administrative distances

Routing information source	Administrative distance
Directly connected interface	0
Static route	1
External BGP	20
Internal EIGRP	90
IGRP	100
OSPF	110
IS-IS	115
RIP	120
EGP	140
External EIGRP	170
Internal BGP	200
Unknown	255

Table 8-1 shows that a route learned by a static route is preferred over a route learned by IGRP. And of course, a route to a network attached to a directly connected interface is the most preferred route.

Variable-Length Subnet Masks (VLSM) and Classless Routing

You can also divide interior routing protocols into two groups based on whether they are classful or classless. A classful protocol relies on the historical distinction between Class A, B, and C networks to interpret addresses. The router itself can use subnet masks associated with its interfaces, but the routing protocol has no way to tell other routers about the masks. The protocol assumes that the subnet mask is a constant throughout the network. In contrast, a classless protocol communicates information about subnet masks explicitly, which allows you to design much more efficient network-addressing schemes.

The biggest drawback of a classful routing protocol is the waste of IP addresses. For example, if you are building a network with a Class C address and a subnet mask of 255.255.255.224, and you need to provide a point-to-point link between two routers, you must assign a whole subnet to that link. This subnet wastes 28 IP addresses: 255.255.255.224 has a total of 32 addresses, of which 2 are not usable (the broadcast address and the subnet address) and 2 are used by the routers at the endpoints of the link; the remaining 28 are not used.

If we use a different subnet mask on this link, the wasted IP addresses can be reclaimed. In this situation, VLSM is the solution. VLSM allows us to assign a smaller subnet mask to the link itself (255.255.255.252). This mask creates an address block that has only four addresses, none of which are wasted.

 Another solution for links like this is to use the `ip unnumbered` command. See Chapter 5 for an example of how this command saves you from wasting IP addresses.

VLSM solves most IP-address issues, but it requires a classless routing protocol, i.e., a routing protocol that can explicitly exchange information about subnet masks, rather than inferring the network mask from the address class. The routing protocols that support VLSM (i.e., the classless protocols) are RIP Version 2, OSPF, EIGRP, and IS-IS. (Using static routes is, of course, consistent with VLSM because static routes don't require a routing protocol. Static routes are covered in detail in the next section.)

Protocol Comparison

Table 8-2 provides a summary of all the interior routing protocols covered in this book. (BGP isn't included because it's an exterior protocol.)

Table 8-2. Features of common interior routing protocols

	RIP	RIPv2	IGRP	EIGRP	OSPF	IS-IS
VLSM support	No	Yes	No	Yes	Yes	Yes
Convergence	Slow	Slow	Medium	Fast	Fast	Fast
Configuration	Easy	Easy	Medium	Medium	Hard	Medium
Bandwidth use	High	High	High	Low	Low	Low
Scalability	Poor	Poor	Good	Good	Good	Good
Interoperability	Yes	Yes	No	No	Yes	Yes

Static Routes

Static routes are routes you assign in the router configuration. These routes don't change until you reconfigure them yourself. You might ask, "Why not just use static routes and forget all this routing stuff?" Well, if all you had were static routes and something changed—perhaps you had to add another subnet, or you changed your Internet service provider—you would have to reconfigure every router to conform to the network changes. It would be impossible to react to short-term changes, such as equipment failures, in all but the simplest networks.

Static routes do have their place in a modern network. They are appropriate for default routes, routes to the null interface, routes to stub networks, and other situations in which the possibility of change is minimal.

To define a static route to network 192.168.11.0 via the router 192.168.5.1, you would use the command:

```
ip route 192.168.11.0 255.255.255.0 192.168.5.1
```

Default Static Routes

Static routes are commonly used for the default route. A default route is used when a router does not have a specific route to a certain address. The Internet gateway is always a good default route. For example, if our gateway router's IP address is 192.168.2.1, our default route might look like this:

```
ip route 0.0.0.0 0.0.0.0 192.168.2.1
```

On the gateway router, the static route could point to the interface that is connected to the Internet:

```
ip route 0.0.0.0 0.0.0.0 serial 0
```

The 0.0.0.0 0.0.0.0 route establishes a default only for the current router and the RIP routing protocol. Other routing protocols, such as IGRP and EIGRP, can learn a default route either from another protocol or from an explicit ip default-network command. This command tells IGRP and EIGRP to distribute the default route to other routers. To create a default network, use the ip default-network command. This route is usually created in tandem with the 0.0.0.0 0.0.0.0 route for completeness, as in this example:

```
! Define the default route for this router
ip route 0.0.0.0 0.0.0.0 192.168.2.1
! Define the default network
ip default-network 192.168.2.0
```

A Static Route to the Null Interface

A static route can be used in conjunction with the null interface to filter unwanted traffic. If we want to drop traffic to the 192.168.3.0 network, we can add a command like this to our router's configuration:

```
ip route 192.168.3.0 255.255.255.0 null0
```

This command defines a route for the 192.168.3.0 network to the null interface. The null interface discards all incoming traffic. This method of disposing of unwanted traffic is much more efficient than using an access list.

Backup Static Routes

Static routes are often used to create backup routes that come into effect when a communications link fails. To create backup static routes, you need to use the administrative distance option to the ip route command.

Normally, static routes have an administrative distance of 1, which means they are used in preference to routes learned from a routing protocol. (See Table 8-1 for a complete list of administrative distances.) This isn't how we want a backup route to behave: we want it to be used only as a last resort. Therefore, our backup route should have a higher administrative distance than our primary routes.

Let's assume that our routing protocol is RIP, which has an administrative distance of 120. We want to assign the backup route an administrative distance that's higher than the routing protocol's—we'll choose 125. Here is a configuration with a backup static route to 192.168.9.1 being redistributed into RIP:

```
! Define our backup static route with a distance of 125
ip route 192.168.11.0 255.255.255.0 192.168.9.1 125
! Configure the RIP information
router rip
  network 192.168.11.0
  network 192.168.9.0
```

Notice that we are not advertising our backup static route through RIP. (There is no redistribute command.) As a general rule, backup static routes should not be advertised; you'll want to use them only when the routes learned from the dynamic routing protocol (RIP, in this case) are unavailable.

For more information on redistributing routing information, see "Route Redistribution" later in this chapter.

Split Horizon

Split horizon is designed to stop one of the greatest routing evils, routing loops. Routing loops occur when a loop is formed between two or more routers. For example, say Router 1 has a network route to 192.168.1.0 via Router 2. Router 2 has a route to the same network, but it is back through Router 1. Therefore, Router 1 sends packets for 192.168.1.0 to Router 2, which then sends the packets back to Router 1. This looping continues until the time to live (TTL) on the packet expires.

Split horizon helps stop routing loops by telling the router not to advertise routes out the same interface from which the route was originally learned. In other words, if a router learns about a route on a particular interface, it does not broadcast that route information out that interface. Split horizon can't prevent routing loops involving three or more routers, but it's effective at preventing loops between two routers.

Split horizon is enabled by default on most interfaces. It can be disabled with the following command:

```
no ip split-horizon
```

You would want to disable split horizon on a multipoint subinterface. (See Chapter 5 for more information on subinterfaces.) An important note is that routing protocols can often work out routing loops on their own; however, split horizon solves the problem more efficiently because it prevents the loops from developing in the first place.

Passive Interfaces

The passive-interface command tells an interface to listen to RIP or IGRP routes but not to advertise them. By disabling routing announcements on an interface, we tell the router to "listen but don't talk." This feature can reduce routing load on the CPU by reducing the number of interfaces on which a protocol needs to communicate. For OSPF and EIGRP, this command completely disables route processing for that interface. Use this command only if you know for sure that the routing protocol doesn't need to talk to anything on the specified interface.

In Figure 8-2, Router 1 and Router 2 can be optimized with the passive-interface command. Without getting into the routing protocol specifics, we want to say, "Keep the EIGRP routing on the serial links and keep the RIP routing on the Ethernet interfaces." Here's how:

```
router eigrp 300
 network 192.168.10.0
 passive-interface ethernet0
```

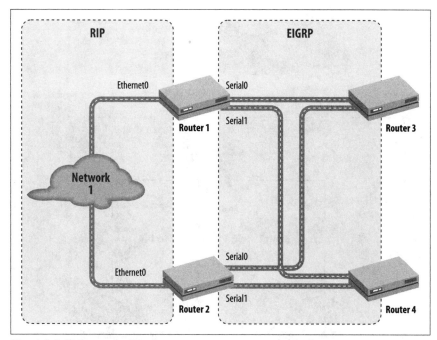

Figure 8-2. Using passive interfaces

```
router rip
  network 192.168.10.0
  passive-interface serial0
  passive-interface serial1
```

This configuration tells Router 1 and Router 2 not to send any EIGRP updates over the Ethernet interface and not to send RIP updates over the serial links. It doesn't solve the problem of getting routing information from our EIGRP process into RIP and vice versa. We will solve this problem using route redistribution.

EIGRP normally multicasts route information to neighbor routers. But we put EIGRP into passive mode, which turned off all EIGRP processing. If this were IGRP, we could use the neighbor command in conjunction with the passive-interface command to establish the relationship we wanted. The neighbor command tells RIP to send unicast updates to a particular group of routers instead of broadcasting the updates on the link; it allows us to specify which routers should receive updates. (EIGRP ignores the neighbor command—it exists only for backward compatibility with IGRP and has no effect.)

The neighbor command has greater purposes, which we'll explore in Chapter 10.

Route Redistribution

If a router is running two or more routing processes, the processes don't automatically share their routing information. Route redistribution is a particular issue when different routing protocols are involved, but it also comes up when you have two different processes using the same protocol. Figure 8-3 shows a network that uses both RIP and EIGRP.

IP Routing

Figure 8-3. Using route redistribution

Table 8-3 shows what the routing table for each router might look like.

Table 8-3. Incomplete routing tables without redistribution

Router 1	Router 2	Router 3
192.168.2.0/24 → serial1	192.168.1.0/24 → ethernet0	192.168.2.0/24 → router1
192.168.3.0/24 → serial0	192.168.2.0/24 → serial0	192.168.3.0/24 → serial1
192.168.1.0/24 → router2	192.168.3.0/24 → router1	192.168.4.0/24 → ethernet0
192.168.4.0/24 → router3		
Default → 172.30.1.2		

Router 1 knows how to get everywhere in our network. However, the other routers don't have enough information to reach all the destinations. These routing tables have three problems: Router 2 cannot get to Network 2, Router 3 cannot get to Network 1, and neither Router 2 nor Router 3 can get to the Internet.

To look at this correctly, here is the output of show ip route on each router:

```
Router1#show ip route
Codes: C - connected, S - static, I - IGRP, R - RIP, M - mobile, B - BGP
       D - EIGRP, EX - EIGRP external, O - OSPF, IA - OSPF inter area
```

```
Gateway of last resort is 172.30.1.2 to network 0.0.0.0

      172.168.0.0/24 is subnetted, 1 subnets
C        172.30.1.0 is directly connected, Ethernet0
D     192.168.4.0/24 [90/2195456] via 192.168.3.2, 00:02:00, Serial0
R     192.168.1.0/24 [120/1] via 192.168.2.2, 00:00:08, Serial1
C     192.168.2.0/24 is directly connected, Serial1
C     192.168.3.0/24 is directly connected, Serial0
S*    0.0.0.0/0 [1/0] via 172.30.1.2

Router2#show ip route
Codes: C - connected, S - static, I - IGRP, R - RIP, M - mobile, B - BGP
       D - EIGRP, EX - EIGRP external, O - OSPF, IA - OSPF inter area

Gateway of last resort is not set

C     192.168.1.0/24 is directly connected, Ethernet0
C     192.168.2.0/24 is directly connected, Serial0
R     192.168.3.0/24 [120/1] via 192.168.2.1, 00:00:26, Serial0

Router3#show ip route
Codes: C - connected, S - static, I - IGRP, R - RIP, M - mobile, B - BGP
       D - EIGRP, EX - EIGRP external, O - OSPF, IA - OSPF inter area

Gateway of last resort is not set

C     192.168.4.0/24 is directly connected, Ethernet0
D     192.168.2.0/24 [90/2681856] via 192.168.3.1, 00:09:35, Serial1
C     192.168.3.0/24 is directly connected, Serial1
```

We can fix our routing problem in a couple of ways. One option is to run RIP on the EIGRP side of Router 1 and then set static routes on Router 2 and Router 3 to point to the Internet connection. The drawback is that we are relying on static routes; worse, we have static routes to the same destination on two routers. If our Internet connection changes, we'll have to change the configuration on both Router 2 and Router 3. In this example, changing the static routes wouldn't be too much work. But what if there were 20 routers?

The second option, route redistribution, is a much better solution. To implement route redistribution across all the routing protocols on our network, we change Router 1's configuration to use redistribution between RIP and EIGRP:

```
! Define the static default route for this router and RIP
! We don't use 172.30.1.1 because that is our interface; we want to use
! the IP address of the router at the other end
ip route 0.0.0.0 0.0.0.0 172.30.1.2
!
router rip
 network 192.168.1.0
 network 192.168.2.0
 redistribute static
 redistribute eigrp 100
 passive-interface ethernet0
 default-metric 10
!
```

```
router eigrp 100
  network 192.168.3.0
  network 192.168.4.0
  redistribute static
  redistribute rip
  passive-interface serial0
  default-metric 1000 250 255 1 1500
```

With this configuration, all the routes learned on Router 1 are shared among all the routing protocols. This sharing allows Router 2 and Router 3 to learn how to reach each other's networks and the Internet. Table 8-4 shows that our routing tables are complete. The default-metric statement tells each routing process how to interpret the routes it is receiving from other sources. For example, the default-metric statement for RIP tells it to assign the metric of 10 to routes it receives through redistribution. Since these routes are coming from other protocols, they won't have metrics that make sense to RIP. Likewise, the more complicated default-metric statement for EIGRP tells EIGRP how to interpret the routes it is receiving.

Table 8-4. Routing tables completed by redistribution

Router 1	Router 2	Router 3
192.168.2.0/24 → serial1	192.168.1.0/24 → ethernet0	192.168.3.0/24 → serial1
192.168.3.0/24 → serial0	192.168.2.0/24 → serial0	192.168.4.0/24 → ethernet0
192.168.1.0/24 → router2	192.168.3.0/24 → router1	192.168.2.0/24 → router1
192.168.4.0/24 → router3	192.168.4.0/24 → router1	192.168.1.0/24 → router1
Default → 172.30.1.2	Default → 172.30.1.2	Default → 172.30.1.2

The only thing left to do is to configure some filters to prevent routing loops from occurring; we'll do that in the next section.

> The default-metric command is required for most redistribution to occur. It tells the other protocols what weight to give the learned routes. Without this command, redistribution occurs only between IGRP and EIGRP processes sharing the same process number (in which case, redistribution is automatic). Also, static routes do not require a default-metric in order to redistribute.

Here is the result of show ip route for each router, showing the new routing tables:

```
Router1#show ip route
Codes: C - connected, S - static, I - IGRP, R - RIP, M - mobile, B - BGP
       D - EIGRP, EX - EIGRP external, O - OSPF, IA - OSPF inter area
       N1 - OSPF NSSA external type 1, N2 - OSPF NSSA external type 2
       E1 - OSPF external type 1, E2 - OSPF external type 2, E - EGP
       i - IS-IS, L1 - IS-IS level-1, L2 - IS-IS level-2, * - candidate default
       U - per-user static route, o - ODR

Gateway of last resort is 172.30.1.2 to network 0.0.0.0
```

```
                172.30.0.0/16 is variably subnetted, 2 subnets, 2 masks
S                  172.30.0.0/16 [1/0] via 172.30.1.0
C                  172.30.1.0/24 is directly connected, Ethernet0
D         192.168.4.0/24 [90/2195456] via 192.168.3.2, 00:23:26, Serial0
R         192.168.1.0/24 [120/1] via 192.168.2.2, 00:00:07, Serial1
C         192.168.2.0/24 is directly connected, Serial1
C         192.168.3.0/24 is directly connected, Serial0
S*        0.0.0.0/0 [1/0] via 172.30.1.2
```

Router2#**show ip route**
```
Codes: C - connected, S - static, I - IGRP, R - RIP, M - mobile, B - BGP
       D - EIGRP, EX - EIGRP external, O - OSPF, IA - OSPF inter area
       N1 - OSPF NSSA external type 1, N2 - OSPF NSSA external type 2
       E1 - OSPF external type 1, E2 - OSPF external type 2, E - EGP
       i - IS-IS, L1 - IS-IS level-1, L2 - IS-IS level-2, * - candidate default
       U - per-user static route, o - ODR

Gateway of last resort is 192.168.2.1 to network 0.0.0.0

R     172.30.0.0/16 [120/10] via 192.168.2.1, 00:00:19, Serial0
R     192.168.4.0/24 [120/10] via 192.168.2.1, 00:00:20, Serial0
C     192.168.1.0/24 is directly connected, Ethernet0
C     192.168.2.0/24 is directly connected, Serial0
R     192.168.3.0/24 [120/1] via 192.168.2.1, 00:00:20, Serial0
R*    0.0.0.0/0 [120/10] via 192.168.2.1, 00:00:20, Serial0
```

Router3#**show ip route**
```
Codes: C - connected, S - static, I - IGRP, R - RIP, M - mobile, B - BGP
       D - EIGRP, EX - EIGRP external, O - OSPF, IA - OSPF inter area
       N1 - OSPF NSSA external type 1, N2 - OSPF NSSA external type 2
       E1 - OSPF external type 1, E2 - OSPF external type 2, E - EGP
       i - IS-IS, L1 - IS-IS level-1, L2 - IS-IS level-2, * - candidate default
       U - per-user static route, o - ODR

Gateway of last resort is 192.168.3.1 to network 0.0.0.0

D EX 172.30.0.0/16 [170/3136000] via 192.168.3.1, 00:00:34, Serial1
C     192.168.4.0/24 is directly connected, Ethernet0
D EX 192.168.1.0/24 [170/3136000] via 192.168.3.1, 00:00:34, Serial1
D     192.168.2.0/24 [90/2681856] via 192.168.3.1, 00:22:01, Serial1
C     192.168.3.0/24 is directly connected, Serial1
D*EX 0.0.0.0/0 [170/3136000] via 192.168.3.1, 00:00:34, Serial1
```

Filtering Routes

We can use access lists to get better control over route redistribution. Access lists
define filters that control which routes the router will listen to or advertise,
depending on the distribute-list command. The distribute-list command
specifies the direction (in or out) and the access list to use. The access list is then
applied to the route redistribution process. To put it another way, the access list
allows us to say "Allow routes from here" and "Don't send routes here."

Filtering incoming routes

To filter incoming routes, the `distribute-list` command is followed by the `in` option. In other words, we are filtering routes that the router hears. The following example applies access list 10 to all incoming RIP routes. If the incoming routes do not match access list 10, they are dropped into a bit bucket:

```
access-list 10 permit 192.168.1.0 0.0.0.255
router rip
 network 192.168.1.0
 network 192.168.2.0
 distribute-list 10 in
```

No matter where the update comes from, any route that does not match network 192.168.1.0 is ignored by RIP. We can take this a step further and say "Any route that arrives via the ethernet0 interface will be checked with access list 10":

```
access-list 10 permit 192.168.1.0 0.0.0.255
router rip
 network 192.168.0.0
 distribute-list 10 in ethernet0
```

Filtering outgoing routes

The `distribute-list` command can also be applied to information the router sends. Just as `distribute-list` in controls what the router can hear, `distribute-list` out controls what the router can announce. In other words, we are filtering outgoing routes. If an outgoing route does not match the access list, it will not be sent. For example:

```
access-list 10 permit 192.168.1.0 0.0.0.255
router rip
 network 192.168.1.0
 network 192.168.2.0
 distribute-list 10 out
```

This configuration globally applies the `distribute-list` to all outgoing RIP routes. The result is that our router won't tell any other routers about routes that don't match the 192.168.1.0/24 network. And in the same way as before, we can apply the access list to one interface (ethernet0):

```
access-list 10 permit 192.168.1.0 0.0.0.255
router rip
 network 192.168.1.0
 network 192.168.2.0
 distribute-list 10 out ethernet0
```

The addition of ethernet0 says that the router applies access list 10 only to routes announced through the ethernet0 interface. The access list doesn't apply to routes advertised through other interfaces—any other interfaces are allowed to announce any routes that are available.

Filtering updates during redistribution

We can do one more thing with the outgoing `distribute-list` command: control the redistribution of routes from one protocol into another protocol. In the example we have been using, we are redistributing into RIP. Now we add the `distribute-list` command to ensure that RIP ignores routes from EIGRP that originated from RIP. `distribute-list 10 out eigrp 100` means "Apply access list 10 to announced routes that were derived from EIGRP 100."

```
access-list 10 deny 192.168.1.0 0.0.0.255
access-list 10 permit any
!
router rip
 network 192.168.1.0
 network 192.168.2.0
 default-metric 10
 redistribute eigrp 100
 distribute-list 10 out eigrp 100
```

Filtering routes that are redistributed from one protocol into another helps to eliminate routing loops by preventing a protocol from learning its own routes from another source.

Revisiting the example

Now let's put all the pieces together. Figure 8-3 shows a network with a routing problem that we solved by redistributing EIGRP into RIP. EIGRP is smart enough to handle the RIP routes and label them as such. RIP is not that smart, so we want to control its redistribution by adding an access list that filters the routes originating from RIP before they are added back into the RIP routing table. Our final configuration adds the necessary filtering to prevent routing loops from forming:

```
! Define the static route for this router and RIP
ip route 0.0.0.0 0.0.0.0 172.30.1.2
!
! Define the RIP process
!
router rip
 network 192.168.1.0
 network 192.168.2.0
 redistribute static
 redistribute eigrp 100
 passive-interface ethernet0
 default-metric 10
 ! Add the distribute-list command with access list 10
 distribute-list 10 out eigrp 100
!
! Define the EIGRP process
!
router eigrp 100
 network 192.168.3.0
 network 192.168.4.0
 redistribute static
 redistribute rip
```

```
    passive-interface serial0
    default-metric 1000 250 255 1 150
    distribute-list 11 out rip
    !
    ! Define access list 10
    ! We want to deny routes from EIGRP that are RIP routes
    ! but permit everything else
    access-list 10 deny 192.168.1.0 0.0.0.255
    access-list 10 permit any
    ! Define access list 10
    ! We want to permit the RIP routes into EIGRP and
    ! deny everything else
    access-list 11 permit 192.168.1.0 0.0.0.255
    access-list 11 deny any
```

Route Maps

Route maps allow you to influence network traffic by changing the attributes of a route based on its characteristics. We can use a route map to modify metrics, the next-hop address, the default interface, and other attributes. This feature becomes increasingly important in BGP and OSPF route redistribution because of the complexity of these protocols.

A route map comprises a list of match criteria, followed by a list of set instructions. The match criteria are similar to access list entries: they describe the incoming routing updates we want to modify. This match can in fact be based on whether a route passes an access list (i.e., matches can be based on an IP address), but it also allows you to select updates based on other criteria, such as route metrics and route tags. The set instructions tell the router what to do with the route once it has a match. In our first example, we change a route's metric based on the source IP address of the packet.

In this example, we define a route map using access list 10. The route map is given the name our-example-map. Route-map names (or *tags*, as they are also called) can be anything you want. After defining the map name, we say that the map uses access list 10 to match a route's destination IP address. (There are many other things we could match. For example, we could match the route's next-hop address, using the command match ip next-hop; or we could match the address of the router from which the route came by using the command match ip route-source. See Chapter 17 for a complete list of match items for route maps.) If any route's destination address matches access list 10, we set the route's metric to 20.

```
    ! Define the route map named "our-example-map"
    route-map our-example-map
      match ip address 10
      set metric 20
    !
    ! Define the access-list that is used in the route-map
    access-list 10 permit 192.168.1.0 0.0.0.255
```

In the OSPF section of Chapter 9, route maps are used to control redistribution between RIP and OSPF. In that redistribution, we want to take the external routes from OSPF and redistribute them into RIP. The only way to achieve that granularity of routing control is to use route maps.

Enforcing routing policy with route maps

Route maps allow us to enforce routing policies. We'll start with an example in which we use a route map to control redistribution. We want to give a redistributed RIP route from certain routers a higher metric than a route coming from other routers. In other words, we are going to trust some routers more than others. We may make this decision for political reasons, or we could just know that one router has better routes, for reasons the routing protocol can't determine.

In this example, we will use two additional features of route maps. First, a route map can contain the permit or deny keyword, which gives us finer control over which routes match. Second, a route map can have a sequence number, which lets us build chains of route maps.

Here's how the permit and deny keywords and sequence numbers are used. If a route map includes the permit keyword, the following occurs when a route arrives:

1. The route is tested against the access list. If it does not match, the next route map in the sequence is tried. If there are no more maps in the sequence, the route is not redistributed.

2. If the route does match the access list, the route map's set options are applied, and the route is redistributed. No more maps in the sequence are processed.

If the route map includes the deny keyword and the route matches the map's access list, the route is not redistributed and no other route maps in the sequence are used.

If a map doesn't contain either deny or permit, the map is part of a policy. The operation specified by the set command is applied if there is a match. In any case, after this map is processed, processing proceeds to the next map in the sequence. No filtering takes place (all routes going through a policy map are eventually redistributed, since no routes are denied), but the route's properties may be changed.

Here is a configuration that redistributes routes from RIP into EIGRP using route maps. The example uses two route maps with the name rip-to-eigrp, but with different sequence numbers (10 and 15). The sequence numbers determine the order in which the two maps are processed: first map 10, then map 15.

 It's a good idea to avoid using consecutive sequence numbers when you're first writing a policy. In our example, we used sequence numbers 10 and 15. If we later need to add a map that's processed after 10 and before 15, we can assign it number 12. If we used consecutive sequence numbers, it would be much harder to add a map to the sequence at a later time.

```
! EIGRP configuration
router eigrp 99
  network 10.0.0.0
  default-metric 1000 250 255 1 1500
  ! Set up redistribution of RIP routes into EIGRP using the route-map
  ! named rip-to-eigrp
  redistribute rip route-map rip-to-eigrp
!
! RIP configuration
```

```
router rip
 network 10.0.0.0
 !
 ! Define our route-maps
route-map rip-to-eigrp permit 10
   match ip route-source 2
   set metric 1000 100 250 100 1500
route-map rip-to-eigrp permit 15
   match ip route-source 3
   set metric 500 100 250 100 1500
 !
 ! Define the access lists that are used in the route maps
access-list 2 permit 10.11.1.1 0.0.0.0
access-list 3 permit any
```

In this example, routes are first processed by the map named rip-to-eigrp, which consists of two submaps, numbered 10 and 15. Map 10 uses access list 2 to select routes that were learned from the router at 10.11.1.1. These routes are given the default metric, which has a bandwidth parameter of 1000. If the route matches, processing ends, and the route is redistributed with the default metric. If the route doesn't match, processing continues with route map 15. This route map uses access list 3, which matches all IP addresses. Therefore, the route map gives all routes that reach it the bandwidth metric of 500, instead of the default; the other parameters are the same. Therefore, we are saying that the 10.11.1.1 router knows about routes that have more bandwidth available than any other routers. Consequently, EIGRP computes a better (lower) metric for them and uses them in preference to routes learned from other routers.

Enforcing routing policy with the ip policy command

In the previous example, we relied on the redistribute command to enforce our redistribution policy. Routing policies can also be enforced on the interface level using the command ip policy, which applies route maps to packets arriving at that interface. The ip policy command can be extremely CPU-intensive, so use it with care. Another tool for enforcing routing policies is the ip local policy route-map command. Unlike the ip policy command, which defines a policy (route map) to be applied to routes coming in an interface, ip local policy route-map is a global configuration command that applies the route maps to all routing packets generated by the router.

In this example, we want to assign specific routes based on the packet's destination IP address. The routes are assigned if there are no default routes for the addresses we are matching. We accomplish this by configuring the serial0 interface to use the route map called examplemap. Our route map implements the following rules for packets arriving on serial0:

1. Packets to the 172.30.10.0 network are sent to router 172.30.100.1.
2. Packets to the 172.30.15.0 network are sent to router 172.30.200.1.
3. Rules 1 and 2 apply only if the packets arrive on interface serial0 and no default route already exists for that destination.
4. All other routes coming in serial0 are passed along as usual.

The router configuration would look like this:

```
! Configure the interface serial0
interface serial0
  ip policy route-map examplemap
  ip address 172.30.1.1 255.255.255.0
!
! Set up the first part of the route map
route-map examplemap permit 10
  match ip address 1
  set ip default next-hop 172.30.100.1
!
! Set up the second part of the route map
route-map examplemap permit 15
  match ip address 2
  set ip default next-hop 172.30.200.1
!
! Define the access lists for use in the route maps
access-list 1 permit 172.30.10.0 0.0.0.255
access-list 1 deny any
access-list 2 permit 172.30.15.0 0.0.0.255
access-list 2 deny any
```

Route maps are explored again in Chapters 9 and 10.

Fast Switching and Process Switching

Whether you use fast switching or process switching can affect the way your routes behave. In one project with which I was involved, the administrators wanted to balance traffic across two T1 lines using EIGRP to perform load balancing. They observed that a daily file transfer always used a single line, which wasn't what they wanted. The problem was that EIGRP's load balancing is session-based, not packet-based. Therefore, once the file transfer started, it was able to use only one of the lines. The solution was to configure the router for process switching rather than fast switching, because process switching is able to load balance on a per-packet basis.

Before looking at this example further, let's look more closely at the difference between fast switching and process switching and the effect each has on routing.

Fast Switching

When the first packet of a session is going out an interface, a route is selected and placed in a route cache. This route cache entry is used for all packets belonging to this specific destination, which means that all packets belonging to the session take the same route. An entry remains in the route cache until the route cache is flushed, the route changes, or the cache overflows. (When a cache overflows, the entry that was least recently used is removed.)

A session is a communication on a port to a specific host. For example, if Host A is FTPing to Host B, each file is transferred in a single session. Successive file transfers require new sessions—i.e., different connections between the client and the server, using different ports. Looking back at the load-balancing problem we discussed at the beginning of this section, we can see that EIGRP would have been able to perform load balancing across the T1 lines if there were multiple file transfer sessions. Since there was only one file transfer, there was only one session, and there was nothing EIGRP could do. There was no way to put the second line to use.

A route cache eliminates the need for the router to select a new route for each packet of a session. Since selecting a route takes time, the route cache saves processing time and lessens the packet's time inside the router. The first packet of the session determines the route; this route is used for every packet for this destination for as long as the route remains in the route cache.

In Figure 8-4, Router 3 has chosen to send the first packet of a file transfer via Router 1; therefore, this route was added to the route cache. The server, Host B, produces a great deal of traffic for this session, all of which goes across the serial0 interface (i.e., to Router 1). Load sharing when using fast switching is session-oriented, not packet-oriented, so Router 3 will use serial0 for the entire file transfer even if there is no traffic on serial1.

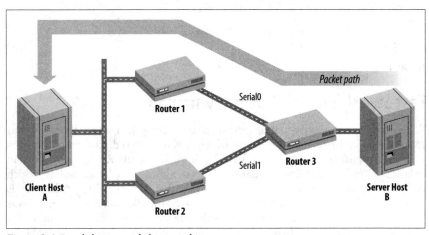

Figure 8-4. Load sharing with fast switching

Process Switching

Process switching is the opposite of fast switching. Every packet that comes into the router is handled independently and can take a different path to its destination. Process switching therefore allows *load sharing* across links that might otherwise not be utilized. Load sharing is not the same as load balancing; load balancing requires more thought on the router's part than simply picking a route for every packet.

Process switching presents two problems: the CPU has to do more work because each packet has to be processed, and sending packets via different routes might cause the packets to arrive at the destination out of sequence. If the packets arrive out of sequence, the destination host needs to do more work to place the packets back together in the correct sequence, which burns up more CPU time and possibly degrades performance.

To enable process switching on an interface, use the no ip route-cache command, which disables the route cache on an interface. A new route must be selected for every packet of a session.

For example, let's revisit Figure 8-4. If the main purpose of the remote site were to transfer data every few hours across our T1s, and nothing else, we might want to optimize the router's configuration so that it uses both T1 lines for these file transfer sessions. To do so, we would add the following to Router 3's configuration:

```
! disable route cache on both interfaces
interface serial0
 no ip route-cache
!
interface serial1
 no ip route-cache
```

Now both lines are used to transmit that session's data. Since there is no route cache, load sharing will be handled on a per-packet basis, spreading the load of the file transfer across the two T1s. This feature works well in this example because of the nature of our network and the requirements of our application. In many other environments, disabling the route cache would be a bad idea. For example, a real-time video feed would require a lot of bandwidth and could benefit from load balancing—but the application probably couldn't tolerate packets arriving out of sequence. In other situations, the additional overhead of process switching might degrade the router's performance so much that the actual throughput wouldn't be satisfactory.

Useful show Commands

The most useful show command for IP routing is show ip route, which we used earlier when talking about redistribution. Here is an example of its output:

```
Router1#show ip route
Codes: C - connected, S - static, I - IGRP, R - RIP, M - mobile, B - BGP
       D - EIGRP, EX - EIGRP external, O - OSPF, IA - OSPF inter area
       N1 - OSPF NSSA external type 1, N2 - OSPF NSSA external type 2
       E1 - OSPF external type 1, E2 - OSPF external type 2, E - EGP
       i - IS-IS, L1 - IS-IS level-1, L2 - IS-IS level-2, * - candidate default
       U - per-user static route, o - ODR

Gateway of last resort is 172.30.1.2 to network 0.0.0.0

     172.30.0.0/24 is subnetted, 1 subnets
C       172.30.1.0 is directly connected, Ethernet0
D    192.168.4.0/24 [90/2195456] via 192.168.3.2, 00:00:47, Serial0
R    192.168.1.0/24 [120/1] via 192.168.2.2, 00:00:20, Serial1
C    192.168.2.0/24 is directly connected, Serial1
C    192.168.3.0/24 is directly connected, Serial0
S*   0.0.0.0/0 [1/0] via 172.30.1.2
```

In this example, we have three connected routes, which are listed with a C. We have one EIGRP route for network 192.168.4.0/24, which is listed with a D. And finally, the R tells us that we have one RIP route for the network 192.168.1.0/24.

We can take this one step further by adding a network to the end of the command to get specific information for that route. For example:

```
Router1#show ip route 172.30.1.0
Routing entry for 172.30.1.0/24
   Known via "connected", distance 0, metric 0 (connected)
   Routing Descriptor Blocks:
   * directly connected, via Ethernet0
        Route metric is 0, traffic share count is 1

Router1#show ip route 192.168.1.0
Routing entry for 192.168.1.0/24
   Known via "rip", distance 120, metric 1
   Redistributing via eigrp 100, rip
   Advertised by eigrp 100
   Last update from 192.168.2.2 on Serial1, 00:00:03 ago
   Routing Descriptor Blocks:
   * 192.168.2.2, from 192.168.2.2, 00:00:03 ago, via Serial1
        Route metric is 1, traffic share count is 1
```

The last two commands ask for specific route information for the 172.30.1.0 and 192.168.1.0 networks. Given the output, we can see how the router learned the route, which is "connected" in the first example and "rip" the second example. We can see that the 192.168.1.0 network is redistributed into EIGRP, which also advertises it. Finally, we can see when the last routing update occurred.

show ip route summary

A useful option to show ip route is summary. Our router gives us the following output:

```
Router1#show ip route summary
Route Source   Networks   Subnets   Overhead   Memory (bytes)
connected      2          1         156        552
static         1          0         52         184
eigrp 100      1          0         52         184
rip            1          0         52         184
internal       1                               138
Total          6          1         312        1242
```

This output shows us all the different route sources (connected, internal, static, eigrp, and rip) that are currently configured and running on our router. For each route source, this command shows the total number of networks it has reported and the total number of subnets. The Overhead and Memory columns aren't particularly meaningful. Taken together, they represent the total amount of memory required by these routes. It's not clear what you could do with this information, except possibly to determine that you need to buy memory expansion if your routing table includes a particularly large number of routes.

clear ip route

The clear ip route command allows you to remove entries from the router's routing table. With an IP address as an argument, it clears routes for that particular address. With * as an argument, it clears the entire routing table:

```
Router#clear ip route *
```

show ip protocols

The command show ip protocols gives us a detailed account of each routing protocol that is currently running on the router. Most of the output from this command should look familiar if you know the routing protocols you're using. Here is the output from a router running EIGRP and RIP:

```
Router1#show ip protocols
Routing Protocol is "eigrp 100"
  Outgoing update filter list for all interfaces is
  Incoming update filter list for all interfaces is
  Default networks flagged in outgoing updates
  Default networks accepted from incoming updates
  EIGRP metric weight K1=1, K2=0, K3=1, K4=0, K5=0
  EIGRP maximum hopcount 100
  EIGRP maximum metric variance 1
  Default redistribution metric is 1000 250 255 1 1500
  Redistributing: static, eigrp 100, rip
  Automatic network summarization is in effect
  Automatic address summarization:
    192.168.4.0/24 for Serial0
  Routing for Networks:
    192.168.3.0
    192.168.4.0
  Passive Interface(s):
    Serial1
  Routing Information Sources:
    Gateway         Distance      Last Update
    192.168.3.2           90      00:21:33
  Distance: internal 90 external 170

Routing Protocol is "rip"
  Sending updates every 30 seconds, next due in 14 seconds
  Invalid after 180 seconds, hold down 180, flushed after 240
  Outgoing update filter list for all interfaces is
  Incoming update filter list for all interfaces is
  Default redistribution metric is 10
  Redistributing: static, eigrp 100, rip
  Default version control: send version 1, receive any version
    Interface        Send  Recv  Key-chain
    Serial1            1     1 2
  Routing for Networks:
    192.168.1.0
    192.168.2.0
  Passive Interface(s):
    Serial0
  Routing Information Sources:
    Gateway         Distance      Last Update
    192.168.2.2          120      00:00:06
  Distance: (default is 120)
```

9

Interior Routing Protocols

This chapter discusses interior routing protocols including Routing Information Protocol (RIP), the Interior Gateway Routing Protocol (IGRP) and the newer Enhanced IGRP (EIGRP), Open Shortest Path First (OSPF), and Intermediate System–to–Intermediate System (IS-IS).

RIP

The Routing Information Protocol (RIP) is the oldest routing protocol that is still widely used. It has a large support base and a simple configuration. However, it also has a major drawback: poor route determination. RIP is a distance-vector protocol that looks only at the number of route hops (i.e., the number of routers crossed in traveling from one network to another) in computing the best route. For example, let's say that there are two routes to a destination. The first route crosses two separate 56K links, for a metric of 2; the second route crosses three T1 links, for a metric of 3. RIP always selects the first (two-hop) route, even though it is obvious that the second route is better under almost all circumstances. It's possible to use offset lists to force RIP to choose the better route, but that's merely adapting to the problem, not fixing it.

Another problem with RIP is that it can't scale to large networks. There are two scaling issues. First, routers using RIP periodically broadcast the entire routing table to the network. These broadcasts can eat precious bandwidth on lines that often can't afford it. Second, RIP considers any route past 15 hops unreachable. In addition, RIP does not support Variable-Length Subnet Masks (VLSM), an important technique for conserving IP-address space. Nor does it have any mechanism for authenticating other routers; it isn't difficult to trick RIP into believing bogus routing information. And it isn't particularly quick at settling on a new set of routes after the network is disrupted.

RIPv2 tried to solve some of RIP's shortcomings by introducing support for VLSM, bandwidth calculations (a more sophisticated metric for determining the best route), and route authentication. However, it is still limited by the basic scaling problem of its predecessor, the 15-hop limit. Any route that exceeds 15 hops is still considered unreachable.

With all of RIP's drawbacks, which are only partially addressed in Version 2, why would you consider RIP at all? You might find that RIP suits your needs if you have a small network and would like a routing protocol that is easy to manage. It's also supported by just about every piece of network hardware in existence, so you may be forced to use RIP if you have a large installed base that you can't afford to replace. In short, while RIP works well in small environments with only a handful of routers, most networks today require a more sophisticated and scalable routing protocol. Still, despite its drawbacks, RIP will be with us for the foreseeable future.

Basic RIP Configuration

Figure 9-1 shows a network configuration in which we want to enable RIP on Router 1, Router 2, and Router 3.

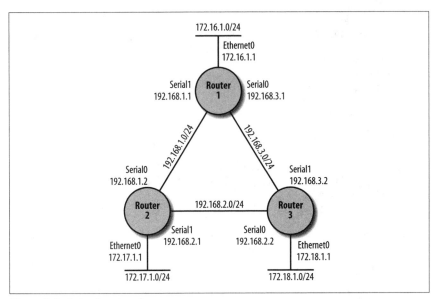

Figure 9-1. A simple network

To enable RIP on the routers, we use the router rip command followed by the network command, which lists the networks that are directly connected to each router and that are participating in RIP. We don't have to list networks that aren't directly connected—RIP's job is to find out about these. Likewise, we don't need to list networks that aren't running RIP; if there are any (and there aren't in this example), we'll have to handle them through route redistribution.

For Router 1, the configuration looks like this:

```
interface Ethernet0
 ip address 172.16.1.1 255.255.255.0
 !
```

```
interface Serial0
 ip address 192.168.3.1 255.255.255.0
 !
interface Serial1
 ip address 192.168.1.1 255.255.255.0
 !
router rip
 version 2
 network 172.16.0.0
 network 192.168.1.0
 network 192.168.3.0
```

Here's the configuration for Router 2:

```
interface Ethernet0
 ip address 172.17.1.1 255.255.255.0
 !
interface Serial0
 ip address 192.168.1.2 255.255.255.0
 !
interface Serial1
 ip address 192.168.2.1 255.255.255.0
 !
router rip
 version 2
 network 172.17.0.0
 network 192.168.1.0
 network 192.168.2.0
```

For Router 3, the configuration is:

```
interface Ethernet0
 ip address 172.18.1.1 255.255.255.0
 !
interface Serial0
 ip address 192.168.2.2 255.255.255.0
 !
interface Serial1
 ip address 192.168.3.2 255.255.255.0
 !
router rip
 version 2
 network 172.18.0.0
 network 192.168.2.0
 network 192.168.3.0
```

Remember that RIP (as well as IGRP and EIGRP) is a classful routing protocol. Therefore, we need to be careful about our network statements. For example, on Router 1 we specify 172.16.0.0 (the classful address), not 172.16.1.0.

After the routers are configured, show ip route shows that everything is working nicely:

```
Router1#show ip route
Codes: C - connected, S - static, I - IGRP, R - RIP, M - mobile, B - BGP
       D - EIGRP, EX - EIGRP external, O - OSPF, IA - OSPF inter area
       N1 - OSPF NSSA external type 1, N2 - OSPF NSSA external type 2
```

```
        E1 - OSPF external type 1, E2 - OSPF external type 2, E - EGP
        i - IS-IS, L1 - IS-IS level-1, L2 - IS-IS level-2, * - candidate default
        U - per-user static route, o - ODR

Gateway of last resort is not set

R    172.17.0.0/16 [120/1] via 192.168.1.2, 00:00:09, Serial1
     172.16.0.0/24 is subnetted, 1 subnets
C       172.16.1.0 is directly connected, Ethernet0
R    172.18.0.0/16 [120/1] via 192.168.3.2, 00:00:03, Serial0
C    192.168.1.0/24 is directly connected, Serial1
R    192.168.2.0/24 [120/1] via 192.168.3.2, 00:00:03, Serial0
                    [120/1] via 192.168.1.2, 00:00:10, Serial1
C    192.168.3.0/24 is directly connected, Serial0
```

From this output, we can see that Router 1 knows how to get to the 172.17.0.0/16 network through Serial1. Note that RIP has summarized 172.17.1.0/24 into a classful network boundary. It has done the same for 172.16.0.0/16 and 172.18.0.0/16. Automatic summarization is enabled by default in most protocols. To disable this behavior, use the no auto-summary command. In our little network, summarization works. (If we had subnetted differently, summarization could have been a big problem. See "EIGRP" later in this chapter for a complete example of how auto-summarization can affect a network.) The output from show ip route also shows that Router 1 knows two paths to the 192.168.2.0/24 network.

Now, let's ping to make sure that our network is functional. From Router 1, ping Router 2's Ethernet interface:

```
Router1#ping 172.17.1.1

Type escape sequence to abort.
Sending 5, 100-byte ICMP Echos to 172.17.1.1, timeout is 2 seconds:
!!!!!
Success rate is 100 percent (5/5), round-trip min/avg/max = 28/29/32 ms
```

Now ping Router 3's Ethernet interface:

```
Router1#ping 172.18.1.1

Type escape sequence to abort.
Sending 5, 100-byte ICMP Echos to 172.18.1.1, timeout is 2 seconds:
!!!!!
Success rate is 100 percent (5/5), round-trip min/avg/max = 28/30/32 ms
```

While the pings were successful, this isn't a true test of our routing configuration—it only tests connectivity to the router. Still, ping is an extremely useful tool for showing that your hosts are on the network and reachable.

Enabling RIPv2 on the Network

By default, a Cisco router automatically listens to both Versions 1 and 2 of RIP. However, it sends only Version 1 packets. If you want to use RIPv2, you must enable it by using the version 2 command, as we did in the previous example. To get finer control over which version of RIP you're using, you can use the ip rip command to enable or disable Version 2 at the interface level. This command allows the router to talk Version 2 out one interface and Version 1 out another. See the ip rip command in Chapter 17 for more information.

Redistributing Other Routing Protocols into RIP

Many networks use two or more routing protocols; often, a second protocol is needed at the interface between one network and another. Less often, two protocols will be used within one network, possibly to accommodate older equipment. This raises a problem with metrics: one protocol's route metric might not translate to the metric used by another protocol. We use the default-metric command to assign a default metric value to routes received from other protocols. In the following example, we need to redistribute routes learned from EIGRP into RIP. However, these protocols have incompatible metrics. To solve this problem, we assign a default metric of 10, which is given to all routes that don't otherwise have a metric—i.e., routes learned from other protocols (in this case, all routes learned from EIGRP):

```
router rip
  network 10.0.0.0
  default-metric 10
  redistribute eigrp 100
```

In this case, the EIGRP process number is 100. Depending on the routing protocol being redistributed, a process number may or may not be required.

RIPv2 Authentication

RIPv2 authentication provides some basic security to the routing updates. Since RIP automatically listens to anyone on the network who is also using RIP, a malicious user could easily intercept and corrupt the routing tables by injecting false information. RIPv2's authentication provides a password-like mechanism called a key to authenticate the routes from other machines.

The default authentication method is text, which means the passwords are exchanged in clear text. The keys will appear in every RIPv2 packet, so clear text is not secure. Anyone with a packet-sniffing program (such as *ethereal* or *snoop*) can discover what the passwords are by scanning all the RIP packets on a network. However, the authentication mode can easily be changed to use the MD5 message-digest algorithm, as in the following example. While MD5 is not true encryption, the passwords are no longer exchanged in clear text.

In this example, we configure the key chain and the authentication mode. The key chain is a series of passwords we are willing to accept. The final step is to enable RIPv2 authentication for an interface, which in this case is ethernet1. (For more information on key configuration, see Chapter 15.)

```
interface ethernet1
  ip rip authentication key-chain group1
  ip rip authentication mode md5
  !
key chain group1
  key 1
  key-string authme1
```

```
  key 2
  key-string authme2
!
router rip
  version 2
  network 10.0.0.0
```

In this configuration, all RIP updates going in and out of ethernet1 are subject to
RIPv2 authentication, which requires the key authme1 or authme2.

IGRP

Like RIP, the Interior Gateway Routing Protocol is a distance-vector routing
protocol. Today, IGRP has been superseded by Enhanced IGRP (EIGRP), which
has many new features and is covered later in this chapter. The two protocols are
fundamentally similar, configuration-wise, and this section serves as an introduction for both.

IGRP and EIGRP have a compound metric that takes into account several factors,
such as link bandwidth and latency. As such, IGRP is superior to RIP, which takes
into account only the hop count, and RIPv2, which uses both hop count and
bandwidth. In addition to the compound metric, which allows better route selection, IGRP tends to have better convergence times, meaning that routing stabilizes
more quickly after a network disruption. In addition, although it is more difficult
to configure than RIP, configuration is still relatively easy.

The biggest drawback of IGRP and EIGRP is that they are proprietary, which
means they are implemented only by Cisco routers. If all you have on your
network are Cisco devices, using IGRP is not a problem. However, if you have a
multivendor environment, you'll be forced to use multiple routing protocols or to
agree on a protocol (such as RIP or OSPF) that is supported by all your vendors.
Another disadvantage is that IGRP (like RIP) broadcasts the entire routing table,
which can consume a lot of network bandwidth. In addition, like RIP, IGRP does
not support VLSM. If you use VLSM—and you probably should—you need to
use EIGRP.

Basic IGRP Configuration

For this example, we will reuse the network diagram in Figure 9-1. We want to
enable IGRP on Router 1 and Router 2. We'll add the bandwidth command on the
serial interfaces because IGRP uses bandwidth for the route metric calculation.
The bandwidth command is necessary on the serial interfaces because the router is
unable to determine a default bandwidth for them. The Ethernet interface does
not need a bandwidth command since the router will supply a reasonable default.

The IGRP commands for Router 1 look like this:

```
interface Ethernet0
 ip address 172.16.1.1 255.255.255.0
!
interface Serial0
 bandwidth 125
```

```
  ip address 192.168.3.1 255.255.255.0
  !
interface Serial1
 bandwidth 125
 ip address 192.168.1.1 255.255.255.0
 !
router igrp 101
  network 172.16.0.0
  network 192.168.1.0
  network 192.168.3.0
```

For Router 2, they look like this:

```
interface Ethernet0
 ip address 172.17.1.1 255.255.255.0
 !
interface Serial0
 bandwidth 125
 ip address 192.168.1.2 255.255.255.0
 !
interface Serial1
 bandwidth 125
 ip address 192.168.2.1 255.255.255.0
 !
router igrp 101
  network 172.17.0.0
  network 192.168.1.0
  network 192.168.2.0
```

And for Router 3, they look like this:

```
interface Ethernet0
 ip address 172.18.1.1 255.255.255.0
 !
interface Serial0
 bandwidth 125
 ip address 192.168.2.2 255.255.255.0
 !
interface Serial1
 bandwidth 125
 ip address 192.168.3.2 255.255.255.0
 !
router igrp 101
  network 172.18.0.0
  network 192.168.2.0
  network 192.168.3.0
```

These commands configure IGRP on the proper networks with a local-AS number of 101. The local-AS number is essentially a process number that serves to identify the routers that will exchange routing information. The actual value you pick is immaterial, as long as all the routers running IGRP on the network use the same value. If they do not, they won't share routing information.

Let's run show ip route and send a few pings to make sure everything is running well:

```
Router1#show ip route
Codes: C - connected, S - static, I - IGRP, R - RIP, M - mobile, B - BGP
       D - EIGRP, EX - EIGRP external, O - OSPF, IA - OSPF inter area
       N1 - OSPF NSSA external type 1, N2 - OSPF NSSA external type 2
       E1 - OSPF external type 1, E2 - OSPF external type 2, E - EGP
       i - IS-IS, L1 - IS-IS level-1, L2 - IS-IS level-2, * - candidate default
       U - per-user static route, o - ODR

Gateway of last resort is not set

I    172.17.0.0/16 [100/82100] via 192.168.1.2, 00:01:05, Serial1
     172.16.0.0/24 is subnetted, 1 subnets
C       172.16.1.0 is directly connected, Ethernet0
I    172.18.0.0/16 [100/82100] via 192.168.3.2, 00:00:02, Serial0
C    192.168.1.0/24 is directly connected, Serial1
I    192.168.2.0/24 [100/84000] via 192.168.1.2, 00:01:06, Serial1
                    [100/84000] via 192.168.3.2, 00:00:02, Serial0
C    192.168.3.0/24 is directly connected, Serial0
```

From Router 1, ping Router 2's Ethernet interface:

```
Router1#ping 172.17.1.1

Type escape sequence to abort.
Sending 5, 100-byte ICMP Echos to 172.17.1.1, timeout is 2 seconds:
!!!!!
Success rate is 100 percent (5/5), round-trip min/avg/max = 28/31/32 ms
```

From Router 1, ping Router 3's Ethernet interface:

```
Router1#ping 172.18.1.1

Type escape sequence to abort.
Sending 5, 100-byte ICMP Echos to 172.18.1.1, timeout is 2 seconds:
!!!!!
Success rate is 100 percent (5/5), round-trip min/avg/max = 28/31/32 ms
```

Once again, the ping shows only that a working path exists between two hosts. It is by no means a complete test of our routing configuration.

IGRP's metric

Previously, we called the metric used by IGRP a *compound* metric, which means it uses more than one value to decide which route to use. The factors IGRP uses to calculate a metric are bandwidth, load, delay, and reliability. Before we examine the formula used to compute the metric, you should understand each of the variables:

bandwidth
> The speed of the line. The bandwidth of any particular link is a configuration item—it isn't derived from the hardware itself. However, there are defaults for almost all media types except serial links. Ethernet, FDDI, token ring, etc., all have default bandwidth settings. Bandwidth is measured in 1-Kbps units; thus, the bandwidth for an Ethernet link is 10,000 Kbps.

delay

The total delay for the path in 10-microsecond units. To get the delay for the entire route, the delay values for all the route's links are added together and the result is divided by 10.

load

A number between 1 and 255, which is a fraction of 255 that reflects the link's usage. A fully loaded link has the value of 255 (which equals 100%); a link with no load is assigned the value 1, which is the lowest possible value. If the loading were at 50%, the load value would be 128 (128/255).

reliability

Like load, reliability is a fraction of 255, where 255 represents 100% reliability and 1 represents the lowest reliability.

In all its gory detail, the metric equation is:

$$Metric = (K1 \times bandwidth) + \frac{(K2 \times bandwidth)}{(256 - load)} + (K3 \times delay)$$

If K5 is greater than 0, you need to apply this second step:

$$Metric = Metric \times \frac{K5}{(reliability + K4)}$$

K1 through K5 are constants used to control the equation's behavior. By varying these constants, you can give a higher or lower priority to different variables. By default, K1 and K3 equal 1, and K2, K4, and K5 equal 0. This means that, in effect, the metric calculation is much simpler:

$$Metric = bandwidth + delay$$

As with any distance-vector protocol, the route with the smallest metric (think in terms of weight) is the best route for the packet to travel.

Despite all this talk about a compound metric, it's apparent that IGRP's default metric is really quite simple and depends only on the bandwidth and the delay. What's the use of having a great compound metric if you set up the constants so that most of the interesting features of that metric are discarded? Well, it is possible to adapt the metric for use in special situations. The command for changing the constants is metric weights *tos k1 k2 k3 k4 k5*. (The tos is a value that is not used; refer to Chapter 17 for an explanation.)

Making intelligent decisions about how to change the constants is beyond the scope of this book. It's easy to make a change that has side effects you don't want. For example, we could tell the router to use the load factor by setting K2 to 1. However, in most networks, this change would have a serious side effect. A link's load can increase and decrease fairly quickly. Each change to the load would cause the link's metric to change and a route update to occur. As metrics change, routing updates and broadcasts also change. This can be an important fact when dealing with a state-driven protocol such as EIGRP. For example, using load and reliability might cause unstable routing tables, because they tend to oscillate based on small changes in traffic volume.

There may be situations in which you want this behavior, but on most networks, you don't want to send routing updates more frequently than necessary. Whatever the reasons, changing the K values should be done cautiously, if at all. It's best not to change the metrics.

Packet size

IGRP also keeps track of the Maximum Transmission Unit (MTU) on every path it knows about. The MTU is the largest packet that can be sent without fragmentation. The MTU for an entire route is the smallest MTU of any of the links in that route.

Modifying the range of the network

Like RIP, IGRP also keeps track of hop counts, although they aren't used in computing the routing metric. Hop counts are used to decide when a network has become unreachable. By default, the maximum hop count is 100; however, you can set it to be as high as 255 using the command metric maximum hops:

```
router igrp 101
  metric maximum-hops 200
```

Note that the maximum hop count of IGRP allows it to support much larger networks than RIP, which supports only 15 hops as a maximum.

IGRP's load balancing

IGRP performs either *equal-cost* load balancing or *unequal-cost* load balancing. Load balancing means that IGRP distributes the network traffic load across more than one link. However, IGRP (and EIGRP) do load balancing on a session-oriented basis. Load balancing is not packet-oriented; therefore, once a session has been started with a host somewhere on the network, all packets in that session will be sent through the same interface.

In equal-cost load balancing, a router can have up to four routes to a particular destination, as long as all the routes have the same (equal) metric. For example, let's assume that a route has a metric of 9,000, and another route to the same destination comes along. The new route is added to the route table, but it is used for load balancing only if its metric is also 9,000. If the metric of the new route is less than 9,000, it will be used for all the traffic, and the original route won't be used. On the other hand, if the new route has a metric greater than 9,000, the router will know of its existence but won't use it to handle any traffic.

Unequal-cost load balancing requires the use of a metric multiplier, which is called a variance. The variance allows other routes to be added to the routing table even if their metrics are not equal. Before any new route is added to the table, however, two rules must be met:

- The new router's metric to the destination must be less than our router's current metric to the destination. Or more simply, the new router must be closer than our router.
- The variance multiplied by our router's metric must be equal to or greater than the new route. Or more simply, our route multiplied by some number (variance) must be larger than the new route's metric. So we are willing to accept an alternate route if its metric is within some fraction of our current metric.

As with equal-cost load balancing, the router keeps up to four routes to a destination in its routing table. If more than four routes are available, only the best four are used. If you understood the two rules, you realized that equal-cost load balancing is nothing more than unequal-cost load balancing with a variance of 1, which is the default value. So the router performs equal-cost load balancing by default; you can set the variance to another value using the variance command. Increasing the variance allows traffic to be distributed over links with unequal metrics. This means that if our primary link is becoming loaded, we can distribute some of the load across the otherwise unused, slower links.

These rules are admittedly confusing; it will help to look at an example. Figure 9-2 shows a simple network with three routers. Our router is Router 1, and we are interested in routes to Router 2. Normally, we would send all our traffic over Route 1, which is a T1 link with a metric of 8,000. Of the routes we have available, this route is clearly the best. But let's see what happens with unequal-cost load balancing. Imagine that the variance is 4. Now notice that Router 3 has a route to Router 2 that is also a T1 link with a metric of 8,000. So Router 3's route to Router 2 is as good as ours, thus meeting the first of the two criteria. Furthermore, the total metric for a route from Router 1 to Router 2 via Router 3 is 11,000. That isn't as good as ours, but it is better than our metric times the variance (11,000 is less than 8,000 × 4). So if our variance is 4, we will add this second route via Router 3 to our routing table and start using it to carry traffic.

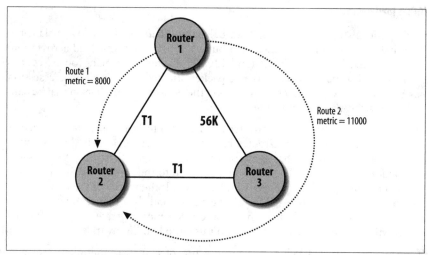

Figure 9-2. An example of unequal-cost load balancing

While we used a variance of 4 to illustrate our example, it's not advisable to use a variance of more than 1.5, because the slower link will have a much larger latency due to transmission time. For example, a 56k link takes .21 seconds to transmit a 1,500-byte packet, and a T1 takes .001 seconds.

With unequal-cost load balancing, traffic is distributed across all possible routes in the route table (there are four maximum routes). We can change this behavior so that the best route is used all the time, and extra routes are used only when the best route becomes unavailable. The command that controls this feature is traffic-share, which by default is set to balanced. In the following example, we change traffic sharing to min (minimum), which sends all traffic to the route with the best metric. We also specify a variance of 2:

```
router igrp 100
    network 10.0.0.0
    variance 2
    traffic-share min across-interfaces
```

The advantage of this configuration is that the extra routes are held in the routing table and are immediately available if the primary route goes down, but there is no attempt at load balancing between routes of unequal quality.

You can perform load balancing on a per-packet basis by using process switching, which is discussed in Chapter 8. Process switching is more CPU-intensive but may be a better solution in some applications.

Redistributing Other Protocols into IGRP

When redistributing RIP into IGRP, you must define a default metric that tells IGRP how to assign metrics for the routes it learns from RIP. The following example uses the redistribute command and the default-metric command:

```
! Define the IGRP routing process
router igrp 100
    network 10.0.0.0
    redistribute rip
    default-metric 10000 100 255 1 1500
! Define the RIP process
router rip
    network 192.168.1.0
```

The default-metric command is required for redistributing most nonstatic routes. In this example, we specify the values that are the input for IGRP's metric computation. The values indicate bandwidth (10,000, which is 10,000 Kbps), delay (in units of tens of microseconds—100 equals a delay of 1 millisecond), reliability (1 to 255), load (1 to 255), and the MTU (1500 bytes). These are all reasonable values for a 10 Mbps Ethernet. A reasonable default metric for a serial link might be:

```
default-metric 1000 100 250 100 1500
```

EIGRP

Enhanced IGRP, like IGRP, is a proprietary Cisco protocol; other vendors' routers cannot support EIGRP, but that's about the only disadvantage. EIGRP provides excellent performance, easy configuration, VLSM support, and support for IPX and AppleTalk. It is a distance-vector protocol that also contains the characteristics of a link-state protocol. EIGRP uses the same compound metric as its predecessor, IGRP. And unlike IGRP, which is prone to routing loops, EIGRP is pretty much loop-free. The most unique feature of EIGRP is its dual finite state machine, which provides an extremely fast convergence time. Other features are partial routing table updates (less bandwidth and CPU are used on routing updates), automatic discovery of neighbors, and increased scalability.

Enabling EIGRP on the Network

Here are the EIGRP configurations for Router 1, Router 2, and Router 3 in Figure 9-1. By now, these configurations should look familiar—they're almost identical to the IGRP configurations, except for the name of the protocol.

The configuration for Router 1 is:

```
interface Ethernet0
 ip address 172.16.1.1 255.255.255.0
!
interface Serial0
 bandwidth 125
 ip address 192.168.3.1 255.255.255.0
!
interface Serial1
 bandwidth 125
 ip address 192.168.1.1 255.255.255.0
!
router eigrp 101
  network 172.16.0.0
  network 192.168.1.0
  network 192.168.3.0
```

For Router 2, the configuration is:

```
interface Ethernet0
 ip address 172.17.1.1 255.255.255.0
!
interface Serial0
 bandwidth 125
 ip address 192.168.1.2 255.255.255.0
!
interface Serial1
 bandwidth 125
 ip address 192.168.2.1 255.255.255.0
!
router eigrp 101
  network 172.17.0.0
  network 192.168.1.0
  network 192.168.2.0
```

And for Router 3, the configuration is:

```
interface Ethernet0
 ip address 172.18.1.1 255.255.255.0
!
interface Serial0
 bandwidth 125
 ip address 192.168.2.2 255.255.255.0
!
interface Serial1
 bandwidth 125
 ip address 192.168.3.2 255.255.255.0
```

```
!
router eigrp 101
  network 172.18.0.0
  network 192.168.2.0
  network 192.168.3.0
```

Let's do some simple testing on Router 1 to make sure the routes are good:

```
Router1#show ip route
Codes: C - connected, S - static, I - IGRP, R - RIP, M - mobile, B - BGP
       D - EIGRP, EX - EIGRP external, O - OSPF, IA - OSPF inter area
       N1 - OSPF NSSA external type 1, N2 - OSPF NSSA external type 2
       E1 - OSPF external type 1, E2 - OSPF external type 2, E - EGP
       i - IS-IS, L1 - IS-IS level-1, L2 - IS-IS level-2, * - candidate default
       U - per-user static route, o - ODR

Gateway of last resort is not set

D    172.17.0.0/16 [90/21017600] via 192.168.1.2, 00:00:05, Serial1
     172.16.0.0/16 is variably subnetted, 2 subnets, 2 masks
D       172.16.0.0/16 is a summary, 00:00:03, Null0
C       172.16.1.0/24 is directly connected, Ethernet0
D    172.18.0.0/16 [90/21017600] via 192.168.3.2, 00:00:03, Serial0
C    192.168.1.0/24 is directly connected, Serial1
D    192.168.2.0/24 [90/21504000] via 192.168.1.2, 00:00:05, Serial1
                    [90/21504000] via 192.168.3.2, 00:00:05, Serial0
C    192.168.3.0/24 is directly connected, Serial0
```

From Router 1, ping Router 2's Ethernet interface:

```
Router1#ping 172.17.1.1

Type escape sequence to abort.
Sending 5, 100-byte ICMP Echos to 172.17.1.1, timeout is 2 seconds:
!!!!!
Success rate is 100 percent (5/5), round-trip min/avg/max = 28/28/32 ms
```

From Router 1, ping Router 3's Ethernet interface:

```
Router1#ping 172.18.1.1

Type escape sequence to abort.
Sending 5, 100-byte ICMP Echos to 172.18.1.1, timeout is 2 seconds:
!!!!!
Success rate is 100 percent (5/5), round-trip min/avg/max = 28/30/32 ms
```

From the output, you can see that Router 1's routing table has the expected routes. And the pings establish that Router 1 knows how to get to the Ethernet interfaces on both Router 2 and Router 3.

Comparing the output of show ip route to our previous examples, we see a new summary route for network 172.16.0.0/16 pointing to Null0. EIGRP creates this route by default; it helps to prevent possible black holes when default and summary routes are used. In our network from Figure 9-1, this summarization isn't a problem, due to our subnetting design.

EIGRP and Route Summarization

Figure 9-3 shows a network on which we are going to use EIGRP as a routing protocol. It's almost identical to the network in Figure 9-1; it differs primarily in that we are going to conserve some address space by using a /30 subnet on our shared serial links. We've also connected each router to a /24 subnet of the 172.16.0.0 network, which (to a classful routing protocol) has a 16-bit netmask. This network will allow us to demonstrate how EIGRP can handle classless routing, in addition to showing how it handles automatic route summarization.

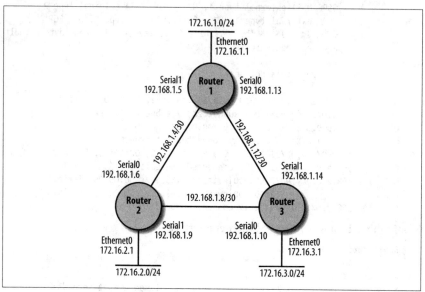

Figure 9-3. A simple network using EIGRP

Here are the initial configurations for our three routers. The interface commands are included to better illustrate the entire configuration.

Here's the configuration for Router 1:

```
interface Ethernet0
 ip address 172.16.1.1 255.255.255.0
 !
interface Serial0
 bandwidth 125
 ip address 192.168.1.13 255.255.255.252
!
interface Serial1
 bandwidth 125
 ip address 192.168.1.5 255.255.255.252
!
router eigrp 100
 network 172.16.0.0
 network 192.168.1.0
!
ip classless
```

For Router 2, the configuration is:

```
interface Ethernet0
 ip address 172.16.2.1 255.255.255.0
!
interface Serial0
 bandwidth 125
 ip address 192.168.1.6 255.255.255.252
!
interface Serial1
 bandwidth 125
 ip address 192.168.1.9 255.255.255.252
!
router eigrp 100
 network 172.16.0.0
 network 192.168.1.0
!
ip classless
```

Here's the configuration for Router 3:

```
interface Ethernet0
 ip address 172.16.3.1 255.255.255.0
!
interface Serial0
 ip address 192.168.1.10 255.255.255.252
!
interface Serial1
 ip address 192.168.1.14 255.255.255.252
!
router eigrp 100
 network 172.16.0.0
 network 192.168.1.0
!
ip classless
```

This looks correct. We didn't need to specify classless routing explicitly, because it's the default for EIGRP, but it never hurts to make it clear how you expect your network to behave. However, if we look at the output from show ip route and a few pings, we will see that something is wrong:

```
Router1#show ip route
Codes: C - connected, S - static, I - IGRP, R - RIP, M - mobile, B - BGP
       D - EIGRP, EX - EIGRP external, O - OSPF, IA - OSPF inter area
       N1 - OSPF NSSA external type 1, N2 - OSPF NSSA external type 2
       E1 - OSPF external type 1, E2 - OSPF external type 2, E - EGP
       i - IS-IS, L1 - IS-IS level-1, L2 - IS-IS level-2, * - candidate default
       U - per-user static route, o - ODR

Gateway of last resort is not set

     172.16.0.0/16 is variably subnetted, 2 subnets, 2 masks
D       172.16.0.0/16 is a summary, 00:00:02, Null0
C       172.16.1.0/24 is directly connected, Ethernet0
     192.168.1.0/30 is subnetted, 3 subnets
D       192.168.1.8 [90/21504000] via 192.168.1.14, 00:00:02, Serial0
                    [90/21504000] via 192.168.1.6, 00:00:02, Serial1
```

```
C       192.168.1.12 is directly connected, Serial0
C       192.168.1.4 is directly connected, Serial1
```

From Router 1, try to ping Router 2's Ethernet interface:

```
Router1#ping 172.16.2.1

Type escape sequence to abort.
Sending 5, 100-byte ICMP Echos to 172.16.2.1, timeout is 2 seconds:
.....
Success rate is 0 percent (0/5)
```

From Router 1, try to ping Router 3's Ethernet interface:

```
Router1#ping 172.16.3.1

Type escape sequence to abort.
Sending 5, 100-byte ICMP Echos to 172.16.3.1, timeout is 2 seconds:
.....
Success rate is 0 percent (0/5)
```

Our attempts to ping the Ethernet interfaces of the other routers from Router 1 failed. If you look closely at the routing table, you can see why. EIGRP has summarized the entire 172.16.0.0/16 network for us and pointed the route to the null interface:

```
        172.16.0.0/16 is variably subnetted, 2 subnets, 2 masks
D           172.16.0.0/16 is a summary, 00:00:02, Null0
C           172.16.1.0/24 is directly connected, Ethernet0
```

This is actually how EIGRP is supposed to behave, strange as it may seem; the summary route is created because of the way we subnetted 172.16.0.0/16. The same summary route exists on Router 2:

```
Router2#show ip route
...
Gateway of last resort is not set

        172.16.0.0/16 is variably subnetted, 2 subnets, 2 masks
D           172.16.0.0/16 is a summary, 00:05:57, Null0
C           172.16.2.0/24 is directly connected, Ethernet0
        192.168.1.0/30 is subnetted, 3 subnets
C           192.168.1.8 is directly connected, Serial1
D           192.168.1.12 [90/21504000] via 192.168.1.5, 00:05:57, Serial0
C           192.168.1.4 is directly connected, Serial0
```

And we'd see the same thing on Router 3 if we took the time to look. Although EIGRP can handle classless addresses, it automatically summarizes routes to classful addresses and creates a summary route that points to the Null0 interface. EIGRP points the summary route to Null0 in order to prevent routing loops.

Route summarization occurs only on:

- Routes that are directly connected to this router
- Routes other than the current interface's network

The solution for this network is to disable auto-summary in EIGRP by adding the no auto-summary command to the EIGRP configuration on each router.

For Router 1, the EIGRP configuration now looks like this:

```
router eigrp 100
 network 172.16.0.0
 network 192.168.1.0
 no auto-summary
```

After making this change on every router, we can do a show ip route on Router 1, which should look better. The summary route to Null0 is gone:

```
Router1#show ip route
...

Gateway of last resort is not set

     172.16.0.0/24 is subnetted, 3 subnets
C       172.16.1.0 is directly connected, Ethernet0
D       172.16.2.0 [90/21017600] via 192.168.1.6, 00:00:23, Serial1
D       172.16.3.0 [90/21017600] via 192.168.1.14, 00:00:03, Serial0
     192.168.1.0/30 is subnetted, 3 subnets
D       192.168.1.8 [90/21504000] via 192.168.1.6, 00:00:03, Serial1
                    [90/21504000] via 192.168.1.14, 00:00:03, Serial0
C       192.168.1.12 is directly connected, Serial0
C       192.168.1.4 is directly connected, Serial1
```

Now we can ping Router 2's Ethernet interface from Router 1:

```
Router1#ping 172.16.2.1

Type escape sequence to abort.
Sending 5, 100-byte ICMP Echos to 172.16.2.1, timeout is 2 seconds:
!!!!!
Success rate is 100 percent (5/5), round-trip min/avg/max = 28/31/32 ms
```

Router 3's Ethernet interface is also now reachable from Router 1:

```
Router1#ping 172.16.3.1

Type escape sequence to abort.
Sending 5, 100-byte ICMP Echos to 172.16.3.1, timeout is 2 seconds:
!!!!!
Success rate is 100 percent (5/5), round-trip min/avg/max = 28/29/32 ms
```

Enabling route summarization on a specific interface

Route summarization can also be controlled at the interface level. On ethernet0, we can apply the following command to summarize any route we want:

```
interface ethernet0
 ip summary-address eigrp 100 10.101.1.0 255.255.255.0
```

When advertised out ethernet0, the 10.101.1.0 summary route is given the administrative distance of 5, which supersedes other EIGRP routes. Consult Chapter 8 for more information on administrative distances.

EIGRP Authentication

EIGRP's authentication prevents unauthorized routers from injecting routes on the network. Here's an example that shows how to enable authentication. First, we create a key-chain, which is a series of passwords we are willing to accept. We specify that these passwords have an infinite lifetime—i.e., they will never expire. After the keys are defined, we can enable EIGRP authentication. Here's a configuration that defines a key-chain named group1, and then uses this key-chain for EIGRP process 100:

```
interface ethernet0
  ip authentication mode eigrp 100 md5
  ip authentication key-chain eigrp 100 group1
!
key-chain group1
  key 1
  key-string authme1
  accept-lifetime 00:00:00 1 jan 1999 infinite
  key 2
  accept-lifetime 00:00:00 1 jan 1999 infinite
  key-string authme2
!
router eigrp 100
  network 10.10.0.0
```

In this configuration, all EIGRP updates are subject to authentication, which requires the key authme1 or authme2. We used MD5 so the keys won't be transmitted in clear text.

EIGRP Metrics

EIGRP metrics are identical to IGRP metrics, including the K values in the metric equation. The only difference between the two is that EIGRP's metric is multiplied by 256, which makes it a 32-bit integer instead of a 24-bit integer. Consult "IGRP'S metric" earlier in this chapter for more information on the metric calculation.

Tuning EIGRP

By default, EIGRP allows itself to use, at most, 50% of a link's maximum bandwidth. In some instances, you might want to change this value; for example, a change might be appropriate if for some reason you told a router that the link's bandwidth was something other than its actual bandwidth. To change the bandwidth usage, use the ip bandwidth-percent eigrp command. In this example, we change the bandwidth EIGRP can use to 65% (100 is the local-AS number, or process number, for the EIGRP process):

```
interface ethernet0
  ip bandwidth-percent eigrp 100 65
```

Hello packets are sent out to discover new EIGRP devices. For most types of links, the default hello interval is five seconds. However, a longer interval might be appropriate for a slower link. To change the hello interval, use the ip hello-interval eigrp command:

```
interface ethernet0
  ip hello-interval eigrp 100 10
```

By default, the time an EIGRP route is held is three times the hello interval (i.e., 15 seconds). Increasing the hold time can be beneficial if there is a great deal of latency on a network. However, changing the hold time is not generally recommended as a solution. The following command increases the hold time to 30 seconds:

```
interface ethernet0
  ip hold-time eigrp 100 30
```

EIGRP show Commands

There are several show commands for EIGRP that are not available for other protocols. Here are some of the more useful commands.

show ip eigrp neighbors

This command shows us the EIGRP neighbors that our router knows about. On our network, Router 1 sees Routers 2 and 3. The Interface column shows which interface received the hello from the neighbor. Hold shows the hold time (in seconds) that the router waits to hear from the neighbor before declaring the neighbor down. Uptime is the amount of time elapsed since we first learned of this neighbor. Smooth Round Trip Time (SRTT) is the number of milliseconds it takes for the router to send an EIGRP packet to the neighbor and for the neighbor to respond. RTO indicates the retransmission timeout, which is the time (in milliseconds) that the router will wait before retransmitting a packet to the neighbor. Q Cnt is the number of queued EIGRP packets that the router is waiting to send. Finally, Seq Num shows the sequence number of the last packet received from the neighbor:

```
Router1#show ip eigrp neighbors
IP-EIGRP neighbors for process 100
H   Address          Interface    Hold Uptime   SRTT   RTO  Q  Seq
                                  (sec)         (ms)       Cnt Num
1   192.168.1.14     Se0          11 15:40:05    32   1164  0  7
0   192.168.1.6      Se1          10 15:40:22   434   2604  0  9
```

The EIGRP neighbor counters can be cleared with the command:

```
clear ip eigrp neighbors
```

Logging can be enabled with the following command:

```
eigrp log-neighbor-changes
```

Any neighbor changes are written to a log file, which means that you must have a valid syslog configuration if you enable logging.

show ip eigrp topology

This command gives us the router's view of the EIGRP network topology. Each entry in the topology has an associated state, which can be Passive, Active, Update, Query, Reply, or Reply Status. Passive means that no EIGRP computations are being used. Active means that EIGRP is performing calculations for this destination. Update, Query, and Reply simply mean that a packet of the indicated type has been sent to the destination. Reply Status means that a reply packet has been sent and the router is waiting for a reply.

The last piece of information needed to decode this table is feasible distance (FD). This number is used in the feasibility calculation. For each entry, the FD number is followed by a slash (/) and another number. The second number is the reported distance of the neighbor. If the reported distance is less than the feasible distance, that path becomes the feasible successor for the route.

```
Router1#show ip eigrp topology
IP-EIGRP Topology Table for process 100

Codes: P - Passive, A - Active, U - Update, Q - Query, R - Reply,
       r - Reply status

P 192.168.1.8/30, 2 successors, FD is 21504000
        via 192.168.1.14 (21504000/20992000), Serial0
        via 192.168.1.6 (21504000/20992000), Serial1
P 192.168.1.12/30, 1 successors, FD is 20992000
        via Connected, Serial0
P 192.168.1.4/30, 1 successors, FD is 20992000
        via Connected, Serial1
P 172.16.1.0/24, 1 successors, FD is 281600
        via Connected, Ethernet0
P 172.16.2.0/24, 1 successors, FD is 21017600
        via 192.168.1.6 (21017600/281600), Serial1
P 172.16.3.0/24, 1 successors, FD is 21017600
        via 192.168.1.14 (21017600/281600), Serial0
```

show ip eigrp traffic

This command simply outputs the hellos, updates, queries, replies, and acks that the EIGRP routing process has sent. For each type of packet, the first number is the number sent and the second number is the number received.

```
Router1#show ip eigrp traffic
IP-EIGRP Traffic Statistics for process 100
  Hellos sent/received: 24728/24704
  Updates sent/received: 23/19
  Queries sent/received: 1/1
  Replies sent/received: 1/1
  Acks sent/received: 12/15
```

EIGRP Redistribution

On a multiprotocol network, you need to define default metrics to handle routes redistributed into EIGRP from other protocols.

RIP

Redistributing RIP into EIGRP is as easy as defining the default metric for the incoming RIP routes. Here's an example:

```
! Define the RIP process
router rip
  network 192.168.1.0
! Define the EIGRP process and include the learned RIP routes
```

```
router eigrp 100
  network 10.0.0.0
  default-metric 1000 250 255 1 1500
  redistribute rip
```

This is almost identical to the earlier example that showed how to redistribute RIP routes into IGRP. That shouldn't be surprising, since IGRP and EIGRP use the same metric computation. We are redistributing in only one direction in this example—from RIP into EIGRP. You must be careful when redistributing in both directions, in which case you'll want to filter the routers to prevent routing loops. See Chapter 8 for an example.

IGRP

When mixing IGRP and EIGRP on a router, redistribution is automatic if the process numbers for the RIP and EIGRP routing processes are the same. If they are different, you must use the redistribute command. In this example, redistribution occurs automatically because both routing protocols use the same process number (100):

```
! Define the IGRP routing process
router igrp 100
  network 10.0.0.0
! Define the EIGRP with same number as IGRP so the redistribution between
! the two is automatic
router eigrp 100
  network 10.0.0.0
```

In the next example, the routing process numbers differ, so route redistribution is not automatic and we need to use the redistribute command. Since both IGRP and EIGRP use the same metrics, the default-metric command is not required.

```
! Define the IGRP routing process
router igrp 100
  network 10.0.0.0
! Define the EIGRP process and redistribute the igrp routes
router eigrp 109
  network 10.0.0.0
  redistribute igrp 100
```

Converting an IGRP Network to EIGRP

It's simple to convert a network from IGRP to EIGRP using an incremental approach. In the previous examples, we showed how EIGRP and IGRP share routes automatically if they share the same process numbers. Using this fact, any IGRP network can be converted to EIGRP incrementally, without much downtime.

Figure 9-4 shows a simple network of 10 routers using IGRP. We start the conversion by picking a place to begin. We will start with Router 1, which is the center of the network. We pick this router because, as we convert the other networks, it will pull in routes and redistribute them for us.

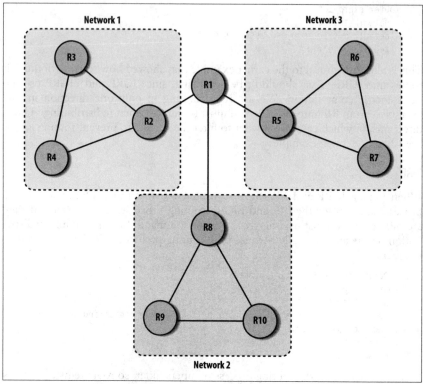

Figure 9-4. An IGRP network to be converted to EIGRP

By enabling IGRP and EIGRP on Router 1, we can slowly migrate Networks 1, 2, and 3 to EIGRP. First we configure Router 1:

```
router igrp 100
  network 10.0.0.0
router eigrp 100
  network 10.0.0.0
```

Now we start with the other networks. Let's start with Network 3, which consists of Routers 5, 6, and 7. We implement the same configuration on each:

```
router igrp 100
  network 10.0.0.0
router eigrp 100
  network 10.0.0.0
```

Once all three routers have this configuration, we remove all IGRP commands. Now Network 3 is using EIGRP exclusively. The process is repeated for Networks 1 and 2. When you have reconfigured all three networks (Routers 2-10), you can remove the IGRP commands from Router 1. At this point, none of the other routers are running IGRP, so running IGRP on Router 1 is only wasting CPU power. We are left with a network that is 100% EIGRP.

OSPF

Open Shortest Path First is a link-state protocol. It's a good choice for networks that need a more sophisticated routing protocol than RIP but are not standardized on a single router vendor and therefore have problems using EIGRP. It has a number of significant advantages, most of which it shares with EIGRP: it doesn't use a lot of network bandwidth, it supports VLSM, and it converges quickly when the network's state changes. Its biggest advantage over EIGRP is that it is an open standard and is supported by almost all router vendors.

OSPF has a reputation for being very complex and, to some extent, this reputation is deserved. However, in small networks it can be configured quickly. This book does not give a comprehensive look at OSPF or its capabilities.

As you'll see, OSPF forces you to use a certain topological design. OSPF divides your network into areas; area 0 is the "backbone" to which all other areas must connect. While this design fits many (perhaps even most) networks, and while there are some tools for giving you additional flexibility, you might reasonably object to using a routing protocol that limits your network's flexibility in the future. However, some people feel that this aspect of OSPF is an advantage, as it forces the use of decent network-design practices.

One possible disadvantage of OSPF is that it tends to use a lot of CPU time on the router because the OSPF LSA maintenance algorithms are CPU-intensive. This tendency to be a CPU hog can be controlled by restricting the number of routers per area, another good network-design practice.

OSPF Concepts

Before saying anything significant about OSPF, it's important to introduce the basic building blocks. Again, I won't try to explain all the details—just enough of the important concepts to get you started.

Areas

An area is a group of routers; a good design should have no more than 50 routers per area (or 100 interfaces). Each area is assigned a number, starting at 0. Area 0 is the backbone area; it must exist in any OSPF network. Figure 9-5 shows how the areas of a network must be ordered in a topological design.

In Figure 9-5, area 0 is the backbone area, with all other areas connecting to it. Areas allow summarization of network addresses, which in turn allows for smaller routing tables. Smaller routing tables mean faster convergence, less routing-protocol bandwidth, and better route determination. However, using a large number of relatively small areas can also mean a more difficult configuration.

Router types

An OSPF router can be classified as one of the following types:

ASBR (autonomous system border router)
    A router with one or more interfaces connected to an external network or a network with a different local-AS number.

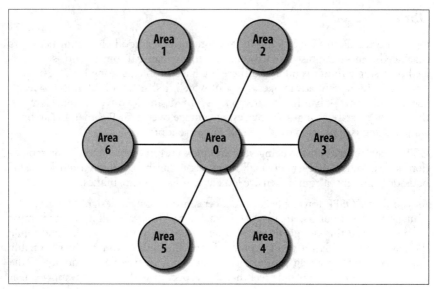

Figure 9-5. OSPF area topology

ABR (area border router)
> A router with one or more interfaces connected to different areas. Information about each area that it is connected to is stored within this router.

Area-internal
> A router whose interfaces are all within the same area.

Backbone
> A router with one or more interfaces connected to the OSPF backbone area. The backbone area is area 0.

Link-state advertisements (LSAs)

Before we discuss the different types of OSPF areas, let's look at how updates are sent between areas. These updates are called "link-state advertisements," or LSAs. An LSA is an OSPF multicast that describes a routing change or routing update to other routers or areas.

There are six different types of LSAs. An LSA's type defines the type of route that is being advertised and how the announcements are processed. LSAs are sent every 30 minutes or at every link-state change. Here are the different LSA types:

Type 1—Router Link
> Type 1 LSAs are flooded (i.e., broadcast to all routers) within an area. These LSAs contain all the link-state information.

Type 2—Network
> Type 2 LSAs contain network-specific information. The designated router of the OSPF network (discussed later) broadcasts this LSA to all area routers.

Type 3—Internal Summary
Type 3 LSAs contain route information for internal networks. This information is broadcast by the ABR to all backbone routers.

Type 4—External Summary
Type 4 LSAs contain route information for ASBR routers.

Type 5—Autonomous System
Type 5 LSAs contain route information about external networks. Only ASBR routers send these LSAs.

Type 6—Multicast OSPF (MOSPF)
Type 6 LSAs multicast specific information. A Cisco router will ignore this type and generate a syslog entry if it does receive one. To suppress the syslog message, use the command `ignore lsa mospf`.

Type 7—NSSA External LSA
Type 7 LSAs are used by NSSAs (not-so-stubby areas).

Area types

There are several possible area types in an OSPF network:

Backbone
All OSPF designs require a backbone area that connects multiple areas together. The backbone area is always area 0.

Standard
A standard area connects to the backbone area and accepts both internal and external LSAs.

Stub
A stub area doesn't need all the routes other areas receive; all it needs is a default route and summary LSAs. It doesn't receive external routes. A stub area generally contains, at most, 50 routers, and its addresses can easily be summarized to areas above it. All areas, except for area 0, can be stubby if they don't contain an ASBR. To create a stub network, use the `stub` command (for example, `area 1 stub`).

Totally stubby
A totally stubby area does not accept external or summary LSAs. It's just like a stub area, except that it doesn't receive any summary information at all; it receives only a default route. To configure a totally stubby area, add the `no-summary` command to the area configuration (for example, `area 1 stub no-summary`).

Not-so-stubby
A not-so-stubby area (NSSA) is like a stub area, but it shares routing information with an external network that uses a different routing protocol. In other words, it is a regular stub area, but it has an ASBR router. The remote network becomes an area of our OSPF network, eliminating the need to implement the different routing protocol within the OSPF network. The ASBR of our NSSA area injects routes redistributed from the other routing protocol and passes them back into the area 0 backbone. To define a network as an NSSA, use the command `area 1 nssa`.

Totally stubby not-so-stubby

Yep, you read that name correctly. As if the area names weren't confusing enough, this command comes along. Basically, to create this area, we add the command no-summary to the end of the nssa command. By doing this, we block type-3 and type-4 LSAs into our NSSA area. So the command now looks like area 1 nssa no summary.

Router ID

Each OSPF router must have a unique router ID to identify it to the OSPF network. By default, the router ID is the address of its loopback interface. If no loopback address is defined, the router ID is the highest IP address of any active interface. Remember that the loopback interface of a Cisco router is an interface that is always up by definition and that has an IP address that is unique on the network (i.e., not 127.0.0.1).

Designated router (DR)

Each network segment needs a designated router, known as the DR, before it can exchange routing information. OSPF elects a DR on each multi-access segment. When an OSPF broadcast arrives at the DR, it is the job of the DR to multicast the update to all routers within its area. This keeps OSPF traffic to a minimum, because each router communicates with only the DR to get the routing information. If this didn't happen, the broadcast would have to go to each router, which would in turn broadcast again until every router got the message. In other words, the DR gives us a one-to-many relationship instead of a many-to-many relationship. With DR routers, there is only one place to send an update and one router that updates all the routers within the segment.

A backup designated router (BDR) must also be selected. This router becomes the DR if the DR becomes unavailable. If both the DR and BDR are unavailable, new ones are chosen automatically.

Enabling OSPF on the Network

You configure OSPF much like you configure other routing protocols: use the router command to establish the protocol and a process number, and use the network command to tell the router which networks it's responsible for. It's easy to become confused: with OSPF the network command takes a wildcard mask, not a subnet mask. For more information on wildcard masks, see Chapter 7. Here's an example:

```
router ospf  99
  network 10.10.1.0 0.0.0.255 area 0
```

Here, we establish an OSPF routing process with the process ID 99. This routing process is responsible for the network 10.10.1.0/24, which belongs to area 0. Therefore, this router is part of the OSPF backbone area. Do not confuse the process ID (99) with the area ID (0).

OSPF will run over all interfaces that match the network commands.

Sample OSPF Configurations

Figure 9-6 shows a network in which the backbone consists of one router. There are three other areas, each with a single router. In this configuration, Router 1 is the backbone router, and Router 2, Router 3, and Router 4 are area border routers (ABRs) with interfaces in different areas. One interface for each of these routers connects to the backbone area.

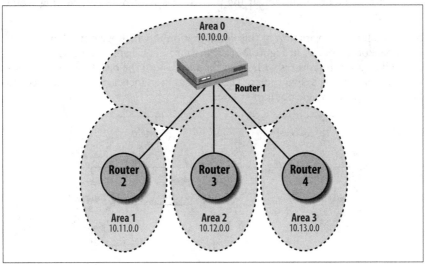

Figure 9-6. An OSPF network with a single backbone router

Router 1 is configured like this:

```
router ospf  99
    network 10.10.0.0 0.0.255.255 area 0
```

The configuration for Router 2 is:

```
router ospf  99
    network 10.10.0.0 0.0.255.255 area 0
    network 10.11.0.0 0.0.255.255 area 1
```

The configuration for Router 3 is:

```
router ospf  99
    network 10.10.0.0 0.0.255.255 area 0
    network 10.12.0.0 0.0.255.255 area 2
```

And here's the configuration for Router 4:

```
router ospf  99
    network 10.10.0.0 0.0.255.255 area 0
    network 10.13.0.0 0.0.255.255 area 3
```

Each router has a network statement for every area in which it participates. Router 1 needs a network statement only for area 0, because it doesn't have interfaces in areas 1, 2, and 3; its only area is the 10.10.0.0 network (area 0). It's important to understand that it's interfaces, not routers, that belong to areas.

The rest of the routers (Router 2, Router 3, and Router 4) are all area border routers, and they need two network statements because they each participate in two areas. Each network statement specifies the subnet that is associated with the area. Therefore, Router 2, Router 3, and Router 4 specify 10.10.0.0 0.0.255.255 for area 0, which is their backbone connection, and they each have an entry for their own areas (1, 2, and 3). Also note that the routers have the same OSPF process ID (99). Unlike local-AS numbers in IGRP and EIGRP, the process ID has no effect outside of the router. If the process IDs were different, routing would still occur.

Now let's look at a variation of this configuration in which we don't have a dedicated backbone router. In Figure 9-7, all three routers share area 0, which makes them all area border routers with no backbone router. The backbone still exists— it just doesn't have its own router. This configuration increases reliability because there's no longer a single point of failure.

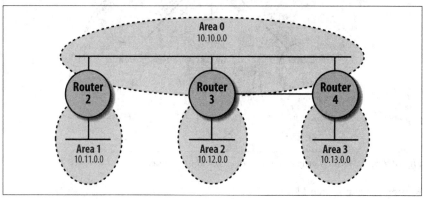

Figure 9-7. An OSPF network with a backbone across three ABRs

Here are the configurations. Not much has changed, except that we have dropped Router 1 from the configuration, and Router 2, Router 3, and Router 4 are all connected on one network segment.

The configuration for Router 2 is:

```
router ospf 99
    network 10.11.0.0 0.0.255.255 area 1
    network 10.10.0.0 0.0.255.255 area 0
```

The configuration for Router 3 is:

```
router ospf 99
    network 10.12.0.0 0.0.255.255 area 2
    network 10.10.0.0 0.0.255.255 area 0
```

And the configuration for Router 4 is:

```
router ospf 99
    network 10.13.0.0 0.0.255.255 area 3
    network 10.10.0.0 0.0.255.255 area 0
```

Route Summarization in OSPF

As with any routing protocol, route summarization helps reduce the routing table size. OSPF distinguishes between two summarization types: inter-area and external.

Inter-area summarization

Inter-area summarization occurs when the ABR summarizes an area's routes. An ABR can summarize routes within its area and beyond, as long as all the subnets are contiguous (bitwise) and summarizable. Just because areas are adjacent doesn't mean their addressing is set up to be summarizable.

To enable inter-area summarization, use the area range command. For example, on Router 2 in Figure 9-7, we can summarize the 10.11.0.0 network in the following manner:

```
router ospf 99
  network 10.11.0.0 0.0.255.255 area 1
  network 10.10.0.0 0.0.255.255 area 0
  ! summarize the areas for this router
  area 1 range 10.11.0.0 255.255.0.0
```

We can do this because we know that all the 10.11.0.0 networks are below this router. In an upcoming example, we will use this exact scenario and show the routing tables to prove that they actually get smaller as the router summarizes.

External summarization

External summarization occurs at ASBRs, where the entire network is summarized. We can use external summarization when we are injecting external routes into OSPF. To enable external summarization, use the summary-address command. For example:

```
summary-address 10.0.0.0 255.0.0.0
```

We're summarizing the entire network (10.0.0.0/8). Later, in the redistributing example, we will use this command to summarize the EIGRP routes that get redistributed into OSPF.

Virtual Backbone Links

There may be times when it's not possible to have a contiguous backbone, perhaps for political or even design issues. Although OSPF requires a single connected backbone, it includes a mechanism that lets you create a backbone out of two separate areas. Such a backbone is called a "virtual link."

Figure 9-8 shows a network that requires a virtual link. In OSPF, all areas must be *contiguous*, meaning that they must physically be connected to each other. When two areas are not contiguous, we solve the problem by creating a virtual link.

In this example, we want to make Router 1 and Router 2 part of area 0, even though they are not contiguous. Since they share area 5, we can mend the partitioned area 0 by adding a virtual link to tunnel area 0 (the backbone) across area 5. This tunneling brings the two distant routers together to act as though they are actually connected.

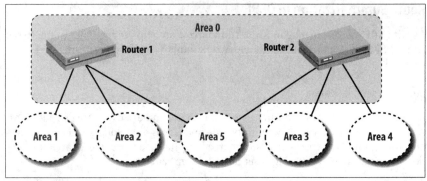

Figure 9-8. An OSPF network with a partitioned Area 0

The virtual link affects the configuration of Routers 1 and 2. First, we should define a loopback interface, which we use as an unambiguous identifier for the router. (Remember that a loopback interface is always up, has a unique address, and is not associated with any hardware.) Then we must create the virtual link with the area command.

Here is Router 1's configuration:

```
interface loopback0
    ip address 10.10.7.4 255.255.255.0
router ospf 99
    network 10.10.1.0 0.0.0.255 area 0
    network 10.10.7.0 0.0.0.255 area 0
    network 10.10.2.0 0.0.0.255 area 1
    network 10.10.3.0 0.0.0.255 area 2
    network 10.10.6.0 0.0.0.255 area 5
    ! Create the virtual link to Router2's ID
    area 5 virtual-link 10.10.8.5
```

And here's the configuration for Router 2, which is very similar:

```
interface loopback0
    ip address 10.10.8.5 255.255.255.0
router ospf 99
    network 10.10.1.0 0.0.0.255 area 0
    network 10.10.9.0 0.0.0.255 area 0
    network 10.10.4.0 0.0.0.255 area 3
    network 10.10.5.0 0.0.0.255 area 4
    network 10.10.6.0 0.0.0.255 area 5
    ! Create the virtual link to Router1's ID
    area 5 virtual-link 10.10.7.4
```

The major rule to remember is that virtual links cannot cross more than one area.

Interoperability with Other Vendors

Cisco routers use bandwidth as the cost of OSPF links. Other vendors might select another method for calculating the cost value. The ospf cost command allows you to define a cost value for OSPF links when talking to another router. A general rule for calculating cost is to take 10^8 (100,000,000) and divide it by the bandwidth. So a T1 link would have a cost of 100,000,000/1,544,000, which is about 64.

```
interface serial0
  ip ospf cost 64
```

Default Routes in OSPF

With the `default-information` command, an ASBR can generate a default route into an OSPF domain. In this example, the ASBR is told to propagate its default route (172.168.10.1) into the OSPF domain:

```
ip route 0.0.0.0 0.0.0.0 172.168.10.1
router ospf 99
  network 10.1.1.0 0.0.0.255 area 0
  default-information originate
```

NSSAs (Not-So-Stubby Areas)

Before NSSAs existed, if a remote site on your network ran another routing protocol, it was difficult to provide full routing and also take advantage of stub areas. But with an NSSA, redistribution within a stub area is possible.

Here's a configuration that uses an NSSA to incorporate a remote network that is using RIP as its routing protocol. Router 2 is an offsite router running RIP; we want to incorporate it into our OSPF network. Router 1 is connected to our OSPF backbone. Area 2 joins Router 1 and Router 2 with an address of 192.168.44.0, and will be our NSSA.

Here's the configuration for Router 1, which is our main office router. It's a simple OSPF configuration, merely specifying that area 2 is an NSSA.

```
router ospf  99
  network 192.168.42.0 0.0.0.255 area 0
  network 192.168.43.0 0.0.0.255 area 1
  network 192.168.44.0 0.0.0.255 area 2
  area 2 nssa
```

Router 2 is the remote office router running RIP:

```
router rip
  network 10.0.0.0
!
! add OSPF and redistribute the RIP routes into it
router ospf  99
  redistribute rip subnets
  network 192.168.44.0 0.0.0.255 area 2
  area 2 nssa
```

This router needs to run both OSPF and RIP, but we have managed to shield Router 1 and the rest of our network from knowing about RIP. The `redistribute` command brings the RIP information into the OSPF process; we have a simple `network` command to define area 2; and we specify that area 2 is not so stubby.

OSPF Configuration Example

Figure 9-9 shows an OSPF network consisting of four areas. Area 0 has two ABR routers. Router 1 is the ABR for areas 1 and 2, while Router 4 is the ABR for area 3.

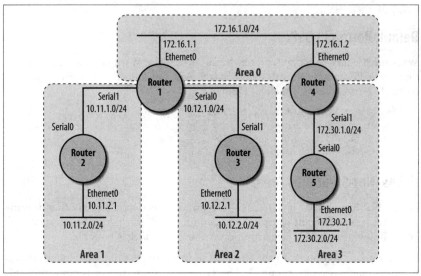

Figure 9-9. An OSPF network

The configuration for Router 1 is:

```
hostname Router1
!
interface Ethernet0
 ip address 172.16.1.1 255.255.255.0
!
interface Serial0
 ip address 10.12.1.1 255.255.255.0
!
interface Serial1
 ip address 10.11.1.1 255.255.255.0
!
router ospf 100
 network 10.11.0.0 0.0.255.255 area 1
 network 10.12.0.0 0.0.255.255 area 2
 network 172.16.1.0 0.0.0.255 area 0
```

The configuration for Router 2 is:

```
hostname Router2
!
interface Ethernet0
 ip address 10.11.2.1 255.255.255.0
!
interface Serial0
 ip address 10.11.1.2 255.255.255.0
```

```
!
router ospf 100
 network 10.11.0.0 0.0.255.255 area 1
```

The configuration for Router 3 is:

```
hostname Router3
!
interface Ethernet0
 ip address 10.12.2.1 255.255.255.0
!
interface Serial1
 ip address 10.12.1.2 255.255.255.0
!
router ospf 100
 network 10.12.0.0 0.0.255.255 area 2
```

The configuration for Router 4 is:

```
hostname Router4
!
interface Ethernet0
 ip address 172.16.1.2 255.255.255.0
!
interface Serial1
 ip address 172.30.1.1 255.255.255.0
!
router ospf 100
 network 172.16.0.0 0.0.255.255 area 0
 network 172.30.0.0 0.0.255.255 area 3
```

And the configuration for Router 5 is:

```
hostname Router5
!
interface Ethernet0
 ip address 172.30.2.1 255.255.255.0
!
interface Serial0
 ip address 172.30.1.2 255.255.255.0
!
router ospf 100
 network 172.30.0.0 0.0.255.255 area 3
```

To test our configuration, we will run a few commands on Router 1 and Router 4. First, let's look at the output from the show ip route command on Router 1:

```
Router1#show ip route
Codes: C - connected, S - static, I - IGRP, R - RIP, M - mobile, B - BGP
       D - EIGRP, EX - EIGRP external, O - OSPF, IA - OSPF inter area
       N1 - OSPF NSSA external type 1, N2 - OSPF NSSA external type 2
       E1 - OSPF external type 1, E2 - OSPF external type 2, E - EGP
       i - IS-IS, L1 - IS-IS level-1, L2 - IS-IS level-2, * - candidate default
       U - per-user static route, o - ODR

Gateway of last resort is not set

     172.16.0.0/24 is subnetted, 1 subnets
```

```
C        172.16.1.0 is directly connected, Ethernet0
     172.30.0.0/24 is subnetted, 2 subnets
O IA    172.30.2.0 [110/84] via 172.16.1.2, 00:03:59, Ethernet0
O IA    172.30.1.0 [110/74] via 172.16.1.2, 00:03:59, Ethernet0
     10.0.0.0/24 is subnetted, 4 subnets
C        10.11.1.0 is directly connected, Serial1
O        10.11.2.0 [110/74] via 10.11.1.2, 00:08:25, Serial1
O        10.12.2.0 [110/74] via 10.12.1.2, 00:08:25, Serial0
C        10.12.1.0 is directly connected, Serial0
```

In this output, we see that we have routes to all networks in our diagram. Routes to networks that are directly connected to Router 1 are noted by a "C" in the left-hand column. All the OSPF routes are noted by an "O". Of course, we have four OSPF routes for the four networks that are not directly connected to Router 1.

Now let's look at the output of show ip ospf neighbor:

```
Router1#show ip ospf neighbor

Neighbor ID    Pri   State       Dead Time   Address       Interface
172.30.1.1      1    FULL/DR     00:00:37    172.16.1.2    Ethernet0
10.12.2.1       1    FULL/ -     00:00:35    10.12.1.2     Serial0
10.11.2.1       1    FULL/ -     00:00:30    10.11.1.2     Serial1
```

Here we have three routers listed: Router 2, Router 3, and Router 4. Router 5 is not in this list because it is not a neighbor of Router 1. Finally, to test connectivity, we will ping the other routers:

```
Router1#ping 10.11.2.1
Type escape sequence to abort.
Sending 5, 100-byte ICMP Echos to 10.11.2.1, timeout is 2 seconds:
!!!!!
Success rate is 100 percent (5/5), round-trip min/avg/max = 28/29/32 ms
Router1#ping 10.12.2.1
Type escape sequence to abort.
Sending 5, 100-byte ICMP Echos to 10.12.2.1, timeout is 2 seconds:
!!!!!
Success rate is 100 percent (5/5), round-trip min/avg/max = 32/32/32 ms
Router1#ping 172.30.2.1
Type escape sequence to abort.
Sending 5, 100-byte ICMP Echos to 172.30.2.1, timeout is 2 seconds:
!!!!!
Success rate is 100 percent (5/5), round-trip min/avg/max = 32/32/36 ms
```

Putting route summarization to use

Everything looks good so far. But now let's look at the output of show ip route on Router 4:

```
Router4#show ip route
Codes: C - connected, S - static, I - IGRP, R - RIP, M - mobile, B - BGP
       D - EIGRP, EX - EIGRP external, O - OSPF, IA - OSPF inter area
       N1 - OSPF NSSA external type 1, N2 - OSPF NSSA external type 2
       E1 - OSPF external type 1, E2 - OSPF external type 2, E - EGP
       i - IS-IS, L1 - IS-IS level-1, L2 - IS-IS level-2, * - candidate default
       U - per-user static route, o - ODR
```

```
Gateway of last resort is not set

     172.16.0.0/24 is subnetted, 1 subnets
C       172.16.1.0 is directly connected, Ethernet0
     172.30.0.0/24 is subnetted, 2 subnets
O       172.30.2.0 [110/74] via 172.30.1.2, 00:18:15, Serial1
C       172.30.1.0 is directly connected, Serial1
     10.0.0.0/24 is subnetted, 4 subnets
O IA    10.11.1.0 [110/74] via 172.16.1.1, 00:10:17, Ethernet0
O IA    10.11.2.0 [110/84] via 172.16.1.1, 00:10:17, Ethernet0
O IA    10.12.2.0 [110/84] via 172.16.1.1, 00:10:08, Ethernet0
O IA    10.12.1.0 [110/74] via 172.16.1.1, 00:10:08, Ethernet0
```

While there is nothing wrong with this configuration, you should notice that there are four routes pointing to 172.16.1.1 for the various 10.*x.x.x* networks. We can simplify the routing table by changing the configuration on Router 1. Let's change the configuration on Router 1 to use the area range command we discussed earlier in the section "Inter-area summarization":

```
hostname Router1
!
interface Ethernet0
 ip address 172.16.1.1 255.255.255.0
!
interface Serial0
 ip address 10.12.1.1 255.255.255.0
!
interface Serial1
 ip address 10.11.1.1 255.255.255.0
!
router ospf 100
 network 10.11.0.0 0.0.255.255 area 1
 network 10.12.0.0 0.0.255.255 area 2
 network 172.16.1.0 0.0.0.255 area 0
 ! Add the commands to summarize the 10.11.0.0 and 10.12.0.0 networks
 area 1 range 10.11.0.0 255.255.0.0
 area 2 range 10.12.0.0 255.255.0.0
```

The addition of the two area range commands changed the way the areas are summarized. Running the show ip route command on Router 4 proves that the routing table is smaller:

```
Router4#sh ip route
Codes: C - connected, S - static, I - IGRP, R - RIP, M - mobile, B - BGP
       D - EIGRP, EX - EIGRP external, O - OSPF, IA - OSPF inter area
       N1 - OSPF NSSA external type 1, N2 - OSPF NSSA external type 2
       E1 - OSPF external type 1, E2 - OSPF external type 2, E - EGP
       i - IS-IS, L1 - IS-IS level-1, L2 - IS-IS level-2, * - candidate default
       U - per-user static route, o - ODR

Gateway of last resort is not set

     172.16.0.0/24 is subnetted, 1 subnets
C       172.16.1.0 is directly connected, Ethernet0
     172.30.0.0/24 is subnetted, 2 subnets
```

```
O        172.30.2.0 [110/74] via 172.30.1.2, 00:21:41, Serial1
C        172.30.1.0 is directly connected, Serial1
         10.0.0.0/16 is subnetted, 2 subnets
O IA     10.11.0.0 [110/74] via 172.16.1.1, 00:01:22, Ethernet0
O IA     10.12.0.0 [110/74] via 172.16.1.1, 00:01:13, Ethernet0
```

Now you see only two routes for the 10.11.0.0 and 10.12.0.0 networks. In this example, the savings aren't really significant. But on a real network with much larger routing tables, simplifying the tables by using summarization can have a significant impact on your network's performance.

Redistributing Other Protocols into OSPF

Instead of listing how each protocol can be redistributed into OSPF, I'll concentrate on one example with more detail. Look at Figure 9-9 and imagine that area 3 is an EIGRP network instead of an OSPF area; i.e., Router 4 runs EIGRP on interface Serial1, and Router 5 runs EIGRP exclusively. The challenge is getting redistribution between OSPF and EIGRP working. Let's start by modifying the configuration on Router 4 to support OSPF and EIGRP with redistribution:

```
hostname Router4
!
interface Ethernet0
 ip address 172.16.1.2 255.255.255.0
!
interface Serial1
 ip address 172.30.1.1 255.255.255.0
!
router eigrp 100
 ! List the EIGRP network
 network 172.30.0.0
 ! Disable EIGRP on the Ethernet0 interface
 passive-interface Ethernet0
 ! Redistribute our static route into EIGRP
 redistribute static
 ! Stop EIGRP from summarizing routes
 no auto-summary
!
!
router ospf 100
 network 172.16.0.0 0.0.255.255 area 0
 ! Use the summary-address command because we are injecting a route into
 ! OSPF (not the area range command, which summarizes OSPF internal
 ! routes)
 summary-address 172.30.0.0 255.255.0.0
 ! Redistribute EIGRP into OSPF
 redistribute eigrp 100 subnets
 default-metric 10
!
! Status default route for EIGRP
ip route 0.0.0.0 0.0.0.0 172.16.1.1
```

Things are much simpler on Router 5. We just need to configure our interfaces and start up EIGRP:

```
hostname Router5
!
interface Ethernet0
 ip address 172.30.2.1 255.255.255.0
!
interface Serial0
 ip address 172.30.1.2 255.255.255.0
!
router eigrp 100
 network 172.30.0.0
```

To verify our configuration, let's look at the route table on Router 1:

```
Router1#show ip route
Codes: C - connected, S - static, I - IGRP, R - RIP, M - mobile, B - BGP
       D - EIGRP, EX - EIGRP external, O - OSPF, IA - OSPF inter area
       N1 - OSPF NSSA external type 1, N2 - OSPF NSSA external type 2
       E1 - OSPF external type 1, E2 - OSPF external type 2, E - EGP
       i - IS-IS, L1 - IS-IS level-1, L2 - IS-IS level-2, * - candidate default
       U - per-user static route, o - ODR

Gateway of last resort is not set

     172.16.0.0/24 is subnetted, 1 subnets
C       172.16.1.0 is directly connected, Ethernet0
O E2 172.30.0.0/16 [110/10] via 172.16.1.2, 00:07:12, Ethernet0
     10.0.0.0/24 is subnetted, 5 subnets
C       10.11.1.0 is directly connected, Serial1
O       10.11.2.0 [110/74] via 10.11.1.2, 00:07:51, Serial1
O       10.12.2.0 [110/74] via 10.12.1.2, 00:07:51, Serial0
C       10.12.1.0 is directly connected, Serial0
O       10.0.0.0 is a summary, 00:07:45, Null0
Router1#
```

The route to the EIGRP router is there. And since we used the summary-address command, there is only one route to the 172.30.0.0/16 network. To verify connectivity, we ping Router 5:

```
Router1#ping 172.30.2.1

Type escape sequence to abort.
Sending 5, 100-byte ICMP Echos to 172.30.2.1, timeout is 2 seconds:
!!!!!
Success rate is 100 percent (5/5), round-trip min/avg/max = 32/33/36 ms
```

And everything looks good.

OSPF show Commands

The following show commands are particularly useful when you're working with OSPF. We've already seen some of them in this chapter.

show ip ospf border routers

This command shows the border routers that this router knows about:

```
Router1#show ip ospf border-routers

OSPF Process 100 internal Routing Table

Codes: i - Intra-area route, I - Inter-area route

i 172.30.1.1 [10] via 172.16.1.2, Ethernet0, ABR, Area 0, SPF 28
```

show ip ospf neighbor

This command gives you a list of OSPF neighbors that are directly connected to the router:

```
Router1#show ip ospf neighbor

Neighbor ID    PRI  State        Dead Time   Address      Interface
172.30.1.1      1   FULL/DR      00:00:37    172.16.1.2   Ethernet0
10.12.2.1       1   FULL/  -     00:00:35    10.12.1.2    Serial0
10.11.2.1       1   FULL/  -     00:00:30    10.11.1.2    Serial1
```

The Neighbor ID is the OSPF router ID for the neighbor. A router's ID is either the highest IP address of any interface on the router or the IP address of the loopback interface (if it has been defined). PRI indicates priority. Priorities are used to establish the DR router; the router with the highest priority is the DR router. The State column reports the state of the connection to the neighbor. The state can be FULL, DOWN, or 2-WAY. FULL means that the routers are fully adjacent. Dead Time is the amount of time the router will wait without hearing a hello from the router before changing the neighbor's state to DOWN. Address is the IP address of the interface to which the neighbor is connected, and Interface shows the interface through which the neighbor is reached.

show ip ospf database

This command is very verbose, as it displays the entire OSPF database for the router. For each entry, there is a Link ID, ADV Router (short for "advertising router"), Age, Seq#, and Checksum. Some entries have Link and Count information as well.

```
        OSPF Router with ID (172.16.1.1) (Process ID 100)


                Router Link States (Area 0)

Link ID        ADV Router     Age      Seq#       Checksum Link Count
10.10.5.2      10.10.5.2      2484     0x8000008D 0xAAC3   3
10.10.5.3      10.10.5.3      2526     0x8000008D 0xDE8A   3
172.16.1.1     172.16.1.1     1617     0x80000002 0xF239   1
172.30.1.1     172.30.1.1     1549     0x80000002 0xE727   1


                Net Link States (Area 0)
```

```
Link ID          ADV Router      Age         Seq#         Checksum
172.16.1.2       172.30.1.1      1550        0x80000001 0xEE33

                 Summary Net Link States (Area 0)

Link ID          ADV Router      Age         Seq#         Checksum
10.11.0.0        172.16.1.1      149         0x80000001 0x65C3
10.12.0.0        172.16.1.1      140         0x80000001 0x59CE
172.30.1.0       172.30.1.1      70          0x80000002 0xC0A2
172.30.2.0       172.30.1.1      70          0x80000002 0x1A3E
```

This command can be expanded to provide even more information by adding the router, network, or summary keywords.

show ip ospf interface

This command provides a wealth of OSPF information on a per-interface basis:

```
Router1#show ip ospf interface
Ethernet0 is up, line protocol is up
  Internet Address 172.16.1.1/24, Area 0
  Process ID 100, Router ID 172.16.1.1, Network Type BROADC*, Cost: 10
  Transmit Delay is 1 sec, State BDR, Priority 1
  Designated Router (ID) 172.30.1.1, Interface address 172.16.1.2
  Backup Designated router (ID) 172.16.1.1, Interface address 172.16.1.1
  Timer intervals configured, Hello 10, Dead 40, Wait 40, Retransmit 5
    Hello due in 00:00:00
  Neighbor Count is 1, Adjacent neighbor count is 1
    Adjacent with neighbor 172.30.1.1  (Designated Router)
  Suppress hello for 0 neighbor(s)
Serial0 is up, line protocol is up
  Internet Address 10.12.1.1/24, Area 2
  Process ID 100, Router ID 172.16.1.1, Network Type POINT_TO_POINT, Cost: 64
  Transmit Delay is 1 sec, State POINT_TO_POINT,
  Timer intervals configured, Hello 10, Dead 40, Wait 40, Retransmit 5
    Hello due in 00:00:00
  Neighbor Count is 1, Adjacent neighbor count is 1
    Adjacent with neighbor 10.12.2.1
  Suppress hello for 0 neighbor(s)
Serial1 is up, line protocol is up
  Internet Address 10.11.1.1/24, Area 1
  Process ID 100, Router ID 172.16.1.1, Network Type POINT_TO_POINT, Cost: 64
  Transmit Delay is 1 sec, State POINT_TO_POINT,
  Timer intervals configured, Hello 10, Dead 40, Wait 40, Retransmit 5
    Hello due in 00:00:09
  Neighbor Count is 1, Adjacent neighbor count is 1
    Adjacent with neighbor 10.11.2.1
  Suppress hello for 0 neighbor(s)
Serial2 is administratively down, line protocol is down
  OSPF not enabled on this interface
Serial3 is administratively down, line protocol is down
  OSPF not enabled on this interface
```

IS-IS

Depending on whom you ask, early on, IS-IS was deployed because OSPF had not matured enough for interconnecting BGP systems. Whether that is true or not is debatable. Today, OSPF is used without any such worries. However, IS-IS continues to be popular among service providers (ISPs) as a way of interconnecting BGP networks.

Another reason for its early popularity might be that it routes both IP and Connectionless Network Service (CLNS). OSPF can route only IP. In fact, even if you are not using CLNS, you must use Network Service Address Point (NSAP) addresses on the router to enable IS-IS. CLNS has the added advantage of keeping IP layer problems, such as duplicate IP addresses, from disrupting the router protocol functions.

IS-IS is a link state protocol that provides an array of features:

- It provides very fast convergence.
- It is relatively easy to configure.
- It is classless.
- It is scalable.
- It is supported by most vendors.
- It can carry MPLS information.

Another advantage is that IS-IS generally allows for larger areas than OSPF. While that might be true, OSPF has a lot of nice features in other areas that IS-IS doesn't.

People often think IS-IS is hard to configure. (It might be those pesky NSAP addresses scaring them off.) But as you'll see, just like any routing protocol—with the exception of BGP—you'll find IS-IS easy to use. Before we start configuring it, we need to review a few IS-IS concepts.

IS-IS Concepts

In order to perform a basic IS-IS configuration, we need to understand levels, NSAP addressing, and enabling an interface for IS-IS.

Level 1 and level 2

IS-IS is broken into a hierarchy with two levels—level 1 and level 2. Level-1 and level-2 routers exist in groups called areas. Level 1 routers can route only within their area. They have no knowledge of routes outside their own area. When a level-1 system needs to send a packet to another area, it sends it to the nearest level-2 router in its area. Level-2 routers can route between areas.

Routers can be defined as level 1, level 2, or both. In our illustrations, we abbreviate these designations as L1, L2, and L1/L2.

Under OSPF, Area 0 is the backbone. In an IS-IS network, contiguous level-2 area routers form the backbone. As shown in Figure 9-10, each area has a level-2 router (really it's a combination level-1 and level-2 router) that connects to another level-2 router, which forms our contiguous backbone. Since level-2 routers are members of one and only one area, unlike OSPF where ABR is a member of Area 0 as well as a "leaf" area, the area boundaries occur "on the line" as illustrated by the area circles in Figure 9-10.

Since level-2 routers interconnect areas, IP summarization occurs only on level-2 routers.

NSAP addressing

For TCP/IP networks, IP addresses must be unique. IS-IS is part of the OSI standard, and a Network Service Address Point (NSAP) address is the equivalent of an IP address for an OSI network; it must be unique throughout the IS-IS network in question. An NSAP address is a hexadecimal address with a length of up to 40 hexadecimal digits. It defines the address of the device (the system ID) and the link to the upper layer (the area number). NSAP addresses are used in ATM, as discussed in Chapter 6.

Table 9-1 shows how Cisco uses the NSAP address bytes in IS-IS.

Table 9-1. Cisco's use of NSAP address bytes for IS-IS

Area ID	System ID	NSEL
1–13 bytes	6 bytes	1 byte

For a device, the Area ID is the router's IS-IS area and the System ID is the router identifier. On routers, the NSAP Selector (NSEL) is almost always set to 00.

Since our IS-IS network is small and not connected to others, we use a simplified addressing scheme designed to correspond to the way Cisco uses the address bytes. For our addresses, we'll convert and use our loopback IP address for our router. So, if our IP address was 192.168.21.1 (think of it as 192.168.021.001), our NSAP addresses look like this:

    49.000N.1921.6802.1001.00

Where N is the area number (1, 2, or 3), and the rest of the NSAP is our IP address (1921.6802.1001). This works for us because device numbers are unique across areas. Another way of creating unique NSAP address is to use the Media Access Control (MAC) address.

Using the loopback naming convention is strictly our own way to help us in selecting the net addresses that we add to the configuration file. Since these addresses look like IP addresses, they serve as bridges between IS-IS and our IP addressing.

 The 49 indicates that the address is labeled a private address, which won't be advertised to other CLNS networks. (It's like the 192.168.0.0/16 address space in IPv4.)

We configure the IS-IS network using the net command:

```
router isis
  net 49.0001.1921.6802.1001.00
```

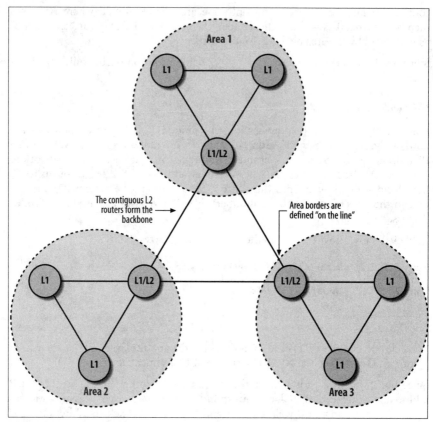

Figure 9-10. IS-IS areas

Since a router is never in more than one area, you shouldn't need to define more than one net address for each router using IS-IS. Adding multiple area net addresses causes the areas to converge into one area. The rule is that you should never have more than one net address defined per router. And as always, there are exceptions to this rule. If you are merging or renumbering your areas, you will need to have multiple net addresses. But after the merger or renumbering is complete, you should be back to one net address defined for your IS-IS router.

Enabling an interface for IS-IS

IS-IS configuration is unique in that you define a routing process, then apply it to an interface instead of a network address. An interface will not participate in IS-IS routing unless configured to do so. In our example, we need to add the passive-interface loopback0 command so the loopback address is advertised via IS-IS, but the loopback interface does not participate in IS-IS advertisements:

```
router isis
  ! Build our NSAP address from the loopback's IP which is 172.16.1.7
  net 49.0001.1720.1600.1007.00
  passive-interface loopback0
```

```
!
interface ethernet0
  ip address 192.168.1.1 255.255.255.0
  ip router isis
```

IS-IS configuration example

Our sample configuration builds on an earlier example. In Figure 9-11, we can see the network with the area boundaries. This is the same network we used in our EIGRP example in Figure 9-3. However, this time we want to drop EIGRP from our network and run IS-IS only.

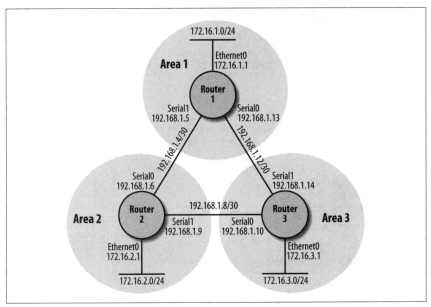

Figure 9-11. Network diagram of IS-IS sample configuration

Here's the configuration for Router 1:

```
hostname router1
!
!
interface loopback0
  ip address 172.16.5.1 255.255.255.0
!
interface Ethernet0
  ip address 172.16.1.1 255.255.255.0
  ip router isis
!
interface Serial0
  bandwidth 125
  ip address 192.168.1.13 255.255.255.252
  ip router isis
!
```

Interior Routing

```
interface Serial1
 bandwidth 125
 ip address 192.168.1.5 255.255.255.252
 ip router isis
!
router isis
 net 49.0001.1720.1600.5001.00
!
ip classless
```

Here's the configuration for Router 2:

```
hostname router2
!
interface loopback0
 ip address 172.16.6.1 255.255.255.0
!
interface Ethernet0
 ip address 172.16.2.1 255.255.255.0
 ip router isis
!
interface Serial0
 bandwidth 125
 ip address 192.168.1.6 255.255.255.252
 ip router isis
!
interface Serial1
 bandwidth 125
 ip address 192.168.1.9 255.255.255.252
 ip router isis
!
router isis
 net 49.0002.1720.1600.6001.00
!
ip classless
```

And here's the configuration for Router 3:

```
hostname router3
!
interface loopback0
 ip address 172.16.7.1 255.255.255.0
!
interface Ethernet0
 ip address 172.16.3.1 255.255.255.0
 ip router isis
!
interface Serial0
 bandwidth 125
 ip address 192.168.1.10 255.255.255.252
 ip router isis
!
interface Serial1
 bandwidth 125
 ip address 192.168.1.14 255.255.255.252
 ip router isis
```

```
!
router isis
 net 49.0003.1720.1600.7001.00
!
ip classless
```

If we do some show commands on Router 1, we can see the network is functioning, as we would expect:

```
router1#show ip route
Codes: C - connected, S - static, I - IGRP, R - RIP, M - mobile, B - BGP
       D - EIGRP, EX - EIGRP external, O - OSPF, IA - OSPF inter area
       N1 - OSPF NSSA external type 1, N2 - OSPF NSSA external type 2
       E1 - OSPF external type 1, E2 - OSPF external type 2, E - EGP
       i - IS-IS, L1 - IS-IS level-1, L2 - IS-IS level-2, ia - IS-IS inter area
       * - candidate default, U - per-user static route, o - ODR
       P - periodic downloaded static route

Gateway of last resort is not set

     172.16.0.0/24 is subnetted, 3 subnets
C       172.16.1.0 is directly connected, Ethernet0
i L2    172.16.2.0 [115/20] via 192.168.1.6, Serial1
i L2    172.16.3.0 [115/20] via 192.168.1.14, Serial0
     192.168.1.0/30 is subnetted, 3 subnets
i L2    192.168.1.8 [115/20] via 192.168.1.14, Serial0
                    [115/20] via 192.168.1.6, Serial1
C       192.168.1.12 is directly connected, Serial0
C       192.168.1.4 is directly connected, Serial1
```

Show Commands

The first command we'll use is show isis topology, which displays the IS-IS network topology as our current router sees it.

```
router1#show isis topology

IS-IS paths to level-1 routers
System Id       Metric  Next-Hop      Interface      SNPA
router2         **
router1         --

IS-IS paths to level-2 routers
System Id       Metric  Next-Hop      Interface      SNPA
router2         10      router2       Se1            *HDLC*
router1         --
router3         10      router3       Se0            *HDLC*
```

The second command we'll look at is show isis database, which shows all the IS-IS information we currently have. If you are troubleshooting your IS-IS network, you might want to look at show isis database detail, which—as the name suggests—provides a greater degree of detail.

```
router1#show isis database
 IS-IS Level-1 Link State Database:
 LSPID                 LSP Seq Num   LSP Checksum   LSP Holdtime      ATT/P/OL
 router2.00-00         0x00000003    0x7ABD         654               0/0/0
 router1.00-00       * 0x00000002    0xBEE7         1091              1/0/0
 IS-IS Level-2 Link State Database:
 LSPID                 LSP Seq Num   LSP Checksum   LSP Holdtime      ATT/P/OL
 router2.00-00         0x00000051    0xEB34         1123              0/0/0
 router1.00-00       * 0x00000005    0xA9D4         1175              0/0/0
 router2.00-00         0x00000003    0xDF9D         1177              0/0/0
 router3.00-00         0x00000005    0x84E6         1176              0/0/0
```

In this output, there are a few terms we should explain. First, the LSPID is the LSP
Identifier, which the first six octets form the System ID of the router that originated the LSP. The Seq Num allows other systems to tell if they have the latest
information from the source. The checksum is, of course, the checksum of the
LSP packet. The holdtime is the amount of seconds that the LSP will remain valid.
A value of zero means that the LSP has expired and is currently being purged from
the router's databases. ATT is the attach bit, which indicates that the router is a
level-2 router. Level-1 routers use this bit to find the nearest level-2 router. P
stands for "repair partitions," which is a feature not supported by Cisco although
it's reported here. Finally, the OL bit stands for "overload," which signals that the
IS is congested. If the OL bit is set, other IS-IS routers will not use that router as a
transit router. And only packets for devices directly connected to the overloaded
router are sent to it.

Finally, show clns route shows the routing table from the CLNS point of view.

```
Router1#show clns route
Codes: C - connected, S - static, d - DecnetIV
       I - ISO-IGRP,  i - IS-IS,  e - ES-IS

C  49.0001.1111.1111.1111.00 [1/0], Local IS-IS NET
C  49.0001 [2/0], Local IS-IS Area
```

Authentication

We can enable IS-IS authentication by providing, directly on the interface, an IS-IS
password for each level directly. The command isis password specifies the passwords for each level, as in this example:

```
interface serial0
  isis password ourAreaOnePasswd level-1
  isis password ourAreaTwoPasswd level-2
```

Now, our router cannot communicate via IS-IS until all its adjacent neighbors are
configured with the same IS-IS passwords. You can also assign passwords to the
area and the domain with the area-password and domain-password commands.

Metric Tuning

Other routing protocols assign a metric to an interface by using a calculation based on bandwidth or some other cost. IS-IS normally just gives every interface a metric of 10. In order to change this metric, you can provide an IS-IS metric directly on the interface with the rather obviously named isis metric command.

You can assign a metric value between the values 0 to 63. These values can be assigned to level 1, level 2, or both. For example, let's configured a metric of 23 for level 1 on Serial 0, and a metric of 25 for both on Serial 1.

```
interface serial0
  isis metric 23 level-1
interface serial1
  isis metric 25
```

Injecting a Default Route

The default-information originate command designates a given router as the default route for the network and announces that information to other routers in the network . For example, if we perform the command on Router 1:

```
router isis
  default-information originate
```

Now, the default route has been injected into the IS-IS routing. If we do a show ip route, we can see that the gateway of last resort, which is the default route to Router 1, is now set on Router 3. To put it another way, what you are seeing here is that we told Router 1 to become the default route for our network. This information has propagated via IS-IS to all our other routers. And now Router 3 has a default route, which is shown in the bolded output below. Before, Router 3 would not have a default route set.

```
router3#show ip route
Codes: C - connected, S - static, I - IGRP, R - RIP, M - mobile, B - BGP
       D - EIGRP, EX - EIGRP external, O - OSPF, IA - OSPF inter area
       N1 - OSPF NSSA external type 1, N2 - OSPF NSSA external type 2
       E1 - OSPF external type 1, E2 - OSPF external type 2, E - EGP
       i - IS-IS, L1 - IS-IS level-1, L2 - IS-IS level-2, ia - IS-IS inter area
       * - candidate default, U - per-user static route, o - ODR
       P - periodic downloaded static route

Gateway of last resort is 192.168.1.13 to network 0.0.0.0

     172.16.0.0/24 is subnetted, 3 subnets
i L2    172.16.1.0 [115/20] via 192.168.1.13, Serial1
i L2    172.16.2.0 [115/20] via 192.168.1.9, Serial0
C       172.16.3.0 is directly connected, Ethernet0
     192.168.1.0/30 is subnetted, 3 subnets
C       192.168.1.8 is directly connected, Serial0
C       192.168.1.12 is directly connected, Serial1
i L2    192.168.1.4 [115/20] via 192.168.1.9, Serial0
                    [115/20] via 192.168.1.13, Serial1
i*L2 0.0.0.0/0 [115/10] via 192.168.1.13, Serial1
```

IS-IS Route Leaking

Route leaking sounds bad doesn't it? We'd better talk about how to plug those route leaks. Actually, it's more about route distribution than leaking. We've talked about how level-1 routers use level-2 routers to route packets that are outside their own area. A level-1 router knows about its own area and level-2 routers know how to connect their own area and the all the other areas.

Route leaking (or distributing) provides a way of letting level-1 areas know about level-2 routing information. The route information is "leaked" from level 2 to level 1. By having this information, the level-1 router can make better decisions as to which level-2 router to use to access outside areas.

Route leaking was added in IOS 12.1. Here's a sample route leaking configuration:

```
router isis
  redistribute isis ip level-2 into level-1 distribute-list 110
  metric-style wide
!
access-list 110 permit ip 172.16.0.0 0.0.255.255 any
access-list 110 permit ip 192.168.1.0 0.0.0.255 any
```

100 is the access list that defines the routes we want to leak. The `metric-style wide` command is optional, but Cisco highly recommends it.

Leaked routes appear in the route table with the **ia** notation (ia stands for "interarea"):

```
i ia 172.16.100.0/8 [115/138] via 192.168.1.13, Serial1
```

Now that this router has a "leaked" route, it can make better decisions about which level-2 router to access in order to reach the 172.16.100.0/8 subnet.

10

Border Gateway Protocol

Fortunately, this is a Nutshell book, so I don't have to do anything more than give a brief introduction to the Border Gateway Protocol (BGP), one of the most complex topics in network routing. Covering BGP in any detail could easily require hundreds of pages. Unlike the other routing protocols we've discussed, BGP is an exterior routing protocol, which means it routes traffic between different autonomous systems. Its primary use is on the Internet backbone; it shouldn't be used on most networks that are connected to the Internet. However, if you have more than one Internet service provider or your network is multihomed, you must use BGP.

BGP is a successor to EGP, which had many limitations. BGP's main new feature was Classless Interdomain Routing (CIDR), which rescued the almost-exhausted Internet IP address space. The current version of BGP is BGP4; it's unlikely that you'll need to know about earlier versions.

Introduction to BGP

We can run two types of BGP routing on our network:

Internal BGP (iBGP)
> iBGP exchanges BGP information within an autonomous system. Internal BGP sounds counterintuitive, since BGP is supposed to be an "external" routing protocol. The point of internal BGP is to distribute your BGP information between your external BGP routers. Your external routers are usually not close together; iBGP allows them to communicate across your internal network. iBGP is necessary in networks that have multiple paths to the Internet. It provides a consistent view of routes to and from the Internet.

External BGP (eBGP)
> eBGP distributes your BGP routing information to other autonomous systems. For example, external BGP is used for routing between your local network and two different ISPs.

Many people make BGP out to be the ultimate solution for advanced routing problems. It isn't, and using BGP successfully requires careful planning and design. Therefore, before deciding that you need BGP, you should think carefully about your options and what you're trying to accomplish. Here are some guidelines for when you should avoid BGP:

- If you can accomplish the same thing with a static route, use it; don't use BGP.
- If you have only one connection to the Internet and your network is small, you don't need BGP.

Once you decide that you need BGP, keep in mind that BGP becomes complex quickly. Keeping things as simple as possible is preferable for both operation and troubleshooting. (Isn't that true for all network protocols?) Furthermore, BGP requires (or demands) that routing policies exist for your network. For example, if you have two ISPs, you need to think about which link to prefer. Should you use the closest link? Should you suppress routes from your ISP? If so, which routes? We examine these configuration items later in this chapter.

How BGP Selects Routes

Before we jump into BGP configuration, you should understand the routing metrics it uses. BGP uses more information than other routing protocols to select routes. The most important parameters that go into route selection are:

Weight
Weight is a purely local measure of which route to prefer. A weight is given to a route on a particular router (via a route map, for example) and is used only within that router. The weight is never given to other routers. The higher the weight of a route, the better the route is. Weight is configurable and can be used to select one route over another.

Local preference
Local preference is another measure of which route to prefer. Unlike weight, local preferences are shared among iBGP routers. However, they are not shared with external BGP routers. The default local preference is 100. As with weight, higher numbers indicate better routes.

Multi-exit discriminator (MED)
MED values describe our routes to external routers. Unlike preference and weight, MED actually leaves our network and tells our neighbor routers which link we want them to talk to. And unlike the other metric values, the lower the MED value, the better the route. The default MED value is zero (0).

The name "multi-exit discriminator" is unfortunate and makes the concept unnecessarily confusing. The BGP designers were thinking from the point of view of your ISP: which exit from the ISP's network should be used to reach you? As a result, the MED will make much more sense if you turn it around and think of it as a "multi-entrance discriminator." That is, you use the MED to tell your ISPs which of several entrances to your network they should use. You should use MED values only if you are multihomed to a single provider.

AS path

BGP routing is based on the list of autonomous systems that are traversed in order to reach a destination. This list is called an AS path. Shorter AS paths are preferred, but there are many ways to filter routes based on their AS paths. AS paths allow BGP to detect routing loops.

BGP selects only one route for a destination; this route is added to the route table and distributed to BGP peers. Here's the process by which a route is selected:

1. Drop the route immediately if its next hop isn't accessible.

2. If there are two routes with different weights, pick the route with the largest (heaviest) weight.

3. If weight values are equal, choose the route with the largest local preference value.

4. If local preference values are equal for multiple routes, choose the route that originated with BGP on this router.

5. If none, or all, of the routes originated on this router, choose the route with the shortest AS path.

6. If all the AS path lengths are the same, choose the path with the lowest origin type. Origin refers to whether the route originated via an internal gateway protocol (IGP) or an external gateway protocol (EGP). Routes that have entered the BGP domain by redistribution are considered incomplete. IGP is lower than EGP, and EGP is lower than incomplete.

7. If all the origin types are the same, choose the path with the lowest MED value.

8. If all the MED values are the same, choose an external route over an internal route.

9. If all the routes are the same, choose the path with the closest IGP neighbor.

10. If the distances to the closest IGP neighbor are the same, choose the path with the lowest BGP router ID. A router's ID is the IP address assigned to the loopback interface or the highest IP address on an active interface at boot time.

Basic Configuration Commands

Basic configuration relies on a number of familiar commands, such as router, network, and neighbor. However, the BGP versions of these commands are a little more complex than for other routing protocols. This section covers the basic configuration items.

The router and network commands

We start our configuration by giving our autonomous system number in the router bgp command. Here, 500 is our AS number:

```
router bgp 500
  network 10.0.0.0
```

In other protocols, such as EIGRP and OSPF, we chose the AS numbers pretty much however we pleased—we were required only to be consistent within our own network. In fact, although they are frequently called AS numbers, the numbers associated with EIGRP and OSPF routing processes are really just process IDs. With BGP, you're dealing with true AS numbers, and each AS number must fit into the rest of the global BGP design. This number is given to you by your service provider and must be used appropriately.

In this example, we'll advertise a route to the network 10.10.2.0. This network doesn't have to be directly connected to the router in order for us to advertise it. We don't provide a network mask, as BGP assumes the old classful addressing scheme when a mask isn't provided explicitly. If this is not what you want, you need to add the mask option to specify a classless network. The following network command advertises the network 10.10.2.0/23:

```
router bgp 500
  network 10.10.2.0 mask 255.255.254.0
```

The neighbor command

Next, we need to define our routing peers with the neighbor command. This step also defines whether we are using iBGP or eBGP. If our neighbor router has the same AS number, we are using iBGP. If our neighbor has a different AS number, we are configuring eBGP. In this case, we configured a neighbor with a different AS number, meaning that we are using eBGP. Most configurations will have several neighbor commands.

```
router bgp 500
  neighbor 192.168.1.5 remote-as 400
```

Neighbors don't have to be in an equivalent network statement. For example, we can have the neighbor 192.168.1.5 and not have a network equivalent or subnet of 192.168.1.0/24. Our IGP routing protocol might have the route we need to access that neighbor. We are using the neighbor command only to specify our peers.

When configuring BGP, you often need to list several neighbor commands for each neighboring router. The neighbor command can take a number of optional keywords, including default-originate and next-hop-self, both of which are discussed later.

 If your BGP neighbors aren't communicating, make sure they can actually reach each other. BGP neighbors will not peer if they can't reach each other.

Local-AS numbers

Just as there are private Class C IP addresses (e.g., 10.0.0.0/8 and 192.168.0.0/16), there are private AS numbers to be used for internal networks. This means that it is possible to use BGP for internal routing or routing between you and your ISP even if you're not involved with the Internet backbone. Situations in which you'd want to do this are rare, but you might consider it if you were managing an extremely large network with a number of connections to a single ISP. The AS numbers reserved for local use range from 64512 to 65535. Just as with private IP addresses, your network provider should filter these AS numbers so that they never appear outside your network.

Synchronization

In BGP, synchronization means that a BGP router is not allowed to advertise a route that is learned from another BGP peer until the router knows about the route via an IGP. Synchronization can take time, and in most cases it isn't needed. Disabling synchronization removes this rule. Although disabling synchronization adds the possibility of dropped packets, it can improve convergence time for your routers. To disable synchronization, add the command no synchronization to the BGP configuration.

Synchronization can be disabled safely under either of two conditions: if your network doesn't pass traffic from one AS to another (i.e., other networks do not route their traffic through you), or if all your border routers are running BGP. Disabling synchronization is an absolute must for running iBGP, which is described in the next few sections.

Automatic summary

By default, BGP summarizes routes on class boundaries. There are many situations in which you don't want summarization to follow class boundaries. For example, say you're given the IP address space of 172.30.5.0/24, 172.30.6.0/24, and 172.30.7.0/24. When BGP announces your route, it will try to summarize the route to the classful route 172.30.0.0/16. This behavior is almost certainly not what you want.

If your ISP is worth anything, it will block announcements from you that don't match your network. However, you shouldn't rely on your ISP to prevent you from advertising misleading information. Configuring no auto-summary disables automatic summarization.

default-originate

default-originate (a keyword that can be appended to the neighbor command) causes the BGP router to advertise a default route to other BGP routers, even if it doesn't have a default route defined for itself. (A default route has the address 0.0.0.0 0.0.0.0.)

next-hop-self

When an iBGP router advertises a route, it advertises the next hop of the route as it learned it. The next-hop-self keyword (used with the neighbor command) tells the router to rewrite the route's next hop as itself. For example, if you have next-hop-self configured from Router 1 to Router 2, Router 1 tells Router 2 that it is the next hop for the routes that it sends to Router 2.

BGP route dampening

Route dampening controls the effect that a flapping route has on the network. Route flapping occurs when a route changes state (up to down, or down to up) repeatedly. This can happen when a router has a bad interface or some other problem exists. Flapping is a problem for any routing protocol, BGP included: when a route changes state, BGP tries to propagate this information to the other routers, consuming a lot of CPU time and network bandwidth in addition to distributing unreliable information.

BGP handles route flapping with the bgp dampening command. When this feature is activated, the router tolerates only a certain number of state changes for a route within a certain amount of time. If the state-change threshold (tolerance) is reached, the route is placed in a hold-down (ignored) state for a period. After the hold-down time passes, the route is again allowed into the routing table to see if it behaves. Dampening doesn't stop the route from receiving unstable routes; rather, it prevents the routing from forwarding what it considers to be unstable routes.

You can set the hold-down time and tolerance values with the dampening command; if these values are not set, the router uses default values.

iBGP checklist

There are two ways to get iBGP to work correctly. The first is to redistribute all external routes into all of your iBGP routers. This method is not a good idea; the routing table might be large, and some of your routers may not be able to handle it. A much better way to implement iBGP is to:

1. Disable synchronization. Remember that synchronization prevents a router from taking a route that was learned via an iBGP neighbor and entering it into the routing table, unless the route is first learned via an interior routing protocol.

2. Make sure all your iBGP routers are fully meshed, i.e., that each iBGP router has a neighbor command for every other iBGP router. A full mesh ensures that all routers along the AS path know how to forward packets to the destination router.

3. Make sure all networks and subnets that connect iBGP routers are known— that is, that a route exists between all of your routers and that your interior routing protocol is doing its job and distributing those routes. If the routers cannot talk to one another, they won't be able to peer.

The example in the next section takes care of all three requirements.

A Simple BGP Configuration

In this section, we'll look at a simple BGP configuration that includes both eBGP and iBGP configurations. A realistic example would be much more complex (particularly for the ISP), but this will help you see how things work. Figure 10-1 shows the sample network. There are two office routers (office-r1 and office-r2); office-r1 connects to the Internet via an ISP, whose router is named (logically enough) "ISP".

Figure 10-1. A simple BGP network

Here's the configuration for office-r1:

```
hostname office-r1
!
interface Ethernet0
 ip address 192.168.1.1 255.255.255.0
!
interface Serial0
 ip address 172.16.1.2 255.255.255.0
!
interface Serial1
 ip address 192.168.3.1 255.255.255.0
!
! Configure BGP for our local-AS 3000
router bgp 3000
 ! We disable synchronization for our iBGP peers
 no synchronization
 ! The networks we want to advertise
 network 192.168.1.0
 network 192.168.3.0
 ! Our EBGP peers
 neighbor 172.16.1.1 remote-as 100
 ! For our IBGP peers, we'll set us as the default-originate
 ! And we'll set us as the next hop using the next-hop-self command
 neighbor 192.168.3.2 remote-as 3000
 neighbor 192.168.3.2 next-hop-self
 neighbor 192.168.3.2 default-originate
!
! Our iBGP peers expect us to be the default route, so we need a local
! default route
ip route 0.0.0.0 0.0.0.0 172.16.1.1
```

The configuration for office-r2 is:

```
hostname office-r2
!
interface Ethernet0
 ip address 192.168.2.1 255.255.255.0
!
interface Serial0
 ip address 192.168.3.2 255.255.255.0
!
! Our BGP configuration
router bgp 3000
 ! Once again, no synchronization for iBGP
 no synchronization
 ! Only one network to define
 network 192.168.2.0
 ! Only one neighbor to define
 neighbor 192.168.3.1 remote-as 3000
```

The configuration for ISP is:

```
! If this were a real ISP configuration, we would be fired!
! But it shows the concepts.
hostname ISP1
 !
 interface Loopback0
 ip address 172.16.3.1 255.255.255.0
!
interface Ethernet0
 ip address 10.1.1.1 255.255.255.0
!
interface Serial1
 ip address 172.16.1.1 255.255.255.0
 clockrate 64000
!
router bgp 100
 network 172.16.0.0
 neighbor 10.1.1.2 remote-as 200
 neighbor 172.16.1.2 remote-as 3000
```

To demonstrate some of the BGP show commands, let's look at the office-r2 router. show ip route gives us a quick look at what's going on:

```
office-r2#show ip route
Codes: C - connected, S - static, I - IGRP, R - RIP, M - mobile, B - BGP
       D - EIGRP, EX - EIGRP external, O - OSPF, IA - OSPF inter area
       N1 - OSPF NSSA external type 1, N2 - OSPF NSSA external type 2
       E1 - OSPF external type 1, E2 - OSPF external type 2, E - EGP
       i - IS-IS, L1 - IS-IS level-1, L2 - IS-IS level-2, * - candidate default
       U - per-user static route, o - ODR

Gateway of last resort is 192.168.3.1 to network 0.0.0.0

B    172.16.0.0/16 [200/0] via 192.168.3.1, 00:03:10
B    192.168.1.0/24 [200/0] via 192.168.3.1, 00:03:15
C    192.168.2.0/24 is directly connected, Ethernet0
```

```
C    192.168.3.0/24 is directly connected, Serial0
B*   0.0.0.0/0 [200/0] via 192.168.3.1, 00:03:16
```

Everything here should be familiar. The gateway of last resort is set, because we have default-originate set on the office-r1 router (192.168.3.1). Note that the route for 172.16.0.0/16 is via 192.168.3.1. This route is set to office-r1's interface, because we used the next-hop-self option in one of the neighbor commands for 192.168.3.2 on office-r1. Therefore, office-r1 rewrote the BGP route for 172.16.0.0, making itself the next hop. If we hadn't put that command in, the route would have looked like this:

```
B    172.16.0.0/16 [200/0] via 172.16.1.1, 00:00:17
```

In this configuration, this route would work as well as the route to 192.168.3.2 because the default route tells our router how to get to that address. If we didn't have the default route, we would have to add an extra network statement, defining 172.16.0.0, to office-r1's configuration. next-hop-self makes the configuration a little easier.

Next, let's look at the output of show ip bgp on office-r2:

```
Office-r2#show ip bgp
BGP table version is 7, local router ID is 192.168.3.2
Status codes: s suppressed, d damped, h history, * valid, > best, i -
internal
Origin codes: i - IGP, e - EGP, ? - incomplete

      Network          Next Hop         Metric LocPrf Weight Path
*>i0.0.0.0           192.168.3.1                100      0 i
*>i172.16.0.0        192.168.3.1           0    100      0 100 i
*>i192.168.1.0       192.168.3.1           0    100      0 i
*> 192.168.2.0       0.0.0.0               0         32768 i
*>i192.168.3.0       192.168.3.1           0    100      0 i
```

The output from this show command gives us a lot of useful information. The left-hand side lists the known networks with different codes (see Table 10-1), indicating the route's status. > indicates the best route to the given network. Then we have the next-hop address, the metric, the local preference (LocPrf), the weight, and finally the AS path.

Table 10-1. Route status codes

Key	Route status
s	Suppressed
d	Damped
*	Valid
h	History
>	Best
i	Internal

The Path column is particularly important. Most of the entries in this column have a path of i, which means that the route was learned through an interior protocol and therefore doesn't cross autonomous system boundaries. The only exception is the 172.16.0.0 network, which is in another autonomous system (AS 100). For this route to reach office-r1, BGP must learn the route from some sort of interior protocol. Therefore, the path for this network is 100 i. AS paths can obviously be much more complex. For a slightly more complex example, imagine that network 172.30.0.0 is attached to the ISP router and has an AS number of 200. The route might look like this:

```
Office-r2#show ip bgp
...
*>i172.30.0.0      192.168.3.1             100     0 100 200 i
...
```

This path shows that to reach 172.30.0.0, you must cross AS 100, then enter AS 200, which learned the route through an interior protocol such as RIP. Therefore, you don't need to cross any more AS boundaries.

Route Filtering

A big part of working with BGP is filtering routes; that's how you control how your network traffic is carried and how you implement routing policies. You might want to filter routes coming from the outside into your network, or filter routes you advertise to other networks. No matter what your reason for filtering, there are basically three ways to do it: AS path filtering, community filtering, and aggregate filtering.

AS Path Filters

A lot of what you do with BGP is based on building AS path filters. Filters let you select specific paths (routes) through the network. AS path filters work like access lists, but with a twist: they support regular expression (regex) pattern matching. Here's an example of a simple AS path filter:

```
ip as-path access-list 70 deny ^100_
ip as-path access-list 70 permit .*
```

Like access lists, AS paths have the following rules:

- Each line is a permit or a deny.
- The first match wins.
- An implicit "deny all" is added to the end of the list.

In this case, we want to deny any AS path that starts with AS 100 and permit everything else. We've assigned the filter number 70 (with the ip as-path access-list 70 command), which we use when we reference the filter in other parts of the configuration. The last part of each line is the regular expression that determines whether or not a path matches the list. Note that the number assigned to the AS path filter has nothing to do with the numbers assigned to regular IP access lists; there's no concept of regular or extended lists, so you can use any number you want. You can even use the same numbers you used for your IP access lists, although this would probably be confusing.

Table 10-2 shows some of the expressions that can be used in an AS path. A path is nothing more than a list of autonomous systems. The first autonomous system in the path (the AS with which the path originates) is on the right; as the path crosses AS boundaries, new autonomous systems are added on the left. Therefore, the leftmost entry in an AS path is the autonomous system from which we heard the path. An underscore is used to separate AS numbers in the path. ^ matches the start of the path; $ matches the end. * matches any repetition of a character, and . matches any character.*

Table 10-2. AS path regular expressions

Regular expression	Meaning
.*	Matches all (i.e., any AS path).
^$	Matches an empty path. The only routes that can have an empty path are routes that originated within our local AS.
^100$	Specifies a path that consists of the single AS, AS 100. The ^ matches the beginning of the path; the $ matches the end.
^(100|200|300)$	Specifies a path that consists of a single AS, which can be either 100, 200, or 300. The vertical bar (|) means "or;" the parentheses are for grouping.
^100_	All paths that start with AS 100.
_100_	All paths with 100 anywhere in the path.
_100$	All paths that end with 100.

Community Filters

The community attribute allows routing policies to be applied to a destination. They are applied to routes using a set command in a route map. Later, you can use the community strings to perform various kinds of filtering. Three special community strings are defined and cause the router to take some action. Table 10-3 lists the three predefined communities.

Table 10-3. Predefined communities

Community	Action
no-export	Do not advertise to eBGP peers.
no-advertise	Do not advertise to any peer.
internet	Advertise to the Internet community (all routers belong to it).

In this example, we define a route map named Community1 that matches IP addresses from list 1. This map sets the community string of any matches to the no-advertise community:

```
access-list 1 permit 0.0.0.0 255.255.255.255
!
route-map Community1
```

---

* For more information about regular expressions, see *Mastering Regular Expressions* by Jeffrey Friedl (O'Reilly).

```
    match ip address 1
    set community no-advertise
  !
  ! Now we use the community in the neighbor command
  router bgp 500
    neighbor 10.1.1.1 remote-as 200
    neighbor 10.1.1.1 send-community
    neighbor 10.1.1.1 route-map Community1 out
```

By applying the route map in the neighbor command, we use it to check all the route updates we send to neighbor 10.1.1.1. However, the route map matches any route destination (because of access list 1) and sets the route's community string to no-advertise. This means that all routes we send to 10.1.1.1 via BGP will have the no-advertise community. Therefore, when 10.1.1.1 receives a route update from us, it will not advertise any of our routes.

We can assign our own community values to outgoing routes. Our neighbors can then implement filters based on the community values we have set and act appropriately. Consider two routers, Router 1 and Router 2. Router 1 belongs to the 10.1.0.0 network (AS 500), while Router 2 belongs to the 10.2.0.0 network (AS 600). Router 1 sends all routes to Router 2 with a community of 100. Router 2 looks for any routes with a community of 100 and sets the weight to 10.

The configuration for Router 1 is:

```
  ! Router1 sends all its outgoing routes to neighbor 10.2.0.0 with
  ! a community value of 100
  !
  router bgp 500
    network 10.0.0.0
    neighbor 10.2.0.0 remote-as 600
    neighbor 10.2.0.0 send-community
    ! the route-map is set to OUT
    neighbor 10.2.0.0 route-map SET100 out
  !
  ! Define our route map, setting the community to 100
  route-map SET100 permit 10
    match ip address 1
    set community 100
  !
  ! Match all IP addresses
  access-list 1 permit 0.0.0.0 255.255.255.255
```

The configuration for Router 2 is:

```
  ! Router 2 looks for any route with a community of 100 and sets the
  ! weight to 10
  router bgp 600
    network 10.2.0.0
    neighbor 10.1.0.0 remote-as 500
    ! The route map is used to check incoming routes
    neighbor 10.1.0.0 route-map CHECK100 in
  !
  ! Define our route map, looking for community 100
```

```
route-map CHECK100 permit 10
  match community 1
  set weight 10
!
! Here is our community-list command. It acts like an access-list. This
! time we are looking for a community of 100
ip community-list 1 permit 100
```

It's easy to get confused by the many layers of indirection. The neighbor statement refers to a route map by name; the match statements inside the route map
refer to community lists or access lists by number, and the community list itself
finally checks the community.

Note that the predefined communities are mutually exclusive. In contrast, user-
defined communities can be made additive by placing the additive keyword on the
set community command. A route may therefore belong to several communities.

Aggregate Filters

Aggregate filters allow several different routes to be expressed in one simple (but
equivalent) route, thus reducing the size of the routing table. Aggregates can be
used only when the routes can be summarized into a single (aggregate) route.

The aggregate-address command controls route aggregation and reduces the
number of outgoing BGP routes. Let's assume that we own several networks,
192.168.1.0/24 through 192.168.254.0/24. There is no need to advertise all of
these networks separately. Instead, we can generate a single route summary for
the entire network space:

```
router bgp 600
  network 10.0.0.0
  aggregate-address 192.168.1.0 255.255.0.0 summary-only
```

The summary-only keyword tells the router to advertise only the aggregate route. If
we leave off summary-only, the router will advertise all of our routes plus the aggregate, which is not our intention.

Aggregate routes also allow us to suppress certain addresses from the aggregate
list. In this example, we want to advertise our aggregate route and our other
routes, but we also want to suppress route 192.168.5.0:

```
router bgp 600
  network 10.1.0.0
  aggregate-address 192.168.1.0 255.255.0.0 suppress-map MAP1
!
! Define our route map
route-map MAP1 permit 1
  match ip address 1
!
! Define our access list to deny 192.168.5.0/24 and permit everything else
access-list 1 deny 192.168.5.0 0.0.0.255
access-list 1 permit 0.0.0.0 255.255.255.255
```

In this case, we use the route map MAP1 to determine which networks we want to
suppress. This route map is based on access list 1.

Now that we've introduced a lot of the concepts, let's look at a complete configuration for a network.

An Advanced BGP Configuration

Figure 10-2 shows a network that consists of two offices connected to two different ISPs. The offices run OSPF between themselves and use BGP to exchange routes with the ISPs. The two offices are part of a single autonomous system, AS 3000. Each ISP has its own AS number (100 and 200). Office 1 has a single router, which takes care of all its needs. Office 2 has two routers: office2-r1 runs OSPF only and is responsible only for interior routing; office2-r2 provides the connection to the outside world through ISP2. On office1-r1, we need to configure eBGP to exchange routes with ISP1. Likewise, we must configure office2-r2 to exchange routes with ISP2. We want to implement a simple routing policy that prevents the ISPs from using our network to send packets to other autonomous networks. That is, we don't want transit traffic flowing through our site—we want only traffic that is destined for our network.

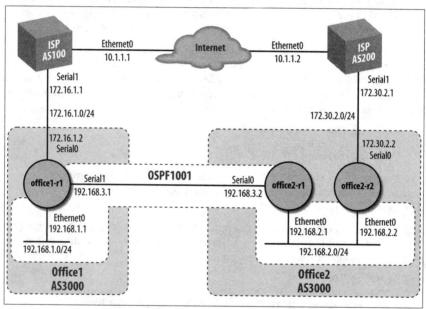

Figure 10-2. BGP network with two service providers

The transit-traffic filtering is accomplished by using AS path filters, which we discussed in a previous section. On both routers, the filtering takes place in AS path access list 1. This is a simple access list: all we need to do is permit routes that originated within our local autonomous system. Our AS number happens to be 3000, but that's not important for writing the filter—we just need to realize that the regular expression ^$ matches routes that originated within our autonomous system, and no others.

Here's the configuration for office1-r1. It runs OSPF (process ID 1001) for communicating with the other office, and it sets up an eBGP connection to AS 100 (ISP1) and an iBGP connection to the office2-r2 router (AS 3000). The filter list that prevents transit traffic is applied to outbound updates destined for ISP1. If we don't tell ISP1 about any routes that don't originate from our own AS, ISP1 will be unable to route transit traffic through our network.

```
hostname office1-r1
!
! Configure our interfaces
interface Ethernet0
 ip address 192.168.1.1 255.255.255.0
!
interface Serial0
 ip address 172.16.1.2 255.255.255.0
!
interface Serial1
 ip address 192.168.3.1 255.255.255.0
 clockrate 64000
!
! We are running OSPF as our IGP
router ospf 1001
 network 192.168.1.0 0.0.0.255 area 1
 network 192.168.3.0 0.0.0.255 area 0
 ! We want to tell other OSPF routers that we are the default router
 default-information originate
!
! Our BGP configuration
router bgp 3000
 no synchronization
 bgp dampening
 network 172.16.1.0
 ! Configuration for ISP1 with an outbound filter list. This list assures
 ! that we will announce only routes that originated within our AS
 neighbor 172.16.1.1 remote-as 100
 neighbor 172.16.1.1 filter-list 1 out
 ! Our neighbor office2-r2
 neighbor 192.168.2.2 remote-as 3000
 neighbor 192.168.2.2 next-hop-self
 no auto-summary
!
! A static route is needed because we are advertising that we are the
! default route for the network, but we need to tell local route traffic
! where the default is for us. (Not required if you have a full routing
! table.)
ip route 0.0.0.0 0.0.0.0 172.16.1.1
!
! The following is a simple AS regular expression. This AS access
! list will permit only routes that originated within our AS
ip as-path access-list 1 permit ^$
```

office2-r1 has a simple OSPF configuration:

```
hostname office2-r1
!
```

```
interface Ethernet0
 ip address 192.168.2.1 255.255.255.0
!
interface Serial0
 ip address 192.168.3.2 255.255.255.0
!
! Nothing new here
router ospf 1001
 network 192.168.2.0 0.0.0.255 area 0
 network 192.168.3.0 0.0.0.255 area 0
```

The configuration for office2-r2 is similar to the configuration for office1-r1.
Again, this router needs an OSPF process for interior routing. The process
number is 1001, which matches the process number on the other routers. For
BGP, we set up an eBGP connection to the ISP2 router (AS 200) and an iBGP
connection to office1-r1 (AS 3000). The route filtering is identical.

```
hostname office2-r2
!
interface Ethernet0
 ip address 192.168.2.2 255.255.255.0
!
interface Serial0
 ip address 172.30.2.2 255.255.255.0
!
router ospf 1001
 network 192.168.2.0 0.0.0.255 area 0
 default-information originate
!
router bgp 3000
 no synchronization
 bgp dampening
 network 172.30.2.0
 neighbor 172.30.2.1 remote-as 200
 neighbor 172.30.2.1 filter-list 1 out
 neighbor 192.168.3.1 remote-as 3000
 neighbor 192.168.3.1 next-hop-self
 no auto-summary
!
ip route 0.0.0.0 0.0.0.0 172.30.2.1
!
ip as-path access-list 1 permit ^$
```

To prove that our configuration works, we can do a show ip bgp from both
office1-r1 and office2-r2. Here are the results:

```
office1-r1#show ip bgp
BGP table version is 50, local router ID is 192.168.3.1
Status codes: s suppressed, d damped, h history, * valid, > best, i - internal
Origin codes: i - IGP, e - EGP, ? - incomplete

   Network          Next Hop          Metric LocPrf Weight Path
*> 172.16.0.0       172.16.1.1            0           0 100 i
*>i172.30.0.0       192.168.2.2          0    100    0 200 I
```

```
office2-r2#show ip bgp
BGP table version is 3, local router ID is 192.168.2.2
Status codes: s suppressed, d damped, h history, * valid, > best, i - internal
Origin codes: i - IGP, e - EGP, ? - incomplete

   Network          Next Hop        Metric LocPrf Weight Path
*>i172.16.0.0       192.168.3.1          0    100      0 100 i
*>  172.30.0.0      172.30.2.1           0             0 200 i
```

This output shows that both routers recognize each other via BGP. The output of show ip route on office2-r2 also shows that the routes are there as expected:

```
office2-r2#sh ip route
Codes: C - connected, S - static, I - IGRP, R - RIP, M - mobile, B - BGP
       D - EIGRP, EX - EIGRP external, O - OSPF, IA - OSPF inter area
       N1 - OSPF NSSA external type 1, N2 - OSPF NSSA external type 2
       E1 - OSPF external type 1, E2 - OSPF external type 2, E - EGP
       i - IS-IS, L1 - IS-IS level-1, L2 - IS-IS level-2, * - candidate default
       U - per-user static route, o - ODR

Gateway of last resort is 172.30.2.1 to network 0.0.0.0

B    172.16.0.0/16 [200/0] via 192.168.3.1, 00:03:15
     172.30.0.0/16 is variably subnetted, 2 subnets, 2 masks
C       172.30.2.0/24 is directly connected, Serial0
B       172.30.0.0/16 [20/0] via 172.30.2.1, 00:03:06
O IA 192.168.1.0/24 [110/84] via 192.168.2.1, 00:49:56, Ethernet0
C    192.168.2.0/24 is directly connected, Ethernet0
O    192.168.3.0/24 [110/74] via 192.168.2.1, 00:49:57, Ethernet0
S*   0.0.0.0/0 [1/0] via 172.30.2.1
```

Finally, to make sure both links work, we can run a quick test on office2-r1. This test is limited, in that it really tests only our OSPF configuration, but it gives us more confidence that the network as a whole is running. First, show ip route on office2-r1 shows that it prefers office2-r2 as its default router:

```
office2-r1#show ip route
Codes: C - connected, S - static, I - IGRP, R - RIP, M - mobile, B - BGP
       D - EIGRP, EX - EIGRP external, O - OSPF, IA - OSPF inter area
       N1 - OSPF NSSA external type 1, N2 - OSPF NSSA external type 2
       E1 - OSPF external type 1, E2 - OSPF external type 2, E - EGP
       i - IS-IS, L1 - IS-IS level-1, L2 - IS-IS level-2, * - candidate default
       U - per-user static route, o - ODR

Gateway of last resort is 192.168.2.2 to network 0.0.0.0

O IA 192.168.1.0/24 [110/74] via 192.168.3.1, 00:08:06, Serial0
C    192.168.2.0/24 is directly connected, Ethernet0
C    192.168.3.0/24 is directly connected, Serial0
O*E2 0.0.0.0/0 [110/1] via 192.168.2.2, 00:07:20, Ethernet0
```

If we shut down the serial0 link on office2-r2, show ip route on office2-r1 shows that it has recalculated its routes and selected office1-r1 as the default router:

```
office2-r1#show ip route
Codes: C - connected, S - static, I - IGRP, R - RIP, M - mobile, B - BGP
       D - EIGRP, EX - EIGRP external, O - OSPF, IA - OSPF inter area
       N1 - OSPF NSSA external type 1, N2 - OSPF NSSA external type 2
       E1 - OSPF external type 1, E2 - OSPF external type 2, E - EGP
       i - IS-IS, L1 - IS-IS level-1, L2 - IS-IS level-2, * - candidate default
       U - per-user static route, o - ODR

Gateway of last resort is 192.168.3.1 to network 0.0.0.0

O IA 192.168.1.0/24 [110/74] via 192.168.3.1, 00:08:48, Serial0
C    192.168.2.0/24 is directly connected, Ethernet0
C    192.168.3.0/24 is directly connected, Serial0
O*E2 0.0.0.0/0 [110/1] via 192.168.3.1, 00:00:05, Serial0
```

Adding a Preference

Figure 10-2 shows a network with links to two different providers. We've already seen configurations that get the network up and running. Now, we would like to give one provider preference over the other for outbound traffic. Let's assume that ISP1 is more reliable so, whenever possible, we want to send our traffic over its network. To do this, we use a route map to modify the local preference metric so that we prefer routes to ISP1. Remember that the local preference metric stays local to our network—that is, we never send the local preference outside of our AS—but is shared among the routers within our AS.

In office2-r2, we add a route map named CHANGE_LOCAL_PREF. This map sets the local preference for routes through ISP2 to 50, making ISP1 more preferable than ISP2. (The default local preference is 100, and higher preferences are better.) The configuration change means that even if we have to traverse our WAN link between the offices, we will use ISP1 rather than ISP2. Here are the changes to the configuration for office2-r2:

```
! While we're at it, we need to make sure OSPF picks the right ISP as
! well, so we'll increase the metric for the default route here
! to 1000.
router ospf 1001
 network 192.168.2.0 0.0.0.255 area 0
 default-information originate metric 1000
!
! In our BGP configuration, the only change is the addition of the route
! map for neighbor 172.30.2.1. Everything else is the same as it was
! before.
router bgp 3000
 neighbor 172.30.2.1 route-map CHANGE_LOCAL_PREF in
!
! Finally, we create our route map to change the local preference for
! neighbor 172.30.2.1
route-map CHANGE_LOCAL_PREF permit 10
 set local-preference 50
```

show ip bgp on office2-r2 shows that the local preference for the route has indeed changed:

```
office2-r2#show ip bgp
BGP table version is 3, local router ID is 192.168.2.2
Status codes: s suppressed, d damped, h history, * valid, > best, i - internal
Origin codes: i - IGP, e - EGP, ? - incomplete

   Network          Next Hop         Metric LocPrf Weight Path
*>i172.16.0.0       192.168.3.1           0    100      0 100 i
*> 172.30.0.0       172.30.2.1            0     50      0 200 i
```

Finally, let's do a show ip route on office2-r1 and see which default route it prefers:

```
office2-r1>show ip route
Codes: C - connected, S - static, I - IGRP, R - RIP, M - mobile, B - BGP
       D - EIGRP, EX - EIGRP external, O - OSPF, IA - OSPF inter area
       N1 - OSPF NSSA external type 1, N2 - OSPF NSSA external type 2
       E1 - OSPF external type 1, E2 - OSPF external type 2, E - EGP
       i - IS-IS, L1 - IS-IS level-1, L2 - IS-IS level-2, * - candidate default
       U - per-user static route, o - ODR

Gateway of last resort is 192.168.3.1 to network 0.0.0.0

O IA 192.168.1.0/24 [110/74] via 192.168.3.1, 01:51:25, Serial0
C    192.168.2.0/24 is directly connected, Ethernet0
C    192.168.3.0/24 is directly connected, Serial0
O*E2 0.0.0.0/0 [110/1] via 192.168.3.1, 01:40:24, Serial0
```

Neighbor Authentication

As with other protocols, we can force BGP to authenticate other routers with a password. All passwords are scrambled using an MD5 message digest. On the network in Figure 10-1, we can enable password authentication between office-r1 and office-r2 by adding the password command to our BGP configuration. On office-r1, we add the neighbor...password command after the neighbor...remote-as command. You must configure the same password on both routers, or they can't communicate with BGP. Here's the configuration for office-r1:

```
router bgp 3000
   neighbor 192.168.3.2 remote-as 3000
   neighbor 192.168.3.2 password letmein
```

The same goes for office-r2:

```
router bgp 3000
   neighbor 192.168.3.1 remote-as 3000
   neighbor 192.168.3.1 password letmein
```

Peer Groups

When working with BGP, you will find that many routers require the same neighbor statements in their configurations. No matter what kind of routing policy you're implementing and how you're implementing it, if you want the same policy lists applied to a group of neighbors, you'll end up giving the same parameters on all the neighbor statements. This process can be error-prone and confusing.

Peer groups eliminate redundant configuration lines by allowing you to define a group and then make each neighbor a part of that group. For example, assume that you have a route map that enforces some routing policy. Instead of applying that route map separately on each neighbor, you can add all the neighbors to a peer group and then apply the route map for the group as a whole.

In Figure 10-3, we have a network (AS 500) with three BGP routers. Instead of defining the same route maps for each neighbor in Router 1's configuration, we create a peer group called policy1. This peer group defines the non-unique configuration items. We then make Router 2 and Router 3 members of this peer group. Here is the BGP configuration for Router 1:

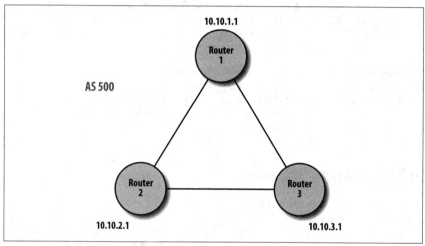

Figure 10-3. iBGP network with peer-group configuration

```
router bgp 500
    ! Define our peer group and apply the configuration items to it
    neighbor policy1 peer-group
    neighbor policy1 remote-as 500
    neighbor policy1 next-hop-self
    neighbor policy1 route-map map1 in
    ! Now define our neighbors as part of peer group policy1
    neighbor 10.10.2.1 peer-group policy1
    neighbor 10.10.3.1 peer-group policy1
```

We can use the same peer-group configuration on Router 2 and Router 3. Unfortunately, we'll still have to type almost identical configurations on each router, but at least we've reduced the amount of duplication on the individual routers. We still have to keep our router configurations in sync, but the peer-group concept makes it easier to keep the configuration uniform within a router.

Route Reflectors

BGP does not advertise a route learned from one iBGP router to another. A route is advertised via iBGP only if it is learned from the iBGP router that first advertised it. For example, assume that Router A advertises a route, and Router B learns about that route. Router B cannot advertise that route to Router C; Router C must learn the route from Router A. In other words, an iBGP router cannot advertise a route it learned from another iBGP router to a third iBGP router. Because of this restriction, if you have multiple routers connected to different AS networks, all of the routers must be fully "meshed."

One solution to this problem is to use route reflectors. Route reflectors ease the advertisement restriction by allowing a BGP router to reflect BGP routes it learns about to a third BGP router. Let's assume we don't have a link between Router 2 and Router 3 in Figure 10-3. The following configuration shows how to set up a route reflector on Router 1 that propagates iBGP routes between Router 2 and Router 3:

```
router bgp 500
   neighbor 10.10.2.1 remote-as 500
   neighbor 10.10.2.1 route-reflector-client
   neighbor 10.10.3.1 remote-as 500
   neighbor 10.10.3.1 route-reflector-client
```

With this configuration, Router 1 can advertise Router 2's iBGP routes to Router 3 and Router 3's routes to Router 2.

BGP Confederacies

A confederacy is a group of cooperating autonomous systems working together as a single AS. Confederacies allow you to divide an AS into smaller, more manageable pieces. The main reason for doing so is the meshing requirement for iBGP. With 10 to 20 routers, meshing is pretty manageable. However, as your network grows larger, managing all the peer relationships can get very complicated. Confederacies allow you to break up your network into little autonomous systems, making it easier to handle. Inside each little AS, all the iBGP routers are fully meshed. Outside, all the little autonomous systems are fully meshed to each other.

Figure 10-4 shows a network on which we'd like to use confederacies. AS 500 has seven BGP routers: R1, R2, R3, R4, R5, R6, and R7. If we didn't use confederacies, all seven routers would have to be fully meshed, or we would have to use route reflectors. In this network, route reflectors would be a problem: we would need more than one reflector, and managing them could easily get out of control. However, we can use confederacies to make a more manageable network. They are particularly important for large ISPs, but can also be useful for very large corporate networks.

We can divide AS 500 into three smaller pieces, each of which is connected to a remote AS. Since they are interconnected as neighbors, they will be able to advertise their routes. Now only our three main routers (R1, R2, and R3) are fully meshed with each other, while all our other BGP routers are meshed within their respective confederacies. Although each confederacy has its own AS number, outside networks still see us as AS 500.

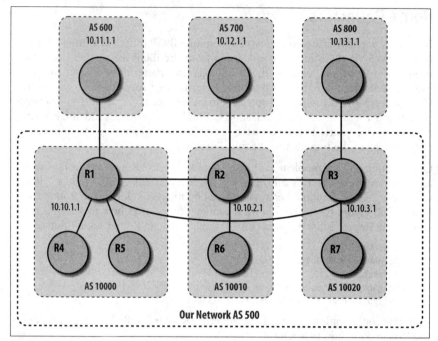

Figure 10-4. BGP confederacies

Here's how to set up confederacies.

On Router 1:

```
router bgp 10000
  bgp confederation identifier 500
  bgp confederation peers 10010 10020
  neighbor 10.10.2.1 remote-as 10010
  neighbor 10.10.3.1 remote-as 10020
  neighbor 10.11.1.1 remote-as 600
```

On Router 2:

```
router bgp 10010
  bgp confederation identifier 500
  bgp confederation peers 10000 10020
  neighbor 10.10.1.1 remote-as 10000
  neighbor 10.10.3.1 remote-as 10020
  neighbor 10.12.1.1 remote-as 700
```

On Router 3:

```
router bgp 10020
  bgp confederation identifier 500
  bgp confederation peers 10000 10010
  neighbor 10.10.1.1 remote-as 10000
  neighbor 10.10.2.1 remote-as 10010
  neighbor 10.13.1.1 remote-as 800
```

BGP TTL Security

In IOS 12.4, Cisco added a feature to BGP that you might want to implement: TTL checking between peers. Although I've never heard of it happening, it is possible for a rogue router to hijack a BGP peer connection and inject bogus routes. To prevent this, you can use TTL checking between peers.

This feature takes advantage of the fact that it is thought to be impossible to forge the TTL count of an IP packet without internal access to the source or destination network. Since it's extremely difficult or impossible to forge TTL counts, we can apply a rule that only accepts IP packets with a TTL count tht is equal to our configured hop-count. (TTL can be considered a hop-count.)

This command is not supported for iBGP (internal) peers. It applies only to eBGP (external) peers.

For example, if the BGP peer was directly connected, we could set the hop-count (TTL) to 2, and our BGP process accepts only packets with that hop-count from that neighbor's IP address.

```
neighbor 10.10.1.1 ttl-security hops 2
```

With this setting, if the hop-count is less than 253, the packet is dropped. (You get 253 by subtracting our hop-count of 2 from 255.) The only TTL values that will be accepted are 254 and 253.

11

Quality of Service

Quality of Service, or QoS, enables you to tell the router (or switch) how to handle packets in times of network congestion. With QoS, we can either tell the router how to deal with network congestion when it occurs, how to try to avoid the congestion in the first place, or a combination of both. A typical example of QoS is giving certain important applications—namely, voice over IP (VoIP)—a much higher priority on your network than other less important traffic (such as the latest peer-to-peer file-sharing program).

When do you need QoS? Well, if you are throwing more bandwidth at your network latency problems, you might want to consider developing a QoS policy to improve your network performance. Setting up QoS is far cheaper than upgrading network bandwidth. It may only delay your need for additional bandwidth, but it will also improve performance for your highest priority applications.

While a properly configured QoS environment improves the speed of important network applications, it does nothing for a poorly designed network. If your network problems are caused by a poor network design, QoS is nothing more than a bandage and might even compound the problem. Evaluate your network design before implementing QoS.

Methods for implementing QoS include congestion management, congestion avoidance, traffic shaping, and traffic policing. Cisco has introduced some advanced tools for QoS management as well: Modular QoS CLI (MQC), Class-Based Weighted Fair Queuing (CBWFQ), and Network-Based Application Recognition (NBAR). These new tools are covered in this chapter.

For now, before we start looking at different QoS methods, we need to understand how a router marks a packet, which designates it for QoS services.

Marking

Marking allows us to identify a packet so that other routers within our network won't have to repeat the steps of identifying the packet. Preferably, this marking occurs on our edge routers, which do the heavy work of identifying and classifying packets. Once classified, the packets can be marked with an IP precedence value that our downstream routers can use for their QoS features, like WFQ or WRED. Marking occurs in the packet's type of service (ToS) byte, also called the IP Precedence value.

Different Types of ToS

An IPv4 packet header includes one byte of ToS information. The ToS byte is *usually* set on the edge routers of a network to be used by internal routers on the network.

IPv4 ToS Byte

Inside the ToS byte, bits 0 through 2 are the Precedence values and bits 3 through 5 are the Type of Service values, while bit 7 is always zero. Table 11-1 shows the values of the bits.

Table 11-1. ToS Precedence values

Bits 0–2	Precedence name (value)	Bits 3–5	Type of service
111	Network control (7)	Bit 3	Delay (0 = Normal; 1=Minimize)
110	Internetwork control (6)	Bit 4	Throughput (0 = Normal; 1= Maximize)
101	Critical (5)	Bit 5	Reliability (0 = Normal; 1=Maximize)
100	Flash Override (4)	Bit 6	Monetary Cost (0 = Normal; 1 = Minimize)
011	Flash (3)		
010	Immediate (2)		
001	Priority (1)		
000	Routine (0)		

Differentiated Services Codepoint (DSCP)

Differentiated Services Codepoint (DSCP), also known as DiffServ, is a new model of QoS. DSCP redefines the ToS byte to a DSCP field. In IP Precedence, the first three bits of the ToS byte are typically assigned priorities in IP. With DSCP, the first six bits assign the Precedence value. This redefining of the precedence size allows DSCP values to be backward-compatible with IP Precedence values by matching the three most significant bits. For example, IP Precedence value 4 (100) maps to IP DSCP value 100 000.

There are 64 standard DSCP values (0–63). The default DSCP value is 000 000. These values can be organized into categories as shown in Table 11-2.

Table 11-2. DSCP Precedence categories

Precedence level	Description
7	Link layer and routing protocol keepalive
6	Used for IP routing protocols
5	Express Forwarding (EF)
4	Class 4
3	Class 3
2	Class 2
1	Class 1
0	Best Effort

Assured Forwarding

Assured Forwarding service was defined in RFC 2697, which developed the idea of predefined levels and classes of traffic. Although the numbers are confusing, you can see in Table 11-3 that we assign traffic levels (low, medium, and high) for each AF value. For example, AF11 has a low drop precedence and AF12 has a medium drop precedence, which means AF11 is "better" than AF12. All the values for AF define levels of network service above the Best Effort service, which of course is 0. The corresponding DSCP number is in parentheses.

Table 11-3. AF values for DSCP with corresponding drop precedences

Drop precedence	Class 1	Class 2	Class 3	Class 4
Low	AF11 (DSCP 10)	AF21 (DSCP 18)	AF32 (DSCP 26)	AF41 (DSCP 34)
Medium	AF12 (DSCP 12)	AF22 (DSCP 20)	AF32 (DSCP 28)	AF42 (DSCP 36)
High	AF13 (DSCP 14)	AF23 (DSCP 22)	AF33 (DSCP 30)	AF43 (DSCP 38)

Expedited Forwarding

Another option for marking packets is EF, which stands for Expedited Forwarding (High Priority) and has a DSCP value of 46. This allows service providers to expedite traffic by offering this traffic the highest queue sizes and other settings to guarantee forwarding of this expedited traffic.

DSCP example

You can see the DSCP values by looking at the possible values for a match:

```
Router(config)#class-map match-all classmap1
Router(config-cmap)#match dscp ?
  <0-63>   Differentiated services codepoint value
  af11     Match packets with AF11 dscp (001010)
  af12     Match packets with AF12 dscp (001100)
  af13     Match packets with AF13 dscp (001110)
```

```
af21     Match packets with AF21 dscp (010010)
af22     Match packets with AF22 dscp (010100)
af23     Match packets with AF23 dscp (010110)
af31     Match packets with AF31 dscp (011010)
af32     Match packets with AF32 dscp (011100)
af33     Match packets with AF33 dscp (011110)
af41     Match packets with AF41 dscp (100010)
af42     Match packets with AF42 dscp (100100)
af43     Match packets with AF43 dscp (100110)
cs1      Match packets with CS1(precedence 1) dscp (001000)
cs2      Match packets with CS2(precedence 2) dscp (010000)
cs3      Match packets with CS3(precedence 3) dscp (011000)
cs4      Match packets with CS4(precedence 4) dscp (100000)
cs5      Match packets with CS5(precedence 5) dscp (101000)
cs6      Match packets with CS6(precedence 6) dscp (110000)
cs7      Match packets with CS7(precedence 7) dscp (111000)
default  Match packets with default dscp (000000)
ef       Match packets with EF dscp (101110)
```

By using DSCP, we can assign values to our traffic classes in our policy map. This allows us to mark our traffic for further QoS handling later in our network by other routers. In this example, we assign our class1 traffic a DSCP value of 8 and our class2 traffic a DSCP value of 40. This means that now that the DSCP value has been set on our edge routers, all our intermediate routers can identify packets by simply looking at the DSCP value in order to determine QoS actions such as providing low-latency treatment to voice packets.

```
! Create our policy map
policy-map policy1
  class class1
    bandwidth 50
    ! set this traffic to DSCP 8
    set dscp 8
  class class2
    bandwidth 80
    ! set this traffic to DSCP 40
    set dscp 40
```

Older Queuing Methods

Older versions of IOS offered only a few congestion management tools. Before we cover the newer QoS features (especially MQC), let's review the older QoS methods, including first-in-first-out (FIFO), priority queuing, custom queuing, and weighted fair queuing. These methods are the easiest to understand, and the newer tools are best understood in comparison to these more basic methods.

FIFO

In a first-in-first-out (FIFO) queue, the first packet on your interface is the first packet out your interface. There aren't any queuing decisions going on here: the packets are simply lined up as they come in and processed as quickly as possible.

If you have several high-bandwidth connections (such as HTTP or FTP), these connections can hog the queue by filling it with their packets. When the queue is full, and a lower-bandwidth connection such as telnet comes along, the telnet packets are forced to wait for the other connection's packets. Forcing the later connection to wait just because it is less demanding is unfair and results in bandwidth-intensive traffic starving well-behaved network traffic.

FIFO is the default setting on connections greater than 2.048 Mbps.

Priority Queuing

Priority lists allow the router to sort and process incoming packets based on priorities you assign. These lists should be used only on WAN links that occasionally become congested; during congested periods, we want to give mission-critical packets top priority. If the link is always congested, using priority lists isn't recommended, for reasons we'll soon explain.

Priority queuing (PQ) handles all high-priority queues before handling any lower-priority queues. On networks that have brief intermittent congestion, Priority queuing is a fantastic way to handle some real-time applications such as VoIP because those applications can't stand queuing delays. In a network with severe congestion, however, the lower-priority queues really suffer with priority queuing, which causes significant network performance problems. In that case, if you want to ensure low latency queuing for real-time applications (such as VoIP), Low-Latency Queuing (LLQ) might be better.

With priority lists, we assign different queue levels to entire protocols or to particular ports. Packets are handled depending on the queue to which they are assigned: low, medium, normal, or high. Each one of these queues is handled individually as a FIFO queue, which means each queue is emptied completely before the next queue is handled. This reiterates the point that busy flows at the higher-priority level can starve well-behaved flows at lower-priority levels.

For example, in Figure 11-1, the users on Network 2 access the web server on Network 1 across the WAN link. The web server is the primary application for our users, and it is the interface to the company database. During times of congestion, web traffic should have top priority. We give telnet medium priority, which allows our telnet sessions to get through, and give all other traffic normal priority.

Figure 11-1. Using a priority list

The configuration for this priority list is:

```
! Give web access the highest priority
priority-list 1 protocol ip high tcp 80
! Give telnet medium priority
priority-list 1 protocol ip medium tcp 23
! Everything else is default traffic
priority-list 1 default normal
```

To complete the example, we apply the priority list to serial0 on Router 1 with the following commands:

```
interface serial0
  priority-group 1
```

Monitoring priority queueing

To display the queue list, use the command show queuing priority.

```
Router#show queueing priority
Current DLCI priority queue configuration:
Current priority queue configuration:

List   Queue  Args
1      high   protocol ip        tcp port www
1      medium protocol ip        tcp port telnet
```

Custom Queuing

Priority lists let us assign a priority to different protocols. Custom Queueing (CQ) lets us specify queue lists with certain characteristics. Queue lists are similar to priority lists in that they allow you to prioritize traffic across a WAN link.

With CQ, however, we create queues of various sizes, then process each queue individually for a certain amount of time before going on to the next queue. A round-robin algorithm is still used for queue processing, but this time, a byte count specifies the amount of data that should be delivered from a queue before moving on to the next queue. While PQ says "process this type of queue completely before moving onto the next," CQ says "process this amount of data in the queue before moving on to the next queue." If we again process web traffic at the highest priority, assign telnet a medium priority, and then all other IP traffic low priority, with this type of queuing we specify that the network should process a large chunk of web traffic, then a medium chunk of telnet traffic, followed by a small chunk of everything else, and then repeat this process. Now let's talk about exactly how we specify that.

Setting the queue size

The queue size is the number of packets the queue can hold at any time. We are going to set two different values: the limit and the byte-count.

The limit is the number of packets that the router is allowed to stuff into a queue at any one time. We can set the queue from 0 to 32,767 queue entries. A value of 0 means that the queue can be of unlimited size.

In the following example, we set the limit for Queue 1 to 100 packets and the limit for Queue 2 to 50 packets.

```
queue-list 1 queue 1 limit 100
queue-list 1 queue 2 limit 50
```

The second value we are going to set is the byte-count, which is the number of bytes the router is allowed to process from the queue in each cycle. Remember that CQ doesn't empty the entire queue before moving on to the next like PQ but instead processes a certain number of packets from the queue before moving on. This "certain number of packets" is set by the byte-count.

Computing the queue size isn't difficult. If you are calculating IP packet size across a link, you might guess that the maximum packet size is 1,500 (the link's MTU). We add 20 to this number to take care of packet headers, which gives us a total of 1,520 bytes per packet.

For example, if we want the highest priority queue to process 10 packets, we set its byte-count to 15,200 bytes (10 x 1,520). Likewise, if we want to process 5 packets in a lower priority queue, we set its byte-count to 7,600 bytes. Here's how to construct a queue list with these two queues:

```
queue-list 1 queue 1 byte-count 15200
queue-list 1 queue 2 byte-count 7600
```

This byte-count is just a guide; the router is still going to process whole packets each cycle. If it goes over the byte-count for one cycle, it will remember that value and subtract it from the limit at the next cycle. In other words, if the queue had to use a few extra bytes in one cycle in order to process a whole packet, it would subtract those few bytes from the limit the next time through the cycle.

Applying a queue to an interface

We can apply the queue list to an interface with the command custom-queue-list:

```
interface serial0
  custom-queue-list 1
```

Assigning packets to queues by protocol type

Now all we need to do is describe what kinds of packets we want to send into each queue. Let's use the same example we used earlier (in Figure 11-1): high priority for web access, medium priority for telnet access, and some sort of default priority for all other IP traffic. The custom queue list equivalent of the priority list would look like this:

```
queue-list 1 protocol ip 1 tcp 80
queue-list 1 protocol ip 2 tcp 23
queue-list 1 default 3
queue-list 1 queue 1 byte-count 7600
queue-list 1 queue 2 byte-count 4560
queue-list 1 queue 3 byte-count 1520

interface serial0
  custom-queue-list 1
```

Again, we use the show queueing command to display our queue information.

```
Router#show queueing custom
Current custom queue configuration:

List    Queue   Args
1       3       default
1       1       protocol ip           tcp port www
1       2       protocol ip           tcp port telnet
1       1       byte-count 7600
1       2       byte-count 4560
1       3       byte-count 1520
```

Weighted Fair Queuing (WFQ)

Instead of paying attention to the most demanding protocols, Weighted Fair Queuing (WFQ) views all incoming packets as part of a "network flow" (also called a "conversation") between two network nodes. It can use the source and destination IP addresses, TCP/UDP ports, or anything else to determine the flow to which the packets belong. Once it knows which packets belong to which flows, WFQ can provide all conversations with equal access to the interface.

WFQ uses IP Precedence to weight the traffic flows and then handle those with the highest weights preferentially. The fact that WFQ uses IP Precedence is one of its advantages. Another advantage is that it ensures that an extremely busy flow will starve itself before causing dropped packets in other more well-behaved flows.

Figure 11-2 illustrates how the flows are treated in WFQ. In this diagram, we have three conversations: a telnet session and two HTTP sessions (A and B). Assume that three packets arrive at the interface and are placed in the queue. T1 is forwarded out first, regardless of the number of packets in the queue for HTTP A and HTTP B, because T1 is a telnet packet. We don't want a telnet session to wait for our HTTP traffic. After T1 has gone out, the remaining packets are sent out based on their flows and timestamps.

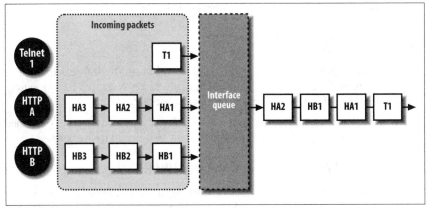

Figure 11-2. Weighted Fair Queuing with three separate conversations

By default, WFQ is enabled for all interfaces whose bandwidth is less than or equal to 2.048 Mbps. Otherwise, FIFO is the default queuing mechanism.

You can disable WFQ with the following command:

```
interface serial0
  no fair-queue
```

The setting we want to look at is the congestive discard threshold, which is the number of packets (queue size) allowed for each flow. The default value is 64; it can range from 16 to 4,096 and must be a power of 2. When this queue size has been reached, all incoming packets for that flow will be discarded.

In this example, we set the congestive discard threshold for each queue on the serial0 interface to 300.

```
interface serial0
  fair-queue 300
```

When would you want to disable WFQ? For some HSSI interfaces, disabling WFQ dramatically improves fast switching rates. See this URL for details: *http://www.cisco.com/univercd/cc/td/doc/product/software/ios113ed/113t/113t_3/hssi3600.htm#4641*.

Monitoring WFQ

Use the show queue command to examine your current queues and their performance. Here we look at the queue for serial0 with the command show queue serial0.

```
Router#show queue serial0
  Input queue: 0/75/0 (size/max/drops); Total output drops: 0
  Queueing strategy: weighted fair
  Output queue: 0/1000/64/0 (size/max total/threshold/drops)
     Conversations  0/1/256 (active/max active/max total)
     Reserved Conversations 0/0 (allocated/max allocated)
```

Modern IOS QoS Tools

Cisco has made QoS a great deal more flexible and useful by introducing a few new IOS features: Modular QoS CLI (MQC), Class-Based Weighted Fair Queuing (CBWFQ), and Network-Based Application Recognition (NBAR).

First, we'll look at what NBAR can do for us. NBAR helps us identify types of traffic, which is useful for deciding which QoS type to apply to different traffic types.

Network-Based Application Recognition (NBAR)

NBAR stands for Network Based Application Recognition. In a nutshell, so to speak, NBAR allows you to identify packets by application (OSI layers 4 through 7). This can be used to identify traffic for classification in our QoS policies.

NBAR helps us classify traffic using sophisticated methods. Not only can it match an application's usual network ports, but NBAR can use regular expressions to match characteristics like HTTP URLs.

Table 11-4 shows configuration commands that accept NBAR.

Table 11-4. QoS types that can use NBAR

QoS type	Configuration command
Class-based marking	set
CBWFQ	bandwidth, queue-limit
LLQ	priority
Policing	police
Shaping	shape

NBAR in action

Suppose for a moment that a new virus has just been detected on the Internet. We know that it infects a machine when the browser downloads a file called *reallybad-worm.exe*. While we are waiting for our favorite vendor to release a patch, we could do something useful, such as block the URL right on our router by using NBAR. To do so, we can create a class map that looks for that specific file:

```
class-map match-any virusblocker
  match protocol http url "*reallybadworm.exe*"
```

Later, we'll see how we can configure MQC to discard incoming packets that match our "virusblocker" class.

For a more detailed example, see how people were (and still are?) blocking the CodeRed worm:

http://www.cisco.com/warp/public/63/nbar_acl_codered.shtml

NBAR protocol discovery

With the command ip nbar protocol-discovery, we can enable NBAR protocol discovery on an interface. This command tells the router to keep application-level statistics for the interface. NBAR uses its database of known applications to classify the traffic.

Here we enable NBAR protocol discovery on interface serial0:

```
interface serial0
  ip nbar protocol-discovery
```

Once enabled, you can view the gathered application statistics with the command show ip nbar protocol-discovery. With the output of this command, you can see what applications are flowing across your network and adjust your QoS policies accordingly.

```
Router# show ip nbar protocol-discovery interface serial0
  Serial0
                        Input                   Output
     Protocol           Packet Count            Packet Count
                        Byte Count              Byte Count
                        5 minute bit rate (bps) 5 minute bit rate (bps)
  ---------------------  -----------------------  -----------------------
     eigrp               114302                  0
                         13861488                0
                         1200                    0
     ntp                 41437                   44367
                         1101231                 119213
                         1000                    0
```

Modular QoS CLI (MQC)

Modular QoS CLI (MQC) makes QoS much easier to configure. Basically, we configure QoS in three steps that define which packets we are going to match and classify, what we will do with them, and where we will implement this QoS policy. In a bit more detail, the three steps look like this:

1. Create the class maps, which define *which* packets we are going to match.

2. Define our QoS policy, which is *what* are we going to do.

3. Apply the QoS policy to an interface, which is *where* we are going to handle the QoS

Step One: Defining the class maps

The first part of the configuring QoS with MQC is telling the router or switch which packets we are going to classify for our QoS policy. To do this, we use the command class-map, which basically acts as a matching access-list. In other words, if a packet matches the criteria in the class-map, we are going to classify that packet.

Options to the class-map command are match-any and match-all. match-any means that if any of the criteria in the class-map is matched, the packet is marked, sort of like a binary OR. If match-all is used, all the criteria in the class map must be met before the packet is marked, which is like a binary AND. match-all is the default if no option is specified.

In this example, we are going to call our class-maps "premium," "mid-grade," and "low-grade," reflecting the level of service the packets will receive. For the premium service, either of the statements must match (match-any). For the mid-grade service, all of the statements in the class map must match. And finally, for the low-level service, only one statement must match.

```
class-map match-any premium
  match protocol ipsec
  match access-group 101
!
class-map match-all mid-grade
  match access-group 102
  match access-group 103
```

```
!
class-map low-level
    match access-group 104
```

In this example, you see two different types of match statements: protocol and access-group. There are many more options. Table 11-5 lists the available matching options and provides a brief description. Consult the Quick Reference (Chapter 17) for more information on each of these options.

Table 11-5. Valid match commands for our MQC class-map

Match command	Description
access-group	Match an access number or name.
any	Match all packets.
class-map	Match another class map. This handy feature is illustrated in the example following this table.
cos	Match IEEE 802.1Q/ISL CoS values. Up to four values can be listed in one match statement.
destination-address	Match the destination MAC address.
discard-class	Match discard class (a value from 0 to 7).
dscp	Match a specific IP differentiated service code point.
fr-dlci	Match a frame relay DLCI (data-link connection identifier).
input-interface	Match the input interface of the packet.
ip dscp	Defunct—use dscp command instead .
ip precedence	Defunct—use the precedence command listed below.
ip rtp	Match a Real Time Protocol (RTP) port range.
match not	Match everything but the listed item. For example, match not protocol ip matches all protocols except IP.
packet length	Match the packet header's Layer 3 packet length.
precedence	Match the IP precedence value.
protocol	Match the protocol name (e.g., cdp, ip, ipv6, ipx, etc.) See the Quick Reference for a complete listing. Can also use NBAR to match.
qos-group	Match a specific QoS group value.
source-address mac	Match the source MAC address.

This example uses more of the matching features for two new class maps. Notice that the class map 2 uses the class-map command, which actually nests class map 1 inside it. This feature (match class-map) makes configuring maps much easier because we can break our maps into smaller chunks, which can be nested as necessary.

```
!
class-map match-any map1
    match protocol ip
    match access-group 101
!
class-map match-all map2
    match class-map map1
    match fr-dlci 500
    match destination-address mac 00:00:00:00:AE:01
```

Step Two: Defining the QoS policy

Now that we have defined our class maps, we need to apply a policy to each of our classes: premium, mid-grade, low-level. This policy specifies what we are going to do with the packets we classified in step one.

To start, we use the `policy-map` command, which puts us into the pmap (policy map) configuration mode. From this mode, we can define the policies for each of our classes:

```
policy-map policy1
    class premium
        bandwidth 5000
```

In this example, we set the bandwidth for the premium class, which determines how the queue is handled. In this case, the queue is handled in a way that ensures that the class receives its designated share of the bandwidth. We'll revisit this in the next section.

Table 11-6 lists all the policy map commands. For now, we are going use only the bandwidth command in our examples. The rest of this chapter touches on the other commands in the appropriate sections.

Table 11-6. Policy-map commands

Policy-map command	QoS type	Traffic direction	Description
bandwidth	CBWFQ	Output	Assigns a slice of the bandwidth in kilobits per second or as a percentage.
queue-limit	CBWFQ	N/A	Defines a queue size (in packets), which is the number of packets that can be queued before packets are dropped.
random-detect	WRED	Output	Enables Weighted Random Early Detection (WRED) instead of tail-drop for dropping packets.
shape	Shaping	Output	Enables traffic shaping.
police	Policy	Input/Output	Defines a committed access rate.
priority	LLQ	Output	Enables low-latency queuing.
set	Marking	Input/Output	Enables class-based packet marking.

We can now finish our configuration for step two, which defines the bandwidth for each of our grades of services. Notice that the class-default command defines a policy setting for any traffic that doesn't match one of our class criteria.

```
policy-map policy1
    class premium
        bandwidth 5000
    class mid-grade
        bandwidth 2000
    class low-grade
        bandwidth 500
    class class-default
        bandwidth 200
```

Now that we have configured our policies, we need to apply them, which takes us to step three.

Step 3: Defining where to apply the service policy

This step, which defines where we are going to define our policy, is the easiest to configure. All we have to do is apply our service policy to an interface. The service-policy command applies our class-based QoS policy directly to an interface:

```
interface ethernet0
    ! apply our policy-map policy1 to the outbound traffic
    service-policy output policy1
```

Implementing Class-Based Weighted Fair Queuing with MQC

Class-Based Weighted Fair Queuing (CBWFQ) extends WFQ by allowing the user to define traffic classes based on various matching criteria and apply different WFQ settings to each class of traffic, which provides significant scalability. The older method of WFQ applied to the entire interface, so you could apply only one type of QoS. On the other hand, CBWFQ is more flexible, can run on higher speed interfaces, and allows more than one type of QoS, such as WRED, which prevents network congestion. Without CBWFQ, you'd be able to run WFQ or WRED on an interface but not both. To enable CBWFQ, we use the bandwidth and queue-length policy commands.

In our previous example, we defined several classes that related to a different level of service for our packets. In the policy definitions, we assigned a bandwidth to each of these classes. Essentially, the bandwidth is the guaranteed bandwidth for the class in times of network congestion.

Another option to CBFWQ is the queue-limit command, which allows you to change the queue sizes. Bigger queues mean fewer tail drops, but they require more memory utilization and potentially greater queuing delays.

Usually, the default queue size is 64 packets (it may be higher depending on the hardware type—for example, 2,600, 3,600, or 7,200 packets—but we can change this value and allot a much larger queue size for certain classes:

```
! Define our class of traffic
class-map match-any class1
  match protocol ipsec
  match access-group 101
!
! Create our policy map
policy-map qos1
  class class1
    bandwidth 10000
    queue-limit 500
  class class-default
    ! Set WFQ for our default class
    fair-queue
    fair-queue queue-limit 200
!
! Apply our policy map to the interface
interface ATM2/0/0.110 point-to-point
  service-policy output qos1
```

Low-Latency Queuing (LLQ)

Low-latency queuing (LLQ) was first called "PQCBWFQ," which is quite a mouthful but describes exactly what LLQ is; CBWFQ with a priority queue (PQ). Basically, LLQ creates a separate queue (the low-latency queue) that has priority over all other queues.

This exhaustive, priority queue is given the maximum share of the bandwidth that it can use. By doing this, a certain amount of bandwidth is reserved for the lower-priority queues so they aren't starved by the higher-priority queues. For this reason, LLQ has all the advantages of regular priority queuing for low latency and limiting jitter in real-time applications (such as VoIP) but doesn't have the same problems that priority queuing does. (Priority queuing was covered earlier in this chapter in "Older Queuing Methods.") And its major flaw is that on highly congested networks, the demanding applications will starve the less-demanding and well-behaved network traffic. LLQ works in much the same way except that it provides a certain amount of bandwidth to our priority queue instead of allowing the priority queue to hog all the bandwidth. The major use of LLQ is for VoIP traffic.

To configure LLQ, we use the priority command described in Table 11-6. The priority command takes a bandwidth value either in kbps or as a percentage.

```
! demonstrates the bandwidth in kbps
policy-map voiceservice
  class voice
     priority 240
!
! demostrates the bandwidth in percentages
policy-map voiceservice2
  class voice2
     priority percentage 20
```

Congestion Avoidance

So far we've talked about how devices should behave when the network is congested. But what if we can prevent network congestion from happening? What are our options for avoiding network congestion in the first place?

Weighted Random Early Detection (WRED)

WRED attempts to avoid network congestion by selectively dropping packets based on IP Precedence. Packets with a higher Precedence value are more likely to get through the router during periods of network congestion while packets with a lower Precedence value are more likely to get dropped. Another way to think of this is to replace the word Detection with Drop, because that's what WRED is all about—dropping packets. By dropping packets, the router hopes to cause the network device that is transmitting the packets to decrease its transmission rate. It's similar, in a sense, to not answering when someone calls your name. With TCP, the device receiving packets sends an acknowledgement of each packet. The transmitting then knows that the packet was actually received. By dropping packets (and also not acknowledging them), the transmitting device will eventually discover that its packets are being dropped or lost and *should* automatically decrease its transmission rate as a result.

On the other hand, for real-time streaming applications that use UDP instead of TCP, dropping packets won't affect the transmission rate.

Configuring WRED on an interface

To enable WRED, we use the command random-detect.

```
interface Serial0
 ip unnumbered Ethernet0
 random-detect
```

We can verify that it's working by reading the output from the show interface command. The relevant line in the output, highlighted in bold, says Random Early Detection (RED), which to the router is the same thing as WRED.

```
Router>show interface serial0
Serial0 is down, line protocol is down
  Hardware is HD64570
  Interface is unnumbered. Using address of Ethernet0 (192.168.2.1)
  MTU 1500 bytes, BW 1544 Kbit, DLY 20000 usec,
     reliability 255/255, txload 1/255, rxload 1/255
  Encapsulation HDLC, loopback not set
  Keepalive set (10 sec)
  Last input never, output 50w5d, output hang never
  Last clearing of "show interface" counters never
  Input queue: 0/75/0/0 (size/max/drops/flushes); Total output drops: 0
  Queueing strategy: random early detection(RED)
```

Using WRED instead of Tail-drop in CBWFQ

In the CBWFQ section, we claimed that an advantage of CBWFQ is that it allows you to use WRED along with it. And in Table 11-3, we noted that we could use WRED instead of tail-drop. Tail-drop is the default packet dropping mechanism; it does not differentiate among various packet types.

A router drops packets during periods of network congestion when it has filled up its queues. And with tail-drop, once the queues are full, the router simply starts dropping packets of any traffic type. Obviously, it's best to drop less important packets, so WRED is far superior to tail-drop.

To make WRED a part of your CBWFQ routing policy, we use the same command (random-detect) in our policy-map.

```
policy-map policy1
  class low-priority-class
    bandwidth 50
  random-detect
```

Traffic Policing

We've just discussed how to avoid congestion, basically through dropping packets so that transmission of lower priority traffic slows down. Traffic policing can be as simple as dropping packets or it can be more complex, as when setting a new IP Precedence value for the packet.

To police traffic, assign a Committed Access Rate (CAR). There are two methods for doing so: MQC CAR and assigning a CAR directly to an interface. If the traffic exceeds our assigned access rates, we perform actions on the traffic, such as dropping certain types of packets or changing their IP Precedence values.

First, let's look at policing in an MQC configuration.

MQC Policing

To add policing with MQC, we use the `police` command. With this command, we assign an average rate, a normal burst rate, and a maximum burst rate for our traffic. To make things a little confusing, the average rate is specified in bits per second while the normal burst size and maximum burst size is in bytes. The average rate sets the long-term transmission rates for traffic. Any traffic that is equal to or below this rate conforms to our policing. The normal burst size determines how big normal traffic bursts can be before the rate limit is exceeded. And finally, the maximum burst size determines how big the burst traffic can be before traffic exceeds the rate limit.

After we configure the rates and burst sizes, we assign actions that tell the router what to do if those sizes are being conformed to, exceeded, or being violated. A conform action is used when the traffic conforms to our values. An exceed action is taken when the traffic exceeds our values. And finally, a violate action (which is optional) is taken if the traffic violates our normal and maximum burst sizes.

In a nutshell, traffic policing allows you to control the maximum rate of traffic received or transmitted on an interface. It is usually enabled on interfaces that are on the edge of your network, allowing you to control traffic rates coming in and going out of your network. In most traffic policing configurations, traffic that falls within the rate parameters is transmitted while traffic that exceeds the parameters is dropped or transmitted with a lower priority. You decide what to do with the traffic by assigning policing actions, which can be drop, transmit with different precedences, and so on.

Table 11-7 lists the valid actions that can be taken as part of traffic policing.

Table 11-7. Valid actions for MQC police command

Police action	Description
`drop`	Drop the packet.
`set-prec-transmit`	Set the IP Precedence value and transmit the packet.
`set-qos-transmit`	Set the QoS group value for the packet and transmit it.
`set-dscp-transmit`	Set the differentiated services code point (DSCP) value for the packet and transmit it.
`transmit`	Transmit the packet.

The following example shows policing configured on class1 in the policy map named `policy-police-example`. We set an average rate of 5,000 bits per second, a normal burst rate at 1,000 bytes, and the excess burst size at 1,000 bytes for all packets leaving our interface. Our conform action is to transmit with no modifications. Our exceed action is to set the QoS group value for the packet before transmitting it. And finally, our violate action is to drop the packet.

```
policy-map policy-police-example
  class class1
    police 5000 1000 2000 conform-action transmit exceed-action
    set-qos-transmit 1 violate-action drop
!
interface fastethernet 0/1
  service-policy output policy-police-example
```

Committed Access Rate (CAR)

We enable a committed access rate (CAR) directly on an interface with the rate-limit command. We can apply the limits in either direction: inbound or outbound. The rate-limit command looks almost identical to the MQC police command. And the actions are similar as well, as you can see in Table 11-8.

Table 11-8. Valid CAR actions

Action	Description
continue	Evaluate the next rate-limit command.
drop	Drop the packet.
set-dscp-continue	Set the differentiated services codepoint (DSCP) and continue to next rate-limit command.
set-dscp-transmit	Set the differentiated services codepoint (DSCP) and transmit the packet without further processing.
set-mpls-exp-imposition-continue	Set the multiprotocol label switching experimental bits and continue to next rate-limit command.
set-mpls-exp-imposition-transmit	Set the multiprotocol label switching experimental bits and transmit the packet without further processing.
set-prec-continue	Set the IP Precedence value (0-7) and continue to next rate-limit command.
set-prec-transmit	Set the IP Precedence value (0-7) and transmit the packet without further processing.
set-qos-continue	Set the QoS group ID (1-99) and continue to next rate-limit command.
set-qos-transmit	Set the QoS group ID (1-99) and transmit the packet without further processing.
transmit	Transmit the packet.

Rate-limit example

In this example, we are going to permit www traffic to have a CAR rate of 20,000,000 bps, with burst rates of 24,000 and 32,000 over that. If the traffic exceeds our values, we drop the packets.

```
! match www traffic
access-list 101 permit tcp any any eq www
!
! limit our www traffic to 256kpbs with bursts
interface Hssi0/0/0
  ip address 192.168.1.250 255.255.255.252
  !
  rate-limit input rate-limit access-group 101 20000000 24000 32000
  conform-action transmit exceed-action drop
```

We can even use the rate-limit command to curb ICMP denial-of-service attacks:

```
! Capture ICMP traffic
access-list 101 permit icmp any any
!
interface serial 1/0
  rate-limit input access-group 101 256000 8000 8000 conform-action transmit
  exceed-action drop
```

Traffic Shaping

An even more proactive approach to handling traffic is traffic shaping. By using traffic shaping, we can ensure a certain amount of bandwidth for certain traffic. With the shape command, we can assign a CIR value, which is the committed information rate in bits per second.

Some optional keywords for the shape command are average, peak, bc-value, and be-value. Table 11-9 lists keywords for this command.

```
shape {average | peak} cir-value [bc-value] [be-value]
```

Table 11-9. Shape command keywords

Shape keyword	Description
average	Specifies the average rate, which ensures an expected bandwidth.
peak	Specifies the peak rate, which allows the traffic to peak to if there is enough bandwidth available.
cir-value	The committed information rate in bits per second, which is used to define our average or peak values.
bc-value	The committed burst size, in bits.
be-value	The excess burst size, in bits.

Traffic Shaping Example

In this example, we attempt to ensure that our traffic can have at least 300 Kbps, but we are going to allow it to peak to 512 Kbps if there is enough bandwidth available on the interface.

```
policy-map policy1
  class premium
    bandwidth 300
    shape peak 512000
```

Frame-Relay Shaping

For frame-relay, we can apply traffic shaping commands directly to the interface with the command `traffic-shape`. For more information and examples, see Chapter 6.

AutoQoS

What if you wanted to enable QoS for your new VoIP phones on your network? And after reading the QoS chapter, you've decided that QoS is fairly confusing and you now have doubts about deploying it. What if I told you that you could deploy QoS with one simple command? Perhaps you don't believe it because it sounds too good to be true. Well, in some ways, you might be right. But if your network only calls for VoIP QoS, AutoQoS might be exactly what you are looking for.

AutoQoS is Cisco's answer to the growing complexity of QoS configurations. With one command on your interfaces, you can enable VoIP QoS automatically on low-speed (768 kbps or lower) interfaces. Okay, it's not just one command—you need to use the bandwidth command as well.

```
interface Serial1
  bandwidth 256
  ip address 192.168.1.1 255.255.255.0
  auto qos voip
```

With AutoQoS, you get the following features:

- Dedicated bandwidth for VoIP
- Automatic congestion avoidance and congestion management
- Traffic priorities for certain network applications
- Traffic shaping that conforms to inconsistencies in ingress/egress speeds

What Does AutoQoS Enable?

What is AutoQoS doing behind the scenes? For the complete details, see Cisco's page on this topic (*http://www.cisco.com/en/US/tech/tk543/tk759/technologies_white_paper09186a00801348bc.shtml*), but here is a quick overview that hits the highlights, paraphrased from that page.

AutoQoS classifies voice traffic—that is, traffic with a real-time protocol and audio codec payload, as VoIP traffic. It then marks the traffic with a high-priority class of service (DSCP EF) and marks VoIP signaling traffic as AF31. Further, AutoQoS puts VoIP traffic into a strict priority LLQ with guaranteed bandwidth. VoIP control traffic is put into a nonpriority queue with a minimum bandwidth guarantee to ensure that there is no packet loss.

What happens to all the other traffic? To further differentiate VoIP, all other traffic is downgraded to best effort (except for important items like routing protocol updates). If traffic is not marked DSCP EF or AF31, AutoQoS marks it as DSCP 0, which, as we mentioned earlier, is synonymous with best effort.

By putting VoIP traffic on the fast track, so to speak, you get good performance for VoIP traffic with little effort expended in tuning QoS for your site. Your needs may be more complex than this, but AutoQoS is certainly worth a try.

AutoQoS Command Usage

To enable AutoQoS, your network must have the following:

1. Cisco devices at both ends of your link.
2. Interface with a "low-speed" link (768 Kbps or lower).
3. An IP address configured on the interface.
4. The bandwidth command configured for the interface.
5. Cisco Express Forwarding (CEF) must be enabled.
6. Cisco Discovery Protocol (CDP) must be enabled. (It's enabled by default so unless you disabled it, you don't need to worry about it.)
7. AutoQoS needs to be enabled on both sides of the link.

Command syntax

The AutoQoS command options are:

```
auto qos voip [trust] [fr-atm]
```

The optional keyword trust tells the device to trust the DSCP packet markings when classifying traffic for QoS. By default, the device does not trust DSCP markings and uses NBAR for identifying VoIP traffic.

The other optional keyword fr-atm is used on frame relay–to–ATM internet-working. This command only applies to low-speed frame relay links.

In most cases, simply apply the auto qos voip command to both sides of a low-speed link (768 Kbps or lower), and you're done.

AutoQoS discovery

Starting with 12.3(7)T, Cisco implemented an auto discovery feature that extends AutoQoS beyond just VoIP. By running AutoQoS in discovery mode for a few days (or weeks), the router collects traffic utilization via NBAR. The data that is collected is used to produce more advanced AutoQoS settings.

To enable AutoQoS discovery, use the auto discovery qos command on the interface. As data is collected, you can view the collection progress with the show auto discovery qos command.

```
interface Serial1
  auto disovery qos
```

Once you are satisfied that enough time has passed to collect enough data to auto produce a relevant QoS policy (a few days at a minimum), you stop the collection with the no auto discovery qos command and then apply the new policy with the auto qos command.

```
interface Serial1
  ! disable collection
  no auto discovery qos
  ! start auto qos process
  auto qos
```

AutoQoS show command

To display the configurations created by AutoQoS, use the command show auto qos. The output of this command can be very verbose depending on the number of interfaces and types of hardware on your device.

QoS Device Manager

Cisco offers QoS Device Manager (QDM) as a free download from its web site. QDM can dramatically increase your understanding of QoS configurations and can help you to make your way through the maze of configuring QoS on your router. By playing with this application and seeing how it manages QoS on your router, you can learn more about QoS configurations.

If you're new to QoS and want to use QoS for more than just VoIP traffic, this application might be for you.

You can download QDM from Cisco's web site. Once you download it, install it in on your router in flash memory. After that, you can point your web browser to your router. (You also need to configure http services on your router with the command ip http server.) The QDM application runs as a Java applet inside your browser, which allows you to graphically configure and monitor all QoS features inside your router. For more information, see:

*http://www.cisco.com/en/US/products/sw/netmgtsw/ps2063/products_release_
and_installation_notes09186a00800a99c5.html.*

12

Dial-on-Demand Routing

Dial-on-demand routing (DDR) is useful in applications that don't require a permanent connection between two sites. This is often the case for small offices or home users who can't justify the expense of a permanent connection. Instead, communication is through some sort of dial-up terminal server using standard telephone service (either analog or ISDN). The router places a call when it has traffic to send and establishes an IP connection using PPP. When the connection is idle, the router should hang up automatically.*

DDR is also useful for backup links; a router can establish a dial-up connection if a permanent, leased-line connection fails. It's also useful if you need to make connections to many sites through a limited number of modems or asynchronous ports.

Cisco's IOS support for dial-on-demand routing falls into two categories:

Legacy DDR

In legacy DDR, all the DDR commands are tied to a specific interface. This includes commands to set up dialer scripts, timeouts, dialer groups ("interesting" traffic), and other DDR information. Legacy DDR is supported from the earliest of IOS versions.

Dialer profiles

Dialer profiles allow you to create a single profile that contains all the DDR information necessary. The profile can then be applied across many dialer interfaces.

I'll cover both types in this chapter. But first, let's examine the basic DDR commands.

---

* Newer services, such as xDSL and cable modems, could potentially reduce the need for dial-on-demand routing. Both of these services establish permanent connections at low cost. However, dial-up services will be with us for the foreseeable future, especially as a backup when DSL or cable service is down.

Configuring a Simple DDR Connection

Let's start by configuring a simple dial-up connection to a remote office. The connection will be made only if there is "interesting" traffic for the network at the remote office. For the connection, we'll use an async interface with an analog modem attached to it.

First, we need to define the dialer script (also called a *chat script*) for the modem. Chat scripts define the process by which the router communicates with the modem and logs into the remote site. The script is organized as a sequence of "expect" and "send" strings, that is, strings the router expects to receive and strings the router sends. For example, here's a simple script that dials the number (410) 555-1111 and waits for a connection:

```
chat-script usr-modem "" "atdt 4105551111" TIMEOUT 60 "CONNECT"
```

After the chat-script command, we have the name usr-modem, which identifies the script in other parts of the configuration. Then we start the expect-send pairs. First, we expect nothing ("") and send the familiar modem dialing command, atdt 4105551111. We specify a 60-second timeout, during which we expect to receive the string CONNECT. The default timeout is 5 seconds.

Next, we'll start configuring the interface. We set up PPP as the encapsulation mode, and specify the authentication procedure (in this case, CHAP) and the username and password to be used for authentication to the remote office. And of course, we need to specify an IP address for this end of the connection. (There are alternatives to providing an explicit IP address—we'll see them later.)

```
! Set up username and password for CHAP authentication on remote router
username office1 password letmein
!
! Async interface
interface async 1
  description DDR link to the remote office
  encapsulation ppp
  ppp authentication chap
  ip address 10.10.3.1 255.255.255.0
```

Now back to setting up DDR. We need to enable DDR on the interface by using the dialer in-band command. (This command is not required for BRI interfaces because they are automatically set for dialing.) We specify that the connection should hang up if there is no traffic for 300 seconds (5 minutes). Next, we specify a dialer group. The dialer group corresponds to a dialer list, which in turn points us to an access list that defines the traffic for which the router will establish the connection:

```
! Enable DDR for this interface
dialer in-band
! Extend the idle period to 5 minutes
dialer idle-timeout 300
! This next command specifies that this interface is part of dialer group 2,
! which is defined below with the dialer-list command
dialer-group 2
! Select the correct chat script
dialer map ip 10.10.3.2 modem-script usr-modem
```

Now we need to tell the router when to dial the link by providing a dialer list. The dialer list defines the traffic that we consider interesting. In this case, we use an extended IP access list to state that we're interested in any traffic using the IP protocol. (A dialer list can also specify the allowed protocols directly, without using an access list.) In the following commands, we define dialer list 2, which matches the previous `dialer-group` command. The dialer list points to access list 101:

```
! Define a dialer list for dialer group 2
dialer-list 2 list 101
access-list 101 permit ip any any
```

Access list 101 permits all IP traffic; in this context, it means that IP traffic will cause the router to dial. After the link is established, this access list does nothing to block any traffic traversing the link; it merely controls when the link is dialed.

Finally, we need to create routes to send traffic to the remote office:

```
! Define a static route for the remote-office IP addresses
ip route 10.10.4.0 255.255.255.0 10.10.3.2
ip route 10.10.5.0 255.255.255.0 10.10.3.2
```

Without the static routes, the router would never know the address space of the remote office because no routing protocol can run across a link that is down. With these routes, any traffic bound for the 10.10.4.0 or 10.10.5.0 subnets is routed via the async1 interface. If the interface is down, the connection is automatically dialed. If the connection is idle for more than 300 seconds, the link is disconnected. This example is fairly simple; in most cases the access list needs to be more restrictive to stop unwanted traffic or routing updates from causing our link to come up. Remember that the access list should describe only "interesting" traffic, and most sites using dial-on-demand routing should not consider routing updates interesting—if for no other reason than that routing updates will tend to keep the link up all the time.

Sample Legacy DDR Configurations

One common application for DDR is a dial-up connection to the Internet. Here's a configuration that dials an ISP any time there is traffic that needs to go to the Internet:

```
! Define the chat scripts
chat-script modem1 "" "atz\r" OK "atdt \T" TIMEOUT 30 CONNECT \c
chat-script login1 TIMEOUT 20 login: "bob\r"  password: "mypassword\r"
!
! Set up the dialer interface
interface async1
    ! We are going to let the router negotiate its IP address through PPP
    ip address negotiated
    encapsulation ppp
        ! Enable dialing on this interface
    dialer in-band
        ! Set the idle timeout
    dialer idle-timeout 600
    ! Map our provider's IP address
    dialer map 172.168.1.20 modem-script modem1 system-script login1 14105551212
    dialer-group 2
```

```
!
! Assign the dialer group to an access list
dialer-list 2 list 101
access-list 101 permit ip any any
!
! Set a default route
ip route 0.0.0.0 0.0.0.0 async1
```

In some respects, this is a simpler configuration than the previous one. We use a negotiated IP address (i.e., an address assigned to us by the ISP) rather than specifying the address explicitly. We specify PPP encapsulation, but don't do any special authentication; authentication is handled by a simple login sequence, which we implement in the chat scripts. This is typical of many ISP connections.

Note that we have separated the chat script into two parts, a modem script and a system script, both of which are specified in our dialer map. This separation allows us to divide the parts of the script that configure the modem from the parts that deal with the ISP (i.e., perform a login). These two parts are specified by the dialer map command, which associates an IP address (in this case, the IP address of the ISP's end of the connection) with an actual phone number. The chat scripts also use a number of abbreviations, such as \T, which stands for the phone number. Table 12-1 shows some common abbreviations.

Table 12-1. Common chat script abbreviations

Abbreviation	Meaning
\c	Suppress newline character
\d	Two-second delay
\K	Send a break
\n	Newline character
\p	1/4-second delay
\r	Return character
\s	Space
\t	Tab character
\T	Phone number
\\	Backslash
BREAK	Send a break.
EOT	EOT character
""	Expect a null string

DDR Backup Links

Dial-on-demand is frequently used to provide a backup link for a permanent connection. There are two methods for dial backup: backup interface commands and floating static routes. Backup interface commands are relatively easy to configure, can provide bandwidth on demand, and stay idle until brought online. On the other hand, they are dependent on encapsulation, and they provide only one backup interface per "permanent" interface.

A floating static route is simply a static route whose administrative distance has been raised so that it is less desirable than the primary route. We covered backup static routes and administrative distances in Chapter 8, so this should be familiar. Floating static routes are convenient if you require multiple backup interfaces or backup routes that are encapsulation-independent. But floating static routes are somewhat difficult to configure, require the use of a routing protocol, and require that the "interesting traffic" access list actually cause the backup interface to be dialed.

First let's look at the backup interface commands and what they can do for us. Then we will revisit the example using a floating static route.

Backup interface commands

In this example, the ISDN interface bri0 is defined as a backup to our serial link. If the serial link goes down, the bri0 interface is dialed and the connection is made. Once the serial link has been restored for a period of time, the bri0 link is disconnected. The first number in the backup delay command tells the router to wait 5 seconds before bringing the bri0 interface up after serial1 goes down; the second number tells the router to wait 30 seconds after serial1 comes back online before switching back. These delay values try to ensure that the serial1 link is really up or down before switching over to the backup interface.

```
interface serial1
  description T1 to Baltimore
  ip address 10.10.2.1 255.255.255.0
  ! The backup for this link is bri0. When serial1 goes down, bri0 comes up
  backup interface bri0
  ! Set delay values. Wait 5 seconds before bringing bri0 up
  ! and wait 30 seconds after serial1 comes back up before switching back
  backup delay 5 30
!
interface bri0
  ip address 10.10.3.1 255.255.255.0
  encapsulation ppp
  dialer map ip 10.10.3.2 name baltimore-rtr broadcast 4105552323
  dialer-group 1
!
isdn switch-type basic-5ess
username baltimore-rtr password hello123
!
! Configure the dialer list
dialer-list 1 protocol ip permit
```

DDR bandwidth on demand with backup interface commands

In the previous example, bri0 acts as a backup for serial1. However, the ISDN link is used only as a backup. In this example, we'll take things a bit farther and use bri0 to provide some additional bandwidth, helping out serial1 during periods of congestion. In particular, we will bring up bri0 when the load on serial1 is greater than 70%, using the backup load command. When the load on serial1 drops back to 15%, we drop the bri0 link.

This configuration does not use an explicit access list to specify what traffic is interesting. Instead, it uses a variant of the `dialer list` command that incorporates a simple access list saying "Any IP traffic is permitted." If your requirements are simple, this approach is often clearer and more straightforward than using a separate access list.

```
interface serial1
  description T1 to Baltimore
  ip address 10.10.2.1 255.255.255.0
  ! Set the backup interface to bri0
  backup interface bri0
  ! Use bri0 when load hits 70, take offline when load drops back to 15
  backup load 70 15
!
interface bri0
  ip address 10.10.3.1 255.255.255.0
  encapsulation ppp
  dialer map ip 10.10.3.2 name baltimore-rtr broadcast 4105552323
  dialer-group 1
!
isdn switch-type basic-5ess
username baltimore-rtr password hello123
!
! Configure the dialer list for dialer-group 1
dialer-list 1 protocol ip permit
```

DDR backup with floating static routes

It's easy to write our backup interface example using a floating static route. In order for this example to work properly, we also need to configure a routing protocol—in this case, we'll use EIGRP. So, to get our floating static route to work, we need to set the administrative distance for the static route higher than EIGRP's distance. The default administrative distance for EIGRP routes is 170 (for external routes), so we'll use a distance of 200 for our backup route. The rest is straightforward.

```
! Almost the same serial configuration as before except no backup commands.
interface serial1
  description T1 to Baltimore
  ip address 10.10.2.1 255.255.255.0
  ! We are going to tweak EIGRP so our backup dialer link comes online
faster
  ! the 100 is our EIGRP AS number
  ip hello-interval eigrp 100 3
  ip hold-time eigrp 100 10
!
interface bri0
  ip address 10.10.3.1 255.255.255.0
  encapsulation ppp
  dialer map ip 10.10.3.2 name baltimore-rtr broadcast 4105552323
  dialer-group 1
!
isdn switch-type basic-5ess
username baltimore-rtr password hello123
```

```
!
! Configure EIGRP
router eigrp 100
  network 10.0.0.0
!
! Configure our floating/backup static route, setting the administrative
! distance to 200
ip route 10.10.5.0 255.255.255.0 10.10.3.2 200
!
! Configure the dialer list; this time use an access list to block
! EIGRP traffic from bringing up our link
dialer-list 1 protocol ip list 101
!
! Finally, our access list. This list blocks EIGRP and permits everything else.
! REMEMBER: This list is used only to identify interesting traffic. It
! does nothing to block traffic once the link is established.
access-list 101 deny eigrp any any
access-list 101 permit ip any any
```

Dialer Maps

Dialer maps allow IP addresses to be mapped directly to phone numbers and dialer scripts. With this feature, one interface can be configured to dial several different sites, or to dial the same site using different phone numbers, based on the IP address.

The most basic form of this command

In the following example, we use the dialer map command to configure the two B channels of an ISDN interface bri0:

```
interface bri0
  ip address 10.10.3.1 255.255.255.0
  encapsulation ppp
  dialer map ip 10.10.3.2 name ROUTER1 broadcast 4105552323
  dialer map ip 10.10.3.4 name ROUTER2 broadcast 4105552333
  ppp authentication chap
  ppp multilink
  dialer-group 1
!
dialer-list 1 protocol ip permit
```

The dialer map commands map the remote device's IP address, its device name (for authentication), and a dial string (phone number). Optionally, we can also set the speed (56 or 64) and whether or not we want to allow broadcasts. The broadcast keyword says that we will allow broadcasts, such as routing updates. By default, broadcasts aren't allowed.

Dialer maps are the preferred way to configure dialing of a link. They are used throughout this chapter.

A more complicated use of dialer maps

In this example, we want to set up a router to communicate with two remote offices through a single serial interface. Office 1's local network is 10.10.2.0/24; Office 2's network is 10.10.4.0/24. To create this configuration, we map the IP address 10.10.1.2 and the phone number 555-1111 to the chat script that dials Office 1; we map 10.10.1.4 and 555-1112 to the chat script for Office 2. To do so, we use two dialer map commands, plus several chat-script commands for setting up the scripts. Both connections are handled by the same interface and the same modem. The static routes set the routes to the proper office network.

In this configuration, it's impossible for both offices to be connected at the same time because we are using a single analog modem. With ISDN, this wouldn't be a problem. BRI interfaces have two B channels, which enable one interface to dial two different locations at once.

Once a connection has been made to either destination, the connection remains up until it has been idle for a certain timeout period. To make this configuration more flexible, we use two different idle timeout periods. The normal timeout, set by the dialer idle-timeout command, is 300 seconds; this timeout is used if there is no traffic waiting for the other office. If there is traffic waiting, the configuration specifies a shorter timeout of 15 seconds, using the dialer fast-idle command.

```
! Set up the chat script for the modem (we have only one type of modem)
chat-script usr ABORT ERROR "" "at z" OK "atdt \T" TIMEOUT 20
!
! Set up the login script for office1
chat-script office1 ABORT invalid TIMEOUT 10 name: frank word: letmein ">"
!
! Set up the login script for office2
chat-script office2 ABORT invalid TIMEOUT 10 name: saul word: letme ">"
!
interface async 3
  description DDR connection to remote offices
  ip address 10.10.1.1 255.255.255.0
  dialer in-band
  ! Create the map for this interface to office1
  dialer map ip 10.10.1.2 modem-script usr system-script office1 555-1111
  ! Create the map for this interface to office2
  dialer map ip 10.10.1.4 modem-script usr system-script office2 555-1112
   ! Set the idle timeouts
  dialer idle-timeout 300
  dialer fast-idle 15
  dialer-group 1
!
! Set a static route to office1
ip route 10.10.2.0 255.255.255.0 10.10.1.2
! Set a static route to office2
ip route 10.10.4.0 255.255.255.0 10.10.1.4
!
! Set up the dialer groups
access-list 110 deny icmp any any
access-list 110 permit ip any any
dialer-list 1 protocol ip list 110
```

We've made one additional improvement to our earlier configurations: we added a deny rule that blocks ICMP traffic to access list 110. Since this rule is used in a dialer list, it prevents a ping from bringing up the connection. We don't want the line to be dialed every time someone pings the remote site. However, we don't actually block pings: this access list isn't applied to the traffic going into or out of an interface. If the line is up, the ping will succeed.

This configuration assumes that a routing protocol is not in use. A routing protocol would bring up the links each time it sends routing updates to adjacent routers, and this is almost certainly undesirable. If you do use a routing protocol in a configuration like this one, make the DDR interface a passive interface. In the following statements, we start a RIP routing process and specify that the interface async3 is passive:

```
router rip
  network 10.0.0.0
  passive-interface async3
```

Dialer Interfaces (Dialer Profiles)

So far, we have applied all the DDR-specific configuration items directly to a physical interface. This method of configuring DDR is called "legacy DDR." The problem with legacy DDR is that it forces an interface to use the same parameters for all connections, incoming or outgoing. In the previous example, we set up a dialer map that called two different destinations through the same interface; all the other configuration items for the two destinations were the same. With dialer profiles, we can move the DDR information into the virtual dialer interface, which allows us to create rotary groups, dialer pools, or maps to different DDR information on the same physical interface.

The configuration of a dialer interface is no different from any other interface configuration:

```
interface dialer 1
  ip address 10.10.1.5 255.255.255.0
  encapsulation ppp
  dialer string 4105551212
```

Dialer interfaces can be applied to physical interfaces in two ways: via rotary groups or dialer pools.

Rotary Groups

Rotary groups allow a group of interfaces to act as one to make or receive calls. This grouping is accomplished by mapping a single virtual dialer interface to many physical interfaces. Rotary groups are useful when you have one router that needs to call several destinations at the same time. Using a rotary group lets you avoid the most important limitation of our previous configuration: only one of the remote sites could be connected at a time.

In this example, we create a rotary group that supports three remote offices, using three async interfaces:

```
! First, we configure the dialer interface
interface dialer1
  description DDR connection to remote offices
  ip address 10.10.1.1 255.255.255.0
  dialer in-band
  ! Create the map for this interface to office2
  dialer map ip 10.10.1.2 modem-script usr system-script office2 555-1111
  ! Create the map for this interface to office3
  dialer map ip 10.10.1.3 modem-script usr system-script office3 555-1112
  ! Create the map for this interface to office4
  dialer map ip 10.10.1.4 modem-script usr system-script office4 555-1113
  ! Set the idle timeouts
  dialer idle-timeout 300
  dialer-group 1
!
! Set up the chat script for the modem (we have only one type of modem)
chat-script usr ABORT ERROR "" "at z" OK "atdt \T" TIMEOUT 20
chat-script office2 ABORT invalid TIMEOUT 10 name: frank word: letmein ">"
chat-script office3 ABORT invalid TIMEOUT 10 name: saul  word: letme ">"
chat-script office4 ABORT invalid TIMEOUT 10 name: bob   word: letmeback ">"
!
! Now configure the physical interfaces. Each interface is a member of
! rotary-group 1
! Note that the rotary-group number is the same as our dialer interface
interface async 1
  no ip address
  dialer rotary-group 1
interface async 2
  no ip address
  dialer rotary-group 1
interface async 3
  no ip address
  dialer rotary-group 1
!
! Set a static route to office2
ip route 10.10.2.0 255.255.255.0 10.10.1.2
! Set a static route to office3
ip route 10.10.3.0 255.255.255.0 10.10.1.3
! Set a static route to office4
ip route 10.10.4.0 255.255.255.0 10.10.1.4
!
! Set up the dialer groups
! (Since we left "broadcast" off the dialer maps, denying EIGRP and ICMP
! isn't completely necessary. However, it is here as a reminder.)
access-list 110 deny icmp any any
access-list 110 deny eigrp any any
access-list 110 permit ip any any
dialer-list 1 protocol ip list 110
```

DDR

In this configuration, we use the dialer rotary-group command to collect three async interfaces into rotary group 1. This group is automatically associated with the interface dialer1; the rotary group number *must* match the dialer interface number. The async interfaces don't have their own IP addresses; the IP addresses are assigned to the dialer interface, which eliminates the need to know which interface will call which office.

We also modified access list 110 to prevent EIGRP traffic from bringing up any of the links. Again, this doesn't prevent EIGRP traffic from being sent over the links, provided that they are already up. Denying ICMP and EIGRP explicitly isn't necessary because we didn't use the broadcast keyword in the dialer map command. However, had we added the broadcast keyword, we would need these lines in our access list. It's a good idea to make your assumptions explicit so that the router won't suddenly change behavior if you later decide that you have to allow broadcast traffic.

Dialer Pools

Dialer pools first appeared in IOS 11.2. They are a bit like rotary groups, but they map many physical interfaces to many virtual interfaces. To best illustrate this feature, consider Figure 12-1, which shows four BRI interfaces that are assigned to three pools. Note that we can assign one interface to two or more pools. The physical interfaces are used as needed by the dialer interfaces you create.

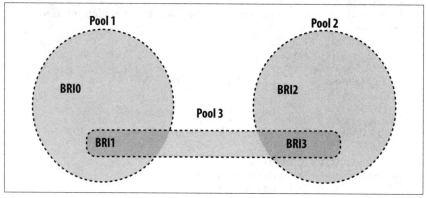

Figure 12-1. Dialer pools

Configuring a dialer pool consists of two steps: assigning a pool number to the dialer interface and making the physical interfaces pool members. Here's the pool configuration for Figure 12-1:

```
interface dialer1
   ip address 10.10.1.5 255.255.255.0
   encapsulation ppp
   dialer in-band
   dialer pool 1
!
interface dialer2
   ip address 10.10.2.5 255.255.255.0
```

```
  encapsulation ppp
  dialer in-band
  dialer pool 2
!
interface dialer3
  ip address 10.10.3.5 255.255.255.0
  encapsulation ppp
  dialer pool 3
!
interface bri0
  encapsulation ppp
  dialer pool-member 1
!
interface bri1
  encapsulation ppp
  dialer pool-member 1
  dialer pool-member 3
!
interface bri2
  encapsulation ppp
  dialer pool-member 2
!
interface bri3
  encapsulation ppp
  dialer pool-member 2
  dialer pool-member 3
```

dialer1 can use any of the interfaces that belong to pool 1; likewise, dialer2 can use any of the interfaces in pool 2, and so on. Note that bri1 and bri3 are both members of two pools, pool 1 and pool 3, so these two interfaces can be used by either dialer1 or dialer3. The result is an extremely flexible relationship between the dialers and the actual interfaces.

Multilink PPP

Multilink PPP (MLP) allows connections over multiple links to have the same remote network address, therefore allowing packet fragmentation and dynamic load balancing across the links. MLP can be configured for async, bri, and pri interfaces. In this example, we have two ports (modems) dedicated to one connection. The traffic is distributed across both links, resulting in a higher bandwidth connection. We use the dialer load-threshold command to tell the router to bring up the second link whenever the first link is at 100% capacity. In this case, it says to bring up the other link whenever either one of the interfaces reaches 100% capacity (the load threshold, which represents a utilization percentage, is a number between 1 and 255, where 255 is 100 percent):

```
interface async 1
  no ip address
  encapsulation ppp
  dialer rotary-group 1
!
interface async 2
  no ip address
  encapsulation ppp
  dialer rotary-group 1
```

```
!
interface dialer 1
  ip unnumber ethernet 0
  encapsulation ppp
  dialer in-band
  dialer load-threshold 100 either
  ppp authentication chap
  ppp multilink
```

Multilink PPP is commonly used to tie the two channels of a BRI ISDN line into a single 128 Kbps connection. Here's what that configuration looks like. We define two ISDN interfaces (one for each B channel), we place those interfaces in the same rotary group, and then we configure a dialer interface for the rotary group using PPP encapsulation. The dialer interface has the multilink command, which allows you to use both BRI interfaces simultaneously (the load threshold of 77 in the example below represents a utilization percentage of 30%):

```
interface BRI0
  no ip address
  encapsulation ppp
  dialer idle-timeout 300
  dialer rotary-group 1
  dialer load-threshold 77 either
!
interface BRI1
  no ip address
  encapsulation ppp
  dialer idle-timeout 300
  dialer rotary-group 1
  dialer load-threshold 77 either
!
! We configure Dialer1 because BRI0 and BRI1 have been
! configured to use rotary group 1 (dialer1)
!
interface Dialer1
  ip address 10.1.1.2 255.255.255.0
  encapsulation ppp
  dialer in-band
  dialer idle-timeout 500
  dialer map ip 10.1.1.1 name baltimore broadcast 55512340101
  dialer load-threshold 77 either
  dialer-group 1
  ppp authentication chap
  ppp multilink
```

Snapshot DDR

In all the previous dial-up examples, we used static routes to define the routing tables for dial-up connections. On small networks, static routes are easily managed, but on larger networks they can quickly get out of hand. However, running a routing protocol in the presence of DDR is a problem because normal routing protocols would keep DDR links up forever with their constant route updates. In some situations this might be acceptable, but it begs the question of why you're using DDR in the first place.

Snapshot routing was designed to allow the use of routing protocols across DDR connections without keeping the line active constantly. As the name implies, snapshot routing means that the routing protocols are allowed to take a "snapshot" of the network's state at specified intervals rather than sending and receiving constant updates. Therefore, dial-up links come up only at a configurable interval, which saves the headache of static route management and keeps the dial-up link's usage to a minimum. Snapshot routing is compatible with RIP (IP and IPX), EIGRP, IGRP, RTMP (AppleTalk), and RTP (Vines), all of which are distance-vector protocols.

Configuring a link for snapshot routing requires one end to be a snapshot server and the other end to be a snapshot client. In this example, Office 1 has the local network 10.10.0.0 and serves as the snapshot server; Office 2 has the local network 10.11.0.0 and is the snapshot client. There are two dialer maps at each site: one for the normal traffic (map this address to this phone number) and another for the snapshot routing protocol.

Here's the configuration for Office 1:

```
hostname office1
!
interface ethernet0
  ip address 10.10.1.1 255.255.0.0
!
! Set the ISDN switch type
isdn switch-type basic-ni1
!
interface BRI0
  ! Don't need an IP address because we are using the dialer interface
  no ip address
  encapsulation ppp
  dialer rotary-group 0
  ! Our local SPIDs for our ISDN lines
  isdn spid1 014105551212111 5551212
  isdn spid2 014105551213111 5551213
!
! Configure the dialer interface
interface dialer 0
  ip unnumbered ethernet0
  encapsulation ppp
  dialer in-band
  dialer idle-timeout 300
  dialer map snapshot 1 name office2 speed 56
  ! Map the IPs to the phone numbers at office2
  ! There are two maps, one for each ISDN channel
  ! Broadcast is required here because we are doing routing
  dialer map ip 10.11.1.1 name office2 speed 56 broadcast 14105551312
  dialer map ip 10.11.1.1 name office2 speed 56 broadcast 14105551313
  dialer-group 1
  ! Enable snapshot server, updates every 30 minutes
  snapshot-server 30
  ! Disable CDP for this interface
  no cdp enable
  ! PPP CHAP authentication
```

```
  ppp authentication chap
  ! Enable multilink for the PPP (2 channels)
  ppp multilink
!
username office1 password letmein
!
dialer-list 1 protocol ip permit
!
! Enable RIP
router rip
  network 10.0.0.0
  version 2
  no validate-update source
```

Here's the configuration for Office 2:

```
hostname office2
!
interface ethernet0
  ip address 10.11.1.1 255.255.0.0
!
! Set the ISDN switch type
isdn switch-type basic-ni1
!
interface BRI0
  ! Don't need an IP address because we are using the dialer interface
  no ip address
  encapsulation ppp
  dialer rotary-group 0
  ! Our local SPIDs for our ISDN lines
  isdn spid1 0141055551312111 5551312
  isdn spid2 0141055551313111 5551313
!
! Configure the dialer interface
interface dialer 0
  ip unnumbered ethernet0
  encapsulation ppp
  dialer in-band
  dialer idle-timeout 300
dialer map snapshot 1 name office1 speed 56
  ! Map the IPs to the phone numbers at office1
  ! Broadcast is required here because we are doing routing
  dialer map ip 10.10.1.1 name office1 speed 56 broadcast 14105551212
  dialer map ip 10.10.1.1 name office1 speed 56 broadcast 14105551213
  dialer-group 1
  ! Enable snapshot client, updates every 30 minutes
  snapshot client 30 600 suppress-statechange-update dialer
  ! Disable CDP for this interface
  no cdp enable
  ! PPP CHAP authentication
  ppp authentication chap
  ! Enable multilink for the PPP (2 channels)
  ppp multilink
!
username office2 password letmein
```

```
!
dialer-list 1 protocol ip permit
!
! Enable RIP
router rip
  network 10.0.0.0
  version 2
```

In this configuration, Office 2 is the snapshot client. Office 2 can exchange routing information whenever the BRI interfaces come up. If the snapshot timeout expires (the timeout is set to 30 minutes), the router is allowed to bring the BRI interface up to exchange routing information even if there is no "interesting" traffic.

Useful show Commands

Here are some show commands that are useful for monitoring DDR on your router.

show dialer

This command can be very verbose. It provides detailed information about all your DDR interfaces; to limit the output, you can specify the name of a particular dialer interface.

```
Router1#show dialer
Dialer0 - dialer type = DIALER PROFILE
          Idle timer (120 secs), Fast idle timer (20 secs)
          Wait for carrier (30 secs), Re-enable (15 secs)
          Dialer state is data link layer up

          Dial String    Successes   Failures   Last called   Last status
          5552323                0          1    00:00:33           failed

BRI0 - dialer type = ISDN

          Dial String        Successes   Failures    Last called   Last status
          0 incoming call(s) have been screened.
          0 incoming call(s) rejected for callback.

BRI0:1 - dialer type = ISDN
          Idle timer (180 secs), Fast idle timer (20 secs)
          Wait for carrier (30 secs), Re-enable (15 secs)
          Dialer state is data link layer up
          Dial reason: ip (s=192.168.1.1, d=10.1.1.2)
          Interface bound to profile Dialer0
          Time until disconnect 148 secs
          Current call connected 00:00:33
          Connected to 5552323 (Router2)

BRI0:2 - dialer type = ISDN
          Idle timer (120 secs), Fast idle timer (20 secs)
          Wait for carrier (30 secs), Re-enable (15 secs)
          Dialer state is idle
```

The output shows that this router has a Dialer0 interface and a BRI0 interface. Table 12-2 describes a few of the more confusing fields in this output.

Table 12-2. Description for values from show dialer

Field	Meaning
Timers (Idle/Fast idle/Wait/Re-enable)	The time, in seconds, for each of the timers. If you don't set any timers in the configuration, these fields reflect the default values.
Dial string	The dial string (essentially, the phone number) of any logged calls.
Successes/Failures/Last called/Last status	The number of successful calls; the number of failed calls; the time of the last call; the status of the last call.
Screened/Rejected	The number of incoming calls that have been screened, and the number of calls that have been rejected by the screening process. A dialer profile can be set up to screen incoming calls and handle them in different ways. The most typical way to handle a screened call is to use caller ID callback. If the callback fails, the call is rejected.
Dialer state	data link layer up means that the call connected properly. Any other message means there is a problem with the call.
Dial reason	The source (S) and destination (D) IP addresses for the packet that caused the link to come up.

show dialer map

This command lists all the dialer maps that are defined:

```
Router1#show dialer map
Static dialer map ip 10.1.1.1 name office2 on Dialer1
Static dialer map ip 10.1.1.2 name office3 on Dialer1
```

show isdn active

This command is limited to ISDN interfaces. It provides some valuable information about active ISDN calls:

```
Router1#show isdn active
--------------------------------------------------------------------------
                         ISDN ACTIVE CALLS
--------------------------------------------------------------------------
History table has a maximum of 100 entries.
History table data is retained for a maximum of 15 Minutes.
--------------------------------------------------------------------------
Call  Calling or Called  Remote    Seconds Seconds Seconds  Recorded Charges
Type  Phone number       Node Name Used    Left    Idle     Units/Currency
--------------------------------------------------------------------------
Out              5552323  Router2   88      105     5        0
--------------------------------------------------------------------------
```

show snapshot

This command displays information about snapshot routing:

```
Router#show snapshot bri0

Bri0 is up, line protocol is up, snapshot up
```

```
Options: dialer support
Length of each activation period: 3 minutes
Period between activations:       30 minutes
Retry period on connect failure:  5
For dialer address 0
 Current queue: active, remaining active time: 1 minutes
 Updates received this cycle: ip
For dialer address 1
 Current queue: client quiet, time until next activation: 27 minutes
```

Everything in this output should be straightforward except for the dialer address. The dialer address number refers to the rotary group number. Therefore, in this example, we're seeing snapshot information for rotary groups 0 and 1.

13

Specialized Networking Topics

This chapter covers a number of IP configuration topics that won't find their way into simple configurations. However, they are becoming more prevalent in corporate networks: you never know what features you're going to need the next time you redesign your network. In particular, we cover:

Bridging
So far, we've used routers as routers, which make intelligent decisions about where to send packets based on their IP addresses and information gathered by routing protocols. Cisco routers can also be configured as bridges, which make routing decisions based on MAC addresses (e.g., Ethernet addresses).

Hot standby routing
Cisco's Hot Standby Routing Protocol (HSRP) enables routers to serve as backups for one another.

Network Address Translation (NAT)
Increasingly, the IP addresses visible outside a network are different from the addresses actually in use inside the network. Translating from a small external address space to a much larger internal space conserves addresses (you can have a large network but use a small block of external addresses) and gives you more control over which hosts in your network are visible to the outside world. In these configurations, the router relies on NAT to map your internal addresses to your external addresses.

Tunneling
Tunneling means establishing a TCP/IP connection to another location and then running other protocols through that connection. It can be used as a means of propagating protocols that can't be routed or that don't belong to the TCP/IP family; encrypted tunnels can also be used as part of a security strategy. Dynamic Multipoint VPN (DMVPN) allows easier configuration of secure tunnels.

Multicast is a means of delivering a single packet to multiple hosts. An example would be a video or web broadcast. The sending machine sends only one packet that is delivered to all the hosts that are watching the broadcast (instead of sending the same packet to each host, which wastes time and networking resources).

MPLS

Multiprotocol Label Switching has become more popular in the last few years. It combines the advantages of switching with the intelligence of routing. In a nutshell, the first router in an MPLS cloud makes the routing decision and tags the packet. After that, all other routers in the cloud need to examine only the MPLS label in order to route the packet.

Bridging

Bridging is a technique for transferring packets between local networks based on their Layer 2 (MAC) addresses rather than their Layer 3 (IP) addresses. A typical bridge between two Ethernets would notice which Ethernet addresses are in use on each Ethernet and selectively transfer packets from one Ethernet to the other, based on the packets' destination Ethernet addresses. Bridges use their own set of protocols to communicate with each other, preventing the equivalent of routing loops and helping them learn how to handle packets for hosts that aren't connected directly to one of their ports.

Bridging is useful in a number of situations:

- Before routers were commodity products, bridging was a way of extending a network beyond the limits of a single physical medium. In other words, it's a way to connect local networks into a larger network without the complexity of routing.

- Many protocols, such as NetBIOS, can't be routed. If you have to deal with protocols that can't be routed, you may want to consider bridging as a way of propagating those protocols across a larger network. Note, however, that many nonroutable protocols (including NetBIOS) can be encapsulated within IP, which effectively makes them routable. Encapsulating nonroutable protocols within IP may be a better solution than bridging them.

- Bridging is often used to connect remote networks to an ISP, particularly when using ADSL modem or cable modem. The ADSL or cable modem is often configured as a bridge, which is often less expensive than using a full-fledged router.

Bridging usually does not scale as well as routing, and it takes much more of the router's CPU and memory.

The type of bridging covered in this section is called *transparent bridging*. There is another type of bridging, called *source-routing bridging* (SRB), that has a narrower focus and is not discussed here.

Creating a bridge between two routers is as simple as selecting which spanning-tree bridge protocol to use (almost always ieee) and then enabling a bridge group on the interfaces. In this example, Router 1 and Router 2 are connected via their serial interfaces (serial1); we create a bridge between the Ethernet interfaces on both routers. Here's the configuration for Router 1:

```
bridge 1 protocol ieee
!
interface ethernet1
 ip address 10.10.1.1 255.255.255.0
 bridge-group 1
!
interface serial1
 ip address 10.10.2.1 255.255.255.0
 bridge-group 1
```

And here's the configuration for Router 2:

```
bridge 1 protocol ieee
!
interface ethernet1
 ip address 10.10.3.1 255.255.255.0
 bridge-group 1
!
interface serial1
 ip address 10.10.2.2 255.255.255.0
 bridge-group 1
```

Now the two Ethernet segments are bridged using the serial links. The bridge numbers you assign are significant only to the local router—they do not have to match across routers. However, keeping the numbers consistent across routers will keep your configurations simpler.

In this example, the routers will route IP but bridge everything else. By default, IP traffic is routed unless it is explicitly bridged. All other protocols are bridged unless explicitly routed. You must use the global command no ip routing to force IP to be bridged, which is probably not what you want. The first way around this problem is Concurrent Routing and Bridging.

Concurrent Routing and Bridging (CRB)

Concurrent Routing and Bridging (CRB) allows the router to route and bridge the same protocol. However, routing and bridging remain separate islands in the router and aren't allowed to interact. In other words, routing can be enabled on some interfaces, and bridging can be enabled on some other interfaces, but the two groups cannot interact. Each interface can either bridge a protocol or route a protocol, but not both; packets will never be transferred from the bridged interfaces to the routed interfaces. The next section discusses Integrated Routing and Bridging (IRB), which allows more interaction and is usually a better solution.

To configure CRB, we use the global command bridge crb. Once enabled, we list the protocols to bridge with the command bridge 1 route ip, where 1 is the bridge group number and ip is the name of the protocol we want to bridge. Obviously, you can use this command to select other protocols; for example, the command bridge 1 route appletalk bridges the AppleTalk protocol. The following example bridges IP traffic between the Ethernet interfaces ethernet0 and ethernet1 and routes IP traffic between the router's other interfaces, serial1 and serial2:

```
interface ethernet0
  ip address 10.1.1.1 255.255.255.0
  bridge-group 1
!
interface ethernet1
  ip addess 10.1.2.1 255.255.255.0
  bridge-group 1
!
interface serial1
  ip address 10.1.3.1 255.255.255.0
!
interface serial2
  ip address 10.1.4.1 255.255.255.0
!
bridge crb
bridge 1 route ip
bridge 1 protocol ieee
```

Remember that the routed traffic is isolated to the routed interfaces while the bridged traffic stays on the bridged interfaces. In other words, a packet can't make its way from ethernet1 to serial1, no matter where it ought to go.

Integrated Routing and Bridging (IRB)

CRB was a nice step toward Integrated Routing and Bridging, which allows routing and bridging to cooperate. IRB allows the router to route and bridge any protocol. In order to do this, we need a special interface called a BVI, which stands for Bridge-Group Virtual Interface. We create a BVI for each bridge group. The BVI is routable and handles all routing tasks for the entire bridge group. Our bridge group interfaces work at Layer 2 while the BVIs work at Layer 3. The router can now happily route and bridge our IP traffic at the same time, in accordance with the bridge-group configurations.

To enable IRB, we use the command bridge irb. Once this command has been issued, we can create a bridge group and specify which spanning-tree protocol to use (ieee). We specify that this bridge group is supposed to route IP. Then we configure the Ethernet interface without an IP address and place it in our bridge group. Finally, we configure the BVI1 interface, which has an IP address. In a more complex configuration, the BVI would also have commands for packet filtering, address translation, and other Layer 3 tasks. Here is an example of IRB in action.

The configuration for Router 1 looks like this:

```
hostname Router1
!
! Enable Integrated Routing and Bridging
bridge irb
! Allow routing of IP for bridge group 1
bridge 1 protocol ieee
  bridge 1 route ip
!
```

```
interface Ethernet0
 no ip address
 bridge-group 1
!
! Configure our BVI for bridge group 1
interface BVI1
 ip address 10.1.1.1 255.255.255.0
```

For Router 2, the configuration is:

```
hostname Router2
!
! Enable Integrated Routing and Bridging
bridge irb
bridge 1 protocol ieee
! Allow routing of IP for bridge group 1
 bridge 1 route ip
!
interface Ethernet0
 no ip address
 bridge-group 1
!
! Configure our BVI for bridge group 1
interface BVI1
 ip address 10.1.1.2 255.255.255.0
```

Now we can ping Router 1's BVI from Router 2:

```
Router2#ping 10.1.1.1

Type escape sequence to abort.
Sending 5, 100-byte ICMP Echos to 10.1.1.1, timeout is 2 seconds:
!!!!!
Success rate is 100 percent (5/5), round-trip min/avg/max = 4/4/8 ms
```

Bridging show Commands

Depending on how your bridging is configured, most of the following show commands will be useful.

show bridge

This command displays the bridging table for each bridge group. This table includes the MAC addresses of the interfaces in the group, the interfaces associated with the addresses, and some other counters:

```
Router2#show bridge

Total of 300 station blocks, 299 free
Codes: P - permanent, S - self

Bridge Group 1:

    Address     Action   Interface    Age   RX count   TX count
0010.7b3a.f659  forward  Ethernet0     0         16          0
```

show bridge group

This command gives you more detailed information about a particular bridge group.

```
Router2#show bridge group

Bridge Group 1 is running the IEEE compatible Spanning Tree protocol

    Port 2 (Ethernet0) of bridge group 1 is forwarding
```

You can get even more detail using the verbose option:

```
Router2#show bridge group verbose

Bridge Group 1 is running the IEEE compatible Spanning Tree protocol

    Acquisition of new addresses is enabled
    LAT service filtering is disabled

    Port 2 (Ethernet0) of bridge group 1 is forwarding
        LAT compression is not set
        Input LAT service deny group code list is not set
        Input LAT service permit group code list is not set
        Output LAT service deny group code list is not set
        Output LAT service Permit group code list is not set
        Access list for input filtering on type is not set
        Access list for input filtering for LSAP is not set
        Access list for input address filter is not set
        Access list for input pattern is not set
        Access list for output filtering on type is not set
        Access list for LSAP is not set
        Access list for output address filter is not set
        Access list for output pattern filter is not set
        Packets too large for translational bridging: 0 input, 0 output
```

DLSw+

DLSw+ stands for Data-Link Switching Plus, which is Cisco's proprietary extension to the open standard protocol DLSw Version 1. The second iteration of the open standard, DSLw Version 2, implements much of the same functionality as DLSw+. Fortunately, all three versions of DLSw interoperate fairly well because the first thing two peers do when connecting is to establish a common set of features, which they then use.

DLSw+ provides a method of transporting SNA (Systems Network Architecture) and other unroutable protocols such as NetBEUI over a different type of backbone, which in our case is IP.

Basically, we use the dlsw peer commands to define our local peer address and the remote peer address. Other than that, our example configuration looks much like our previous bridging example, which sets up a peer relationship for tunneling bridged traffic between the two endpoints.

Here's the configuration for Router 1:

```
bridge 1 protocol ieee
!
! Define our dlsw configuration
dlsw local-peer peer-id 10.10.2.1
dlsw remote-peer 0 tcp 10.10.2.2
dlsw bridge-group 1
!
interface ethernet1
 ip address 10.10.1.1 255.255.255.0
 bridge-group 1
!
interface serial1
  ip address 10.10.2.1 255.255.255.0
  bridge-group 1
```

Here's the configuration for Router 2:

```
bridge 1 protocol ieee
!
! Define our dlsw configuration
dlsw local-peer peer-id 10.10.2.2
dlsw remote-peer 0 tcp 10.10.2.1
dlsw bridge-group 1
!
interface ethernet1
  ip address 10.10.3.1 255.255.255.0
  bridge-group 1
!
interface serial1
  ip address 10.10.2.2 255.255.255.0
  bridge-group 1
```

Two important show commands for DLSw are show dlsw peers and show dlsw reachability. In show dlsw peers, the output shows the status of the DLSw remote peers because without a connection between the remote peers, DLSw won't work. The show dlsw reachability command shows the router's reachability cache, which it uses when it wants to initiate a connection to a report peer.

If the state is not CONNECT in the show dlsw peers command, check your IP connectivity before trying to debug DLSw setups.

The status in show dlsw reachability might be Found, Searching, Not_Found, Unconfirmed, and Verify. Found means the peer has sent or received a broadcast. Searching means the router has sent a broadcast to the peer and is awaiting a response. Not_Found means that negative caching is occurring and the peer has not responded to queries. Unconfirmed means that the peer is configured but DLSw has yet to verify it. Verify means that the cache information is about to expire, so the information is being verified.

```
router2#show dlsw peers

Peers:          state   pkts rx  pkts tx  type  drops  ckts  TCP  uptime
TCP 10.10.2.1   CONNECT 11       11             0      0     51
0:00:04:42
```

```
router2#show dlsw reachability
DLSw MAC address reachability cache list
Mac Addr        status      Loc.   peer/port    rif
0000.e341.109a  SEARCHING   LOCAL
0000.6a9a.7bea  FOUND       LOCAL  TokenRing0/0 0CB0.0011.3E71.A041.0DE5.0640
0800.5a4b.10f0  SEARCHING   LOCAL
```

Another great feature of DLSw+ is the ability to bridge SDLC to Ethernet or Token Ring, which makes the serial device look like a network device. By doing that, you save a whole lot of FEP (Front End Processor) interfaces in a mainframe network. SDLC stands for Synchronous Data link Control, which is a protocol for transferring data over a serial line.

Hot Standby Routing Protocol (HSRP)

In this book, several examples dealt with creating backup links for use in case some other link fails. But routers themselves fail—so how do you implement backup routers? You might think that this shouldn't be a problem: after all, if you have two routers connecting your site to the external world, and one fails, your own routing protocols should eventually route around the failure. However, it's not that simple. If the individual hosts on your network aren't running some sort of routing protocol (such as RIP) or router discovery protocol (such as IRDP), they'll never find out about the failure. And in most cases, you don't want to be running a routing protocol on individual hosts; you want to set up each host with a simple default route and leave it at that. Furthermore, when a router fails, it can take some time for a protocol such as RIP to converge on a new route.

That's the overall picture. More concretely, the top illustration in Figure 13-1 shows a larger network comprising two smaller networks. There are two routers, both connected to the external gateway. Let's assume that you want to configure the hosts on Network 1 and Network 2 with static default routes. To which router should these default routes point? All the hosts on both networks can reach either router, but each host can have only one default route. What happens if the router a particular host is using fails? How does that host find out about the other router, aside from an administrator manually changing its default route?

The elegant solution is HSRP. The second part of Figure 13-1 shows a new router, Router 3. Router 3 is a *virtual router*, meaning that there's no such physical piece of equipment: it's an illusion created by the use of HSRP on Router 1 and Router 2. However, although Router 3 is an illusion, it has a unique IP address and a unique MAC address that is configured between Router 1 and Router 2.

Configuring HSRP is as simple as using the standby command on the appropriate interfaces. In the following configuration, we apply the standby command to the ethernet1 interfaces of both routers. Router 1 has the standby preempt command, which tells the routers that Router 1 should be the active router for the standby group, but only when Router 1 has the higher priority. We ensure it has a higher priority by setting the value explicitly to 120 with the priority command. If Router 1 goes down, Router 2 becomes the standby router and takes over the routing duties for our virtual Router 3. If Router 1 comes back up, it will automatically take over because it has the higher priority and the preempt command in its configuration. The standby ip command provides the IP address for the virtual router.

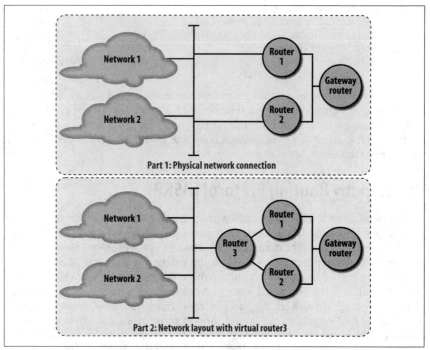

Figure 13-1. HSRP layout

Here's the configuration for Router 1:

```
interface ethernet1
    ! A real IP address is still required for this interface
    ip address 10.10.28.1 255.255.255.0
    standby preempt
    standby priority 120
    ! The IP address for the virtual Router3 is 10.10.28.3
    standby ip 10.10.28.3
```

Here's the configuration for Router 2:

```
interface ethernet1
    ! A real IP address is still required for this interface
    ip address 10.10.28.2 255.255.255.0
    ! The IP address for the virtual Router3 is 10.10.28.3
    standby ip 10.10.28.3
```

With this configuration, all the nodes in Networks 1 and 2 can use 10.10.28.3 as their default gateway address. This is the IP address for the virtual router, Router 3; hosts on the two networks can communicate with Router 3 as if it were a real device. Initially, Router 1 acts as Router 3 and handles packets sent to the virtual router's address. If Router 1 fails, Router 2 takes over immediately. The switchover happens so quickly that the network devices never know that anything has happened; they can continue to use Router 3 as their default router.

It's worth mentioning that the routers adopt a common virtual MAC address as well as a virtual IP address. You don't have to configure the virtual MAC address;

the routers do this for you. A virtual MAC address ensures that the ARP caches remain valid when HSRP switches over to another router.

Tracking Another Interface

With the HSRP track command, we can tell our HSRP process to watch another interface and decrement our priority if the other interface goes down. This feature would be useful in our examples to track the interface on each router going to the gateway router. Let's assume that Router 1 and Router 2 both use serial0 to connect to the gateway router as shown in Figure 13-1. All we need to do to our previous configuration is add the track command.

Here's the configuration for Router 1:

```
interface ethernet1
    ip address 10.10.28.1 255.255.255.0
    standby preempt
    standby priority 120
    standby track serial0
    standby ip 10.10.28.3
```

And here's the configuration for Router 2:

```
interface ethernet1
    ip address 10.10.28.2 255.255.255.0
    standby track serial0
    standby ip 10.10.28.3
```

Naming Our HSRP Configuration

We can also assign a name to our HSRP configuration. As we will see later in the NAT configuration, we'll use this for stateful NAT. The command is simply standby name followed by the name you would like to use.

```
interface ethernet1
    standby name hsrpname1
```

Multiple-Group Hot Standby Routing

HSRP allows you to create multiple virtual routers, each supported by a number of physical routers, by using the concept of router groups in the standby commands. Multiple standby groups are supported only by newer router models and high-end routers. The 2500-series routers do not support this function (Lance Ethernet chipset).

Our previous example didn't specify a group number, meaning that both routers were in the default group (group 0). In this example, we'll use three physical routers to create three virtual routers, using three router groups. Here's how we'll organize the routers:

Router 1
    Active for group 1 and standby for group 3

Router 2
    Active for group 2 and standby for group 3

Router 3

Active for group 3 and standby for group 1 and group 2

The virtual router for group 1 has the address 10.10.1.11; group 2 has the address 10.10.1.12; and group 3 has the address 10.10.1.13.

Here's the configuration for Router 1:

```
interface ethernet1
  ip address 10.10.1.1 255.255.255.0
  standby 1 priority 120
  standby 1 preempt
  standby 1 ip 10.10.1.11
  standby 3 ip 10.10.1.13
```

Here's the configuration for Router 2:

```
interface ethernet1
  ip address 10.10.1.2 255.255.255.0
  standby 2 priority 120
  standby 2 preempt
  standby 2 ip 10.10.1.12
  standby 3 ip 10.10.1.13
```

And here's the configuration for Router 3:

```
interface ethernet1
  ip address 10.10.1.3 255.255.255.0
  standby 3 priority 120
  standby 3 preempt
  standby 3 ip 10.10.1.13
  standby 1 ip 10.10.1.11
  standby 2 ip 10.10.1.12
```

HSRP groups help your switches behave reasonably as different routers are enabled. Remember that the router automatically generates a virtual MAC address for each HSRP router. If you have your HSRP routers connected to a single switch (or multiple switches VLANed together), the switch will see the same MAC address on different ports as the HSRP routers become active. With HSRP groups, the routers use a unique MAC address for each HSRP group. So, if you do have your HSRP routers plugged into a single switch, you can use multiple HSRP groups to enforce the use of different MAC addresses on different ports, which keeps switches happy.

Load Sharing with Hot Standby

You can use HSRP for a form of load sharing. Think back to Figure 13-1. In this network, we gave all the hosts a default route to the virtual router (10.10.28.3) and configured Router 1 to act as the virtual router unless it failed. This is clearly inefficient, since most of the time Router 2 was doing nothing: all the traffic flowed through Router 1, and Router 2 just waited for Router 1 to break.

In this example, we configure the networks so that Network 1 uses Router 1 as its default route, and Network 2 uses Router 2. To do so, we create two virtual routers, each with its own IP address. Each physical router is the primary router for one of the virtual routers and the backup for the other. With this configuration, Network 1 can use the virtual Router 1 (10.10.28.3) for its default route, and Network 2 can use the virtual Router 2 (10.10.28.4). In this way, they both carry traffic until one of the routers goes down, and then the other router takes over all the traffic.

Here's the configuration for Router 1:

```
interface ethernet1
  ip address 10.10.28.1 255.255.255.0
  standby 1 preempt
  standby 1 priority 120
  standby 1 ip 10.10.28.3
  standby 2 ip 10.10.28.4
```

Here's the configuration for Router 2:

```
interface ethernet 1
  ip address 10.10.28.2 255.255.255.0
  standby 2 preempt
  standby 2 priority 120
  standby 2 ip 10.10.28.4
  standby 1 ip 10.10.28.3
```

Devices within Network 1 use 10.10.28.3 as their default router, and devices within Network 2 use 10.10.28.4 as their default router. This configuration provides a primitive form of load sharing across the two networks. If either router goes down, the other takes over.

HSRP show Commands

The command show standby displays all the HSRP information that the router knows about. In this configuration, we can see that HSRP is configured only on Ethernet0:

```
Router1#show standby
Ethernet0 - Group 0
  Local state is Active, priority 120, may preempt
  Hellotime 3 holdtime 10
  Next hello sent in 00:00:02.564
  Hot standby IP address is 192.168.1.3 configured
  Active router is local
  Standby router is unknown expires in 00:00:04
  Standby virtual mac address is 0000.0c07.ac00
```

Network Address Translation (NAT)

Network Address Translation provides a method for mapping an internal IP address space to an external IP address space. This mapping is beneficial for making smooth transitions to different ISPs, hiding internal IP addresses, and conserving IP addresses.

To better understand what NAT does, consider Figure 13-2. NAT is configured on our gateway. The serial0 interface is configured with our global Internet address (from the address space given to our network by our ISP). This is the *outside* portion of NAT. The ethernet0 interface, and any devices that are connected to this Ethernet, have addresses that are invisible to the outside world; this is the *inside* portion of NAT.

Figure 13-2. NAT example

There are two methods of performing NAT: *static* and *dynamic*. With static translation, each inside address is mapped to a specific outside address. With dynamic translation, possible outside addresses are collected into an address pool and are selected from the pool on an as-needed basis.

Let's look at how to implement the address translation used in Figure 13-2. In this example, the internal network has the address space of 10.10.1.0/24. We need to map these addresses to the external address space, 172.168.1.0/24. First, let's look at the configuration with the static mapping:

```
! Assign IP address for NAT for IP addresses .2 through .10
! (Skip 172.168.1.1 because that is our serial0 interface)
ip nat inside source static 10.10.1.2 172.168.1.2
ip nat inside source static 10.10.1.3 172.168.1.3
ip nat inside source static 10.10.1.4 172.168.1.4
ip nat inside source static 10.10.1.5 172.168.1.5
ip nat inside source static 10.10.1.6 172.168.1.6
ip nat inside source static 10.10.1.7 172.168.1.7
ip nat inside source static 10.10.1.8 172.168.1.8
ip nat inside source static 10.10.1.9 172.168.1.9
ip nat inside source static 10.10.1.10 172.168.1.10
ip nat inside source static 10.10.1.11 172.168.1.11
!
interface ethernet 0
  ip address 10.10.1.1 255.255.255.0
  ip nat inside
!
interface serial 0
  ip address 172.168.1.1 255.255.255.0
  ip nat outside
```

The static configuration configures only the first 10 IP addresses in our address space, but it's easy to see how to use the rest. Remember that we can't map 172.168.1.1 because that's the address of the serial0 interface.

Here's the configuration for dynamic NAT. This time, we use our entire global address space, 172.168.1.1 through 172.168.1.254:

```
! Define the IP address pool
! (Leave out 172.168.1.1 because that is our serial 0 interface)
ip nat pool poolone 172.168.1.2 172.168.1.254 netmask 255.255.255.0
ip nat inside source list 20 pool poolone
!
interface ethernet0
  ip address 10.10.1.1 255.255.255.0
  ip nat inside
!
interface serial0
  ip address 172.168.1.1 255.255.255.0
  ip nat outside
!
! Access list for our pool, which is used above to select which IP
! addresses can be translated
access-list 20 permit 10.10.0.0 0.0.255.255
```

Static and dynamic mappings can be combined; just don't include your statically mapped internal addresses in your address pool. This allows you to specify some hosts (such as mail servers) that have a fixed external address but belong to your internal network, while allowing other hosts to be assigned their external address dynamically.

If you're using a bridged configuration, remember that your BVI is the outside interface of your NAT configuration.

Overloading NAT Address Space

If you use the overload command, the pooled NAT address space will be shared among as many internal hosts as possible by multiplexing the ports. In the previous dynamic configuration, changing the third line to the following enables overloading:

```
ip nat inside source list 20 pool poolone overload
```

For example, if an FTP session to an Internet host is started from 10.10.1.3, the outbound connection might be mapped to 172.168.1.3. While that connection is going, a telnet connection is started from 10.10.1.4 to another Internet host. This connection might also be mapped to 172.168.1.3. This means you could have one public IP address shared by hundreds of internal private IP addresses. The router keeps track of what packets belong to what sessions and makes sure that all the packets reach the appropriate destination. This is often called Port Address Translation (PAT) because the router uses the port number to distinguish between different connections using the same address.

In this example, we have one public IP address (172.168.1.2) that is shared by all our hosts on the 10.10.1.0/24 private network:

```
! Define the IP address pool
! (Leave out 172.168.1.1 because that is our serial 0 interface)
ip nat pool poolone 172.168.1.2 172.168.1.2 netmask 255.255.255.0
! Add the overload command
ip nat inside source list 20 pool poolone overload
!
interface ethernet0
  ip address 10.10.1.1 255.255.255.0
  ip nat inside
!
interface serial0
  ip address 172.168.1.1 255.255.255.0
  ip nat outside
!
! Access list for our pool, which is used to select which IP addresses
! should be translated
access-list 20 permit 10.10.0.0 0.0.255.255
```

The previous configuration, which creates an explicit external address pool and then uses it to map inside addresses, is the most common way to set up address translation. But in this case, where you're creating a pool that has only a single IP address, there's a shortcut. You can omit the ip nat pool command and instead tell the ip nat inside command to use the IP address of your serial interface for translations. The result looks like this:

```
! Define IP address translation (PAT) without using an address pool
ip nat inside source list 20 interface serial0 overload
!
interface ethernet0
  ip address 10.10.1.1 255.255.255.0
  ip nat inside
!
interface serial0
  ip address 172.168.1.1 255.255.255.0
  ip nat outside
!
! Access list for our pool, which is used to select which IP addresses
! should be translated
access-list 20 permit 10.10.0.0 0.0.255.255
```

Mapping incoming ports to different NAT addresses

One of the drawbacks of having all your internal IP addresses mapped to one external address is that you don't have room for adding external services. That is, if you want to run a web server or any other public service, that machine's address must be visible to the outside world. With the kinds of dynamic address translation we've seen so far, that isn't the case—a host isn't visible to the outside world until it initiates a connection, and even then, its address might be shared. If someone from the Internet tries to start a connection to an internal server using a shared address, how will the router know which machine should receive the packets?

Let's take this example a step further. What if you want to run a web server and a mail server? You could put both on the same machine and create one static mapping to a single external address. Or you could put the mail and web servers on different machines and create static mappings to two external addresses. But what if you want the servers on different machines but you want only one external address?

The solution to this problem is static PAT. To do the port-based translation, we use the keyword extendable, which allows us to map UDP and TCP ports to internal addresses. In this example, we have one unique global IP address (172.168.1.1) mapped to our internal network (10.10.1.0/24) using the overload keyword. We want our incoming email traffic (port 25) to go to 10.10.1.5, and our incoming web traffic (port 80) to go to 10.10.1.4. The following configuration handles this:

```
! Use PAT to overload our internal IP space 10.10.1.0/24 to
! one external IP address 172.168.1.1 (serial0's IP address)
ip nat inside source list 20 interface Serial0 overload
! Map incoming mail (port 25) to device 10.10.1.5
ip nat inside source static tcp 10.10.1.5 23 172.168.1.1 25 extendable
! Map incoming web (port 80) to device 10.10.1.4
ip nat inside source static tcp 10.10.1.4 80 172.168.1.1 80 extendable
!
access-list 20 permit 10.10.0.0 0.0.255.255
```

By changing the port type, you can do translations based on UDP ports as well:

```
ip nat inside source static udp 10.10.1.6 172.168.1.1 69 extendable
```

NAT show Commands

show ip nat statistics and show ip nat translations are the two most helpful show commands for NAT. The statistics show the total number of translations, the interfaces configured for NAT, the hits (the number of times the router looked in the NAT table and found a match), the misses (the number of times the router looked in the NAT table and didn't find an entry), and the number of translations that have expired:

```
Router1#show ip nat statistics
Total translations: 1 (0 static, 1 dynamic; 0 extended)
Outside interfaces: Serial0
Inside interfaces: Ethernet0
Hits: 9  Misses: 1
Expired translations: 0
Dynamic mappings:
-- Inside Source
access-list 20 pool poolone refcount 1
 pool poolone: netmask 255.255.255.0
        start 172.168.1.2 end 172.168.1.2
        type generic, total addresses 1, allocated 1 (100%), misses 1
```

show ip nat translations simply shows all the NAT translations that occur.

```
Router1#show ip nat translations
Pro Inside global     Inside local      Outside local    Outside global
--- 172.168.1.2       10.10.1.1         ---              ---
```

This output shows the inside mapping of the local address 10.10.1.1 to the outside global address of 172.168.1.2.

There's one other essential command. It's possible for dynamic address translation to get confused. When this happens, translated traffic stops flowing through the router. There's a simple fix: clear ip nat translations *. The asterisk means to clear all dynamic translations. You can replace it with the address of a particular translation, but that usually isn't worth the effort.

Stateful NAT (SNAT)

As network downtime becomes less and less tolerable, we need new ways to support immediate network failover. For NAT, a new feature called Stateful NAT or SNAT provides increased IP resiliency. SNAT allows two or more routers to perform NAT. One router is the active NAT router while the other device or devices serve as the backup. The active router continuously sends NAT state changes to the backup devices. If a failover does occur, the backup device can immediately take over NAT.

SNAT is designed to work in concert with HSRP to detect failover. However, you can configure SNAT to work on its own.

The first release of SNAT (in IOS 12.2(13)T) offered limited protocol support (there was no FTP support, for example). IOS 12.4 added a feature that broadens SNAT's protocol support: embedded addressing. With embedded addressing, the NAT process learns ports from the application itself. This new feature allows SNAT to support VoIP, FTP, and DNS applications.

Configuring SNAT with HSRP

In our first example, we are going to configure SNAT to work with HSRP. To do this, we use the ip nat stateful command. This command takes three important options; id, redundancy, and mapping-id. The id simply identifies the router to the SNAT protocol (each router should be configured with a unique id value). The redundancy option identifies the HSRP process that we are going to use for our configuration. In this example, we have given our HSRP configuration the name SNATHSRP. And finally, the mapping-id option identifies which NAT translations are sent to SNAT peers. In this case, we have chosen a mapping id of 10, which means that any translations created in our NAT rule (the ip nat inside command) will have an id of 10 associated with them. These translations are then identified—by the mapping id—as ones to send to our peer router. You can have multiple mapping-ids that form a mapping list.

Here's the configuration for Router 1:

```
!
Interface ethernet0
  ip address 10.10.1.1 255.255.255.0
  ip nat inside
  ! enable HSRP
  standby name SNATHSRP
  standby preempt
  standby priority 120
  standby ip 10.10.1.3
!
! Enable Snat for the group (id is 1 for router 1)
```

```
! Any NAT translations with a mapping id of 10 are sent
! to our peer
ip nat stateful id 1 redundancy SNATHSRP mapping-id 10
!
! Define our NAT POOL
ip nat pool poolone 172.168.1.1 172.168.1.254 prefix-length 24
!
! Configure our NAT translation;don't forget the mapping-id
! that identifies what translations we want to tell our peer about
ip nat inside source list 20 pool poolone mapping-id 10 overload
!
access-list 20 permit 10.10.0.0 0.0.255.255
```

And here's the configuration for Router 2:

```
!
Interface ethernet0
  ip address 10.10.1.2 255.255.255.0
  ip nat inside
  ! enable HSRP
  standby name SNATHSRP
  standby ip 10.10.1.3
!
! Enable Snat for the group (id is 2 for router 2)
! Any NAT translations with a mapping id of 10 are sent
! to our peer
ip nat stateful id 2 redundancy SNATHSRP mapping-id 10
!
! Define our NAT POOL
ip nat pool poolone 172.168.1.1 172.168.1.254 prefix-length 24
!
! Configure our NAT translation; don't forget the mapping-id
! that identifies what translations we want to tell our peer about
ip nat inside source list 20 pool poolone mapping-id 10 overload
!
access-list 20 permit 10.10.0.0 0.0.255.255
```

One important configuration note: we configured NAT pools on both routers. Had we configured a NAT pool only on Router 1 and Router 1 failed, Router 2 would continue to support already translated addresses but would not be able to create new sessions without the pool command. In order to support new sessions in the event of a failover, it's important to specify the pool command on both routers.

Configuring SNAT without HSRP

It is possible to configure SNAT without the benefit of HSRP by using a static primary and peer relationship. To do this, we use the primary command, which defines the interface and IP address to use for SNAT.

Here's the configuration for Router 1:

```
ip nat stateful id 1 primary 10.10.1.1 peer 10.10.1.2 mapping-id 10
```

Here's the configuration for Router 2:

```
ip nat stateful id 2 primary 10.10.1.2 peer 10.10.1.1 mapping-id 10
```

Tunnels

Tunnels take packets from one network, encapsulate them within an IP protocol, and transfer them to another network. This sounds inefficient, and in a sense it is. Why would you want to take perfectly good packets, wrap them up in some other protocol, send them to another location, and unwrap them? For two reasons. First, many protocols can't be routed. If you want to connect two sites using nonroutable protocols, the only way to do so is to wrap the nonroutable protocols within a routable protocol, such as IP. Second, it's increasingly common to use the Internet to connect remote sites to a central office. But this connection has its perils, the most significant of which is security. Do you really want corporate data flowing over the public Internet? To minimize security problems, you can establish a tunnel between the offices and then encrypt all the traffic on the tunnel.

In this section, we'll first look at how to establish a tunnel, then at how to encrypt the traffic traveling over the tunnel. We won't discuss encapsulating nonroutable protocols within IP in any detail. Figure 13-3 shows two offices connected by an ISP. The ISP has assigned two IP addresses for our use: 192.168.1.1 and 192.168.2.1. The network numbers used by Offices 1 and 2 are 10.10.1.0/24 and 10.10.2.0/24, respectively.

Here's the configuration for Office 1:

Figure 13-3. A tunnel through an ISP

```
hostname Office1
!
! Configure the interface tunnel
interface tunnel1
    ! Use an unnummbered IP address to stay in sync with serial0 and make our
    ! configuration easier
    ip unnumbered serial0
    ! Set up the tunnel's source IP and destination IP, and enable checksums
    tunnel source serial0
    tunnel destination 192.168.2.1
    tunnel checksum
```

```
! GRE IP is the default tunnel mode, so this command is optional
! GRE IP stands for Generic Route Encapsulation over IP
tunnel mode gre ip
no shutdown
!
! Configure the serial interface
interface serial0
  ip address 192.168.1.1 255.255.255.0
  no shutdown
!
! Our ISP is our default route
ip route 0.0.0.0 0.0.0.0 192.168.1.2
! Set up a static route to the other side of the tunnel
ip route 10.10.2.0 255.255.255.0 tunnel1
```

The trickiest part of the configuration is the routing. We set up a static default route, and then set up a more specific static route that sends any traffic destined for 10.10.2.0 through the tunnel.

Here's the configuration for Office 2; it's very similar to that for Office 1:

```
hostname Office2
!
! Configure the interface tunnel
! We used a different name here (tunnel2) just to show that they
! don't have to match.
interface tunnel2
    ! Use an unnummbered IP address to stay in sync with serial0 and make our
    ! configuration easier
    ip unnumbered serial1
    ! Set up the tunnel's source IP and destination IP, and enable checksums
    tunnel source serial1
    tunnel destination 192.168.1.1
    tunnel checksum
    ! GRE IP is the default tunnel mode, so this command is optional
    ! GRE IP stands for Generic Route Encapsulation over IP
    tunnel mode gre ip
    no shutdown
!
! Configure the serial interface
interface serial1
    ip address 192.168.2.1 255.255.255.0
!
! Default route
ip route 0.0.0.0 0.0.0.0 192.168.2.2
! Set up a static route to the other side of the tunnel
ip route 10.10.1.0 255.255.255.0 tunnel1
```

We can ping Office 2 from Office 1 using the tunnel:

```
Office1#ping 10.10.2.1

Type escape sequence to abort.
Sending 5, 100-byte ICMP Echos to 10.10.2.1, timeout is 2 seconds:
!!!!!
Success rate is 100 percent (5/5), round-trip min/avg/max = 68/68/68 ms
```

show Commands for Tunnels

The most useful show commands for tunnels are two that we've already seen: show ip route and show interface. This makes sense—tunnels are really just special interfaces, and the most difficult problem with creating tunnels is getting the routing to work correctly.

The command show ip route shows that we have an active route for the 10.10.2.0 network through the tunnel1 interface:

```
office1#show ip route
Codes: C - connected, S - static, I - IGRP, R - RIP, M - mobile, B - BGP
       D - EIGRP, EX - EIGRP external, O - OSPF, IA - OSPF inter area
       N1 - OSPF NSSA external type 1, N2 - OSPF NSSA external type 2
       E1 - OSPF external type 1, E2 - OSPF external type 2, E - EGP
       i - IS-IS, L1 - IS-IS level-1, L2 - IS-IS level-2, * - candidate default
       U - per-user static route, o - ODR

Gateway of last resort is 192.168.1.2 to network 0.0.0.0

     10.0.0.0/24 is subnetted, 2 subnets
C       10.10.1.0 is directly connected, Ethernet0
S       10.10.2.0 is directly connected, Tunnel1
C    192.168.1.0/24 is directly connected, Serial0
S*   0.0.0.0/0 [1/0] via 192.168.1.2
```

The command show interface tunnel1 gives results like any other show interface command. We see that the interface is up, the hardware associated with the interface is Tunnel (i.e., this is a virtual interface rather than a specific hardware interface), the encapsulation is TUNNEL, and the source and destination ports are properly set.

```
office1#show interface tunnel 1
Tunnel1 is up, line protocol is up
  Hardware is Tunnel
  Interface is unnumbered.  Using address of Serial0 (192.168.1.1)
  MTU 1514 bytes, BW 9 Kbit, DLY 500000 usec, rely 255/255, load 1/255
  Encapsulation TUNNEL, loopback not set, keepalive set (10 sec)
  Tunnel source 192.168.1.1 (Serial0), destination 192.168.2.1
  Tunnel protocol/transport GRE/IP, key disabled, sequencing disabled
  Checksumming of packets enabled,   fast tunneling enabled
  Last input never, output never, output hang never
  Last clearing of "show interface" counters never
  Queueing strategy: fifo
  Output queue 0/0, 0 drops; input queue 0/75, 0 drops
  5 minute input rate 0 bits/sec, 0 packets/sec
  5 minute output rate 0 bits/sec, 0 packets/sec
     0 packets input, 0 bytes, 0 no buffer
     Received 0 broadcasts, 0 runts, 0 giants, 0 throttles
     0 input errors, 0 CRC, 0 frame, 0 overrun, 0 ignored, 0 abort
     0 packets output, 0 bytes, 0 underruns
     0 output errors, 0 collisions, 0 interface resets
     0 output buffer failures, 0 output buffers swapped out
```

Encrypted Tunnels

In the previous example, we created a tunnel that could carry traffic between routers, but we didn't do anything to secure that traffic: the traffic went through the tunnel without any sort of encryption, so anyone with a packet sniffer and access to our network could see what was traveling through the tunnel. Since one of the biggest applications for tunneling is increased security, cryptography is essential. In this section, we'll explore two ways to encrypt the traffic flowing through the tunnel. First, we will use DSS and DES on a router running Version 11.3 of IOS. Depending on the feature set of your IOS, this form of encryption might be all that's available. (If other encryption methods, such as RSA, are available on your router, the configuration should be the same.) Next, we will look at encryption using IPSec, which is a security protocol that belongs to the TCP/IP protocol suite. The IPSec examples assume that you are using IOS Version 12.0 (or greater).

Tunnel Encryption with DSS and DES

Regardless of the type of encryption you use, an encrypted tunnel requires the generation of public and private keys, some form of authentication and key exchange (each end of the tunnel has to prove that it is who it says it is), and something to encrypt the actual traffic. In this example, we will use DSS (the Digital Signature Standard) for authentication and key exchange. Each host must generate private and public keys, and the hosts must exchange their public keys before traffic can flow. We use DES (the Digital Encryption Standard) for encryption. DES is now considered a relatively weak form of encryption, but it's still useful if your security needs aren't that great. In the IPSec section, we will use Triple DES (3DES) encryption, which is much more secure.

Generating keys

DSS requires us to generate public and private keys on each router. The routers at each end of the tunnel must share their public keys, which are used to encrypt and decrypt the messages sent across the tunnel. The private keys, of course, are never sent anywhere.

To generate a key pair, you must first use the zeroize command to erase any keys that are currently in the router's memory. (zeroize breaks any encryption that has already been configured. If you already have a key pair, skip this process and use the show command to display your public key.) Then use the command crypto key generate to generate the key pair:

```
office1(config)#crypto key zeroize dss
Warning! Zeroize will remove your DSS signature keys.
Do you want to continue? [yes/no]: yes
% Keys to be removed are named office1.
Do you really want to remove these keys? [yes/no]: yes
% Zeroize done.
office1(config)#crypto key generate dss office1
Generating DSS keys ....
  [OK]
```

Now use the command show crypto key mypubkey dss to display the key:

```
office1#show crypto key mypubkey dss
Key name: office1
 Serial number: 10609455
 Usage: Signature Key
 Key Data:
  E3F9ECB2 73841C55 42DBFFF4 10245836 0291EC42 8F97FF5E FA2B0314 AF29E520
  407004D5 70AA888C 88B25313 FACD03B6 6608D9EB F0F7C4D0 A679F408 F7E90C5F
```

You must generate a key for each router that will use this encryption method. Before going any further, save your keys by doing a copy running-config startup-config. If you don't, you will lose your keys the next time you reboot.

Configuring encryption on the tunnel

To encrypt our tunnel, we need a crypto map. Defining the map is relatively simple. We give it a name, an encryption method, and an access list. The name allows us to apply the map to the desired interfaces, the encryption method specifies how we want to perform encryption, and the access list ensures that we encrypt only traffic headed to the destination. In this example, we don't want to encrypt all the traffic that goes out the serial interface; we want to encrypt only traffic for the remote office.

The trickiest part of this configuration is to remember that you have to apply the crypto map both to the physical interface the tunnel uses and to the tunnel interface itself.

Here is the configuration for Office 1, with encryption enabled:

```
hostname office1
!
! Define office2's public key using the pubkey-chain command. Older versions
! of the IOS use only the crypto public-key command.
crypto key pubkey-chain dss
 named-key office2 signature
  serial-number 06897848
  key-string
   91A48507 2AC44FB3 C0EDBA3C B87C8F14 E2729110 6734DE5F 509C4476 1117E427
   B157882D B240CD84 2105C0FA 7F00C6B8 2493C4A7 A5C036A8 9E408D91 D5B73870
  quit
!
! Define our crypto map. We named it tunnelmap. The 5 is just
! a sequence number.
crypto map tunnelmap 5
 set peer office2
 ! Encrypt with 40-bit DES, our only choice on this router's IOS version
 set algorithm 40-bit-des
 ! Only encrypt traffic for the tunnel with access list 101
 match address 101
!
interface Tunnel1
 ip unnumbered Serial0
 tunnel source Serial0
 tunnel destination 192.168.2.1
```

```
  tunnel checksum
  ! Apply the crypto map to the tunnel
  crypto map tunnelmap
  !
interface Ethernet0
  ip address 10.10.1.1 255.255.255.0
  !
interface Serial0
  ip address 192.168.1.1 255.255.255.0
  ! Don't forget to apply the crypto map here
  crypto map tunnelmap
  !
  ! Static route to our provider
  ip route 0.0.0.0 0.0.0.0 192.168.1.2
  ! Route all tunnel traffic through the tunnel
  ip route 10.10.2.0 255.255.255.0 Tunnel1
  !
  ! Our access list is only one line long. Optionally, we could have used the
  ! keyword "ip" instead of "gre". This access list says encrypt tunnel traffic
  ! from our host to the destination
  access-list 101 permit gre host 192.168.1.1 host 192.168.2.1
```

And here is the configuration for Office 2:

```
hostname office2
  !
  ! Define office1's public key using the pubkey-chain command. Older versions
  ! of the IOS use only the crypto public-key command.
  crypto key pubkey-chain dss
   named-key office1 signature
    serial-number 10609455
    key-string
     9FFA2039 F4642B77 21A6FBA7 5179E1D8 211DD211 DA96699C 2045730D AB033253
     8A101977 B6580054 FEDBA12E 97F6B1BE 0D40EFB1 6F62ABBC 952F6DAF BB87BE60
    quit
  !
  ! Define our crypto map. We named it tunnelmap. The 5 is just
  ! a sequence number.
  crypto map tunnelmap 5
   set peer office1
   ! Encrypt with 40-bit DES, our only choice on this router's IOS version.
   set algorithm 40-bit-des
   ! Only encrypt traffic for the tunnel with access list 101
   match address 101
  !
interface Tunnel1
   ip unnumbered Serial1
   tunnel source Serial1
   tunnel destination 192.168.1.1
   ! Apply the crypto map to the tunnel
   crypto map tunnelmap
  !
interface Ethernet0
   ip address 10.10.2.1 255.255.255.0
  !
```

```
interface Serial1
 ip address 192.168.2.1 255.255.255.0
 clockrate 64000
 ! Don't forget to apply the crypto map to this interface
 crypto map tunnelmap
!
! Static route to our provider
ip route 0.0.0.0 0.0.0.0 192.168.2.2
!
! Route all tunnel traffic through the tunnel
ip route 10.10.1.0 255.255.255.0 Tunnel1
!
! Our access list is only one line long. Optionally, we could have used the
! keyword "ip" instead of "gre". This access list says encrypt tunnel traffic
! from our host to the destination
access-list 101 permit gre host 192.168.2.1 host 192.168.1.1
```

This configuration requires you to create the keys, and then cut and paste them into your router's configuration. That's clearly an awkward, error-prone process. It's possible to perform the key exchange automatically. Take the following steps:

1. On one router, start the key exchange in passive mode. After you press Enter to confirm, the router will wait for another router to initiate a key exchange connection:

   ```
   office1(config)#crypto key exchange dss passive
   Enter escape character to abort if connection does not complete.
   Wait for connection from peer[confirm]
   Waiting....
   ```

2. On the other router, start the key exchange in active mode, supplying the IP address of the first router and the name of the key you want to send to the other router. This is the name given to the key when it was created. After sending the key, the router asks you whether it should wait for a key from the first (passive) router; press Enter to confirm. In the following example, we initiate a key exchange to 192.168.1.1 and send the key named office2:

   ```
   office2(config)#crypto key exchange dss 192.168.1.1 office2
   Public key for office2:
   Serial Number 06897848
   Fingerprint   91A4 8507 2AC4 4FB3

       Wait for peer to send a key[confirm]
       Waiting ....
   ```

3. The first (passive) router receives the key sent by the active router, then asks whether you want to send a key in return. If you have more than one key configured on this router, it will ask you to select which key to send. In this example, we send the key office1 back to the active router:

   ```
   Send peer a key in return[confirm]<Enter>
   Which one?
       some-other-key? [yes]: n
       office1? [yes]:<Enter>
       Public key for office1:
         Serial Number 06897848
         Fingerprint   91A4 8507 2AC4 4FB3
   ```

4. The second (active) router confirms that it has received the key from the first router.

```
Public key for office1:
Serial Number 10609455
Fingerprint   E3F9 ECB2 7384 1C55
Add this public key to the configuration? [yes/no]: y
```

Now you have configured the keys on each of your routers without having to cut and paste the long key values.

DES Tunnel show Commands

When you're working with DES tunnels, a few show commands are particularly useful.

show crypto engine connections active

This command shows all active encrypted connections:

```
office2#show crypto engine connections active
ID   Interface    IP-Address    State   Algorithm     Encrypt  Decrypt
13   Serial1      192.168.2.1   set     DES_40_CFB64   10       0
```

Or if you are using Triple DES (3DES), which is more secure that regular DES, the output reflects that choice:

```
office2#show crypto engine connections active
ID Interface    IP-Address    State  Algorithm           Encrypt  Decrypt
13 Serial1      192.168.2.1   set    HMAC_MD5+3DES_56_C   10        0
```

The ID is useful for the clear crypto connection command, which allows you to remove a connection from the map. Clearing a connection is sometimes useful when you suspect that things aren't working when you are first configuring encryption. After you issue a clear, the connection is re-established, which causes the key exchange to occur again.

show crypto engine configuration

This command summarizes the currently running encryption:

```
office2#show crypto engine configuration
crypto engine name:   office2
crypto engine type:   software
serial number:        06897848
crypto engine state:  dss key generated
crypto lib version:   10.0.0

platform:             rp crypto engine

Encryption Process Info:
input queue top:   103
input queue bot:   103
input queue count: 0
```

IPSec Tunneling

IPSec has significant advantages over the other available tunneling methods. Some of these advantages are:

- multivendor support
- automatic key management, which makes it much more scalable
- compression before encryption

IPSec consists of four components. You really don't need to understand all of these pieces, but it is good to know what they mean when you see them in the configuration. The components are:

AH (Authentication Headers)
Provides strong cryptographic checksums for packets.

ESP (Encapsulating Security Payload)
Guarantees that your packet wasn't intercepted in transit.

IPcomp (IP Compression)
Compresses packets prior to encryption.

IKE (Internet Key Exchange)
Manages the keys.

In this section, we configure IPSec tunneling for the network in Figure 13-3. Although it looks more complex, this configuration is really quite similar to the configuration of the previous section. Some new items are configuring the IKE policy, setting the key, and setting the transform set.

To configure the IKE policy, we use the command `crypto isakmp policy`. The argument to this command is a priority value; the lower the number, the higher the policy's priority. In this example, the priority isn't important, but it is conceivable that a router will have several policies to choose from (possibly because it creates tunnels to different destinations). In this case, the router will use the highest-priority policy that both ends of the tunnel can agree on. The policy itself does two things: it sets the authentication hash algorithm to MD5, and it sets the authentication method to pre-share. The default hashing algorithm is SHA (Secure Hash Algorithm), but it doesn't matter which hash algorithm you use as long as both ends of the tunnel agree. Pre-share tells the router that it should use pre-shared keys.

To configure pre-shared keys, we use the command `crypto isakmp key`. This command is simple; we provide a name for the key (officekey, in this case) followed by the peer's IP address (the address of office2). Remember that this key must be the same on both routers.

To configure the transform set, we use the command `crypto ipsec transform-set`. This command defines the protocols used in the set. In this example, we use the transform set `esp-des esp-md5-hmac`, which specifies DES for ESP and MD5 for the authentication algorithm. Other protocol combinations that can be used are `ah-md5-hmac`, `esp-des`, `esp-3des`, `esp-md5-hmac`, `ah-sha-hmac`, `aesp-des`, and `comp-lzs`. Again, the crucial thing isn't the actual protocols you use, but that the protocols on either end of the tunnel agree. The transform set is assigned a name, which in this case is `office1-to-office2`. In our example, we used the same name for the transform set on each router—this will help you to preserve your sanity.

Finally, we create a crypto map, which specifies the `ipsec-isakmp` protocol, the peer address, the transform set, and the access list. Then we create a tunnel interface, to which we apply the crypto map.

Here's the configuration for Office 1:

```
hostname office1
!
! First we define the IKE policy. We are going to use MD5 and a pre-shared
! key that will be defined on both routers.
crypto isakmp policy 25
 hash md5
 encr 3des
 authentication pre-share
!
! This command defines the pre-shared key we mentioned.
! This key must be the same on both routers. The IP address is
! that of the peer (office2, in this case).
crypto isakmp key officekey address 192.168.2.1
!
! This command sets the transform set we are going to use. The name can be
! different on each router, but the protocol list must be the same.
crypto ipsec transform-set office1-to-office2 esp-3des esp-md5-hmac
!
! Define the crypto map. Since we are using IKE, this map is fairly simple
crypto map tunnelmap 10 ipsec-isakmp
 set peer 192.168.2.1
 ! Point to the transform set we configured earlier
 set transform-set office1-to-office2
 match address 101
!
interface Tunnel1
 ip unnumbered Serial0
 tunnel source Serial0
 tunnel destination 192.168.2.1
 tunnel checksum
 crypto map tunnelmap
!
interface Ethernet0
 ip address 10.10.1.1 255.255.255.0
!
interface Serial0
 ip address 192.168.1.1 255.255.255.0
 clockrate 64000
 crypto map tunnelmap
!
ip route 0.0.0.0 0.0.0.0 192.168.1.2
ip route 10.10.2.0 255.255.255.0 Tunnel1
!
access-list 101 permit gre host 192.168.1.1 host 192.168.2.1
```

Here's the configuration for Office 2:

```
hostname Office2
!
! First we define the IKE policy. We are going to use MD5 and a pre-shared
```

```
! key that will be defined on both routers.
crypto isakmp policy 25
 hash md5
 encr 3des
 authentication pre-share
!
! This command defines the pre-shared key we mentioned above.
! This key must be the same on both routers. The IP address is
! that of the peer (office1, in this case).
crypto isakmp key officekey address 192.168.1.1
!
! This command sets the transform set we are going to use. The name can be
! different on each router, but the protocol list must be the same.
crypto ipsec transform-set office1-to-office2 esp-3des esp-md5-hmac
!
!
! Define the crypto map. Since we are using IKE, this map is fairly simple
crypto map tunnelmap 10 ipsec-isakmp
 set peer 192.168.1.1
 set transform-set office1-to-office2
 match address 101
!
interface Tunnel1
 ip unnumbered Serial1
 tunnel source Serial1
 tunnel destination 192.168.1.1
 tunnel checksum
 crypto map tunnelmap
!
interface Ethernet0
 ip address 10.10.2.1 255.255.255.0
!
interface Serial1
 ip address 192.168.2.1 255.255.255.0
 crypto map tunnelmap
!
ip route 0.0.0.0 0.0.0.0 192.168.2.2
!
ip route 10.10.1.0 255.255.255.0 Tunnel1
!
access-list 101 permit gre host 192.168.2.1 host 192.168.1.1
```

To show that our IPSec configuration is working, we use the show crypto engine command:

```
office2#show crypto engine connections active

  ID Interface   IP-Address    State  Algorithm         Encrypt  Decrypt
  22 Serial1     192.168.2.1   set    HMAC_MD5+3DES_56_C     10        0
```

In this output, we can see the encrypted connection and the algorithm used to do the encryption.

Dynamic Multipoint VPN

In the previous section, we showed how to create an IPSec tunnel between two sites, which was not terribly complicated. However, if you have multiple routers—and most of us do—you might need to configure IPSec tunnels between all of them. If you do a hub and spoke configuration, your hub's configuration will quickly grow. As each new spoke is added to the system, the hub router needs additional configuration to accommodate the new spoke. On top of all that, if we decide to configure tunnels between our spokes (spoke-to-spoke), we add another layer of complexity to the configurations of all the routers.

To solve this problem, Cisco has introduced the DMVPN feature, which stands for Dynamic Multipoint VPN. Basically, this feature combines GRE Tunnels, IPSec encryption, and Next Hop Resolution Protocol (NHRP) to provide a better way to implement large-scale IPSec VPNs. The main features are:

- Reduced configuration on the hub router. The hub needs to be configured only once. As more spokes are added, the hub router configuration remains the same as NHRP learns about new spokes.
- Automatic IPSec encryption
- Support for dynamically addressed spoke routers such as cable and DSL spokes.
- Dynamic tunnel creation for spoke-to-spoke communication.

Figure 13-4 shows our DMVPN network. We have one hub router and two spoke routers.

Figure 13-4. DMVPN network diagram

In this configuration, each spoke has a permanent IPSec tunnel to the hub router. The spoke-to-spoke tunnels are dynamically—and temporarily—created.

When a spoke router wants to communicate with another spoke router, the router asks the NHRP server (the hub) for the real address of the destination spoke. After it has this address, dynamic IPSec tunnels are created. These dynamic spoke-to-spoke tunnels allow traffic to flow directly between the spokes instead of being relayed through the hub routers. After a certain amount of inactivity, these tunnels are shut down to conserve resources.

Configuring DMVPN

To configure this feature, we need to accomplish three main tasks: configure an IPSec profile, enable the hub for DMVPN, and enable each spoke for DMVPN.

Configuring an IPSec profile. The commands for creating the IPSec profile are identical to the crypto map commands we used in the previous section. However, since this is a profile, only a few of the commands are used. Basically, we set up the crypto transformation set along with various options. In this example, we just create the profile like this:

```
! Use Triple-DES
crypto ipsec transform-set set1 esp-3des esp-md5-hmac
!
! This is the profile, the name we are using is dmvpn-exmample, which
! we will use in the next configuration step
crypto ipsec profile dmvpn-example
  set transform-set set1
  set security association lifetime seconds 60
```

This part of the configuration is done on the hub and every spoke router.

Configuring the hub for DMVPN. To configure the hub, we want to set up our tunnel for Multipoint GRE tunnels and NHRP. In previous examples, we used the ip unnumbered command for the IP address of the tunnel in order to reduce the number of subnets we used. However, for DMVPN, this can make debugging more difficult. So for our DMVPN configurations, we apply an IP address to our tunnels.

The main commands we will use are ip nhrp, tunnel mode greSmultipoint, and tunnel protection ipsec profile. Each of these commands is documented in the following configuration example.

Here's the configuration for our HUB router:

```
!
hostname hubrouter
!
! Configure our tunnel interface.
interface tunnel 100
  ip address 10.1.1.1 255.255.255.0
  ip mtu 1416
  ! Set up NHRP authentication string. This string must match on all
  ! routers that are participating in NHRP
  ip nhrp authentication ournhrpstring
```

```
! Configure NHRP to add our spoke routers to the NHRP mappings
ip nhrp map multicast dynamic
! Enable NHRP on the interface with a network-id. This id must
! match on all routers
ip nhrp network-id 1000
! Configure our tunnel source, which is ethernet0
tunnel source ethernet0
! Set a key for our tunnel
! This must be identical on all routers within our DMVPN network
tunnel key 10000
! Enable Multipoint GRE (mGRE)
tunnel mode gre multipoint
! Enable IPSec by associating an IPSec profile. This profile name is
! the same one we created earlier
tunnel protection ipsec profile dmvpn-example
! We need to disable split-horizon for the tunnel. In this case, we are
! using EIGRP.
no ip split-horizon eigrp 100
delay 1000
bandwidth 1000
!
interface Ethernet0
  ip address 172.16.1.1 255.255.255.0
  no shutdown
!
interface Ethernet1
  ip address 192.168.1.1 255.255.255.0
  no shutdown
!
interface Ethernet2
 ip address 172.16.2.1 255.255.255.0
  no shutdown
!
router eigrp 100
  network 10.1.1.0 0.0.0.255
  network 192.168.1.0 0.0.0.255
  no auto-summary
!
! Don't forget our IPSec Profile from earlier
crypto ipsec transform-set set1 esp-3des esp-md5-hmac
crypto ipsec profile dmvpn-example
  set transform-set set1
  set security association lifetime seconds 60
```

 We lowered the MTU to 1416 so that packets are fragmented before encryption. Otherwise, the receiving router would have to reassemble the packet.

Configuring a spoke router for DMVPN. On our spoke routers, the configuration is pretty much the same as the hub. We will add some simple NHRP mappings back to the hub router with the ip nhrp map command. The ip nhrp map multicast command is needed because there is more than one destination for multicast packets in our multipoint tunnel.

Here's the configuration for the Spoke 1 router:

```
!
hostname spoke1
!
! Configure our tunnel interface.
interface tunnel 100
  ip address 10.1.1.2 255.255.255.0
  ip mtu 1416
  ! Setup NHRP authentication string. This string must match on all
  ! routers that are participating in NHRP
  ip nhrp authentication ournhrpstring
  ! Map the tunnel ip to the HUB's physical address
  ip nhrp map 10.1.1.1 172.16.1.1
  ! Map multicast packets to the HUB's physical address
  ip nhrp map multicast 172.16.1.1
  ! Configure the hub router as the NHRP server
  ip nhrp nhs 10.0.0.1
  ! Enable nhrp on the interface
  ip nhrp network-id 1000
  ! Configure our tunnel source, which is ethernet0
  tunnel source ethernet0
  ! Set a key for our tunnel
  tunnel key 10000
  ! Enable Multipoint GRE (mGRE)
  tunnel mode gre multipoint
  ! enable IPSec by associating an IPSec profile. This profile name is
  ! the same one we created earlier
  tunnel protection ipsec profile dmvpn-example
  ! We need to disable split-horizon for the tunnel. In this case, we are
  ! using EIGRP.
  no ip split-horizon eigrp 100
  delay 1000
  bandwidth 1000
!
interface Ethernet0
  ip address 172.16.1.2 255.255.255.0
  no shutdown
!
interface Ethernet1
  ip address 192.168.2.1 255.255.255.0
  no shutdown
!
router eigrp 100
  network 10.1.1.0 0.0.0.255
  network 192.168.2.0 0.0.0.255
  no auto-summary
!
! Don't forget our IPSec Profile from earlier
crypto ipsec transform-set set1 esp-3des esp-md5-hmac
crypto ipsec profile dmvpn-example
  set transform-set set1
  set security association lifetime seconds 60
```

On Spoke 2's router, the configuration is identical with the exception of the IP addresses. No new configuration is required on the hub router as we add new spoke routers, which makes DMVPN such a nice feature.

Verifying DMVPN configuration. We can verify our configuration with the commands show ip route and show ip nhrp.

```
Hub#show ip nhrp
  10.1.1.2/32 via 10.1.1.2, Tunnel00 created 00:00:17, expire     00:05:43
    Type: dynamic, Flags: authoritative unique registered
    NBMA address: 172.16.2.1
```

Multicast Routing

Besides the fact that multicast packets have more than just one destination, they differ from most other technologies in one important way: multicast packets are routed based on their source address rather than their destination address. In the Appendix, we say that the multicast range is 224.0.0.0 through 239.255.255.255, which is also the class D address space. Packets destined for these addresses are flooded through the portion of our network where we configure multicast routing.

Multicast routing has two major configuration modes: dense mode and sparse mode. Before we discuss the two mode types and how they work, we need to review a few multicast concepts.

IGMP

IGMP stands for Internet Group Management Protocol. It is used by network hosts to tell the routers which multicast groups they would like to join by sending Join messages. The routers keep track of these multicast groups in a table. When hosts want to leave a group, they send a Leave message. The router manages this table efficiently. It doesn't keep track of every host that's interested in a multicast group. Rather, it keeps track of the fact that at least one node on the network wants packets from the requested multicast group. Since the router doesn't keep track of the number of hosts in a particular multicast group, it must respond a little differently to Leave messages. When a host sends a Leave message to the router, the router then asks all hosts on the network if anyone is still interested in that group. If no hosts respond to that request, the router removes that group from the list of forwarded multicast groups.

Later in this chapter, we'll review two other IGMP concepts when discussing multicasting with switches: IGMP snooping and Cisco Group Management Protocol (CGMP).

Reverse Path Forwarding

RPF stands for Reverse Path Forwarding. The main function of RPF is loop avoidance, which it achieves by applying several rules when dealing with multicast packets:

- An RPF interface is one that represents the best route back to the source IP address.
- If the router receives a packet on an interface that is the RPF interface back to the source of this packet, it forwards the packet to all other multicast interfaces.
- If the router receives a multicast packet on any other interface, it drops the packet.

By following these rules, the router attempts to avoid multicast loops.

Now we are ready to look at the modes of multicast routing: dense mode, sparse mode, and sparse-dense mode, which is far less confusing than it sounds.

Dense Mode

For the dense mode, a "push" model is used to flood multicast traffic through the network. Dense mode assumes everyone wants to receive multicast packets, so it floods the packets down all interfaces that are configured for multicast support. It then prunes the ones that explicitly reject a given group. This push and pruning method is used to develop source-based delivery trees.

Dense mode is suited to local LANs and high-bandwidth connections. However, it can be run on low-bandwidth networks if the multicast application is economical or if a large part of the network is expected to join the group.

Configuring multicast for dense mode

To configure multicasting routing, we first need to enable it on the router with the global ip multicast-routing command. This command is required for both dense and sparse mode.

Before we examine the router configurations, let's look at the example network. Figure 13-5 shows our humble network.

After configuring the router with multicast routing, we configure each interface we want to participate in multicast sessions. To do this, we'll use the ip pim dense-mode command (pim indicates "Protocol Independent Multicasting"). And in our network, we want every interface to participate in multicasting. So the configurations will look like this:

```
hostname router1
!
ip multicast-routing
!
interface serial0
  ip pim dense-mode
  ip address 192.168.2.1 255.255.255.0
!
interface serial1
```

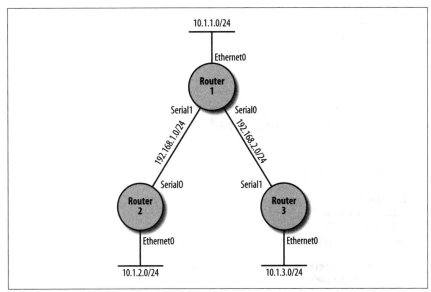

Figure 13-5. Example multicast network

```
ip pim dense-mode
ip address 192.168.1.1 255.255.255.0
!
interface ethernet0
ip pim dense-mode
ip address 10.1.1.1 255.255.255.0
!
router eigrp 100
  network 10.0.0.0
  network 192.168.1.0
  network 192.168.2.0
```

For Router 2 and Router 3, we are going to use an additional command: ip igmp join-group because we have no hosts on our network to demonstrate the joining of groups. In other words, there are no hosts sending IGMP messages, so we need this command to make the routers join the groups explicitly and make our show command output meaningful in this example. This command causes our router to respond as a multicast host on its own interface. By doing this, we'll be able to ping the multicast address and verify that multicast routing is indeed working.

Here's the configuration for Router 2:

```
hostname router2
!
ip multicast-routing
!
interface serial0
  ip pim dense-mode
  ip address 192.168.1.2 255.255.255.0
  !
interface ethernet0
```

```
      ip pim dense-mode
      ip address 10.1.2.1 255.255.255.0
      ip igmp join-group 239.0.0.0
    !
    router eigrp 100
      network 10.0.0.0
      network 192.168.1.0
      network 192.168.2.0
```

And here's the configuration for Router 3:

```
    hostname router3
    !
    ip multicast-routing
    !
    interface serial1
      ip pim dense-mode
      ip address 192.168.2.2 255.255.255.0
      clockrate 64000
    !
    interface ethernet0
      ip pim dense-mode
      ip address 10.1.3.1 255.255.255.0
      ip igmp join-group 239.0.0.0
    !
    router eigrp 100
      network 10.0.0.0
      network 192.168.1.0
      network 192.168.2.0
```

To show that multicast is working, we can ping a multicast address and see who responds:

```
    router1#ping 239.0.0.0

    Type escape sequence to abort.
    Sending 1, 100-byte ICMP Echos to 239.0.0.0, timeout is 2 seconds:

    Reply to request 0 from 192.168.1.2, 24 ms
    Reply to request 0 from 192.168.2.2, 36 ms
```

This works because of the ip igmp join-group command we added to Router 2 and Router 3. If we didn't use this command, those interfaces would not respond to this ping. A router isn't normally a multicast client except for routing protocols that use multicast for distributing routing information. In our little network, we have no multicast clients to ping, so this trick makes our simple example work. You wouldn't need this command in a normal environment. Also, be aware that join-group is considered a dangerous command because it can lead to multicast routing loops if not used with care. If you configure a static IGMP join on an interface, the router will always forward packets for that group out that interface, even if the router would normally prune this interface from the RPF tree. But as we said, we needed it for this example to demonstrate multicasting packets.

Two major show commands that display the state of our multicast configuration are show ip pim interface and show ip pim neighbor. The show ip pim interface command displays the interfaces that are enabled for multicast. (**D** in the following output indicates dense mode.) And the neighbor commands show the multicast neighbors for this router.

```
router1#show ip pim interface
```

Address	Interface	Ver/ Mode	Nbr Count	Query Intvl	DR Prior	DR
10.1.1.1	Ethernet0	v2/D	0	30	1	10.1.1.1
192.168.2.1	Serial0	v2/D	1	30	1	0.0.0.0
192.168.1.1	Serial1	v2/D	1	30	1	0.0.0.0

```
router1#show ip pim neighbor
PIM Neighbor Table
```

Neighbor Address	Interface	Uptime/Expires	Ver	DR Priority	
192.168.2.2	Serial0	00:36:28/00:01:20	v2	1	(BD)
192.168.1.2	Serial1	00:37:47/00:01:31	v2	1	(BD)

```
router1#
```

Finally, the show ip mroute command displays the multicast routing table. In this output, we can see which multicast networks are being used and the various flags. In this output, all our interfaces are in dense mode:

```
router1#show ip mroute
IP Multicast Routing Table
Flags: D - Dense, S - Sparse, B - Bidir Group, s - SSM Group, C - Connected,
       L - Local, P - Pruned, R - RP-bit set, F - Register flag,
       T - SPT-bit set, J - Join SPT, M - MSDP created entry,
       X - Proxy Join Timer Running, A - Advertised via MSDP, U - URD,
       I - Received Source Specific Host Report
Outgoing interface flags: H - Hardware switched
Timers: Uptime/Expires
Interface state: Interface, Next-Hop or VCD, State/Mode

(*, 224.0.1.40), 00:19:08/00:00:00, RP 0.0.0.0, flags: DJCL
  Incoming interface: Null, RPF nbr 0.0.0.0
  Outgoing interface list:
    Ethernet0, Forward/Dense, 00:19:08/00:00:00
    Serial0, Forward/Dense, 00:19:08/00:00:00
    Serial1, Forward/Dense, 00:19:08/00:00:00

(*, 239.0.0.0), 00:12:10/00:02:59, RP 0.0.0.0, flags: D
  Incoming interface: Null, RPF nbr 0.0.0.0
  Outgoing interface list:
    Serial0, Forward/Dense, 00:12:10/00:00:00
    Serial1, Forward/Dense, 00:12:10/00:00:00

(192.168.1.1, 239.0.0.0), 00:02:19/00:01:10, flags: T
  Incoming interface: Serial1, RPF nbr 192.168.1.2
  Outgoing interface list:
    Serial0, Forward/Dense, 00:02:19/00:00:00
```

```
(192.168.2.1, 239.0.0.0), 00:01:34/00:01:55, flags: T
    Incoming interface: Serial0, RPF nbr 192.168.2.2
    Outgoing interface list:
      Serial1, Forward/Dense, 00:01:34/00:00:00
```

Another entry that you see in the output of this command is RPF, which we described earlier.

Sparse Mode

Unlike dense mode, sparse mode forwards multicast packets only to receivers that have actually joined the multicast group. (Dense mode just assumes everyone wants the packets and floods them everywhere until it receives rejection requests from clients and they are pruned from the tree.) So how do receivers join the multicast group? Once again, the hosts use IGMP to communicate with the router. But this time the router sends multicast traffic to a designated Rendezvous Point (RP).

An RP is a selected router on the network that all the other routers will use for multicast traffic. When a node sends a Join message to a router, the router will send that Join message to the nearest RP router. The RP router keeps track of the host and the multicast group in a shared source tree. When multicast traffic enters the network, the router that receives it forwards the traffic to the RP. The RP looks at its shared source tree and forwards the packet to all routers on the network with hosts that have joined the packet's multicast group. This shared source tree method is different from dense mode, in which each router maintains a separate tree of sources and multicast groups.

There can be multiple RPs on a multicast network. And RPs can defined statically or dynamically. For our first configuration, we'll look at static RP definitions.

Configuring multicast for sparse mode

Just as with dense mode, we'll need to enable multicast routing globally on the router with the ip multicast-routing command. After that, each interface gets ip pim sparse-mode command, which is much like our dense mode configuration. The only new item for sparse mode is defining the RP, which we are doing statically. For this configuration, we have selected Router 1 as the RP. No extra configuration is required on Router 1 to make it the RP because any router assumes that it is an RP once it starts receiving incoming join messages that contain one of its own multicast-enabled interfaces.

All we need to do is define the RP on Router 2 and Router 3 with the ip pim rp-address command. We will use Ethernet0 as the address on Router 1. Also, the interface we choose must have ip pim sparse-mode configured, even loopback interfaces.

Here's the configuration for Router 1:

```
hostname router1
!
ip multicast-routing
!
interface serial0
  ip pim sparse-mode
  ip address 192.168.2.1 255.255.255.0
```

```
!
interface serial1
  ip pim sparse-mode
  ip address 192.168.1.1 255.255.255.0
!
interface ethernet0
  ip pim sparse-mode
  ip address 10.1.1.1 255.255.255.0
!
router eigrp 100
  network 10.0.0.0
  network 192.168.1.0
  network 192.168.2.0
```

Here's the configuration for Router 2:

```
hostname router2
!
ip multicast-routing
!
! Define our RP for our network
ip pim rp-address 10.1.1.1
!
interface serial0
  ip pim sparse-mode
  ip address 192.168.1.2 255.255.255.0
  !
interface ethernet0
  ip pim sparse-mode
  ip address 10.1.2.1 255.255.255.0
  ip igmp join-group 239.0.0.0
!
router eigrp 100
  network 10.0.0.0
  network 192.168.1.0
  network 192.168.2.0
```

And here's the configuration for Router 3:

```
hostname router3
!
ip multicast-routing
!
! Define our RP for our network
ip pim rp-address 10.1.1.1
!
interface serial1
  ip pim sparse-mode
  ip address 192.168.2.2 255.255.255.0
!
interface ethernet0
  ip pim sparse-mode
  ip address 10.1.3.1 255.255.255.0
  ip igmp join-group 239.0.0.0
```

```
!
router eigrp 100
  network 10.0.0.0
  network 192.168.1.0
  network 192.168.2.0
```

The output for show ip mroute lists our defined RP:

```
router1#show ip mroute
IP Multicast Routing Table
Flags: D - Dense, S - Sparse, B - Bidir Group, s - SSM Group, C - Connected,
       L - Local, P - Pruned, R - RP-bit set, F - Register flag,
       T - SPT-bit set, J - Join SPT, M - MSDP created entry,
       X - Proxy Join Timer Running, A - Advertised via MSDP, U - URD,
       I - Received Source Specific Host Report
Outgoing interface flags: H - Hardware switched
Timers: Uptime/Expires
Interface state: Interface, Next-Hop or VCD, State/Mode

(*, 224.0.1.40), 00:04:24/00:00:00, RP 10.1.1.1, flags: SJCL
  Incoming interface: Null, RPF nbr 0.0.0.0
  Outgoing interface list:
    Serial0, Forward/Sparse, 00:04:24/00:03:23
    Serial1, Forward/Sparse, 00:01:25/00:02:30

(*, 239.0.0.0), 00:01:36/00:03:25, RP 10.1.1.1, flags: S
  Incoming interface: Null, RPF nbr 0.0.0.0
  Outgoing interface list:
    Serial1, Forward/Sparse, 00:01:36/00:02:30
    Serial0, Forward/Sparse, 00:00:04/00:03:25

router1#ping 239.0.0.0

Type escape sequence to abort.
Sending 1, 100-byte ICMP Echos to 239.0.0.0, timeout is 2 seconds:

Reply to request 0 from 192.168.1.2, 56 ms
Reply to request 0 from 192.168.1.2, 112 ms
```

Auto-RP configuration and sparse-dense mode

Statically defining the RP in our little network is fine, but for larger networks, static defining anything isn't really a good idea. Luckily for us there is Auto-RP, which allows the routers to learn who the RP is dynamically. All we do is configure the router we want to be the RP and let it announce itself to other routers.

In order to use Auto-RP, we need to change all our modes from sparse mode to sparse-dense mode. Sparse-dense mode isn't as contradictory as it might sound. Basically, it allows the interface to operate in dense mode until an RP is selected. Once the RP is selected, the group begins operating in sparse mode and our interface switches to sparse mode as well. In other words, dense mode is needed to accept the RP announcements. Once the RP is selected, we are back to sparse mode.

Now, on Router 1 we are going to define a loopback interface and then let the router announce itself as the RP.

```
interface loopback0
  ip address 10.2.1.1 255.255.255.0
  ip pim sparse-dense-mode
!
! Set the auto-rp announcements to have a scope of 16.
! The scope is the Time-To-Live, which limits how far
! they can travel. Choose a number large enough to cover
! your pim domain.
ip pim send-rp-announce loopback0 scope 16
ip pim send-rp-discovery scope 16
```

On all other routers, make sure our interfaces are in sparse-dense mode:

```
interface serial0
  ip pim sparse-dense-mode
```

In order for the RP selection to begin, we need to start our multicast software. In this case, all we need to do is ping 239.0.0.0:

```
router1#ping 239.0.0.0

Type escape sequence to abort.
Sending 1, 100-byte ICMP Echos to 239.0.0.0, timeout is 2 seconds:

Reply to request 0 from 192.168.2.2, 64 ms
Reply to request 0 from 192.168.1.2, 100 ms
```

Now, we can see the RP selection for 239.0.0.0:

```
router1#show ip mroute
IP Multicast Routing Table
Flags: D - Dense, S - Sparse, B - Bidir Group, s - SSM Group, C - Connected,
       L - Local, P - Pruned, R - RP-bit set, F - Register flag,
       T - SPT-bit set, J - Join SPT, M - MSDP created entry,
       X - Proxy Join Timer Running, A - Advertised via MSDP, U - URD,
       I - Received Source Specific Host Report
Outgoing interface flags: H - Hardware switched
Timers: Uptime/Expires
Interface state: Interface, Next-Hop or VCD, State/Mode

(*, 239.0.0.0), 00:01:39/00:02:59, RP 10.5.1.1, flags: S
  Incoming interface: Null, RPF nbr 0.0.0.0
  Outgoing interface list:
    Serial0, Forward/Sparse-Dense, 00:00:40/00:02:49
    Serial1, Forward/Sparse-Dense, 00:00:39/00:02:50
```

BSR

Bootstrap Router (BSR) was introduced in PIMv2. It operates much like Auto-RP except that BSR is an open standard while Auto-RP is proprietary to Cisco. Also, with BSR, you need only sparse mode. There is no need for sparse-dense mode with BSR.

You can use BSR instead of Auto-RP just by using the following commands:

```
ip pim bsr-candidate loopback 0 1
ip pim rp-candidate loopback 0
```

In this case, we configured the BSR and RP to be the same router. You can configure them on different routers.

Cisco Group Management Protocol (CGMP)

CGMP works with switches to limit the forwarding of multicast packets to the ports with multicast clients. As clients join and leave multicast groups, the switch dynamically updates its database of multicast ports. The major advantage of this—besides keeping multicast configuration simpler on the switch side—is that this protocol reduces the amount of multicast traffic on user segments by sending multicast packets only to the ports that actually require it.

Without CGMP, a switch has to listen to every single IGMP packet using what's called IGMP snooping. In IGMP snooping, the switch listens for every IGMP packet and analyzes it in order to determine how to switch the packet. To do this, the switch's management module has to be a member of every multicast group all the time, which can result in significant overhead for the switch.

CGMP takes advantage of the fact that the router has to listen to IGMP anyway. The router can use CGMP to just pass local membership information over to the switch, which eliminates the need for the switch to perform IGMP snooping.

In the end, the goal of CGMP and IGMP snooping is to allow the switch to know how to forward multicast packets to specific devices that are members of the multicast groups.

CGMP is a proprietary Cisco protocol that requires both Cisco routers and Cisco (Catalyst) switches. On almost all Cisco switches, CGMP is enabled by default. There is one notable exception, however; the 5000 series requires the following command to enable CGMP:

```
set cgmp enable
```

On the router side, you configure CGMP and IGMP with the following commands:

```
ip cgmp
ip igmp
```

Multiprotocol Label Switching (MPLS)

Multiprotocol Label Switching (MPLS) integrates layer 2 information with layer 3 routing, which means that MPLS offers the performance of switching with all the intelligence of routing.

MPLS Terminology

Before we start talking about the advantages of MPLS and how it operates, we need to define a few terms:

MPLS domain
> A group of routers in an MPLS "cloud," that is, where all are running MPLS.

LSR
> Label Switching Router. A router within our MPLS domain that is running MPLS.

LSP
> Label Switched Path. The path the packet will take along our MPLS routers.

Ingress router
> The first router in the MPLS domain. It attaches the MPLS tag to our packet.

Egress router
> The last router in the MPLS domain for a packet's path. The egress router strips the MPLS tag from the packet before forwarding it to its final destination.

How Does It Work?

An MPLS domain is a group of LSR routers, as shown in Figure 13-6. By using MPLS, the routers are able to route and switch packets based on the label (tag) that the packet has been given. (This label is appended to the packet by the ingress router and removed by the egress router.) This label identifies the flow between the two endpoints in the MPLS domain. In this case, the path is from Customer A Site 1 to Customer A Site 2.

So, you might be asking, what's the big deal? It attaches labels to packets; so what? Well, here is the big deal: as a packet travels along the path, the routers do not need to examine or process the IP header of the packet nor do the routers need to make routing decisions for each packet. The routers simply look at the packet's label to make the "routing decision." Before we were using MPLS, each router had to examine the packet's IP information and then look up the routing tables, which is a waste of resources. Why have each router repeat the same steps?

One common analogy used to explain MPLS compares it to the post office. (I almost hate to use it here because I see it so often, but I can't think of a better analogy.) When the post office receives a piece of mail, it's processed just once at the first sorting facility that it reaches. At this facility, the letter is scanned and labeled with a tag. This tag identifies the path this letter will take to its destination. As the letter travels to a new facility, the letter doesn't need to be reread and routed; only the tag needs to be processed. The tag points to a path from the one facility to the next. If each sorting facility reread the letter's address, mail delivery would be highly inefficient. The same thing goes for MPLS: having each router along the MPLS domain reread the packet's IP address information and make a routing decision is a waste. MPLS saves routing resources by making the decision once and letting routers farther down the path make routing decisions based solely on a simple label.

To better understand, we could look at the MPLS process. The first LSR router in our MPLS domain is the one that examines the packet's IP information and attaches the MPLS tag to the packet. As each LSR router along the path receives the labeled packet, the following steps occur:

1. The MPLS label is examined in the packet.
2. The packet is forwarded to the next LSR.
3. If this is the last router in the MPLS domain (the egress router), the MPLS label is stripped and the packet is forwarded to its destination.

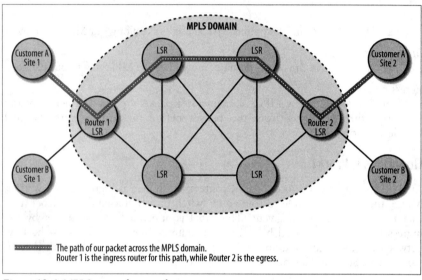

Figure 13-6. MPLS network example

Configuring MPLS

There isn't much to a simple MPLS configuration; we just need to enable CEF (Cisco Express Forwarding) on the router with the global command ip cef and enable MPLS with the older interface command tag-switching ip.

```
! Enable Cisco Express Forwarding
ip cef
!
! Enable interface for MPLS
interface fastethernet0/1
    tag-switching ip
```

As of IOS version 12.0, the mpls command replaces the tag-switching command. So our configuration becomes:

```
! Enable Cisco Express Forwarding
ip cef
!
! Enable interface for MPLS
interface fastethernet0/1
    mpls ip
```

Incrementally deploying MPLS

If you want to deploy MPLS slowly, you can do so two routers at a time. For example, we can start our migration to MPLS by adding the following configurations on just two of our interconnected routers. After we have the two routers running MPLS, we can move out and configure the next connected router on our path. We'll start at the core with two adjacent routers. Each time we move out and implement MPLS on more routers, we are defining new ingress and egress routers and expanding our core.

Here's the configuration for Router 1:

```
ip cef
! Connection to Router 1
interface fastethernet0/1
    mpls ip
```

Here's the configuration for Router 2:

```
ip cef
! Connection to Router 2
interface fastethernet0/2
    mpls ip
```

Now just keep going to the next router until the entire MPLS domain is complete.

Verifying the MPLS configuration

We can verify our MPLS configuration with the following commands: show mpls interfaces, which displays all the MPLS information for interfaces configured for MPLS, and show mpls forwarding-table, which displays the contents of the MPLS forwarding information base. In the following output, we can see which interfaces have MPLS enabled.

```
router# show mpls interfaces
Interface        IP          Tunnel  Operational
Ethernet0/1/1    Yes (tdp)   No      No
Ethernet0/1/2    Yes (tdp)   No      No
Ethernet0/1/3    Yes (tdp)   Yes     Yes
POS2/0/0         Yes (tdp)   No      No
ATM0/0.1         Yes (tdp)   No      No           (ATM labels)
ATM1/0.1         Yes (ldp)   No      Yes          (ATM labels)
```

And with the show mpls forwarding-table command, we can see the local tag and the outgoing tag. The outgoing tag is the label assigned by the next hop router. It is either untagged or pop tag. Untagged means there is no label for the destination from the next hop or that label switching isn't available on the outgoing interface. Pop tag means that the next hop advertised an implicit NULL label for the destination, which made this router pop the top label.

```
Router# show mpls forwarding-table
Local  Outgoing    Prefix        Bytes tag  Outgoing    Next Hop
tag    tag or VC   or Tunnel Id  switched   interface

26     Untagged    10.1.0.0/16   0          Et0/1/1     192.168.32.4
28     1/30        10.2.0.0/16   0          AT0/0.1     point2point
29     Pop tag     10.3.0.0/16   0          Hs5/0       point2point
```

Networking Topics

MPLS VPN

As if MPLS were not already a big-enough feature, there is one more major part to describe: MPLS VPNs. These VPNs allow you to create totally separate VPNs across an MPLS domain. These VPNs are seen as private intranets within each domain, so there is no concern about one customer's traffic mixing with another's.

MPLS VPNs are connectionless, scaleable, easy to create, and support technologies such as multicast, QoS, and VoIP. Since they are connectionless, the biggest advantages are that they are easier to build and manage versus conventional VPNs, take up less CPU and memory on the routers, and offer faster switching. For an MPLS VPN to operate, we need to understand some VPN router types, as shown in Table 13-1.

Table 13-1. VPN router types

Router type	Meaning
P	Provider's core router
PE	Provider's edge router
CE	Customer's edge router
C	Customer's router

Our network diagram in Figure 13-6 shows PE routers Router 1 and Router 2. All the other LSR routers in our Domain are Ps. The CE and C routers would be at the customer site. For our example configuration, we configure only the PE routers for the VPNs.

Each MPLS VPN is associated with a VPN routing/forwarding (VRF) instance. A VRF defines the VPN membership of a remote site to the PE router. For each VRF, a separate routing table and CEF table is managed, which keeps the outside traffic from entering our VPN and information leaving our VPN.

For this example, let's assume our BGP AS is 1000 and that Router 1 has IP address 10.1.1.4 and Router 2 has 10.1.1.6. To set up our VPNs, we are going to define the VPN with the VRF command and then configure BGP.

On our PE routers (Router 1 and Router 2), we need to define our VPNs. To do this, we create two VRFs with the ip vrf command and apply these VRFs to our interfaces with the ip vrf forwarding command. The route distinguisher is our AS number followed by another number, which in this case is 1 for Customer A and 2 for Customer B.

```
hostname router1
!
! Required for MPLS
ip cef
!
! Define our VPN routing instance for customerA
ip vrf customerA
  rd 1000:1
  route-target both 1000:1
!
! Define our VPN Routing instance for customerB
```

```
ip vrf customerB
  rd 1000:2
  route-target both 1000:2
!
! Set up interface as a VRF link to customer router (CE)
interface fastethernet0/0
  ip vrf forwarding customerA
  ip address 172.16.1.1 255.255.255.0
!
! Set up interface as a VRF link to customer router (CE)
interface fastethernet0/1
  ip vrf forwarding customerB
  ip address 172.16.4.1 255.255.255.0
```

For our BGP configuration, we simply use the address-family ipv4 vrf command, which allows us to define what is to be redistributed. In this case, we are just redistributing the connected information, but it could be static routes, RIP, OSPF, and so on.

```
! Configure BGP for this router
router bgp 1000
  bgp log-neighbor-changes
  neighbor 10.1.1.6 remote-as 1000
  !
  address-family vpnv4
  neigbor 10.1.1.6 activate
  neighbor 10.1.1.6 send-community both
  exit-address-family
  !
  address-family ipv4 vrf customerA
  redistribute connected
  no auto-summary
  no synchronization
  exit-address-family
  !
  address-family ipv4 vrf customerB
  redistribute connected
  no auto-summary
  no synchronization
  exit-address-family
```

For Router 2, the configuration would be identical except for the IP addresses:

```
bostname Router2
!
! Required for MPLS
ip cef
!
! Define our VPN routing instance for customerA
ip vrf customerA
  rd 1000:1
  route-target both 1000:1
!
! Define our VPN Routing instance for customerB
ip vrf customerB
```

```
  rd 1000:2
  route-target both 1000:2
!
! Set up interface as a VRF link to customer router (CE)
interface fastethernet0/0
  ip vrf forwarding customerA
  ip address 172.16.2.1 255.255.255.0
!
! Set up interface as a VRF link to customer router (CE)
interface fastethernet0/1
  ip vrf forwarding customerB
  ip address 172.16.5.1 255.255.255.0
!
! Configure BGP for this router
router bgp 1000
  bgp log-neighbor-changes
  neighbor 10.1.1.4 remote-as 1000
  !
address-family vpnv4
neigbor 10.1.1.4 activate
neighbor 10.1.1.4 send-community both
exit-address-family
!
address-family ipv4 vrf customerA
redistribute connected
no auto-summary
no synchronization
exit-address-family
!
address-family ipv4 vrf customerB
redistribute connected
no auto-summary
no synchronization
exit-address-family
```

To verify our MPLS VPN configuration, we can use the following commands:

`show ip vrf`
Shows which VRFs have been defined and what interface they are on.

`show ip vrf interface`
Shows the interface information for our VRFs.

`show ip route vrf CustomerA`
Our VPNs should appear in the BGP routes.

Let's look at those commands with their output.

```
Router1#show ip vrf
  Name               Default RD        Interfaces
  CustomerA          1000:1            FastEthernet0/0
  CustomerB          1000:2            FastEthernet0/1

Router1#show ip vrf interfaces
Interface           IP-Address        VRF          Procotol
FastEthernet0/0     172.16.1.1        CustomerA    up
FastEthernet0/1     172.16.4.1        CustomerB    up
```

14

Switches and VLANs

Switches are enhanced versions of bridges. Bridges were introduced in the mid-1980s to improve network performance. They solved a basic network problem: reducing network collisions by segmenting networks. On an Ethernet segment, only one machine may transmit at once. If more than one machine tries to communicate, a collision occurs on the segment. When a collision occurs, the machines that were trying to communicate go into a random wait period before attempting to transmit again. As the number of devices on a segment increases, so does the number of collisions. And the more collisions on a segment, the worse the network performs. By using a bridge, a network is separated into segments called *collision domains*, which reduce the number of devices—and collisions— per segment.

Switches improve on bridges in one important way; switches allow the network to be partitioned into logical smaller segments called Virtual LANs or VLANs. These VLANs allow you to create even smaller domains, decreasing the likelihood of collisions and improving network performance.

Bridges and switches act almost the same way when it comes to learning MAC addresses and forwarding packets based on those addresses. Both switches and bridges implement a loop prevention protocol called *spanning tree*, described later in this chapter.

When switches were first introduced, the companies selling switches announced the death of the router! We now know that switches and routers must work together in a modern network, a fact that is confirmed by Cisco's continued purchase and development of switching technology. This chapter describes Cisco switches, with an emphasis on IOS-enabled switches.

Switch Terminology

Before we delve into the details on switches, we need to define some basic terminology.

Layer-2 and Layer-3 Switching

Most of this chapter focuses on the functionality of a layer-2 switch, a switch that operates at the Data Link layer of the OSI networking model (see the appendix for more details on the OSI model). In other words, it switches frames at the MAC address level.

However, a new switch technology is coming to its own, layer 3 switching. From the name, it's easy to guess that these switches operate at the Networking layer of the OSI model, which means it switches based on IP address. As you can see, the line between routers and switches is becoming even less defined. However, you must remember that just because a switch can operate at layer 3 and above, that doesn't make it a router. In most cases, it means that the switch can do more advanced things, like filtering based on IP access lists. However, as we said earlier, Cisco has been releasing new devices that have both routing and switching capabilities; the lines between these devices are indeed blurring.

Learning MAC Addresses

In order to improve network performance, a switch needs to discover which hosts are connected to each port. Once it has that information, it can send the traffic for a specific host out only one interface instead of clogging the rest of the ports with unnecessary traffic. In other words, the switch sends traffic only to the host that needs it.

In order to do so, the switch must learn which port a host is on. It does this by taking the source MAC address of incoming packets. As the switch learns new MAC addresses, it adds them to the address table, which you can view with the command `show mac-address-table`.

When a switch doesn't know which port a host is on, it sends the traffic out all its active ports. It continues flooding traffic out all ports until the host finally replies. At that point, the switch can add the host's MAC address to its port table. Once the host is in the table, all traffic destined for that host is sent out only that port. Each port can support multiple MAC addresses. For example, if you have a hub plugged into a port, the switch will continue to store MAC addresses for all devices on the hub.

VLAN

A VLAN is a virtual local area network, a network segment defined by a switch or router. The switch connects all ports associated with a VLAN by its internal backbone, which is located inside the switch's hardware.

You can assign any series of ports on a switch to a VLAN. For example, on a 12-port switch, we could assign ports 1–6 to VLAN 2 and ports 7–12 to VLAN 3.

Without extra configuration, these VLANs are logically separated. Devices in VLAN 2 cannot access devices in VLAN 3 and vice-versa. Each VLAN is basically a separate subnet.

Every VLAN is assigned a number, which identifies it with not only the local switch but other switches on the network. In the example we just mentioned, we said we had VLAN 2 and VLAN 3. When we talk about trunking later in this chapter, we'll see that two or more switches can be joined together and share VLAN information as if they were all on one switch.

Broadcast Domain

By default, a router doesn't forward broadcast packets. Since they don't forward broadcast packets, routers create broadcast domains. A broadcast domain is the area to which a broadcast is limited. Switches, by contrast, do forward broadcasts. A VLAN is by definition a broadcast domain, so even though a switch forwards broadcasts among devices in a particular VLAN, it doesn't forward them to other VLANs.

Collision Domain

As described earlier, a collision domain is defined by the number of devices on a particular network segment. The more devices you have on a segment, the more collisions that will occur. Luckily, each port of a switch is considered a separate collision domain. If you add only one device per switch port, this works very well. However, if you plug a hub into a switch port and then plug multiple devices into the hub, you just created a collision domain among the hosts on the segment, and the switch can't do anything to prevent collisions.

Spanning Tree Protocol

Switches and bridges implement the spanning tree protocol (STP). This protocol has one primary purpose: loop prevention. A loop is basically a network transmission that keeps getting forwarded to other segments until it comes back to the original switch, which in turn forwards it again.

 Throughout the explanation of spanning tree, you'll see the name bridge. That's because spanning tree was first developed for bridges. For the purposes of our discussion, whenever you see the word "bridge," substitute the word "switch."

To better illustrate a loop, consider the diagram in Figure 14-1, which shows Switch 1 forwarding a broadcast.

Without STP, loops can easily occur because switches have no knowledge of which frames they've already forwarded. In this example, Switch 1 forwards the broadcast to Switch 2 and Switch 3. These switches forward the broadcast back out every port except for the port on which the broadcast was originally received. The broadcast then makes it back to Switch 1, which happily broadcasts the same frame because it has no way of knowing it has already sent that broadcast out. As the cycle repeats, more copies of the same broadcast are flooded onto the network. This scenario is called a broadcast storm.

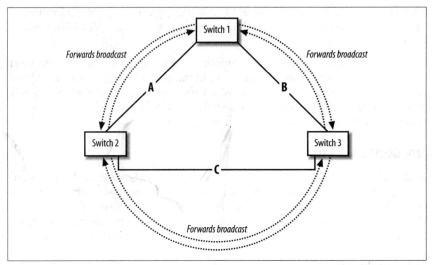

Figure 14-1. Broadcast storm

STP prevents this very situation. In a nutshell, STP builds a tree structure out of our network by removing redundant links. At the logical center of this new tree structure is the *root bridge*. Every switch on the network can access any nonlocal MAC address by forwarding frames toward the *root switch*. This tree structure—with its removal of redundant links—provides us with a loop-free network.

To understand how STP achieves this—from a very high level—we must first explain some STP terminology, including Port States and BPDUs.

Spanning Tree Port States

Consider that every active switch port can have one of the following states:

- Disabled
- Blocking
- Listening
- Learning
- Forwarding

A port is considered disabled if it has no link status or has been shut down with an IOS command. Once a port is enabled (e.g., a cable is plugged in), the port is immediately placed into the blocking state, which allows the network to stabilize before making any changes to the network.

In the blocking state, the port does not participate in frame forwarding. The port remains in the blocking state for the duration of the forward-delay timer, which is 20 seconds. If the port does not hear any messages from another switch during this period, the port switches to the listening state.

Once in the listening state, port learning and frame forwarding are still both disabled. Instead, the switch is listening for messages from other switches in order to try to determine how the network topology is configured. The listening state lasts for 15 seconds, after which the switch moves to the learning state.

In the learning state, the switch listens for station location information to add into its Filtering Database (MAC address table.). Once this state is complete, the switch port goes into the forwarding state, which is the normal operating mode of a switch in which it forwards frames.

Here are the possible transitions of port states:

- initialization → blocking
- blocking → listening or disabled
- listening → learning or disabled
- learning → forwarding or disabled
- forwarding → disabled

As you can see from this list, the disabled state can occur at any time. When a change occurs on the network, each port repeats the blocking → listening → learning → forwarding cycle. The switch cannot place a port into the disabled state by itself. Only the administrator can move a port into and out of the disabled state.

Have you ever unplugged your laptop from the network and then plugged it back in a few moments later, only to find that your network connection won't come back for about a minute? Chances are, you are plugging into a switch. That delay is STP doing its work on your port, moving it from blocking to listening to learning to forwarding. Once the port goes back into the forwarding state, your network connection is back. You can get around this delay, however; see the description of portfast later in this section.

Bridge Protocol Data Units

Every switch that speaks STP uses Bridge Protocol Data Units (BPDUs). BPDUs are messages that switches (and bridges) pass back and forth to each other in order to discover the STP network topology. Every switch sends out one of these multicast messages approximately every 2 seconds. These communications continue even after the STP network topology has been determined. If a change is detected on the network, the switches need to reconfigure the STP network.

With BPDUs, the switches establish (or *elect*) a few things on the network:

- root bridge
- root port
- designated port

STP selects the root bridge

Selecting the *root bridge* is an important process. All switches (like nearly all people) start out thinking they are the root bridge. As switches send out BPDUs, they attach their associated Bridge ID (BID). The switch with the lowest BID wins and becomes the root bridge. Part of the BID message contains the switch's MAC address and a configurable priority value. If left to the default, the switch with the lowest MAC address has the winning BID. However, you can force a switch to win the election by simply setting its priority value to a lower number than the other switches.

The root bridge selection is important because all other STP calculations are based on that choice. The root bridge becomes the logical center of our new tree structure. And as we already said, any switch on the network can reach any nonlocal MAC address by forwarding frames toward this root bridge.

Selecting a root port and a designated port

Every switch that is not the root bridge must elect a root port. The root port is the port with the lowest "cost" back to the root bridge. Table 14-1 shows the costs associated with various link types.

Table 14-1. Sample path costs

Link type	Cost
Gigabit Ethernet	4
Fast Ethernet	19
Ethernet	100

One problem with the selection of the root port is that this might not be the best or closest path to your intended destination, as we will see. In other words, just because the selected path is closest to the root bridge doesn't mean it's the closest to where you want to go.

A single *designated port* is elected for each LAN segment. One port on one switch is selected as the best path back to the root bridge. Unlike the root port, which is selected for every non-root switch, only one designated port is selected per segment. Basically, this port is the one that is placed in a forward state for the segment while the other ports on the segment are placed in blocking state. All ports that do not fall into the category of *root port* or *designated port* are put into blocking mode. By doing this, every segment (or LAN) is connected to every other segment on the network by only one path.

In Figure 14-2, the previous example has been updated with the root bridge, root ports, and designed ports. As you can see, the port connected to Switch 2 from Segment C is in forward state while the port connected to Switch 3 from Segment C is in the blocking state. This gives us only one path from Switch 2 to Switch 3, which is shown with the dotted line. Like we said before, we have only one path to the root bridge, and it's not exactly the best path to our destination, which in this case is Switch 3.

To put it another way, in order to get to our intended destination (Switch 3), we have to take the longer path to follow STP rules. While this isn't the best path, it's a small price to pay for a loop-free network.

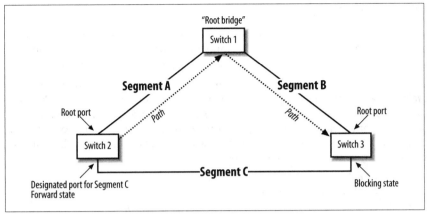

Figure 14-2. Loop-free network, thanks to spanning tree

Remember, even though Switch 3 is blocking on the Segment C port, it's still able to listen to BPDUs from Switch 2. The BPDU that it "hears" lets Switch 3 know that Switch 1 is the root bridge. And in order to get to the root bridge, Switch 2 has the best (designated) port on the segment that they share.

In summary, STP calculates three things to ensure a loop-free network:

- Root bridge election
- Root port on each non-root switch
- Designated port on each segment

By doing this, STP removes redundant links from our network. STP selects a root bridge and tells every other switch how to get back to it. Every switch can access any other nonlocal address simply by forwarding frames toward the root switch. These frames traverse the tree until they reach the final destination on our network.

In the next section, we'll learn how STP recovers if something breaks in our network. With convergence, STP rebuilds our network tree if a link goes down. In other words, one of the previously disabled redundant links will automatically become active.

Convergence in STP

Although our STP network topology has been selected, the switches keep communicating with BPDUs in case something changes. If something does change, like a switch is added or a current switch goes down, STP repeats the state cycle in order to converge the network. For example, if Switch 2 went down, Switch 3 would detect this and repeat the blocking, learning, listening state cycle, which would result in Switch 3 putting its port into the forwarding state. Once that happened, traffic would again flow from Segment C. The downside is that it takes about 50 seconds for this convergence to occur. (That works out to be 20 seconds in the blocking state if the root bridge can no longer be reached, 15 seconds for the listening state, and 15 more seconds for the learning state.)

Speeding up STP convergence

To most people, waiting 50 seconds for the switches to converge during a network change is unacceptable, so Cisco has provided a few methods to speed up STP convergence. The two methods that we cover are portfast and uplinkfast.

The portfast command tells the switch to enter the forwarding state immediately, bypassing the listening and learning states. This command should be used only on ports that are directly connected to a single device such as a server, workstation, or other end-user device (e.g., a network printer.) You should never use this on a port that connects to another switch because doing so will definitely break STP by introducing bridging loops.

```
interface fa0/11
   description port to bobs PC
   spanning-tree portfast
```

On the (older) 1900 and 2820 series switches, the portfast command is called spantree start-forward, which is actually more descriptive of what the command does by putting the switch immediately into the forwarding state.

The uplinkfast command causes an immediate switchover to another available root port when the current root port fails. The new root port is immediately switched from the blocking state to the forwarding state. By doing this, we bypass the STP calculation of selecting a new root port. This command should be used only on switches that will never be selected as the root bridge because the command changes the bridge priority to 19152, a value that assures that it will never be selected as the root bridge.

```
interface fa0/11
   spanning-tree uplinkfast
```

On the 1900 and 2820 series switches, this command is called spantree uplink-fast.

show spanning-tree

The show spanning-tree command gives you the output and status of spanning tree for the switch. In the highlighted sections of the sample output, we can see that the selected root port is port 8. If this switch were the root bridge, this line would read "We are the root of the spanning tree" because there is no root port on the root bridge. Why? Since the root port is always the port that leads toward the root bridge, we won't find any such ports on the root bridge itself.

As for the interface listing, we can see that Interface Fa0/1 is in the forwarding state. Other states you might see are disabled and blocking. Finally, the other important item is the BPDU counter, which tells us the number of BPDUs that were sent and received on this interface.

```
switch2#show spanning-tree
Spanning tree 1 is executing the IEEE compatible Spanning Tree protocol
   Bridge Identifier has priority 32768, address 0030.80ae.ce40
   Configured hello time 2, max age 20, forward delay 15
   Current root has priority 32768, address 0030.809b.9f80
```

Root port is 8, cost of root path is 19
Topology change flag not set, detected flag not set, changes 15
Times: hold 1, topology change 35, notification 2
          hello 2, max age 20, forward delay 15
Timers: hello 0, topology change 0, notification 0

Interface Fa0/1 (port 1) in Spanning tree 1 is FORWARDING
Port path cost 100, Port priority 128
Designated root has priority 32768, address 0030.809b.9f80
Designated bridge has priority 32768, address 0030.80ae.ce40
Designated port is 1, path cost 19
Timers: message age 0, forward delay 0, hold 0
BPDU: sent 211437, received 0

IOS on Switches

All Cisco switches use either IOS or CatOS as the user interface. IOS-enabled switches include the 2900XL, 2950, 3550, and 1900 series devices. These devices use the same IOS interface that routers use, with a few slight differences.

On the 1900 series (which is at the end of its product lifecycle), you must take an extra step to get to the IOS interface, navigating through a menu prompt. You press K to get to the IOS interface. For example:

```
Catalyst 1900 Management Console
Copyright (c) Cisco Systems, Inc.  1993-1998
All rights reserved.
Enterprise Edition Software
Ethernet Address:       00-B0-64-A7-85-00

PCA Number:            73-3121-04
PCA Serial Number:     FAB040231K4
Model Number:          WS-C1924-A
System Serial Number:  FAB0403VOKG
Power Supply S/N:      PHI03430376
PCB Serial Number:     FAB040231K4,73-3121-04
-------------------------------------------------

1 user(s) now active on Management Console.

        User Interface Menu

    [M] Menus
    [K] Command Line

Enter Selection:  K


        CLI session with the switch is open.
        To end the CLI session, enter [Exit].

switch1>
```

Many higher-end Catalyst series switches (4000, 5000, 5500, 6000, 6500) still run the CatOS (Catalyst OS). This interface is only vaguely similar to IOS. Like IOS, CatOS has an enable mode and show commands. However, that's where the similarities end. The CatOS uses set commands to configure the router. For example:

```
switch> (enable) set system name switch2
switch2> (enable) set ip route 0.0.0.0/0.0.0.0 172.16.1.3
switch2> (enable)
```

As you can see, the enable mode is a bit different. However, most of the commands will be familiar although their syntax and naming is totally different in most places. The good news is that Cisco is working on IOS capability for the newer models of CatOS switches. For example, the 6500 series can be configured with your choice of either CatOS or IOS. (You can easily guess which choice I would make.)

Basic Switch Configuration

Commands for IOS-enabled switches (e.g., 2900XL, 2950, 1900, and 3550) are almost identical to those on the IOS routers, which makes them fit nicely into the scope of this book. To connect a switch to the network, we must first configure the management port, as described next.

Configuring the Management Port (VLAN 1)

In order to access a switch remotely with telnet (SSH is not yet available on switches), ping, or SNMP, we need to supply a few basic pieces of information, including the IP address, subnet mask, and a default gateway.

We won't be applying the IP address to an interface; in fact, you should never configure a physical switch interface with an IP address unless it's a layer 3 switch. Instead, we apply the address to a logical interface. If you look at a default configuration of one of the IOS-based switches that we mentioned previously, you will see the physical ports, such as interface fastethernet0/1 through interface fastethernet0/24. You will also see interface VLAN 1. This does not correspond to a physical port; it is a logical port. By default, VLAN 1 is the management VLAN. Different protocols, which help to manage the network between devices such as CDP or VTP, travel over the management VLAN. When we assign an IP address to a switch, we configure it on the logical VLAN interface. You can configure the default management VLAN 1 with an IP address; however, any VLAN to which you assign an IP address becomes the management VLAN.

Figure 14-3 illustrates a very simple network, consisting only of a router and a switch. In our example network, you can imagine that we just replaced a hub with our new switch. Now that we have swapped our hub for a new switch, we need to configure it.

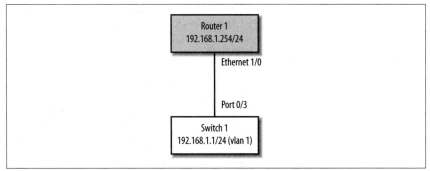

Figure 14-3. Basic switch connection to the network

Simple Switch Configuration

In this configuration, we are going to set VLAN 1 (the management VLAN for the switch) to 192.168.1.1/24 and our default gateway to the IP address of the router, which is 1921.68.1.254/24.

Here's the configuration file for Switch 1 from Figure 14-3:

```
! Set the hostname
hostname switch1

! Configure the management VLAN interface
interface VLAN1
   description Our management VLAN for the switch
   ip address 192.168.1.1 255.255.255.0
   no shutdown
!
! Set the default gateway
ip default-gateway 192.168.1.254
!
! Configure the port that connects to router1
interface fastethernet 0/3
   description Connection to router1
   no shutdown
```

No matter how trivial they may seem, interface descriptions are always important. Configuring an interface always requires a good description, not for the switch's sake but for your own sanity.

Now that we have our management VLAN configured, we can ping back and forth from the router to the switch.

```
switch1#ping 192.168.1.254

Type escape sequence to abort.
Sending 5, 100-byte ICMP Echos to 192.168.1.254, timeout is 2 seconds:
!!!!!
Success rate is 100 percent (5/5), round-trip min/avg/max = 1/2/6 ms
```

The output of the show VLAN brief command shows all the interfaces currently in VLAN 1, which is what we'd expect since we haven't yet configured them into different VLANs:

```
switch1#show VLAN brief
VLAN Name                              Status   Ports
---- -------------------------------- -------------------------------------
1    default                          active   Fa0/1, Fa0/2, Fa0/3, Fa0/4,
                                               Fa0/5, Fa0/6, Fa0/7, Fa0/8,
                                               Fa0/9, Fa0/10, Fa0/11, Fa0/12,
                                               Fa0/13, Fa0/14, Fa0/15, Fa0/16,
                                               Fa0/17, Fa0/18, Fa0/19, Fa0/20,
                                               Fa0/21, Fa0/22, Fa0/23, Fa0/24
```

The show mac-address-table command displays all the MAC addresses the switch has learned so far, which, in this case, is the MAC address of the router:

```
switch1#show mac-address-table
Dynamic Address Count:                 1
Secure Address Count:                  0
Static Address (User-defined) Count:   0
System Self Address Count:             47
Total MAC addresses:                   48
Maximum MAC addresses:                 2048
Non-static Address Table:
Destination Address  Address Type  VLAN  Destination Port
-------------------  ------------  ----  --------------------
00b0.64f3.5ae0       Dynamic         1   FastEthernet0/3
```

Auto Detection

On our interfaces, we have the ability to leave the speed and duplex settings in auto negotiate, which means that the device will try to detect and set them automatically. Unfortunately, these auto-sensing features are notoriously bad at choosing the correct setting. Furthermore, an incorrect duplex setting can result in serious network latency and intermittent connectivity.

At half duplex, it is possible for both devices to sense that the wire is available and to transmit at the exact same time, which results in a collision. Collisions are considered normal. However, more than a one percent ratio of errors to total traffic signals indicates that something else might be wrong.

At full duplex, the collisions counter is not active. A duplex mismatch causes impaired collision handling. It's always a good idea to set these values explicitly in interface configuration with the speed and duplex commands.

```
interface fastethernet 0/3
  speed 100
  duplex full
```

To verify the settings, use the show interface command, just as you would on a router:

```
switch#show interface fastethernet0/3
FastEthernet0/3 is up, line protocol is up
  Hardware is Fast Ethernet, address is 0030.809b.9f83 (bia 0030.809b.9f83)
```

```
MTU 1500 bytes, BW 100000 Kbit, DLY 100 usec, rely 255/255, load 1/255
Encapsulation ARPA, loopback not set, keepalive not set
Full-duplex, 100Mb/s, 100BaseTX/FX
ARP type: ARPA, ARP Timeout 04:00:00
...
```

 If a device is slowing down your network, check the speed and duplex settings for the switch and the device. If you see increasing CRC errors, alignment errors, or runts on your network, it could be a duplex mismatch.

Sample VLAN Configuration

In our previous example, we configured only the management VLAN for the switch (VLAN 1). To make our network more realistic, let's split our network up into four VLANs: VLAN 1, VLAN 2 (Human Resources), VLAN 3 (Development), and VLAN 4 (Sales).

Figure 14-4 shows how these VLANs will be configured in our network.

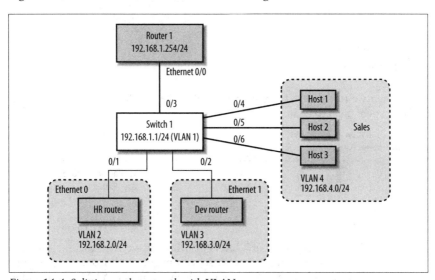

Figure 14-4. Splitting up the network with VLANs

As you can see, VLAN 2 (Human Resources) and VLAN 3 (Development) each have routers for their subnets while VLAN 4 (Sales) is simply composed of three hosts that are directly connected to the switch.

VLAN Interface Commands

To make an interface a member of a VLAN, use the switchport access command on each interface. In very simple terms, this command assigns an interface to each VLAN. The following configuration shows the switch commands for the network illustrated in Figure 14-4:

```
!
interface FastEthernet0/1
 description HR router (VLAN 2)
 switchport access VLAN 2
!
interface FastEthernet0/2
 description Development router (VLAN 3)
 switchport access VLAN 3
!
! This is our router connection from before
! no VLAN setting here - yet!
interface FastEthernet0/3
 description Connection to Router1
!
interface FastEthernet0/4
 description Sales1 (VLAN 4)
 switchport access VLAN 4
!
interface FastEthernet0/5
 description Sales2 (VLAN 4)
 switchport access VLAN 4
!
interface FastEthernet0/6
 description Sales3 (VLAN 4)
 switchport access VLAN 4
!
```

Now, when we run show VLAN brief, we see that the interfaces are in the VLANs that we expect them to be in:

```
Switch1#show VLAN brief
VLAN Name                             Status    Ports
---- -------------------------------- --------- -------------------------------
1    default                          active    Fa0/3, Fa0/7, Fa0/8, Fa0/9,
                                                Fa0/10, Fa0/11
2    VLAN0002                         active    Fa0/1
3    VLAN0003                         active    Fa0/2
4    VLAN0004                         active    Fa0/4, Fa0/5, Fa0/6
```

That's great! We've configured our VLANs just the way we want them. However, there's a big problem with this network. As you might recall from our previous discussion, each VLAN is a separate subnet, which means that VLANs 2, 3, and 4 are all logically separated. Router 1 can access only VLAN1 in this configuration, which means that the other VLANs can't access each other or Router 1. So what do we do? We need to make Router 1 a member of all VLANs. To do that, we need to employ trunking.

Trunking

Trunking allows us to connect two devices so that they can share each other's VLANs. For example, suppose you have more than one switch on your network, and you want to configure each switch so that it has ports in VLANs 1, 2, and 3. One (unrecommended) way you could accomplish this is to run a cable for each VLAN to each switch. In this way, each interface would have a port in all the

VLANs. Not only is this a waste of ports and cables, but it's terribly confusing. A much better method is to use trunking between the switches, which allows the devices to share their VLAN information easily.

Consider our previous example, with four VLANs configured on our switch. Like we just said, we could use a separate interface on the router for each VLAN. However, trunking makes this much cleaner. To better understand this concept, look at Figure 14-5.

Figure 14-5. The benefits of trunking

Figure 14-5 shows two options for connecting our VLANs to the router. On the left side, which is labeled "without trunking," you can see that we have used an extra interface and cable on the router to connect to each of the VLANs. What a mess. The much cleaner side, which is labeled "with trunking," shows that we can use subinterfaces on the already used FastEthernet 0/1 interface and enable a trunk to the switch. Each subinterface on the router is given a VLAN id. The router tags outgoing packets with the appropriate VLAN id before sending them out the trunk. When the switch receives the packets on the trunk port, it can identify the VLAN tag and easily forward to the correct VLAN.

There are two trunking protocols that we can use:

ISL
> Inter-Switch Link is a Cisco proprietary protocol, which means it only works on Cisco devices. ISL works on Ethernet, FDDI and Token Ring networks.

802.1Q
> This protocol is an industry standard that works well in mixed environments.

 Trunking works only on ports with speeds of 100 Mbps or greater, which means you can't run trunking on a 10 Mbps Ethernet connection.

By default, all ports on a switch are access ports. In order to use a port as a trunk, you must configure it with the `switchport mode trunk` command. We can also set the encapsulation type with the `switchport trunk encapsulation` command, which is set to ISL by default:

```
! This is our router connection from before
interface FastEthernet0/3
  description Connection to router 1
```

```
switchport mode trunk
! Set the trunking to 802.1q instead of ISL
switchport trunk encapsulation dot1q
!
```

Restricting VLANs on a Trunk

By default, VLANs 1–1005 for ISL and 1-4095 for 802.1q are allowed to pass over
a trunk. If you want to restrict which VLANs traverse the trunk port, you can use
the following commands to add and remove VLANs from the allowed list:

```
switchport trunk allowed VLAN remove
switchport trunk allowed VLAN add
```

In a sense, the allowed list behaves like an access-list. We can verify the allowed
VLAN list with the command show interface switchport allowed-VLAN. Here we
can see that all VLANs are automatically allowed:

```
switch1#show interface fa0/8 switchport allowed-VLAN
"ALL"
```

If we had VLANs 2–200 but we only wanted allow VLANs 150–155 through the
trunk, we could set it up like this:

```
interface fastethernet0/8
  switchport mode trunk
  switchport trunk allowed VLAN remove 2-200
  switchport trunk allowed VLAN add 150-155
```

These commands first remove all our defined VLANs from the list. We add the
VLANs we want to permit. We can now verify that this is the truly the case with
the show command:

```
switch1#show interface fa0/8 switchport allowed-VLAN
"1,150-155,201-1005"
```

VLAN 1 and VLANs 1002–1005 are reserved and cannot be
removed. The switch automatically adds those VLANs to the
allowed list.

Finishing Our Previous Network

In the previous section, we configured our switch for the multiple VLANs shown
in Figure 14-4. Now that we know about trunking, we can finish our example by
enabling trunking on the router, which allows the router to have a subinterface in
each of the switch's VLANs. This configuration is often referred to a "router on a
stick."

Here is Router 1's configuration:

```
hostname Router1
!
interface FastEthernet0/0
 no ip address
!
interface FastEthernet0/0.1
```

```
 description VLAN1 - management VLAN
 encapsulation isl 1
 ip address 192.168.1.254 255.255.255.0
 no ip redirects
!
interface FastEthernet0/0.2
 description HR VLAN 2
 encapsulation isl 2
 ip address 192.168.2.254 255.255.255.0
 no ip redirects
!
interface FastEthernet0/0.3
 description Development VLAN 3
 encapsulation isl 3
 ip address 192.168.3.254 255.255.255.0
 no ip redirects
!
interface FastEthernet0/0.4
 description Sales VLAN 4
 encapsulation isl 4
 ip address 192.168.4.254 255.255.255.0
 no ip redirects
```

Here is Switch 1's configuration. The only thing that has changed in the enabling of the trunk on FastEthernet0/3 interface, highlighted in bold. The rest of the configuration is shown for completeness.

```
hostname switch1
!
interface VLAN1
 ip address 192.168.1.1 255.255.255.0
 no ip route-cache
!
interface FastEthernet0/1
 description HR router (VLAN 2)
 switchport access VLAN 2
!
interface FastEthernet0/2
 description Development router (VLAN 3)
 switchport access VLAN 3
!
interface FastEthernet0/3
 description ISL trunk back to Router1
 switchport mode trunk
!
interface FastEthernet0/4
 description Sales1 (VLAN 4)
 switchport access VLAN 4
!
interface FastEthernet0/5
 description Sales2 (VLAN 4)
 switchport access VLAN 4
!
interface FastEthernet0/6
 description Sales3 (VLAN 4)
 switchport access VLAN 4
```

To verify our configuration, we can ping the HR and Development routers from Router 1:

```
Router1#ping 192.168.2.1

Type escape sequence to abort.
Sending 5, 100-byte ICMP Echos to 192.168.2.1, timeout is 2 seconds:
!!!!!
Success rate is 100 percent (5/5), round-trip min/avg/max = 4/4/4 ms
Router1#ping 192.168.3.1

Type escape sequence to abort.
Sending 5, 100-byte ICMP Echos to 192.168.3.1, timeout is 2 seconds:
!!!!!
Success rate is 100 percent (5/5), round-trip min/avg/max = 4/4/4 ms
```

On the switch, we can verify that the port to Router 1 is indeed trunking:

```
switch1#show interface fastethernet0/3 switchport
Name: Fa0/3
Switchport: Enabled
Administrative mode: trunk
Operational Mode: trunk
Administrative Trunking Encapsulation: isl
Operational Trunking Encapsulation: isl
Negotiation of Trunking: Disabled
Access Mode VLAN: 0 ((Inactive))
Trunking Native Mode VLAN: 1 (default)
Trunking VLANs Enabled: ALL
Trunking VLANs Active: 1-4
Pruning VLANs Enabled: NONE
```

Added Port Security

One method to secure a port is to limit the number of MAC addresses that can be detected. This feature keeps users from plugging in extra devices (with the use of a hub or switch).

To enable this feature on a 2900 or 3500 series switch, use the port security and port security max-mac-count commands. In the following example, we restrict the port to only 1 MAC address:

```
interface FastEthernet 0/2
  port security
  port security max-mac-count 1
```

We can verify our settings with the following command:

```
switch1#show port security fa0/2
Secure Port     Secure Addr    Secure Addr  Security    Security Action
                Cnt (Current)  Cnt (Max)    Reject Cnt
--------------- -------------  -----------  ----------  --------------------
FastEthernet0/2 1              1            0           Send Trap
```

To take this example a little further, we could have the switch automatically send us an SNMP trap (assuming we have SNMP set up to forward to our network management station). Or, we could have the switch just shut down the port:

```
interface FastEthernet 0/2
  port security
  port security max-mac-count 1
  port security action shutdown
  port security action trap
```

On enable port security on a 2950 or 3500 switch, the commands are a bit different:

```
interface FastEthernet 0/2
  ! enable port security
  switchport port-security
  ! set the number of mac addresses
  switchport port-security maximum 1
  ! set the action to shutdown  (other options are protect and restrict)
  switchport port-security violation shutdown
```

VLAN Trunking Protocol

VLAN Trunking Protocol (VTP) allows switches to communicate about VLANs across trunk ports (see Figure 14-6). VTP makes administration of multiple switches much easier. Once you configure a switch for a VTP domain and set its mode (to either client or server), the switches automatically begin sharing VLAN information from the server.

Figure 14-6. Trunks between switches with VTP management

VTP Modes

Switches configured with VTP have three modes: server, client, and transparent. All switches default to server mode when they are first configured for VTP. A VTP server switch can add, remove, and modify VLANs in the VLAN database. Once a change is made on a VTP server, the change is sent to all other VTP switches inside the VTP domain.

A VTP client switch pretty much just does what it's told by the VTP server switch, as long as the server is in the same VTP domain. A client cannot add, remove, or modify VLANs in the VLAN database.

In transparent mode, the switch acts as a go-between. The switch passes along VTP updates received by server switches, but the switch does not process them. A transparent switch is allowed to add, modify, and delete VLANs, but these changes remain local to the switch and are not sent out to other members of the VTP domain.

VLAN Database

To access the VLAN database and to configure VTP, use the VLAN database global command, which places you in VLAN configuration mode. In other words, this command is issued at the global command level, not in configuration mode, as this example shows:

```
switch1#VLAN database
switch1(VLAN)#?
VLAN database editing buffer manipulation commands:
  abort  Exit mode without applying the changes
  apply  Apply current changes and bump revision number
  exit   Apply changes, bump revision number, and exit mode
  no     Negate a command or set its defaults
  reset  Abandon current changes and reread current database
  show   Show database information
  VLAN   Add, delete, or modify values assoicated with a single VLAN
  vtp    Perform VTP adminsitrative functions.

switch1(VLAN)#
switch1(VLAN)#exit
APPLY completed.
Exiting....
switch1#
```

Notice two important things in this example. First, when we exited VLAN configuration mode, our changes were immediately applied. Second, we entered that command from global command (enable) mode, not configuration mode.

Why from global command level? In short, I don't understand Cisco's rationale for this choice. Maybe it's the same reason that VLAN database configuration commands are not kept with the rest of the router configuration. It doesn't make a lot of sense; you just have to know that's where it is.

As I said, VLAN database configurations are not stored with the regular configuration commands, which are stored in the startup configuration. On a 2900 series router, you can see a *VLAN.dat* file in the output of a dir command on the flash contents:

```
switch1#dir flash:
Directory of flash:

    2  -rwx      4388  Mar 01 2004 00:31:53  VLAN.dat
    8  -rwx       656  Mar 01 2004 00:29:08  config.text
```

You also see the *config.text* file, which is the switch's startup configuration. *VLAN.dat* is the file in which our VLAN configurations are actually stored.

While this state of affairs is a bit confusing, it is changing. On newer devices and newer versions of IOS, Cisco has begun to move VTP settings into the regular configuration mode. For example, on the newer 3550 switches, you get this message when you type in the vlan database command:

```
% Warning: It is recommended to configure VLAN from config mode, as VLAN
database mode is being deprecated.
```

Configuring VTP

The following are the most commonly used VTP configuration commands. All of these are demonstrated in the configuration example later in this section.

Setting the VTP mode

Every device starts out thinking it's a VTP server. It's up to you to tell it whether it's client, server, or transparent with the vtp server, vtp client, or vtp transparent commands.

Setting the VTP domain

All VTP devices operate only within their domain. For clients and servers to talk to each other, you need to configure the VTP domain with the vtp domain command.

Setting the VTP password

Setting the VTP password is optional. However, it provides a bit of security so that someone on your network can't hook up a Cisco switch and start creating havoc with your VTP databases. The command to use is vtp password.

Creating a VLAN

You can create a VLAN by simply using the VLAN *id* name *text* command. *id* is the VLAN number and *text* is the name you wish to give to the VLAN.

Configuration example

In our network in Figure 14-4, we had only one switch. However, let's say we wanted to hook up another switch to our network called Switch 2. Switch 2 will have VLANs 3 and 4 on it. We'll connect these switches together using port 0/8 on both switches. Then we'll configure those two ports as trunks.

Set port 0/8 to trunking on both switches:

```
int fastethernet 0/8
  switchport mode trunk
  no shutdown
```

And on Switch 2, we'll configure the VLAN 1 interface:

```
switch2(config)#interface VLAN1
switch2(config-if)#ip address 192.168.1.2 255.255.255.0
switch2(config-if)#no shutdown
```

When we first connect the switches, they both think that they are VTP servers. On Switch 1, we'll set it as server (which it already is) and configure the VTP domain.

```
switch1#VLAN database
switch1(VLAN)#vtp server
Device mode already VTP SERVER.
switch1(VLAN)#vtp domain xyzcorp
Changing VTP domain name from NULL to xyzcorp
switch1(VLAN)#vtp password vtppass
Setting device VLAN database password to vtppass.
switch1(VLAN)#exit
APPLY completed.
Exiting....
```

Now, configure and name the VLANs on the VTP Server, which is Switch 1:

```
switch1#VLAN database
switch1(VLAN)#VLAN 2 name HR
VLAN 2 modified:
    Name: HR
switch1(VLAN)#VLAN 3 name Development
VLAN 3 modified:
    Name: Development
switch1(VLAN)#VLAN 4 name Sales
VLAN 4 modified:
    Name: Sales
switch1(VLAN)#exit
APPLY completed.
Exiting....
```

After configuring the VLANs in the database, the output of show VLAN brief now displays the names we just assigned:

```
switch1#show VLAN brief
VLAN Name                             Status    Ports
---- -------------------------------- --------- ----------------------------
1    default                          active    Fa0/7, Fa0/9, Fa0/10, Fa0/11,
                                                Fa0/12
2    HR                               active    Fa0/1
3    Development                      active    Fa0/2
4    Sales                            active    Fa0/4, Fa0/5, Fa0/6
```

Next, we'll configure Switch 2 as a VTP client using pretty much the same commands as we used for Switch 1. The only major difference is that this switch is a client.

```
switch2#VLAN database
switch2(VLAN)#vtp client
Setting device to VTP CLIENT mode.
switch2(VLAN)#vtp domain xyzcorp
Changing VTP domain name from NULL to xyzcorp
switch2(VLAN)#vtp password vtppass
Setting device VLAN database password to vtppass.
switch2(VLAN)#exit
In CLIENT state, no apply attempted.
Exiting....
```

Now, when we run show VLAN brief on Switch 2, we find that the VLAN names have propagated:

```
Switch2#show VLAN brief
VLAN Name                          Status    Ports
---- ------------------------------ --------- ---------------------------
1    default                       active    Fa0/1, Fa0/2, Fa0/3, Fa0/4,
                                             Fa0/5, Fa0/6, Fa0/7, Fa0/9,
                                             Fa0/10, Fa0/11, Fa0/12
2    HR                            active
3    Development                   active
4    Sales                         active
```

VTP works only over trunks. Therefore, if you see the VLANs come across to the second switch, you know that you must have a valid trunk. The command is the best test of our trunking configuration. Also, as you can see, we haven't configured any ports for the VLANs yet, so everything is still in VLAN 1.

Finally, a good VTP show command:

```
switch2#show vtp counters
VTP statistics:
Summary advertisements received   : 3
Subset advertisements received    : 2
Reuqest advertisements received   : 0
Summary advertisements transmitted : 4
Subset advertisements transmitted  : 2
Request advertisements transmitted : 2
Number of config revision errors  : 0
Number of config digest errors    : 0
Number of V1 summary errors       : 0

VTP pruning statistics:
Trunk           Join Transmitted Join Received    Summary advts received from
                                                  non-pruning-capable device
-------------- ---------------- ---------------- ---------------------------
Fa0/8           0                0                0
```

Backing Up the VLAN Database

Earlier, we described how the VLAN database is stored separately from the device's starting configuration in a file called *VLAN.dat*. Even though this will probably change in the future, you can use it to your advantage now. If you want to, you can back up your VLAN database before you make any changes. If you want to revert to the previous configuration, use the following commands.

To back up the VLAN database:

```
switch2#copy flash:VLAN.dat flash:VLAN.bak
Source filename [VLAN.dat]?
Destination filename [VLAN.bak]?
4388 bytes copied in 0.131 secs
```

To recover a backed up version:

```
switch2#copy flash:VLAN.bak flash:VLAN.dat
Source filename [VLAN.bak]?
Destination filename [VLAN.dat]?
4388 bytes copied in 0.131 secs
switch2#reload
```

Switch Monitor Port for IDS or Sniffers

In order to configure an Intrusion Detection System (IDS) such as Snort (*http://www.snort.org*) or a sniffer for a switch, you need to select the interfaces or VLANs that you want to monitor. This monitoring is done with Switch Port Analyzer or (SPAN).

While the setup of SPAN differs by switch model, the same concepts are common to all switches. You select the interfaces or VLANs that you want the current port to "monitor." Any traffic sent and received out the monitored interfaces or VLANs should also be sent to your monitor port.

For example, let's assume we want to plug an IDS box into our switch on port fastethernet0/9. Our incoming Internet connection from the firewall is plugged into fastethernet0/1. This means that we want to send all incoming and outgoing traffic for fastethernet0/1 out to our IDS, which is on fastethernet0/9.

For the 2900xl/3500xl series devices, this is fairly straightforward:

```
interface FastEthernet0/9
  port monitor FastEthernet0/1
```

With this configuration, any packet transmitted or received by fastethernet0/1 is copied (mirrored) out interface fastethernet0/9. That way, our IDS box can listen to all incoming and outgoing packets and look for signs of intrusion.

We can verify this with show port monitor:

```
switch2#show port monitor
Monitor Port        Port Being Monitored
------------------  --------------------
FastEthernet0/9     FastEthernet0/1
```

On 2940, 2950, 2955, 2970, 3550, 3560, 3750 and most other series switches, you need to employ the global monitor command:

```
! Set up fastEthernet 0/1 as our SOURCE port
monitor session 1 source interface fastEthernet 0/1
! Setup fastEtherent 0/9 as our DESTINATION port
monitor session 1 destination interface fastethernet 0/9
```

On a 2950, we can have only one monitor session and we can monitor only source interfaces.

To see the monitor configuration, use the show monitor command

```
# show monitor session 1
Session 1
---------
```

```
Source Ports:
    RX Only:      None
      TX Only:       None
      Both:          Fa0/1
Destination Ports: Fa0/9
```

Troubleshooting Switches

Here are some common troubleshooting techniques to try when configuring VLANs:

- Verify physical connections and layer 2 (data link layer).
  - Is the cable plugged into the correct port?
  - Is the link light on, and if so, what color is it? (green = forwarding, yellow = blocking, blinking yellow = error)
  - Use show interface command to verify link state (up or down).
  - Verify duplex and speed settings. (Remember that autonegotiation is unreliable.)
  - Use CDP to see if the Cisco devices can see each other (see Chapter 3 for details).
  - Verify that VLAN 1 has been configured and that a default gateway has been configured.
- If your VLANs can't see each other or your edge routers, verify your router and switch configurations.
  - Is the router a member of all VLANs?
  - Do you need trunking?
  - If you have a router in each VLAN, verify the router's configuration.
- Verify VLAN configuration.
  - Is the port in the correct VLAN?
  - Is there an "allowed" statement in the trunking configuration?
  - Use show VLAN.
  - Use show interface switchport.
  - Use show spanning-tree.
- If two switches don't seem to be sharing VLAN information or are not forwarding frames, verify the VTP configuration.
  - Is trunking enabled between the two switches?
  - Are both switches using the same trunk encapsulation (ISL, dot1q, etc.)?
  - Use the show interface fastethernet0/1 switchport command to verify the trunk encapsulation.
  - Use the vtp status command to verify the domain name and revision number.

15

Router Security

Before deploying a router, you should secure it: that is, you should do everything you can to prevent the router from being misused, either by people within your own organization or by intruders from the outside. This chapter describes the first simple steps you can take toward router security; however, it's not a complete discussion by any means. I don't do anything more than point you in the right direction. For more security review and hints, you might want to look at some O'Reilly titles, especially *Hardening Cisco Routers* by Thomas Akin and *Cisco Cookbook* by Kevin Dooley and Ian J. Brown.

Securing Enable Mode Access

One of the basic security items you need to protect is access to the enable mode, which allows a user access to the router's configuration and boot information. You want to protect this mode as much as possible and give access only to people who really need it and who know what they are doing. For this section, we'll look at setting the enable password, the enable secret command (which provides additional security), and enable privilege levels.

Setting the Enable Password

The enable password grants the user access to your complete router configuration. It's much like the superuser or root password on a Unix system or like the Administrator password on Windows. It must be guarded carefully. In Chapter 3, I showed how to set the enable password:

```
Router(config)#enable password mypassword
```

The problem with setting the password this way is that mypassword is your actual password; anyone looking over your configuration files can see the password, and at that point, it's no longer a secret. Generally speaking, the accepted wisdom for managing passwords is that they should never be written down in clear text—not even in a configuration file that you think no one has access to. Obviously, there are plenty of ways for a clear-text password to leak out: for example, you might print the configuration file so you can take it home to think through some arcane route-redistribution problem and forget that the password is clearly visible to anyone hanging around the printer.

The solution to this problem is to use some sort of encryption. The simplest way to activate encryption is to use the command service password-encryption:

```
service password-encryption
enable password some-password
```

Now when you do a show configuration, your password is no longer visible in clear text:

```
Router#show configuration
version 11.3
service password-encryption
!
hostname Router1
!
enable password 7 095F41041C480713181F13253920
```

Now your password isn't clearly visible to anyone casually looking over your shoulder. However, you haven't accomplished as much as you might have hoped. The 7 in the enable password command, as it appears in the configuration file, indicates that the password has been encrypted with type 7 encryption, which is very weak. Type 7 encryption uses a simple exclusive-OR algorithm that protects the password from casual observers but does nothing to stop a determined attacker. O'Reilly's *Cisco Cookbook* includes a Perl script that easily decrypts passwords of this type, which demonstrates how easy this encryption is to defeat.

The More Secure enable secret Command

The problem with the enable password is that the encryption is so weak. Cisco soon realized that people were expecting too much from type 7 encryption and that people would post or email their configurations with the passwords intact. And as we said, the original purpose of type 7 encryption was just to keep people from glancing over your shoulder and reading the password. Today, several web sites offer password-decoding utilities that quickly decrypt type 7 encoding.

Cisco responded to this need with the enable secret command:

```
enable secret some-password
```

This command sets an enable password with a much stronger form of encryption.

 What if you've already set the enable password? In this case, when you enter the enable secret command, the router forces you to set a different password. This new password overrides the existing enable password.

Now, when we look at the configuration, we see a slightly different take on our enable password:

```
enable secret 5 $1$TbpU$nvC0m4OInOhvguatfNq5m0
```

The encrypted form of the password looks equally inscrutable. But this time, the password is encrypted using an MD5 hash (indicated by the number 5 in the configuration). This algorithm should be resistant even to determined intruders. However, don't relax. It's possible to crack the encryption used here with a brute-force dictionary attack. It's still a good idea to prevent others from seeing the encrypted password. So, for example, if you're trying to solve a problem by asking a question in a newsgroup or mailing list and you want to include your configuration, it's a good idea to remove the hashed password.

As you can see from the output of show tech-support, Cisco heeds its own advice by removing passwords from the output before you send them out:

```
hostname router1
!
enable secret 5 <removed>
!
username admin password 0 <removed>
memory-size iomem 10
```

Privilege Levels for enable access

Privilege levels allow certain users to have access to certain exec commands. Allowing users to have access to certain commands, without giving them access to everything, is often useful: for example, you can allow some users to clear a line that is hung without giving them the ability to delete the entire router configuration.

To get a better understanding of privilege levels, consider that normal user exec commands are level 1 while privileged exec mode commands (enable commands) are level 15.

To set up a privilege level, first create an enable password with a privilege level assigned to it:

```
enable secret password level 10 ourpassword
```

This command assigns the password ourpassword to privilege level 10. Next, assign commands for this level with the privilege command:

```
privilege exec level 10 clear line
privilege exec level 10 show running
privilege exec level 1 show
```

Now users can enter privilege level 10 by giving the following command, followed by the correct password when they are prompted:

```
Router>enable 10
```

After entering the password, a user can give the commands clear line and show running, but not other privileged mode commands.

Routine Security Measures

Now that we examined how we can protect enable mode, it's time to look at securing the rest of the router. If the router is directly connected to the Internet, there are many, many security items we need to review. If the router is connected to a neighbor's network—but not fully trusted—there are still quite a few security items to consider. In this section, we'll review features that should be disabled or enabled for security reasons.

Features to Disable

A gateway router is the most vulnerable to attacks, especially if it sits outside your firewall. Table 15-1 lists a number of services that should be disabled to heighten security. The Level column shows whether the command is part of the global configuration or needs to be applied to specific interfaces.

Table 15-1. Features to disable on the router for heightened security

Command	Level	Resulting action
no cdp enable	Interface	Disables CDP at the interface level. You don't want untrusted networks to learn any extra information about your router. CDP is very helpful, so disable it only on interfaces that are connected to untrusted networks.
no ip proxy-arp	Interface	Ignores incoming ARP requests for hosts within the network.
no ip directed-broadcast	Interface	Disables translations of directed broadcasts to physical broadcasts.
no ip unreachables	Interface	Disables ICMP unreachable messages on an interface.
no ip redirects	Interface	Disables redirect messages. A redirect message is generated to another device when a datagram is sent out over the same interface through which it was received. The redirect message tells the sending host that it should have been able to get to the destination without going through the router. Redirects have played a role in a number of attacks, so it's safest to disable them.
no ip source-route	Global	Causes the router to discard any packet with source-route information. Presumably, we don't want hosts telling our router how to route the traffic.
no service finger	Global	Disables the finger daemon on the router. Finger has always been a problem source; it lets attackers know who is logged in and provides the user's real username. Now all they need is a password!
no service udp-small-servers no service tcp-small-servers	Global	Disables all small UDP and TCP services on your router (*echo*, *chargen*, and some others). These are services that outsiders shouldn't see anyway.

Features to Enable

As we said before, a gateway router—one that connects to the Internet or one that connects to another untrusted network—needs more security than an internal router. In the previous section, we looked at features to disable in order to increase security.

Table 15-2 lists the features you might want to enable on your router.

Table 15-2. Features to enable on the router for heightened security

Command	Level	Resulting action
`exec-timeout`	Line	Kills idle VTY sessions. Default is 10 minutes.
`ip http authentication` `ip http access-class`	Global	If you are using the http configuration on the router, you should protect it with authentication and an access list that restricts which machines can access the HTTP server. Or even easier, you can just shut down the http configuration altogether with the `no ip http` command.
`ip verify unicast reverse-path`	Interface	Verifies that a packet's return path is the same as the interface it arrived on. This attempts to stop IP address spoofing. However, be careful; this might cause problems in networks with asymmetric paths. (Requires CEF; see Chapter 17 for more details.)
`ip route 0.0.0.0 0.0.0.0` `null 0 255`	Global	A static route that quickly throws away packets with invalid destinations.
`scheduler-interval` `scheduler allocate`	Global	Allows time for important router processes during time of floods.
`service password-encryption`	Global	Provides some password protection.
`service tcp-keepalives-in`	Global	Attempts to kill orphaned or inactive sessions to the router.
`snmp-server community <password>`	Global	For years, people have been using "public" and "private" as their SNMPv1 passwords. Set both the read and write password to something unique. Or better yet, use SNMPv3.
`spanning-port portfast`	Switch Interfaces	If you know a switch port is always going to be connected to an end-user device, you can configure this command, which keeps the port from going through spanning tree. Although this isn't technically a security command, it does provide a degree of switch security by keeping users from starting an STP cycle.
`transport input`	Line	Controls which protocols can be used to connect to VTY or TTY ports. (Use SSH, as described later in this chapter.)

Deny local IP addresses coming from outside

If we get a packet from outside our network that bears a local IP address (see RFC 1918), we know that, at best, it's invalid and, at worst, it's forged. Either way we should drop such packets. A simple access list will throw these away:

```
! See warning about this list in the next paragraph
access-list 110 deny ip 172.16.0.0 0.15.255.255 any
access-list 110 deny ip 192.168.0.0 0.0.255.255 any
access-list 110 deny ip 10.0.0.0 0.255.255.255 any
access-list 110 permit ip any any
!
interface serial 1
  Ip access-group 100 in
```

This access list is just an example of denying the local IP addresses. As a security example, however, this access list is extremely deficient because it allows all traffic into our network. For a real example of providing a decent access list on your edge router, see "Building a Gateway Router" in Chapter 7.

Use a warning banner

To properly secure a machine, you need to supply a warning banner. The banner doesn't actually do anything to protect the router, but it does warn people who are connecting to the router that unauthorized access is taken seriously. That way, they can't use the excuse that they didn't know. It's a good idea to ask for legal help in crafting an appropriate message.

The following commands create a warning banner:

```
! Apply a warning banner.
! Seek legal advice to craft a banner to properly protect your network
banner login ^C
          #### WARNING ####
          Authorized Access ONLY!
All connections are logged and monitored. Any unauthorized
use will be prosecuted to the fullest extent of the law. If
you do not agree to these conditions, disconnect now.
^C
```

AutoSecure: Letting the Router Do the Work

With the release of IOS 12.3, Cisco has provided a command that essentially locks down your router with a simple command. When you run the auto secure command, the router asks a series of questions and then modifies the configuration as it sees fit, applying as many security enhancements as it can.

```
Router#auto secure
              --- AutoSecure Configuration ---

*** AutoSecure configuration enhances the security of
the router but it will not make router absolutely secure
from all security attacks ***

All the configuration done as part of AutoSecure will be
shown here. For more details of why and how this configuration
is useful, and any possible side effects, please refer to Cisco
documentation of AutoSecure.
At any prompt you may enter '?' for help.
Use ctrl-c to abort this session at any prompt.

Gathering information about the router for AutoSecure

Is this router connected to internet? [no]: yes
Enter the number of interfaces facing internet [1]: 1
Interface              IP-Address      OK? Method Status
Protocol
Ethernet0/0            192.168.0.100   YES NVRAM  up
up
```

```
Loopback0                   192.168.1.1      YES NVRAM  up
up
Enter the interface name that is facing internet: ethernet0/0

Securing Management plane services..
Disabling service finger
Disabling service pad
Disabling udp & tcp small servers
Enabling service password encryption
Enabling service tcp-keepalives-in
Enabling service tcp-keepalives-out
Disabling the cdp protocol
Disabling the bootp server
Disabling the http server
Disabling the finger service
Disabling source routing
Disabling gratuitous arp
Enter the new enable password:
Confirm the enable password:
Configuring aaa local authentication
Configuring console, Aux and vty lines for
local authentication, exec-timeout, transport
Securing device against Login Attacks
...
```

This sample is only a small portion of the command's output. To review the output later, use the command show auto secure config, which displays all the configuration changes that AutoSecure made on the router. For a production router, I don't recommend running this command. But if you have a new router, you might want to use AutoSecure as a starting place for your new configuration. In this way, you know you'll be starting out with the most secure router configuration possible.

To see the entire list of what AutoSecure will configure on your router, see Cisco's AutoSecure web page at *http://www.cisco.com/en/US/products/sw/iosswrel/ps5187/products_feature_guide09186a008017d101.html#wp1027184.*

Restricting Access to Your Router

The ability to remotely administer your router is a very important feature. However, you want to restrict access as much as possible to keep intruders out. Aside from configuring your firewall to deny access to routers, we can configure the router to allow access only in specific ways. Sometimes the people you want to keep off your routers are users on your local network. We'll examine user authentication and passwords to restrict access to the router.

Virtual Terminal Access

The virtual terminal (VTY) configuration on your router defines how incoming connections to your router are handled. For example, we can configure the types of protocols are allowed (telnet versus SSH) to connect to our devices.

Protecting VTY with an access list

When you telnet or ssh to your router, you connect to a VTY. This terminal lets you configure your router over the network without a physical connection to the console port. This capability is extremely useful but also dangerous: if you can configure your router over the network, so can anyone else with the appropriate password. One way to make the router more secure is to apply an access list to the VTY ports. This list should allow connections only from certain hosts. The following commands restrict telnet access to the 192.168.1.5 machine (we'll talk about SSH in the next section). We also apply an exec-timeout, which disconnects idle connections:

```
! Define the access list
access-list 5 permit 192.168.1.5 0.0.0.0
access-list 5 deny any log
!
line vty 0 4
  ! Only allow telnet
  tranport input telnet
  ! Apply our access list for incoming connections
  access-class 5 in
  ! Finally, apply an exec-timeout, which will disconnect an idle connection
  ! The timeout is 10 minutes and 0 seconds
  exec-timeout 10 0
```

 Here's a cool tip. The line in bold logs all failed authorization attempts to your router. The log will contain the user's IP address, which is pretty useful if you want to track down who's trying to access your router without permission.

Allowing SSH connections to the router

In the previous example, we used the command `transport input telnet`, which allowed only telnet access to our router. Once this was quite acceptable, but times have changed and telnet's security limitations are now well known. SSH is now the standard method for connecting to remote devices.

Enabling SSH

To enable SSH on our router (in this case, running IOS 12.2), we need to enable SSH, configure RSA keys, set a hostname, and set the IP domain name. After SSH is enabled, we are going to restrict our VTY access to SSH only.

First we enable SSH and set the hostname and domain name:

```
Router(config)#ip ssh
Router(config)#hostname router1
router1(config)#ip domain-name xyz.com
```

Next we create the RSA keys:

```
router1(config)#crypto key generate rsa
The name for the keys will be: router1.xyz.com
Choose the size of the key modulus in the range of 360 to 2048 for your
  General Purpose Keys. Choosing a key modulus greater than 512 may take
  a few minutes.
```

Router
Security

```
How many bits in the modulus [512]:
Generating RSA keys ...
[OK]

router1(config)#end
router1#
00:18:57: %SSH-5-ENABLED: SSH 1.5 has been enabled
00:18:59: %SYS-5-CONFIG_I: Configured from console by console
```

We can verify our SSH configuration with the show ip ssh command.

```
router1#show ip ssh
SSH Enabled - version 1.5
Authentication timeout: 120 secs; Authentication retries: 3
```

All that's left is to restrict our VTY access to SSH:

```
line vty 0 4
 login
 password somepassword
 transport input ssh
```

Users and Authentication

Usernames are optional: many routers by default have no usernames and only a single password, which is given to everyone who needs access to the router. However, doing without usernames has obvious problems: you can never tell who is logged in, who just rebooted the router, or who is responsible for the configuration changes that broke your Internet connection. Usernames and passwords make it possible to trace who has done what; they add a sense of accountability and allow more fine-grained control over what individuals are allowed to do.

There are several methods for adding users; the more advanced methods allow accounting (tracking what a particular user actually did) as well as authorization (merely verifying that a user has permission to do something). First, let's look at the easiest way to add users to a router's configuration.

Adding users with the user command

Throughout this book, we have added username and password pairs to the router configuration itself. For example, we can add the users Patty and Pete to the router's configuration with the username command:

```
! First, enable password encryption to "hide" the
! clear-text passwords in the configuration
service password-encryption
! Now define the passwords
username patty password patty1
username pete password pete2
```

Patty's password is now patty1, and Pete's password is pete2.*

---

* These passwords are clearly weak and are used here only for clarity of the illustration. You would use a stronger password to protect your routers and educate users to do likewise.

When we display the router's configuration, we see the passwords in their encrypted form:

```
username pete password 7 0831495A0C4B
```

To tell the VTY to use the usernames that you have listed with the username command, we need to use the login local command. This command is considered the old way of enabling local authentication. The new way is with the AAA commands, which we cover in the next section.

```
! this is the old way of enabling local authentication.
line vty 0 4
 login local
 ! restrict inbound connections to ssh only
 transport input ssh
```

For reference, the AAA equivalent command for the above example is:

```
aaa new-model
aaa authentication login default local
```

Now that the passwords are in the configuration, Patty and Pete can log in when they connect to the router. That was certainly simple. But this method doesn't scale—it's not manageable if you need to work with more than a few users and one or two routers. What if you're managing a worldwide corporate network with hundreds of routers and dozens of administrators? What if you're managing an ISP with thousands of dial-up users? In either case, you have a long list of usernames and passwords that needs to be maintained on several different machines. How do you keep the lists in sync? How would you even keep them up to date?

There is a better way. Make a central authentication repository using an authentication protocol, and configure the router to use the authentication server. There are several different protocols that you can use, but the most popular are TACACS+ and Radius, both of which use the AAA framework.

Using the AAA framework

The authentication, authorization, and accounting model (AAA) is a framework for providing authentication and accounting services across a network. It requires the support of another protocol—typically, Radius or TACACS+. Radius is an open standard that is supported by a wide range of devices and vendors. Both Radius and TACACS+ encrypt sensitive data.

Radius and TACACS+ are both supported by the CiscoSecure product. If you wish to use that product for your AAA configurations, you can find out more information on Cisco's website. Or you can use a Radius server, which you should be able to find in both free and commercial versions. For example, for a Linux box, you could look at *http://www.freeradius.org* (other free Radius servers are also available). Windows 2000 and Windows Server 2003 include a Radius server. For other platforms, a quick Google search will lead you to several Radius servers.

The rest of this section deals with the configuration on the router side using AAA to communicate with a Radius or TACACS+ server.

User management with AAA

The first step is to enable AAA on the router with the command aaa new-model:

```
! This is required to use the AAA method
aaa new-model

! Configure the Radius server
radius-server host 10.10.1.2
radius-server key somepassword
```

Next we set up the list of authentication services we want to use with the command aaa authentication. In this example, we are setting the name of the list to the default, which tells the router to use this list for all lines and interfaces. If we assign a name other than the default, we must explicitly reference that name in the line configuration (we will do this in an upcoming example). In this list, we tell the router to attempt to authenticate with the Radius server. If it can't connect, it should use the enable password as a backup:

```
aaa authentication login default radius enable
```

The next step defines the authorization for the user, specifying what the person is allowed to do on the system. In this case, we are going to grant the user access to the router's command line with the command exec:

```
aaa authorization exec default group radius none
```

The final piece is the accounting, which can log user activity to the Radius server. In this example, we are going to log the starting and stopping of any commands performed by the user. The value 15 is the privilege level of the commands to log.

```
aaa accounting commands 15 default start-stop group radius
```

Restricting dial-in user access with AAA

While we are reviewing AAA access to our devices, we should consider using it for our dial-in configurations as well. In this sample configuration, we show a group of eight lines configured for dial-in access. The AAA configuration items are highlighted in bold. The rest of the configuration is here for completeness. Refer to Chapter 17 for more information on those commands.

```
! Configure AAA
aaa new-model
aaa authentication login default radius local
aaa authentication ppp default if-needed radius
aaa authorization network radius
!
! Define our pool of addresses for dialup users
ip local pool pool1 10.10.1.100 10.10.1.108
!
!
interface Group-Async1
 ip unnumbered Ethernet0
 encapsulation ppp
 async mode interactive
 peer default ip address pool pool1
```

```
! Take our security advice on disabling CDP on interfaces
! that don't need it
no cdp enable
ppp authentication chap
group-range 1 8
!
!
! Configure the lines connected to the modes
line 1 8
 autoselect ppp
 autoselect during-login
 modem dialin
 transport input all
 stopbits 1
 rxspeed 115200
 txspeed 115200
 flowcontrol hardware
```

16

Troubleshooting and Logging

This chapter includes a grab bag of techniques for troubleshooting and monitoring your router. The two tasks are closely related: it's impossible to figure out what's going wrong if you don't have good logs that show what the router was trying (or failing) to do. We'll start with ping and trace, two tools that are available on virtually any computer that can connect to a network.

ping

ping tests network connectivity by sending an ICMP echo-request message to the remote machine. The remote machine must respond with an ICMP reply message. The ping command takes a single argument: the address or hostname of the remote system. It prints various statistics about the responses it receives:

```
Router>ping 10.10.1.2
Type escape sequence to abort
Sending 5, 100-byte ICMP Echos to 10.10.1.2, timeout is 2 seconds:
!!!!!
Success rate is 100 percent (5/5), round-trip min/avg/max = 1/2/4 ms
Router>
```

Each exclamation point indicates that the router has successfully received a response from the remote host. On a local network, you would expect a success rate very close to 100%. Across the Internet, you would tolerate some failures, but they should still be relatively rare. Many sites configure their routers to block ICMP traffic because it has been used in a number of denial-of-service attacks. Therefore, you can't count on the ability to ping an arbitrary host on the Internet.

 If ping locks up, you can abort by typing Ctrl+^ then x.

If you don't give the hostname on the command line, the router prompts you for it, and for other information. You can specify the number of packets to send, the number of seconds to wait for a response before assuming that the ping has failed, the amount of data to include in the packet, and more:

```
Router>ping
  Protocol [ip]: ip              We are doing IP only
  Target IP address: 10.10.1.    The host we want to ping
2
  Repeat count [5]: 10           Number of pings to be sent to the
                                 destination
  Datagram size [100]:           The actual size of the packet in bytes
  Timeout in seconds [2]:        Timeout value
  Extended commands [n]:         See the Privileged Ping Commands
  Sweep range of sizes [n]:      Changes the packet size as it pings

Type escape sequence to abort.
Sending 10, 100-byte ICMP Echos to 10.10.1.2, timeout is 2 seconds:
!!!!!!!!!!
Success rate is 100 percent (10/10), round-trip min/avg/max = 1/3/4 ms
```

Here we changed the repeat count to 10, which sent 10 ping packets to our destination.

Ping the Broadcast Address

If you want to discover what hosts are active on your subnet, you can ping the network's broadcast address. All nodes on the subnet should respond. Since this tool can be used for malicious purposes, it is available only from the privileged level. For example, if our ethernet0 interface were on the 192.168.1.0/24 subnet, we could ping the broadcast address of that network:

```
Router#ping 192.168.1.255
```

The output will show the responses from all the hosts on the subnet. Another way to find out which hosts the router knows about is to display its ARP table:

```
Router#show ip arp
```

This command lists all the machines from which the router has seen packets.

Extended ping

Extended ping provides more options than the basic ping command. These options can be used to better diagnose a network connectivity problem. To enter the extended ping mode, type the ping command, then type y at the "Extended commands" prompt:

```
Extended commands [n]: y
Source address or interface: 192.168.1.1
Type of service [0]:
Set DF bit in IP header? [no]:
Validate reply data? [no]:
Data pattern [0xABCD]:
Loose, Strict, Record, Timestamp, Verbose[none]:
```

```
Sweep range of sizes [n]:
Type escape sequence to abort.
Sending 5, 100-byte ICMP Echos to 192.168.1.1, timeout is 2 seconds:
!!!!!
Success rate is 100 percent (5/5), round-trip min/avg/max = 4/4/4 ms
```

The most useful of the extended commands is Source address or interface. This command lets you specify the source address that will be used in constructing the packet; you can specify either the IP address or the name of the interface from which the IP address will be taken. Normally, the router sets the packet's source IP address to the interface that was used to send the ICMP packet, based on the routing table.

What can we test with the source address?

Setting the source address of the ICMP packet allows you to test network connectivity more thoroughly. The host that receives the ICMP packet must reply to the source address given in the packet. This generally means that the remote host replies to the address of the interface through which the packet was sent. But by setting another source address, we can direct the ICMP reply to another address. Consider Figure 16-1.

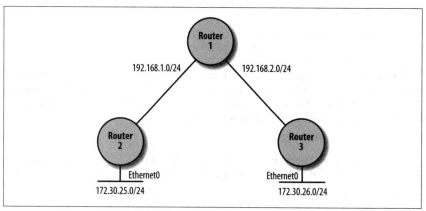

Figure 16-1. Using the source address in extended pings

If Router 2 pings Router 3, the source address of the ICMP packet defaults to the address of the interface closest to Router 3—i.e., the interface on the 192.168.1.0/24 network. If this ping succeeds, we know Router 3 can get to the 192.168.1.0 network. But what if we want to test whether Router 3 knows how to get to the 172.30.25.0/24 subnet? To execute this test, we perform an extended ping on Router 2 while using the source address on ethernet0:

```
Router#ping
Protocol [ip]:
Target IP address: 172.30.26.1
Repeat count [5]:
Datagram size [100]:
Timeout in seconds [2]:
Extended commands [n]: y
```

```
Source address or interface: ethernet0
Type of service [0]:
Set DF bit in IP header? [no]:
Validate reply data? [no]:
Data pattern [0xABCD]:
Loose, Strict, Record, Timestamp, Verbose[none]:
Sweep range of sizes [n]:
Type escape sequence to abort.
Sending 5, 100-byte ICMP Echos to 172.30.26.1, timeout is 2 seconds:
!!!!!
Success rate is 100 percent (5/5), round-trip min/avg/max = 4/4/4 ms
```

This successful ping proves two things. First, the pings obviously made it to 172.30.26.1. This shows that routing is working on Router 2, at least to a minimal extent. If routing were not working, Router 2 wouldn't know how to send a packet to 172.30.26.1, to which it doesn't have a direct connection. Second, the pings also made it back to Router 2's ethernet0 interface, which is on the 172.30.25.0/24 subnet. This proves that some form of routing is working on Router 3—otherwise, it wouldn't know how to get to the 172.30.25.0/24 subnet. If this test failed, it would indicate that either Router 2 did not know how to get to Router 3's network, or Router 3 did not know how to get to Router 2's network.

While this test is useful, it isn't perfect. Even if the packet returns, we really don't know how it made it back. In a more complex network, there may be many ways for a packet to make it from Router 3 back to Router 2. Using the source address doesn't actually prove that a certain network is up or down, but it's helpful as a quick test.

trace

trace (also known as "traceroute" on Unix systems or "tracert" on Windows systems) tries to discover the actual path a packet takes to a selected destination. On Unix, it accomplishes this by using the TTL (time to live) field of a UDP packet. On Microsoft platforms, ICMP is used instead of UDP. The TTL is the number of hops a packet is allowed to take before the network gives up the delivery attempt and returns an error message to the sender. Each hop through a router decrements the TTL counter until the TTL hits 0, at which time the router returns the packet to the originator with a "TTL expired" error. Three packets are sent for each TTL because there's no guarantee that all will make the journey.

trace starts by sending a packet to a UDP port on the destination with a TTL of 1. The UDP port is unimportant as long as it's not being used by the destination. Cisco routers pick a default port of 33434. When the packet hits the first router, it is returned. The host from which the packet was returned (the source address of the returned packet) is the first gateway between your router and the destination. trace then sends out a second packet with a TTL of 2. This packet will make it to the second router along the path to the destination, which then returns it. This router is the second gateway in our trace. This process is repeated until the destination is reached and a "port unreachable" message is returned. Figure 16-2 shows this process.

Figure 16-2. Using TTLs to trace the route to a destination

Here's what the output from a trace command looks like:

```
Router#trace sphinx
Tracing the route to sphinx (10.10.3.1)
  1 rtr1 (10.10.1.1) 8msec 8msec 4msec
  2 rtr2 (10.10.2.1) 8msec 8msec 4msec
  3 sphinx (10.10.3.1) 10msec 10msec 10msec
```

Debugging

Almost every aspect of the router's configuration can have debugging enabled. For example, we could say:

```
debug chat
```

With debugging on, any chat script activity is logged to the router's console (or to the syslog server, if configured). To disable logging, use the undebug command:

```
undebug chat
```

If you forget what debugging you turned on, use the undebug all command to turn all debugging off:

```
undebug all
```

There is a debug all command, but—unless you have major problems—there is rarely a good need for it. When it is executed, all debug information possible is flooded to your screen. You'll be overwhelmed with data, even if logging is enabled. The best practice is to activate debugging only for the items in which you're interested.

Using Debugging in Practice

The debug command is an extremely powerful troubleshooting tool. Assume that you have a serial interface on a router named Baltimore. At the other end of this interface is a router named New-York with an IP address of 10.1.2.55. You are having trouble communicating with the New-York router. One strategy for analyzing the problem is to enable IP packet debugging on the Baltimore router to see if packets from New-York are arriving. To do so, use the command debug ip packet:

```
baltimore#debug ip packet
IP packet debugging is on
baltimore#
IP: s=10.1.2.55 (Serial0), d=255.255.255.255, len 72, rcvd 2
IP: s=10.1.2.29 (Serial1), d=255.255.255.255, len 72, rcvd 2
IP: s=10.1.2.97 (local), d=255.255.255.255 (Ethernet0), len 72, sending
broad/multicast
IP: s=10.1.2.66 (local), d=255.255.255.255 (Serial0), len 72, sending
broad/multicast
IP: s=10.1.2.93 (local), d=255.255.255.255 (Serial1), len 72, sending
broad/multicast
IP: s=10.1.2.55 (Serial0), d=255.255.255.255, len 72, rcvd 2
IP: s=10.1.2.29 (Serial1), d=255.255.255.255, len 72, rcvd 2
baltimore#undebug ip packet
```

 This command is very dangerous: it produces a great deal of output and could render a busy router useless. The problem arises because logging debug messages takes priority in IOS. To get around this problem, we could use an access list to limit which packets are displayed. We will cover that trick in a moment.

The s field in the output indicates the source of the packets. This short transcript shows that we've received packets from a number of hosts, including two packets from the New-York router's IP address. Therefore, we are capable of receiving from the other end. Now that we have confirmed that we have communication between the two sites, we can troubleshoot other items, such as our routing configuration.

A safer way to use this command—one that doesn't risk overwhelming the router with its logging duties—is to combine the debug command with an access list that limits which packets get displayed. In the following example, we set up an access list that controls which packets are logged:

```
baltimore(config)#access-list 1 permit 10.1.2.0 0.0.0.255
baltimore(config)#end
baltimore#debug ip packet 1
IP packet debugging is on for access list 1
```

This command is still somewhat dangerous because you still don't know how much traffic will make it through the access list. But it's significantly less likely to cause problems than enabling packet debugging without some form of access control. Other debug commands aren't as dangerous; we can enable them with some level of confidence that the router won't be overworked. For example, let's debug RIP packets:

```
baltimore#debug ip rip
RIP protocol debugging is on
1d07h: RIP: sending v1 update to 255.255.255.255 via Ethernet0 (10.1.2.97)
1d07h:       subnet 10.1.2.192, metric 1
1d07h:       subnet 10.1.2.64, metric 1
1d07h: RIP: sending v1 update to 255.255.255.255 via Serial0 (10.1.2.66)
1d07h:       subnet 10.1.2.192, metric 1
1d07h:       subnet 10.1.2.96, metric 1
```

```
1d07h: RIP: sending v1 update to 255.255.255.255 via Serial1 (10.1.2.93)
1d07h:      subnet  10.1.2.96, metric 1
1d07h:      subnet  10.1.2.64, metric 1
baltimore#undebug ip rip
RIP protocol debugging is off
```

This output shows that we are sending RIP updates from each of our active interfaces. The next step is to see whether the end routers are receiving the updates. To check, you can turn on debugging on the remote routers, continuing until you have discovered the problem.

There are debug commands for just about everything within the router. When you need help, use the debug ? command to get you started. If you forget what you enabled, always remember that undebug all disables all debug output.

The debug list command

The debug list command allows us to apply an access list or interface to a specific debug command. It's an effective way to control the load debugging places on your router and to limit the amount of debugging output you have to look through. This command takes an access list number or an interface name as an argument; it applies to the next debug statement. For example, assume that we're using EIGRP for routing and we're having problems communicating with the router at 10.1.1.1. We could use the command debug ip eigrp, but that would bombard us with output for all the EIGRP routers. Instead, we first create an access list that permits traffic from 10.1.1.1. We then use the debug list command to apply the access list to the following debug statement. Finally, we can give the command debug ip eigrp:

```
router1#undebug all
router1#config terminal
router1(config)#access-list 10 permit host 10.1.1.1
router1(config)#exit
router1#debug list 10
router1#debug ip eigrp
IP-EIGRP Route Events debugging is on
          for access list: 10
```

The router responds by saying that EIGRP route event debugging is enabled for access list 10.

The debug list command can also apply to specific interfaces. In the next example, we limit the output from the debug ip eigrp command to EIGRP traffic through ethernet0:

```
router1#undebug all
router1#debug list ethernet0
router1#debug ip packet
IP-EIGRP Route Events debugging is on
          for interface: ethernet0
```

You can apply a debug list to just about any debugging command.

Logging

The router can display logging messages on the terminal, store them in a buffer on the router, or send them to a log server using syslog (syslog is standard on Unix systems, and available for Windows*). You can control how much logging information is collected by using severity levels. For example, you can say that all messages should be sent to the log server regardless of severity, but that only critical messages should be displayed on a console.

Configuring Logging

By default, logging is disabled. If you want to log the router's activity, you must start by enabling logging:

```
logging on
```

We can now configure the syslog server. On a Unix system, you configure syslog by editing the /etc/syslog.conf file. On Windows, the configuration process depends on the software you use. No matter what operating system you run it on, each log file is associated with a facility and a severity. For example, the syslog.conf file might contain the following entry:

```
local5.debug        /var/adm/local5.log
```

This means that messages coming from the user-defined facility local5, with a severity debug (or greater), should be saved in the file /var/adm/local5.log. Since debug is the lowest possible severity, this statement means that we will log all messages from the local5 facility. On the router, the following commands start logging:

```
! Enable timestamps for all log messages and debug with a time and date
stamp.
! The localtime keyword lists the time in local time instead of UTC
service timestamps log datetime localtime
service timestamps debug datetime localtime
! Set the syslog server's IP address
logging host 10.10.1.2
! Limit the log messages to informational and higher
logging trap informational
! Set the facility name on the syslog server
logging facility local5
```

The final two commands are the most important. The logging trap command says that we're interested in messages with a severity of informational or higher. The logging facility command says that, when the router generates a message, it should be tagged with the facility local5. The facility name you use must match one of the facilities configured on the server.

* One source for syslog for Windows is Kiwi Syslog Daemon (*http://www.kiwisyslog.com*). Search on "syslog and Windows" at *http://www.download.com* to find a number of others.

Severity Levels

Syslog keeps track of messages using eight severity levels, listed in Table 16-1. If you set logging to any particular level, all messages at that level and above will be logged.

Table 16-1. Severity levels

Level	Name	Syslog translation	What it means to you
0	Emergencies	LOG_EMERG	System unusable
1	Alerts	LOG_ALERT	Immediate action required
2	Critical	LOG_CRIT	Critical condition
3	Errors	LOG_ERR	Error condition
4	Warnings	LOG_WARNING	Warning
5	Notifications	LOG_NOTICE	Normal significant conditions
6	Informational	LOG_INFO	Just FYI messages
7	Debugging	LOG_DEBUG	Debugging output

Buffering Logging and Debug Output

Some other logging commands provide control over how log messages are handled. The first one we will look at is logging buffered, which gives us some control over chatty debug output. For example, if you enable debugging for EIGRP with the command debug ip eigrp, you're in for a lot of logging in the console window. However, you can disable console logging and enable buffered logging with the following commands:

```
router#config terminal
router(config)#no logging console
router(config)#logging buffered
```

Now when you enable debugging, all the log messages will be stored in the logging buffer instead of scrolling past on the screen. The default size of the logging buffer is platform-specific, but you can change the size by adding a byte count to the end of the logging buffered command. The buffer size can be from 4,096 to 4,294,967,295 bytes, but sizes toward the upper end of this range are obviously impractical.

To view the buffer, use the show logging command:

```
router#show logging
Syslog logging: enabled (0 messages dropped, 0 flushes, 0 overruns)
    Console logging: disabled
    Monitor logging: level debugging, 0 messages logged
    Buffer logging: level debugging, 65356 messages logged
    Trap logging: level informational, 86 message lines logged

Log Buffer (4096 bytes):
1w5d: IP: s=10.1.5.1 (local), d=224.0.0.10 (BRIO), len 60, sending
broad/multicast
```

```
1w5d: IP: s=10.1.5.1 (local), d=224.0.0.10 (BRIO), len 60, encapsulation
failed
1w5d: IP: s=10.1.3.1 (Serial0), d=224.0.0.10, len 60, rcvd 2
```

If the log buffer fills up with too much junk, you can clear it with the command
clear logging:

```
router#clear logging
```

This command clears the buffer, which allows you to start over.

XML Output of Logging Messages

Starting with IOS 12.2(15)T, syslog messages can be formatted in XML, which is
convenient for parsing log messages with other software. As we have seen, our
logging messages usually look like this:

```
1w0d: %SYS-5-CONFIG_I: Configured from console by console
```

With XML formatting, our log messages look like this:

```
<ios-log-msg><facility>SYS</facility><severity>5</severity><msg-id>CONFIG_I
</msg-id><time>1w0d</time><args><arg id="0">console</arg></ios-log-msg>
```

To enable XML logging to the buffered logs on the router, use these commands:

```
Router#config terminal
Router(config)#logging buffered xml
Router(config)#end
```

We can verify the setting with the show logging xml command, which shows the
logging settings and our buffered log messages. The two logging messages shown
here are highlighted in bold.

```
Router#show logging xml
<syslog-logging status="enabled" msg-dropped="0" msg-rate-limited="1"
flushes="0" overruns="0"><xml>enabled</xml><filter>disabled</filter>
</syslog-logging>
    <console-logging level="debugging" messages-logged="9"><xml>disabled
</xml><filter>disabled</filter></console-logging>
    <monitor-logging level="debugging" messages-logged="0"><xml>disabled
</xml><filter>disabled</filter></monitor-logging>
    <buffer-logging>disabled<xml messages-logged="2">enabled</xml><filter>
disabled</filter></buffer-logging>
    <logging-exception size="4096 bytes"></logging-exception>
    <count-and-timestamp-logging status="disabled">
</count-and-timestamp-logging>
    <trap-logging level="informational" messages-lines-logged="13">
</trap-logging>

<log-xml-buffer size="4096 bytes"></log-xml-buffer>

<ios-log-msg><facility>SYS</facility><severity>5</severity><msg-id>CONFIG_I
</msg-id><time>00:00:55</time><args><arg id="0">console</arg><arg id="1">
console</arg></args></ios-log-msg>
<ios-log-msg><facility>SYS</facility><severity>5</severity><msg-id>CONFIG_I
</msg-id><time>00:01:44</time><args><arg id="0">console</arg><arg id="1">
console</arg></args></ios-log-msg>
```

The "Troubleshoot" text appears as a sidebar tab.

Troubleshoot

To enable XML logging to a Syslog host, just use the logging host command as you normally would with the addition the XML option. In this example, our syslog host is 192.168.0.5 and it's prepared to handle the XML form of our logging.

```
Router(config)#logging host 192.168.0.5 xml
```

17

Quick Reference

aaa accounting   global

aaa accounting {auth-proxy | system | network | exec | connection |
    commands *level*} {default | list-name} [vrf *vrf-name*] {start-stop |
    stop-only | none} [broadcast] group *group-name*

no aaa accounting {auth-proxy | system | network | exec | connection |
    commands *level*} {default | list-name} [vrf *vrf-name*] {start-stop |
    stop-only | none} [broadcast] group *group-name*

Configures   AAA Accounting

Default   Disabled

Description

This command enables accounting, which can be used for billing and security
purposes.

auth-proxy
    Provides information about all authenticated proxy user events.

system
    Enables accounting for all system events that are not associated with a user (such
    as a reload).

exec
    Enables accounting for EXEC-level commands.

connection
    Provides information about all outbound connections, such as telnet, LAT, rlogin
    and SSH.

commands level
    Enables accounting for the specified privilege level (0 to 15).

default
    Uses the listed accounting methods that follow this argument as the default list
    for accounting services

`list-name`
> Specifies the AAA accounting protocol to use (radius or tacacs+).

`vrf vrf-name`
> Optional. Specifies a virtual route forwarding (VRF) configuration.

`start-stop`
> Creates an accounting entry at the start and end of the command.

`stop-only`
> Sends an accounting entry only when the command has completed execution.

`none`
> Disables accounting services on this line or interface.

`broadcast`
> Optional. Enables the sending accounting records to multiple AAA servers.

`group group-name`
> Specifies the AAA accounting protocol to use for the specified server group (group radius and group tacacs+).

Example

The following configuration statements enable AAA accounting for commands at level 5. An accounting entry is generated when the command is initiated and when it is terminated; the command doesn't execute until the server has received the message and the TACACS+ protocol is used to send the entries to the accounting server.

```
aaa new-model
aaa accounting command 5 default group tacacs+
```

---

aaa accounting delay-start   global

```
aaa accounting delay-start
no accounting delay-start
```

Configures   Delays accounting start records until the user's IP address is established

Default   Disabled (no delay)

Description

The default behavior is to start accounting as soon as the user connects, even before her IP address has been established. The command delays the accounting until the IP address has been established.

---

aaa accounting gigawords   global

```
aaa accounting gigawords
no aaa accounting gigawords
```

Configures   Enables 64-bit counters within AAA

Default   Enabled

Description

The command is enabled by default and only shows up in the configuration if the no version is used. The high-capacity counters provide greater counter capacity but use 8 percent of CPU memory for 24,000 sessions running under the ready state. If you do disable this with the no form of the command, you must reload the router to have it take effect.

---

aaa accounting nested   global

```
aaa accounting nested
no aaa accounting nested
```

Configures   Nesting network records within EXEC start and stop records

Default   Disabled

Description

This commands keeps EXEC start and stop records together—or nested—for PPP users who start EXEC terminal sessions. Such nesting can be helpful for certain billing practices.

---

aaa accounting resource   global

```
aaa accounting resource method-list start-stop [broadcast] group group-name
no accounting resource method-list start-stop [broadcast] group group-name
aaa accounting resource method-list stop-failure [broadcast] group group-name
no accounting resource method-list stop-failure [broadcast] group group-name
```

Configures   Accounting for the starting or stopping of a connection

Default   N/A

Description

The start-stop version of this command enables the accounting of a user's connection at the start of the call and at the end. The stop-failure command enables the generation of a stop record if the user's call is terminated.

method-list
> Method used for accounting services. You can set this to default or provide a list of accounting methods.

broadcast
> Optional. Enables the sending of accounting records to multiple AAA servers.

group group-name
> Specifies the AAA accounting protocol to use (group radius or group tacacs+).

Example

```
aaa accounting resource default start-stop group radius
aaa accounting resource default stop-failure group radius
```

aaa accounting send stop-record authentication failure
global

```
aaa accounting send stop-record authentication failure
no aaa accounting send stop-record authentication failure
```

Configures   Stop records for users who fail to authenticate

Default   Disabled

Description

If the user fails a login or session negotiation, this command causes a stop record to be generated for this connection attempt.

aaa accounting session-duration ntp-adjusted
global

```
aaa accounting session-duration ntp-adjusted
no accounting session-duration ntp-adjusted
```

Configures   Use of NTP clock to calculate Radius session time

Default   Disabled

Description

By default, the Radius attribute acct-sess-time is calculated on a 64-bit monotonically increasing counter, which is not Network Time Protocol–adjusted. This command causes the attribute to be calculated based on the NTP clock.

aaa accounting suppress null-username
global

```
aaa accounting suppress null-username
no aaa accounting suppress null-username
```

Configures

Stopping the sending of accounting messages when the username is NULL

Default   Disabled

Description

This command prevents the creation of accounting records with usernames of NULL.

aaa accounting update
global

```
aaa accounting update [newinfo] [periodic minutes [jitter {maximum max-value}]]
no accounting update
```

Configures   Periodic interim accounting records

Default   Disabled

Description

Enables periodic interim accounting records to be sent to the accounting server. If the newinfo option is used, periodic reports are sent only when there is new information to report.

newinfo

> Optional. Causes periodic information to be sent whenever there is new information about the user.

periodic

> Optional. Specifies the number of minutes between periodic updates.

jitter

> Optional. Allows the setting of the maximum jitter value.

maximum

> Required for the jitter command. Sets the number of seconds for the maximum jitter in a periodic update. A value of 0 disables jitter. The default is 300 seconds.

---

aaa authentication attempts login global

```
aaa authentication attempts login number
no aaa authentication attempts login
```

Configures   The maximum number of login failures

Default   Three attempts

Description

This command sets the number of login attempts that will be permitted before the connection is dropped. *number* is the maximum value, which can be 1 to 25.

---

aaa authentication banner global

```
aaa authentication banner delimiter
no aaa authentication banner
```

Configures   A banner to be displayed at user login

Default   None

Description

Like all banner commands, this one takes a *delimiter*, which marks the end of the following banner string. This banner is displayed to the user at login.

Example

```
aaa new-model
aaa authentication banner * Welcome to our system. Unauthorized access is
prohibited *
aaa authentication login default group radius
```

aaa authentication enable default

global

```
aaa authentication enable default method ... method
no aaa authentication enable default method ... method
```

Configures   Authentication for privileged command level

Default   None

Description

This command configures the router to use AAA to determine whether a user can access the privileged command set. The *method* parameter can be any of the following: enable, line, none, group tacacs+, or group radius. Each method describes where to get the password for authentication. If more than one method is listed, the methods are tried in order until one succeeds or all fail. This command does not work with TACACS or Extended TACACS (XTACACS).

aaa authentication fail-message

global

```
aaa authentication fail-message delimiter
no aaa authentication fail-message
```

Configures   A failed login attempt banner message

Default   Disabled

Description

Like all banner commands, this one takes a delimiter, which marks the end of the following banner string. This banner is displayed to the user at a failed login attempt.

aaa authentication local-override

global

```
aaa authentication local-override
no aaa authentication local-override
```

Configures   The use of local usernames and passwords

Default   Disabled

Description

This command tells the router to check its own username and password database for a match before using any other authentication methods. It is useful if you have a small set of administrators who need access to the router even when the AAA server is down.

aaa authentication login

```
aaa authentication login {default | listname} method ... method
no aaa authentication login
```

Configures   AAA authentication method for login

Default   local

Description

This command defines a named list of authentication methods that can be used when a user logs into the device. The *listname* parameter specifies the name of the list; the login authentication command is used to apply a list. default is a special list name; the default list specifies the authentication methods to be used by default (i.e., in the absence of explicit login authentication commands). *method* describes where to get the password for authentication. If more than one method is listed, the methods are tried in order until one succeeds or all have failed. The valid *method*s are: enable, krb5, line, local, local-case, none, group radius, group tacacs+, and krb5-telnet. The local-case option uses case-sensitive local usernames.

Example

The following command defines the default list of login authentication methods. Because this is the default list, it applies to all users, even if there is no login authentication command. The router first attempts to use the tacacs+ method for authentication, then the enable method. Therefore, the enable password is used to authenticate users if the device cannot contact the TACACS+ server.

```
! Set authentication for login
aaa authentication login default group tacacs+ enable none
```

aaa authentication password-prompt

```
aaa authentication password-prompt string
no aaa authentication password-prompt
```

Configures   Password prompt for logins

Default   Password:

Description

This command sets the text displayed for a user's password prompt to *string*.

Example

```
aaa authentication password-prompt "What is your password?"
```

aaa authentication ppp

global

```
aaa authentication ppp {default | listname} method ... method
no aaa authentication ppp
```

Configures   AAA authentication method for PPP

Default   local

Description
This command defines a named list of authentication methods that can be used when a user starts a PPP session. The `listname` parameter specifies the name of the list; the `login authentication` command is used to apply a list. `default` is a special list name; the `default` list specifies the authentication methods to be used by default (i.e., in the absence of explicit `login authentication` commands). `method` describes where to get the password for authentication. If more than one method is listed, they are tried in order until one succeeds or all fail. The valid `method`s are `enable`, `krb5`, `line`, `local`, `local-case`, `none`, `group radius`, `group tacacs+`, and `krb5-telnet`.

Example
The following command defines the default list of authentication methods for PPP users. Because this is the default list, it applies to all PPP users, even if there is no `login authentication` command. The router attempts to use the `tacacs+` method for authentication; if the device cannot contact the TACACS+ server, no other authentication is attempted, and the connection is rejected.

```
! Set authentication for ppp
aaa authentication ppp default tacacs+ none
```

aaa authentication username-prompt

global

```
aaa authentication username-prompt string
no aaa authentication username-prompt string
```

Configures   Username prompt for AAA authentication

Default   Username:

Description
Like the `password-prompt` command, this command sets the text used to prompt for a username when using AAA authentication. The prompt is set to `string`.

aaa authorization

global

```
aaa authorization {network | exec | command level} method ... method
no aaa authorization {network | exec | command level}
```

Configures   Authorization for actions

Default   Disabled

Description

This command sets the authorization method for different command sets.

`network`

> Sets the authorization method used for network commands.

`exec`

> Sets the authorization method for any EXEC-level command.

`command level`

> Sets the authorization method for commands at the given privilege level. Privilege levels range from 0 to 15, inclusive.

`method ... method`

> Specifies where the device looks up the authorization information for a user. *method* describes where to get the password for authentication. If more than one method is listed, the methods are tried in order until one succeeds or all have failed. The valid method types are group `tacacs+`, `if-authenticated`, `none`, `local`, group `radius`, and `krb5-instance`.

Example

The following commands require TACACS+ authentication for users giving commands at level 8.

```
aaa new-model
aaa authorization command 8 group tacacs+ none
```

---

aaa authorization config-commands   global

```
aaa authorization config-commands
no aaa authorization config-commands
```

Configures   Authorization for config level access

Default

Disabled, unless the aaa authorization command has been given, in which case all config-commands require authorization

Description

This command enables authorization of config-commands (i.e., any command that requires you to give the `conf terminal` command to enter configuration mode). Here's a scenario in which you might use it: if you give the aaa authorization command, AAA authorization will be required for all commands. To disable authorization of config-commands, you can give the command `no aaa authorization config-commands`.

Example

```
aaa new-model
aaa authorization command 8 tacacs+ none
no aaa authorization config-commands
```

aaa authorization reverse-access

global

```
aaa authorization reverse-access {group tacacs+ | group radius}
no aaa authorization reverse-access
```

Configures   Authorization for reverse telnet access

Default   Disabled (no authorization for reverse telnet)

Description

This command enables authorization for a user who is requesting reverse telnet access. If specified, group tacacs+ or group radius is used for authentication.

aaa authorization template

global

```
aaa authorization template
no aaa authorization template
```

Configures   Local or remote customer templates

Default   Disabled

Description

This command enables the use of customer templates for VPN or VPN Routing and Forwarding (VRF).

aaa configuration route

global

```
aaa configuration route username string [password string]
no aaa configuration route username string [password string]
```

Configures

Username and password for downloading static routes from Radius server

Default   Username is hostname and password is cisco

Description

This command allows for the definition of a username and password other than the defaults for downloading static route information from a Radius server.

aaa group server radius

global

```
aaa group server radius group-name
no aaa group server radius group-name
```

Configures   A group of Radius servers

Default   None

Description

This command defines a group of Radius servers. To add a Radius server to the group, use the server command, followed by the IP address of the server. If the auth-port and acct-port are not defined, the default ports of 1645 and 1646 are used.

Example

```
aaa group server radius myradiusgroup
  server 10.1.1.1
  server 10.1.2.1 auth-port 1700 acct-port 1701
```

aaa group server tacacs+   global

```
aaa group server tacacs+ group-name
no aaa group server tacacs+ group-name
```

Configures   A group of TACACS+ servers

Default   None

Description

This command defines a group of TACACS+ servers. To add a TACACS+ server to the group, use the server command, followed by the IP address of the server.

Example

```
aaa group server tacacs+ mytacacsplusgroup
  server 10.1.1.1
  server 10.1.2.1
```

aaa new-model   global

```
aaa new-model
no aaa new-model
```

Configures   Enables AAA access control

Default   Disabled

Description

By default, the AAA model is not enabled, and you cannot use the AAA configuration commands. This command enables AAA and allows you to configure it.

absolute-timeout   line

```
absolute-timeout number-of-minutes
no absolute-timeout
```

Configures   Amount of time a connection can be open

Default   None

Description

This command sets the interval before closing a connection to *number-of-minutes*. Unlike the other timeouts, this command sets a hard limit for the connection time; it is not an idle timeout. The connection will be closed at this time even if the connection is not idle. Use the no form of the command to disable the timeout.

---

access-class   line

```
access-class access-list [in | out]
no access-class access-list
```

Configures   Applies an access list to a line

Default   None

Description

This command specifies which access list to apply to this line (*access-list*), and in what direction the list should be applied (in or out). For more information on creating access lists, see Chapter 7.

Example

The following commands apply access list 10 to outgoing traffic on virtual terminals 0–4.

```
access-list 10 permit host 10.10.1.2
! Apply the access-list to the virtual lines 0-4
line vty 0 4
  access-class 10 out
```

---

access-enable   command

```
access-enable [host] [timeout minutes]
```

Configures   Creates an entry in a dynamic access list

Default   None

Description

This command enables the Lock and Key feature. It allows an entry to be made in a dynamic access list for the current session. The host keyword is optional; it tells the access list to allow access only from the host that initiated the session. The timeout option specifies the time in *minutes*, after which the access list entry is deleted if no traffic matching the entry is seen. In other words, if the connection is idle for the given time, the entry in the access list is deleted and the user must re-authenticate.

access-enable is often used with autocommand to create a dynamic access list for an incoming telnet session.

Example

This example creates a dynamic access list for the host that made the connection. The access list times out after five minutes.

```
autocommand access-enable host timeout 5
```

To make use of this entry, there must be an extended access list like the following:

```
access-list 110 dynamic incoming-user timeout 5 permit ip any any
```

This list must be applied to any interfaces that support dial-in users. The permit part of the statement controls the incoming user's access to network resources. The timeout in the access-list command is absolute; the temporary entry exists only for the given number of minutes. It overrides the timeout in the access-enable command.

---

access-list   global

Standard:

```
access-list number {permit | deny} src-address-spec
```

Extended:

```
access-list number {permit | deny} protocol src-address-spec [operator port]
    dest-address-spec [operator port] [established] [precedence value]
    [tos value] [log]
```

Named:

```
ip access-list {standard | extended} name
```

All access list types:

```
no access-list number
```

Configures   An access list

Default   None

Description

Access lists are an extremely general method for controlling access to the router, the traffic flowing in and out of the router, and even the routes accepted by the router. This command defines an entry in an access list.

number

A number that identifies the list and list type. Table 17-1 shows the ranges assigned to each list type. This book covers only standard and extended IP access lists, plus named and reflexive access lists.

Table 17-1. Access list numbers

List type	Numeric range
Standard IP access lists	1–99
Extended IP access lists	100–199
Ethernet type code	200–299
DECnet	300–399
XNS	400–499
Extended XNS	500–599

Table 17-1. Access list numbers (continued)

List type	Numeric range
AppleTalk	600–699
Ethernet address	700–799
Novell	800–899
Extended Novell	900–999
Novell SAP	1000–1099
Additional standard IP access lists	1300–1999
Additional extended IP access lists	2000–2699
Named access lists	None
Reflexive access lists	None

permit|deny
> Specifies if the line is to permit or deny matched traffic.

protocol
> Specifies the protocol to which the access list entry applies. For IP access lists, this option can be ip, tcp, udp, igmp, or icmp.

src-address-spec dest-address-spec
> The source and destination addresses or networks can be expressed in a number of ways: any, a single host address, or an entire network address, as follows:

> any
>> Matches any address. This command is shorthand for the IP address and wild-card mask of 0.0.0.0 255.255.255.255. (See Chapter 7 for more information.)

> host ip-address
>> Matches a single host, identified by its IP address.

> ip-address wildcard-mask
>> Matches any address in the set specified by the IP address and the wildcard mask. For example, 10.10.1.0 0.0.0.255 matches the address range 10.10.1.0 through 10.10.1.255. Wildcards are covered in Chapter 7.

operator port
> These options, *operator* and *port*, allow you to specify services or groups of services. The operator must be one of the following:

> lt
>> Less than

> gt
>> Greater than

> eq
>> Equal

> neq
>> Not equal

> range
>> The range between two port numbers

> Ports can be specified either by number or by the name of a service (smtp, telnet, www, ftp, etc.).

If a port expression follows the source address in an access list, packets must have a source port that matches the expression in order to pass the access list. Likewise, if a port expression follows the destination address, packets must have a destination port that matches the expression to pass the access list.

precedence value
> Optional. This command allows packets to be filtered on IP precedence level. The value can be 0 to 7.

tos value
> Optional. TOS stands for Type of Service. Packets can be filtered by the IP Type of Service, with a value of 0 to 15.

log
> This keyword causes the router to write a log message to the console for packets that match this line. It logs the first packet that matches the line and then repeats only every few minutes, which prevents a flood of log messages. Console logging must be enabled before messages appear.

established
> This keyword matches TCP packets that have ACK or RST bits set, i.e., packets that belonged to an established connection. It is used to prevent hosts from outside the local network from starting connections to hosts within the network, while allowing packets from an established connection back into the network.

icmp-type value
> ICMP packets can be filtered based on their type, which is a value from 0 to 255.

igmp-type value
> IGMP packets can be filtered based on their type, which is a value from 0 to 15.

Many different kinds of statements are used to apply an access list. The most common are ip access-group, which applies an access list to incoming or outgoing traffic on an interface, and access-class, which applies an access list to incoming or outgoing traffic on a line.

Note that the no form of this command deletes the entire access list, *not* just a single entry.

Named Access Lists (IOS 11.0 and greater)

IOS 11.0 introduced a new method of creating and editing IP access lists, called *named access lists*. As the name implies, named access lists are assigned a string-based name, rather than a number. Otherwise, they are essentially identical to standard and extended IP access lists but with the added ability to do some basic editing.

To create a named access list, start with the ip access list command:

    ip access-list {standard | extended} name

The keyword standard indicates that this is a standard IP access list; extended indicates that this is an extended IP access list. name is the name of the list; it must be a unique alphanumeric string. You may then enter a series of permit and deny commands. For standard access lists, these commands have the following syntax:

    {permit | deny} src-address-spec

For an extended list, the syntax is:

    {permit | deny} protocol src-address-spec [operator port] dest-address-spec
    [operator port] [established] [precedence value] [tos value] [log]

The parameters for the permit and deny commands in named access lists are the same as for extended access lists.

Named access lists cannot always be used in the same places that numbered access lists can, though this is slowly being corrected as IOS evolves.

As of IOS 12.4, you can enter noncontiguous ports on a single line within a named access list. Before, you would write such an access list like this:

```
ip access-list extended acllist1
  permit tcp any host 192.168.1.1 eq telnet
  permit tcp any host 192.168.1.1 eq www
  permit tcp any host 192.168.1.1 eq smtp
  permit tcp any host 192.168.1.1 eq pop3
```

With noncontiguous port support, you can write it more tersely:

```
ip access-list extended acllist1
  permit tcp any host 192.168.1.1 eq telnet www smtp pop3
```

Example

Here are examples of several types of access list elements. We assume that these access lists are used to restrict incoming traffic on an interface. First, a standard IP access list that permits traffic from the network 10.0.1.0:

```
access-list 5 permit 10.0.1.0 0.0.0.255
```

This access list element permits HTTP traffic from any source to reach the server at 10.1.2.3:

```
access-list 105 permit tcp any host 10.1.2.3 eq http
```

And this element permits TCP traffic to enter the router from any destination, provided that the session was initiated by a host "behind" the router:

```
access-list 105 permit tcp any any established
```

Remember that all access lists end with an "implicit deny," which rejects all traffic not permitted by a statement in the access list.

---

access-list rate-limit   global

```
access-list rate-limit access-list {precedence | exp | mac-address |
  mask precedence-mask}
no access-list rate-limit access-list
```

Configures   An access list for Committed Access Rate (CAR)

Default   None

Description

This command selects packets for CAR policies based on IP precedence or MAC addresses. There can only be one command per access list. If you need to assign more than one precedence level to a single access list, use the mask keyword. The access list is used to classify packets. For IP, use any number from 1 to 99; for MAC, use any number from 100 to 199; and for the MPLS experimental field, use any number from 200 to 299.

precedence

The IP precedence level to apply to the access list.

exp

MPLS experimental field. Valid values are number from 0 to 7.

mac-address

The MAC address to apply to the access list.

mask precedence-mask

The precedence mask to apply to the access list. To calculate the mask, convert the precedence value to an eight-bit mask. A precedence of 0 is encoded as 000000001; a precedence of 1 is 00000010. Then AND all the bit values together to get a single mask. For example, the mask that covers a precedence of 1 through 3 would be 00001110. When you have the binary mask, convert it to a two-digit hexadecimal number; for this example, the mask would be 0E.

Example

```
! This command assigns a CAR access-list of 10 to packets with an IP
! precedence of 1 through 3.
access-list rate-limit 10 mask 0E
```

---

access-template   command

access-template [*access-list*] [*temp-list*] [*source*] [*destination*] [timeout *minutes*]

Configures   An entry in a temporary access list

Default   None

Description

This command creates an entry in a temporary access list on the router to which you are connected.

access-list

The name or number of the dynamic access list.

temp-list

The name of the temporary list within the access list.

source

The usual source address specification (the host and any keywords are allowed).

destination

The usual destination address specification (the host and any keywords are allowed).

timeout minutes

The maximum time, in *minutes*, that the entry will remain in the list.

For more information about how source and destination addresses are specified, see the description of the access-list command and Chapter 7.

activation-character line

```
activation-character ascii-number
no activation-character
```

Configures   The activation character for an idle terminal session

Default   Return character (13)

Description

This command specifies which key initiates a session at an idle terminal. *ascii-number* is the decimal value of the activation character you wish to set. To disable this command and return to the default, use the no form.

Example

These commands set the activation character for a terminal connected to line 2 to ASCII character 13 (Return or Enter):

```
Router(config)# line 2
Router(config-line)# activation-character 13
```

aggregate-address router, BGP

```
aggregate-address address mask [as-set] [summary-only] [suppress-map map]
    [advertise-map map] [attribute-map map]
no aggregate-address address mask [as-set] [summary-only] [suppress-map map]
    [advertise-map map] [attribute-map map]
```

Configures   BGP route aggregation

Default   Disabled

Description

This command configures route aggregation when using BGP. An aggregate route is generated by combining several different routes. The new route covers all the smaller routes with a single route, making the routing table smaller and easier to manage.

address
> The IP address of the destination network for the aggregate route.

mask
> The network mask for the aggregate route.

as-set
> Optional. Generates AS-SET path information.

summary-only
> Optional. This keyword causes routes that are more specific than the aggregate address to be suppressed.

suppress-map map
> Optional. The map to use to select routes to be suppressed.

```
advertise-map map
```
Optional. The map to use to select routes to create AS-SET origin communities.
```
attribute-map map
```
Optional. The map to use to set the attributes of the aggregate route.

Example

Say that we're configuring a router for the network 10.10.0.0. Instead of advertising all the routes within this network that we know about (10.10.1.0, 10.10.2.0, etc.), we want to advertise an aggregate address for the whole 10.10.0.0 network:

```
! BGP configuration
router bgp 100
  neighbor 10.1.1.1 remote-as 100
  neighbor 10.2.2.2 remote-as 200
  network 10.10.0.0
  ! Without the summary-only keyword, the router would continue to advertise
  ! the component networks of this summary route.
  aggregrate-address 10.10.0.0 255.255.0.0 summary-only
```

---

alias   global

```
alias mode alias-name command
```

Configures   Command aliases

Default   None

Description

This command allows you to configure an alias, or abbreviation, for any IOS command.
```
mode
```
The mode to which the alias and the command that you are aliasing belong. It can be any of the configuration modes: configuration (for global commands), user, exec, hub, interface, line, map-class, map-list, route-map, router, etc.
```
alias-name
```
The name to be assigned to the alias.
```
command
```
The IOS command represented by the alias.

Example

To assign the shorthand t1 to the command telnet 10.1.1.1 2001, use the following command:

```
alias exec t1 telnet 10.1.1.1 2001
```

area authentication

```
area area-id authentication [message-digest]
no area area-id authentication
```

Configures   OSPF authentication

Default   No authentication

Description
This command enables simple password authentication for an OSPF network. All routers within the OSPF area must be configured to use the same password. The authentication password is set by the ip ospf authentication-key command.

area-id
> The area to which this command applies.

message-digest
> Enables MD5 authentication for the area.

Example
The following configuration starts an OSPF process using authentication for area 0. The authentication key is letmein.

```
! Set the OSPF key on interface serial 0 to letmein
interface serial 0
  ip address 10.100.1.1 255.255.2255.0
  ip ospf authentication-key letmein
!
router ospf 99
  network 10.0.0.0 0.255.255.255 area 0
  area 0 authentication
```

area default-cost

```
area area-id default-cost cost
no area area-id default-cost
```

Configures   The OSPF cost for a default summary route

Default   1

Description
This command is used only for an Area Border Router (ABR) to a stub area.

area-id
> The area to which the default-cost applies.

cost
> The value of the cost. Any 24-bit number can be used.

area nssa

```
area area-id nssa [no-redistribution] [default-information-originate]
no area area-id nssa
```

Configures   An OSPF NSSA

Default   None

Description

A not-so-stubby area (NSSA) is just like a stub area, but shares routing information with an external network that is using a different routing protocol. In other words, it is a stub area with an ASBR router. The remote network becomes an area to your OSPF network, eliminating the need to implement the different routing protocol within the OSPF network. See the OSPF section in Chapter 9 for more information.

```
area-id
```
    The area to which this command applies.

```
no-redistribution
```
    Optional. Disables redistribution of normal area routes into the NSSA.

```
default-information-originate
```
    Optional. Generates type-7 default routes into the NSSA.

area-password

```
area-password password
no area-password
```

Configures   IS-IS area authentication password

Default   No password authentication

Description

This command enables password authentication for an IS-IS area. The *password* is transmitted in clear text; it thus provides very little security but may help prevent misconfiguration.

area range

```
area area-id range address mask
no area area-id range address mask
```

Configures   OSPF route summarization

Default   None

Description

This command tells the OSPF routing process to summarize selected routes for an area. A single route to the given address is generated, instead of separate routes for the individual networks.

area-id
> The area to be summarized.

address
> The IP address of the network to summarize.

mask
> The mask for the IP address, showing which routes to include in the summary.

Example

The following OSPF configuration summarizes all routes for area 2 into a single route for network 10.0.0.0/8:

```
router ospf  99
  network 10.0.0.0 0.255.255.255 area 2
  area 2 range 10.0.0.0 255.0.0.0
```

area stub   router, OSPF

area *area-id* stub [no-summary]
no area *area-id* stub

Configures   An OSPF stub area

Default   None

Description

This command defines an area to be a stub area. A stub area receives a default summary route from the ABR for destinations outside the autonomous system. The no-summary option makes the area a Totally Stubby network, which restricts LSA Type-3 packets (intra-area summaries) from entering the stubby area.

area-id
> The area to define as a stub.

no-summary
> Prevents summary link advertisements from entering the stub area.

area virtual-link   router, OSPF

area *area-id* virtual-link *router-id* [hello-interval *seconds*]
    [retransmit-interval *seconds*] [transmit-delay *seconds*]
    [dead-interval *seconds*] [authentication-key *key*]
    [message-digest-key *keyid* md5 *key*]
no area *area-id* virtual-link *router-id*

Configures   An OSPF virtual link

Default   None

Description

This command establishes a virtual link that connects a broken OSPF backbone; in OSPF, the backbone must be contiguous. It is useful when a contiguous backbone is not possible. Virtual links can also be used to create an area that does not have a direct link to the backbone (area 0).

area-id
>   The ID of the area being crossed by the virtual link.

router-id
>   The ID of the router at the other end of the virtual link.

hello-interval seconds
>   Optional. The time in seconds between transmission of hello messages by the router over the virtual link. The default is 10 seconds. All routers participating in the same area must have the same hello interval.

retransmit-interval seconds
>   Optional. The time in seconds that a router waits before retransmitting a link-state announcement (LSA). The default is five seconds. When setting this value, you need to ensure that the time includes the entire round trip of the packet.

transmit-delay seconds
>   Optional. This is the estimated time, in seconds, that the interface will take to transmit the packet. An LSA's age is decremented by this value before transmission. The default is one second.

dead-interval seconds
>   Optional. A router is considered down if a hello packet isn't received from it within this interval. All routers participating in the area must have the same dead-interval. The default is 40 seconds.

authentication-key key
>   Optional. This is the authentication password used for OSPF routing if authentication is enabled. The key can be up to eight bytes long. If you want to use authentication, all routers in the OSPF network must have authentication enabled, and all neighbor routers must use the same key.

message-digest-key keyid md5 key
>   Optional. This is the authentication key and password to be used by neighboring OSPF routers. The *keyid* is a number between 1 and 255, and is used to identify this key in subsequent commands. The *key* is essentially a password; it is a string up to 16 characters long. All neighbor routers must use the same *keyid* and *key*.

---

arp (global)   global

arp *ip-address mac-address type* [alias]
no arp *ip-address mac-address type* [alias]

Configures   Adds a static entry to the ARP table

Default   No static ARP entries are made

Description

This command allows you to place a static entry in the ARP table, which is a dynamic table that maps IP addresses to the corresponding MAC (hardware) addresses. The *ip-address* and *mac-address* are simply the IP address and the hardware address for the entry you wish to create. The *type* argument is the encapsulation type (arpa for Ethernet, smds for SMDS, snap for FDDI and token ring, etc.). The optional alias keyword tells the router to respond to ARP requests as if it were the requested device itself; i.e., the router responds to an ARP request for an aliased device with its own IP address.

arp (interface)   interface

```
arp {arpa | frame-relay | probe | snap}
no arp {arpa | frame-relay | probe | snap}
```

Configures   Interface-specific handling of ARP requests

Default   ARPA (Ethernet)

Description

This command allows you to specify the type of encapsulation to use for ARP packets on this interface. The types are arpa (Ethernet, the default), frame-relay (ARP over Frame Relay encapsulation), probe (HP Probe protocol), and snap (RFC 1042).

arp timeout   interface

```
arp timeout seconds
no arp timeout seconds
```

Configures   The lifetime of an ARP entry in the ARP table

Default   14400 seconds

Description

This command allows you to set the time that an entry will remain in the ARP table. The default is 4 hours.

async-bootp   global

```
async-bootp keyword [:hostname] value
no async-bootp keyword [:hostname] value
```

Configures   BOOTP parameters for async dial-up lines

Default   Disabled

Description

This command assigns a *value* to a given BOOTP *keyword*. Table 17-2 shows the BOOTP parameters and their values. Normally, all BOOTP parameters are sent to dial-up hosts requesting BOOTP information. Adding :*hostname* to a keyword applies the BOOTP variable to a specific requesting host. Other hosts that request BOOTP parameters will not be sent this keyword.

Table 17-2. BOOTP keywords and values

Keyword	Value	Meaning
bootfile	*filename*	Server boot file to be downloaded
subnet-mask	*mask*	The subnet mask to be used
time-offset	*offset*	The offset time in seconds from the Coordinated Universal Time (UTC)
gateway	*address*	The IP address of the default gateway
time-server	*address*	The IP address of the time server
nbns-server	*address*	The IP address of the Windows NT server
dns-server	*address*	The IP address of the DNS server
log-server	*address*	The IP address of the MIT-LCS log server
quote-server	*address*	The IP address of the QOTD (quote of the day) server
lpr-server	*address*	The IP address of the LPR print server
bootfile-size	*size*	The size of the bootfile in terms of 512-byte blocks

Example

The following commands define the DNS server, subnet mask, and NBNS server to be sent to hosts requesting BOOTP information:

```
! Configure our bootp items
async-bootp subnet-mask 255.255.255.0
async-bootp dns-server 10.1.1.1
async-bootp nbns-server 10.1.1.2
```

async default ip address
interface

```
async default ip address address
no async default ip address address
```

Configures   The IP address used by the connecting (remote) system

Default   None

Description   This command is defunct. Use peer default ip address instead.

async default routing
interface

```
async default routing
no async default routing
```

Configures   Routing on async interfaces

Default   Disabled

Description

By default, routing protocols like RIP, IGRP, EIGRP, and OSPF are not enabled on asynchronous interfaces. This command allows all the routing protocols to be enabled on these interfaces. It can be used to route between offices that are linked by traditional analog modems. Use the no form to disable routing on this interface.

Example

The following commands set up default routing for a dedicated async line:

```
interface async  2
  encapsulation ppp
  async mode dedicated
  async default routing
```

---

async dynamic address   interface

```
async dynamic address
no async dynamic address
```

Configures   Dynamic IP addresses on async interfaces

Default   Disabled

Description

Dynamic addressing means that a user connecting to the router for a PPP or SLIP session is allowed to select the interface's IP address using the EXEC mode commands. This feature can be used only when the async mode is interactive.

---

async dynamic routing   interface

```
async dynamic routing
no async dynamic routing
```

Configures   Dynamic routing on an async interface

Default   Disabled

Description

Dynamic routing means that remote users who connect to this asynchronous interface can enable routing over their PPP or SLIP connections. By default, no dynamic routing is done on an asynchronous interface.

Example

```
interface async 5
  ip tcp header-compression passive
  async dynamic routing
  async dynamic address
```

async mode

```
async mode {dedicated | interactive}
no async mode {dedicated | interactive}
```

Configures   The mode the user receives when connecting to an async interface

Default   Disabled

Description
The mode can be either dedicated or interactive.

dedicated
> The interface is reserved for PPP and SLIP connections. No user prompt ever appears on a dedicated line when a user connects. Instead, the connection parameters are negotiated automatically.

interactive
> Users are given a prompt when they connect to this interface. It is up to the user to start PPP or SLIP, or to interact directly with the router from the command prompt. The autoselect command can be used to detect PPP packets on an interactive async line and start PPP automatically. autoselect is not needed on dedicated mode async lines.

Example
On the first interface (async1), we set up a dedicated interface, which means that an IOS prompt doesn't appear when a user connects to the router through this interface. We make the second interface interactive, allowing the user to enter IOS commands and requiring her to start PPP or SLIP manually.

```
interface async1
  peer default ip address 10.10.1.1
  async mode dedicated
  encapsulation ppp
!
interface async2
  peer default ip address 10.10.1.2
  async mode interactive
```

atm address

```
atm address address
no atm address
```

Configures   An ATM address

Default   An automatically generated ATM address is assigned

Description
This command assigns a full (20-byte) ATM address or a partial (13-byte) address. Multiple ATM addresses are allowed. The first address in the list is the active address.

atm arp-server
interface

```
atm arp-server {self [timeout minutes] |nsap nsap-address}
no atm arp-server {self [timeout minutes] | nsap nsap-address}
```

Configures   An ARP server for the network

Default   No ATM ARP server

Description
This command assigns an ARP server for the ATM network. The self keyword identifies the current device as the ARP server. The timeout *minutes* option specifies the amount of time that an ARP entry is listed before the server tries to verify the entry; the default timeout value is 20 minutes. The nsap *nsap-address* parameter specifies the NSAP address of the ATM ARP server if the current device isn't acting as the server.

atm esi-address
interface

```
atm esi-address esi.selector
no atm esi-address
```

Configures   End station ID and selector fields of the ATM NSAP address

Default   None

Description
This command specifies the end station ID (ESI) and the selector byte fields of an ATM address. The ESI is 12 hexadecimal characters; the selector byte field is 2 hexadecimal characters.

atm lecs-address
interface

```
atm lecs-address lecs-address[sequence-number]
no atm lecs-address
```

Configures   The LECS address to be advertised

Default   None

Description
This command configures the address of the LAN Emulation Configuration Server (LECS) for the current interface. If this command isn't in the interface's configuration, the LECS defaults to the server given by atm lecs-address-default. The *lecs-address* is the NSAP address of the server. The *sequence-number* provides the position in the address in the LECS table.

atm lecs-address-default

atm lecs-address-default *lecs-address*[*sequence-number*]

no atm lecs-address-default *lecs-address*

Configures   The LECS address to be advertised

Default   None

Description

This command configures the address of the LECS. It is a global command; the server specified here is overridden by the interface-specific atm lecs-address command. The *lecs-address* is the NSAP address of the server. The *sequence-number* provides the position in the address in the LECS table.

atm nsap-address

atm nsap-address *address*

no atm nsap-address

Configures   The NSAP ATM end-system address of the interface

Default   None

Description

This command sets the NSAP address of the interface, which consists of 40 hexadecimal characters.

atm pvc

atm pvc *vcd vpi vci encap* [*peak avg* [*burst*]] [inarp [*minutes*]]
    [oam [*seconds*]] [compress]

no atm pvc *vcd vpi vci encap* [*peak avg* [*burst*]] [inarp [*minutes*]]
    [oam [*seconds*]] [compress]

Configures   Creates an ATM PVC

Default   None

Description

This command creates an ATM Permanent Virtual Circuit (PVC). On recent versions of IOS, it's preferable to use the pvc command, if available. ATM commands are highly hardware-dependent, so the commands available on any particular router vary. For more information on creating PVCs, consult Chapter 6.

vcd

A Virtual Circuit Descriptor, which is a unique number used to identify this particular VPI/VCI pair on the router.

vpi

The Virtual Path Identifier of the PVC. This identifier is unique only to the interface. The value can be from 0 to 255.

vci

The Virtual Channel Identifier of the PVC, which is a value from 0 to 1023. 0 to 31 are typically reserved for specific kinds of management traffic. *vpi* and *vci* may not both be 0.

encap

The type of encapsulation used on the line. The encapsulation may be aal5mux (a MUX-type virtual connection), aal5snap (the only encapsulation supported for Inverse ARP), aal1 (used for streaming video), aal5voice (used for voice traffic), ilmi, and qsaal.

peak

Optional, but required for voice circuits. The maximum capacity of the virtual circuit in Kbps. *peak* ranges from 56 to 10,000. The default is the link's maximum capacity.

avg

Optional, but required for voice circuits. The average rate at which data is sent over the virtual circuit. Legal values are hardware-dependent. The default is the link's maximum capacity.

burst

Optional, but required for voice circuits. The maximum number of ATM cells that the circuit can transmit at its peak rate.

inarp minutes

Optional. This option generates inverse ARP packets on this virtual circuit. *minutes* specifies the interval between inverse ARP packets, and ranges from 1 to 60; if omitted, *minutes* defaults to 15.

oam seconds

Optional. This option generates OAM cells on this virtual circuit. *seconds* specifies the interval at which OAM cells are generated, and ranges from 1 to 600; if omitted, *seconds* defaults to 10.

compress

Optional. This option compresses traffic over the circuit; hardware compression is used if it's available.

Example

The following commands set up a permanent virtual circuit on an ATM interface.

```
interface atm0.1
  ! assign our interface's IP address
  ip address 10.10.1.1 255.255.255.0
  ! Create pvc 20 with a VPI of 0 and a VCI of 60
  atm pvc 20 0 60 aal5snap
```

```
ip address atm-vc vci [class class-name] [broadcast] [aal5mux]
no ip address atm-vc vci [class class-name] [broadcast] [aal5mux]
```

Configures   An ATM PVC

Default   None

Description

This command creates an ATM PVC. The `map-list` command places you in the map list configuration mode; you must be in this mode to use the `atm-vc` command.

Note that it is rather bizarre to call this command `atm-vc`; by normal notions of command naming, it should be called `ip`. We're following Cisco's usage; in its defense, there are many commands whose names start with `ip` and have nothing to do with ATM configuration.

address
:   The destination IP address being mapped to this PVC.

vci
:   The Virtual Channel Identifier (VCI).

class class-name
:   Optional. *class-name* is the name of a table that contains encapsulation-specific parameters.

broadcast
:   Optional. This specifies that this entry should be used when broadcast packets need to be sent.

aal5mux
:   Optional. This specifies AAL5 multiplexing encapsulation. The default is snap encapsulation.

Example

The following commands create an ATM map named `atm-map1`. It establishes a virtual channel with a VCI of 20, which is mapped to the IP address 10.10.2.1; this virtual channel can be used for broadcast.

```
map-list atm-map1
   ip 10.10.2.1 atm-vc 20 broadcast
```

---

autobaud   line

```
autobaud [fast]
no autobaud
```

Configures   Automatic baud rate detection

Default   Disabled

Reference
A-B

Description

The autobaud command configures a line to select the incoming baud rate automatically. The baud rate must be between 300 and 115,200. There are two limitations to this command:

- Autobaud cannot be used on a connection at rates higher than 19,200 baud when the parity bit is set.
- This command cannot be used on outgoing connections.

The optional fast keyword detects the baud rate with exactly three carriage returns.

Many routers do not support the higher baud rates.

Example

The following commands enable automatic baud rate detection on line 3:

```
Router(config)#line 3
Router(config-line)#autobaud
```

To disable autobaud and to return to the default, use the no form of this command:

```
Router(config)#line 3
Router(config-line)#no autobaud
```

---

autocommand   line

```
autocommand command-string
no autocommand
```

Configures   Automatic execution of a command upon connection

Default   Disabled

Description

This command forces a specified line command, given by *command-string*, to be executed automatically when a login session is started. The command string can be any valid command. Use the no form to delete the selected autocommand.

Example

The following code starts PPP automatically after a successful login on line 5:

```
Router(config)#line tty 5
Router(config-line)#autocommand ppp
```

---

autodetect encapsulation   interface

```
autodetect encapsulation {lapb-ta | ppp | v120}
no autodetect encapsulation
```

Configures   Automatic detection of encapsulation types

Default   No autodetect

Description

This command enables automatic detection of the encapsulation type for ISDN or point-to-point serial links. The interface changes its encapsulation type if it detects that the remote system is using a different configuration. The valid types are lapb-ta (Link Access Procedure Balanced for ISDN), ppp, and v120 (for V.120 on ISDN B channels).

---

autohangup   line

```
autohangup
no autohangup
```

Configures   Automatic line disconnect

Default   Disabled

Description

This command tells the router to hang up the line automatically after the session is closed.

---

auto discovery qos   QoS

```
auto discovery qos [trust]
no auto discovery qos
```

Configures   Auto QoS Autodiscovery

Default   Disabled

Description

This command enables the disovery and collecting of data for the configuration of AutoQoS. Using NBAR, this command can analyze the traffic on the network in order to produce a more relevant QoS configuration. You should let this command run a few days in order for the data collection to work. Once the system has collected enough data, disable this command with the no auto disovery qos command and then enable AutoQoS with the auto qos command. To view the QoS policy generated by this command, use the show auto qos command. This command was introduced in IOS 12.3(7)T.

trust

Optional. When used, this keyword tells AutoQoS that the DSCP (Differentiated Service Code Point) values of a packet can be trusted for packet classification. If the trust keyword is not used, AutoQoS relies solely on NBAR for DSCP values.

auto qos voip

```
auto qos [voip] [trust] [fr-atm]
no auto qos [voip] [trust] [fr-atm]
```

Configures   The AutoQos VoIP feature on an interface

Default   Disabled

Description

This command enables the AutoQoS VoIP feature on an interface.

trust

> Optional. Indicates that the DSCP markings are to be trusted for classification of voice traffic.

fr-atm

> Optional. Enables this feature for Frame Relay–to–ATM links.

Example

```
interface serial3/1.102 point-to-point
  bandwidth 100
  ip address 192.168.1.2 255.255.255.0
  frame-relay interface-dlci 102
    auto qos voip trust fr-dlci
```

---

auto secure

```
auto secure [management | forwarding] [no-interact]
```

Configures   The router for security automatically

Default   Disabled

Description

By using this command, you are telling the router to try to automatically secure as many IP services as it can in order to configure the router as much as possible. This command reduces the complexity of securely configuring your router. For more information on this command, see Chapter 15.

management

> Optional. Configure only the management level of the router.

forwarding

> Optional. Configure only the packet forwarding part of the router.

no-interact

> Optional. No user prompts on any configuration items.

autoselect

```
autoselect {arap | ppp | slip| during-login}
no autoselect
```

Configures   Automatic selection of session type

Default   ARAP sessions

Description

This command configures a line to start the selected session type automatically. The sessions allowed are arap (AppleTalk remote access), ppp, and slip. during-login means that the username and password prompt are presented without a carriage return, and the user must log in normally before autoselection takes place.

Example

The following commands configure the router to start a PPP session automatically on line 10, but only after the user has successfully logged in:

```
line 10
   autoselect ppp
   autoselect during-login
```

auto-summary

```
auto-summary
no auto-summary
```

Configures   RIP (Version 2), EIGRP, BGP route summarization

Default   Enabled

Description

By default, subnet routes are summarized to "classful" network routes. If you need to advertise subnets across networks, auto-summary must be disabled. To disable auto-summary, use the no form of this command. For more information, consult Chapter 8.

Example

The following configuration disables auto-summary for an EIGRP routing process:

```
router eigrp 110
   network 10.0.0.0
   no auto-summary
```

```
backup interface interface
no backup interface interface


backup delay {enable-time | never} {disable-time | never}
no backup delay {enable-time | never} {disable-time | never}


backup load {enable-load | never} {disable-load | never}
no backup load {enable-load | never} {disable-load | never}
```

Configures   A backup interface

Default   None

Description

This family of commands configures a backup interface for the current interface. The first command, backup interface, specifies the *interface* to be used as the backup. The backup interface is activated when the primary interface goes down or reaches the load specified by the backup load command.

The backup delay command specifies how long the router should wait before activating (*enable-time*) or deactivating (*disable-time*) the backup interface. Both *enable-time* and *disable-time* are in seconds. Use of the backup delay command allows you to prevent routing instability if you have an intermittent interface. The keyword never, when used for the *enable-time* parameter, prevents the backup interface from being activated; when used for the *disable-time* parameter, it prevents the backup interface from being deactivated once it has been activated.

The backup load command specifies the load on the primary interface at which the backup interface should be activated (*enable-load*) or deactivated (*disable-load*). The load is expressed as a percentage of the primary interface's maximum capacity. The keyword never, when used for the *enable-load* parameter, prevents the backup interface from being activated; when used for the *disable-load* parameter, it prevents the backup interface from being deactivated once it has been activated.

Example

This example configures serial1 as a backup interface for serial0. If serial0 goes down for more than five seconds, or if the load on serial0 reaches 70%, the backup interface is activated.

```
interface serial0
   backup interface serial 1
   backup delay 5 20
   backup load 70 20
```

bandwidth (interface)

```
bandwidth rate
no bandwidth rate
```

Configures   The bandwidth value to be used in computing routing metrics

Default   Depends on the interface

Description

This command describes the bandwidth value to the routing protocols that use the bandwidth in computing routing metrics. It does *not* actually set the bit-rate on the interface itself. It does not affect the speed at which data is transmitted over the link, but does affect how the router selects routes and, therefore, how the link is used.

Example

A T1 connection would be:

```
bandwidth 1536
```

A 56K connection would be:

```
bandwidth 56
```

bandwidth (policy-map)

```
bandwidth {rate | remaining percent value | percent value }
no bandwidth {rate | remaining percent value | percent value }
```

Configures   Specifies or modifies the bandwidth allocated for a policy map

Default   None

Description

This command specifies the bandwidth in Kbps to be assigned to the class in a policy map. Alternatively, a percentage of the available bandwidth can be specified. The amount configured should be large enough to accommodate the Layer-2 overhead.

rate

> The amount of bandwidth in Kbps.

`remaining percent`

> Amount of guaranteed bandwidth, based on a relative percentage of remaining bandwidth. Value can be from 1 to 100.

`percent`

> This is the percentage of available bandwidth to be set aside for this class. Value can be from 1 to 100.

Example

```
policy-map policy1
  class class1
    bandwidth percent 80
```

banner exec   global

```
banner exec delimiter message delimiter
no banner exec
```

Configures   The banner that is displayed to the user upon successful login

Default   None

Description

This command specifies the *message* that is displayed after the user has logged in to the
router. It is not displayed for reverse-telnet connections. This command defines only
the banner message; use the exec-banner command to enable or disable the message.
The *delimiter* marks the beginning and the end of the message; it may be any character that isn't used in the message.

Example

Here's an example of a banner:

```
Router(config)# banner exec # Welcome to Pyramid #
```

You can also do multiple lines:

```
Router(config)# banner exec #
Enter TEXT message.  End with the character '#'.
Welcome to Pyramid
   Enjoy your stay
#
```

To delete the banner:

```
Router(config)#no banner exec
```

By default, this banner is automatically active; disabling the banner requires the use of
no exec-banner:

```
Router(config)#no exec-banner
```

Note that disabling the exec-banner also disables the motd-banner.

---

banner incoming   global

```
banner incoming delimiter message delimiter
no banner incoming
```

Configures   The banner message for all incoming reverse telnet connections

Default   None

Description

This command specifies the *message* that is displayed to all incoming reverse telnet
connections (instead of the exec banner). If you want to disable the message, delete the
banner with the no form of this command. The *delimiter* marks the beginning and the
end of the message; it may be any character that isn't used in the message.

Example

Here's how to set a banner:

```
Router(config)#banner incoming # Welcome to Pyramid #
```

You can also do multiple lines:

```
Router(config)#banner incoming #
Enter TEXT message.  End with the character '#'.
Welcome to Pyramid
    Enjoy your stay
#
```

To disable the message, delete it with the following command:

```
Router(config)#no banner incoming
```

---

banner login   global

```
banner login delimiter message delimiter
no banner login
```

Configures   The login banner message

Default   None

Description

This command specifies the *message* that is displayed prior to the login prompt for all connections. This message cannot be disabled. If you do not want it displayed, delete it with the no form of this command. The *delimiter* marks the beginning and the end of the message; it may be any character that isn't used in the message.

Example

Here's an example of a login banner:

```
Router(config)#banner login # Restricted Access #
```

To disable this message, delete it with the following command:

```
Router(config)#no banner login
```

---

banner motd   global

```
banner motd delimiter message delimiter
no banner motd
```

Configures   The banner that is displayed before the login prompt

Default   None

Description

This command specifies the *message* that is displayed as the message of the day, the very first message displayed to an incoming connection. This command defines only the message; the motd-banner command enables or disables the display. The *delimiter* marks the beginning and the end of the message; it may be any character that isn't used in the message.

Example

The following commands create a message-of-the-day banner and enable its display:

```
Router(config)# banner motd  # All routers will be rebooted at Sunday 10AM #
Router(config)# motd-banner
```

The motd-banner command isn't strictly necessary, since the display is enabled by default. To disable the display, use the no motd-banner command:

```
Router(config)#no banner motd
```

bgp always-compare-med

router, BGP

```
bgp always-compare-med
no bgp always-compare-med
```

Configures   BGP route selection

Default   Disabled

Description

This command allows the comparison of the multi-exit discriminator (MED) for paths, regardless of which autonomous system the path comes from.

bgp bestpath as-path ignore

router, BGP

```
bgp bestpath as-path ignore
no bgp bestpath as-path ignore
```

Configures   BGP route selection

Default   Disabled

Description

This command prevents the router from considering the autonomous system path (as-path) when selecting routes.

bgp bestpath med-confed

router, BGP

```
bgp bestpath med-confed
no bgp bestpath med-confed
```

Configures   BGP route selection

Default   Disabled

Description

This command enables MED comparison among paths from confederation peers.

---

bgp bestpath missing-as-worst
router, BGP

```
bgp bestpath missing-as-worst
no bgp bestpath missing-as-worst
```

Configures   BGP route selection

Default   Disabled

Description

By default, routers give a route with a missing MED a value of 1, which causes that route to be considered the best path. This command causes the router to assign a value of infinity to the missing MED, which makes the route the least desirable of all the routes. For more information on MED values, consult Chapter 10.

---

bgp client-to-client reflection
router, BGP

```
bgp client-to-client reflection
no bgp client-to-client reflection
```

Configures   Route reflection

Default   Enabled

Description

A route reflector automatically reflects routes from one BGP client to another. The no form of this command disables route reflection. Route reflection isn't needed if the clients already have fully meshed IBGP connections, because the clients will learn their routes directly from each other.

---

bgp cluster-id
router, BGP

```
bgp cluster-id id
no bgp cluster-id id
```

Configures   Cluster ID of a route reflector

Default   Router ID

Description

This command specifies the cluster ID (*id*) for a BGP router. When you have one route reflector, its cluster ID is normally its router ID. If there is more than one route reflector in a cluster, they must all have the same cluster ID. In this case, you would use the bgp cluster-id command to specify the ID explicitly. A cluster ID is four bytes long.

Example

The following BGP configuration creates a BGP process for autonomous system 10. This router is designated as a route reflector. We set its cluster ID explicitly, because there is presumably more than one route reflector in the cluster.

```
router bgp 10
    network 10.200.200.1 route-reflector
    bgp cluster-id 10000
```

---

bgp confederation identifier
router, BGP

```
bgp confederation identifier as
no bgp confederation identifier as
```

Configures   AS number of the confederation

Default   None

Description

This command specifies the autonomous system (AS) number for a confederation. A confederation is a group of small autonomous systems that appear to the world as a single large autonomous system. The autonomous system number for the confederation is set to *as*.

---

bgp confederation peers
router, BGP

```
bgp confederation peers as [as]
no bgp confederation peers as [as]
```

Configures   A BGP confederation

Default   None

Description

This command lets you list the AS numbers that belong to the confederation.

Example

```
router bgp 1000
    bgp conferation peers 1001 1002 1003 1004
```

---

bgp dampening
global

```
bgp dampening [half-life reuse suppress max-suppress-time] [route-map map]
no bgp dampening [half-life reuse suppress max-suppress-time] [route-map map]
```

Configures   BGP dampening settings

Defaults

half-life, 15 min; *reuse*, 750; *suppress*, 2000; *max-suppress-time*, 60 min

---

Description

This command allows you to specify the route dampening values for BGP. Dampening allows you to control "route flap," which is routing instability that results from a route making repeated transitions.

half-life
> The time in minutes after which a penalty is decreased by half.

reuse
> If the penalty for a flapping route increases to this value, the route can be reused.

suppress
> When the penalty exceeds this limit, the route is suppressed.

max-suppress-time
> The maximum amount of time a route can be suppressed; this should be about four times the half-life.

route-map *map*
> A route map that controls which routes are selected for route dampening.

---

bgp default local-preference   router, BGP

```
bgp default local-preference value
no bgp default local-preference value
```

Configures   BGP local preference

Default   100

Description

This command allows you to set the local preference to *value*. The higher the preference, the better the path. Acceptable values range from 0 to 4,294,967,295.

---

bgp default route-target filter   router, BGP

```
bgp default route-target filter
no bgp default route-target filter
```

Configures   BGP route-target community filtering

Default   Enabled

Description

When the no form of this command is used, all received VPN IPv4 routes are accepted. If the router is an autonomous system border or customer edge router, this is the desired behavior.

bgp deterministic med

```
bgp deterministic med
no bgp deterministic med
```

Configures   BGP route selection

Default   Disabled

Description

By default, the router does not compare the MED values for paths learned from different autonomous systems within the same confederation. This command allows you to enable MED comparison for routes learned from different autonomous systems within the same confederation.

bgp fast-external-fallover

```
bgp fast-external-fallover
no bgp fast-external-fallover
```

Configures   BGP fast failover

Default
Enabled

Description

This command enables the router to reset the BGP sessions of any direct peers immediately if the link that connects the router to the peer goes down.

bgp log-neighbor-changes

```
bgp log-neighbor-changes
no bgp log-neighbor-changes
```

Configures   BGP logging

Default   Disabled prior to IOS 12.1

Description

This command allows you to log changes in the status of BGP neighbors.

bgp-policy

```
bgp-policy {source | destination} {ip-prec-map | ip-qos-map}
no bgp-policy {source | destination} {ip-prec-map | ip-qos-map}
```

Configures   Propagation of policy information via BGP

Default   Disabled

Description

This command allows the propagation of policy information that is based on the IP precedence setting via BGP. To enable this properly, you must also configure a route map to set the IP precedence or QoS (quality of service) group ID by using the set ip precedence or set ip qos-group commands.

source
> Use the precedence or QoS bit from the source address.

destination
> Use the precedence or QoS bit from the destination address.

ip-prec-map
> Use IP precedence as the QoS policy.

ip-qos-map
> Use the QoS group ID as the QoS policy.

bridge acquire   global

bridge *bridge-group* acquire
no bridge *bridge-group* acquire

Configures   Bridge forwarding

Default   Enabled

Description

By default, the router forwards frames from dynamically learned hosts. The no form of this command allows you to change this behavior so that the router only forwards frames from statically configured stations. To create static bridge hosts, use the bridge address command.

bridge address   global

bridge bridge-group address mac {forward | discard} [interface]
no bridge bridge-group address mac

Configures   Static bridge hosts

Default   None

Description

This command allows a bridge group to filter packets based on the MAC address.

bridge-group
> The bridge group to which this command applies. A bridge group can have a value of 1 to 63. On larger routers, the value can be from 1 to 255.

mac
> The MAC address to be filtered.

forward
> This keyword tells the router to forward frames from the given MAC address to other interfaces in the bridge group.

discard
> This keyword tells the router to discard frames from the given MAC address.

interface
> Optional. The interface on which the MAC address can be found.

---

bridge cmf   global

```
bridge cmf
no bridge cmf
```

Configures   Constrained Multicast Flooding (CMF)

Default   Disabled

Description

This command enables CMF for all configured bridge groups.

---

bridge crb   global

```
bridge crb
no bridge crb
```

Configures   Concurrent Routing and Bridging (CRB)

Default   Disabled

Description

This command allows the router to route and bridge a protocol at the same time but on different interfaces. Unlike Integrated Routing and Bridging (IRB), the routed and bridged interfaces cannot communicate with each other.

---

bridge forward-time   global

```
bridge bridge-group forward-time seconds
no bridge bridge-group forward-time seconds
```

Configures   The forward delay interval

Default   30 seconds

Description

This command sets the bridge forwarding delay interval for the interface to *seconds*. The value of *seconds* can be from 10 to 200. (Note: Catalysts use 6–40 seconds.)

---

bridge-group

interface

```
bridge-group bridge-group
no bridge-group bridge-group
```

Configures   Makes an interface part of a bridge group

Default   None

Description

This command makes the interface a member of the given bridge group. Use the no form of this command to remove the bridge group from the interface.

bridge-group aging-time

global

```
bridge-group bridge-group aging-time seconds
no bridge-group bridge-group aging-time
```

Configures   The time that a dynamic entry remains in the bridge table

Default   300 seconds

Description

This command sets the amount of time in *seconds* that a dynamic entry can remain in the bridge table. If the entry is updated, the counter starts over. The value can range from 0 to 1,000,000 seconds.

bridge-group circuit-group

interface

```
bridge-group bridge-group circuit-group circuit-group
no bridge-group bridge-group circuit-group circuit-group
```

Configures   Assigns a circuit group to a bridge group for the interface

Default   None

Description

This command assigns a circuit group for a bridge group. It is used only for HDLC encapsulated interfaces.

bridge-group input-address-list

interface

```
bridge-group bridge-group input-address-list access-list
no bridge-group bridge-group input-address-list access-list
```

Configures   Allows an interface to filter based on an access list

Default   None

Description

This command applies an access list to an interface for a bridge group. This access list must filter based on MAC addresses, which means that the access list must be an Ethernet access list with a number between 700 and 799. By applying an access list, you can permit or deny bridging to hosts based on the MAC addresses.

bridge-group input-lsap-list interface

bridge-group *bridge-group* input-lsap-list *access-list*
no bridge-group *bridge-group* input-lsap-list *access-list*

Configures   An access list for filtering IEEE 802.2 packets

Default   Disabled

Description

This command applies an access list to all IEEE 802.2 packets received on the interface.

bridge-group input-pattern interface

bridge-group *bridge-group* input-pattern *access-list*
no bridge-group *bridge-group* input-pattern *access-list*

Configures   An access list for a bridge group

Default   None

Description

This command applies an access list to incoming packets on an interface for a specific bridge group.

bridge-group input-type-list interface

bridge-group *bridge-group* input-type-list *access-list*
no bridge-group *bridge-group* input-type-list *access-list*

Configures   An access list for a bridge group

Default   None

Description

This command applies an access list to all incoming Ethernet and SNAP frames on an interface for a specific bridge group.

bridge-group output-address-list

interface

```
bridge-group bridge-group output-address-list access-list
no bridge-group bridge-group output-address-list access-list
```

Configures   Filtering based on an access list

Default   None

Description

This command allows you to apply an access list to an interface for a bridge group. This access list can filter based on MAC addresses, which means the access list must be an Ethernet access list numbered 700 through 799. With this command, you can permit or deny bridging to hosts based on the MAC addresses.

bridge-group output-lsap-list

interface

```
bridge-group bridge-group output-lsap-listaccess-list
no bridge-group bridge-group output-lsap-list access-list
```

Configures   An access list for outgoing IEEE 802.2

Default   Disabled

Description

This command applies an access list to all IEEE 802.2 packets leaving the interface.

bridge-group output-pattern

interface

```
bridge-group bridge-group output-pattern access-list
no bridge-group bridge-group output-pattern access-list
```

Configures   An access list for a bridge group

Default   None

Description

This command applies an access list to outgoing packets on an interface for a specific bridge group.

bridge-group output-type-list

interface

```
bridge-group bridge-group output-type-list access-list
no bridge-group bridge-group output-type-list access-list
```

Configures   An access list for a bridge group

Default   None

Reference
A-B

Description

This command applies an access list to all outgoing Ethernet and SNAP frames on an interface for a specific bridge group.

---

bridge-group path-cost interface

```
bridge-group bridge-group path-cost value
no bridge-group bridge-group path-cost value
```

Configures   Changes a bridge group's path cost for an interface

Default   Based on the interface's bandwidth setting

Description

This command changes the path cost for an interface, which is usually calculated as 10,000 ÷ bandwidth, where the bandwidth is the value set by the bandwidth command or the default bandwidth for the interface. The *value* can be from 1 to 65,535. The higher the value, the higher the cost.

---

bridge-group priority interface

```
bridge-group bridge-group priority value
no bridge-group bridge-group priority value
```

Configures   Assigns a priority to a bridge group

Default

32,768 for bridges using the IEEE protocol; 128 for bridges using the Digital spanning-tree protocol

Description

This command assigns a priority to an interface within the given *bridge-group*. *value* specifies the interface's priority; this must be between 0 and 65,535. A higher priority increases the chance that the interface will be selected as the root bridge.

---

bridge-group spanning-disabled interface

```
bridge-group bridge-group spanning-disabled
no bridge-group bridge-group spanning-disabled
```

Configures   Use of the spanning-tree algorithm

Default   Enabled

Description

This command disables the spanning-tree algorithm for the given *bridge-group*. The spanning algorithm can be disabled safely for bridge groups that have no possible loop paths at layer 2.

Example

```
interface ethernet 1
  bridge-group 1
  bridge-group 1 spanning-disabled
```

bridge hello-time   global

bridge *bridge-group* hello-time *seconds*
no bridge *bridge-group* hello-time *seconds*

Configures   The interval between hello packets

Default

2 seconds

Description

This command sets the hello interval for the given *bridge-group* to *seconds*. The value of *seconds* can be from 1 to 10.

bridge irb   global

bridge irb
no bridge irb

Configures   Integrated Routing and Bridging (IRB)

Default   Disabled

Description

Like CRB, IRB allows a router to both route and bridge a single protocol. However, unlike CRB, IRB allows the routed and bridged interfaces to communicate with each other. See also interface bvi.

bridge max-age   global

bridge*bridge-group* max-age *seconds*
no bridge *bridge-group* max-age *seconds*

Configures   The time to save Bridge Protocol Data Units (BPDUs)

Default   15 seconds

Description

This command sets the maximum time that the router will wait to hear from the root bridge for the given *bridge-group*. If the router does not hear from the root bridge within this interval, the spanning tree is recomputed. The value of *seconds* can be from 6 to 200. (Note: Catalysts use 6–40 seconds.)

bridge multicast-source

global

```
bridge bridge-group multicast-source
no bridge bridge-group multicast-source
```

Configures   Bridging to support the forwarding of multicast packets

Default   Disabled

Description
This command permits the given *bridge-group* to forward multicast packets.

bridge priority

global

```
bridge bridge-group priority value
no bridge bridge-group priority value
```

Configures   The priority of an individual bridge

Default   32768 for bridges using the IEEE protocol; 128 for bridges using the Digital spanning-tree protocol

Description
This command assigns a priority to an individual bridge within the given *bridge-group*. *value* specifies the interface's priority; *value* must be between 0 and 65535. A higher priority increases the chance that an interface will be selected as the root bridge. To set an interface to a specific priority, use the bridge-group priority command.

bridge protocol

global

```
bridge bridge-group protocol {ieee | dec}
no bridge bridge-group protocol {ieee | dec}
```

Configures   The spanning-tree protocol

Default   None

Description
This command selects the spanning-tree protocol to use for the *bridge-group*. Possible values are dec, for the Digital spanning-tree protocol, and ieee, for the IEEE spanning-tree protocol. IEEE is the recommend protocol.

bridge route

global

```
bridge bridge-group route protocol {apollo | appletalk | clns | decnet | ip |
    ipx | vines | xns}
no bridge bridge-group route protocol {apollo | appletalk | clns | decnet | ip
    | ipx | vines | xns}
```

Configures   Routing of a protocol in a bridge group

Default   None

Description

This command enables routing of the given *protocol* on a specific bridge group. The protocol parameter may be apollo, appletalk, clns, decnet, ip, ipx, vines, or xns.

Example

This example enables routing of both IP and IPX in a CRB environment:

```
bridge crb
bridge 5 protocol ieee
bridge 5 route ip
bridge 5 ipx
```

busy-message

global

```
busy-message hostname delimiter message delimiter
no busy-message
```

Configures   The message displayed when a connection fails

Default   None

Description

This command sets the message that is displayed when a telnet connection to a specific host (given by the *hostname* parameter) fails. The new *message* replaces the generic "host failed" message. To disable this message, delete it with the no form of this command. This banner is useful when you want to give the user information about the connection failure. The *delimiter* marks the beginning and end of the message; it may be any character that is not used in the message.

Example

```
Router(config)#busy-message sunserver2 # server2 is down,
please contact sysadmin at 555-1234 #
```

cable helper-address   interface

```
cable helper-address ip-address [cable-modem | host ]
no cable helper-address ip-address [cable-modem | host ]
```

Configures   DHCP destination address

Default   Disabled

Description
This command specifies an IP address of a DHCP server to use for UDP broadcasts
from cable modems or other hosts. The cable-modem option specifies that only cable
modem UDP broadcasts are forwarded while the host option specifies that only host
UDP broadcasts are forwarded.

calendar set   command

```
calendar set hh:mm:ss day month year
```

Configures   The system calendar

Description
The calendar is available only on high-end routers. It is an internal clock that
continues to run even when the router is powered off. This command allows you to set
the calendar to a new time. The *month* must be a name, for example, june. The *year*
must be a complete four-digit value, for example, 2000.

callback forced-wait   global

```
callback forced-wait seconds
no callback forced-wait seconds
```

Configures   The time the router waits before a callback

Default   None

Description
This command specifies the amount of time in *seconds* that the router waits before
initiating a callback to a remote modem.

cd   command

```
cd [URL]
```

Description
This command changes the current working directory within the router's filesystem.
The URL is optional; if not provided, the system defaults to the *flash:* directory. See
the copy command for other valid filesystem URLs.

cdp advertise-v2

```
cdp advertise-v2
no cdp advertise-v2
```

Configures   Cisco Discovery Protocol (CDP)

Default   Enabled

Description

This command enables Version 2 of CDP, which provides added information. CDP is available only on Cisco routers.

cdp enable

```
cdp enable
no cdp enable
```

Configures   Cisco Discovery Protocol (CDP)

Default   Enabled

Description

This command enables CDP on a specific interface. CDP provides information about neighboring Cisco routers. It is a proprietary protocol, and therefore isn't implemented by other router vendors. Use show cdp neighbors to see the output.

Example

```
interface ethernet0
  cdp enable
```

cdp holdtime

```
cdp holdtime seconds
no cdp holdtime seconds
```

Configures   CDP holdtime

Default   180 seconds

Description

This command sets the amount of time, in seconds, that the router holds CDP packets before discarding them.

cdp run

global

```
cdp run
no cdp run
```

Configures   Globally enables/disables CDP

Default   Enabled

Description
This command enables CDP on all interfaces.

Example
```
Router(config)#cdp run
```

---

cdp timer

global

```
cdp timer seconds
no cdp timer seconds
```

Configures   CDP update broadcast interval

Default   60 seconds

Description
This command sets the interval, in *seconds*, at which the router transmits CDP updates to its neighbors.

---

channel-group (controller)

controller

```
channel-group channel-number timeslots range [speed kbps]
no channel-group channel-number timeslots range [speed kbps]
```

Configures   T1 or E1 timeslots

Default   None

Description
This command defines the channel timeslots for a fractional T1 or E1 line. Your service provider determines the timeslots for your lines.

channel-number

A number identifying the communication channel you are defining. For T1 lines, the channel number can be from 0 to 23; for E1 lines, 0 to 30.

timeslots range

A list of timeslots that make up this communication channel. The list can be a series of comma-separated timeslot numbers, or a pair of timeslots separated by a dash to indicate a range. Timeslot numbers range from 1 to 24 on a T1 line; 1 to 31 for E1. A timeslot cannot belong to more than one channel group.

speed *kbps*

The speed of a single timeslot in Kbps. Allowable values are 48, 56, and 64. 56 is the default for T1; 64 is the default for E1.

Example

When defining the timeslots range, the value can be a single number or a group of ranges separated by commas and hyphens. For example, the following ranges are all valid:

```
channel-group 3 timeslots 4
channel-group 5 timeslots 4,6-15,24
channel-group 8 timeslots 4-10
```

channel-group (interface)   interface

channel-group *channel-number*
no channel-group *channel-number*

Configures   A Fast EtherChannel group

Default   None

Description

This command allows a Fast Ethernet interface to be part of a Fast EtherChannel group. A Fast EtherChannel group allows multiple point-to-point Fast Ethernet interfaces to act as one logical interface. At most, four Fast Ethernet interfaces can belong to a channel group.

chat-script   global

chat-script *name script-string*
no chat-script *name script-string*

Configures   A chat script for placing a call over a modem

Default   None

Description

The chat-script command defines the script to use for modem communication when dialing to a remote device. *name* identifies the chat script for use in other commands; *script-string* specifies the script itself. The *script-string* contains a series of expect/send characters that communicate with the modem. Table 17-3 shows special characters and escape codes that can be used in chat scripts. Chat scripts are allowed only on asynchronous interfaces like ASYNC and BRI.

Table 17-3. Special values and escape codes for chat scripts

Character or code	Meaning
" "	Null string
ABORT string	The string following the ABORT indicates why the script failed
TIMEOUT timeout	Set the timeout to wait for a response; default is 5 seconds

Table 17-3. Special values and escape codes for chat scripts (continued)

Character or code	Meaning
EOT	End of transmission character
BREAK	Send a BREAK character
\c	Suppress newline at end of string
\d	Cause a two-second delay
\n	Send a newline
\p	Pause for one-fourth of a second
\r	Send a return character
\s	Send a space character
\t	Send a tab character
\\	Send a backslash character
\T	Replaced with phone number

class (frame-relay)

frame-relay

```
class name
no class name
```

Configures   Association of a map class with a DLCI

Default   None

Description

This command associates the map class given by *name* with a Data Link Connection Identifier (DLCI).

class (MPLS)

CoS map, MPLS

```
class class [available | standard | premium | control]
no class class
```

Configures   MPLS

Default   Disabled

Description

This command specifies a class that shows how classes map to Label Switched Controlled Virtual Circuits (LVCs).

class

   The precedence of identified traffic to classify (from 0 to 7).

available

   Optional. Means low precedence.

standard

   Optional. Means next precedence.

```
premium
```
Optional. Means high precedence.
```
control
```
Optional. Means highest precedence.

Example
```
mpls cos-map 50
  Class 1 premium
```

---

class (policy-map)   policy-map

```
class name
no class name
```

Configures   The name of a class within a policy

Default   None

Description
This command identifies the name of the class to change or modify within a policy.
The policy-map command must be used to enter the policy map configuration mode
before entering this command. The maximum number of classes that can be configured for a router is 64.

Example
```
policy-map policy1
  class class1
    bandwidth 1000
    queue-limit 50
  class class2
    bandwidth 2000
    random-detect
```

---

class-map   global

```
class-map name [ match-all | match-any]
no class-map name [ match-all | match-any]
```

Configures   A class map to be used for matching packets to a specified class

Default   None

Description
This command creates a class map, which is used for matching packets with a defined
class. The name is the class's name as defined in the policy-map. match-all means that all
of the following criteria must be met before a packet is marked for the class. match-any
means that if any of the following criteria matches, the packet is marked for the class.

The class map consists of a set of criteria defined by the match command.

Example

```
class-map class1 match-all
    match input-interface ethernet0
    match access-group 100
```

---

clear   command

```
clear command
```

Description

A clear command erases counters for various statistics or performs a reset action. For example, clear line clears an asynchronous line and drops the connection, while clear cdp counters resets the Cisco Discovery Protocol statistics. Table 17-4 summarizes the many clear commands.

Table 17-4. Clear commands

Command	Subcommand	Action
clear access-list	counters	Clears access list statistical information.
clear access-template		Clears the access template.
clear arp-cache		Clears the entire ARP cache.
clear bridge		Resets bridge forwarding cache.
	multicast	Resets multicast group state.
clear bstun		Clears counters displayed in show bstun.
clear cdp		Resets CDP information.
	counters	Clears CDP counters.
	table	Clears the CDP table.
clear counters	*interface*	Clears counters on one or all interfaces.
clear controller		
clear crypto		Resets encryption subsystem.
clear dialer	*interface*	Clears dialer statistics.
clear frame-relay-inarp		Clears inverse ARP entries from the map table.
clear host	*	Deletes all host table entrie.s
	name	Deletes the given host table entry.
clear hub	ethernet *n*	Clears (resets) a hub.
	counters	Clears hub statistics.
clear interface		Clears the hardware logic on an interface.
clear ip access-list counters		Clears access list statistical information.
clear ip access-template		Clears the IP access template.
clear ip accounting		Clears the IP accounting database.
clear ip bgp		Clears BGP connections (resets all connections).
	*	Clears all BGP connections.
	as number	Clears the peer AS number.
	ip address	Clears the IP address of peer.

Table 17-4. Clear commands (continued)

Command	Subcommand	Action
	dampening	Clears route-dampening information.
	flap-statis-tics	Clears route-flap statistics.
	peer-group	Clears connections of a BGP peer group.
clear ip cache		Deletes cache table entries.
clear ip cgmp	*interface*	Resets the Cisco Group Management Protocol (CGMP); if no interface is specified, resets all interfaces.
clear ip drp		Clears director responder counters.
clear ip dvmrp		Clears DVMRP counters.
clear ip eigrp		Clears IP-EIGRP (resets all connections).
	as number	
	neighbors	
clear ip igmp group		Clears IGMP group cache entries.
clear ip mroute		Deletes multicast route table entries.
	*	Deletes all entries.
	IP-address or *name*	Deletes entries for the group name or IP address.
clear ip mtag		Clears multicast tag information base (TIB) entries (resets all connections).
clear ip nat		Clears NAT.
	statistics	
	translation	
clear ip nhrp		Clears the NHRP cache.
clear ip ospf redistribution		Clears OSPF redistribution counters.
clear ip pim	auto-rp	Clears the auto-rp table.
	interface	Clears the PIM packet count for that interface.
clear ip prefix-list		Clears the prefix list.
clear ip redirect		Clears the redirect cache.
clear ip route	*	Deletes all route table entries.
	IP-address	Deletes route to IP addresses.
clear ip rsvp		Clears RSVP (Resource Reservation Protocol).
	reservation	
	sender	
clear ip rtp header-compression		Clears RTP/UDP/IP header compression statistics.
clear ip sdr	*group-ip*	Clears the Session Directory (SDPv2) cache.
clear ip trigger-authentication		Clears trigger-authentication host table.
clear isis		Clears all IS-IS data structures.
clear kerberos creds		Clears Kerberos credentials.
clear line		Resets a terminal line.
clear logging		Clears logging buffer.

Table 17-4. Clear commands (continued)

Command	Subcommand	Action
clear mac-address-table		Removes entries from MAC address table.
clear rif-cache		Clears the entire RIF cache.
clear smrp		Clears Simple Multicast Routing Protocol (SMRP) statistics.
clear snapshot		Clears snapshot timers
clear source-bridge		Clears counters displayed in show source-bridge.
clear tarp		Resets TID Address Resolution Protocol (TARP) information.
clear tcp		Clears a TCP connection or statistics.
	line	Clears TTY line.
	local	Clears local host.
	statistics	Clears TCP protocol statistics.
clear vlan		Deletes a VLAN from a management domain.
clear vpdn		Clears a VPDN entity.
clear x25		Resets X.25 circuits.

client-atm-address name
LANE database

```
client-atm-address atm-address name elan-name
no client-atm-address atm-address
```

Configures   Adds a LANE client address to the database

Default   None

Description

This command adds a LANE client address to the LAN emulation configuration server's database.

atm-address
> Either a complete ATM address or a template that specifies matching ATM addresses. You can create a template by using wildcard characters: an asterisk (*) to match a single character, or an ellipsis (...) to match any number of leading, middle, or trailing characters. A full address is 20 bytes (40 hex characters) long, and is similar to (though not the same as) an NSAP address.

name elan-name
> The name of the emulated LAN. The maximum length of a name is 32 characters.

If you use a template, any name that matches the template is associated with the ELAN. If the given address or template matches addresses that are already in the database, the command has no effect; the database is not changed.

clock calendar-valid

```
clock calendar-valid
no clock calendar-valid
```

Configures   Network Time Protocol (NTP)

Default   Disabled

Description

This command tells the router to consider the RTC calendar in hardware to be a valid source of time. This command is valid only on high-end routers (5000, 6000, 7500, 8500, etc.).

clock rate

```
clock rate bps
no clock rate
```

Configures   Clock rate for serial devices

Default   None

Description

By default, no clock rate is configured for any serial devices. This command specifies the bit rate for DCE serial devices in bps. Possible values for *bps* are 1200, 2400, 4800, 9600, 19200, 38400, 56000, 64000, 72000, 125000, 148000, 500000, 800000, 1000000, 1300000, 2000000, and 4000000.

This command is most useful for connecting routers back-to-back in a lab setting. In this case, the command is required only on the DCE end of the link. You usually don't need this command when connecting to a WAN service because the network provider provides the clockings.

clock read-calendar

```
clock read-calendar
```

Configures   Calendar time

Description

This command manually updates the calendar time into the router's system clock. It is not a configuration command and is not stored in the router's configuration. Normally, the system clock is updated from the calendar during system boot-up. This command is available only on high-end routers (5000, 6000, 7500, 8500, etc.).

clock set

`clock set hh:mm:ss day month year`

Description

This command manually sets the router's internal clock. It is not stored in the router's configuration. The time is specified in terms of a 24-hour clock; the year must be a full four digits (for example, 2001).

---

clock summer-time

`clock summer-time zone recurring [sweek sday smonth shh:mm eweek eday emonth ehh:mm][offset]`

`clock summer-time zone date sday smonth syear shh:mm eday emonth eyear ehh:mm [offset]`

`no clock summer-time`

Configures daylight savings time behavior

Default No daylight savings time

Description

This command tells the router to update for daylight savings time. The `recurring` form of the command specifies that daylight savings time should be observed at the given time every year. The `date` form of the command specifies a specific start date and end date for daylight savings time. Use the `no` form of the command to return to the default, in which daylight savings time is not observed.

zone
> The time zone (EDT, CDT, etc.).

sweek, eweek
> The week of the month (1, 2, 3, 4, 5, last) on which daylight savings time begins (*sweek*) or ends (*eweek*). (This is only used in the `recurring` form of the command.)

sday, eday
> The day on which daylight savings time starts (*sday*) or ends (*eday*). For the `recurring` form of the command, use the actual name of the day (Monday, Tuesday, etc.) For the `date` form of the command, use a numeric date (1–31).

smonth, emonth
> The month in which daylight savings time starts (*smonth*) or ends (*emonth*). Use the actual name of the month (September, October, etc.).

syear, eyear
> All four digits of the year. *syear* is the year in which daylight savings time starts; *eyear* is the year in which it ends (used only in the `date` form of the command).

shh:mm, ehh:mm
> The time in hours and minutes at which daylight savings time starts or ends.

offset
> The number of minutes to add for daylight savings time (optional; the default is 60).

Example

The following command sets the time zone to use U.S. rules in the Eastern time zone:

```
clock summer-time EDT recurring
```

clock timezone

global

```
clock timezone zone hours[minutes]
no clock timezone
```

Configures   The router's time zone

Default   Coordinated Universal Time (UTC)

Description

This command sets the router's time zone and the number of hours from the UTC. *minutes* is optional and is also an offset from the UTC.

zone
> The time zone (PST, EST, etc.).

hours
> The offset from the UTC (a positive or negative integer).

minutes
> Optional. The offset from the UTC in minutes (a positive or negative integer).

clock update-calendar

command

```
clock update-calendar
```

Configures   Updates the calendar

Description

This command manually updates the calendar from the router's system clock. The calendar is a separate internal clock that continuously runs even if the router is powered off. This command is available only on high-end routers (5000, 6000, 7500, 8500, etc.).

compress

interface

```
compress {predictor | stac}
no compress {predictor | stac}
```

Configures   Type of compression used across an interface

Default   None

Description

This command enables compression for the selected interface. Compression can be enabled only for PPP or HDLC encapsulation. Two types of compression are supported:

predictor
> Can be used on PPP connections; consumes more of the router's CPU and memory, but less bandwidth.

stac
> Can be used on HDLC or PPP connections; consumes more bandwidth, but requires less CPU power.

Compression should not be activated on lines where link speeds are very high or most of the data is already compressed. If the data is already compressed, the router spends valuable CPU cycles for no reason.

When using compression, monitor the router's CPU usage. If the CPU usage is consistently high (65%), compression might be hindering the router.

The same type of compression must be enabled on both ends of the link.

Example

The following commands enable stac compression for the serial1 interface, which uses HDLC encapsulation.

```
interface serial1
  encapsulation hdlc
  compress stac
```

---

config-register   global

config-register *value*

Configures   Sets the configuration register

Default   Depends on the product

Description

This command allows the user to change the configuration register. Setting the configuration register is useful for recovering lost passwords and remedying other situations.

value
> The value to set in the configuration register. The register is 16 bits wide, so legal values range from 0x0 to 0xFFFF in hexadecimal (0 to 65,535 decimal). Table 17-5 shows the significance of the bits in the configuration register. (There are some differences in bit assignments on different products; check your documentation.)

Table 17-5. Configuration register settings

Bit number	Value	Action
00	0x0000	Remains at the system bootstrap prompt.
01	0x0001	Boots system image on EPROM.
02,03	0x0002–0x000f	Specifies a Netboot filename, where the filename is in the form cisco-processor_name. The *n* in the filename is taken from the hexadecimal value of these bits.

Table 17-5. Configuration register settings (continued)

Bit number	Value	Action
06	0x0040	Ignores NVRAM contents.
07	0x0080	Enables OEM bit.
08	0x0100	Breaks disabled. If you enable this bit, the break key can cause the router to go to boot ROM at any time. During the first 60 seconds of bootup, the break key is enabled no matter what this bit field is set to.
10	0x0400	Sets the IP broadcast address to all zeros.
05,11,12	0x0020,0x0800, 0x1000	Sets the console line speed. See next table for more information.
13	0x2000	Boots default ROM software if network boot fails.
14	0x4000	IP broadcasts do not have network numbers.
15	0x8000	Enables diagnostic messages.

Since the baud settings are now spread over three different bits (5, 11, and 12), Table 17-6 shows the baud settings for the bits:

Table 17-6. Bit settings for possible baud rates

Speed (bits per second)	Bit 5	Bit 12	Bit 11
115200	1	1	1
57600	1	1	0
38400	1	0	1
19200	1	0	0
9600	0	0	0
4800	0	0	1
2400	0	1	1
1200	0	1	0

configure   command

configure {terminal | memory | network | overwrite-network}

Configures   Enters global configuration mode

Description
The conf terminal command places you in configuration mode. conf memory executes the commands stored in memory (essentially a reload of the startup config). Note that the commands conf network and conf overwrite-network have been deprecated; it is now preferable to use copy tftp running-config.

Example
The following command places you in configuration mode; from there, you can enter global configuration commands.

```
Router#configure terminal
Router(config)# ! I can now enter configuration commands!
```

controller

```
controller {t1 | e1} slot/port
controller {t1 | e1} number
```

Configures   T1 or E1 controllers

Default   None

Description

This command places you in the controller mode, allowing you to configure a controller for a T1 or E1 line. *slot/port* and *number* identify the controller that you are configuring.

copy

```
copy source [destination]
```

Description

This command allows you to copy system images and configuration files. You can copy files within the router's memory (for example, copy running-config startup-config), or you can copy files to or from a TFTP server or an RCP server. Table 17-7 shows possible values for the *source* and *destination* parameters. If you omit the destination, the router will prompt you for it.

Table 17-7. Sources and destinations for the copy command

Sources and destinations	Meaning
running-config	The currently running configuration
startup-config	The configuration that will be loaded when the router boots
tftp	An external TFTP server
rcp	An external RCP server
ftp	An external FTP server
flash	The router's flash filesystem
scp	An external SSH server's secure copy protocol
slot0: slot1:	The router's PCMCIA flash memory cards
disk0: disk1:	The router's internal drives (high-end routers)
bootflash	The internal bootstrap flash memory; only on some devices (4500)

Newer versions of IOS also permit the use of URLs. The syntax of a URL can look like this:

```
tftp:[[//hostname]/path]/filename
ftp:[[//[username[:password]@]hostname]/path]/filename
rcp:[[//[username@]hostname]/path]/filename
scp:[[//[username@hostname]/path]/filename
```

In each of these URLs, the *hostname* is simply the hostname or IP address of the end device. TFTP doesn't require a username or password. FTP and RCP can have an optional username and password, which depends on the server configuration.

To use the URL, simply provide the correct hostname and path in the source or destination.

Example

Here are some accepted uses of the copy command:

```
copy running-config startup-config
copy startup-config tftp
copy running-config tftp
copy flash tftp
copy startup-config rcp
copy running-config rcp
copy flash rcp
copy tftp running-config
copy tftp://ourserver/newconfig running-config
copy ftp://bob:letmein@oursever/newconfig running-config
```

---

crc
interface

crc *length*

no crc

Configures   The length of the CRC checksum

Default   16 bits

Description

This command sets the *length* (in bits) of the CRC (Cyclic Redundancy Check) on FSIP (Fast Serial Interface Processor) and HIP (HSSI Interface Processor) interfaces. These interfaces are found only on the 7500 series routers. The length must be 16 or 32 bits.

---

custom-queue-list
interface

custom-queue-list *list-number*

no custom-queue-list *list-number*

Configures   Applies a custom queue list to an interface

Default   None

Description

This command applies a custom queue to the current interface. The *list-number* must be between 1 and 16. Custom queue lists are used to implement priority-based queuing; they allow you to configure the bandwidth used by a particular type of traffic. To create a queue list, use the queue-list command. If you're configuring a Frame Relay interface, see the frame-relay custom-queue-list command. Queue lists are discussed in Chapter 11.

databits

databits {5 | 6 | 7 | 8}

Configures   Databits per character

Default   8

Description
This command defines the number of databits per character that are interpreted and generated by the hardware. Possible values are 5, 6, 7, and 8.

Example
The following commands configure TTY 3 for seven databits per character:

```
Router(config)#line tty3
Router(config-line)#databits 7
```

data-character-bits

data-character-bits {7 | 8}

Configures   Software databits per character

Default   8

Description
This command defines the number of databits per character that are interpreted and generated by the software. Possible values are 7 and 8.

dce-terminal-timing enable

dce-terminal-timing enable
no dce-terminal-timing enable

Configures   Interface timing

Default   Off (the DCE provides its own clock)

Description
This command prevents phase-shifting of data on high-speed data lines that span long distances. Phase-shifting is prevented by taking the clock from the DTE to provide timing for the DCE. (The DTE's timing is called SCTE.)

debug

debug *level*
undebug *level*
undebug all

Configures   System debugging

Default   Disabled

Description

This command enables debugging at the specified *level*. Just about every configuration item within the IOS has a debug level associated with it. The debug ? command gives you an extensive list that allows you to find the debug level that meets your needs.

Be careful in selecting your debug level; you can easily crash a busy router with the incorrect selection. For example, debug ip packet might render a busy router useless until debugging is disabled. See Chapter 16 for more information on using debug correctly. If you get in trouble, issue the command undebug all, which disables all debug output.

Example

Here is the output from debug ip ?:

```
Router#debug ip ?
   bgp        BGP information
   cache      IP cache operations
   cgmp       CGMP protocol activity
   dvmrp      DVMRP protocol activity
   egp        EGP information
   eigrp      IP-EIGRP information
   error      IP error debugging
   ftp        FTP dialogue
   http       HTTP connections
   icmp       ICMP transactions
   igmp       IGMP protocol activity
   igrp       IGRP information
   mcache     IP multicast cache operations
   mobile     Mobility protocols
   mpacket    IP multicast packet debugging
   mrouting   IP multicast routing table activity
   ospf       OSPF information
   packet     General IP debugging and IPSO security transactions
   peer       IP peer address activity
   pim        PIM protocol activity
   policy     Policy routing
   rip        RIP protocol transactions
   routing    Routing table events
   rsvp       RSVP protocol activity
   sd         Session Directory (SD)
   security   IP security options
   tcp        TCP information
   udp        UDP based transactions
```

Though there is a debug all command, using it is not recommended. It produces so much output that it will overwhelm you and the router. Use it only as a last resort.

The undebug all command disables all debugging that is currently enabled.

---

default-information

```
default-information {in | out} access-list
no default-information {in | out}
```

Configures   Default routing information

Default

EIGRP announces the default route in both incoming and outgoing updates

Description

When redistributing EIGRP into IGRP, you can use this command to allow (or suppress, using the no form of the command) the redistribution of the default routes or exterior routes from EIGRP. By default, all exterior routes (including default routes) are passed between IGRP and EIGRP.

in

Allows the protocol to receive the default route via redistribution.

out

Allows the protocol to propagate the default route via redistribution.

access-list

The number or name of a simple access list that permits or denies the default routes you want to propagate.

Example

The following commands prevent IGRP from receiving exterior or default routes via redistribution from EIGRP.

```
router igrp 109
  network 10.0.0.0
  redistribute eigrp 100
  no default-information in
```

To disable the default routes in outgoing updates, use the no form of the command.

```
router eigrp 100
  network 10.0.0.0
  no default-information out
```

default-information originate router, BGP, OSPF

```
default-information originate [route-map map]
no default information originate
```

BGP:
```
default-information originate
no default-information originate
```

OSPF:
```
default-information originate [always] [metric metric-value] [metric-type type]
   [route-map map]
no default-information originate [always] [metric metric-value]
   [metric-type type] [route-map map]
```

Configures   Redistribution of the default route

Default   Disabled

Description

This command allows the protocol to propagate the default route (0.0.0.0). The use of a route map, *map*, tells the router to inject the default route if the route map's conditions are met.

For OSPF, this command tells an Autonomous System Border Router (ASBR) to inject a default route into the OSPF domain. When used with OSPF, this command has the following additional parameters.

always
> Optional. Specifies to advertise the route even if the software does not have a default route.

metric metric-value
> Optional. The metric value of the default route. The default metric is 10.

metric-type metric-type
> Optional. Defines the link type associated with the default route. Possible values are 1 (Type-1 external route) and 2 (Type-2 external route; the default).

route-map map
> Optional. Defines the route map to use for the default route. The route is advertised only if the route map is successful. This option can be used to set a different default metric depending on the host to which the route is sent.

Example

```
! BGP
router bgp 150
  default-information orginate
!
! Ospf
router ospf 110
  default-information originate metric 100 metric-type 1
```

default-metric

BGP:

    default-metric number
    no default-metric number

RIP:

    default-metric number
    no default-metric

IGRP/EIGRP:

    default-metric bandwidth delay reliability loading mtu
    no default metric bandwidth delay reliability loading mtu

OSPF:

    default-metric number
    no default-metric number

Configures   Default metric for routes learned from a different routing protocol

Default   Depends on the protocol

Description

When redistributing routes from one routing protocol to another, the metrics used by the different protocols are not compatible. This command allows you to set the metric values for routes learned from other protocols.

For RIP and OSPF, this command simply sets the metric value to *number*.

For BGP, this command sets the value for the multi-exit discriminator (MED) metric to *number*.

For IGRP and EIGRP, this command sets the default metric for redistributing other protocols into EIGRP. (Note that IGRP and EIGRP have compatible metrics, so the default metric set by this command is not required when distributing routes between these two protocols.) The default metric is computed using the following parameters:

bandwidth
> The route bandwidth measured in kilobits per second.

delay
> The route delay in microseconds.

reliability
> An estimate of the reliability of packet transmission on this link. It must be a value between 0 and 255; 255 indicates 100% reliability and 0 indicates that the link is completely unreliable (no packets are transferred correctly).

loading
> The effective bandwidth of a route as a fraction of the bandwidth's capacity. This value must be between 0 and 255; 255 indicates 100% loading.

mtu
> The maximum transmission unit for this route in octets.

Example

The following commands assign metric 10 to all routes redistributed from OSPF into RIP:

```
router rip
   network 192.168.1.0
   default-metric 10
   redistribute ospf 110
```

The following commands provide various parameters for computing an EIGRP metric to be used when redistributing routes from RIP into EIGRP:

```
router eigrp 101
  network 10.0.0.0
  redistribute rip
  default-metric 1000 100 250 100 1500
```

---

default-name   LANE database

```
default-name elan-name
no default-name
```

Configures   A default ELAN for clients

Default   None

Description

This command sets the default name for the ELAN (Emulated LAN) in the configuration server's database. This name is used for clients who do not have an explicit name set. The name can be up to 32 characters in length and must already be in the configuration server's database. To put a name in the LANE emulation server database, use the commands lane database and name server-atm-address.

---

delay   interface

```
delay tens-of-milliseconds
no delay
```

Configures   Link delay

Default   Depends on the interface type

Description

This command is used to specify the latency of an interface in tens-of-milliseconds. The value is used as input to route metric calculations; it does not set anything on the interface itself.

delete command

```
delete URL
```

Description
This command marks a file as deleted in the flash filesystem. The actual behavior of this command depends on the type of filesystem implemented for your router. In a Class-A filesystem, deleted files are only marked for deletion, and can be recovered with the undelete command; the squeeze command permanently deletes the marked files. In a Class-B filesystem, files are deleted immediately, but the space they occupied can't be recovered without erasing the entire filesystem. In a Class-C filesystem, files are deleted immediately, and their space is recovered immediately. Filesystems are described in more detail in Chapter 2.

description interface

```
description text
no description
```

Configures   A description for the interface

Default   None

Description
This command provides a description for the interface, letting you build some documentation into your IOS configuration. The description is for informational purposes and does not affect the interface's behavior. The description you give appears in the output of some show commands.

Example
```
interface serial0
    description T1 Connection to Baltimore
```

dialer aaa interface

```
dialer aaa
no dialer aaa
```

Configures   AAA for dial-on-demand routing (DDR)

Default   Disabled

Description   This command enables AAA for a dialer interface.

dialer callback-secure

```
dialer callback-secure
no dialer callback-secure
```

Configures   Callback security

Default   Disabled

Description   This command enables secure callback dialing on the interface.

dialer callback-server

```
dialer callback-server [username] [dialstring]
no dialer callback-server
```

Configures   An interface to return calls

Default   Disabled

Description

This command enables an interface to return calls. The username keyword tells the router to identify the caller by looking up the authenticated hostname in the dialer map command; this is the default behavior for this command. The dialstring keyword tells the router to identify the caller during callback negotiation.

dialer caller

```
dialer caller number [callback]
no dialer caller number [callback]
```

Configures   Caller ID screening

Default   Disabled

Description

This command configures a dialer interface to reject calls that do not match the given number. The number can be any phone number; the character x can be used as a wildcard. The callback keyword enables Caller ID callback; in this case, the incoming call is refused, and the router initiates a call to the Caller ID number. This may help you to manage your telephone charges. This feature is available only on certain routers with special dialer interfaces. A switch that supports Caller ID is also required for this operation. If you enable this feature and do not have the required hardware for Caller ID, all calls are denied.

Example

The following command allows any number from 4,105,554,290 through 4,105,554,299:

```
dialer caller 410555429x
```

dialer dtr

interface

```
dialer dtr
no dialer dtr
```

Configures   Enables DDR and specifies that the modem handles only DTR
signaling

Default   None

Description

Configures interfaces that are connected to modems that require DTR (Data Terminal
Ready), and enables DDR. Interfaces configured with this command cannot receive
calls; they can only make them.

dialer enable-timeout

interface

```
dialer enable-timeout seconds
no dialer enable-timeout
```

Configures   The amount of time the interface remains down

Default   15 seconds

Description

Sets the time in seconds that an interface remains down between calls or failed
connections.

dialer fast-idle

interface, map-class

```
dialer fast-idle seconds
no dialer fast-idle
```

Configures   The amount of idle time when there is contention for the line

Default   20 seconds

Description

This command can apply to interfaces or map-class configurations. When used on an
interface or a map class, it defines the number of *seconds* that must pass before a line is
disconnected when there is contention for the interface, i.e., when there is traffic
waiting for a different destination other than the current connection.

When used for a map class, this command defines the number of seconds to wait
before placing another call, and defaults to the fast-idle setting for the interface.

For regular idle-timeouts for a DDR interface, see the `dialer idle-timeout` command.

Example

Interface configuration:

```
interface async 5
  dialer fast-idle 55
```

Map-class configuration:

```
map-class dialer office
  dialer fast-idle 55
```

dialer-group

```
dialer-group number
no dialer-group number
```

Configures   Associates an interface with a dialer group

Default   None

Description

This command adds the interface to the dialer group specified by *number*. An interface can have only one dialer group associated with it. Each dialer group has an associated access list that defines "interesting" traffic for this interface. If the traffic is permitted by the access list, a call is initiated for the interface if the interface is not already connected.

Example

The following commands add the async1 interface to dialer-group 1. access-list 110 specifies the traffic that causes this interface to initiate a call; in this case, ICMP traffic doesn't bring up the connection, but any other IP traffic does. Note that this access list does not block ICMP traffic once the link is up; it just prevents ICMP traffic from bringing it up in the first place.

```
! Set the interface as part of the dialer group
interface async 1
  dialer-group 1
!
! Set the dialer group to use access-list 110
dialer-list 1 list 110
!
! Configure the access-list for the dialer group
access-list 110 deny icmp any any
access-list 110 permit ip any any
```

dialer hold-queue

```
dialer hold-queue packets timeout seconds
no dialer hold-queue packets timeout seconds
```

Configures   A queue that holds packets until a dial-up connection is established

Default   Disabled

Description

Instructs the interface to queue traffic until the dial-up connection is completed. By default, queuing is not enabled and packets are dropped until the connection is established.

packets
> The number of packets to hold in the queue, waiting for the connection. The value can be set from 0 to 100.

timeout seconds
> The period of time after which the connection attempt is determined to have failed, and the waiting packets are discarded.

---

dialer idle-timeout   interface, map-class

```
dialer idle-timeout seconds
no dialer idle-timeout seconds
```

Configures   The amount of idle time before a connection is disconnected

Default   120 seconds

Description

This command can apply to interfaces or map-class configurations. When used on an interface or a map class, it defines the number of seconds an interface must be idle (no traffic) before the connection is closed. When there is contention for a dialer (i.e., traffic for a destination different from the one to which the interface is currently connected), then the fast idle timeout is used. (See dialer fast-idle.)

Example

Interface configuration:

```
interface async 4
  dialer idle-timeout 300
```

Map-class configuration:

```
map-class dialer office
  dialer idle-timeout 300
```

---

dialer in-band   interface

```
dialer in-band [no-parity | odd-parity]
no dialer in-band
```

Configures   Dial-on-demand routing (DDR)

Default

Disabled; no-parity is the default when the command is issued with no options

Description

This command configures an interface to support DDR.

---

no-parity

Optional. Chat scripts to the modem have no parity.

odd-parity

Optional. Chat scripts to the modem have odd parity.

This is not required on BRI interfaces.

---

dialer isdn

map-class, dialer

```
dialer isdn [speed value] [spc]
no dialer isdn [speed value] [spc]
```

Configures   Bit rate used on the B channel

Default   64

Description

This command is for map-class configurations only. It defines the bit rate for the B channel of an ISDN connection and sets up semipermanent connections for the map class.

speed value

Optional. Defines the bit rate in Kbps for the B channel; either 56 or 64. Default is 64.

spc

Optional. Requires the use of ISDN semipermanent connections for this map class (Germany only).

Example

```
map-class dialer office
  dialer isdn speed 64
```

---

dialer-list

global

```
dialer-list grouplist access-list
dialer-list group protocol protocol {permit | deny | list} access-list
no dialer-list group
```

Configures   Assigns an access list to a dialer group

Default   None

Description

The first version of this command specifies a group number and applies the given access list to that group. The access list defines "interesting" traffic for the dialer group. If traffic matches the access list, it is deemed interesting, and the DDR interface establishes a connection (if one hasn't been already established).

group

The dialer group number.

```
list access-list
```
The access list that defines interesting traffic for this group.

The second version of this command allows you to specify the traffic that brings up the connection without using an external access list. Its parameters are:

```
group
```
The dialer group number.

```
protocol protocol
```
The protocol to allow (or reject): `ip`, `ipx`, etc.

```
permit
```
Permits traffic using this protocol.

```
deny
```
Denies the entire protocol.

```
list access-list
```
Applies an access list to the protocol. Used to single out ports within the protocol.

Examples

The following commands define a dialer group, assign an interface to that dialer group, and specify that the interface should be brought up if traffic matching access list 110 appears on the interface.

```
interface async 5
  dialer-group 10
  !
  ! Define the access-list for group 10
  dialer-list 10 list 110
  !
  ! Define the list ( all IP traffic to 10.10.1.0 network)
  access-list 110 permit ip any 10.10.1.0 0.0.0.255
```

The following commands define a dialer group, assign an interface to that dialer group, and specify that the interface should be brought up for any IP traffic. No access list is used.

```
interface async 5
  dialer-group 10
  !
  ! Define all ip traffic as interesting
  dialer-list 10 protocol ip permit
```

---

dialer load-threshold
interface

```
dialer load-threshold load [{outbound | inbound | either}]
no dialer load-threshold
```

Configures   The threshold for opening an additional connection

Default   None

Description

This command defines the threshold at which the router opens an additional connection to obtain more bandwidth. Another connection can be made only if this interface is part of a rotary group. This command can be used only if the interface belongs to a rotary group.

load
> The utilization at which another connection to the destination is established. The number can be from 1 to 255 (255 = 100% utilization).

outbound
> Optional. Load is considered only for outbound traffic.

inbound
> Optional. Load is considered only for inbound traffic.

either
> Optional. Default. A new connection is established if the utilization exceeds the given load in either the outbound or inbound direction.

---

dialer map
interface

dialer map *protocol destination* [name *hostname*] [class *name*] [broadcast] [spc] [speed {56|64}] [modem-script *script-name*] [system-script *script-name*] [*dial-string*]

no dialer map *protocol destination* [name *hostname*] [class *name*] [broadcast] [spc] [speed {56|64}] [modem-script *script-name*] [system-script *script-name*] [*dial-string*]

Configures   Any non-DTR dialer interface for PPP callback

Default   None

Description

The dialer map command allows an interface to call one or more different sites by mapping a destination address to connection-specific dial strings and connection scripts.

protocol
> Names the protocol to use for the connection. Valid values are ip, appletalk, bridge, decnet, ipx, novell, snapshot, vines, and xns.

destination
> The destination address to use for this map. The next-hop address of a packet is the destination address in map configurations.

name hostname
> Optional. The name of the remote system for the DDR connection.

class name
> Optional. Names a map class to use for this mapping. A map class is defined with the map-class command.

broadcast
> Optional. Allows broadcast packets to be forwarded over this connection.

spc
> Optional. ISDN only; Germany only. Configures a semipermanent connection between the ISDN device and the exchange.

speed speed
> Optional. ISDN only. Defines the speed of an ISDN B channel in Kbps. Valid values are 56 and 64. The default value is 64.

```
modem-script script-name
```
Optional. Names the modem script to use for dialing the connection. Required only if no dialer string is defined for the interface used.

```
system-script script-name
```
Optional. Names the system script to use for logging into the remote system.

```
dial-string
```
Optional. This option must be the last entry on the command line. It defines the telephone number to be sent to the dialing device. For multipoint ISDN connections, append the subaddress to the dial string (separated by a colon).

---

dialer map snapshot   interface

```
dialer map snapshot seq-number dial-string
no dialer map snapshot [seq-number]
```

Configures   Snapshot routing

Default   None

Description
This command configures client snapshot routing on a DDR interface.

```
seq-number
```
Identifies the dialer map. This number can range from 1 to 254.

```
dial-string
```
The telephone number to dial for this snapshot connection.

---

dialer max-link   interface

```
dialer max-link number
no dialer max-link
```

Configures
The maximum number of open links that a dialer profile can have to a destination

Default   255

Description
This command sets the maximum number of links that a dialer profile can have open to a single destination at any time. This command can be used only on dialer interfaces. *number* can be from 1 to 255.

---

dialer pool   interface

```
dialer pool pool-number
no dialer pool pool-number
```

Configures   The dialing pool to use to connect to a specific network

---

Default   None

Description

Specifies the dialer pool to which a `dialer` interface belongs. Pool numbers range from 1 to 255. For more information on dialer pools, consult Chapter 12.

Example

The following code configures a dialer interface with an IP address and PPP encapsulation, and assigns the interface to dialer pool 5.

```
interface dialer1
  ip address 10.10.1.0 255.255.255.0
  encapsulation ppp
  dialer pool 5
```

dialer pool-member   interface

dialer pool-member *pool-number* [priority *value*] [min-link *value*] [max-link *value*]

no dialer pool-member *pool-number*

Configures   Assigns a physical interface to a dialer pool

Default   Disabled

Description

Any interface can belong to a dialer pool. Dialer pools are configured using the `dialer` interface. This command assigns an interface to a pool.

pool-number
  The pool to which the interface is assigned.

priority value
  Optional. This value is the interface's priority within the pool. The interface with the highest priority is selected first for dialing out. This value can be from 0 to 255; the default is 0.

min-link value
  Optional. This is for ISDN lines; it specifies the minimum number of B channels that are reserved on this interface. The value can be from 0 to 255; the default is 0.

max-link value
  Optional. This is for ISDN lines; it specifies the maximum number of B channels that are reserved on this interface. The value can be from 0 to 255; the default is 0.

Example

The following commands assign the ISDN interface BRI1 to dialer pool 1:

```
interface BRI1
  encapsulation ppp
  dialer pool-member 1 priority 50
```

dialer priority

```
dialer priority value
no dialer priority value
```

Configures   The priority of an interface in a rotary group

Default   0

Description

This command sets the priority of the interface within a rotary group. *value* can be from 0 to 255. The highest-priority interface is selected first for dialing.

dialer remote-name

```
dialer remote-name username
no dialer remote-name username
```

Configures   The authentication name for the remote router

Default   None

Description

This command sets the username to use when connecting to a remote system with CHAP or PAP authentication.

dialer rotary-group

```
dialer rotary-group group-number
no dialer rotary-group group-number
```

Configures   Includes the interface as part of a dialer rotary group

Default   None

Description

This command sets the rotary group for an interface to *group-number*. The number of the rotary group must match the number of the dialer interface for which the rotary group is defined. The group number can range from 0 to 255.

dialer rotor

```
dialer rotor {priority | best}
no dialer rotor {priority | best}
```

Configures   The method for selecting the next interface to use to dial out

Default   Disabled

Description

For rotary groups, this command tells the router whether to select the interface with the highest priority (priority) or the interface with the most recent connection success (best).

---

dialer string   interface

```
dialer string string [class dialer-map-name]
no dialer string
```

Configures   Legacy DDR phone numbers

Default   None

Description

Specifies the dial string for the interface's modem. Table 17-8 shows the codes that can be used in the dialer string. This command is used only for legacy DDR; on modern routers, it's more flexible to use dialer pools or dialer map statements, which allow more than one destination to be called. The class option names the dialer map associated with this dialer string.

Table 17-8. Codes for use in legacy DDR

Code	Meaning
T	Tone dialing
P	Pulse dialing
&	Flash
:	Wait tone
= ,	Separators 3 and 4 (for international use)

---

dialer wait-for-carrier-time   interface, map-class

```
dialer wait-for-carrier-time seconds
no dialer wait-for-carrier-time
```

Configures   The amount of time the interface waits for a carrier

Default   30 seconds

Description

This command sets the maximum amount of time in seconds that the router waits for a carrier when bringing up a dialer interface. It can be used on an interface or map-class configuration.

dialer watch-disable

interface

```
dialer watch-disable seconds
no dialer watch-disable
```

Configures   Delay time for the backup interface

Default   Disabled

Description

This command configures the time in seconds to keep the backup link up after the primary link recovers, if the backup link has been brought up by a dialer watch group.

dialer watch-group

interface

```
dialer watch-group group-number
no dialer watch-group group-number
```

Configures   Enables backup DDR for an interface

Default   Disabled

Description

This command is used to configure an interface as a backup DDR link using a watch list. The *group-number* identifies the watch list that triggers calls on this interface; the interface is brought up if the router doesn't have any routes to the networks listed in the watch list. A watch list is created by the dialer watch-list command; the interface must have a dialer map that corresponds exactly to the networks listed in that command.

dialer watch-list

global

```
dialer watch-list group-number ip address mask
no dialer watch-list group-number ip address mask
```

Configures   A watch group number assigned to an IP address range

Default   None

Description

This command allows you to define a group of routes based on IP address and mask, and assign that group to a *group-number*. If no routes to these networks are in the routing table, the router dials a backup connection. Note that this connection is dialed regardless of whether there is any traffic for these destinations; dialing depends only on the existence of a route. This command is used in conjunction with dialer watch-group, dialer watch-disable, and dialer map. Valid group numbers are from 1 to 255.

dir

```
dir [/all] [filesystem:]
```

Description
This command displays the files in the router's filesystem. If you supply a directory as an argument, the command lists the files in that directory; otherwise, it lists the current working directory. Use the /all keyword to list all files, including those marked for deletion.

disable
command

```
disable [level]
```

Description
This command exits privileged mode and returns the user to user mode. The optional level parameter value ranges from 0 through 15. 0 is the normal user mode; 15 is the privileged user mode. If no level is specified, the user is returned to level 0 (user mode). See the privilege command for more information on setting the level values.

Example
```
Router# disable
Router
```

disconnect
command

```
disconnect
```

Description   This command terminates a background telnet session.

disconnect-character
line

```
disconnect-character ascii-number
no disconnect-character
```

Configures   The character to use to disconnect a session

Default   None

Description
This command defines the character that a user types to end an interactive session. As with the activation-character command, the ascii-number is the decimal value of the desired character.

Example
In this example, we set the disconnect character to control-D, which is ASCII number 4, and we inform the users with a banner message.

```
Router(config)# line 2
```

```
Router(config-line)# activation-character 13
Router(config-line)# disconnect-character 4
Router(config-line)# vacant-message #
Router(config-line)#                    ***** Welcome to Sphinx *****
Router(config-line)#        Press the return key to start the connection
Router(config-line)#        Disconnect with a control-D key
Router(config-line)# #
```

disconnect ssh command

```
disconnect ssh session-id
```

Configures   The character to use to disconnect a session

Description
This command terminates a background SSH session. Run show ip ssh to display the
session-id.

dispatch-character line

```
dispatch-character ascii-number
no dispatch-character
```

Configures   The character that causes a packet to be sent

Default   None

Description
This command defines the character that causes a packet to be sent. Setting the
dispatch character causes the router to buffer a group of characters into a packet
before sending them to the remote host. *ascii-number* is the decimal value of the
desired character.

Example
The following example sets the Enter key (ASCII 13) as the dispatch character for
virtual terminals 1 through 4.

```
line vty 1 4
  dispatch-character 13
```

distance router

```
distance distance [address mask] [access-list]
no distance distance [address mask] [access-list]
```

Configures   Administrative distance

Default   Depends on the protocol

Description

The distance command allows you to change the trustworthiness of a route's source relative to other routing protocols. The lower the distance, the more the route's source is trusted. Routes with a distance of 255 are not added to the route table. Chapter 8 discusses how routing protocols use administrative distances and lists the default value for each protocol.

distance

> The administrative distance to be assigned to this protocol (or to routes selected by the other arguments to this command). Administrative distance must be a value from 1 to 255.

address mask

> Optional. If these arguments are present, the administrative distance applies only to routes whose destinations match this address/mask pair.

access-list

> Optional. If this argument is present, the administrative distance applies only to routes that match the given access list.

---

distance bgp
router, BGP

```
distance bgp external-distance internal-distance local-distance
no distance bgp
```

Configures   Administrative distance for BGP

Default   External distance, 20; internal distance, 200; local distance, 200

Description

The distance bgp command allows you to change the trustworthiness of a route's source relative to other routing protocols. The lower the distance, the more the route's source is trusted. Routes with a distance of 255 are not added to the route table. *external-distance* applies to external BGP routes (routes learned from a peer outside your AS); *internal-distance* applies to internal BGP routes (routes learned from a peer within your AS); *local-distance* applies to routes added with the network command. It's usually not a good idea to change BGP's routing distances.

Example

The distance bgp command is often used to change the internal distance so that its value is equal to the external distance, as in the following example:

```
router bgp 101
  distance bgp 20 20 200
```

---

distance eigrp
router, EIGRP

```
distance eigrp internal-distance external-distance
no distance eigrp
```

Configures   Administrative distance for EIGRP

Default   External distance, 170; internal distance, 90

Description

This command sets the internal and external administrative distances for the EIGRP protocol. The administrative distance reflects the trustworthiness of a route's source relative to other routing protocols. The *internal-distance* applies to internal routes, which are routes learned from the current EIGRP routing process (commonly called "autonomous system"). The *external-distance* applies to routes learned from other EIGRP routing processes. *internal-distance* and *external-distance* must be in the range of 1 to 255. Chapter 8 discusses the use of administrative distance and shows the default distances for the different routing protocols.

---

distribute-list in   router

```
distribute-list access-list in [interface]
no distribute-list access-list in [interface]
```

Configures   An access list to filter incoming routing updates

Default   None

Description

This command allows you to apply an access list to incoming route updates to a routing protocol. If no interface is specified, the access list is applied to all incoming route updates. If an interface is specified, the access list is applied only to route updates received on that interface. The access list should be a standard access list.

Example

The following distribute list applies access list 1 to incoming routes:

```
route rip
  network 10.0.0.0
  distribute-list 1 in
!
! Deny network 10.1.1.0
access-list 1 deny 10.1.1.0
! Permit everything else
access-list 1 permit 0.0.0.0 255.255.255.255
```

---

distribute-list out   router

```
distribute-list access-list out [interface | routing-process]
no distribute-list access-list out [interface | routing-process]
```

Configures   A filter list to be applied to outbound routing updates

Default   None

Description

This command applies the given access list to outbound routing updates. The access list must be a standard IP access list; it defines which networks will be denied or permitted. The *interface* name applies the list to routing updates going out a specific

---

interface. (This does not apply to OSPF.) The *routing-process* applies the access list to routes going to another routing process. The connected and static keywords may be used to specify a routing process.

Example

```
route rip
  network 10.0.0.0
  distribute-list 1 out
!
! Deny network 10.1.1.0
access-list 1 deny 10.1.1.0
! Permit everything else
access-list 1 permit 0.0.0.0 255.255.255.255
```

---

domain-password   router, IS-IS

```
domain-password password
no domain-password
```

Configures   Password for IS-IS routing

Default   Disabled

Description

This command assigns a *password* for exchanging L2 routing information for IS-IS. Like the area-password command, this password is transmitted in clear text and provides very little security.

---

downward-compatible-config   global

```
downward-compatible-config version
no downward-compatible-config
```

Configures   Configuration

Default   Disabled

Description

This command generates a configuration that is compatible with an earlier IOS *version*. The version number must be 10.2 or later.

---

down-when-looped   interface

```
down-when-looped
no down-when-looped
```

Configures   Loopback detection

Default   Disabled

Description

This command tells the interface to go down when a loopback is detected. The default behavior is for the interface to remain up when the device is placed in loopback, so you can place a DCE device such as a CSU/DSU in loopback and ping the interface. This allows you to test the cable between the router and the DCE device.

Use the no form of this command to disable this behavior. If this command is given, the interface shuts down when the DCE device (CSU/DSU) is placed in loopback mode.

---

drop
policy-map

```
drop
no drop
```

Configures   A traffic class to discard packets for a specific class

Default   Disabled

Description

This command enables packet discarding for a class. Use the no form of the command to disable packet discarding.

Example

```
policy-map policy1
  class class1
    drop
interface serial1/0
  service-policy output policy1
class-map class1
  match access-group 101
```

---

dte-invert-txc
interface

```
dte-invert-txc
no dte-invert-txc
```

Configures   Inverts TXC clock signal

Default   Disabled

Description

This command inverts the TXC clock signal when the interface is operating as the DTE.

---

early-token-release
interface

```
early-token-release
no early-token-release
```

Configures   Token ring interfaces

Default   Disabled

Description

This command tells the interface to immediately release the token back to the ring after transmitting a packet. Normally, a token ring interface waits for a transmitted packet to return before releasing the token. This command is used only on 16-Mb rings where all devices support it.

---

editing   line

```
editing
no editing
```

Configures   Enhanced editing mode

Default   Enabled

Description

The no form of this command disables the enhanced editing mode for a line: i.e., the support for control keys such as Ctrl-w, which erases a word. The command-line editing keys are discussed in Chapter 1; they should be familiar to users of Unix and Unix-like operating systems.

---

eigrp log-neighbor-changes   router, EIGRP

```
eigrp log-neighbor-changes
no eigrp log-neighbor-changes
```

Configures   Logging for EIGRP neighbor states

Default   Disabled

Description

This command enables logging of changes in the status of EIGRP neighbors. Logging provides information to help you detect routing or connectivity problems.

---

enable   command

```
enable [level]
```

Description

With no arguments, this command takes an interactive session from user EXEC mode to privileged EXEC mode. If the level argument is present, it can be used to enter any of 16 levels, 0 through 15. Level 0 is the normal user mode (user EXEC mode) and 15 is the privileged user mode (privileged EXEC mode). See the privilege command in Chapter 4 for more information on setting the level values.

enable last-resort global

```
enable last-resort {password | succeed}
no enable last-resort {password | succeed}
```

Configures   The action to take if the TACACS servers do not respond

Default   Disabled

Description

This command tells the router what to do if the TACACS server times out, and you are using TACACS for the enable password. The password keyword tells the router to prompt for the enable password that is in the configuration. The succeed keyword tells the router to go to enable mode without further action. The latter behavior is very insecure.

enable password global

```
enable password [level level] password
no enable password
```

Configures   The password for the enable mode

Default   None

Description

This command sets the password for the enable mode. It can also be used to establish passwords for other levels. In the router's configuration, the password is stored in the clear and can be viewed by using show running-config and other commands.

You can encrypt this password as well as other passwords with the command service password-encryption. However, because this encryption uses a very simple XOR algorithm, it is easily cracked.

enable secret global

```
enable secret [level level] password
no enable secret
```

Configures   The password for the enable mode

Default   None

Description

This command sets the password for the enable mode. It can also be used to establish passwords for other levels. In the router's configuration, the password is stored in an encrypted form and is never displayed in the clear.

enable use-tacacs global

```
enable use-tacacs
no enable use-tacacs
```

Configures   TACACS authentication for the privileged (enable) command level

Default   Disabled

Description

This command requires the use of TACACS for the enable password. If you use this command, be sure that you also use the tacacs-server authenticate enable command.

encapsulation (ATM/MPLS) ATM/MPLS

```
encapsulation layer-type
no encapsulation
```

Configures   ATM adaptation layer for Any Transport over MPLS (AtoM)

Default   AAL5

Description

This command configures the ATM adaptation layer for Any Transport over MPLS (AtoM) while in the AtoM VC configuration. The *layer-type* can be aa5 for ATM Adaptation layer 5 or aal0 for ATM adaptation layer 0.

Example

```
! For AtoM we must use the l2transport command with the pvc command
pvc 1/101 l2transport
  encapsulation aal5
```

encapsulation (interface) interface

```
encapsulation type
encapsulation dot1q vlan-id [native]
encapsulation isl vlan-id
no encapsulation
```

Configures   Encapsulation method used by the interface

Default   Depends on interface

Description

This command sets the encapsulation method for this interface. Possible values for the encapsulation type are atm-dxi, bstun (block serial tunnel), dot1q, frame-relay (see Chapter 6), hdlc, isl, lapb, ppp, sde, dlc, and smds.

For Frame Relay interfaces, the options are cisco and ietf. The default is cisco, which is Cisco's proprietary encapsulation method. ietf sets the encapsulation method to the IETF standard, which is used when connecting to another vendor's Frame Relay router or switch.

For interfaces that are compatible, such as Fast Ethernet interfaces, you can enable dot1q to apply a VLAN ID to the interface. native is an optional keyword that sets the VLAN ID value of the port to the value specified by vlan-id. To enable ISL encapsulation on an interface, use the isl keyword followed by the VLAN ID you wish to use. For more information on dot1q and ISL encapsulation, see Chapter 14.

Example

The following code uses hdlc encapsulation on a serial line:

```
interface serial0
  encapsulation hdlc
```

This code uses PPP on an ISDN line:

```
interface bri0
  encapsulation ppp
```

This code sets vlan 101 to a subinterface:

```
interface fastethernet0/1.101
  encapsulation dot1q 101
```

---

end
any configuration mode

end

Description

This command exits the current configuration mode and must be used to mark the end of any configuration file.

Example

```
! lengthy configuration file omitted
! some commands here
! end of configuration file
end
```

---

erase
command

erase [startup-config] [flash]

Description

This command erases the stored configuration (startup-config) or the flash memory (flash) on the router. Flash memory stores the IOS operating system image; obviously, this command is dangerous.

Example

This command erases your stored configuration:

```
Router# erase startup-config
```

This one erases your IOS image:

```
Router# erase flash
```

---

escape-character

```
escape-character ascii-number
no escape-character
```

Configures   The system escape character

Default   Ctrl-^

Description

This command defines the character that terminates a running command. The default, as specified in the hot-key listing, is Ctrl-^ (Control+Shift+6 on most keyboards). *ascii-number* must be the decimal value of the character you want to use. The Break key cannot be used as an escape character.

The no form of the instruction returns the escape character to the default.

Example

The following commands set the disconnect character to Ctrl-C, which has a decimal value of 3:

```
Router(config)# line 2
Router(config-line)# escape-character 3
Router(config-line)# vacant-message #
Router(config-line)#                 ***** Welcome to Sphinx *****
Router(config-line)#                 Escape key is Ctrl-C
Router(config-line)# #
```

exception core-file

```
exception core-file name
no exception core-file name
```

Configures   A core dump filename

Default   *routername-core*

Description

This command sets the *name* of the core file that is generated when a router crashes. Use the exception protocol command to set the protocol that the router uses to transmit the core file.

exception dump

```
exception dump ip
no exception dump
```

Configures   The exception dump server IP address

Default   None

Description
This command sets the IP address of the server to which the router sends a core dump when the router crashes.

---

exception memory   global

```
exception memory {fragment size | minimum size}
no exception memory
```

Configures   Memory parameters that cause a core dump

Default   Disabled

Description
This command causes a core dump if certain memory parameters are exceeded. The fragment size is the minimum contiguous block of memory in the free pool in bytes; the minimum size is the lowest allowable size of the free memory pool in bytes. If these parameters are exceeded, a core dump is generated. For example, if you set the minimum size to 100000 and the memory goes below 100,000 bytes, a core file is generated.

---

exception protocol   global

```
exception protocol {ftp | rcp | tftp}
no exception protocol
```

Configures   Protocol to transmit a core file to a server

Default   tftp

Description
This command sets the protocol to use for transmitting a core file to a server. The protocol can be ftp, rcp, or tftp. Use the exception dump command to set the IP address of the server.

Example
```
exception protocol tftp
exception dump 192.168.1.1
```

---

exception spurious-interrupt   global

```
exception spurious-interrupt [number]
no exception spurious-interrupt
```

Configures   The number of spurious interrupts that generate a core dump

Default   Disabled

Description

This command sets the number of spurious interrupts that will cause the router to generate a core file and reboot. *number* can be from 1 to 4,294,967,295.

---

exec
line

```
exec
no exec
```

Configures   Access to the router command interface

Default   Enabled

Description

The no form of this command disables EXEC processes, which are enabled by default. Disabling EXEC processes is useful for lines on which you do not want users to access the router. For example, you may want to disallow login access on a dial-in line.

---

exec-timeout
line

```
exec-timeout minutes [seconds]
no exec-timeout
```

Configures   The time an EXEC session can be idle

Default   10 minutes

Description

This command sets the amount of time a session waits for user input before timing out and closing the session. *minutes* specifies the number of minutes in the timeout period; *seconds* specifies the number of seconds.

Don't set the EXEC timeout to be extremely short; for example, don't give a command like exec-timeout 0 1. You may never get back into your router without doing a configuration recovery.

Example

The following command sets the timeout period to 4 minutes and 59 seconds:

```
exec-timeout 4 59
```

---

exit
command

```
exit
```

Description

This command closes your current connection if you are in user EXEC mode or privileged EXEC mode. If you are in a subconfiguration mode such as the interface or routing configuration mode, this command takes you to the next higher level (e.g., back to EXEC mode from interface configuration mode).

Example
```
Routerexit
Connection Closed

Routerenable
Router#conf t
Enter configuration commands, one per line.   End with CNTL/Z.
Router(config)#interface serial0
Router(config-if)#exit
Router(config)#
```

---

fair-queue (policy-map class)   policy-map

```
fair-queue [queues]
no fair-queue [queues]
```

Configures   The number of dynamic queues to be reserved for the default class

Default   Depends on interface

Description
This command specifies the number of dynamic queues reserved for the default class
(class-default) only. It can be used with the queue-limit command and or the random-
detect command.

The default number of queues is based on bandwidth: less than 64 Kbps is 16 queues,
64 to 128 Kbps is 32 queues, 128 to 256 Kbps is 64 queues, 256 to 512 Kbps is 128
queues, and more than 512 Kbps is 256 queues.

Example
```
policy-map policy1
   class class-default
      fair-queue 16
      queue-limit 20
```

---

fair-queue (interface)   interface

```
fair-queue [congestive [dynamic [reservable]]]
no fair-queue [congestive [dynamic [reservable]]]
```

Configures   Weighted Fair Queueing

Default
WFQ is enabled for interfaces with bandwidth less than or equal to 2 Mbps; default
values are congestive 64, dynamic 256, reservable 0.

Description
This command enables Weighted Fair Queueing on an interface. For Weighted Fair
Queueing, the options are:

---

congestive
> Optional. The number of messages allowed in each queue past which traffic is discarded. The value can range from 1 to 512.

dynamic
> Optional. The number of queues for best-effort conversations. Valid values are 16, 32, 64, 128, 256, 512, 1024, 2048, and 4096.

reservable
> Optional. The number of queues for reserved conversations. The value can be from 0 to 1,000.

---

fair-queue aggregate-limit interface

```
fair-queue aggregate-limit packets
no fair-queue aggregate-limit
```

Configures   Maximum number of packets for DWFQ

Default   Based on buffer space in the Versatile Interface Processor (VIP)

Description
This command sets the total number of buffered packets allowed before packets are dropped. This is the sum of all packets in buffers for Distributed Weighted Fair Queuing (DWFQ). If the buffered packets stay below this limit, no packets are dropped.

---

fair-queue individual-limit interface

```
fair-queue individual-limit packets
no fair-queue individual-limit
```

Configures   Maximum queue depth for an individual queue

Default   Half of the aggregate queue limit

Description
This command sets the maximum number of *packets* allowed in an individual queue during periods of congestion.

---

fair-queue limit interface

```
fair-queue {qos-group group | tos number} limit class-packet-size
no fair-queue {qos-group group | tos number} limit class-packet-size
```

Configures   Maximum queue depth for a specific DWFQ class

Default
Half the aggregate limit size unless the individual limit is set, in which case that is the default

---

Description

This command sets the queue size for a specific DWFQ. The qos-group number can be from 1 to 99; it is used to match the value set by the Committed Access Rate (CAR) or the BGP policy propagation. The tos value is used to match the two low-order IP precedence bits in the ToS (Type of Service) field. The *class-packet-size* is the maximum number of packets allowed in the queue during periods of congestion.

---

fair-queue qos-group
interface

```
fair-queue qos-group
no fair-queue qos-group
```

Configures   DWFQ based on QoS (Quality of Service) group numbers

Default   Disabled

Description

This command enables DWFQ based on QoS group numbers. The QoS group numbers, which are taken from the CAR or BGP policy propagation, are used to sort traffic into queues. The fair-queue weight and fair-queue limit commands set up the appropriate queues.

---

fair-queue tos
interface

```
fair-queue tos
no fair-queue tos
```

Configures   DWFQ based on ToS (Type of Service) values

Default   Disabled

Description

This command enables DWFQ based on ToS values. The ToS fields in the packet provide two low-order IP precedence bits, which are used to sort packets into queues. The fair-queue weight and fair-queue limit commands set up the appropriate queues.

---

fair-queue weight
interface

```
fair-queue {qos-group group | tos number} weight value
no fair-queue {qos-group group | tos number} weight value
```

Configures   Assigns a specific weight for DWFQ

Default

For qos-group, unallocated bandwidth defaults to group 0; for tos, the default class/weight values are 0/10, 1/20, 2/30, and 3/40

Description

This command allocates a specific weight (percentage of the bandwidth) to each QoS group or ToS type. *value* must be between 0 and 100.

---

fddi burst-count

interface

```
fddi burst-count size
no fddi burst-count
```

Configures   Buffers to allocate to handle extra FDDI traffic

Default   3

Description

This command enables an FDDI interface to allocate extra buffers ahead of time. These buffers are used to handle possible traffic bursts. The buffer *size* can be from 1 to 10; the default is 3.

---

fddi c-min

interface

```
fddi c-min microseconds
no fddi c-min
```

Configures   The C-Min timer

Default   1,600 microseconds

Description

This command sets the C-Min timer on the interface to microseconds.

---

fddi cmt-signal-bits

interface

```
fddi cmt-signal-bits signal-bits [phy-a | phy-b]
no fddi cmt-signal-bits signal-bits [phy-a | phy-b]
```

Configures   CMT transmission bits

Default   None

Description

This command sets the bits to be transmitted during the signal phase of CMT. Changing these values is not recommended and should be done only to debug specific CMT problems. *signal-bits* is the hexadecimal value of the bit fields you wish to set. phy-a and phy-b select the physical sublayer, either a or b. Table 17-9 describes the bit fields.

Table 17-9. Bit values for CMT signals

Bit position	Meaning
0	Escape bit
1–2	Physical type
3	Physical compatibility
4–5	Link confidence test duration
6	MAC for link confidence test
7	Link confidence test failed
8	MAC for local loop
9	MAC on physical output

fddi duplicate-address-check
interface

```
fddi duplicate-address-check
no fddi duplicate-address-check
```

Configures   Duplicate address checking during ring initialization

Default   Disabled

Description
This command enables an FDDI interface to detect duplicate addresses on the ring.

fddi encapsulate
interface

```
fddi encapsulate
no fddi encapsulate
```

Configures   Encapsulation mode

Default   Enabled (SNAP)

Description
This command enables the bridge encapsulating mode for this interface, which is used to interface the CSC-FCIT with other FDDI modules. The CSC-FCIT has bridging enabled by default. no fddi encapsulate disables bridging for this interface.

fddi frames-per-token
interface

```
fddi frames-per-token number
no fddi frames-per-token
```

Configures   Number of frames that an interface transmits per token capture

Default   3 frames

Description

This command sets the number of frames that an interface transmits during a token capture. *number* can be from 1 to 10.

---

fddi smt-frames
interface

```
fddi smt-frames
no fddi smt-frames
```

Configures   Enables SMT frame processing

Default   Enabled

Description

This command enables the interface to process and generate SMT (FDDI Station Management) frames.

---

fddi tb-min
interface

```
fddi tb-min milliseconds
no fddi tb-min
```

Configures   TB-min timer

Default   100 milliseconds

Description

This command sets the TB-min timer in the Physical Connection Management (PCM) for this interface.

---

fddi tl-min-time
interface

```
fddi tl-min-time microseconds
no fddi tl-min-time microseconds
```

Configures   Minimum time to transmit a physical line state

Default   30 microseconds

Description

This command sets the minimum time to transmit a physical line state before transitioning to the PCM state for this interface. Changing this field is not recommended.

fddi token-rotation-time

interface

```
fddi token-rotation-time microseconds
no fddi token-rotation-time microseconds
```

Configures   Ring scheduling

Default   5,000 microseconds

Description

This command sets the time in microseconds for the ring to recover from ring errors. The range can be from 4,000 to 165,000 microseconds.

fddi t-out

interface

```
fddi t-out milliseconds
no fddi t-out
```

Configures   The t-out timer

Default   100 ms

Description   This command sets the t-out timer for the PCM.

fddi valid-transmission-time

interface

```
fddi valid-transmission-time microseconds
no fddi valid-transmission-time microseconds
```

Configures   Time to recover from a transient ring error

Default   2,500 microseconds

Description

This command sets the transmission time for the interface. The range can be from 40 to 1,342,200 microseconds.

flowcontrol

line

```
flowcontrol {none | software [lock] [in | out] | hardware [in | out]}
no flowcontrol {none | software [lock] [in | out] | hardware [in | out]}
```

Configures   Flow control for a line

Default   No flow control

Description

This command defines the serial flow control between the router and the device connected to a serial line.

none
> No flow control.

software
> Sets to software flow control.

lock
> Makes it impossible to turn off flow control.

hardware
> Sets to hardware flow control.

If neither in nor out are specified, flow control is assumed to be in both directions, i.e., the router accepts and sends flow control.

---

format   command

Class C filesystem:

format *filesystem*:

Class A filesystem:

format [spare *number*] *filesystem*:

Configures   A Class C or Class A filesystem

Description

This command formats a flash filesystem. Each filesystem name must be followed by a colon; for example, format slot0:.

The spare option is valid only for Class A filesystems, which allow you to reserve a number of spare sectors. *number* can be from 0 to 16. The default is 0.

---

frame-relay adaptive-shaping   map-class

frame-relay adaptive-shaping {becn | foresight}
no frame-relay adaptive-shaping

Configures   The type of backward notification

Default   Disabled

Description

This command selects the type of backward notification to which the Frame Relay interface should respond. It can be set to becn (backwards explicit congestion notification) or foresight.

frame-relay [bc | be]

map-class

```
frame-relay {bc | be} {in | out} bits
no frame-relay {bc | be} {in | out} bits
```

Configures   The committed and excess burst sizes

Default   7000 bits for both bc and be

Description

This command specifies the incoming (in) or outgoing (out) committed burst size (bc) and the excess burst size (be) for a Frame Relay virtual circuit. The burst size is given in bits.

frame-relay becn-response-enable

map-class

```
frame-relay becn-response-enable
no frame-relay becn-response-enable
```

Configures   The use of BECNs to regulate output traffic

Default   Enabled when frame traffic shaping is in use

Description

This command is enabled when traffic shaping is in use. The use of BECNs (backwards explicit congestion notifications) regulates output traffic. You won't see this command in the configuration when you do a show. Use the no form to disable traffic shaping.

frame-relay broadcast-queue

interface

```
frame-relay broadcast-queue size byte-rate packet-rate
no frame-relay broadcast-queue
```

Configures   Queues for broadcast traffic

Default   Size, 64; byte rate, 256,000 bps; packet rate, 36 packets per second

Description

This command sets the broadcast queue parameters for a Frame Relay interface. A broadcast queue is used for any broadcast packets that have to be replicated for multiple DLCIs on the interface.

size
> The number of packets to hold in the queue. Normally, you want at least 20 for each DLCI on the interface.

byte-rate
> The maximum number of bytes to be transmitted per second. This value should be less than:

- 1/4 the local access rate (in bytes per second)
- N/4 times the minimum remote access rate, where N is the number of DLCIs to which the broadcast should be replicated

packet-rate
> The maximum number of packets to be transmitted per second.

---

frame-relay cir map-class

```
frame-relay cir {in | out} bps
no frame-relay cir {in | out} bps
```

Configures   Incoming or outgoing CIR

Default   56,000 bps

Description
This command sets the Committed Information Rate (CIR) for a Switched Virtual Circuit (SVC) to *bps* (bits per second). The CIR is the guaranteed available bandwidth for the circuit, and may be 0. The in and out keywords specify the direction to which the CIR applies.

---

frame-relay class interface

```
frame-relay class name
no frame-relay class name
```

Configures   Associates a map class with an interface

Default   None

Description
This command applies the map class given by *name* to a Frame Relay interface. The map class may be built from Frame Relay commands used in the map-class context.

Example
In this example, we assign a map class called MAP1 to interface serial1.1:

```
interface serial1.1
   frame-relay class MAP1
!
! Now make the map-class
map-class frame-relay MAP1
   frame-relay cir in 56000
   no frame-relay becn-response-enable
```

frame-relay custom-queue-list

map-class

```
frame-relay custom-queue-list list
no frame-relay custom-queue-list list
```

Configures   The custom queue list to be used for the interface

Default   None (FIFO)

Description

See the queue-list command for information about creating a custom queue list.

---

frame-relay de-group

interface

```
frame-relay de-group group-number dlci
no frame-relay de-group
```

Configures   Discard Eligibility (DE)

Default   None

Description

This command applies a DE group to a DLCI. *group-number* can be from 1 to 10. DE groups are defined with the command frame-relay de-list; they identify traffic that may be discarded if the traffic on the interface exceeds the committed information rate and the Frame Relay switch is congested.

---

frame-relay de-list

global

```
frame-relay de-list list-number {protocol type | interface type number}
    characteristic
no frame-relay de-list list-number {protocol type | interface type number}
    characteristic
```

Configures   Discard Eligibility (DE)

Default   None

Description

This command defines packets that are eligible for discard during times of congestion on a Frame Relay switch. Packets matched by this list have the "discard eligible" bit set in the Frame Relay header.

list-number
> An identifying number. This number identifies the list when it is referenced by other commands, particularly frame-relay de-group. A DE list may be defined by several frame-relay de-list statements with the same number.

protocol type
>Specifies the protocol of the packets to be selected by this list. Possible values are arp, apollo, appletalk, bridge, clns, clns_es, clns_is, compressedtcp, decnet, ip, ipx, vines, and xns.

interface type number
>Specifies the interface of packets to be selected for the list; that is, you can specify that all traffic coming through a certain interface should be marked as discard-eligible. The interface must be a serial interface, an Ethernet interface, or the null interface.

characteristic
>Specifies the characteristics of the packets that are eligible for discard. It must be one of the following: fragments (fragmented packets eligible for discard), tcp *port* (TCP traffic on the specified port), udp *port* (UDP traffic on the specified port), list *access-list* (traffic matched by the given access list), gt *bytes* (packets larger than the given size; make sure to include all headers), or lt *bytes* (packets less than the given size; again, include all headers).

---

frame-relay idle-timer
map-class

frame-relay idle-timer *seconds*
no frame-relay idle-timer *seconds*

Configures   Idle timeout for an SVC

Default   120 seconds

Description
This command sets the idle timeout for a Switched Virtual Circuit (SVC) to *seconds*.

---

frame-relay interface-dlci
interface

frame-relay interface-dlci *dlci* [broadcast] [ietf | cisco]
no frame-relay interface-dlci *dlci* [broadcast] [ietf | cisco]

Configures   DLCI for a Frame Relay subinterface

Default   No DLCI is set as default

Description
Assigns a Data Link Connection Identifier (DLCI) to a Frame Relay subinterface.

dlci
>The DLCI number to be used on the current subinterface.

broadcast
>Allows broadcast packets on this connection.

ietf
>Specifies IETF encapsulation for this connection.

cisco
>Specifies CISCO encapsulation for this connection.

---

frame-relay intf-type

```
frame-relay intf-type [dce | dte | nni]
no frame-relay intf-type
```

Configures   Frame Relay switch type

Default   dte

Description

This command sets the Frame Relay switch type. It is valid only if Frame Relay switching has been enabled with the global frame-relay switching command. The keyword dce causes the router to function as a switch connected to another router; dte is used when the router is connected to a Frame Relay network; nni (Network-to-Network Interface) is used when the router connects to another switch.

frame-relay inverse-arp

```
frame-relay inverse-arp [protocol] [dlci]
no frame-relay inverse-arp [protocol] [dlci]
```

Configures   Inverse ARP for Frame Relay

Default   Enabled

Description

This command configures the use of inverse ARP for associating an IP address with a Frame Relay interface. This command is useful if inverse ARP was globally disabled on the router, but you want to enable inverse ARP for a particular interface or subinterface. To enable or disable inverse ARP for a specific protocol and DLCI pair, use both arguments (protocol and dlci); for all protocols on a DLCI, use only the dlci argument; for all DLCIs, use only the protocol argument.

protocol
    The protocol to support on this interface. Supported protocols include appletalk, decnet, ip, ipx, vines, and xns.

dlci
    One of the DLCI numbers for this interface. The value can be from 16 to 1,007.

frame-relay ip rtp header-compression

```
frame-relay ip rtp header-compression [active | passive]
no frame-relay ip rtp header-compression
```

Configures   RTP header compression on the interface

Default   Disabled

Description

This command enables RTP header compression on the interface. The active keyword tells the device to compress all headers; the passive keyword tells it to compress headers only if the incoming packet had its headers compressed. The default is active.

frame-relay ip tcp header-compression

interface

```
frame-relay ip tcp header-compression [passive]
no frame-relay ip tcp header-compression
```

Configures   Compression of TCP/IP packet headers

Default   Enabled

Description

This command configures an interface so that its PVCs compress IP headers.

passive
> Optional. Performs compression only if the incoming packets are compressed.

frame-relay lmi-type

interface

```
frame-relay lmi-type {ansi | cisco | q933a}
no frame-relay lmi-type {ansi | cisco | q933a}
```

Configures   The LMI

Default   Autosense

Description

This command allows you to set the Local Management Type (LMI) of the Frame Relay switch the router is talking to. Setting the LMI type explicitly deactivates autosensing. Use the keepalive command with this command.

Example

```
interface serial0
    encapulation frame-relay
    frame-relay lmi-type cisco
    keepalive 20
```

frame-relay local-dlci

interface

```
frame-relay local-dlci number
no frame-relay local-dlci
```

Configures   The local DLCI

Default   None

Description

This command sets the local DLCI. It is rarely needed because LMI is normally used to set the local DLCI. If you don't use LMI, this command allows you to set the local DLCI explicitly.

---

frame-relay map

interface

```
frame-relay map protocol protocol-address dlci [broadcast] [ietf | cisco]
   [payload-compress {packet-by-packet | frf9 stac [hardware-options]}]
no frame-relay map protocol protocol-address
```

Configures   Frame Relay connection parameters

Default   None

Description

This command defines a mapping between a protocol-specific destination address and the DLCI to use for connections to that destination.

protocol
> One of appletalk, decnet, dlsw, ip, ipx, llc2, rsrb, vines, or xns.

protocol-address
> The destination address.

dlci
> The DLCI to use.

broadcast
> Optional. Activates forwarding of broadcasts to this address when multicast is not enabled.

ietf
> Optional. Use IETF encapsulation on this interface.

cisco
> Optional. Use Cisco's encapsulation method on this interface. If neither ietf nor cisco is specified, the interface uses the encapsulation specified by the encapsulation frame-relay command.

payload-compress packet-by-packet
> Optional. Activates packet-by-packet compression using the Stacker method. Packet-by-packet compression is a proprietary Cisco feature and won't interoperate with other vendors' equipment.

payload-compress frf9 stac
> Optional. Activates FRF.9 compression using the Stacker method.

hardware-options
> Optional. Can be distributed, software, or csa. distributed causes compression to be performed in a VIP2; software causes compression to occur in the IOS software on the main processor; csa csa-number specifies the CSA to use for a particular interface (available only on 7200 series routers).

frame-relay map bridge

```
frame-relay map bridge dlci[broadcast] [ietf]
no frame-relay map bridge dlci [broadcast] [ietf]
```

Configures   Broadcast forwarding

Default   None

Description

This command specifies that broadcasts are to be forwarded.

dlci
> The DLCI to use for bridging on this interface.

broadcast
> Optional. Forwards broadcasts when multicast is not enabled.

ietf
> Optional. Forces the use of IETF encapsulation, which is used when talking to a non-Cisco device.

frame-relay map clns

interface

```
frame-relay map clns dlci [broadcast]
no frame-relay map clns dlci [broadcast]
```

Configures   Broadcast forwarding for ISO CLNS routing

Default   None

Description

This command causes broadcasts to be forwarded when ISO CLNS is used for routing.

dlci
> The DLCI to use for CLNS broadcast forwarding.

broadcast
> Optional. Causes broadcasts to be forwarded when multicast is not enabled.

frame-relay map ip compress

interface

```
frame-relay map ip address dlci [broadcast] compress
frame-relay map ip address dlci [broadcast] nocompress
```

Configures   Compression for both RTP and TCP headers

Default   Disabled

Description

This command enables compression for both RTP and TCP packet headers.

address
> The IP address of the destination or next hop.

dlci
> The DLCI number.

broadcast
> Optional. Forwards broadcasts to the specified IP address.

---

frame-relay map ip rtp header-compression   interface

frame-relay map ip rtp *address* *dlci* rtp header-compression [active | passive]

no frame-relay map ip rtp *address* *dlci* rtp header-compression [active | passive]

Configures   Compression for RTP headers per DLCI

Default   Disabled

Description
This command enables RTP compression for a specific *dlci* on a link. The active keyword means that the router should always compress the RTP headers (this is the default). The passive keyword specifies that the router should compress packets only when the incoming packet was compressed.

---

frame-relay map ip tcp header-compression   interface

frame-relay map ip *address* *dlci* [broadcast] [cisco| ietf] [no compress] tcp header-compression {active | passive}

no frame-relay map ip *address* *dlci* [broadcast] [cisco| ietf] [no compress] tcp header-compression {active | passive}

Configures   Compression methods for a map

Default   None

Description
This command maps a Frame Relay DLCI to an IP address, enabling TCP header compression for this connection. It's useful if header compression isn't the default for the interface.

address
> The IP address.

dlci
> The DLCI to use.

broadcast
> Optional. Causes broadcasts to be forwarded.

cisco
> Optional. Uses Cisco's encapsulation method.

ietf
> Optional. Uses RFC 1490 encapsulation.

```
no compress
```
Optional. Disables compression.
```
active
```
Causes every TCP/IP packet header to be compressed.
```
passive
```
Compresses packet headers only if the incoming packet was compressed.

frame-relay mincir interface

```
frame-relay mincir {in | out} bps
no frame-relay mincir {in | out} bps
```

Configures   The CIR

Default   56,000 bps

Description

This command sets the minimum incoming (in) or outgoing (out) committed information rate (CIR) that you are willing to accept, in bits per second (*bps*).

frame-relay multicast-dlci interface

```
frame-relay multicast-dlci dlci
no frame-relay multicast-dlci
```

Configures   The DLCI to be used for multicasts

Default   None

Description

This command defines a *dlci* for multicasts. This command is used for testing Frame Relay configurations and is not required in a production configuration.

frame-relay payload-compress packet-by-packet interface

```
frame-relay payload-compress packet-by-packet
no frame-relay payload-compress packet-by-packet
```

Configures   Payload compression

Default   Disabled

Description

This command enables compression on the link, using a proprietary compression protocol that will not work with other vendors' equipment.

frame-relay priority-dlci-group

```
frame-relay priority-dlci-group group-number high-dlci medium-dlci normal-
    dlci low-dlci
```

Configures   Assigns a priority to different DLCIs

Default   Disabled

Description
This command sets the priority levels for DLCIs in the group specified by *group-number*. Within a group, there are four priority levels (high, medium, normal, and low); one DLCI is assigned to each priority level (*high-dlci* to the high-priority level, etc.). If fewer than four DLCIs are given, the last DLCI is assigned to the remaining priority levels.

frame-relay priority-group

```
frame-relay priority-group list-number
no frame-relay priority-group list-number
```

Configures   Applies a priority list to a Frame Relay virtual circuit

Description
This command is similar to the priority-group command for the interface, except that it applies the priority list to a Frame Relay virtual circuit.

list-number
    The priority list number. Priority lists are defined with the priority-list command.

Example
The following example applies priority-list 1 to the Frame Relay configuration:

```
interface serial 0
    encapsulation frame-relay
    frame-relay interface-dlci 200
    frame-relay priority-group 1
!
priority-list 1 protocol ip high
```

frame-relay route

```
frame-relay route in-dlci out-interface out-dlci
no frame-relay route in-dlci out-interface out-dlci
```

Configures   Static routes for PVC switching

Default   None

Description
This command allows you to assign a static route based on DLCIs.

Example

In the following configuration, packets from DLCI 100 received by the serial0 interface are routed out through DLCI 200 on serial1. Likewise, packets received from DLCI 101 on serial0 are routed out through DLCI 201 on serial1.

```
interface serial0
    frame-relay route 100 interface Serial1 200
    frame-relay route 101 interface Serial1 201
```

---

frame-relay svc   interface

```
frame-relay svc
no frame-relay svc
```

Configures   SVC operation on the interface

Default   Disabled

Description

This command enables Switched Virtual Circuit (SVC) processing on the interface and all its subinterfaces.

---

frame-relay switching   global

```
frame-relay switching
no frame-relay switching
```

Configures   Enables PVC switching

Default   Disabled

Description

This command enables Permanent Virtual Circuit (PVC) switching on the router.

---

frame-relay traffic-rate   map-class

```
frame-relay traffic-rate average [peak]
no frame-relay traffic-rate average [peak]
```

Configures   Traffic shaping for a virtual circuit

Default   The bandwidth of the line

Description

This command allows you to configure traffic shaping for a virtual circuit. It doesn't provide the granularity of other commands that configure traffic shaping; it lets you specify only average and peak traffic rates.

---

average

The average rate in bits per second, which is the same as the contracted CIR.

peak

Optional. The peak rate expected for this interface in bits per second. If this option is omitted, the default value is the line rate calculated from the bandwidth command.

---

frame-relay traffic-shaping

interface

```
frame-relay traffic-shaping
no frame-relay traffic-shaping
```

Configures   Traffic shaping

Default   Disabled

Description   This command enables traffic shaping for the interface.

---

fsck

command

```
fsck [/nocrc] filesystem:
```

Configures   Checks and repairs a Class C filesystem

Description

This command checks the given *filesystem*, which must be a Class C filesystem, and repairs any problems it finds. The /nocrc option forces fsck to skip CRC checks. The filesystem name must be followed by a colon.

---

ftp-server enable

global

```
ftp-server enable
no ftp-server enable
```

Configures   Enables FTP server

Default   Disabled

Description

This command enables FTP services on the router; the router runs an FTP server that can be used to upload and download files in the router's filesystem. To use this feature, you must also configure the ftp-server topdir command.

---

ftp-server topdir   global

```
ftp-server topdir directory
no ftp-server topdir
```

Configures   The directory to which FTP clients have read/write access

Default   None (all read and write operations are denied)

Description
This command sets the *directory* in the router's filesystem that FTP clients are allowed to access. Access is also allowed to subdirectories of this directory. If this command has not been given or if no ftp-server topdir has been given, no access is allowed via FTP.

Example
The following commands enable the router's FTP server and allow it to access the directory *disk1:/logs* and all its subdirectories.

```
ftp-server enable
ftp-server topdir disk1:/logs
```

full-duplex   interface

```
full-duplex
no full-duplex
```

Configures   Full-duplex mode

Default   Half-duplex

Description   This command enables full-duplex mode on interfaces that support it.

full-help   line configuration

```
full-help
no full-help
```

Configures   Full help for a line

Default   Disabled

Description   This command enables full help on a line configuration.

group-range

group-range *start* *end*
no group-range *start* *end*

Configures   An interface group

Default   None

Description
This command specifies a range of interfaces that are treated as a group for the purposes of configuration. It is used in conjunction with the interface group-async command. *start* and *end* are the beginning and ending numbers of the interfaces that are configured as a group.

Example
The following commands group the async interfaces 1 through 7. Once a group has been defined, specific interfaces can be singled out for special treatment with the member command: for example, specific IP addresses can be applied to each interface.

```
interface group-async 0
  group-range 1 7
  ip unnumbered ethernet0
  async mode interactive
  member 1 peer default ip 10.10.1.1
  member 2 peer default ip 10.10.1.2
  member 3 peer default ip 10.10.1.3
  member 4 peer default ip 10.10.1.4
  member 5 peer default ip 10.10.1.5
  member 6 peer default ip 10.10.1.6
  member 7 peer default ip 10.10.1.7
```

half-duplex

half-duplex
no half-duplex

Configures   An SDLC interface for half-duplex

Default   Disabled

Description   This command configures an SDLC interface for half-duplex mode.

half-duplex controlled-carrier

half-duplex controlled-carrier
no half-duplex controlled-carrier

Configures   Controlled carrier mode versus constant carrier mode

Default   Constant carrier mode

Description

Low speed serial interfaces use constant carrier mode by default. This command places the interface in controlled carrier mode; it can be used only on interfaces that have been configured for half-duplex.

---

help   command

`help`

Description

Displays a brief listing of user-level commands. To get more verbose help, use the `full-help` command.

---

history   global

`history [number-of-lines]`
`no history`

Configures   History buffer size

Default   10 lines

Description

This command enables the user interface's history mechanism. A history is a listing of commands that have been executed in the current session. This command is stored in the router's configuration and applies to all user sessions. *number-of-lines* is the size of the history buffer and must be in the range of 0–256. If omitted, the buffer size is set to the default value.

Use the no version of this command to disable the history mechanism; use the show history command to view the current history buffer. If you want to activate a history buffer only for your current session, use the command terminal history.

Example

```
Router# history 255
Router# no history
Router# show history
```

---

hold-character   line

`hold-character ascii-number`
`no hold-character`

Configures   The character that suspends output

Default   None

Description

This command sets the character that suspends output to a terminal screen. *ascii-number* is the value of the character in decimal. Having a pause key benefits users who need to scroll through a lot of text; pressing any character resumes output to the screen.

Example

```
Router(config)# line 2
Router(config-line)# hold-character 19
Router(config-line)# vacant-message #
Router(config-line)#             ***** Welcome to Sphinx *****
Router(config-line)#      Press the return key to start the connection
Router(config-line)#              Suspend with Ctrl-S
Router(config-line)# #
```

---

hold-queue   interface

hold-queue *packets* {in | out}
no hold-queue *packets* {in | out}

Configures   Size of the hold queue

Default   Input queue, 75 packets; output queue, 40 packets

Description

This command specifies the length of the input queue (in) or the output queue (out) in *packets*. Slower links require smaller queue sizes than faster links.

Example

```
interface Async4
    ip unnumbered Ethernet0
    hold-queue 20 out
    async default ip address 192.101.187.164
    async mode interactive
```

---

hostname   global

hostname *name-string*
no hostname

Configures   The hostname of the router

Default   Factory-assigned "Router"

Description   This command sets the hostname of the router.

hssi external-loop-request
interface

```
hssi external-loop-request
no hssi external-loop-request
```

Configures   Support for CSU/DSU

Default   Disabled

Description
This command enables support for CSU/DSUs that provide the LC signal. The LC signal allows the CSU/DSU to request loopback from the router.

hssi internal-clock
interface

```
hssi internal-clock
no hssi internal-clock
```

Configures   Use of the internal clock

Default   Disabled

Description
This command configures an HSSI interface to provide a 45 MHz master clock. It is used when two HSSI interfaces are connected via a null modem cable; one of the two interfaces must provide a clock signal on the link. Both interfaces cannot provide clocks, so use this command only on one side of the link.

hub
global

```
hub ethernet hub-number first-port [last-port]
```

Configures   Hub configuration mode

Default   None

Description
The hub command enters hub configuration mode, in which you can enter commands that configure a hub. It is applicable only to routers that are equipped with hub interfaces. *hub-number* is the number of the hub that you are configuring. *first-port* is the beginning of a range of consecutive ports to be configured as part of the hub; *last-port* is the last port in the range. If you omit *last-port*, this command adds a single port to the hub.

Example
To configure one port of a hub:

```
hub ethernet 0 1
  source-address 00:00:0c:ff:d0:04
```

To configure all ports of a hub:

```
hub ethernet 0 1 7
  no link-test
  auto-polarity
```

ignore-dcd

interface

```
ignore-dcd
no ignore-dcd
```

Configures   Determination of a link's status

Default   A DTE serial interface monitors the DCD signal

Description

This command tells the interface to ignore the DCD signal and use the DSR signal to determine whether the link is up or down. By default, all DTE serial interfaces monitor the DCD signal for the link's status.

interface

global

```
interface interface.subinterface [{point-to-point | multipoint}]
```

Configures   Allows configuration of a given interface

Default   None

Description

This command enters the interface configuration mode for the given *interface* and *subinterface*. The interface most commonly consists of an interface type followed by the number of the particular interface (for example, ethernet0). A space is allowed (and commonly used) between the interface type and the number. Table 17-10 shows the most common interface types. On more complex routers, the interface number can be specified in a number of different ways: as a *slot/port* combination, as a *slot/adapter/port* combination, or as a *slot/port:channel-group* combination. The appropriate form depends on the hardware you're dealing with. The interface specification can include a subinterface number; subinterfaces are most common when using protocols like Frame Relay or ATM, which can package a number of communications channels on a single physical connection. The point-to-point keyword indicates that a subinterface is logically connected to a single remote node; multipoint indicates that it is logically connected to a number of remote nodes. multipoint and point-to-point are most commonly used on Frame Relay and ATM interfaces.

Table 17-10. Common interface types

Type	Description
async	An asynchronous interface (a standard terminal or modem line)
atm	ATM
bri	ISDN BRI (2 B channels)

Table 17-10. Common interface types (continued)

Type	Description
dialer	Dial-on-demand interface (see the `interface dialer` command)
ethernet	Ethernet
fastethernet	100-Mbps Ethernet
fddi	FDDI
gigabitethernet	Gigabit Ethernet
group-async	A logical grouping of asynchronous interfaces to which all configuration commands apply (see the `interface group-async` command)
hssi	High-speed serial interface
lex	LAN extender
loopback	The internal software virtual interface
null	Null interface; packets sent to this interface are discarded
pos	OC-3/SONET
serial	Serial interface (used for leased line, T1, and T3)
tokenring	Token ring
tunnel	A virtual interface for a tunnel configuration

interface bvi   global

```
interface bvi bridge-group-number
no interface bvi bridge-group-number
```

Configures   Bridging

Default   None

Description
The Bridge-Group Virtual Interface (BVI) becomes available on routers when the bridge irb command has been given. This interface allows the router to route and bridge the same protocol over the same interface. The *bridge group-number* must match the bridge group defined for the bridge.

Example
In this configuration, serial0 and serial1 are bridged, and traffic is routed through those interfaces out through ethernet0:

```
bridge irb
bridge 1 protocol ieee
!
interface serial0
 bridge-group 1
!
interface serial
  bridge-group 1
!
interface ethernet 0
  ip address 10.11.1.1 255.255.255.0
!
```

```
! Configure the virtual bvi interface with a bridge group number of 1
interface bvi 1
   ip address 10.10.3.1 255.255.255.0
!
! Now configure the routing for the bridge
bridge 1 route ip
```

interface dialer   global

```
interface dialer number
no interface dialer number
```

Configures   A dialer configuration

Default   None

Description
This command allows you to define a virtual dialer configuration that can be applied
to a set of physical interfaces. Once you configure this interface, you can make other
interfaces use this configuration by using the `dialer rotary-group` command. *number* is
the virtual interface number, and can be a value from 0 to 9.

Example
```
interface dialer 0
   encapsulation ppp
   dialer in-band
   dialer map ip 10.1.1.1 name bob 5551111
!
interface async 1
   dialer rotary-group 0
```

interface group-async   global

```
interface group-async number
no interface group-async number
```

Configures   A group of interfaces that can share configuration parameters

Default   None

Description
This command allows you to create a group of async interfaces to which you can apply
commands. Actual interfaces that belong to the group inherit the settings you apply to
this virtual interface. The `group-range` command defines which physical async interfaces are included in the group. A physical interface can belong only to one group.

Example
The following commands define a group-async interface that includes async interfaces
1 through 7. The `ip` `unnumbered` and `async` `mode` commands apply to all the interfaces
in the group.

```
interface group-async 0
  group-range 1 7
  ip unnumbered ethernet0
  async mode interactive
```

ip access-group
interface

```
ip access-group access-list [in | out]
no ip access-group access-list [in | out]
```

Configures   Assigns an access list to an interface

Default   No access lists defined

Description
This command applies the given access list to the interface in the direction specified (in or out). Access-list commands are discussed in Chapter 7. Each interface can support only one access list in either direction.

Example
The following commands apply access list 110 to filter incoming packets on the serial1 interface, and access list 111 to filter outgoing packets:

```
interface serial1
  ip access-group 110 in
  ip access-group 111 out
```

To remove an access list from an interface, use the no form of this command:

```
interface serial1
  no ip access-group 111 out
```

If you use the no access-list command, your access list will be deleted. Be sure to use no ip access-group when removing lists from interfaces.

ip access-list
global

```
ip access-list {standard | extended} name
```

Configures   Named access lists

Default   None

Description
This command allows you to create a named access list. A named access list is really no different from a numbered access list as defined by the access-list command, except that it is identified by a logical name. A named access list may be either standard or extended. This command is followed by permit and deny commands that specify the access-list rules. For more about access lists, see Chapter 7 and the discussion of the access-list command.

Example

The following commands define a named access list that allows HTTP traffic from any host to the server at 10.1.2.3 and permits all other TCP traffic that has the SYN flag set. Remember that all access lists end with an implicit deny, which rejects all traffic not permitted by a statement in the access list.

```
ip access-list extended bogus-firewall
  permit tcp any host 10.1.2.3 eq http
  permit tcp any any established
```

As of IOS 12.4, you can enter noncontiguous ports on a single line within a named access list. Before, you would write such an access list like this:

```
ip access-list extended acllist1
  permit tcp any host 192.168.1.1 eq telnet
  permit tcp any host 192.168.1.1 eq www
  permit tcp any host 192.168.1.1 eq smtp
  permit tcp any host 192.168.1.1 eq pop3
```

With noncontigious port support, you can write it more tersely:

```
ip access-list extended acllist1
  permit tcp any host 192.168.1.1 eq telnet www smtp pop3
```

---

ip accounting   interface

```
ip accounting [access-violations]
no ip accounting [access-violations]
```

Configures   IP accounting for an interface

Default   Disabled

Description

This command enables IP accounting based on the source and destination IP addresses that are passing through this router. Traffic that terminates at the router is not logged. The access-violations option enables logging based on access lists. For an access list to log information, the log keyword must be specified at the end of the access-list command.

Example

The following interface has IP accounting enabled and logs access-list violations:

```
interface serial 1
  ip address 10.10.2.3 255.255.255.0
  ip access-group 110 in
  ip accounting access-violations
! Deny telnet to the outside and log it when someone tries
access-list 110 deny tcp 10.10.2.0 0.0.0.255 any eq 23 log
access-list 110 permit ip any any
```

ip accounting-list

global

```
ip accounting-list address mask
no ip accounting-list address mask
```

Configures   An accounting filter

Default   None

Description

This command defines an IP *address* and wildcard *mask* for use as an accounting filter. Once a filter has been created, traffic is logged only if it matches the filter. If an IP address fails to match this filter, it is considered a transit IP packet and is logged to a separate table. See ip accounting-transits.

Example

The following command logs traffic to and from the 10.10.0.0 network:

```
ip accounting-list 10.10.0.0 0.0.255.255
```

ip accounting-threshold

global

```
ip accounting-threshold log-size
no ip accounting-threshold log-size
```

Configures   The IP accounting log table

Default   512 entries

Description

This command sets the size of the IP accounting table to *log-size* bytes. Each entry takes up to 26 bytes. Therefore, an accounting table defined at 100 entries could consume up to 2600 bytes of memory. This calculation should be kept in mind when defining new thresholds, as memory usage has adverse affects on the router.

Example

To double the accounting buffer:

```
ip accounting-threshold 1024
```

ip accounting-transits

global

```
ip accounting-transits number
no ip accounting-transits
```

Configures   The table used for logging transit IP addresses

Default   None

Description

This command sets the size of the table for transit IP accounting to *number* entries. A transit IP packet is any packet with a source or destination that does not match the filter defined in the ip accounting-list command. If no accounting filters are defined, there are no transit IP packets.

Example

To set the transit table to 200 entries:

```
ip accounting-transits 200
```

---

ip address   interface

```
ip address address subnet-mask [secondary]
no ip address address subnet-mask [secondary]
```

Configures   The IP address for an interface

Default   No IP address

Description

This command sets the IP address for the interface to *address*; the network mask used on the network is *subnet-mask*. The secondary keyword is used to apply a second (or third, or fourth...) address to an interface. It is allowed only if the interface allows multiple IP addresses.

Example

This command sets the IP address of the ethernet0 interface to 10.10.1.1 and the subnet mask to 255.255.255.0:

```
interface ethernet0
  ip address 10.10.1.1 255.255.255.0
```

The following commands use the secondary keyword to add a second IP address to the ethernet0 interface:

```
interface ethernet0
  ip address 10.10.1.1 255.255.255.0
  ip address 10.10.2.1 255.255.255.0 secondary
```

This interface will now answer and provide routing for both the 10.10.1.0/24 and 10.10.2.0/24 subnets.

---

ip address negotiated   interface

```
ip address negotiated
no ip address negotiated
```

Configures   PPP address negotiation

Default   Disabled

Description   This command configures an interface to obtain its IP address via PPP.

---

ip address-pool

```
ip address-pool [dhcp-proxy-client | local]
no ip address-pool
```

Configures   Default address pooling

Default   Disabled

Description

This command provides an IP address pool to be used on dial-in or ISDN interfaces.

dhcp-proxy-client
> Optional. The router works as a proxy between the dial-in peers and the DHCP server to provide the address pool.

local
> Optional. Tells the router to use the local address pool.

ip alias

```
ip alias ip-address port
no ip alias ip-address
```

Configures   IP address mapping for reverse telnet

Default   None

Description

This command allows you to provide aliases in the form of IP addresses for various ports on the router. This feature is helpful if you are configuring a communication server with reverse telnet.

ip-address
> The IP address of the port for which you want to establish an alias.

port
> The port that you want to use as an alias for the IP address.

Example

Say we have a communication server (router) with three ports to which we allow reverse telnet access: 2001, 2002, and 2003. Instead of requiring users to type the router's IP address and the port every time, we assign (alias) an available IP address to each of our ports. The following commands create three IP address aliases (172.30.1.1, 172.30.1.2, and 172.30.1.3):

```
ip alias 172.30.1.1 2001
ip alias 172.30.1.2 2002
ip alias 172.30.1.3 2003
```

ip as-path access-list

global

```
ip as-path access-list access-list {permit | deny} as-regex
no ip as-path access-list access-list {permit | deny} as-regex
```

Configures   A BGP access list

Default   None

Description

This command allows you to build an access list for BGP autonomous system (AS) paths. These lists can be applied to a neighbor with the `filter-list` option to the `neighbor` command. `access-list` is a number that identifies the list; `as-regex` is a regular expression that matches AS paths. For more information on valid regular expressions for BGP, see Chapter 10.

Example

The following commands create an AS-path access list that denies (blocks) routes that include AS 111. This access list is then applied to routes that are sent to the BGP neighbor 11.1.1.1.

```
ip as-path access-list 1 deny _111_

router bgp 120
  network 10.1.0.0
  neighbor 11.1.1.1 remote-as 200
  neighbor 11.1.1.1 filter-list 1 out
```

ip authentication

interface

```
ip authentication key-chain eigrp as-number key-chain
no ip authentication key-chain eigrp as-number key-chain


ip authentication mode eigrp as-number md5
no ip authentication mode eigrp as-number md5
```

Configures   Authentication of EIGRP packets

Default   None

Description

The `ip authentication key-chain` command defines the key chain to be used for authenticating EIGRP packets. It is used with the `ip authentication mode eigrp` command, which applies the key chain to the correct EIGRP process. Key chains are defined with the global `key chain` command.

as-number
　The EIGRP process to which this key applies.

key-chain
　The name of an EIGRP key chain.

Example

```
interface ethernet0
  ip authentication key-chain eigrp 100 key1
  ip authentication mode eigrp 100 md5
```

---

ip bandwidth-percent eigrp
interface, EIGRP

ip bandwidth-percent eigrp *as-number percent-value*

Configures   The bandwidth that EIGRP is allowed to use

Default   50 percent

Description

This command sets the bandwidth percentage that EIGRP is allowed to consume on a link. It is particularly useful if the link's bandwidth has been set to a fake value for some reason (such as metrics).

as-number
> The EIGRP process whose bandwidth is being limited.

percent-value
> The percentage of the interface's total bandwidth that can be used by EIGRP. The interface's bandwidth is defined by the bandwidth command and may not be the same as the actual bandwidth available on the link. Note that *percent-value* may be greater than 100; this is useful if the bandwidth has been set to an artificially low value and doesn't reflect the actual capacity of the link.

---

ip bgp-community new-format
global

ip bgp-community new-format
no ip bgp-community new-format

Configures   Display of the BGP communities

Default   Disabled

Description

This command changes the display of BGP communities from NN:AA to AA:NN.

---

ip bootp server
global

ip bootp server
no ip bootp server

Configures   Use of a BOOTP server from the network

Default   Enabled

Description

This command enables or disables the router's BOOTP server. Disabling this feature prevents hosts from accessing the BOOTP service on the router; that is, the router won't act as a BOOTP server.

---

ip broadcast-address

interface

ip broadcast-address *address*
no ip broadcast-address *address*

Configures   A broadcast address for an interface

Default   Depends on the settings in the config-register

Description

This command specifies the interface's broadcast address. All hosts on the network to which the interface is connected must use the same broadcast address. Broadcast addresses are usually formed by setting the "host address" portion of the IP address to 1, which is the default for the router and most modern computer systems. Some old systems may form the broadcast address by setting the host portion to 0, and may be incapable of using the "1" form. In this case, you must explicitly set the broadcast address of the router interface (and all other hosts on the network) to use the older form.

Example

The following code changes the broadcast IP address for serial 0 to 10.10.10.255:

```
interface serial 0
    ip broadcast-address 10.10.10.255
```

---

ip cef

global

ip cef [distributed]
no ip cef

Configures   Cisco Express Forwarding (CEF)

Default   Depends on the hardware; usually disabled

Description

This command enables CEF on the router. CEF is a Layer 3 switching technology that increases network performance for certain types of network traffic.

The optional distributed keyword enables distributed CEF (dCEF), which distributes CEF information to line cards on the router.

ip cef traffic-statistics

global

```
ip cef traffic-statistics [load-interval seconds] [update-rate seconds]
no ip cef traffic-statistics
```

Configures Time intervals that control when NHRP creates or destroys an SVC

Default `load-interval` is 30 seconds; `update-rate` is 10 seconds

Description

This command sets the intervals that NHRP uses when building or tearing down an SVC. The `load-interval` is used in conjunction with the `ip nhrp trigger-svc` command; its value can range from 30 to 300 seconds. The `update-rate` is the frequency, in seconds, at which the port adapter sends statistics to the route processor (RP). When using NHRP in distributed CEF switching mode, the update rate must be set to 5 seconds.

ip cgmp

interface

```
ip cgmp [proxy | router-only]
no ip cgmp
```

Configures Cisco Group Management Protocol (CGMP)

Default Disabled

Description

This command enables CGMP on an interface, which is useful when the interface is connected to a Cisco Catalyst family switch.

proxy

   Optional. Enables CGMP and the CGMP proxy function.

router-only

   Optional. Enables the router to send only CGMP self-join and CGMP self-leave messages.

ip classless

global

```
ip classless
no ip classless
```

Configures IP classless routing for the router

Default Depends on the IOS version

Description

This command enables routing based on "classless" addresses. With classless routing, packets can be routed if the router knows a route for a supernet of the addressee.

Without classless addressing, the packet is discarded if it arrives at the router and there is no network route for its destination. Assume that a packet arrives with the destination of 10.10.1.5, but we have routes only for 10.10.2.0/24, 10.10.3.0/24, and 10.10.0.0/16. With IP classless routing enabled, the router forwards the packet to the 10.10.0.0/16 network because 10.10.0.0/16 is the best matching supernet of 10.10.1.5.

ip community-list
global

```
ip community-list number {permit | deny} community
no ip community-list number
```

Configures   A community list for BGP

Default   None

Description

This command defines a community list, which is basically an access list for a BGP community. A community list can be used with the match community command in a route-map configuration.

number

A value identifying the community list that this command belongs to. Values can be 1 to 99.

permit | deny

Permits or denies the given community.

community

The community to permit or deny. This parameter may be a community number between 1 and 99, or one of the default community names (internet, no-export, no-advertise).

Example

```
ip community-list 1 permit internet
```

ip default-gateway
global

```
ip default-gateway address
no default-gateway address
```

Configures   The default gateway for the router

Default   None

Description

This command establishes *address* as the router's default gateway, which is the gateway to which nonlocal packets are forwarded in the absence of a better route. It is useful if the no ip routing command has been issued or if you are running from boot mode, in which IP routing is disabled. This command allows you to forward traffic to the default gateway when routing is disabled. Use the no form of this command to remove the entry from the router's configuration.

ip default-network

global

```
ip default-network network
no ip default-network network
```

Configures   Gateway of last resort

Default   None

Description

This command defines a gateway of last resort. The *network* argument is a network address; any route to the network becomes the default route. For RIP, this is the 0.0.0.0 route; for OSPF, it is an external route.

ip dhcp-server

global

```
ip dhcp-server address
no ip dhcp-server address
```

Configures   The DHCP server for the router

Default   None

Description

Specifies the *address* of the DHCP server for this router. You can provide the hostname of the DHCP server instead of its IP address. This DHCP server is then used for creating address pools with the `ip address-pool` command.

ip directed-broadcast

interface

```
ip directed-broadcast [access-list]
no ip directed-broadcast
```

Configures   Broadcast forwarding

Default   Enabled (disabled for IOS 12.0 and later)

Description

By default, the router automatically translates directed broadcasts to physical broadcasts within your network. In other words, Layer 3 broadcasts to the IP broadcast address (10.10.1.255 for the subnet 10.10.1.0/24) are translated into Layer 2 broadcasts with an address appropriate for the interface (e.g., ff:ff:ff:ff:ff:ff for an Ethernet interface).

While this can be useful, an interface that is configured to the outside world could allow a potential hacker to flood your network by pinging the broadcast address on your interface. It is recommended that directed-broadcast is disabled on your external interfaces to prevent this attack from occurring. Directed broadcast is also the primary mechanism used for the "smurf" attack. It is recommended that you disable directed broadcast on all your interfaces unless you have a very good reason to use it.

Example

To disable directed broadcasts:

```
interface serial 0
    no ip directed-broadcast
```

---

ip domain-list   global

```
ip domain-list domain
no ip domain-list domain
```

Configures   Domain name completion

Default   None

Description

This command allows you to define a series of domain names to be used (in turn) to complete an unqualified domain name. It behaves just like the domain-name command except that it allows you to list a series of domains.

Example

These commands set the domain list to mydomain.com, com.com, and mycom.com:

```
ip domain-list mydomain.com
ip domain-list com.com
ip domain list mycom.com
```

Use the no form of the command to delete an entry:

```
no ip domain-list com.com
```

---

ip domain-lookup   global

```
ip domain-lookup
no ip domain-lookup
```

Configures   DNS lookups for hostnames

Default   Enabled

Description

This command enables the DNS lookup feature. To disable DNS, use the no form of this command. Disabling this feature is useful because you don't usually want the router trying to perform a DNS lookup on every word that you type at the command prompt. (You can accomplish the same thing by enabling transport preferred none on all lines.) Furthermore, if you are having network problems, you may not be able to reach any DNS servers to perform lookups.

Example

To disable DNS lookups:

```
no ip domain-lookup
```

---

ip domain-name
global

```
ip domain-name domain
no ip domain-name domain
```

Configures   Domain name completion

Default   None

Description

This command sets the domain name that the router will use to complete any unqualified domain names. See also ip domain-list.

Example

Here, all unqualified hostnames are taken to be in the mydomain.com domain:

```
ip domain-name mydomain.com
```

---

ip dvmrp accept-filter
interface

```
ip dvmrp accept-filter access-list [distance] [neighbor-list access-list]
no dvmrp accept-filter access-list
```

Configures   Incoming filter for DVMRP reports

Default   All reports are accepted with a distance of 0

Description

This command applies an access list to incoming DVMRP reports. The lower the distance, the higher the precedence of the route when computing the Reverse Path Forwarding value.

access-list
> The number of a standard IP access list (0–99). Routes matching the access list are assigned the given administrative distance. If the access list number is 0 (which is not a legal access list number), all reports are accepted with the given administrative distance.

distance
> Optional. The administrative distance to be assigned to routes matching the filter. Default is 0.

neighbor-list list
> Optional. The number of a standard IP access list (1–99). DVMRP reports are accepted only from neighbors who match this access list.

ip dvmrp auto-summary

```
ip dvmrp auto-summary
no ip dvmrp auto-summary
```

Configures   DVMRP auto summarization

Default   Enabled

Description

Auto summarization occurs when a route is summarized into a classful network route. Use the no form of this command to disable it, which you will want to do if you are using the ip dvmrp summary-address command.

ip dvmrp default-information

```
ip dvmrp default-information {originate | only}
no dvmrp default-information
```

Configures   Advertises a default route to DVMRP neighbors

Default   Disabled

Description

This command causes the default route (0.0.0.0) to be advertised to DVMRP neighbors.

originate
  Routes more specific than 0.0.0.0 can be advertised.

only
  Only the default route is advertised.

ip dvmrp metric

```
ip dvmrp metric metric [list access-list] [[protocol process-id] | [dvmrp]
no ip dvmrp metric
```

Configures   Metrics for DVMRP

Default   1

Description

This command lets you specify a metric to be used with the DVMRP routing protocol. The specified metric is assigned to multicast destinations that match the access list.

metric
  The metric associated with DVMRP reports; it can range from 0 to 32. means the route is not advertised; 32 means that the route's destination is unreachable.

list access-list
  Optional. If used, this metric is assigned only to multicast destinations that match the access list.

protocol
  Optional. bgp, eigrp, igrp, isis, ospf, rip, static, or dvmrp.

process-id
  Optional. The process ID of the routing protocol, if required.

dvmrp
  Optional. Allows routes from the DVMRP routing table to be advertised with the
  configured metric route map.

ip dvmrp metric-offset   interface

```
ip dvmrp metric-offset [in | out] value
no ip dvmrp metric-offset
```

Configures   Metrics of advertised DVMRP routes

Default   in; the default value for in is 1, for out is 0

Description
This command allows you to increment the metric for DVMRP routes. The given
value is added to either metrics received (in) or metrics sent (out) by the router.

ip dvmrp output-report-delay   interface

```
ip dvmrp output-report-delay milliseconds [burst-packets]
no ip dvmrp output-report-delay
```

Configures   Interpacket delay of a DVMRP report

Default   100 milliseconds; 2 burst packets

Description
This command sets the number of milliseconds that elapse between packets of a
DVMRP report.

milliseconds
  Number of milliseconds between transmission of packets.

burst-packets
  Optional. The number of packets in the set being transmitted.

ip dvmrp reject-non-pruners   interface

```
ip dvmrp reject-non-pruners
no ip dvmrp reject-non-pruners
```

Configures   Peering with DVMRP non-pruners

Default   Disabled

Description

When enabled, this feature tells the interface not to peer with DVMRP hosts that do not support pruning. By default, the router will peer with all DVMRP neighbors.

---

ip dvmrp routehog-notification   global

```
ip dvmrp routehog-notification route-count
no ip dvmrp routehog-notification
```

Configures   Number of routes accepted before a syslog message is generated

Default   10,000

Description

This command sets the number of DVMRP routes that can be accepted within one minute to *route-count*. If more than this number of routes is accepted within a minute, the router generates a syslog message. This usually helps capture any router that is misconfigured and injecting too many routes.

---

ip dvmrp route-limit   global

```
ip dvmrp route-limit count
no ip dvmrp route-limit count
```

Configures   Number of advertised DVMRP routes

Default   7,000

Description

This command sets the limit on the number of DVMRP routes that can be advertised over an interface to *count*.

---

ip dvmrp summary-address   interface

```
ip dvmrp summary-address address mask [metric value]
no ip dvmrp summary-address address mask
```

Configures   A summary DVMRP route

Default   None

Description

This command configures a summary DVMRP route to be advertised over an interface.

address
> The IP address of the summary route.

mask
> The network mask of the summary route.

metric *value*
> Optional. The metric to be assigned to the summary address. Default is 1.

---

ip dvmrp unicast-routing interface

```
ip dvmrp unicast-routing
no dvmrp unicast-routing
```

Configures   DVMRP unicast routing

Default   Disabled

Description   This command enables DVMRP unicast routing on the interface.

---

ip forward-protocol global

```
ip forward-protocol {udp [port] | any-local-broadcast | spanning-tree |
   turbo-flood}
no ip forward-protocol
```

Configures   Forwarding of broadcast packets for certain services

Default   Enabled with the ip helper-address command

Description

When the ip helper-address command is configured for an interface, the router "helps" hosts find certain UDP services by forwarding the packets. These services are BOOTP (DHCP), DNS, TFTP, TACACS, TIME, and NetBIOS name and datagram servers. This command allows you to define additional UDP ports that you want forwarded automatically to the helper IP address.

port
> Optional. Without this parameter, all the default UDP ports listed here are forwarded. This keyword allows you to forward a specific port. You can disable a default port with the no version of this command.

any-local-broadcast
> Forwards any broadcasts including local subnet broadcasts.

spanning-tree
> Forwards IP broadcasts that meet the following criteria: First, it must be a MAC level broadcast; second, it must be an IP level broadcast; and third, it must be TFTP, DNS, NetBIOS, ND, TIME, BOOTP, or any other UDP packet specified by an ip forward-protocol udp command.

turbo-flood

> Speeds up the flooding of UDP datagrams when using the spanning-tree algorithm. This command should be used in conjunction with the ip forward-protocol spanning-tree command.

Example

To forward port 21000 for a specific application:

```
ip forward-protocol udp 21000
```

ip ftp passive   global

```
ip ftp passive
no ip ftp passive
```

Configures   Passive FTP mode

Default   Disabled (normal FTP)

Description

This command configures the router to use passive FTP. Passive FTP is often used when connecting through firewalls or access lists that block normal FTP connections. With passive FTP, the file transfer session originates from the client, not the server, which makes firewalls more likely to allow it. You may need to use passive FTP when copying a file or image to an FTP server.

ip ftp password   global

```
ip ftp password [encryption-level] password
no ftp password
```

Configures   The FTP password

Default   *username@routername.domain*

Description

This command sets the password to be used for FTP connections. The default password is appropriate for anonymous FTP connections. If you do not use anonymous FTP, you must use this command to provide an appropriate secret password. The *encryption-level* allows you to encrypt the password within the router's configuration, so people who have access to the configuration file won't learn it. The *encryption-level* may be 0 or 7; 0 does not encrypt the password, while 7 uses a proprietary (but not particularly strong) encryption scheme.

ip ftp source-interface   global

```
ip ftp source-interface interface
no ip ftp source-interface
```

Configures   The FTP source address

Default   The IP address of the interface closest to the destination

Description

This command sets the source address for FTP connections to the IP address of the given *interface*.

---

ip ftp username   global

```
ip ftp username username
no ip ftp username
```

Configures   The FTP username

Default   anonymous

Description

This command sets the username for FTP connections. If no username is supplied, the router attempts an anonymous FTP file transfer.

Example

The following commands configure the router to use passive FTP with the username saul and the password pleaseletmein.

```
ip ftp passive
ip ftp username saul
ip ftp password pleaseletmein
```

---

ip hello-interval eigrp   interface

```
ip hello-interval eigrp as-number seconds
no ip hello-interval eigrp as-number seconds
```

Configures   Hello interval for EIGRP

Default   five seconds

Description

This command sets the interval at which EIGRP hello discovery packets are sent out on a link. The default value for the hello interval is 5 seconds. On links where latency is high, changing this value to a higher number can be advantageous.

as-number
> The EIGRP process number (frequently called an AS number).

seconds
> The interval between hello discovery packets.

ip helper-address interface

```
ip helper-address address
no ip helper-address address
```

Configures   IP address to which certain broadcast UDP packets are forwarded

Default   Disabled

Description

This command sets the helper address to *address*. The helper address should be the address of a host that can answer UDP requests from other hosts. The router sees these requests broadcast on a LAN interface and forwards them to the helper address (generally a unicast address) if one is defined. A helper is particularly useful for DHCP requests; without some kind of forwarding, DHCP requires you to have a separate server on every subnet. By itself, this command forwards packets for the BOOTP (DHCP), DNS, TFTP, TACACS, TIME, and NetBIOS name and datagram services. The ip forward-protocol command can be used to forward additional UDP services.

Example

To configure interface ethernet0 to have a helper address:

```
interface ethernet0
    ip address 10.10.1.2 255.255.255.0
    ip helper address 10.10.2.5
```

ip hold-time eigrp interface

```
ip hold-time eigrp as-number seconds
no ip hold-time eigrp as-number seconds
```

Configures   Hold time for EIGRP networks

Default   15 seconds

Description

This command defines the number of seconds that a route is held before hearing from a neighbor router. If the router doesn't hear from a neighbor within this time, the routes from that neighbor are considered invalid. The default holdtime is three times the hello interval, which is 15 seconds on most links. Slower links might have a holdtime of 180 seconds and a hello interval of 60 seconds.

as-number
    The EIGRP process number (frequently called an AS number).

seconds
    The holdtime for this EIGRP process.

ip host

```
ip host name [tcp-port] address [address]
no ip host name address
```

Configures   A static hostname that maps to one or more IP addresses

Default   None

Description

This command allows you to define an IP address for a hostname. Each hostname can have up to eight IP addresses associated with it. This is similar to a host file on a workstation (for example, the */etc/hosts* file on Unix).

name
> The name of a host.

tcp-port
> Optional. The port to connect to on the host when using the telnet command.

address
> The address assigned to the host.

Example

The following commands define two IP hosts; the second one has two IP addresses:

```
ip host gateway1 10.10.1.1
ip host gateway2 10.10.1.2 10.10.1.3
```

ip http

```
ip http server
no ip http server


ip http access-class access-list
no ip http access-class access-list


ip http authentication method
no ip http authentication method


ip http port port
no ip http port port
```

Configures   Web IOS interface

Default   Disabled; when enabled, listens on port 80

Description

This command configures support for the Web IOS interface software. This feature enables an HTTP server on the router and allows you to configure the router by pointing any web browser at this server. The access-class option lets you specify an access list that limits access to the HTTP server. The port option lets you specify the port on which the server listens.

The acceptable authentication methods are enable, local, tacacs, and aaa.

Example

The following commands enable the web browser interface and specify a non-default port:

```
ip http server
ip http port 8008
```

---

ip identd   global

```
ip identd
no ip identd
```

Configures   Identification support

Default   Disabled

Description

This command enables the IDENTD identification protocol. To disable IDENTD, use the no form of the command.

---

ip igmp access-group   interface

```
ip igmp access-group access-list version
no ip igmp access-group access-list version
```

Configures   Controls multicast groups

Default   All groups are enabled; default version is 2

Description

This command allows you to set an *access-list* that controls which groups are available on the interface for hosts to join. If a host is in the access list, it will be allowed to join multicast groups. The *version* parameter changes the IGMP version.

---

ip igmp explicit-tracking   interface

```
ip igmp explicit-tracking
no ip igmp explicit-tracking
```

Configures   Explicit tracking for IGMPv3

Default   Disabled

Description

This command enables explicit tracking of hosts, groups, and channels for IGMP v3. Explicit tracking allows the router to individually track IGMP membership states of all reporting hosts. To view the information, use the show ip igmp membership command.

---

ip igmp helper-address   interface

ip igmp helper-address *ip-address*
no ip igmp helper-address *ip-address*

Configures   Forwards IGMP messages to another IP address

Default   Disabled

Description

This command causes all IGMP Host Reports and Leave messages to be sent to the host specified by the *ip-address* parameter.

---

ip igmp join-group   interface

ip igmp join-group *group-address*
no ip igmp join-group *group-address*

Configures   Has the router join a multicast group

Default   None

Description

This command causes the router to join the multicast group specified by the IP group address on the interface.

---

ip igmp query-interval   interface

ip igmp query-interval *seconds*
no ip igmp query-interval *seconds*

Configures   Query message interval

Default   60 seconds

Description

This command configures the router to send IGMP host-query messages at the specified interval. Changing this value may affect multicast forwarding.

ip igmp query-max-response-time

```
ip igmp query-max-response-time seconds
no ip igmp query-max-response-time seconds
```

Configures   Response time advertised in IGMP query packets

Default   10 seconds

Description
This command sets the time in *seconds* that the responder has to respond to a query before the router deletes the group. This command works only with IGMP Version 2.

ip igmp query-timeout

```
ip igmp query-timeout seconds
no ip igmp query-timeout seconds
```

Configures   Query timeout

Default   two times the query interval

Description
This command sets the query timeout period in *seconds*. This is the time that the router waits after the last querier stops querying, and takes over as the querier.

ip igmp static-group

```
ip igmp static-group group-address
no ip igmp static-group group-address
```

Configures   A static *igmp* group for the router

Default   Disabled

Description
This command enrolls the router in the multicast group specified by the *group-address*. Unlike the `ip igmp join-group` command, this command allows packets to the group to be fast-switched out the interface.

ip igmp version

```
ip igmp version {1 | 2 | 3}
no ip igmp version
```

Configures   The IGMP version type

Default   2

Description

This command sets the version number of IGMP supported by the router (1, 2, or 3). Make sure that your hosts support the same version. Version 3 was introduced in 12.1(5)T.

ip irdp

```
ip irdp [multicast | holdtime seconds | maxadvertinterval seconds |
    minadvertinterval seconds | preference value | address ip-address
    [preference]]
no ip irdp
```

Configures   IRDP

Default   Disabled

Description

This command enables ICMP Router Discovery Protocol (IRDP) on an interface. Other hosts on the network can use this protocol to negotiate a default router based on the preference parameter.

This command has many options. Instead of writing a single long command, it's often more convenient to issue a number of shorter commands, each setting one option.

multicast
  Optional. Tells the router to use the multicast address instead of the broadcast address for IRDP.

holdtime seconds
  Optional. The time in seconds that advertisements are held. By default, this value is three times the maxadvertinterval.

maxadvertinterval seconds
  Optional. Sets the maximum interval in seconds between advertisements. The default is 600 seconds.

minadvertinterval seconds
  Optional. Sets the minimum interval in seconds between advertisements. The default is the maximum interval.

preference value
  Optional. Sets the preference value for this router, which is used by the routers running IRDP to select the default gateway. The default preference is 0. The higher the preference, the more preferred this router is to hosts.

address ip-address [preference]
  Optional. Tells the router to generate proxy advertisements for the given ip-address. If you specify a preference, it is associated with the given ip-address. This allows routers that do not run IRDP to participate in router discovery.

Example

```
interface ethernet0
  ! Enable IRDP on this interface
  ip irdp
  ! make this router preferred
  ip irdp preference 10
```

ip load-sharing interface

```
ip load-sharing [per-packet] [per-destination]
no ip load-sharing [per-packet] [per-destination]
```

Configures   Cisco Express Forwarding (CEF)

Default   per-destination

Description

This command enables load sharing for Cisco Express Forwarding (CEF). By default, CEF uses per-destination load sharing, in which all traffic for a given destination is sent through the same interface. The per-packet keyword changes the behavior of CEF so that packets for the same destination may be sent through different interfaces. This approach makes load sharing more effective because it increases the effective bandwidth between the router and the destination. However, packets might arrive at the destination out of order, requiring the destination host to reassemble them.

ip local policy route-map global

```
ip local policy route-map map
no ip local policy route-map map
```

Configures   Policy routing

Default   None

Description

This command enables local policy routing. In brief, policy routing means using criteria other than the shortest path to the destination (as computed by a routing protocol) for route selection. The *map* parameter is the name of a route map that specifies the routing policy. Unlike the ip policy command, which applies a routing policy to a single interface, this command applies the policy to traffic originating on the router.

Example

In this example, a route map named map1 states that any traffic that matching access list 101 will be routed to the 10.1.1.1 router. Access list 101 matches all IP traffic destined for network 10.1.5.0/24. The ip local policy command is used to apply this route map, effectively routing all traffic for 10.1.5.0 through 10.1.1.1 regardless of what the routing protocols might tell the router to do. There are many possible reasons for this policy—for example, the traffic for 10.1.5.0 might be highly confidential, and we want to make sure that it passes only through trusted routers.

```
access-list 101 permit ip 10.1.5.0 0.0.0.255 any
!
ip local policy route-map map1
!
route-map map1
  match ip address 101
  set ip next-hop 10.1.1.1
```

ip local pool global

```
ip local pool {default | poolname} low-ip-address [high-ip-address]
no ip local pool {default | poolname}
```

Configures   A pool of IP addresses

Default   None

Description
This command allows you to create a pool of IP addresses that are used when a remote system connects to one of your interfaces. The default pool is the one used if no name is given on the interface.

default
> Default pool configuration.

poolname
> The name of the pool you are configuring.

low-ip-address
> The starting (lowest) IP address in the address pool.

high-ip-address
> The ending (highest) IP address in the pool. This is optional. If omitted, the only IP address in the pool is the low-ip-address.

Example
```
! Assign a pool called dialins1 that goes from 172.30.25.10 to 172.30.25.100
ip local pool dialins1 172.30.25.10 172.30.25.100
```

ip mask-reply interface

```
ip mask-reply
no mask-reply
```

Configures   Responses to ICMP mask request messages

Default   Disabled

Description
By default, the router does not respond to ICMP mask requests. This command enables responses through the interface.

Example
```
interface ethernet 1
  ip mask-reply
```

ip mroute global

ip mroute *source mask* [protocol *as-number*] {*rpf-address* | *interface*} [*distance*]

no ip mroute *source mask* [protocol *as-number*] {*rpf-address* | *interface*}
    [*distance*]

Configures   A multicast static route

Default   None

Description   This command adds a static multicast route.

source
    The source IP address.

mask
    Network mask for the source address.

protocol as-number
    Optional. The unicast routing protocol you are using, followed by the protocol's
    process number or autonomous system number, if applicable.

rpf-address
    The address of the incoming interface for the multicast route. This address can be
    a host address or a network address.

interface
    The incoming interface for the route (e.g., serial0).

distance
    Optional. This value is used to decide if a unicast, DVMRP, or static route should
    be used for RPF lookup.

ip mroute-cache interface

ip mroute-cache

no ip mroute-cache

Configures   IP multicast fast switching

Default   Enabled

Description

This command enables fast switching for multicast routing, which is analogous to the
route cache for unicast routing. If disabled with the no form of the command, every
packet is switched at the process level.

ip mtu interface

ip mtu *bytes*

no ip mtu *bytes*

Configures   Maximum Transmission Unit (MTU) for the interface

Default   Depends on the interface's media type

Description

This command sets the MTU for the interface to *bytes*. The MTU is the largest packet size that can be sent over the interface. The default MTU depends on the media type; Table 17-11 shows default MTU values for some common media. This command allows you to modify the MTU for any interface. Larger MTU values are more efficient with highly reliable networks; lower MTU values can help if an interface is unreliable, or in situations where protocols do not support fragmentation.

Table 17-11. Default MTU values

Interface type	Default MTU
Ethernet/Serial	1500
HSSI/ATM/FDDI	4470

Example

```
interface ethernet 0
  ip mtu 1250
```

ip multicast boundary   interface

```
ip multicast boundary access-list
no ip multicast boundary
```

Configures   A multicast boundary

Default   None

Description

The *access-list* defines the multicast boundary, which is used to keep multicast packets from being forwarded out the interface.

ip multicast cache-headers   global

```
ip multicast cache-headers
no ip multicast cache-headers
```

Configures   Buffers multicast packet headers

Default   Disabled

Description

This command enables the router to cache IP multicast packet headers. These headers can be viewed with the show ip mpacket command.

ip multicast helper-map

interface

```
ip multicast helper-map group-address broadcast-address access-list
no ip multicast helper-map group-address broadcast-address access-list

ip multicast helper-map broadcast multicast-address access-list
no ip multicast helper-map broadcast multicast-address access-list
```

Configures   Multicast tunneling

Default   None

Description

Use this command to send broadcast packets through a multicast network that connects two or more broadcast-capable networks. At one multicast network, you convert the multicast packets to broadcast packets and send them through the broadcast network, which converts them back to multicast packets at the other end.

group-address
  Multicast group whose traffic is to be converted to broadcast traffic.

broadcast
  Specifies that the traffic is going to be converted from broadcast to multicast.

broadcast-address
  When using the *group-address* parameter, this parameter specifies the IP address to which to send the broadcast traffic.

multicast-address
  When using the broadcast option, this variable specifies the multicast address to which converted traffic is sent.

access-list
  An extended access list that uses the UDP port number to control which broadcast packets will be converted.

Example

The following configuration converts multicast traffic for the multicast group 224.1.1.2 to broadcast traffic using the broadcast address 10.1.1.255 and UDP port 5000:

```
interface ethernet 0
  ip multicast helper-map 224.1.1.2 10.1.1.255 101
  ip pim dense-mode
!
! Convert to UDP port 5000
access-list 101 permit any any udp 5000
access-list 101 deny any any udp
!
! Forward UDP port 5000
ip forward-protocol udp 5000
```

The next configuration is the other end of the tunnel. It converts broadcast traffic on UDP port 5000 to multicast traffic:

```
interface ethernet 0
  ip multicast helper-map broadcast 224.1.1.2 101
  ip pim dense-mode
!
! Use access list to convert traffic to UDP
! port 5000
access-list 101 permit any any udp 5000
access-list 101 deny any any udp
!
! Forward udp port 5000
ip forward-protocol udp 5000
```

ip multicast rate-limit   interface

ip multicast rate-limit {in | out} [video | whiteboard] [group-list *access-list*] [source-list *access-list*] *kbps*

no ip multicast rate-limit {in | out} [video | whiteboard] [group-list *access-list*] [source-list *access-list*] *kbps*

Configures   The rate at which a sender can send to a multicast group

Default   No rate limit

Description

This command controls the rate at which hosts matching a source list can send multicast packets to a multicast group.

in
> The limit applies only to incoming packets.

out
> The limit applies only to outgoing packets.

video
> Optional. Rate limit applies only to video traffic.

whiteboard
> Optional. Rate limit applies only to whiteboard traffic.

group-list *access-list*
> Optional. The rate limit applies only to multicast groups that match the access list.

source-list *access-list*
> Optional. The rate limit applies only to hosts sending multicast traffic that match the access list.

kbps
> The total bandwidth, in Kbps, that is used for multicast traffic that matches the preceding parameters. Traffic in excess of this rate is discarded. If the rate is set to 0, no traffic is permitted.

ip multicast-routing
global

```
ip multicast-routing
no ip multicast-routing
```

Configures   IP multicast routing

Default   Disabled

Description

By default, the router does not forward multicast packets. This command enables multicast routing.

ip multicast ttl-threshold
interface

```
ip multicast ttl-threshold ttl
no ip multicast ttl-threshold
```

Configures   TTL threshold of forwarded packets

Default   0

Description

This command configures the TTL threshold for packets that are being forwarded out the interface. Only packets with TTL values greater than the threshold are forwarded. The default value is 0, which means all packets are forwarded. The value of *ttl* can be from 0 to 255.

ip name-server
global

```
ip name-server address [address]
no ip name-server address
```

Configures   DNS server name

Default   None

Description

This command sets the name servers that the router uses for DNS queries. You can specify the *address*es of up to 6 different DNS servers on one command line. Because you are configuring domain name service, be sure to use an IP address and *not* a hostname for the server!

Example

The first line configures one name server; the second line configures six name servers:

```
ip name-server 10.10.2.5
ip name-server 10.10.1.5 10.10.2.5 10.10.3.5 10.10.4.5 10.10.5.5 10.10.6.5
```

ip nat

```
ip nat {inside | outside} [log {translations syslog}]
no ip nat {inside | outside} [log {translations syslog}]
```

Configures   IP Network Address Translation (NAT)

Default   Disabled

Description

This command configures an interface for NAT. The translation can occur for inside or outside addresses.

Example

In the following configuration, ethernet0 is our internal network with the internal IP address; serial0 is our external interface to the Internet. The NAT translation should be inside on ethernet0 and outside on serial0. The optional log command enables NAT logging. translations enables NAT logging translation. The syslog keyword enables syslog logging for NAT.

```
interface ethernet0
  ip address 10.10.1.1 255.255.255.0
  ip nat inside
interface serial0
  ip address 192.168.1.1 255.255.255.0
  ip nat outside
```

ip nat inside destination

```
ip nat inside destination [list access-list] pool pool-name
no ip nat inside destination [list access-list] pool pool-name
```

```
ip nat inside destination [list access-list] static global-ip local-ip
no ip nat inside destination [list access-list] static global-ip local-ip
```

Configures   Enables NAT for inside destination IP addresses

Default   Disabled

Description

This command enables the mapping of internal (inside) destination addresses to global destination addresses.

list *access-list*
     Optional. Defines an access list for the translation. If an address is not blocked by the access list, it is translated.

pool *pool-name*
     The name of the address pool for allocating global IP addresses.

static *global-ip local-ip*
     A static mapping of a global IP address to a local IP address.

ip nat inside source global

```
ip nat inside source {list access-list | route-map name}
  {interface interface-name | pool pool-name} [overload]
no ip inside source {list access-list] pool pool-name [overload]


ip nat inside source static local-ip global-ip
no ip nat inside source static local-ip global-ip
```

Configures   Enables NAT for inside source IP addresses

Default   None

Description

This command enables the mapping of internal (inside) source addresses to global addresses.

list *access-list*
> Optional. Defines an access list for the translation. If an address is not blocked by the access list, it is translated. You can use an access list number or name.

route-map *name*
> Specifies a named route map.

interface *interface-name*
> Specifies the name of an interface to be used for selecting the global IP address.

pool *pool-name*
> The name of an address pool to be used for selecting global IP addresses.

overload
> Optional. Allows many local IP addresses to share a few global IP addresses by multiplexing the ports.

static *local-ip global-ip*
> A static mapping of a local IP address to a global IP address.

---

ip nat outside source global

```
ip nat outside source {list access-list | route-map name} pool pool-name
no ip nat outside source {list access-list} pool pool-name


ip nat outside source {list access-list}static global-ip local-ip
no ip nat outside source {list access-list} static global-ip local-ip
```

Configures   Enables NAT for outside source IP addresses

Default   None

Description

This command enables the mapping of external (outside) source addresses to internal addresses.

---

list *access-list*
> Optional. Defines an access list for the translation. If an address is not blocked by the access list, it is translated. You can use an access list number or name.

pool *pool-name*
> The name of the address pool for allocating global IP addresses.

route-map *name*
> Specifies a named route map.

static *global-ip local-ip*
> A static mapping of a global IP address to a local IP address.

---

ip nat pool global

ip nat pool *name starting-address ending-address* [netmask *value* | prefix-length *length*] [type rotary]

no ip nat pool *name starting-address ending-address* [netmask *value* | prefix-length *length*] [type rotary]

Configures   The IP address pool to be used in the NAT configuration

Default   None

Description
This command defines a sequential range of IP addresses to use with NAT configurations.

name
> Name of the address pool.

starting-address
> The beginning of the pool's IP address range.

ending-address
> The last IP address in the pool.

netmask *value*
> Specifies the netmask for the pool address range.

prefix-length *length*
> Specifies the number of ones in the bitmask.

type rotary
> Optional. Specifies that the range of IP addresses corresponds to real hosts for which load distribution should occur. This means that the pool is defined as a round-robin set of address for load balancing. As new TCP connections are made, a new address is selected from the pool. Non-TCP traffic passes through without translation.

---

ip nat stateful id global

ip nat stateful id *id-number* {redundancy *name* | {{primary *ip-primary* | backup *ip-backup*} peer *ip-peer*} mapping-id *map-number*}

no ip nat stateful id *id-number* {redundancy *name* | {{ primary *ip-primary* | backup *ip-backup*} peer *ip-peer*} mapping-id *map-number*}

Configures   Stateful Network Address Translation (SNAT)

Default　　　None

Description

This command enables Stateful NAT, providing failover capabilities. For a complete explanation, see the NAT section in Chapter 13.

id-number

　A unique number given to the stateful translation group.

redundancy name

　Establishes HSRP as the method for redundancy.

primary ip-primary

　Manually sets the IP address of the primary router.

backup ip-backup

　Manually sets the IP address of the backup router.

peer ip-peer

　Manually sets the IP address of the peer router in the translation group.

mapping-id map-number

　Specifies whether the local stateful NAT translation router will distribute a set of locally created entries to the peer SNAT router.

---

ip nat translation   global

```
ip nat translation [max-entries number] {timeout | udp-timeout | dns-timeout |
   tcp-timeout | finrst-timeout | icmp-timeout | pptp-timeout | syn-timeout |
   port-timeout} seconds
no ip nat translation [max-entries number] {timeout | udp-timeout | dns-timeout |
   tcp-timeout | finrst-timeout | icmp-timeout | pptp-timeout | syn-timeout |
   port-timeout} seconds
```

Configures　　　None

Default　　　See description

Description

This command specifies different timeouts for NAT translations.

max-entries number

　Optional. Specifies the maximum number of NAT entries. Default is unlimited.

timeout seconds

　The timeout on all translations except overloads. Default is 86,400 seconds.

udp-timeout seconds

　The timeout on UDP port translations. Default is 300 seconds.

dns-timeout seconds

　The timeout on DNS (Domain Name Service). Default is 60 seconds.

tcp-timeout seconds

　The timeout on TCP ports. Default is 86400 seconds.

`finrst-timeout` *seconds*
: The timeout on Finish and Reset TCP packets. Default is 60 seconds.

`icmp-timeout` *seconds*
: The timeout for ICMP flows. Default is 60 seconds.

`pptp-timeout` *seconds*
: The timeout for NAT Point-to-Point Protocol flows. Default is 86,400 seconds.

`syn-timeout` *seconds*
: The timeout for TCP flows immediately after a SYN (synchronous transmission) message. The default is 60 seconds.

`port-timeout` *seconds*
: The timeout that applies to TCP/UDP ports. The default is 0 (never).

---

ip nbar pdlm   global

```
ip nbar pdlm name
no ip nbar pdlm name
```

Configures   Network-Based Application Recognition (NBAR)

Default   None

Description

This command specifies a Packet Description Language Module (PDLM) file, which the router uses to extend its NBAR capabilities. The PDLM is a collection of items used by NBAR to identify protocols. A list of PDLM files is on Cisco's web site (*http://www.cisco.com/pcgi-bin/tablebuild.pl/pdlm*; note that this URL is available only to those with a Cisco service agreement).

Example

```
ip nbar pdm flash://somefilename.pdlm
```

---

ip nbar port-map   global

```
ip nbar port-map name [tcp | udp] port-number
no ip nbar port-map name [tcp | udp] port-number
```

Configures   Network-Based Application Recognition (NBAR)

Default   None

Description

This command configures NBAR to look for a protocol on a specified port other than the well-known port. *port-number* can be a value from 0 to 65,535 and up to 16 ports can be listed on one line.

Example

```
! we run our ssh on different ports
ip nbar port-map ssh tcp 6000 60002
```

---

ip nbar protocol-discovery

```
ip nbar protocol-discovery
no ip nbar protocol-discovery
```

Configures   Network-Based Application Recognition (NBAR)

Default   None

Description

This command enables traffic statistics for an interface using all protocols known to NBAR. Use the show ip nbar protocol-discovery command to view the statistics.

Example

```
interface ethernet 1/1
   ip nbar protocol-discovery
```

ip netmask-format

```
ip netmask-format [bitcount | decimal | hexadecimal]
no ip netmask-format [bitcount | decimal | hexadecimal]
```

Configures   How subnets are displayed by the show command

Default   Decimal format (255.255.255.0)

Description

This command determines the format that the show commands use for displaying subnet masks. Table 17-12 shows the possibilities.

Table 17-12. Netmask formats

Format name	Example
decimal	255.255.255.0
bitcount	10.10.1.0/24
hexadecimal	0xffffff00

ip nhrp authentication

```
ip nhrp authentication string
no ip nhrp authentication
```

Configures   Authentication for NHRP

Default   Disabled

Description

This command sets an authentication *string* for Next-Hop Resolution Protocol (NHRP). By default, no authentication is performed. The string can be up to eight characters in length. All routers within the NBMA (Non-Broadcast Multi-Access) must use the same authentication string.

ip nhrp holdtime

```
ip nhrp holdtime seconds
no ip nhrp holdtime
```

Configures   NHRP holdtime

Default   7200 seconds

Description

This command sets the number of *seconds* to advertise to other routers that they should keep NHRP information.

ip nhrp interest

```
ip nhrp interest access-list
no ip nhrp interest
```

Configures   Which packets should trigger NHRP requests

Default   All non-NHRP packets trigger NHRP requests

Description

This command specifies an *access-list* that the router uses to select which packets should generate NHRP traffic.

ip nhrp map

```
ip nhrp map ip-address nbma-address
no ip nhrp map ip-address nbma-address
```

Configures   A static NBMA-to-IP address mapping

Default   None

Description

This command allows you to define a static *ip-address* to *nbma-address* mapping. The NBMA address can be a MAC address for Ethernet or an NSAP address for ATM. For NHRP, you usually need to configure one static mapping to get to the next-hop server.

ip nhrp map multicast

```
ip nhrp map multicast
no ip nhrp map multicast
```

Configures   An NBMA address for broadcast or multicast packets

Default   None

Description

This command defines a nonbroadcast multi-access (NBMA) address to which to send broadcast or multicast traffic. An NBMA address is a MAC address for Ethernet networks or an NSAP address for ATM networks. A configuration may include several of these commands, each defining another NBMA address. This command allows you to send multicast traffic through a tunnel that crosses networks that do not support IP multicasting. It may be used only on tunnel interfaces.

ip nhrp max-send

```
ip nhrp max-send packet-count every interval
no ip nhrp max-send
```

Configures   Frequency of NHRP packets

Default   packet-count is 5; interval is 10 seconds

Description

This command controls the rate at which NHRP packets can be sent. At most, *packet-count* packets can be sent every *interval* seconds. *packet-count* can be from 1 to 65,535; *interval* can be from 10 to 65,535. NHRP traffic cannot exceed this rate. Both locally generated and forwarded traffic count toward the total.

ip nhrp network-id

```
ip nhrp network-id id
no ip nhrp network-id id
```

Configures   Enables NHRP

Default   Disabled

Description

This command enables NHRP on an interface by assigning a unique identifier for the network. All hosts participating in NHRP on a logical NBMA network must use the same network ID. *id* can be from 1 to 4,294,967,295.

ip nhrp nhs

```
ip nhrp nhs ip-address [network mask]
no ip nhrp nhs ip-address [network mask]
```

Configures   The NHS address

Default   None

Description

This command configures the *ip-address* of the next-hop server (NHS). Optionally, you can provide a *network* address and *mask* that specify the network that the NHS serves. To specify multiple networks for a single NHS, enter this command multiple times with different *network* and *mask* parameters.

When NHS servers are configured, they override the normal NHRP forwarding table.

---

ip nhrp record

```
ip nhrp record
no ip nhrp record
```

Configures   The use of forward and reverse record options in NHRP packets

Default   Enabled

Description

The no form of this command disables the forward and reverse record options in NHRP request and reply packets. These options provide loop detection.

---

ip nhrp responder

```
ip nhrp responder interface
no ip nhrp responder interface
```

Configures   The IP address to use as the source of NHRP reply packets

Default   The IP address of the interface that received the NHRP request

Description

This command specifies the *interface* whose IP address is used as the source for NHRP reply packets. Normally, the IP address of the interface that received the NHRP packet is used. This command is useful on next-hop servers because it allows a form of loop detection: the server can look for its own unique IP address.

ip nhrp server-only

```
ip nhrp server-only [non-caching]
no ip nhrp server-only
```

Configures   NHRP on an interface acting in server mode only

Default   Disabled

Description

This command enables NHRP on an interface in server mode only. In server mode, an interface does not originate NHRP requests. The optional non-caching keyword disables the cache of NHRP information.

ip nhrp trigger-svc

```
ip nhrp trigger-svc trigger-threshold teardown-threshold
no ip nhrp trigger-svc
```

Configures   The thresholds for building an SVC based on traffic rates

Default   Trigger threshold, 1 Kbps; teardown threshold, 0 Kbps

Description

This command sets the thresholds for traffic rates that define when an SVC is built or destroyed. The *trigger-threshold* is the average traffic rate at (or above) which NHRP will create an SVC for a destination. The *teardown-threshold* is the traffic rate at (or below) which NHRP will tear down an SVC. Both parameters are in Kbps; they are calculated during the load interval.

The load interval is the length of time over which the router calculates the interface's throughput for comparison with the trigger and teardown thresholds. It is always a multiple of 30 seconds and is set by the ip cef traffic-statistics command.

ip nhrp use

```
ip nhrp use count
no ip nhrp use
```

Configures   A usage count that defers NHRP requests for some number of packets

Default   1

Description

By default, when the router has a packet that is eligible for NHRP address resolution, the router sends the NHRP request immediately. This command allows you to defer the NHRP request until *count* packets have been sent to the destination. The packet count can be from 1 to 65,535.

The packet count is destination-based. If the count was set to 3 and the router received five packets, two for destination 1 and three for destination 2, the router would generate an NHRP request only for destination 2.

ip ospf authentication
interface

```
ip ospf authentication [message-digest | null]
no ip ospf authentication
```

Configures   OSPF authentication

Default   No authentication

Description
This command enables OSPF authentication for an interface, to be used if the area authentication command is not enabled. If you enable this command with no options, specify the password with the ip ospf authentiation-key command. If you use the message-digest option, specify the password with the ip ospf message-digest-key command. The null option can be used to disable authentication for this interface if authentication of the entire area has already been configured.

ip ospf authentication-key
interface

```
ip ospf authentication-key password
no ip ospf authentication-key
```

Configures   A password to authenticate OSPF neighbors

Default   None

Description
This command assigns a *password* for communicating with neighboring routers to this interface. All adjacent routers should be configured with the same authentication key. The password can be from 1 to 8 bytes in length.

ip ospf cost
interface

```
ip ospf cost value
no ip ospf cost value
```

Configures   A default OSPF cost for packets sent out on this interface

Default 10^8 / bandwidth

Description
This command sets the cost of sending an OSPF packet on an interface to *value*. By default, Cisco routers use the bandwidth to determine the link's cost; high-speed links have a lower cost and are therefore more preferred. Other vendors may have alternative methods for cost calculation. This command can be used as needed to set the cost

appropriately in a multivendor environment, or to change the preference of two links of the same type. By default, OSPF attempts load balancing across links of the same type; this command changes that behavior by modifying the cost associated with each link.

Example

In this example, there are two FDDI links. The second link has a higher cost, causing the router to prefer the first.

```
interface fddi0
    ip ospf cost 2
interface fddi1
    ip ospf cost 5
```

---

ip ospf dead-interval   interface

```
ip ospf dead-interval seconds
no ip ospf dead-interval
```

Configures   The interval that can pass between hello packets

Default   four times the hello interval

Description

This command specifies the length of time in seconds that must pass before receiving a hello packet. If the time passes without a hello packet from a neighbor router, the router is marked down.

---

ip ospf demand-circuit   interface

```
ip ospf demand-circuit
no ip ospf demand-circuit
```

Configures   Dial-on-demand behavior

Default   Disabled

Description

This command tells OSPF that this interface is a demand circuit (i.e., an interface configured for dial-on-demand routing). OSPF will suppress verbose traffic (such as periodic hello packets), thus preventing the circuit from being kept up all the time.

Example

This example configures an ISDN interface as a DDR link for OSPF:

```
interface bri0
    ip address 10.12.1.5 255.255.255.0
    encapsulation ppp
    ip ospf demand-circuit
```

ip ospf hello-interval

interface

```
ip ospf hello-interval seconds
no ip ospf hello-interval
```

Configures   The interval between hello packets

Default   10 seconds

Description

This command sets the number of seconds between hello packets on a given interface. All nodes on a network must have the same hello interval. If you change the interval on one router, you must change it on all routers within the area.

ip ospf message-digest-key

interface

```
ip ospf message-digest-key keyid md5 key
no ip ospf message-digest-key keyid md5 key
```

Configures   MD5 authentication

Default   Disabled

Description

This command enables MD5 password authentication for the interface. The *keyid* can be from 1 to 255; the *key* can be up to 16 bytes in length.

ip ospf name-lookup

global

```
ip ospf name-lookup
no ip ospf name-lookup
```

Configures   DNS lookups for OSPF show commands

Default   Disabled

Description

This command enables DNS name lookups for all OSPF show commands. By default, show commands display IP addresses in numeric form.

ip ospf network

interface

```
ip ospf network {broadcast | non-broadcast | point-to-multipoint |
  point-to-point}
no ip ospf network
```

Configures   The type of OSPF network

Default   Depends on the interface type

Description

Given the interface's type, the OSPF process selects a default network type. This command allows the default network type to be changed.

broadcast
>   The interface is connected to a broadcast network.

non-broadcast
>   The interface is connected to a nonbroadcast network, i.e., a network with no effective way of dealing with broadcast packets. One example is a point-to-point network.

point-to-multipoint
>   The interface is connected to a point-to-multipoint network.

point-to-point
>   The interface is connected to a point-to-point network.

Example

By default, a serial interface is point-to-point. The following commands configure a serial subinterface as part of a broadcast network:

```
interface serial0.1
    ip ospf network broadcast
```

---

ip ospf priority   interface

```
ip ospf priority priority
no ip ospf priority priority
```

Configures   OSPF priority

Default   1

Description

This command sets the priority for the router within the OSPF area to which the interface is connected. The *priority* determines which routers are selected as the area's DR and BDR, and can range from 0 to 255. Routers with a priority of 0 are excluded from the selection process; the router with the highest priority is selected.

Example

```
interface serial0
    ip ospf priority 10
```

---

ip ospf retransmit-interval   interface

```
ip ospf retransmit-interval seconds
no ip ospf retransmit-interval seconds
```

Configures   The interval between LSAs

Default   5 seconds

Description

This command sets the interval (in seconds) at which link-state advertisements (LSAs) are sent to adjacent routers via the interface. The interval can range from 1 to 65,535 seconds.

Example

```
interface serial0
   ip ospf retransmit-interface 3
```

ip ospf transmit-delay   interface

```
ip ospf transmit-delay seconds
no ip ospf transmit-delay seconds
```

Configures   Estimated time to send a link update on the interface

Default   1 second

Description

This command lets you estimate the number of seconds required to transmit a link-state advertisement through this interface. It's most useful on slow interfaces where it may take a significant amount of time to transmit the announcement. The estimate is used in computing the packet's age; its value can range from 1 to 65,535 seconds.

Example

```
interface serial0
   ip ospf transmit-delay 3
```

ip pim   interface

```
ip pim {sparse-mode | dense-mode | sparse-dense-mode}
no ip pim
```

Configures   IP multicast routing on the interface

Default   Disabled

Description

This command enables PIM (Protocol-Independent Multicast) and IGMP on the interface.

sparse-mode
   In this mode, the router forwards multicast packets only if it has received a join message from a downstream router or if it has group members directly connected to this interface.

dense-mode
   In this mode, the router forwards multicast packets until it can determine whether there are group members or downstream routers. Unlike sparse-mode, it doesn't wait for a join message to begin sending multicast packets.

sparse-dense-mode

This mode allows the router to operate in both sparse-mode and dense-mode, depending on what the other routers in the multicast group are using.

ip pim accept-rp

global

ip pim accept-rp {*address* | auto-rp} [*access-list*]
no ip pim accept-rp {*address* | auto-rp} [*access-list*]

Configures   Processing of multicast join and prune messages

Default   Disabled

Description

By default, all join and prune messages are processed. This command lets you tell the router to process join and prune messages destined for a specific Rendezvous Point (RP) or a specific list of groups.

address

The RP allowed to send messages to the multicast groups specified by the group access list.

auto-rp

Accepts only messages from RPs in the auto-rp cache.

access-list

Optional. An access list that defines the multicast groups for which we want to process join and accept messages.

ip pim message-interval

global

ip pim message-interval *seconds*
no ip pim message-interval *seconds*

Configures   Interval for join/prune messages

Default   60 seconds

Description

In sparse-mode operation, this command allows you to control the interval in *seconds* for sending join and prune PIM messages. A router is pruned if it is not heard from in three times this interval. The interval's value can be from 1 to 65,535 seconds.

ip pim minimum-vc-rate

interface

ip pim minimum-vc-rate *packets-per-second*
no ip pim minimum-vc-rate

Configures   Which VCs are eligible for idling

Default   0 (all VCs)

Description

This command sets the packet rate at which ATM virtual circuits (VCs) can be idled. A VC is idled if its traffic rate falls below *packets-per-second*, which can range from 0 to 4,294,967,295. This command applies only to ATM interfaces in PIM sparse mode.

ip pim multipoint-signalling

interface

```
ip pim multipoint-signalling
no ip pim multipoint-signalling
```

Configures   PIM's ability to open ATM SVCs for multicast groups

Default   Disabled

Description

This command enables an ATM interface to open multipoint SVCs for each PIM multicast group that it joins.

ip pim nbma-mode

interface

```
ip pim nbma-mode
no ip pim nbma-mode
```

Configures   NBMA mode

Default   Disabled

Description

This command sets the interface for nonbroadcast multi-access (NBMA) mode and is used on nonmulticast interfaces such as Frame Relay and ATM. Use this command only with ip pim sparse-mode.

ip pim neighbor-filter

interface

```
ip pim neighbor-filter access-list
no ip pim neighbor-filter access-list
```

Configures   A method to filter (deny) PIM packets from other routers

Default   None

Description

This command allows you to specify a standard IP *access-list* to control which routers receive PIM packets. The standard access list denies PIM packets from the source, preventing the router from joining PIM.

ip pim query-interval

```
ip pim query-interval seconds
no ip pim query-interval
```

Configures   The frequency of PIM query messages

Default   30 seconds

Description

This command sets the query interval to *seconds*. The query message is used to determine which router on the subnet will be the designated router. The designated router sends IGMP messages to the rest of the routers on the LAN; it also sends messages to the rendezvous point when operating in sparse-mode. The query interval defaults to 30 seconds and can be set to a value between 1 and 65,535 seconds.

ip pim rp-address

```
ip pim rp-address ip-address [group-access-list] [override]
no ip pim rp-address ip-address
```

Configures   Defines the RP for a group

Default   None

Description

This command specifies the Rendezvous Point (RP) for a particular multicast group.

ip-address
    IP address of the PIM rendezvous point.

group-access-list
    Optional. Defines the multicast groups for which this RP address should be used. If there is no access list, the RP address is used for all groups.

override
    Optional. If the rendezvous point address defined by this command conflicts with the rp-cache, the override option causes this command to override the auto-rp cache.

ip pim rp-announce-filter

```
ip pim rp-announce-filter rp-list access-list group-list access-list
no ip pim rp-announce-filter rp-list access-list group-list access-list
```

Configures   A filter for incoming RP announcements

Default   All announcements are accepted

Description

RP routers periodically send out auto-rp announcement messages. This command controls which of these messages are accepted.

rp-list *access-list*
> A standard access list that defines the list of allowable RP addresses for the group list.

group-list *access-list*
> A standard access list that defines the multicast groups that the RPs serve.

---

ip pim send-rp-announce   global

ip pim send-rp-announce *interface* scope *ttl* group-list *access-list*
no ip pim send-rp-announce *interface* scope *ttl* group-list *access-list*

Configures   The auto-rp cache

Default   Disabled

Description

This command tells the router to use the auto-rp cache to define the multicast groups for which the router is willing to become the RP. You normally use this command in the router that you wish to become the RP.

interface
> The interface that identifies the RP address.

scope *ttl*
> Time-to-Live value for announcements. TTL is roughly equivalent to a hop count.

group-list *access-list*
> An access list that defines the groups for which this router should be the RP.

---

ip pim send-rp-discovery   global

ip pim send-rp-discovery scope *ttl*
no ip pim send-rp-discovery scope *ttl*

Configures   The router to be the RP mapping agent

Default   Disabled

Description

This command configures the router to be the RP mapping agent for the PIM domain. The time-to-live value (*ttl*) should be large enough to cover the entire domain.

ip pim vc-count

interface

```
ip pim vc-count number
no ip pim vc-count
```

Configures   The number of VCs that PIM can open

Default   200 VCs per ATM interface or subinterface

Description

This command sets the maximum *number* of virtual circuits (VCs) that PIM can open. *number* must be between 1 and 65,535.

ip pim version

interface

```
ip pim version {1 | 2}
no ip pim version
```

Configures   PIM version to use on an interface

Default   2

Description

This command sets the PIM version to use for an interface. The version can be 1 or 2.

ip policy-list

policy map mode

```
ip policy-list name { permit | deny }
no ip policy-list name
```

Configures   A policy list for use in a route map

Default   None

Description

This command allows you to create a policy list for use in a BGP route map. The *name* is the name of the policy map. permit and deny establish what to do with traffic that matches the policy list conditions.

Example

```
ip policy-list out-policy permit
  match as-path 10
  match metric 12
```

ip policy route-map interface

```
ip policy route-map map
no ip policy route-map map
```

Configures   Policy routing

Default   None

Description

This command enables policy routing for an interface. In brief, policy routing means using criteria other than the shortest path (as computed by a routing protocol) for route selection. The *map* parameter is the name of a route map that specifies the routing policy. The map applies only to traffic arriving on the interface.

Example

The following configuration applies the route map map1 to packets arriving on the serial1 interface. This route map selects packets that match access list 101 and sends them to the router at 10.1.1.1 for further routing, regardless of other information in the routing table.

```
access-list 101 permit ip 10.1.5.0 0.0.0.255 any
!
interface serial 1
  ip policy route-map map1
!
route-map map1
  match ip address 101
  set ip next-hop 10.1.1.1
```

ip proxy-arp interface

```
ip proxy-arp
no ip proxy-arp
```

Configures   The proxy-arp feature for an interface

Default   Enabled

Description

ARP allows machines to find hardware addresses (MAC addresses) using the corresponding IP addresses. The router's proxy-arp feature helps the machines find each other across subnets. When a host sends an ARP packet requesting information about a host that can't receive the ARP broadcast, the router helps out by responding to the ARP packet on behalf of the requested host.

While proxy-arp is often useful, it can be a burden on the router in large networks. Disabling proxy-arp and relying on proper subnetting is a better solution than relying on proxy-arp to solve subnetting problems.

Example

The following commands disable proxy-arp on ethernet0. All hosts on this subnet must have the proper subnet mask because proxy-arp isn't there to help them.

```
interface ethernet0
    ip address 10.10.1.64 255.255.255.224
    no ip proxy-arp
```

---

ip radius source-interface   global

```
ip radius source-interface interface
no ip radius source-interface interface
```

Configures   Radius

Default   Disabled

Description

This command configures the device to send all outgoing Radius packets using the IP address of the named interface.

---

ip rarp-server   interface

```
ip rarp-server address
no ip rarp-server address
```

Configures   RARP

Default   Disabled

Description

This command enables a router's interface to act as a Reverse Address Resolution Protocol (RARP) server. The *address* parameter is the address to be used in responses to RARP queries.

---

ip rcmd rcp-enable   global

```
ip rcmd rcp-enable
no ip rcmd rcp-enable
```

Configures   RCP to the router

Default   Disabled

Description

This command allows remote users to use the Remote Copy Protocol (RCP) to transfer files to and from the router, and RSH to access the router. For security reasons, RCP is disabled by default.

---

ip rcmd remote-host

ip rcmd remote-host *local-username* {*ip-address* | *hostname*} *remote-username*
   [enable [*level*]]

no ip rcmd remote-host *local-username* {*ip-address* | *hostname*} *remote-username*
   [enable [*level*]]

Configures   Which users can access the router via RSH and RCP

Default   None

Description
This command defines a local and remote username pair that allows remote users to perform remote shell tasks (RSH and RCP).

local-username
   A locally defined username or the router's hostname. The user must provide a local username to perform an operation via RSH or RCP.

ip-address or hostname
   The remote host from which the router accepts remote shell commands.

remote-username
   The username on the remote host from which the router accepts remote shell commands.

enable *level*
   Optional. Provides the remote user the ability to execute privileged commands via the remote shell. *level* specifies a privilege level; the user may execute commands up to and including that level. For more information about privilege levels, see Chapter 4 and the privilege level command.

ip rcmd remote-username

ip rcmd remote-username *username*

no ip rcmd remote-username *username*

Configures   The username to use when performing remote copy commands

Default   The username for the session or the router's hostname

Description
This command sets the *username* that the router uses when connecting to remote hosts to execute remote copy commands. By default, the router uses the username of the current session. If that username isn't valid, the router uses the router's hostname.

ip rcmd rsh-enable

ip rcmd rsh-enable

no ip rcmd rsh-enable

Configures   Remote shell access by remote users

Default   Disabled

Description

This command enables remote shell access to the router via the rsh command. For security reasons, remote shell access is disabled by default.

---

ip redirects interface

```
ip redirects
no ip redirects
```

Configures   ICMP redirects for interfaces

Default   Enabled

Description

An ICMP redirect packet is generated by a router to inform a host of a better route to some specific destination. The recipient of an ICMP redirect overrides its route table with the information given in the redirect packet. This command configures the sending of ICMP redirects for an interface. The router never processes received ICMP redirects while IP routing is enabled.

Redirects are enabled by default on all interfaces unless Hot Standby Routing Protocol (HSRP) is configured.

Example

To avoid sending ICMP redirect packets out the ethernet0 interface:

```
interface ethernet 0
  no ip redirects
```

---

ip rip authentication interface

```
ip rip authentication key-chain name
no ip rip authentication key-chain name

ip rip authentication mode {md5 | text}
no ip rip authentication mode {md5 | text}
```

Configures   RIP route authentication

Default   Default mode is clear text

Description

This command specifies a key chain to be used for authentication of RIP routing updates. *name* is the name of the key chain to be used. Once the key chain is applied, the interface expects to authenticate any incoming RIPv2 routes. The key chain must be defined separately with the key command.

The mode version of this command specifies the authentication mode for an interface: either text (clear text) or md5.

Example

The following commands specify that RIP routes should be authenticated using MD5 encryption with the key chain defined in group1:

```
interface ethernet 1
  ip rip authentication key-chain group1
  ip rip authentication mode md5
!
key chain group1
  key 1
  key-string authme1
  key 2
  key-string authme2
```

---

ip rip receive version
interface

```
ip rip receive version {1 | 2 | 1 2}
no ip rip receive version
```

Configures   Version of RIP to receive on an interface

Default   The version in the router configuration

Description

This command tells an interface which RIP version to listen for. This version can be 1, 2, or both (1 2). By default, the router listens for the version specified by the version command in the router configuration.

Example

This configuration accepts only Version 2 packets on ethernet0:

```
interface ethernet0
  ip rip receive version 2
```

---

ip rip send version
interface

```
ip rip send version {1 | 2 | 1 2}
no ip rip send version
```

Configures   The version of RIP to send

Default   The version in the router configuration, or 1 if no version specified

Description

This command tells an interface which RIP version to use when sending RIP packets. This version can be 1, 2, or both (1 2). By default, the router uses the version specified by the version command in the router configuration.

Example

This configuration sends only Version 2 packets on ethernet0:

```
interface ethernet0
  ip rip send version 2
```

ip rip triggered
interface

```
ip rip triggered
no ip rip triggered
```

Configures   RIP routing

Default   Disabled

Description

This command enables triggered extensions to RIP, which causes routing updates to be sent on a WAN link only if one of the following conditions is met:

- A specific request for a routing update is received by the router.
- Routing information from another interface modifies the routing database.
- The interface comes up or down.
- The router first powers on or resets.

ip rip v2-broadcast
interface

```
ip rip v2-broadcast
no ip v2-broadcast
```

Configures   RIP routing

Default   Disabled

Description

This command enables RIPv2 update packets to be sent as broadcast packets (255. 255.255.255). Normally, RIPv2 update packets are multicast (244.0.0.9).

ip route
global

```
ip route network mask {next-hop-address|interface} [distance] [permanent]
  [track number] [tag tag]
no ip route network mask {next-hop-address|interface} [distance] [permanent]
  [track number] [tag tag]
```

Configures   A static route for a network

Default   None

Description

This command defines a static route to the destination network specified by its *network* address and *mask*. *next-hop-address* is the IP address of the router to which traffic for this destination network should be sent. Instead of the *next-hop-address*, you can specify the *interface* that can be used to reach the network. *distance* is an optional administrative distance that allows you change the way the static route behaves. If the distance is high enough, it can be overwritten by dynamic protocols. See Chapter 8 for more information about administrative distances. The permanent keyword tells the router to keep the route in the route table even if the interface goes down. The router normally removes static routes that are invalid because the interface is down.

The track keyword is optional. It associates a track object with this route. Valid values for the track number are 1 to 500.

The tag keyword applies a value that can be used to match the route in route maps, which is useful for controlling redistribution.

Example

The following commands create two static routes. The first route sends traffic for the 192. 168.1.0/24 network to 10.1.1.1; the second route sends traffic for the 192.168.2.0/24 network to 10.2.2.2.

```
ip route 192.168.1.0 255.255.255.0 10.1.1.1
ip route 192.168.2.0 255.255.255.0 10.2.2.2
```

Here is another example of using an interface instead of a *next-hop-address*:

```
ip route 192.168.3.0 255.255.255.0 serial0
```

---

ip route-cache   interface

```
ip route-cache [cbus] [flow] [same-interface] [cef] [distributed]
no ip route-cache
```

Configures   The route cache for an interface

Default   Enabled for most interfaces

Description

A route cache stores a route in a temporary table for the duration of a network session. When the session is completed or the session times out, the routing entry is removed from the route cache. The no form of this command disables the route cache, which causes the router to look up the route for each packet of the network session. In some applications, this can be the desired behavior; see Chapter 8.

cbus
    Optional. Enables fast switching and autonomous switching.

flow
    Optional. Enables the Route Switch Processor to perform flow switching.

same-interface
    Optional. Enables fast switching packets back out the interface on which they arrived.

cef
> Optional. Enables Cisco Express Forwarding on an interface after it has been
> disabled globally.

distributed
> Optional. Enables VIP distributed switching.

Example

The route cache can be disabled with the no form of this command.

```
interface serial 0
  no ip route-cache
```

---

ip route-cache policy   interface

```
ip route-cache policy
no ip route-cache policy
```

Configures   Fast-switch Policy Based Routing (PBR)

Default   Disabled

Description

This command enables fast-switch policy-based routing (PBR). If Cisco Express
Forwarding (CEF) is enabled, this command is not required because PBR packets are
CEF-switched by default. Also, before you can enable this, PBR must be configured.
To enable PBR, use the ip policy route-map command.

---

ip route priority high   router

```
ip route priority high tag-value
no ip route priority high tag-value
```

Configures   IS-IS routing

Default   None

Description

This command assigns a high priority to an IS-IS prefix, which means routes with the
specified tag are marked for faster processing and installation into the global routing
table. This provides faster convergence for applications like Voice over IP. The tag is
the same as that specified in the isis tag command.

Example

```
interface serial1
  ip router isis
  isis tag 101
!
router isis
  ip route priority high tag 101
```

---

ip route profile

```
ip route profile
no ip route profile
```

Configures   IP routing table statistics

Default   Disabled

Description

This command enables IP routing table statistics collection, which helps you to monitor route flapping. To view the collected data, use the show ip route profile command.

ip router isis

```
ip router isis [tag]
no ip router isis [tag]
```

Configures   An interface for IS-IS routing

Default   Disabled

Description

This command identifies an interface to be used for IS-IS routing. The optional *tag* allows you to identify the IS-IS routing process if the process has a tag.

Example

```
interface ethernet 0
   ip router isis
```

ip routing

```
ip routing
no ip routing
```

Configures   IP routing

Default   Enabled

Description   This command enables or disables routing.

ip rtp compression-connections

```
ip rtp compression-connections number
no ip rtp compression-connections number
```

Configures   Real-time Transport Protocol (RTP)

Default   32 connections

Description

This command configures the number of RTP compression connections that can exist on an interface, from 3 to 1,000.

---

ip rtp header-compression   interface

```
ip rtp header-compression [passive]
no ip rtp header-compression [passive]
```

Configures   Real-time Transport Protocol (RTP)

Default   Disabled

Description

This command enables RTP header-compression on the interface. If you use this command without the passive option, all RTP traffic is compressed.

---

ip rtp priority   interface

```
ip rtp priority starting-rtp-port port-number-range bandwidth
no ip rtp priority
```

Configures   Real-time Transport Protocol (RTP)

Default   Disabled

Description

This command reserves a strict priority queue for a set of RTP packet flows belonging to a range of UDP destination ports. This command is most useful for VoIP traffic.

starting-rtp-port

> This option is the starting RTP port for our defined range and can be from 2,000 to 65,535.

port-number-range

> This value is added to the starting-rtp-port value to get the ending port for the range. This value can be from 0 to 16,383.

bandwidth

> This option is the maximum allowed bandwidth in Kbps, which can be from 0 to 2,000.

ip scp server enable

```
ip scp server enable
no ip scp server enable
```

Configures   SCP server-side functionality

Default   Disabled

Description

This command enables a router to support SCP functionality, which allows a user to use SCP to copy a file (image or configuration) to or from the router.

ip source-route

```
ip source-route
no ip source-route
```

Configures   Routing of source-routed packets

Default   Enabled

Description

This command allows the router to route packets that contain source-routing options. (Source routing is an IP option that allows the packet to specify the route it should take to its destination.) Source routing is a potential security problem, so it is best to disable this feature unless required.

Example

To disable IP source routing:

```
no ip source-route
```

ip split-horizon

```
ip split-horizon [as-number]
no ip split-horizon [as-number]
```

Configures   Split horizon for the interface

Default   Varies with the interface type; usually enabled

Description

When split horizon is enabled, any route learned from an interface is not advertised back out the same interface. This rule is intended to stop routing loops with distance-vector protocols. To enable split-horizon for EIGRP, specify the EIGRP *as-number*.

With most interfaces, split horizon is enabled. However, with multipoint interfaces—such as a multipoint Frame Relay interface—split horizon is disabled. See Chapter 8 for more information on split horizon.

ip ssh

global

```
ip ssh { [timeout seconds] | [authentication-retries value] }
no ip ssh { [timeout seconds] | [authentication-retries value] }
```

Configures   SSH values

Default   120 seconds timeout, 3 authentication retries

Description

When SSH is enabled on your router, this command allows you to modify the SSH control parameters. The timeout is the interval that the router waits for the SSH client to respond. The maximum timeout is 120 seconds. authentication-retries is the number of attempts that can be made from the SSH client before it is denied access. The maximum is 5 retries.

ip subnet-zero

global

```
ip subnet-zero
no ip subnet-zero
```

Configures   The zero subnet

Default   Enabled in recent versions of IOS (12.X)

Description

When subnetting a network, the 0 subnet (the subnet whose subnet bits are all 0) is normally not allowed because of potential confusion between the subnet address and the network address. In practice, this confusion is rarely an issue. This command allows the router to use the all-zeros subnet.

Example

The following command enables the zero subnet:

```
ip subnet-zero
```

ip summary-address eigrp

interface

```
ip summary-address eigrp as-number network-address subnet-mask [admin-distance]
no ip summary-address eigrp as-number network-address subnet-mask [admin-
   distance]
```

Configures

A summary aggregate address for an interface.

Default   None

Description

This command configures a summary address for the interface with the supplied network address and subnet mask. Normally, summary addresses are given the administrative distance of 5. However, you can modify this setting with the optional *admin-distance* value, which can be from 0 to 255.

Example

```
interface ethernet1
   ip summary-address eigrp 101 192.168.0.0 255.255.0.0 100
```

---

ip summary-address rip   interface

```
ip summary-address rip
no ip summary-address rip
```

Configures   A summary aggregate address for the interface

Default   None

Description

This command configures a RIP summary aggregate address for the interface.

Example

```
interface ethernet1
   ip address 192.168.1.1 255.255.255.0
   ip summary-address rip 192.168.0.0 255.255.0.0
```

---

ip tcp chunk-size   global

```
ip tcp chunk-size size
no ip tcp chunk-size
```

Configures   The number of bytes that a telnet or rlogin session can read at once

Default   0 (the largest size possible)

Description

This command sets the maximum number of bytes (*size*) that a telnet or rlogin session can read at the same time. A value of 0 means the largest size possible for that connection.

---

ip tcp compression-connections   interface

```
ip tcp compression-connections number
no ip tcp compress-connections number
```

Configures

The maximum number of TCP connections that can use header compression

---

Default   16

Description

This command sets the number of connections through an interface that can use TCP header compression. The *number* of connections can be from 3 to 256. A buffer is allocated for each connection that can be compressed. Both sides of a serial link must have the same number of buffers defined.

---

ip tcp header-compression   interface

```
ip tcp header-compression [passive]
no ip tcp header-compression [passive]
```

Configures   TCP header compression for an interface

Default   Disabled

Description

This command enables TCP header compression on the interface. The passive keyword tells the interface to compress headers only when the incoming packets are compressed.

Example

```
interface serial 0
   ip tcp header-compression passive
```

---

ip tcp mtu-path-discovery   interface

```
ip tcp mtu-path-discovery [age-timer minutes] [infinite]
no ip tcp mtu-path discovery
```

Configures   Path MTU discovery

Default   Disabled for most interfaces; special interfaces use 10 minutes

Description

This command enables or disables path MTU discovery on new TCP connections.

age-timer *minutes*
  Optional. *minutes* specifies the interval after which the router recalculates the MTU; its value must be between 1 and 30.

infinite
  Disables the age timer.

ip tcp queuemax

global

```
ip tcp queuemax packets
no ip tcp queuemax packets
```

Configures   The queue for outgoing TCP packets

Default   5 for TTY (async and console) interfaces; 20 for others

Description
This command sets the size of the outgoing TCP queue to *packets*. The queue is maintained per-connection; i.e., every connection has its own queue.

Example
```
interface serial 0
  ip tcp queuemax 15
```

ip tcp synwait-time

global

```
ip tcp synwait-time seconds
no ip tcp synwait-time seconds
```

Configures   The time the router waits for a TCP connection to open

Default   30 seconds

Description
This command sets the number of *seconds* that the router waits for a TCP connection to open, before it times out. The value must be between 3 to 300. A longer synwait-time can be useful for dial-on-demand connections where you have to wait for the line to be dialed before a connection can open. This setting applies only to traffic originating within the router, not traffic coming through the router.

Example
If you are telneting from the router to a remote site through a DDR connection, you might want to increase the synwait-time to more reasonable level so that telnet does not time out:
```
ip tcp synwait-time 100
```

ip tcp window-size

global

```
ip tcp window-size bytes
no ip tcp window-size bytes
```

Configures   The window size of a TCP connection

Default   2,144 bytes

Description

This command sets the size of the TCP window to *bytes*. Changing the size of the TCP window modifies the size and number of packets that can fit within that window. With the default window of 2,144 bytes, you could buffer two 1,000-byte packets, or 21 100-byte packets. Regardless of the window's size, the number of packets within the window is restricted to the values set by the `ip tcp queuemax` command; they default to 5 for TTY interfaces (async and console interfaces) and 20 for other interfaces. The maximum size of the window is 65,536 bytes.

Example

```
ip tcp window-size 4000
```

---

ip telnet source-interface   global

```
ip telnet source-interface interface
no ip telnet source-interface
```

Configures   The source address for telnet connections

Default   None

Description

This command sets the address used as the source address for outgoing telnet connections to the address of the given *interface*.

---

ip tftp source-interface   global

```
ip tftp source-interface interface
no ip tftp source-interface
```

Configures   The source IP address for TFTP traffic

Default   The IP address of the interface closest to the destination

Description

This command sets the interface from which the router takes the source IP address for all TFTP traffic.

---

ip unnumbered   interface

```
ip unnumbered interface
no ip unnumbered interface
```

Configures   Interface IP address

Default   None

Description

Normally, creating point-to-point links requires dedicating a subnet specifically for the link. This works well if all your equipment supports variable-length subnet masks (VLSM), but can be very wasteful if your equipment doesn't support VLSM. This forces you to assign relatively large subnets to your point-to-point links.

The ip unnumbered command tells the router to use the IP address of the selected *interface* as the address for this link. In other words, the router "borrows" the IP address of the named interface and uses that as the link's address.

Example

Assume that older equipment in our network forces us to use a subnet mask of 255.255.255.0. This means that assigning a subnet to a point-to-point link would use 254 addresses, of which only two are actually doing something. Instead of wasting 252 addresses, we can use the ip unnumbered command to borrow the address of another interface for use on the serial link:

```
interface serial0
 ip unnumbered ethernet0
 encapsulation ppp
 clockrate 1300000
```

Borrowing the address of the loopback interface for an unnumbered interface is often a good idea because the loopback interface is always up. The following configuration uses the loopback interface to provide the IP address for interface async2:

```
interface loopback 0
    ip address 10.10.1.4 255.255.255.0
interface async2
    ip unnumbered loopback0
```

---

ip unreachables   interface

```
ip unreachables
no ip unreachables
```

Configures   Sending of ICMP unreachable messages for an interface

Default   Enabled

Description

ICMP unreachable messages are generated when something about an incoming packet is unknown to the router. For example, an "ICMP host unreachable" message is generated if the router cannot deliver a package to its final destination. There are many different types of ICMP unreachable messages, and they all mean that the packet can't be delivered for some reason. Disabling these messages can improve security because the messages can be used to discover information about your network.

Example

The following commands prevent the router from sending IP unreachable messages through the serial0 interface:

```
interface serial0
  no ip unreachables
```

---

isdn answer1, isdn answer2

```
isdn answer1 [called-party-number][:sub-address]
no isdn answer1 [called-party-number][:sub-address]

isdn answer2 [called-party-number][:sub-address]
no isdn answer2 [called-party-number][:sub-address]
```

Configures   Verification of the called party

Default   None

Description
This command configures the interface to verify that the telephone number being called (which is reported by the ISDN switch as part of call setup) matches the telephone number of the router. By default, calls are processed without verification. If this command is configured, the router verifies the incoming *called-party-number* before allowing the connection. Using this command can reduce the potential for confusion when several ISDN devices share the same ISDN local loop. Use isdn answer2 to verify a second called-party number.

To list a *called-party-number* or a *sub-address*, use any number of digits up to 50; an x specifies a wildcard. You must specify either the *called-party-number* or the *sub-address*, but you are not required to specify both. If you specify only one, the other is taken as a wildcard.

isdn autodetect

```
isdn autodetect
no isdn autodetect
```

Configures   Automatic detection of ISDN SPIDs and switch types

Default   Disabled

Description
This command enables the automatic detection of ISDN SPIDs and switch types on an interface. It works in North America only.

isdn bchan-number-order

```
isdn bchan-number-order {ascending | descending}
no isdn bchan-number-order
```

Configures   ISDN PRI

Default   descending

Description

This command sets the order (ascending or descending) of outgoing B channels. It is for PRI configurations only.

---

isdn busy

interface

```
isdn busy dsl number b_channel number
no isdn busy dsl number b_channel number
```

Configures   A false busy signal on an ISDN B channel

Default   Disabled

Description

This command sets a false busy signal on an ISDN B channel; that is, the ISDN interface reports to the switch that the channel is busy even if it isn't.

dsl *number*
> The digital subscriber loop (DSL) number.

b_channel *number*
> The range of B channels to be set to a busy signal. *number* can range from 0 to 24 on a PRI interface (it isn't clear whether this command applies to BRI interfaces); 0 indicates the entire interface.

---

isdn caller

interface

```
isdn caller phone-number [callback]
no isdn caller phone-number [callback]
```

Configures   ISDN caller ID screening

Default   Disabled

Description

If your ISDN switch supports caller ID, this command lets you specify a *phone-number* from which incoming connections are allowed. If the inbound call does not originate from this number, it will be rejected. You may use the letter x in the phone number as a wildcard character; for example, 458-xxxx means "any number in the 458 exchange." The callback keyword causes the router to reject the call and initiate a callback to the caller's number; this feature may help you manage phone costs.

---

isdn call interface

command

```
isdn call interface interface telephone-number [speed {56 | 64}]
```

Description

This command initiates an ISDN call from the IOS command line in privileged EXEC mode. To make the call, supply the *interface* to use, the *telephone-number* to call, and optionally the line speed (56 or 64 Kbps). The line speed defaults to 64 Kbps.

Example

```
Router# isdn call interface bri0 4105551212
```

---

isdn calling-number
interface

```
isdn calling-number phone-number
no isdn calling-number phone-number
```

Configures　　The phone number of the device making the outgoing call

Default　　None

Description

This command sets the *phone-number* of the ISDN device making an outgoing call. The router presents this number to the switch when placing a call.

---

isdn conference-code
interface

```
isdn conference-code code
no isdn conference-code
```

Configures　　Three-way calling

Default　　60

Description

This command configures a conference code. Conference codes can be used if you have ordered three-way calling as part of your service.

---

isdn disconnect interface
command

```
isdn disconnect interface interface channel
```

Configures　　Disconnects an ISDN call

Default　　None

Description

This command disconnects an ISDN call on the given *interface* without bringing down the interface. The *channel* may be b1 for the first B channel, b2 for the second, or all for both B channels.

isdn fast-rollover-delay   interface

```
isdn fast-rollover-delay seconds
no isdn fast-rollover-delay seconds
```

Configures   Time delay between consecutive dial attempts

Default   Disabled (0 seconds)

Description
If more than one dialer map is provided for an ISDN interface, this command provides the time to wait (in *seconds*) after the first map fails before placing a call using the second map.

isdn incoming-voice   interface

```
isdn incoming-voice {56 | 64}
no isdn incoming-voice {56 | 64}
```

Configures   Accepts calls on the voice lines

Default   Disabled

Description
By default, incoming voice calls on data lines are not answered. This command allows you to use voice lines to transfer data by configuring the router to answer voice calls, which can result in significant savings in some areas. The call speed can be either 56 or 64; if no speed is specified, the speed is set to the incoming call's speed.

isdn leased-line bri 128   global

```
isdn leased-line bri number 128
no isdn leased-line bri number 128
```

Configures   ISDN interface for leased-line service at 128 Kbps

Default   Disabled

Description
This command configures ISDN access over a leased line. There are no phone numbers; both of the line's B channels are combined to provide a single line with a capacity of 128 Kbps. *number* is the number of the BRI interface.

isdn not-end-to-end

```
isdn not-end-to-end {56 | 64}
no isdn not-end-to-end {56 | 64}
```

Configures   Overrides the speed the network reported it will use

Default   64 Kbps

Description

This command forces the speed of an incoming connection. Sometimes, when ISDN ports don't belong to the same network, incorrect speed selection by the router causes the ISDN connection to fail. This command lets you set the speed manually for incoming connections. Valid speeds are 56 and 64 Kbps.

isdn nsf-service

```
isdn nsf-service {megacom | sdn}
no isdn nsf-service
```

Configures   Network-specific facilities (NSF)

Default   Disabled

Description

This command enables NSF on an ISDN PRI for outgoing voice calls. megacom is for AT&T Megacom NSF, and sdn is for AT&T SDN NSF.

isdn outgoing-voice

```
isdn outgoing-voice {info-transfer-capability {3.1kHz-audio | speech}}
no isdn outgoing-voice
```

Configures   Information transfer capability set for outgoing voice calls

Default   None

Description

This command sets the information transfer capability for outgoing voice calls through an interface. It isn't clear what the optional keywords mean; presumably they request different kinds of signal processing adapted for general audio or speech.

isdn overlap-receiving

```
isdn overlap-receiving
no isdn overlap-receiving
```

Configures   ISDN overlap receiving

Default   Disabled

Description

This command enables ISDN overlap receiving for an interface. In this mode, the interface waits for additional information from the switch before establishing the call. This command can be useful when carrying voice traffic through the router.

isdn send-alerting   interface

```
isdn send-alerting
no isdn send-alerting
```

Configures   Sending an Alerting message

Default   Disabled

Description

This command enables the sending of an Alerting message before a Connect message when making ISDN calls. Some types of switches want to receive an Alerting message before a Connect message.

isdn sending-complete   interface

```
isdn sending-complete
no isdn sending-complete
```

Configures   The sending of a Sending Complete element in the Setup message

Default   Disabled

Description

This command configures the router to include the Sending Complete element in the Setup message. Some switches require this message, which tells the switch that it has all the information for the call in the Setup message.

isdn service   interface

```
isdn service dsl number b_channel number state value
no isdn service dsl number b_channel number state value
```

Configures   A B channel range to a specified state

Default   Disabled

Description

This command sets a range of B channels or an entire PRI interface to "in service," "maintenance," or "out of service."

dsl *number*
> The digital subscriber loop number.

b_channel *number*
> The B channel or range of B channels to which the command applies. *number* can range from 0–24, where 0 means the entire PRI interface. A range of consecutive channels is indicated by *n–m*, where *n* and *m* can range from 1–24.

state *value*
> The state to which you wish to set the channels. The state is indicated by a number between 0 and 2; 0 is for "in service," 1 is for "maintenance," and 2 is for "out of service."

---

isdn spid1 (spid2)   interface

isdn {spid1 | spid2} *spid* [*local-directory-number*]
no isdn {spid1 | spid2} *spid* [*local-directory-number*]

Configures   ISDN SPIDs

Default   None

Description
This command provides the service profile identifier (SPID) for the B1 channel (spid1) or the B2 channel (spid2). You can also use this command to specify the *local-directory-number* (optional). Your ISDN carrier (i.e., your phone company) provides the SPIDs and the local directory number. Some carriers and switch types do not require SPIDs (for example, if they are not used in Europe).

---

isdn switch-type   global

isdn switch-type *type*
no isdn switch-type *type*

Configures   ISDN switch type

Default   None

Description
There are many different types of ISDN switches in use. The router must be configured with the appropriate switch *type* in order to interact with the telephone network. While there are exceptions, your geographic location is the best clue to the type of switch in use. Table 17-13 lists common switch types.

Table 17-13. Common ISDN switch types

IOS type	Switch
basic-5ess	AT&T switches (North America)
basic-dms100	Northern Telecom (North America)
basic-ni1	National ISDN-1 (North America)

Table 17-13. Common ISDN switch types (continued)

IOS type	Switch
basic-ts013	Australian
basic-ltr6	German
basic-nwnet3	Net3 switches (Norway)
basic-net3	Net3 switches (Europe/Taiwan)
basic-nznet3	Net3 switches (New Zealand)
vn2	VN2 (French)
vn3	VN3 (French)
ntt	NTT (Japan)

isdn tei global

```
isdn tei [first-call | powerup]
no isdn tei
```

Configures   ISDN endpoint negotiation

Default   powerup

Description
TEI stands for Terminal Endpoint Identifier. This command enables TEI negotiation on the ISDN interface. TEI negotiation occurs at powerup or when it places its first call (first-call).

isdn tei-negotiation global, interface

```
isdn tei-negotiation {first-call | powerup}
no isdn tei-negotiation
```

Configures   When TEI negotiation occurs

Default   powerup

Description
This command sets when TEI negotiation occurs. By default, negotiation takes place when the router is first turned on (powerup). The first-call option states that negotiation should occur when the first ISDN call is placed or received.

isdn transfer-code interface

```
isdn transfer-code code
no isdn transfer-code
```

Configures   Call transferring

Default   61

Description

This command enables call transferring. This feature is available only if your service provider supports it. *code* is supplied by your service provider.

---

isdn twait-disable   interface

```
isdn twait-disable
no isdn twait-disable
```

Configures   Time to wait on startup

Default   Enabled

Description

After a power failure, ISDN interfaces wait a random period of time (1 to 300 seconds) before starting up. This command prevents the interfaces from coming back online at the same time when power is restored and the ISDN devices are restarting. This feature can be disabled with the no form of this command.

---

isdn voice-priority   interface

```
isdn voice-priority ISDN-directory-number {in | out} {always | conditional |
  off}
no isdn voice-priority ISDN-directory-number
```

Configures   The priority of data and voice calls

Default   A data call is never bumped

Description

This command allows you to set the priority of a data call relative to a voice call. *ISDN-directory-number* is the directory number assigned by your telephone company. in and out specify whether the command applies to incoming or outgoing voice calls. always means always bump a data call for a voice call. conditional means bump a data call if there is more than one call to the same destination. off means never bump a data call for a voice call.

---

isis advertise-prefix   interface

```
isis advertise-prefix
no isis advertise-prefix
```

Configures   Advertising of IP prefixes for IS-IS routing

Default   Enabled

Description

By default, IP prefixes of connected networks are advertised in LSP advertisements for IS-IS interfaces. To disable the advertisement of connected networks, use the no form of this command.

isis authentication key-chain interface

```
isis authentication key-chain name [level-1 | level-2]
no isis authentication key-chain name [level-1 | level-2]
```

Configures   Authentication for IS-IS routing

Default   None

Description

This command enables authentication for IS-IS routing on an interface. The *name* of the key-chain specifies the group of valid keys. The optional keywords level-1 and level-2 specify that packets from level-1 or level-2 routers must be authenticated.

isis authentication mode interface

```
isis authentication mode {md5 | text} [level-1 | level-2 ]
no isis authentication mode {md5 | text} [level-1 | level-2]
```

Configures   Authentication for IS-IS routing

Default   Disabled

Description

This command configures the type of authentication for IS-IS routing on a interface. The type can be md5 (Message Digest 5) or text (clear text). The optional keywords level-1 and level-2 specify that packets from level-1 or level-2 routers must be authenticated.

isis authentication send-only interface

```
isis authentication send-only [level-1 | level-2]
no isis authentication send-only [level-1 | level-2]
```

Configures   Authentication for IS-IS routing

Default   Disabled

Description

This command tells the interface that only outgoing IS-IS packets are authenticated. Normally, when authentication is configured for IS-IS, both incoming and outgoing packets are authenticated. The keywords level-1 and level-2 specify that only packets sent from level-1 or level-2 routers must be authenticated.

isis circuit-type   interface

```
isis circuit-type {level-1 | level-1-2 | level-2-only}
no isis circuit-type
```

Configures   Type of IS-IS routing on an interface

Default   level-1-2

Description
This command sets the type of IS-IS routing used on an interface. It is rarely used except for border routers (routers that lie between areas).

isis csnp-interval   interface

```
isis csnp-interval seconds [{level-1 | level-2}]
no isis csnp-interval
```

Configures   CSNP interval

Default   10 seconds

Description
This command sets the interval (in *seconds*) for CSNP packets on border routers. CSNP packets are broadcast at the specified interval to ensure that the routing database is synchronized. This command can be used only in multiaccess interfaces. The level-1 and level-2 keywords are optional; they specify that the interval applies only to the given level of router.

isis hello-interval   interface

```
isis hello-interval seconds [{level-1 | level-2}]
no isis hello-interval
```

Configures   IS-IS hello interval for an interface

Default   10 seconds

Description
This command sets the hello interval for IS-IS routing to *seconds*. By default, the hello interval is the advertised holdtime multiplied by the hello multiplier, which has a default of 3. The optional level-1 and level-2 keywords allow you to apply this command to an individual level; otherwise the interval is applied to both levels.

isis hello-multiplier

```
isis hello-multiplier value [{level-1 |level-2}]
no isis hello-multiplier
```

Configures   The holdtime value multiplier

Default   3

Description

For IS-IS, the holdtime is calculated by taking the hello interval and multiplying it by the hello multiplier. This command sets the hello multiplier to *value*. By changing the hello multiplier, you effectively change the holdtime. The optional level-1 and level-2 keywords allow you to apply this command to an individual level; otherwise the interval is applied to both levels.

Example

The following commands configure IS-IS routing for the interface ethernet 1. The hello interval is set to 5 seconds (for level 1) and the multiplier is set to 5, yielding a holdtime of 25 seconds.

```
interface ethernet 1
  ip router isis
  isis hello-interval 5 level-1
  isis hello-multiplier 5 level-1
```

isis lsp-interval

```
isis lsp-interval milliseconds
no isis lsp-interval
```

Configures   Time delay between LSPs for IS-IS routing

Default   33 milliseconds

Description

This command sets the number of *milliseconds* between IS-IS link state packets (LSPs). If a router has many IS-IS interfaces, it might have trouble sending all the LSPs. This command lets you increase the time between the packets, which should reduce the load on the router's CPU.

isis metric

```
isis metric value [{level-1 | level-2}]
no isis metric
```

Configures   The default IS-IS metric for the interface

Default   10

Description

This command sets the default metric for the interface to *value*. By using the keywords level-1 or level-2, you can specify a metric for a specific routing level. If no level is specified, level-1 is used.

isis password   interface

```
isis password password [{level-1 | level-2}]
no isis password
```

Configures   The authentication password for IS-IS routing

Default   None

Description

This command sets the authentication *password* for IS-IS routing for the interface. All IS-IS communication to other routers through this interface must be authenticated with this password. However, like other password settings for IS-IS, this password is sent out in clear-text, providing little security. The level-1 and level-2 keywords are optional; they allow separate passwords to be applied to each level. If no level is specified, level-1 is used.

isis priority   interface

```
isis priority priority [{level-1 | level-2}]
no isis priority
```

Configures   A priority value for the interface for IS-IS routing

Default   64

Description

This command allows you to set the router's *priority* in an IS-IS network. The priority is used to determine which routers become the designated router (DR) and the backup designated router (BDR). The priority can range from 0 to 127; 127 is the highest. The optional keywords level-1 and level-2 allow you to set a different priority for each level; otherwise the priority value applies to both levels.

isis retransmit-interval   interface

```
isis retransmit-interval seconds
no isis retransmit-interval
```

Configures   The time between link state packet (LSP) retransmissions

Default   5 seconds

Description

This command sets the time (in *seconds*) between LSP retransmissions. It should be used only on point-to-point links.

---

isis retransmit-throttle-interval

```
isis retransmit-throttle-interval milliseconds
no isis retransmit-throttle-interval
```

Configures   Time between retransmissions of LSPs

Default   Calculated from the isis lsp-interval command

Description

This command sets the interval in *milliseconds* between retransmissions of IS-IS LSPs.

---

is-type

```
is-type {level-1 | level-1-2 | level-2-only}
no is-type {level-1 | level-1-2 | level-2-only}
```

Configures   The level at which the IS-IS routing protocol will operate

Default   level-1-2

Description

This command sets the level at which the IS-IS routing protocol operates, which also defines the type of IS-IS router it is (station or area). By default, the router operates at both levels, which means it is both a station router and an area router.

level-1
> The router performs only as a station router.

level-1-2
> The router performs as both a station and an area router.

level-2-only
> The router performs only as an area router.

Example

```
router isis
  is-type level-2-only
```

---

keepalive

```
keepalive seconds
no keepalive
```

Configures   The keepalive interval

Default   10 seconds

Description

The keepalive command specifies the interval (in *seconds*) that the router waits before sending a message on the interface to test the link and determine whether it is up or down. On Ethernet interfaces, the router sends the message to itself. On serial interfaces, the message is sent to the router on the other end of the link.

Keepalive settings can be very sensitive. If the keepalive interval is too low, the keepalive packets might be delayed by other traffic. If the interval is set too high, the router will take longer to update the interface's status, which slows route convergence.

On Frame Relay interfaces, the keepalive value should match (or be less than) the LMI interval configured on the carrier's switch.

Example

```
interface ethernet 1
    keepalive 5
```

---

key   key chain configuration mode

```
key number
no key number
```

Configures   An identification number of a key on a key chain

Default   None

Description

This command applies an identification *number* to an authentication key on a key chain. ID numbers can range from 0 to 2,147,483,647. See the key chain command for more information.

---

key chain   global

```
key chain name
no key chain name
```

Configures   Enters the key chain configuration mode

Default   None

Description

This command enters the key chain configuration mode, which allows you to create authentication keys for routing protocols and other uses. Each key chain must have at least one key defined with the key command. A key chain may have as many as 2,147,483,647 keys.

Example

```
! Create a key chain called "ExampleKeyChain" with two keys
key chain ExampleKeyChain
  key 1
    key-string MyKey1
  key 2
    key-string MyKey2
```

key config-key   global

```
key config-key 1 string
```

Configures   A private DES key for the router

Default   None

Description

This command defines a private DES key for the router. This key can be used to encrypt various parts of the router's configuration with DES. The key itself does not appear in the configuration. If you lose the key, it can't be recovered. The string can be from one to eight alphanumeric characters long.

key-string   key chain configuration mode

```
key-string string
no key-string string
```

Configures   An authentication string for a key

Default   None

Description

This command sets the actual authentication string for a key. *string* can be from 1 to 80 alphanumeric characters in length; the first character cannot be a number. See the key chain command for more information.

lane auto-config-atm-address   interface

```
lane [config] auto-config-atm-address
no lane [config] auto-config-atm-address
```

Configures   Automatic configuration of the configuration server's ATM address

Default   No ATM address

Description

This command specifies that the configuration server address and the client's address should be automatically computed. When the optional config keyword is used, the command applies only to the LANE Configuration Server (LECS).

---

lane bus-atm-address   interface

```
lane-bus-atm-address atm-address
no lane-bus-atm-address
```

Configures   The ATM address of the BUS

Default   Automatic ATM address assignment

Description

This command specifies the ATM address of the broadcast and unknown server (BUS). The *atm-address* can be a complete ATM address or an ATM template. A template may use * as a wildcard to represent any single character, or ... to represent any group of consecutive characters.

---

lane client   interface

```
lane client {ethernet | tokenring} [elan-name]
no lane client {ethernet | tokenring}
```

Configures   Activates a LANE client

Default   None

Description

This command activates a LANE client for the interface. The ethernet and tokenring keywords specify the type of Emulated LAN (ELAN) that the interface is connected to. *elan-name* is optional; it defines which ELAN the client belongs to. If you do not include an *elan-name*, the client contacts the LAN emulation configuration server to find out which ELAN to join.

---

lane client-atm-address   interface

```
lane client-atm-address atm-address
no lane client-atm-address atm-address
```

Configures   The ATM address for the LANE client on the interface

Default   Automatic ATM address

Description

This command specifies the ATM address for the LANE client on the interface. The *atm-address* can be a complete ATM address or an ATM address template.

---

lane config-atm-address

```
lane [config] config-atm-address atm-address
no lane [config] config-atm-address atm-address
```

Configures   The ATM address for the configuration server

Default   None

Description

This command sets the ATM address for the LANE server and the LANE client. If the optional config keyword is used, the ATM address applies only to the configuration server. The *atm-address* can be a complete ATM address or an ATM address template.

lane config database

interface (major only; no subinterface)

```
lane config database name
no lane config database
```

Configures   The LANE database for the LANE configuration server

Default   None

Description

This command specifies the name of the LANE database for the current interface. The database must exist before you give this command. There can be only one LANE database per interface. The LANE database is created with the lane database command.

lane database

global

```
lane database name
no lane database name
```

Configures   A named configuration database

Default   None

Description

This command creates a named configuration database (a LANE database) that is associated with a configuration server.

Example

The following commands create a database named elandatabase1. The lane database command sets up the name and enters the LANE database configuration mode. The remaining commands set up the database by mapping an ELAN name to a LANE emulation server address, and then setting up a default ELAN name.

```
! Define the ELAN database named elandatabase1
lane database elandatabase1
  name elan1 server-atm-address 47.00918100000000613E5D0301.00603E0DE841.01
  ! We set a default lane for LECs that don't know the ELAN they should join
  default-name elan1
```

lane fixed-config-atm-address
interface

```
lane [config] fixed-config-atm-address
no lane [config] fixed-config-atm-address
```

Configures   The LECS used by the ATM address assigned by the ATM forum

Default   No address set

Description
This command sets the address of the ATM server to the default address assigned by the ATM Forum. The NSAP address is 47.007900000000000000000000.00A03E000001.00. The optional config keyword specifies that the address applies to the configuration server only.

lane global-lecs-address
interface

```
lane global-lecs-address address
no lane global-lecs-address address
```

Configures   A list of LECS addresses to use

Default   None

Description
This command specifies a LECS address to use when the ILMI cannot be used. Normally, the router obtains the LECS address from the ILMI. This command can be used as many times as necessary to create a list of LECS addresses.

lane le-arp
interface

```
lane le-arp {mac-address | route-desc segment segment-number bridge bridge-
  number} atm-address
no lane le-arp {mac-address | route-desc segment segment-number bridge
  bridge-number} atm-address
```

Configures   Assigns a static MAC address to an ATM address

Default   None

Description

This command adds a mapping between a static MAC address and an ATM address to the ARP database. You may either specify the MAC address explicitly, or specify a route description using the route-desc keyword. In this case, you must specify a *segment-number* (1–4,095) and *bridge-number* (1–15) instead. ARP entries created by this command do not expire. To remove them from the table, use the no form of this command.

---

lane server-atm-address
interface

```
lane server-atm-address atm-address
no lane server-atm-address atm-address
```

Configures   LANE server ATM address

Default   The server's ATM address is provided by the configuration server

Description

This command sets the ATM address of the configuration server, overriding the address provided by the configuration server itself. The *atm-address* can be a complete ATM address or an ATM address template.

---

lane server-bus
interface

```
lane server-bus {ethernet | tokenring} elan-name
no lane server-bus {ethernet | tokenring} elan-name
```

Configures   Enables a LANE server and a BUS on a subinterface

Default   None

Description

This command enables a LANE server and a BUS on the subinterface. The ethernet and tokenring keywords specify the type of Emulated LAN attached to the interface. The *elan-name* is the name of the ELAN, and can be up to 32 characters in length.

---

line
global

```
line [line-type] line-number [end-line-number]
```

Description

This command enters the line configuration mode. Valid *line-types* are aux, console, tty, or vty. If no *line-type* is given, the *line-number* is treated as an absolute line number. (See the results of a show line command to see absolute line numbers.)

The *line-number* is the number of the first line you want to configure. The *end-line-number* is the last line you want to configure. If you want to configure only a single line, omit *end-line-number*.

Example

The following commands set the password on lines 0 through 4, inclusive, and then set the connection speed on line 5.

```
! change the password on vty 0 4 to vtyin
line vty 0 4
  password vtyin
! Change the speed on tty 5
line tty 5
  speed 38400
```

---

linecode
controller

```
linecode {ami | b8zs | hdb3}
no linecode {ami | b8zs | hdb3}
```

Configures   The line encoding used on a T1/E1 line

Default   ami for T1 lines; hdb3 for E1 lines

Description

This command specifies the line encoding for a T1 or E1 line. ami can be applied to either T1 or E1; b8zs can be used only for T1 lines, and hdb3 only for E1 lines. The encodings used must match at both ends of the line; in practice, this means that the encoding is defined by your carrier.

---

link-test
interface (hub)

```
link-test
no link-test
```

Configures   Link-test functionality on a hub interface

Default
Enabled

Description

This command is specific to Cisco devices with built-in hub interfaces. It enables the port's link-test function. Use the no form to disable the link test.

Example

```
hub ethernet 0 1
  no link-test
```

location

```
location text
no location
```

Configures   The location description for a line

Default   None

Description
This command has no effect on the line's configuration; it simply lets you document the location of the equipment connected to a particular line. This information can be displayed to the user at login by placing the service linenumber command in the configuration.

Example
```
line tty3
  location Router-Room11,port 34
  service linenumber
```

logging

```
logging syslog-server
no logging syslog-server
```

Configures   A server for logging messages

Default   None

Description
This command specifies the hostname or IP address of the log server (syslog-server) to which the router sends log messages. These messages use the standard Unix/Linux syslog facility; there are implementations of this facility for other operating systems (notably Windows NT and Windows 2000).

For syslog configuration on a Unix box, see the */etc/syslog.conf* file and the *syslogd* manpage.

logging buffered

```
logging buffered [size] [level]
no logging buffered
```

Configures   Messages logged to the internal buffer

Default   Depends on the platform; usually enabled

Description
This command enables logging to an internal buffer.

size

Optional. The size of the internal buffer, in bytes. The default size depends on the platform; you can give a buffer size from 4,096 to 4,294,967,295. If you set the buffer size too high, the router will run out of memory for routing tasks.

level

Optional. A numeric severity level or the name of a severity level. Any message at this severity or higher are logged to the internal buffer. Severity levels are: emergencies (0), alerts (1), critical (2), errors (3), warnings (4), notifications (5), informational (6), and debugging (7). Note that the numeric levels are the opposite of what you'd expect: a lower number indicates a higher severity.

logging buffered xml global

```
logging buffered xml [size]
no logging buffered
```

Configures   Messages logged to the internal buffer

Default   Depends on the platform; usually enabled

Description

This command enables logging to an internal buffer using XML-formatted messages.

size

Optional. The size of the internal buffer in bytes. The default size depends on the platform; you can give a buffer size from 4,096 to 4,294,967,295. If you set the buffer size too high, the router will run out of memory for routing tasks.

logging console global

```
logging console level
no logging console
```

Configures   Logging of messages to the console

Default   Debugging (7)

Description

This command enables logging to the console screen, thus setting the severity level of messages that will be displayed. All messages at the given *level* (either a level name or a level number) are logged. By default, all messages are logged.

logging console xml global

```
logging console xml [level]
no logging console
```

Configures   Logging of messages to the console

Default   Debugging (7)

Description

This command enables logging to the console screen using XML-formatted messages.

---

logging count global

```
logging count
no logging count
```

Configures   Error log count capability

Default   Disabled

Description

This command enables error log count capability. You can view the counter and statistics with the command show logging count.

---

logging facility global

```
logging facility facility
no logging facility
```

Configures   The syslog facility to which the messages are sent

Default   local7

Description

A syslog server separates messages according to their facility type. This command states the *facility* to which messages generated by the router belong. Valid facilities are auth, cron, daemon, kern, lpr, mail, news, syslog, local0 through local7, sys9 through sys14, user, and uucp.

Example

The following command configures the router to send syslog messages to the local7 facility:

```
#logging facility local7
```

The behavior of the syslog server depends on its own configuration. With the following line in *syslog.conf*, the server saves local7 messages with a debugging severity to the file */var/log/debug-logfile*:

```
local7.debug        /var/log/debug-logfile
```

logging history

global

```
logging history level
no logging history
```

Configures   The severity levels to be logged

Default   Warnings (4)

Description

This command sets the type of syslog messages that are entered into the syslog history table. These messages are also set to an SNMP management station, if one is configured; all messages at the given level or higher are logged.

Example

The following command logs messages with a severity of errors (3) or greater, i.e., critical (2), alerts (1), and emergencies (0):

```
logging history errors
```

logging history size

global

```
logging history size number
no logging history size
```

Configures   The size of the history table

Default   1

Description

This command sets the size of the history table. *number* is the number of messages saved in the table; the value can be from 1 to 500.

logging host

global

```
logging host machine-name [xml]
no logging host machine-name [xml]
```

Configures   The logging syslog server

Default   Not enabled

Description

This command sets the hostname of the syslog server to which the router should send its system messages. The *machine-name* can be a hostname or IP address of the server. The optional xml keyword specifies that the log messages be sent in XML format.

logging monitor   global

```
logging monitor level
no logging monitor
```

Configures   Messages logged to terminal lines (monitors)

Default   Debugging (7)

Description

This command controls which messages are sent to the console and other terminal lines. *level* can be either the name of a severity level or a number. Messages at the given level and higher are sent to the terminal lines. The default level sends all messages to the terminal lines because debugging is the lowest severity level.

logging on   global

```
logging on
no logging on
```

Configures   Controls all logging

Default   Enabled

Description

This command allows you to enable or disable all logging. Use it with caution, as the router often waits for error messages to be displayed on a console before continuing.

logging source-interface   global

```
logging source-interface interface
no logging source-interface
```

Configures   The interface from which syslog packets are sent

Default   The router uses the interface "closest" to the destination

Description

This command sets the interface that the router uses to send syslog packets, and therefore sets the source IP address for syslog packets that originate from the router. Specifying the source interface allows you to control the path that logging packets take from the router to the network management station, which can be an important security consideration. By default, packets originate from the interface closest to the destination.

logging synchronous line

```
logging synchronous [level severity | all] [limit number-of-messages]
no logging synchronous
```

Configures   Display of log messages

Default

Disabled; when enabled, default severity level is 2 and buffer message limit is 20

Description

This command controls the printing of log messages to a user's terminal. By default, messages are printed at any time, possibly disrupting the user's current command. This command tells the router to wait until the user's current command and its output are completed before displaying any logging messages.

level *severity*

> The severity level that this command affects. All messages with a severity at or below (i.e., with a higher number than) the given level are sent synchronously (i.e., after waiting for the user to complete the current command and the router to generate the requested output).

all

> Equivalent to level emergencies; all messages are sent synchronously.

limit *number-of-messages*

> Specifies the number of messages that will be queued waiting for delivery.

Example

The following commands specify that on terminal lines 0 through 8, log messages at levels 6 and 7 (informational and debugging) will be delivered synchronously.

```
line 0 8
  logging synchronous level 6
```

logging trap global

```
logging trap level
no logging trap
```

Configures   Messages sent to syslog servers

Default   Disabled

Description

This command limits the type of messages that are sent to the syslog servers. Only messages of the given severity level and higher are sent to the server.

login

```
login [local | tacacs]
no login [login | tacacs]
```

Configures   The login authentication method for connections

Default   No authentication

Description

This command tells the line to authenticate the user before allowing access. If you give this command without any arguments, you must use the password command to specify a password for this line. The local keyword tells the router to maintain its own database of users, created using the username command. The tacacs keyword tells the router to authenticate users by contacting a TACACS server.

When using login local, make sure you have at least one username configured before you log out. Otherwise, you will be locked out of the specified lines.

Example

To enable simple authentication using a single password for all access through this line:

```
line vty 0 4
  login
  password letmein
```

These commands enable authentication using a local database of usernames and user-specific passwords; users Bob, Ann, and John are the only ones able to log into this line.

```
username bob password letmein
username ann password letmein2
username john password letmein3
line vty 0 4
  login local
```

---

login authentication

```
login authentication {default | list-name}
no login authentication {default | list-name}
```

Configures   TACACS+ authentication for logins

Default   No authentication

Description

This command configures the login authentication method. The methods used to perform authentication can be taken either from the default list or a named list.

default
     Uses the default list created with the aaa authentication login command.

list-name
     Specifies a list created with the aaa authentication login command.

logout-warning

```
logout-warning seconds
no logout-warning
```

Configures   A warning message before an automatic logout

Default   None

Description

This command activates the logout warning message. This message warns users that a forced logout is about to occur. The *seconds* parameter specifies how much warning time is given; that is, the time that will elapse before the session closes after the warning is issued.

loopback

```
loopback [options]
no loopback
```

Configures   Loopback mode

Default   Disabled

Description

The loopback command sets the equipment at some point between a router interface and the other end of the line to reflect all data back to the router. Loopbacks are extremely useful for troubleshooting. With no options, loopback tests the local interface: all packets sent to the interface are immediately reflected back to the router without being sent to the destination. The various *options* and parameters allow you to place the loopback point farther down the line:

applique
> Sets the internal loopback for an HSSI interface.

dte
> Sets the loopback at the CSU/DSU, which tests the cable between the router (the DTE) and the CSU/DSU. The CSU/DSU must support this option.

line [payload]
> Sets the loopback at the "far end" of the CSU/DSU, which sends the packets completely through the CSU/DSU and back to the router. The CSU/DSU must support this option. On routers with built-in CSU/DSUs (2524 or 2525) you can add the payload keyword, which creates the loopback at the DSU.

remote *option*
> Sets the loopback at the remote CSU/DSU, which sends packets all the way to the remote end of the connection before reflecting them back to the router. This command tests the entire communications link between the router and the far end of the line. The remote CSU/DSU must be configured for remote loopback. Additional options give you more control over the behavior of remote loopback.

The following options are applicable to the `loopback remote` command:

`full`
> Places the loopback at the remote CSU.

`payload`
> Places the loopback on the DSU side of the remote device and transmits a payload request.

`smart-jack`
> Places the loopback at the remote smart-jack connection.

`0in1`
> Transmits an all-zeros test pattern for verifying a B8ZS-encoded line.

`1in1`
> Transmits an all-ones test pattern.

`1in2`
> Transmits alternating test patterns of all ones and all zeros.

`1in5`
> Transmits the standard test pattern for testing lines.

`1in8`
> Transmits a stress-test pattern for testing repeaters and their timing recovery.

`3in24`
> Transmits a test pattern for testing AMI lines.

`qrw`
> Transmits a quasi-random word pattern test to simulate real-world data patterns.

`user-pattern` *value*
> Transmits a pattern defined by the *value* parameter. This pattern is a binary string and can be as long as 24 bits.

`511`
> Transmits a random test pattern that repeats every 511 bits.

`2047`
> Transmits a random test pattern that repeats every 2,047 bits.

Example

The following commands place the remote device in loopback mode and send the qrw test pattern:

```
interface serial 0
  loopback remote full qrw
```

In response, the router produces the following output, reporting that it has changed the line's state to down (because it can't be used for data while it is in loopback mode) and has succeeded in placing the remote CSU/DSU in loopback mode:

```
%LINEPROTO-5-UPDOWN: Line protocol on Interface Serial0, changed state to down
%LINK-3-UPDOWN: Interface Serial0, changed state to down
%SERVICE_MODULE-5-LOOPUPREMOTE: Unit 0 - Remote unit placed in loopback
```

mac-address-table aging-time   global

```
mac-address-table aging-time seconds
no mac-address-table aging-time seconds
```

Configures   Aging time for MAC address es

Default   300 seconds

Description
This command configures the aging time for MAC addresses in the MAC address
table. Valid times are 0 or from 10 to 1,000,000 seconds. A setting of 0 (zero) disables
the aging time.

mac-address-table dynamic   global

```
mac-address-table dynamic mac-address interface {fa | gi} vlan vlan-id
no mac-address-table dynamic mac-address interface {fa | gi} vlan vlan-id
```

Configures   Insertion of dynamic MAC address into the MAC address table

Default   Dynamic addresses are not added to the table

Description
This command adds dynamic MAC addresses to the MAC address table.

mac-address
    The MAC address to be added to (or removed from) the table.
interface
    The interface to which packets for the MAC address are forwarded.
fa
    Specifies FastEthernet.
gi
    Specifies GigabitEthernet.
vlan *vlan-id*
    The vlan parameter specifies where to forward packets for the MAC address.

mac-address-table secure   global

```
mac-address-table secure mac-address interface {fa | gi} vlan vlan-id
no mac-address-table secure mac-address interface {fa | gi} vlan vlan-id
```

Configures   Insertion of secure MAC addresses into the MAC address table

Default   Secure addresses are not added to the table

Description
This command adds secure MAC addresses to the MAC address table.

mac-address
The MAC address to be added to (or removed from) the table.

interface
The interface to which packets for the MAC address are forwarded.

fa
Specifies FastEthernet.

gi
Specifies GigabitEthernet.

vlan *vlan-id*
The vlan parameter specifies where to forward packets for the MAC address.

mac-address-table static   global

```
mac-address-table static mac-address {interface int-type} {vlan vlan-id}
no mac-address-table static mac-address {interface int-type} {vlan vlan-id}
```

Configures   Insertion of static MAC addresses into the MAC address table

Default   Static addresses are not added to the table

Description
This command adds static MAC addresses to the MAC address table.

mac-address
The MAC address to be added to (or removed from) the table.

interface *int-type*
The interface to which packets for the MAC address are forwarded.

vlan *vlan-id*
The vlan parameter specifies where to forward packets for the MAC address.

map-class dialer   global

```
map-class dialer name
no map-class dialer name
```

Configures   A map class for configuring DDR

Default   None

Description
Defines a map class that can be used in dialer map commands. The name of the map class is an alphanumeric string. After you give the map-class command, the router enters the map-class context, in which you can enter commands that configure the map class.

Example

The following code configures a map class named myclass. This map class is used within a dialer command to specify the properties of the telephone line used for the dial-on-demand connection.

```
! Define the map class and its commands
map-class dialer myclass
  dialer isdn speed 64
!
! Configure ISDN interface
interface bri 0
  encapsulation ppp
  dialer map ip 10.10.1.5 name office2 class myclass 014105551234001
```

---

map-class frame-relay   global

```
map-class frame-relay name
no map-class frame-relay name
```

Configures   A map class to define QoS attributes for an SVC or PVC

Default   None

Description

This command creates a special kind of map class used to define QoS attributes for a Frame Relay SVC or PVC. The following frame-relay commands can be applied to the map class:

frame-relay custom-queue-list *list*
:   Specifies a custom queue list for the map.

frame-relay priority-group *list*
:   Specifies a priority queue for the map.

frame-relay adaptive-shaping [becn | foresight]
:   Enables the type of BECN (backwards explicit congestion notification) information that will throttle the transmission rate.

frame-relay cir [in | out] *bps*
:   The inbound or outbound committed information rate. If neither in nor out is specified, the command applies to both directions.

frame-relay mincir [in | out] *bps*
:   The minimum incoming or outgoing committed information rate. If neither in nor out is specified, the command applies to both directions.

frame-relay bc [in | out] *bits*
:   The incoming or outgoing committed burst size. If neither in nor out is specified, the command applies to both directions.

frame-relay be [in | out] *bits*
:   The incoming or outgoing excess burst size. If neither in nor out is specified, the command applies to both directions.

frame-relay idle-time *duration*
:   The idle timeout interval for the map.

Example

The following code defines a Frame Relay map that specifies an incoming and outgoing committed information rate of 56 Kbps:

```
map-class frame-relay map1
  frame-relay cir 56000
```

map-group   interface

```
map-group name
no map-group name
```

Configures   Applies a map list to an interface

Default   None

Description

This command applies a map list to an interface. See the map-list command for an example.

map-list   global

```
map-list map-name src-addr {e164 | x121} source-address dest-addr {e164 | x121}
  destination-address

no map-list map-name src-addr {e164 | x121} source-address dest-addr
  {e164 | x121} destination-address
```

Configures   A map list for a Frame Relay SVC

Default   None

Description

Use this command to define a map list for a Frame Relay SVC.

map-name
   The name of the map.

src-addr {e164 | x121}
   Type of source address; it may be either e164 or x121.

source-address
   The actual source address.

dest-addr {e164 | x121}
   Type of destination address; it may be either e164 or x121.

destination-address
   The actual destination address.

Example

The following commands set up a map list that brings up a Frame Relay SVC in response to IP or AppleTalk traffic. The map list, named map1, is applied to the serial0 interface using a map-group command. The map list itself consists of two statements that specify the protocol and address we're interested in, followed by a map class that specifies the quality of service parameters to be used by the circuit.

```
interface serial0
  ip address 172.30.8.1
  encapsulation frame-relay
  map-group map1
!
map-list map1 source-addr E164 112233 dest-addr E164 445566
  ip 10.1.1.1 class some-map-class
  appletalk 2000.2 class some-map-class
!
map-class frame-relay some-map-class
  frame-relay be out 9000
```

---

match access-group
class-map

```
match access-group access-list
no match access-group access-list
```

Configures   QoS class map match line

Default   None

Description
This command creates an entry in a class map that applies an access list as the match criteria. The *access-list* can be a numbered or named access list.

Example
```
class-map class1
  match access-group 101
```

---

match any
class-map

```
match any
no match any
```

Configures   QoS class map match line

Default   None

Description
This command creates an entry in the class map that causes *all* packets to match.

---

match as-path
route-map

```
match as-path path-list-number
no match as-path path-list-number
```

Configures   BGP route filtering

Default   None

Description

This command allows you to require that any route in a route map pass an AS path access list. Routes that are permitted by the list undergo further processing. You might use this command to create a route map that modifies routing metrics or changes the routes in some way, depending on the routes' AS path. These modifications are applied only to routes matching the AS path access list.

Example

The following code filters all routes to be sent to the neighboring router 10.10.1.1 through the AS path list 1. The AS path list is applied in the route map test-as-path, which adds our AS number (300) to all routes that match this list.

```
route-map test-as-path
  match as-path 1
  set as-path prepend 300
!
ip as-path access-list 1 permit .*
!
router bgp 300
  neighbor 10.10.1.1 route-map set-as-path out
```

---

match class-map   class-map

```
match class-map class-map-name
no class-map class-map-name
```

Configures   QoS class map match line

Default   None

Description

This command tells the current class map to use an entirely different class map as a matching criteria. By using this command, you can nest class maps.

Example

In this example, you can see that class1 uses class2 with this command.

```
class-map match-any class2
  match protocol ip
  match access-group 101
!
class-map match-all class1
  match class-map class2
  match access-group 102
```

match community-list

```
match community-list community-list-number [exact]
no match community-list community-list-number [exact]
```

Configures   BGP route filtering

Default   None

Description
This command lets you build a route map that requires a match to a BGP community list. If the route's community string matches the named list, the **set** commands of the route map are applied. The **exact** keyword states that all the communities within the community list must be present for the route. Without the **exact** keyword, only one match is required.

match cos

```
match cos value [value2 value3 value4]
no match cos value [value2 value3 value4]
```

Configures   QoS class map match line

Default   None

Description
This command configures a match line in a class map that matches a packet's Class of Service (CoS) value. The IEEE 802.1Q/ISL CoS value can be a value from 0 to 7. And you can specify from 1 to 4 values on a single line.

Example
```
class-map voice
  match cos 7
```

match destination-address mac

```
match destination-address mac address
no match destination-address mac address
```

Configures   QoS class map match line

Default   None

Description
This command configures a class-map match statement that causes the packet's MAC address to be compared to the supplied *address*.

match discard-class

```
match discard-class value
no match discard-class value
```

Configures   QoS class map match line

Default   Packets not classified as expected

Description

This command configures a `class-map match` statement that matches the packet's discard class value. The *value* is a number from 0 to 7.

---

match dscp

```
match [ip] dscp value
no match [ip] dscp value
```

Configures   QoS class map match line

Default   None

Description

This command tells a class map to match a packet's Differentiated Service Code Point (DSCP). The `ip` command is optional; it tells the match to work only for IPv4 packets. If you leave ip out, both IPv4 and IPv6 packets are matched. The *value* can be from 0 to 63.

---

match fr-dlci

```
match fr-dlci dlci-number
no match fr-dlci dlci-number
```

Configures   QoS class map match line

Default   None

Description

This command specifies a Frame Relay DLCI value to use in a class map. The *dlci-number* is matched against the packet's DLCI number.

---

match input-interface

```
match input-interface interface-name
no match input-interface interface-name
```

Configures   QoS class map match line

Default   None

Description

This command specifies an input interface to match a packet against. If the packet's input interface matches the *interface-name*, the line matches.

---

match interface
route-map

```
match interface interface [... interface]
no match interface interface [... interface]
```

Configures   Route filtering

Default   None

Description

This command lets you build a route map that selects routes according to the interfaces they use. For the route to match, its next hop must be through one of the interfaces listed. Routes that match are processed according to the other statements in the route map.

Example

In the following route map, all routes must have a next hop through the serial0 or serial1 interface for the route to match.

```
route-map example1
    match interface serial0 serial1
```

---

match ip address
route-map

```
match ip address access-list
no match ip address access-list
```

Configures   Route filtering

Default   None

Description

This command is used to match the IP address of the route's destination. If the destination matches the specified access list, the route is included in the map and processed according to the other statements in the route map. With this command, you can use extended access lists to implement routing policies.

---

match ip dscp
class-map

```
match ip dscp
no match ip dscp
```

Configures   QoS class map match line

Default   None

Description   This command has been replaced with the match dcsp command.

---

match ip next-hop route-map

```
match ip next-hop access-list [... access-list]
no match ip next-hop access-list [... access-list]
```

Configures   Route filtering

Default   None

Description

This command lets you specify that a route's next hop IP address must match the specified access list (or lists) to be included in the map. If a route passes any of the access lists, it is processed according to the other statements in the route map.

match ip precedence class-map

```
match ip precedence
no match ip precedence
```

Configures   QoS class map match line

Default   None

Description

This command has been replaced with the match precedence command.

match ip route-source route-map

```
match ip route-source access-list [... access-list]
no match ip route-source access-list [... access-list]
```

Configures   Route filtering

Default   None

Description

This command lets you specify that a route's source address (i.e., the router that originally advertised the route) must match the given access lists to be included in the map. If a route passes any of the access lists, it is processed according to the other statements in the route map.

match ip rtp class-map

```
match ip rtp starting-port-number end-port-range
no match ip rtp starting-port-number end-port-range
```

Configures   QoS class map match line

Default   None

Description

This command configures a range of ports to match a packet using the Real-Time Protocol (RTP). Any RTP packets that fall within the specified *starting-port-number* and *end-port-range* are matched. The *starting-port-number* can be from 2,000 to 65,535. The RTP *end-port-range* can be from 0 to 16,383.

---

match length   route-map

```
match length min max
no match length min max
```

Configures   Route filtering

Default   None

Description

This command lets you build a route map that selects packets whose size is between *min* and *max*. If a packet's size falls in this range, it is processed according to the other statements in the route map. This command is used with policy routing.

Example

In this example, we want to match packets that are between 10 to 100 bytes long. We then send matching packets out through the serial0 interface.

```
interface ethernet1
  ip policy route-map example1
!
route-map example1
  match length 10 100
  set interface serial0
```

---

match metric   route-map

```
match metric value
no match metric value
```

Configures   Route filtering

Default   None

Description

This command lets you build a route map that selects routes with a certain metric, given by *value*. The metric value can be from 0 to 4,294,967,295. If a route's metric matches the given value, it is processed according to the other statements in the route map.

match mpls experimental

```
match mpls experimental value
no match mpls experimental value
match mpls experimental topmost value
no match mpls experimental topmost value
```

Configures   QoS class map match line

Default   None

Description

This command specifies an MPLS experimental value against which to match packets. The *value* is the experimental MPLS value to match against. Values can be from 0 to 7. The topmost command checks the MPLS packet's topmost field for the value.

match mpls-label

```
match mpls-label
no match mpls-label
```

Configures   Route map

Default   Routes with MPLS labels are not redistributed

Description

This command allows routes with MPLS labels to be redistributed in a route map.

Example

```
route-map mymap permit 1
  match ip address 101
  match mpls-label
```

match not

```
match not match-command
no match not match-command
```

Configures   QoS class map match line

Default   None

Description

This command specifies the not version of a *match-command*. For example, if you wanted to match all protocols except IP, you could use the match protocol command combined with a not.

Example
```
class-map all-but-ip
  match not protocol ip
```

---

match packet length   class-map

```
match packet length max value min value
no match packet length max value min value
```

Configures   QoS class map match line

Default   None

Description
This command tells the class-map to match the layer 3 packet length in the IP header of the packet. You can specify a min value, a max value, or both. If a minimum value is supplied, only packets with a value greater than the minimum are matched. If only a maximum value is supplied, only packets less than the maximum are matched. If both a minimum and maximum are supplied, packets must be within that range in order to be matched.

Valid values for both minimum and maximum are from 1 to 2,000.

---

match precedence   class-map

```
match precedence value
no match precedence value
```

Configures   QoS class map match line

Default   None

Description
This command supplies an IP precedence value to use as match criteria for a map-class. The value can be a precedence value of 0 to 7.

---

match protocol   class-map

```
match protocol name
no match protocol name
```

Configures   QoS class map match line

Default   None

Description
This command supplies a protocol name to use as match criteria for a map class. The protocol name can be any protocol such as aarp, arp, bridge, bstun, cdp, clns, vmns, compressedtcp, decnet, ip, ipv6, ipx, llc2, pad, qllc, rsrb, snapshot, and stun.

Two other protocols, citrix and http, take additional parameters.

Example

Citrix uses an option called app to identify packets:

```
! match citrix application called application1
match protocol citrix app application1
```

http has optional url, host, and mime modifiers:

```
match protocol http host cisco*
match protocol http url index.html*
```

---

match qos-group   class-map

```
match qos-group value
no match qos-group value
```

Configures   QoS class map match line

Default   None

Description

This command specifies a packet's QoS tag to use as a match criterion in a class map. The qos-group value can be from 0 to 99. The command is often used with the set qos-group command, which sets a packet's QoS tag (usually done on another device).

---

match route-type   route-map

```
match route-type {local | internal | external [type-1 | type-2] | level-1 |
    level-2}
no match route-type {local | internal | external [type-1 | type-2] | level-1 |
    level-2}
```

Configures   Route filtering

Default   None

Description

This command lets you build route maps that match routes of a certain type. The types you can match are:

local
> BGP internal routes.

internal
> EIGRP internal routes or OSPF inter-area and intra-area.

external
> EIGRP and OSPF external routes. type-1 and type-2 will only match OSPF type-1 and type-2 routes, respectively.

level-1
> Level 1 IS-IS routes.

level-2
> Level 2 IS-IS routes.

match source-address mac

```
match source-address mac address
no match source-address mac address
```

Configures   QoS class map match line

Default   None

Description

This command specifies a packet's source MAC address to use as a class map match criterion.

match tag

```
match tag tag-value [... tag-value]
no match tag tag-value [... tag-value]
```

Configures   BGP route filtering

Default   None

Description

This command lets you build route maps that match routes with certain tag values. If a route has a tag that matches any given *tag-value*, it is processed according to the other statements in the route map. The *tag-value* parameters can have values from to 4,294,967,295.

maximum-paths

```
maximum-paths number
no maximum-paths number
```

Configures   The maximum number of paths with equal metrics

Default   1 for BGP; 4 for other protocols

Description

This command lets you set the *number* of paths with equal metrics that the router will maintain in its routing table. *number* can range from 1 to 6.

For BGP, the meaning of this command is slightly different, since BGP doesn't have a simple routing metric. For BGP, this command allows you to increase the number of parallel equal-length paths that the router maintains in its tables.

max-reserved-bandwidth interface

```
max-reserved-bandwidth percent-value
no max-reserved-bandwidth
```

Configures   QoS class map match line

Default   75 percent

Description
This command configures the percentage of bandwidth allocated for a given QoS technique, such as CBWFQ or LLC.

media-type interface

```
media-type type
no media-type type
```

Configures   The type of media for specific interfaces

Default   Depends on the interface type

Description
Certain interface types can be associated with several types of ports. For example, the Ethernet module on a 4000 series or an FEIP (Fast Ethernet interface processor) on a 7000/7500 series can be associated with an AUI, 10BaseT, or 100BaseT port. The type depends on the actual interface you are configuring; the possible types are shown in Table 17-14.

Table 17-14. Media types

Type	Meaning
aui	15-pin AUI port
10baset	10BaseT RJ45 port
100baset	100BaseT RJ45 port
mii	Media-independent interface

Example
```
interface fastethernet0/1
  media-type 100baset
```

member interface

```
member number command
no member number command
```

Configures   Applies a configuration to one async interface of a group

Default   None

Description

This command is used in conjunction with the group-range command. It allows a certain command to be applied to one specific interface of a given range. The *number* specifies the group member to which the given *command* should be applied. Only two commands can be applied to an interface using the member command: peer default ip and description. For examples, see the group-range command.

---

menu   global

menu *name* [clear-screen | line-mode | single-space | status-line]
no menu *name*

Configures   Menu display options

Default   None

Description

This command displays the menu with the given *name* and allows you to specify menu display options. Menus can be used to provide simple configuration commands for users connecting to the router through telnet or reverse telnet; the menu itself is defined using the menu command. The available options are:

clear-screen
    Forces a clear screen before displaying the menu.

line-mode
    Allows the user to backspace over a selected item and press Enter to execute a command.

single-space
    Displays the menu single-spaced instead of double-spaced.

status-line
    Displays a status line about the current user.

Menus are constructed using the commands menu command, menu text, and menu title.

---

menu command   global

menu *name* command *number command*

Configures   Commands for user interface menus

Default   None

Description

This command lets you build arbitrary menus for executing configuration commands. The menus are accessible from the router's command-line prompt.

---

name

> The name of the menu. Names cannot be more than 20 characters long.

number

> The selection number associated with the menu entry.

command

> The command to be executed when the given number is selected.

---

menu text

global

menu *name* text *number text*

Configures   Descriptive text for menus

Default   None

Description

This command lets you provide descriptive text to associate with menu items. The menus are accessible from the router's command-line prompt using the menu command, followed by the menu name.

name

> The name of the menu. Names cannot be more than 20 characters long.

number

> The selection number associated with the menu entry.

text

> The text to be displayed for the given menu selection.

Example

The following commands set up a menu called incoming with several selections. If a user types 1, the command telnet 10.1.1.1 is executed; if she types 2, the command telnet 10.1.1.2 is executed; if she types 3, the menu exits.

```
menu incoming command 1 telnet 10.1.1.1
menu incoming text 1 Telnet to New York router (10.1.1.1)
menu incoming command 2 telnet 10.1.1.2
menu incoming text 2 Telnet to San Francisco router (10.1.1.2)
menu incoming command 3 menu-exit
menu incoming text 3 Exit
```

---

menu title

global

menu *name* title *delimiter text delimiter*

Configures   A title for a user interface menu

Default   None

Description
This command allows you to assign a title to the user interface menu identified by *name*. The *text* is the menu's title; the *delimiter* can be any character that does not appear within the *text* that serves to mark the beginning and end of the *text*.

---

metric holddown
router, IGRP

```
metric holddown
no metric holddown
```

Configures   Keeps a route from being used for a given amount of time

Default   Disabled

Description
This command tells IGRP to wait a specific time before implementing new routes. It helps you to avoid routing loops in networks that converge slowly by delaying routing updates. Routing loops are still possible, however, if all routers within the same IGRP domain are not configured the same way. Using this command can result in very slow convergence.

---

metric maximum-hops
router, IGRP, EIGRP

```
metric maximum-hops hops
no metric maximum-hops hops
```

Configures   The maximum number of hops that a route can take

Default   100

Description
This command allows you to change the maximum hop count for EIGRP and IGRP. Routes that exceed the given limit are considered unreachable. The maximum number of hops is 255.

Example
The following commands configure the router to mark routes as unreachable if they require more than 180 hops:

```
router igrp 101
    network 10.10.0.0
    metric maximum-hops 180
```

---

metric weights
router

```
metric weights tos k1 k2 k3 k4 k5
no metric weights
```

Configures   EIGRP and IGRP metric calculation

Default $tos=0$; $k1=1$; $k2=0$; $k3=1$; $k4=0$; $k5=0$

Description

This command allows you to tune the routing metric for EIGRP and IGRP. The metric is calculated as follows:

$$metric = (k1 \times bandwidth) + \frac{(k2 \times bandwidth)}{(256 - load)} + (k3 \times delay)$$

If $k5$ greater than zero, the calculation continues:

$$metric = metric \times \frac{k5}{(reliability + k4)}$$

The tos (Type of Service) parameter is currently unused. It should be set to 0 when you use this command.

Example

The following commands modify the values of $k4$ and $k5$ and set the other values to their defaults:

```
router igrp 100
   network 10.10.0.0
   metric weights 0 1 0 1 2 2
```

---

mkdir   command

```
mkdir directory
```

Description

This command allows you to create a directory on a Class C filesystem.

---

modem

This family of commands is used to configure modems on TTY lines. The discussion is limited to commands that are available for all routers. Terminal servers with manageable modems, such as the AS5200, AS5300, and CS3600 series products, have additional commands.

`modem answer-timeout time`
> Sets the amount of time the router waits for the carrier signal after answering an incoming RING.

`modem autoconfigure discovery`
> The router automatically tries to discover the modem type.

`modem autoconfigure type type`
> Sets the modem to the type known by the router. To view a list of known modems, use the command modem autoconfigure type ?.

`modem callin`
> Enables support of modems that use DTR to control hook-status.

`modem callout`
> Enables reverse connections. (See Chapter 4.)

modem chat-script *script-name*
>   Specifies which chat script to use when the modem is automatically dialing. See Chapter 12 for more information.

modem cts-required
>   Configures a line to require the CTS (clear to send) signal.

modem dialin
>   Configures a modem to accept incoming calls only.

modem dtr-active
>   Configures the modem line to leave the DTR signal low unless there is an active connection.

modem inout
>   Allows both incoming and outgoing connections to the modem. This command enables reverse telnet, so be sure this what you want to do.

---

monitor session   global

monitor session *session-number* {source {interface *interface-name*}}
    [*range* | rx | tx | both]

no monitor session *session-number* {source {interface *interface-name*}}
    [*range* | rx | tx | both]

monitor session *session-number* {destination {interface *interface-name*}} [*range*]

no monitor session *session-number* {destination {interface *interface-name*}}
    [*range*]

monitor session *session-number*

no monitor session *session-number*

Configures   Switched Port Analyzer (SPAN)

Default   None

Description

This command enables the Switched Port Analyzer or SPAN, which allows a port to "monitor" traffic that's sent or received on another port or VLAN. For more information, see Chapter 14. Use the command show monitor to display the SPAN session information.

session-number
>   The SPAN session number. Valid values are 1 and 2.

source
>   Specifies the SPAN source.

destination
>   Specifies the SPAN destination.

interface-name
>   Optional. The interface type and number.

range

Optional. Specifies a list of VLANs to use for SPAN. It can be a list or a range. For example, "100,200,205,305" or "100-300". Valid values are 1 to 1,005.

rx

Optional. Restricts monitor to received traffic only.

tx

Optional. Restricts monitor to transmitted traffic only.

both

Optional. Monitor for both received and transmitted traffic.

---

more   EXEC

more [/ascii | /binary | /ebcdic] *file-url*

Configures   Displays a file's contents

Default   N/A

Description
This command allows you to view a file on the router where the *file-url* can be a file stored in flash or a system URL. See Table 2-6 in Chapter 2 for a list of valid URL prefixes.

Example
To view the startup configuration, you would use this command:

    more nvram:startup-config

---

motd-banner   line

motd-banner
no motd-banner

Configures   Suppresses the message of the day

Default   Enabled

Description
By default, the motd (message-of-the-day) banner is enabled on all lines. This command allows you to suppress the banner on selected lines.

Example

    ! Don't display the motd on lines 5 through 10
    line 5 10
      no motd-banner

mpls atm control-vc

```
mpls atm control-vc vpi vci
no mpls control-vc vpi vci
```

Configures   MPLS

Default   VPI, 3; VCI, 32

Description

This command specifies the VPI (Virtual Path Identifier) and the VCI (Virtual Circuit Identifier) for the initial link to a MPLS peer.

Example

```
interface atm1/0.1 mpls
  mpls ip
  mpls atm control-vc 1 32
```

mpls atm cos

```
mpls atm cos { available | standard | premium | control } weight
no mpls atm cos { available | standard | premium | control } weight
```

Configures   MPLS

Default   available 50%; control 50%

Description

This command changes the configured bandwidth allocation for CoS (Class of Service). You choose a class (available, standard, premium, or control) and then assign a *weight*, which is a value from 1 to 100.

mpls atm disable-headend-vc

```
mpls atm disable-headend-vc
no mpls atm disable-headend-vc
```

Configures   MPLS

Default   Enabled

Description

This command stops the LSC from initiating headend LVCs (label switched controlled virtual circuits), which reduces the number of LVCs in the network.

mpls atm multi-vc

```
mpls atm multi-vc
no mpls atm multi-vc
```

Configures   MPLS

Default   N/A

Description

This command allows an ATM MPLS subinterface to create one or more label switched controlled virtual circuits over which packets of different classes can be transmitted.

mpls atm vpi

```
mpls atm vpi lowvpi [- highvpi] [vci-range lowvci - highvci]
no mpls atm vpi lowvpi [- highvpi] [vci-range lowvci - highvci]
```

Configures   MPLS

Default   VPI is 1 to 1, VCI is 33–65,535

Description

This command configures the range of values to use in the VPI field for label switched controlled virtual circuits.

lowvpi

  Virtual Path Identifier, low end of range (0 to 4,095)

highvpi

  Optional. Virtual Path Identifier, high end of range (0 to 4,095)

vci-range

  Optional. Range of Virtual Channel Identifiers the subinterface can use.

mpls atm vp-tunnel

```
mpls atm vp-tunnel vpi [vci-range lowvci - highvci]
no mpls atm vp-tunnel vpi [vci-range lowvci - highvci]
```

Configures   MPLS

Default   Disabled

Description   This command configures an interface as a Virtual Path tunnel.

vpi

  The Virtual Path Identifier value for the local end of the tunnel.

vci-range

  Optional. Range of Virtual Channel Identifiers the subinterface can use.

mpls cos-map

global

```
mpls cos-map map
no mpls cos-map map
```

Configures   MPLS

Default   None

Description

This command creates a class map that specifies how classes correspond to Virtual
Circuits.

Example

```
mpls cos-map 10
  class 1 premium
```

mpls ip

interface, global

```
mpls ip
no mpls ip
```

Configures   MPLS

Default   Disabled

Description

This command enables label switching of IPv4 packets. The command must be
applied globally and to the interface.

Example

```
mpls ip
interface ethernet 1/1
  mpls ip
```

mpls ip default-route

global

```
mpls ip default-route
no mpls ip default-route
```

Configures   MPLS

Default   Disabled

Description

This command enables distribution of labels associated with the default route.

Example
```
mpls ip
mpls ip default-route
```

mpls ip encapsulate explicit-null

interface

```
mpls ip encapsulate explicit-null
no mpls ip encapsulate explicit-null
```

Configures   MPLS

Default   Disabled

Description

This command enables all packets sent out an interface or subinterface with an explicit NULL label header. To be used on a customer edge router.

mpls ip ttl-expiration pop

global

```
mpls ip ttl-expiration pop labels
no mpls ip ttl-expiration pop labels
```

Configures   MPLS

Default   Packets are forwarded by the original label stack

Description

This command specifies how to forward a packet with an expired time-to-live (TTL) value.

mpls label protocol

global, interface

```
mpls label protocol { ldp | tdp }
no mpls label protocol
```

Configures   MPLS

Default   TDP

Description

This command specifies the label distribution protocol to use for the platform or interface. ldp specifies the Label Distribution Protocol while tdp specifies the Tag Distribution Protocol.

For the interface version of this command, you can specify both, which allows both LDP and TDP. This is useful on interfaces where different peers might use different protocols.

Example

```
mpls label protocol ldp
!
interface ethernet 1/1
  mpls label protocol both
```

---

mpls label range   global

```
mpls label range min max
no mpls label range
```

Configures   MPLS

Default   Minimum 16, Maximum 1,048,575

Description   This command configures the range of local labels available for MPLS.

---

mpls mtu   interface

```
mpls mtu bytes
no mpls mtu bytes
```

Configures   MPLS

Default   The interface's default MTU

Description

This command sets the per-interface maximum transmission unit (MTU) for labeled packets.

---

mpls prefix-map   interface

```
mpls prefix-map map access-list acl cos-map map
no mpls prefix-map map access-list acl cos-map map
```

Configures   MPLS

Default   Disabled

Description

This command applies a QoS map when a label distribution prefix matches the specified access-list (acl).

mpls request-labels for

mpls request-labels for *access-list*
no mpls request-labels for

Configures   MPLS

Default   Disabled

Description
This command applies an access list to restrict the creation of LSPs (Label Switched Paths) on the Label Switch Controller (LSC) or Label Edge Router (LER).

mrinfo

mrinfo [*host*] [*source-interface*]

Configures   Queries a multicast router

Description
This command allows you to query a multicast router. If you provide no arguments to this command, the router queries itself.

host
    Optional. Specifies the IP address or name of the host to query.

source-interface
    Optional. Specifies the IP address or name of the interface to use as the source of the request.

mstat

mstat *source* [*destination*] [*group*]

Configures   Displays multicast statistics

Description
This command displays multicast statistics, including the packet rate and the number of packets lost. If you do not provide arguments to this command, the router prompts you for them.

source
    Specifies the IP address or name of the multicast source.

destination
    Optional. Specifies the IP address or name of the destination. If not provided, the router uses itself as the destination.

group
    Optional. Specifies the IP address or name of the group to display. The default is 224.2.0.1.

mtrace

```
mtrace source [destination] [group]
```

Description

This command provides a trace from the source to the destination for a multicast distribution tree.

source
> Specifies the IP address or name of the multicast source.

destination
> Optional. Specifies the IP address or name of the destination. If not provided, the router uses itself as the destination.

group
> Optional. Specifies the IP address or name of the group to display. The default is 224.2.0.1.

mtu

```
mtu bytes
no mtu bytes
```

Configures   Maximum transmission unit (MTU)

Default

Depends on media type (defaults for some common media are listed in Table 17-11, under the ip mtu command)

Description

This command allows you to modify the MTU for any interface. The default MTU depends on the media you are using (FDDI, Ethernet, etc.); for example, Ethernet has an MTU of 1,500.

Performance considerations may lead you to modify this value; a smaller MTU might give better performance on a lossy or noisy line.

Example

```
interface ethernet0
  mtu 1250
```

name elan-id

```
name name elan-id id
no name name elan-id id
```

Configures   ELAN ID of an ELAN in the LECS database

Default   None

Description

This command sets the *name* and *id* number for an Emulated LAN (ELAN) in the LECS database.

---

name local-seg-id
LANE database

name *elan-name* local-seg-id *segment-number*
no name *elan-name* local-seg-id *segment-number*

Configures   The token ring number of an ELAN

Default   None

Description

This command sets the token ring's ring number of an ELAN. The *segment-number* is the number to be assigned, which can be from 1 to 4,095.

---

name preempt
LANE database configuration (ATM)

name *name* preempt
no name *name* preempt

Configures   Preempt for the ELAN

Default   Disabled

Description

This command allows you to enable preempting of an ELAN. This is useful when a LAN Emulation Server (LES) of a higher priority fails and then comes back online; it allows the higher-priority LES to preempt the lower-priority LES, avoiding network flapping and instability.

---

name server-atm-address
LANE database

name *elan-name* server-atm-address *atm-address* [restricted | un-restricted]
    [index *value*]
no name *elan-name* server-atm-address *atm-address*

Configures   The LANE server's ATM address for the ELAN

Default   None

Description

This command sets the ATM address of the LANE server for the ELAN.

elan-name
    The name of the ELAN.

atm-address
    The LANE server's ATM address.

```
restricted | un-restricted
```
Optional. If restricted, only LANE clients defined in the ELAN's configuration server can be members of the ELAN.

```
index value
```
Optional. This keyword sets a priority for the LANE server. (You can assign multiple LANE servers for fault tolerance.) 0 is the highest priority.

---

neighbor router

RIP/IGRP/EIGRP:

```
neighbor address
```

```
no neighbor address
```

OSPF:

```
neighbor address [priority value] [poll-interval seconds] [cost number]
    [database-filter all]
```

```
no neighbor address [priority value] [poll-interval seconds] [cost number]
    [database-filter all]
```

Configures   A routing neighbor

Default   No neighbors defined

Description

The behavior and syntax of this command depend on the routing protocol you are using.

For RIP, this command specifies a RIP neighbor. This is useful when you have routers that cannot receive RIP broadcasts. In this situation, use the `neighbor` command to specify the IP addresses of routers that should receive RIP packets directly. If you use this command, RIP packets are not broadcast; they are sent only to the specified neighbors. The `neighbor` command is frequently used with the `passive-interface` command, which specifies that the interface should only listen for routing updates.

For IGRP, the command specifies an IGRP neighbor for the router to communicate with. It is often used with the `passive-interface` command. As with RIP, you can use the `neighbor` command together with `passive-interface` to send updates to one or more routers without sending updates to other routers on the network. Multiple `neighbor` commands are allowed.

For EIGRP, the `neighbor` command is accepted by the parser but has no effect on the EIGRP process. It is accepted for backward compatibility with IGRP configurations.

For OSPF, you use the command to define a router's OSPF neighbors explicitly. The OSPF version of this command has the following parameters:

```
address
```
The IP address of the neighbor.

```
priority value
```
Optional. The priority of the neighbor, from 0 to 255. The default is 0.

```
poll-interval seconds
```
Optional. The frequency at which the neighbor is polled. The default is 120 seconds.

cost *number*
> Optional. Assigns a cost to the neighbor. The cost can be from 1 to 65,535. Neighbors that aren't configured with a specific cost assume the cost of the interface based on the ip ospf cost command.

database-filter
> Optional. Filters outgoing link-state advertisements (LSAs) to the neighbor.

Example

In the following configuration, we have an IGRP routing process that we have told not to advertise (broadcast) IGRP updates out interface ethernet0. We use the neighbor command to explicitly tell the routing process to communicate with the router at 10.10.1.5, which happens to be reachable through the ethernet0 interface. We are thus using the neighbor command to control which routers receive IGRP information:

```
router igrp 100
  network 10.0.0.0
  passive-interface ethernet0
  neighbor 10.10.1.5
```

The following commands set up a similar routing configuration using RIP. As in the previous example, we use passive-interface to suppress routing broadcasts out ethernet0, and the neighbor command to list explicitly the routers with which we want to communicate:

```
router rip
  network 10.0.0.0
  passive-interface ethernet0
  neighbor 10.10.1.5
```

In the following example, we create an OSPF routing process and list a priority 1 neighbor explicitly:

```
! OSPF neighbor with a priority of 1
!
router ospf  99
  neighbor 192.168.1.2 priority 1
```

neighbor advertisement-interval   router, BGP

neighbor {*address* | *peer-group*} advertisement-interval *seconds*
no neighbor {*address* | *peer-group*} advertisement-interval *seconds*

Configures   Minimum interval between BGP routing updates

Default   5 seconds for internal peers; 30 seconds for external peers

Description

This command sets the BGP routing update interval. *seconds* can be from 0 to 600. You must specify either the *address* or *peer-group* of a particular peer.

neighbor database-filter

router, OSPF

```
neighbor address database-filter all out
no neighbor address database-filter all out
```

Configures   Filter LSAs to a certain OSPF neighbor

Default   Disabled

Description
Normally, all outgoing LSAs are flooded to all neighbors. This command allows you to disable flooding to a specific neighbor in point-to-multipoint networks. In broadcast, nonbroadcast, and point-to-point networks, you can disable flooding by using the ospf database-filter command.

neighbor default-originate

router, BGP

```
neighbor {address | peer-group} default-originate [route-map map]
no neighbor {address | peer-group} default-originate [route-map map]
```

Configures   Sends the default route to a BGP neighbor

Default   Disabled

Description
This command tells the router to send the default route to a neighbor, identified either by *address* or by *peer-group*. By default, no default route is sent. The use of the route map *map* allows you to place conditions on the sending of the route.

neighbor description

router, BGP

```
neighbor {address | peer-group} description text
no neighbor {address | peer-group} description
```

Configures   A text description of a BGP neighbor or peer group

Default   None

Description
This command allows you to give a text description for a neighbor, identified either by *address* or by *peer-group*. The text can be up to 80 characters. The description is purely for documentation and doesn't affect the router's behavior.

Example
```
router bgp 200
    neighbor 10.200.200.1 description Peer in the pasadena office
```

neighbor distribute-list

neighbor {*address* | *peer-group*} distribute-list {*access-list* | prefix-list
  name} {in | out}

no neighbor {*address* | *peer-group*} distribute-list {*access-list* | prefix-list
  name} {in | out}

Configures   Applies a distribute list to a neighbor or peer group

Default   None

Description

This command applies an access list or a prefix list to filter incoming (in) or outgoing
(out) routes exchanged with the given neighbor (specified by *address* or *peer-group*).

neighbor filter-list

neighbor {*address* | *peer-group*} filter-list *access-list* {in | out}

no neighbor {*address* | *peer-group*} filter-list *access-list* {in | out}

Configures   A filter for BGP

Default   None

Description

This command sets up an AS path access list that filters BGP routes sent to or received
from a specific neighbor. Routes that match the access list are discarded.

address or peer-group
  The address or peer group of the neighbor.

filter-list *access-list*
  The name of an AS path access list defined by the ip as-path access-list
  command.

in
  The filter applies to incoming routes.

out
  The filter applies to outgoing routes.

neighbor maximum-prefix

neighbor {*address* | *peer-group* maximum-prefix *max* [*threshold*] [warning-only]

no neighbor {*address* | *peer-group* maximum-prefix *max* [*threshold*] [warning-only]

Configures   The number of prefixes that can be received from a neighbor

Default   No limit

Description

This command allows you to set a limit on the number of prefixes that the router can receive from the neighbor.

address or peer-group
> The address or peer group of the neighbor.

maximum-prefix *max*
> The maximum number of prefixes you are willing to accept.

threshold
> Optional. The percentage of the maximum number of prefixes at which the router will start generating warning messages. The default is 75%.

warning-only
> Tells the router to generate a warning message about reaching the maximum value, but not to take any other action.

---

neighbor next-hop-self

router, BGP

neighbor {*address* | *peer-group*} next-hop-self
no neighbor {*address* | *peer-group*} next-hop-self

Configures   Next-hop processing of the neighbor router

Default   Disabled

Description

This command forces the router to advertise itself as the next hop to the neighbor. The neighbor router is identified by its IP *address* or *peer-group*.

---

neighbor password

router, BGP

neighbor {*address* | *peer-group*} password *word*
no neighbor {*address* | *peer-group*} password *word*

Configures   MD5 authentication between BGP peers

Default   Disabled

Description

This command requires authentication between BGP peers (identified by *address* or by *peer-group*). The MD5 algorithm is used for authentication. The password, *word*, can be any alphanumeric string up to 80 characters long; spaces are allowed, but the first character cannot be a number.

neighbor peer-group

```
neighbor address peer-group peer-group
no neighbor address peer-group peer-group
```

Configures   Assigns a neighbor to a peer group

Default   None

Description

When configuring BGP, you often want to apply the same set of configuration items to a number of BGP neighbors. Peer groups let you simplify the router configuration by making a neighbor a peer group member. Once you have created a peer group, all configuration items for that group apply to all the members of the group. *address* is the IP address of the neighbor to be added to the peer group; *peer-group* is the name of the peer group.

Example

In this example, we create a peer group called group1 and place all our neighbors into this peer group (179.69.232.53, 54, and 55). Having created the peer group, we can apply neighbor filter-list commands to the group as a whole, rather than to the individual neighbors. We still have to configure the unique features (such as remote AS numbers) of the neighbors individually.

```
router bgp 200
  neighbor group1 peer-group
  neighbor group1 filter-list 100 in
  neighbor group1 filter-list 102 out
  neighbor 171.69.232.53 remote-as 300
  neighbor 171.69.232.53 peer-group group1
  neighbor 171.69.232.54 remote-as 400
  neighbor 171.69.232.54 peer-group group1
  neighbor 171.69.232.55 remote-as 500
  neighbor 171.69.232.55 peer-group group1
```

neighbor prefix-list

```
neighbor {address | peer-group} prefix-list prefix-list-name {in | out}
no neighbor {address | peer-group} prefix-list prefix-list-name {in | out}
```

Configures   Assigns a prefix list to a BGP neighbor

Default   None

Description

This command lets you filter BGP routes by assigning a prefix list to a neighbor instead of using an AS path filter.

address or peer-group
    The address or peer group of the neighbor.

prefix-list *prefix-list-name*
    The name of the prefix list defined by the ip as-path access-list command.

in
> The filter applies to incoming routes.

out
> The filter applies to outgoing routes.

---

neighbor remote-as
router, BGP

```
neighbor {address | peer-group} remote-as as-number
no neighbor {address | peer-group} remote-as as-number
```

Configures   The remote AS number of a BGP neighbor

Default   None

Description
This command specifies a neighbor's AS number. This number is used to determine whether the neighbor is an internal or external BGP router. If the neighbor's AS number is the same as the AS number in the current BGP configuration, the neighbor is an internal BGP router; likewise, if the AS numbers are different, the neighbor is an external BGP router.

address or peer-group
> The address or peer group of the neighbor.

as-number
> The AS number of the neighbor router (or the routers in the peer group).

Example
In this example, the neighbor (10.200.200.3) is an internal BGP router because its AS number is the same as the local AS number:

```
router bgp 100
    neighbor 10.200.200.3 remote-as 100
```

In the following example, the neighbor (10.200.200.4) is an external BGP router:

```
router bgp 100
    neighbor 10.200.200.4 remote-as 200
```

---

neighbor route-map
router, BGP

```
neighbor {address | peer-group} route-map map {in | out}
no neighbor {address | peer-group} route-map map {in | out}
```

Configures   Assigns a route map to a BGP neighbor

Default   None

Description
This command assigns a route map to a BGP neighbor. The route map is used to filter or otherwise modify routes that are sent to or received from the neighbor.

---

address or peer-group
> The address or peer group of the neighbor.

map
> The number of the map used to filter the routes.

in
> The map is applied only to incoming routes.

out
> The map is applied only to outgoing routes.

---

neighbor route-reflector-client router, BGP

```
neighbor address route-reflector-client
no neighbor address route-reflector-client
```

Configures   BGP route reflector

Default   None

Description
This command configures the local router as a route reflector; the neighbor at the specified *address* is a client of the route reflector. Route reflectors allow you to get around the rule that all internal BGP speakers (peers) must be fully meshed. A route reflector passes iBGP routes from one router to another without modification.

---

neighbor send-community router, BGP

```
neighbor {address | peer-group} send-community
no neighbor {address | peer-group} send-community
```

Configures   Community attribute

Default   None

Description
This command tells the router to send the COMMUNITIES attribute to BGP neighbors. The neighbors that receive this attribute are identified either by *address* or by *peer-group*.

---

neighbor send-label router, BGP

```
neighbor {address | peer-group} send-label
no neighbor {address | peer-group} send-label
```

Configures   BGP to send MPLS label

Default   None

Description

This command tells the device to send MPLS labels with BGP routes to the specified BGP neighbor.

---

neighbor shutdown
router, BGP

neighbor {*address* | *peer-group*} shutdown
no neighbor {*address* | *peer-group*} shutdown

Configures   Removes a BGP neighbor from the BGP configuration

Default   None

Description

This command disables the neighbor (specified by *address* or *peer-group*) so that it no longer takes part in the BGP routing protocol or exchanges BGP routing information and tables. Use the no form to reenable the BGP neighbor.

---

neighbor soft-reconfiguration inbound
router, BGP

neighbor {*address* | *peer-group*} soft-reconfiguration inbound
no neighbor {*address* | *peer-group*} soft-reconfiguration inbound

Configures   Storage of received updates

Default   None

Description

This command enables the storage of received updates, which is required for an inbound soft reconfiguration.

---

neighbor ttl-security
·BGP

neighbor ip ttl-security hops hop-count
no neighbor ip ttl-security hops hop-count

Configures   Maximum TTL count for eBGP peers

Default   Disabled

Description

This command enables BGP TTL checking for neighbors. This command is only used on external BGP (eBGP) neighbors. It provides a simple security mechanism for protecting your eBGP routers from possible hijacking attempts. By enabling this feature, only packets with TTL counts that are equal to or higher than the given value are accepted as valid packets. (It is generally considered impossible to forge TTL counts without access to the source or destination network.) If the packet's TTL value is *less* than this value, the router discards the packet without generating any ICMP messages. The idea is that we don't want to generate any error messages that might be sent back to a possible hacker.

neighbor timers

router, BGP

```
neighbor {address | peer-group} timers keepalive holdtime
no neighbor {address | peer-group} timers keepalive holdtime
```

Configures   Timer values for BGP routing information

Default   keepalive is 60 seconds; holdtime is 180 seconds

Description
This command allows you to set the timer information for BGP routes. The *keepalive* parameter specifies the frequency (in seconds) that keepalive messages are sent to the specified neighbor (as identified by *address* or *peer-group*). The *holdtime* parameter specifies the interval (in seconds) within which the router expects to hear a keepalive message from the given neighbor or peer group before declaring the peer dead.

neighbor ttl-security

BGP

```
neighbor ip ttl-security hops hop-count
no neighbor ip ttl-security hops hop-count
```

Configures   Maximum TTL count for eBGP peers

Default   Disabled

Description
This command enables BGP TTL checking for neighbors. This command is only used on external BGP (eBGP) neighbors. It provides a simple security mechanism for protecting your eBGP routers from possible hijacking attempts. By enabling this feature, only packets with TTL counts that are equal to or higher than the given value are accepted as valid packets. (It is generally considered impossible to forge TTL counts without access to the source or destination network.) If the packet's TTL value is less than this value, the router discards the packet without generating any ICMP messages. The idea is that we don't want to generate any error messages that might be sent back to a possible hacker.

neighbor update-source

router, BGP

```
neighbor {address | peer-group} update-source interface
no neighbor {address | peer-group} update-source interface
```

Configures   Best interface to reach a neighbor

Default   The closest interface (sometimes called the best local address)

Description

This command tells the router to use a certain interface for a neighbor (as specified by *address* or *peer-group*) rather than the default. Use this command when other routers are peering to your loopback address.

---

neighbor version

router, BGP

```
neighbor {address | peer-group} version value
no neighbor {address | peer-group} version value
```

Configures The BGP version to use for the neighbor

Default Version 4

Description

This command lets you specify which BGP version to use when talking to the given neighbor (as specified by *address* or *peer-group*). The version number must be 2, 3, or 4. Although Version 4 is the default, the router should dynamically negotiate down to Version 2 if the neighbor doesn't support Version 4.

---

neighbor weight

router, BGP

```
neighbor {address | peer-group} weight value
no neighbor {address | peer-group} weight value
```

Configures The weight metric for a BGP neighbor

Default Routes learned from the local router have a weight of 32,768; routes learned from other BGP peers have a weight of 0

Description

This command lets you assign a weight to routes learned from the given neighbor (as specified by *address* or *peer-group*). Routes with a higher weight are chosen first. You can use this command to tell BGP to prefer routes learned from a given neighbor. This is a Cisco proprietary attribute.

Example

In the following configuration, we assign a weight of 100 to routes learned from the neighbor 10.200.200.3. This weighting causes the router to prefer routes learned from 10.200.200.3 to routes learned from other BGP peers.

```
router bgp 200
    neighbor 10.200.200.3 weight 100
```

net

```
net value
no net value
```

Configures   The NET for an IS-IS routing process

Default   None

Description

In order to configure an IS-IS routing process, you need to define a Network Entity Title (NET). Essentially, a NET serves as the area number and the system ID for the routing process. The NET is an NSAP whose last byte is 0.

Example

Let's assume that we have an IS-IS system ID of 0000.0000.0004 and an area ID of 04.0002. This gives us a NET of 04.0002.0000.0000.0004.00, which is the area ID followed by the system ID followed by the ending zero. The following configuration shows how the net command is used to assign the appropriate value:

```
router isis
  net 04.0002.0000.0000.0004.00
  is-type level-1
!
interface ethernet 0
  ip router isis
  ip address 10.1.1.1 255.255.255.0
```

---

network

BGP:

```
network network-number [mask network-mask]
no network network-number [mask network-mask]
```

IGRP/EIGRP/RIP:

```
network network-address
no network network-address
```

OSPF:

```
network network-address wildcard-mask area area-id
no network network-address wildcard-mask area area-id
```

Configures   The network for which the routing process is responsible

Default   None

Description

The network command provides a way to tell the routing process what networks it is responsible for. With IGRP, EIGRP, RIP, and, to a degree, BGP, all you need to do is list the network addresses (one per line) for the routing process. To remove a network from the routing process, use the no form of the command.

In OSPF, the network command requires three parameters: a *network-address*, a *wildcard-mask*, and an *area-id*. You must include the area ID. The wildcard mask specifies the portion of an IP address that isn't part of the network address; for example, a 24-bit mask subnet would use the wildcard mask 0.0.0.255. An interface can be attached only to a single OSPF area. If the address ranges (i.e., address/mask combinations) of two network commands overlap, the OSPF process takes the first match and ignores the rest.

For BGP, the network address is specified using a subnet mask, not a wildcard mask; for example, an 8-bit subnet would use the subnet mask 255.255.255.0. The mask is optional. If it is omitted, a mask of 255.255.255.0 is assumed.

Example

The following commands define a network for RIP and EIGRP routing processes:

```
router rip
   network 10.0.0.0
!
router eigrp
   network 11.0.0.0
```

The following commands configure OSPF with a process ID of 99 and two areas:

```
router ospf 99
   network 10.10.1.0 0.0.0.255 area 0
   network 10.10.2.0 0.0.0.255 area 1
```

---

network backdoor
router, BGP

network *address* backdoor
no network *address* backdoor

Configures   A backdoor route to a BGP border router

Default   None

Description

This command allows you to give a backdoor route to a BGP router. This route acts like a local network but is not advertised.

---

network weight
router, BGP

network *address* *mask* weight *weight* [route-map *map*]
no network *address* *mask* weight *weight* [route-map *map*]

Configures   An absolute weight to a BGP network

Default   None

Description

This command sets the weight for routes to the given network, overriding any weight value learned by other means (redistribution, etc.).

address mask
> The address of a network, specified as an IP address followed by a subnet mask.

weight *weight*
> The weight to be assigned to these routes. It can have any value from to 65,535.

route-map *map*
> A route map to be applied to these routes.

---

nrzi-encoding   interface

```
nrzi-encoding
no nrzi-encoding
```

Configures   T1 encoding type

Default   Disabled (i.e., B8ZS)

Description

This command enables "Nonreturn to Zero Inverted" encoding on T1 lines. The default encoding for T1 lines is B8ZS.

Example

```
interface serial1
    nrzi-encoding
```

---

ntp access-group   global

```
ntp access-group [condition] access-list
no ntp access-group [condition] access-list
```

Configures   Network Time Protocol (NTP) service

Default   None

Description

This command applies an access list to the router's NTP service.

condition
> Optional. Specifies the type of NTP queries to which the access list applies. Valid values are query-only, serve-only, serve, and peer. query-only allows NTP control requests only; serve-only allows time requests only; serve allows time requests and NTP control requests, but does not allow the router to synchronize its time with another NTP peer; peer allows time requests, NTP control requests, and time synchronization with other NTP peers. If this keyword is omitted, the access list applies to all queries.

access-list
> A standard access list to be applied to NTP connections.

ntp authenticate

```
ntp authenticate
no ntp authenticate
```

Configures   Network Time Protocol (NTP) service

Default   No authentication

Description   This command enables NTP authentication on the router.

ntp authentication-key

```
ntp authentication-key number md5 value
no ntp authentication-key number
```

Configures   Network Time Protocol (NTP) service

Default   None

Description

This command defines the authentication key to be used for NTP. Use the no form of this command to delete this key.

number
    A value that identifies this key (1 to 4,294,967,295).

md5 *value*
    The actual key value.

ntp broadcast

```
ntp broadcast
no ntp broadcast
```

Configures   Network Time Protocol (NTP) service

Default   Disabled

Description

This command tells the router to transmit NTP broadcast packets through the interface.

ntp broadcast client

```
ntp broadcast client
no ntp broadcast client
```

Configures   Network Time Protocol (NTP) service

Default   Disabled

Description
This command tells the router to receive NTP broadcast packets through the interface.

---

ntp broadcastdelay   global

ntp broadcastdelay *microseconds*
no ntp broadcastdelay

Configures   Network Time Protocol (NTP) service

Default   None

Description
This command sets the estimated round-trip delay for NTP broadcast packets in microseconds.

---

ntp disable   interface

ntp disable
no ntp disable

Configures   Network Time Protocol (NTP) service

Default   Enabled on all interfaces if NTP is configured

Description   This command disables the interface's ability to receive NTP packets.

---

ntp master   global

ntp master *stratum*
no ntp master *stratum*

Configures   Network Time Protocol (NTP) service

Default   The router is not a master

Description
This command configures the router as the master NTP server from which other NTP peers can receive their NTP time. (See the ntp peer command for setting peer values.) This command should be used with extreme caution, as it can declare the router's clock to be stratum 1 (most accurate) without any safeguards about how accurate the clock really is.

stratum
    The NTP stratum number for this server. The value can be 1 through 15.

ntp peer

```
ntp peer address [version value] [key keyid] [source interface] [prefer]
no ntp peer address
```

Configures   Network Time Protocol (NTP) service

Default   None

Description

This command defines the address of an NTP peer. The router synchronizes its time with the peer's time and attempts to update the peer's time. Notice how a peer is different from a server. If you specify an NTP server with the ntp server command, the router gets its time from the server but does not attempt to update the server's time.

address
> The IP address of the NTP peer.

version *value*
> The NTP version (1 through 3). The default is 3.

key *keyid*
> Authentication key to use for this peer. The ntp authentication-key command defines the keys and their key IDs.

source *interface*
> The interface the router should use to communicate with this peer.

prefer
> Makes this peer preferred over others.

Example

The following command sets an NTP peer at 10.11.1.2, which is available via the ethernet0 interface.

```
ntp peer 10.11.1.2 version 2 source ethernet0
```

ntp server

```
ntp server address [version value] [key keyid] [source interface]
no ntp server address
```

Configures   Network Time Protocol (NTP) service

Default   None

Description

This command tells the router which NTP server to use. The router derives its time from the server but does not try to update the server's time.

address
> The IP address of the NTP peer.

version *value*
> The NTP version (1 through 3). The default is 3.

key *keyid*
> Authentication key to use for this peer. The ntp authentication-key command defines the keys and their key IDs.

source *interface*
> The interface the router should use to communicate with this server.

Example

The following command sets our NTP server to 10.11.1.5:

```
ntp server 10.11.1.5 version 2
```

ntp source   global

```
ntp source interface
no ntp source interface
```

Configures   NTP source interface

Default   The closest interface to the destination

Description

This command allows you to define the interface to be used as the source interface for generating NTP traffic. By default, the router normally uses the interface closest to the destination as the source interface.

ntp trusted-key   global

```
ntp trusted-key keyid
no ntp trusted-key keyid
```

Configures   Network Time Protocol (NTP) service

Default   None

Description

This command sets the authentication key to use to synchronize with the NTP server.

keyid
> The authentication key to use. The ntp authentication-key command defines the keys and their key IDs.

ntp update-calendar   global

```
ntp update-calendar
no ntp update-calendar
```

Configures   Network Time Protocol (NTP) service

Default   Disabled

Description

On high-end routers (7500, 5000, 6000, 1010, 8500, etc.), this command tells the router to update the calendar using NTP. Normally, the calendar is not updated through NTP; only the system clock is updated.

---

offset-list
router

```
offset-list access-list {in | out} value [interface]
no offset-list access-list {in | out} value [interface]
```

Configures   Adds an offset value to incoming or outgoing routing metrics

Default   None

Description

This command allows you to apply an offset to the metric of incoming or outgoing routes.

access-list
> The offset is applied to routes matching this access list (name or number). 0 means all routes.

in or out
> The direction in which to apply the metric offset. in applies the offset to incoming routes; out applies the offset to outgoing routes.

value
> The amount by which route metrics will be increased. The value must be positive; the acceptable range depends on the routing protocol.

interface
> Optional. The offset will be applied only to routes traveling through the given interface.

Example

The following configuration adds an offset of 10 to routes that match access list 1 (i.e., routes with the destination 10.10.1.0) traveling out through the ethernet0 interface:

```
access-list 1 permit 10.10.1.0 0.0.0.255
!
router eigrp 100
  offset-list 1 out 10 ethernet0
  network 10.10.0.0
```

---

ospf auto-cost reference-bandwidth
router

```
ospf auto-cost reference-bandwidth value
no ospf auto-cost reference-bandwidth value
```

Configures   How OSPF calculates default metrics

Default   100 Mb

Description

The default OSPF metric is calculated by dividing the reference bandwidth by the bandwidth of the interface. The default value of the reference bandwidth is $10^{\wedge}8$ or 100,000,000. Using this formula, the OSPF cost for a T1 is 65 (100,000,000/ 1,544,000). This number is also convenient because it causes the cost of an FDDI link or Fast Ethernet to be 1. This command allows you to modify the reference bandwidth to support interfaces that are faster than 100 Mbps.

---

ospf log-adj-changes
router

```
ospf log-adj-changes
no ospf log-adj-changes
```

Configures   OSPF state change logging

Default   None

Description
This command enables syslog logging of changes in the state of neighbor routers.

---

output-delay
router

```
output-delay value
no output-delay value
```

Configures   Delay between packets in a multipacket route update

Default   0 (no delay)

Description
This command modifies the interpacket delay during RIP updates. *value* specifies the delay in milliseconds between consecutive packets in a multipacket update. A delay is useful when a fast router needs to communicate with a slower one, as it allows the slower router to catch up.

Example
This example sets the output delay of multipacket router updates to 5 milliseconds:

```
router rip
  network 10.10.0.0
  output-delay 5
```

---

padding
line

```
padding ascii-number count
no padding ascii-number
```

Configures   Pads a specific character with NULLs

Default   No padding

Description

This command pads a specific output character with NULL characters. It supports older terminals that require padding after certain characters, such as the Return key. Unless you are using a terminal that requires padding, you will never need this command.

ascii-number
> The decimal value of the character that needs padding.

count
> The number of NULL bytes to send after this character.

---

parity   line

parity {none | even | odd | space | mark}
no parity

Configures   Parity

Default   None

Description

This command defines the parity bit for an asynchronous serial line. Its value may be none, even, odd, space, or mark.

Example

```
Router(config)#line tty 2
Router(config)#parity none
```

---

passive-interface   router

passive-interface *interface*
no passive-interface *interface*

Configures   Disables a routing protocol on a specific interface either partially (RIP, IGRP) or completely (EIGRP, OSPF, etc.)

Default   None

Description

For RIP and IGRP, this command causes the specified *interface* to listen for routing updates but prevents it from sending them. For OSPF, EIGRP, or other "hello-based" routing protocols, this command effectively disables the protocol on that interface (both sending and receiving). These protocols cannot operate without exchanging hello messages.

Example

```
router igrp 100
  network 10.0.0.0
  ! Suppress routing advertisements on serial 1
  passive-interface serial 1
```

---

password   line

```
password value
no password value
```

Configures   A login password for the line

Default   No password

Description

This command allows you to assign a password to any available line. Most lines must also be configured with the login command.

Example

The following example sets the login password to *cisco* for the console and the five VTY lines.

```
! First the console
line con 0
 password cisco
 login
! And the five virtual terminals (for incoming telnets)
line vty 0 5
 password cisco
 login
```

---

peer default ip address   interface

```
peer default ip {address address | dhcp | pool pool}
no peer default ip {address address | dhcp | pool pool}
```

Configures   Address assignment for PPP or SLIP peers

Default   pool

Description

This command allows you to assign an IP address to peers that connect to this interface using PPP or SLIP. There are three ways in which an *address* can be assigned: you can specify a single address to be used whenever a peer connects to this interface; you can specify an address *pool* from which an address is taken; or you can specify that the router should obtain an address for the peer through dhcp. This command overrides the global setting for the default IP address selection.

async-bootp can also be used to provided addresses to dial-up clients.

peer neighbor-route

```
peer neighbor-route
no peer neighbor-route
```

Configures   Generation of neighbor routes for incoming PPP connections

Default   Enabled

Description

The generation of a neighbor route for a new PPP connection is enabled by default. The no form of this command disables that behavior.

physical-layer

```
physical-layer {sync | async}
no physical-layer {sync | async}
```

Configures   Whether the interface is synchronous or asynchronous

Default   sync

Description

This command lets you specify whether a serial interface is synchronous or asynchronous. It is available on low-speed serial interfaces.

ping

```
ping
ping host
```

Description

The ping command sends a sequence of ICMP echo request packets to the specified *host*. It is one of the simplest and most commonly used troubleshooting tools. If you omit the host from the command line and are in privileged EXEC mode, the router prompts you for the rest of the information.

Ping prints a special character for each packet indicating whether the router received the corresponding echo reply. Table 17-15 shows what these special characters mean. Ping also summarizes the success rate and the round-trip times.

Table 17-15. Ping success codes

Character	Meaning
!	Ping successful
.	Timed out waiting for reply
?	Unknown packet
&	TTL of packet was exceeded
A	Access list denied packet

Table 17-15. Ping success codes (continued)

Character	Meaning
C	Network congestion
I	User interrupt (if you hit CTRL+^)
U	Destination unreachable

Example

```
Router# ping 10.10.1.2
Type escape sequence to abort.
Sending 5, 100-byte ICMP Echos to 10.10.1.2, timeout is 2 seconds:
!!!!!
Success rate is 100 percent (5/5), round-trip min/avg/max = 1/3/4 ms
```

police

policy-map

police *bps* [*burst-normal*] [*burst-max*] conform-action *action* exceed-action
   action [violate-action *action*]

no police *bps* [*burst-normal*] [*burst-max*] conform-action *action* exceed-action
   action [violate-action *action*]

Configures   Traffic policing

Default   Disabled

Description

This command configures traffic policing within a map class. By defining the average bit rate (*bps*) and a normal and maximum burst rates, you can define actions for packets that conform to, exceed, or violate those rates.

bps

Defines the average rate in bits per second (bps). The value must be defined in increments of 8 Kbps. The value can be from 8,000 to 2,000,000,000.

burst-normal

Normal burst size in bytes. This value can be from 1,000 to 512,000,000. Default normal burst size is 1,500 bytes.

burst-max

Excess burst-size in bytes. This value can be from 1,000 to 512,000,000.

conform-action

The action to take on packets that conform to the rate limit (see Table 17-16).

exceed-action

The action to take on packets that exceed the rate limit (see Table 17-16).

violate-action

Optional. The action to take on packets that violate the normal and maximum burst sizes (see Table 17-16).

Table 17-16. Traffic policing actions

Action	Meaning
drop	Drop the packet
set-discard-class-transmit	Set the DSCP discard class value and transmit the packet
set-dscp-transmit	Set the DSCP value and transmit the packet
set-frde-transmit	Set the Frame Relay Discard Eligibility bit and transmit the packet
set-mpls-exp-imposition-transmit	Set the MPLS experimental bits and transmit the packet
set-mpls-exp-topmost-transmit	Set the MPLS experimental bits and transmit the packet
set-prec-transmit	Set the IP precedence (0 to 7) and transmit the packet
set-qos-transmit	Set the QoS group ID (1 to 99) and transmit the packet
transmit	Transmit the packet

See Chapter 11 for more details.

policy-map   global

```
policy-map name
no policy-map name
```

Configures   A policy map for QoS

Default   None

Description
This command allows you to create a policy map that can be attached to one or more interfaces. See Chapter 11 for examples of using and creating policy maps.

ppp   command

```
ppp
```

Description
This command is given by a user who wants to establish a PPP session after connecting to one of the router's interfaces (for example, a dial-up serial interface) and logging in using some kind of terminal emulation. Giving this command at the user EXEC command prompt establishes the PPP connection.

ppp authentication   interface

```
ppp authentication {chap | pap} [if-needed] [list] [callin]
no ppp authentication
```

Configures   Enables CHAP or PAP authentication

Default   No authentication

Description
This command enables CHAP or PAP authentication on interfaces. In addition to the type of authentication, this command may have the following parameters:

if-needed
> Optional. Prevents reauthorization if the user has already been authorized at some other point during the session.

list
> Optional. Provides a list of AAA authorization methods. To set up an authorization list, use the command aaa authentication ppp.

callin
> Optional. Tells the interface to authorize incoming (dial-in) connections only.

---

ppp bridge ip
interface

```
ppp bridge ip
no ppp bridge ip
```

Configures   Bridging a PPP connection

Default   Disabled

Description
This command enables half-bridging of IP packets across a serial or ISDN interface.

---

ppp chap
interface

```
ppp chap password password
no ppp chap password password
```

Configures   CHAP authentication

Default   Disabled

Description
This command configures a single *password* for PPP authentication using the CHAP protocol.

---

ppp compress
interface

```
ppp compress {predictor | stac}
no ppp compress {predictor | stac}
```

Configures   Compression

Default   None

Description

This command enables compression for the PPP connection. For compression to work, both ends of the PPP connection must be configured to use the same type of compression.

---

ppp multilink interface

```
ppp multilink
no ppp multilink
```

Configures   Multilink PPP (MLP) over multiple interfaces

Default   Disabled

Description

If you have two or more communications links between the router and the destination, you can use multilink PPP to send traffic over several interfaces in parallel to get higher throughput. Asynchronous serial interfaces, ISDN BRI interfaces, and ISDN PRI interfaces can make use of multilink PPP. Multilink PPP works best on digital lines such as ISDN; it is less effective on low-speed analog connections.

---

ppp quality interface

```
ppp quality percentage
no ppp quality percentage
```

Configures   Quality monitoring

Default   Disabled

Description

This command enables link quality monitoring. Once enabled, the PPP link is shut down if the quality degrades below a certain value. The value, commonly thought of as a *percentage*, is expressed as a number between 1 and 100, with 100 indicating the highest quality.

---

ppp reliable-link interface

```
ppp reliable-link
no ppp reliable-link
```

Configures   LAPB numbered mode negotiation

Default   Disabled

Description

This command enables LAPB numbered mode negotiation, which means that the router will try to negotiate a reliable link, not necessarily build a reliable link. This command is not available on asynchronous interfaces and doesn't work with multilink.

---

ppp use-tacacs
interface

```
ppp use-tacacs
no ppp use-tacacs
```

Configures   TACACS authentication for PPP

Default   Disabled

Description   This command enables the use of TACACS for PPP authentication.

priority-group
interface

```
priority-group list
no priority-group
```

Configures   A priority list for the interface

Default   None

Description
This command applies a priority list to an interface. See the priority-list command for information on constructing priority lists.

Example
The following commands apply priority list 1 to the serial0 interface:

```
interface serial0
  priority-group 1
```

priority-list
global

```
priority-list number default level
no priority-list number default level


priority-list number protocol value level port-type port
no priority-list number protocol value level port-type port


priority-list number queue-limit high-limit medium-limit normal-limit low-limit
no priority-list number queue-limit
```

Configures   Priority lists for priority traffic queuing

Default   None

Description

The priority-list command is a set of three related commands that are used to construct a list. A priority list is a set of four queues, one for each of four priority *levels*: high, medium, normal, and low. Each queue has its own capacity (in packets); the queue sizes are set using priority-list queue-limit, although I recommend that you don't modify the default queue sizes. The priority-list protocol version of the command assigns packets to a queue based on their protocols and, optionally, their ports. The priority-queue default command assigns a queue to all packets that aren't explicitly assigned to a queue (i.e., all packets not associated with a protocol and port specified with the priority-list protocol command).

Once you have created a priority list, use the priority-group command to apply a priority list to an interface. The queues in the list are then used for all traffic going out the interface. The parameters for these commands are:

number
> The number of the priority list you are configuring; it can be a value from 1 to 10.

protocol *value*
> The protocol to prioritize. In mixed-protocol environments, the protocol can be ip, ipx, etc. The examples here all use IP.

level
> The queue you are configuring: low, medium, normal, or high.

port-type
> Either tcp or udp.

port
> A port number.

high-limit, medium-limit, normal-limit, low-limit
> When configuring queue sizes, the number of packets in the high, medium, normal, and low priority queues. The default number of packets for each queue is given in Table 17-17.

Table 17-17. Default sizes for queues in a priority list

Queue	Default size
low	80 packets
normal	60 packets
medium	40 packets
high	20 packets

Example

The following example creates priority list 1, which sends all IP packets to the medium priority queue. Next, all telnet packets (TCP packets with a destination port of 23) are assigned to the high priority queue. Finally, all other traffic (non–IP traffic) is assigned to the normal priority queue:

```
priority-list 1 protocol ip medium
priority-list 1 protocol ip high tcp 23
priority-list 1 default normal
```

The next example changes the size of the queues in the priority list:

```
priority-list 1 queue-list 30 20 15 10
```

---

privilege level (global)

```
privilege mode level level command
no privilege mode level level command
```

Configures   Privilege level information

Default

Level 1 consists of all user EXEC commands; Level 15 consists of all enable commands

Description

The privilege level commands allow you to control access to a set of commands. The first of these commands, where you supply a mode and a command name, is used to set up a privilege level: a group of commands protected by a password. This is a global command—it is used outside of any context. Passwords for privilege levels are defined with the enable password command.

mode

> The configuration mode to which the command belongs. exec is most common; configuration, controller, hub, interface, ipx-router, line, map-class, map-list, route-map, and router are also used.

level

> A number from 0 to 15 indicating the level to which you're assigning the command. Each level is a superset of the previous levels; for example, level 13 automatically includes all the commands for levels 0 through 12.

command

> The command that you are assigning to a level.

Example

The first command in the following configuration assigns the clear command to privilege level 14. The password guessme is assigned to privilege level 14, requiring users to give this password before they can execute any of the clear commands. Since the other enable commands are assigned to level 15, users who know this password are not necessarily allowed to make general changes to the router's configuration; without the enable password, they can give only the clear commands (and any other commands that belong to level 14).

Next, we make privilege level 14 the default privilege level for the aux 0 port. This means that anyone who can access the aux 0 port and knows the password guessme can give the clear command and any other level 14 commands defined.

```
! assign the clear command to level 14
privilege exec level 14 clear
! set the password for level 14 to guessme
enable password level 14 guessme
!
! configure the default level for the aux port
line aux 0
  privilege level 14
```

privilege level (line)

line

privilege level *level*
no privilege level

Configures   Privilege level information

Default

Level 1 consists of all user EXEC commands; Level 15 consists of all enable commands

Description

This form of the privilege command applies a privilege level to a line, and therefore must be used in the context of line configuration. Applying a privilege level to a line means that the given privilege level becomes the default level for the line; anyone who can access the line can run the commands in the default privilege level without giving the enable password. See also privilege level (global).

level
> A number from 1 to 15 indicating the level to which you're assigning the command. Each level is a superset of the previous levels; for example, level 13 automatically includes all the commands for levels 1 through 12.

prompt

global

prompt *string*
no prompt *string*

Configures   The router prompt

Default   %h%p

Description

This command sets the prompt to the specified string. The string can have any combination of characters and escape sequences. The special characters are listed in Table 17-18. Use the no form of this command to set the system prompt to the default value.

Table 17-18. Escape sequences for the router prompt

Escape sequence	Meaning
%%	Percent character
%h	Hostname of the router
%n	TTY number for this EXEC session
%p	The prompt character; either > for user level or # for privileged level
%s	Space character
%t	Tab character

pulse-time
interface

```
pulse-time seconds
no pulse-time seconds
```

Configures   The DTR signal pulse intervals

Default   0 seconds

Description
This command sets the interval between the DTR pulsing signals, in seconds. When a line goes down, the DTR is held inactive for the duration of the pulse-time.

---

pvc
interface

```
pvc [name] vpi/vci [encap]
no pvc [name] vpi/vci [encap]
```

Configures   ATM PVC

Default   None

Description
This command configures a Permanent Virtual Circuit (PVC) on an ATM interface. It isn't supported on all ATM hardware; more sophisticated ATM hardware tends to use the atm pvc command.

name
> Optional. A name to be assigned to this PVC.

vpi/vci
> The Virtual Path Identifier and the Virtual Channel Identifier, separated by a slash. If you omit the slash and the *vci*, it defaults to 0. If *vci* is 0, *vpi* cannot be 0, and vice versa.

encap
> Optional. The type of encapsulation to use on the channel. Possible values are ilmi, qsaal, and smds. ilmi is used to set up a connection for the Integrated Local Management Interface, and is normally used with the VPI/VCI pair 0/16. qsaal sets up a PVC used for setting up and tearing down SVCs (switched virtual circuits), and is normally used with the VPI/VCI pair 0/5. smds is used only for SMDS networks.

---

qos pre-classify
interface

```
qos pre-classify
no qos pre-classify
```

Configures   QoS

Default   Disabled

Description

This command enables QoS (Quality of Service) preclassification and is restricted to tunnel interfaces, virtual templates, and crypto maps. Applies only to IP packets.

---

queue-limit

policy-map class

```
queue-limit size-in-packets
no queue-limit size-in-packets
```

Configures   The DTR signal pulse intervals

Default   64 packets on most platforms

Description

This command allows you to override the default queue size for a class. In WFQ (Weighted Fair Queuing), a queue is created for every class that is defined. If a queue is filled, tail-drop is used for further incoming packets unless WRED is configured (Weighted Random Early Detection). The default of 64 applies on all platforms except those with Versatile Interface Processors (VIPs), where the default is a calculation of bandwidth and buffer memory available.

---

queue-list

global

```
queue-list number protocol value queue-number [port-type port-number]
queue-list number protocol value queue-number [list list-number]
queue-list number interface interface queue-number
queue-list number queue-number byte-count size-in-bytes
queue-list number queue queue-number limit size-in-packets
queue-list number default queue-number
no queue-list number
```

Configures   Custom queuing

Default   None

Description

The queue-list commands define a custom queue list, which is a group of queues that can be used to configure the amount of bandwidth used by specific types of traffic. A custom queue is different from a priority queue in that a priority queue only allows you to set the relative priority of different traffic types. The queue-list byte-count command creates queues within the list and assigns each queue a transmission size. The default transmission size is 1,500 bytes. The queue-list queue command specifies the absolute size of a queue, in packets. The queue-list protocol command assigns traffic for a given protocol and port to one of the queues in a queue list; instead of specifying a protocol and port, you can specify an IP access list. The queue-list interface command assigns traffic arriving for a given interface to one of the queues; and the queue-list default command assigns all otherwise unassigned traffic to one of the queues.

To use a queue list, it must be applied to an interface using the custom-queue-list command.

When sending traffic out an interface, the router works through the queues in order, emptying each queue before moving to the next. Therefore, increasing the size of a queue increases the bandwidth that can be used by the traffic assigned to the queue.

When assigning traffic to a queue, the router processes the queue-list statements in order.

number
> A number identifying the queue list; it can be from 1 to 10.

protocol *value*
> Specifies the protocol to be assigned to the queue. Valid protocols are ip, ipx, dlsw, etc.

interface *interface*
> Used for establishing queuing priorities based on incoming interface for the packet.

queue-number
> The queue within this list that is being described.

port-type port-number
> A port type (tcp or udp) and port number; traffic for this port is assigned to a particular queue within the list. You can specify either a port number, or the name of a well-known port.

list *list-number*
> An access list of an appropriate type for the given protocol. Traffic matching this access list is assigned to the specified queue.

byte-count *size-in-bytes*
> Specifies the queue's transmission size, in bytes. The router works through the list of queues in order, taking *size-in-bytes* bytes of traffic from each queue before proceeding to the next. Therefore, a larger queue size assigns more bandwidth to the protocols that are routed through this queue.

limit *size-in-packets*
> An absolute maximum for the number of packets that can be waiting in the queue. Packets in excess of this limit are discarded. The default limit is 20 packets.

Example

The following commands create a custom queue list (list 5) and apply that queue list to the serial0 interface, where it is used to prioritize the traffic sent out that interface. The queue list consists of four queues with transmission sizes of 1,000, 4,000, 5,000, and 4,000 bytes. Therefore, queue 3 within the list is the highest priority and is allocated the most bandwidth; queue 1 is the lowest priority. Traffic is assigned to the queues as follows:

- Telnet traffic is assigned to queue 1 (low priority)
- Traffic that matches access list 10 (not shown) is assigned to queue 2 (moderate priority)
- Traffic arriving on the interface tunnel1 is assigned to queue 3 (high priority)
- Otherwise-unassigned IP traffic is assigned to queue 4 (moderate priority)
- All remaining traffic (i.e., non-IP traffic) is assigned to queue 4 (moderate priority)

Note that the queue list is processed in order. Therefore, adding another traffic assignment statement after the `queue-list default` statement has no effect.

The effect of this queue is to transmit 1,000 bytes from queue 1, then 4,000 from queue 2, then 5,000 from queue 3, then 4,000 from queue 4, and so on, in round-robin fashion. Even though queue 1 has the lowest priority, it is guaranteed some bandwidth during each queue-processing cycle. In this respect, a custom queue is unlike a priority queue, which always sends the highest-priority packets first and may therefore starve low-priority traffic.

```
interface serial0
  ! apply the custom queue list
  custom-queue-list 5
!
! Define the custom queue list
queue-list 5 protocol ip 1 tcp telnet
queue-list 5 protocol ip 2 list 10
queue-list 5 interface tunnel1 3
queue-list 5 protocol ip 4
queue-list 5 default 4
queue-list 5 queue 1 byte-count 1000
queue-list 5 queue 2 byte-count 4000
queue-list 5 queue 3 byte-count 5000
queue-list 5 queue 4 byte-count 4000
```

radius-server   global

```
radius-server host {hostname | ip-address}
no radius-server host {hostname | ip-address}

radius-server key string
no radius-server key string

radius-server retransmit retries
no radius-server retransmit retries

radius-server timeout seconds
no radius-server timeout seconds
```

Configures   Radius server

Default   None

Description

This set of commands is used to specify a radius server that the router will use for authentication. The `radius-server host` command allows you to specify which radius server to use, either by hostname or IP address. You can define more than one radius server; the router attempts to contact the servers in the order that you specify.

The radius-server key command specifies the encryption string to be used for communication with the radius server. Obviously, this string must match the setting on the radius server. If you use multiple servers, they must all share the same key.

The retransmit and timeout forms of this command specify the number of times the router searches the list of radius servers before giving up, and the amount of time that it will wait for any given server to reply before retrying.

---

random-detect
interface

```
random-detect [dscp-based | prec-based]
no random-detect number
```

Configures   Weighted Random Early Detection (WRED)

Default   Disabled

Description
This command enables WRED on an interface. The options dscp-based and prec-based tell WRED which packet characteristic to use to calculate drop probability. If you don't select either one, the default is used (IP precedence).

dscp-based

>   Optional. Tells WRED to use the packet's DSCP value to calculate drop probability.

prec-based

>   Optional/Default. Tells WRED to use the packet's IP precedence value to calculate drop probability.

---

random-detect discard-class
policy-map

```
random-detect discard-class class-value min-threshold max-threshold mark-
  denominator
no random-detect discard-class class-value min-threshold max-threshold
  mark-denominator
```

Configures   Weighted Random Early Detection (WRED)

Default   None

Description
This command defines the packet thresholds based on the discard class value of a packet.

class-value

>   The discard class value, from 0 to 7.

min-threshold

>   The minimum threshold in number of packets, from 1 to 4,096. If the minimum threshold is reached, WRED randomly drops some packets with the specified IP precedence.

max-threshold

The maximum threshold in number of packets, from 1 to 4,096. When the threshold is reached, WRED drops all packets with the specified IP precedence.

mark-denominator

Denominator for the fraction of packets dropped when the average queue depth is at the maximum threshold. The default is 10, which means that 1 out of every 10 packets is dropped at the maximum threshold.

---

random-detect discard-class-based
policy-map

```
random-detect discard-class-based
no random-detect discard-class-based
```

Configures   Weighted Random Early Detection (WRED)

Default   None

Description

This command configures WRED to work based on the discard class of packets.

---

random-detect dscp
policy-map

```
random-detect dscp dscp-value min-threshold max-threshold mark-denominator
no random-detect dscp dscp-value min-threshold max-threshold mark-denominator
```

Configures   Weighted Random Early Detection (WRED)

Default   None

Description

This command defines the packet thresholds based on the distributed services code point (DSCP) class value of a packet.

dscp-value

The DSCP value, from 0 to 7.

min-threshold

The minimum threshold in number of packets, from 1 to 4,096. If the minimum threshold is reached, WRED randomly drops some packets with the specified IP precedence.

max-threshold

The maximum threshold in number of packets, from 1 to 4,096. When the threshold is reached, WRED drops all packets with the specified IP precedence.

mark-denominator

Denominator for the fraction of packets dropped when the average queue depth is at the maximum threshold. The default is 10, which means that 1 out of every 10 packets is dropped at the maximum threshold.

---

random-detect ecn

policy-map

```
random-detect ecn
no random-detect ecn
```

Configures   Weighted Random Early Detection (WRED)

Default   Disabled

Description   This command enables explicit congestion notification (ECN).

random-detect exponential-weighting-constant

interface

```
random-detect exponential-weighting-constant value
no random-detect exponential-weighting-constant
```

Configures   Weighted Random Early Detection (WRED)

Default   9

Description

This command allows you to change the value of the exponential weight factor, which is used in the average queue size calculation, from 1 to 16.

random-detect flow

interface

```
random-detect flow
no random-detect flow
random-detect flow average-depth-factor scaling-factor
no random-detect flow average-depth-factor scaling-factor
random-detect flow count number
no random-detect flow count number
```

Configures   Weighted Random Early Detection (WRED)

Default   Disabled

Description

The command random-detect flow enables flow-based WRED on an interface. To configure the characteristics of flow-based WRED, use the average-depth-factor and flow-count commands.

random-detect flow average-depth-factor configures the multiplier used in determining the average depth factor for flow-based WRED. The scaling-factor can be a value from 1 to 16. The default is 4.

random-detect flow count configures the flow count for flow-based WRED. The number can be from 16 to 32,768. The default is 256.

rate-limit interface

```
rate-limit {input | output} { bps | access-group acl | [rate-limit]
    rate-limit-acl] dscp dscp-value | qos-group qos-group-number} burst-normal
    burst-max conform-action action exceed-action action
no rate-limit {input | output} { bps | access-group acl | [rate-limit]
    rate-limit-acl] dscp dscp-value | qos-group qos-group-number} burst-normal
    burst-max conform-action action exceed-action action
```

Configures   Committed Access Rate (CAR)

Default   Disabled

Description

This command configures a CAR (Committed Access Rate) policy on an interface. Multiple policies can be implemented on a single interface by repeating this command.

input

> Applies the CAR policy to incoming packets on this interface.

output

> Applies the CAR policy to outgoing packets on this interface.

bps

> Defines the average rate in bits per second (bps). The value must be defined in increments of 8 Kbps and can be from 8,000 to 2,000,000,000.

access-group

> Optional. Applies this CAR policy to the specified access list. Value can be 1 to 2,699.

rate-limit

> Optional. Sets the access-list as a rate-limit access-list. The value can be from 0 to 99.

dscp

> Optional. Applies the rate limit to packets that match this DSCP value. The value can be from 0 to 63.

qos-group

> Optional. Applies the rate limit to any packet that matches the qos-group number. The value can be from 0 to 99.

burst-normal

> Normal burst size in bytes. The minimum is the bps value divided by 2,000. This value can be from 1,000 to 512,000,000.

burst-max

> Excess burst size in bytes. The number can be from 2,000 to 1,024,000,000. Cisco recommends a value of twice the normal burst.

conform-action

> The action to take on packets that conform to the rate limit (see Table 17-19 for valid actions).

exceed-action

> The action to take on packets that exceed the rate limit (see Table 17-19).

Table 17-19. Rate limit actions

Action	Meaning
continue	Evaluate the next rate-limit command on this interface
drop	Drop the packet
set-dscp-continue	Set the DSCP value and evaluate the next rate-limit command
set-dscp-transmit	Set the DSCP value and transmit the packet
set-mpls-exp-imposition-continue	Set the MPLS experimental bits and evaluate the next rate-limit command on the interface
set-mpls-exp-imposition-transmit	Set the MPLS experimental bits and transmit the packet
set-prec-continue	Set the IP precedence (0 to 7) and evaluate next rate-limit command on the interface
set-prec-transmit	Set the IP precedence (0 to 7) and transmit the packet
set-qos-continue	Set the QoS group ID (1 to 99) and evaluate next rate-limit command on the interface
set-qos-transmit	Set the QoS group ID (1 to 99) and transmit the packet
transmit	Transmit the packet

See Chapter 11 for more details.

redistribute

router

```
redistribute {protocol | static} [metric value] [metric-type type] [route-map
    map] [weight weight] [subnets]
no redistribute protocol
```

Configures   Redistribution of routes between protocols

Default   Disabled

Description

This command allows you to redistribute routes from one routing protocol to another.
It also allows you to redistribute static routes into a routing protocol. Some protocols
require you to specify a default metric that will be assigned to external routes. See the
default-metric command and Chapters 8 and 9 for more information.

protocol

This is the protocol from which routes are redistributed. If a process ID or local
AS is required for the protocol, you must provide that as well. Possible values are
bgp, igrp, eigrp, isis, ospf, and rip. You can also redistribute static routes.

metric value

Optional. This keyword sets the metric value for the redistributed route. If you
don't have a value defined here, the router uses the default metric as defined in
the default-metric command. For most redistribution, you must define a default
metric. Exceptions to this rule are static routes and IGRP to EIGRP redistribution.

`metric-type` *type*

> Optional. This keyword applies to OSPF and IS-IS only. For OSPF, this allows you to assign two possible metric type values: 1 (Type 1 external route) and 2 (Type 2 external route). The default type for OSPF is Type 2. For IS-IS, the options are `internal` (the metric is less than 63) and `external` (the metric is greater than 63 but less than 128). The default metric type for IS-IS is `internal`.

`route-map` *map*

> Optional. This keyword allows you to apply a route-map filter to the routes before they are redistributed into the protocol.

`weight` *weight*

> Optional. This keyword is for BGP only; it allows you to assign a BGP weight to the redistributed route.

`subnets`

> Optional. Used for redistributing routes into OSPF. When this keyword is used, it causes OSPF to accept all subnet routes. Without this keyword, OSPF only redistributes routes that are not subnets.

Example

The following example shows redistribution into OSPF of both EIGRP and RIP routes. For EIGRP, we are redistributing routes from `eigrp 1001` and assigning a metric of 100. The subnets keyword tells OSPF to redistribute all subnet routes. As for RIP, we are assigning a much higher metric of 200 to its routes.

```
router ospf 1000
    redistribute eigrp 1001 metric 100 subnets
    redistribute rip metric 200 subnets
```

When you don't use the `metric` command in the redistribute line, you must have a `default-metric` statement defined (except for static route redistribution).

```
router rip
    redistribute eigrp 1002
    default-metric 10
```

---

refuse-message   line

`refuse-message` *delimiter message delimiter*

`no refuse-message`

Configures   The message the user receives when a connection is busy.

Default   None

Description

This command defines the *message* that is displayed when the user attempts to connect a line that is already in use. *delimiter* is a character that marks the beginning and end of the message; it must not appear within the message itself.

Example

In this example, the user is told that the line is busy and to try another one:

```
line 1
  refuse-message # This line is currently busy, please try lines 2-8 #
```

To disable this message, delete it with the no form of this command:

```
line 1
  no refuse-message
```

---

reload

command

```
reload [warm] [in hh:mm] [at hh:mm [month day] [cancel] [text]
show reload
```

Description

This command causes the router to reload the IOS operating system and reboot. You can specify a time for the reload to occur by using the in and at options. The show version of the command gives you the status of any pending reloads.

text
> The reason for the reload; this reason is stored in memory and is used for a show reload command, sending warning messages, or sending messages to syslog servers.

in *hh:mm*
> Tells the router to reload some time from now. For example, to start a reload in two hours, enter in 2:00.

at *hh:mm month day*
> Tells the router to reload at a specific time (*hh:mm*). Optionally, you can specify a month and a day of the month, but the reboot must occur within 24 days.

cancel
> Cancels a scheduled reload.

warm
> This keyword was added in IOS 12.3(2). It allows the user to reload the router without reloading the IOS images. Since the image software is not reloaded, boot time is significantly decreased.

This command can be helpful when you are configuring a router remotely. One problem with working remotely is that if you make a mistake, you can kill your connection to the router, which may leave the router in a state that doesn't allow you to reconnect. Use this command before executing "dangerous" configuration commands remotely. If you make a mistake and haven't saved the configuration, the router will reboot and return to the previous configuration. If you don't make a mistake and your changes work, you can simply cancel the impending reload.

Example

```
Router#reload in 2:00 "IOS upgrade"
Router#reload cancel
Router#show reload
No reload is scheduled.
```

rename
command

```
rename current-name new-name
```

Description
This command allows you to rename a file from *current-name* to *new-name* in a Class C filesystem.

---

ring-speed
interface

```
ring-speed {4 | 16}
no ring-speed {4 | 16}
```

Configures   Token ring interface default speed

Default   16 Mbps

Description
This command sets the speed for a token ring interface to either 4 or 16 Mbps. The default speed is 16 Mbps. Be sure to set the correct speed; specifying an incorrect speed on a token ring interface will cause the ring to go down.

---

rlogin
command

```
rlogin hostname
```

Description
This command allows you to log into the remote machine given by *hostname*. You can specify either a hostname or an IP address. rlogin stands for remote login, which follows the remote shell rules. If this command doesn't work, try telnet.

---

rmdir
command

```
rmdir directory
```

Description
This command allows you to remove a directory from a Class C filesystem.

---

route-map
global

```
route-map tag-name [permit | deny] [sequence-number]
no route-map tag-name [permit | deny] [sequence-number]
```

Configures   A route map for route redistribution or policy routing

Default   None

Description

A route map is a very flexible mechanism for specifying what to do with routes. A route map lets you match certain routes and set various parameters of the matching routes. The route-map command merely defines the list; the match command specifies which routes the map should match (something like an access list); and a number of set commands specify what to do with the matching routes.

A route map is identified by a name (*tag-name*); any number of route-map commands can share the same name. route-map commands with the same name are processed in the order given by the *sequence-number*. Although most route processing is specified by the set commands associated with the map, the permit and deny keywords can be used to specify some very simple processing. permit is the default; it means that normal route processing (as specified by the set commands) takes place for all routes that match the map.

Processing continues with other route maps that share the same sequence number. The deny keyword specifies that if a match occurs, the route is not distributed and no further processing of other route maps takes place.

To delete a route map, use the no form of the command. Note that if you omit the *sequence-number*, this command deletes all maps matching the given *tag-name*.

tag-name
> An identifying name.

permit
> Optional. Specifies that normal route processing should occur when a route matches the map.

deny
> Optional. Specifies that routes matching the map should not be propagated and that no further processing should occur.

sequence-number
> A sequence number that indicates the order in which route maps sharing the same name are processed.

Example

The following commands define a route map named check with a sequence number of 10. The match command selects the routes that match the map; it refers to community list 1, which specifies routes that include community 100. The set command sets the weight of any route matching this community list to 10.

```
route-map check permit 10
  match community 1
  set weight 10

ip community-list 1 permit 100
```

router

RIP:

router rip

no router rip

BGP:

router bgp *as-number*

no router bgp *as-number*

EIGRP:

router eigrp *as-system*

no router eigrp *as-system*

IGRP:

router igrp *as-system*

no router igrp *as-system*

IS-IS:

router isis [tag]

no router isis [tag]

OSPF:

router ospf *as-system*

no router ospf *as-system*

Configures   Enters the routing configuration mode

Default   None

Description
This command starts the configuration of a routing process: it identifies the routing protocol you want to run and other parameters necessary for the routing protocol. The RIP protocol doesn't require additional parameters; BGP requires an AS number; EIGRP, IGRP, and OSPF require process numbers (commonly called AS numbers); and IS-IS can optionally have a tag that defines a name for the routing process.

Example
```
! Configure our rip process
router rip
    network 10.0.0.0
```

rsh

rsh *host* [/user *username*] *command-to-execute*

Description
This command executes a command on a remote host via a remote shell.

host
> The hostname of the machine on which to execute the command.

/user *username*
> The username to use when executing the command.

command-to-execute
> The command to be executed.

Example

The following command executes the command ls on a machine named sun-machine as user bob.

```
rsh sun-machine /user bob ls
```

---

rxspeed

rxspeed *speed*
no rxspeed

Configures   Receive speed

Default   9,600 bps

Description

This command sets the receive speed for this line to *speed*, in bits per second.

---

send

send {*line-number* | * | aux *n* | console *n* | tty *n* | vty *n*} *message*

Description

This command sends a message immediately to one or more terminals. It is not stored in the router's configuration.

line-number
> The line number to which to send the message.

*
> Sends the message to all TTY lines.

aux *n*
> The AUX port to which to send the message.

tty *n*
> The TTY port to which to send the message.

vty *n*
> The VTY port to which to send the message.

console *n*
> The console line to which to send the message.

message
> The message you wish to send. It may span multiple lines, and must be terminated with Ctrl-Z on a line by itself.

Example

The following commands send a message to all TTY lines:

```
Routersend *
Enter message, end with CTRL/Z; abort with CTRL/C:
REBOOTING Router in ten minutes for an emergency repair!
^Z
Send message? [confirm]y
Router

***
***
*** Message from tty19 to all terminals:
***
REBOOTING router in ten minutes for an emergency repair!
```

---

service

```
service service
no service service
```

Configures   Service level items

Default   Depends on the service

Description

The service command disables or enables certain router features. These features range from minor TCP/IP servers to the router's callback behavior. The services controlled by this command are:

config
> Enables autoloading configuration files from a server. This command is required for boot network commands to work.

exec-callback
> Enables the callback feature for clients. A callback tells the router to authenticate a dial-in user, disconnect, and then call the user back at a prearranged number. See Chapter 12 for more information.

exec-wait
> Delays the display of the prompt.

finger
> Allows finger requests to be made to the router (i.e., enables a finger server). For IOS 12.0 and later, this has been superseded by ip finger.

hide-telnet-address
> Hides the IP address of the destination host when a telnet command is issued. When a user executes a telnet command at the EXEC prompt, the IP address of the destination machine is usually displayed with a message like "Trying machinename (10.10.1.4)."

nagle
> Enables the Nagle congestion control algorithm.

`password-encryption`
> Enables password encryption. By default, password encryption is enabled.

`prompt config`
> Enables the display of the (`config`) prompt when in the configuration mode.

`tcp-keepalives-in`
> Enables TCP keepalives on incoming connections (connections initiated by remote hosts).

`tcp-keepalives-out`
> Enables TCP keepalives on outgoing connections (connections initiated by the router).

`tcp-small-servers`
> Enables servers for the so-called "small TCP services" (the *echo*, *discard*, *chargen*, and *daytime* protocols). By default, these services are disabled as of IOS 11.2 and later.

`telnet-zeroidle`
> When enabled, this feature tells the router to set the packet window to zero when a telnet connection is idle.

`udp-small-servers`
> Enables servers for the small UDP services (*echo*, *discard*, and *chargen*). By default, these services are disabled as of IOS 11.2 and later.

---

service compress-config   global

```
service compress-config
no service compress-config
```

Configures   Compression of configurations in memory

Default   Disabled

Description
This command lets you compress the configuration file; this feature is available only on high-end routers (5000, 6000, and 7500 series). To disable compression, use the no form of the command.

---

service linenumber   line

```
service linenumber
no service linenumber
```

Configures   Line number display

Default   Disabled

Description
This command configures the router to display the line number, line location, and hostname after the incoming banner.

service-module 56k

```
service-module 56k parameters
no service-module 56k parameters
```

Configures   Internal 56k (DS0) CSU/DSU

Default   Depends on the command

Description
The service-module commands are for routers that have 56k CSU/DSU modules built into them. These commands set various options on the internal CSU/DSU. The parameters that can be configured are:

clock rate *speed*
> Configures the line speed for a four-wire 56k line. The valid speeds are 2.4, 4.8, 9.6, 19.2, 38.4, 56, and 64. The default is 56.

clock source {line | internal}
> By default, the clock source is the line, which is provided by the carrier. This command allows you to switch to the internal clock source on the module.

data-coding {normal | scrambled}
> normal data coding is the default behavior for service modules. scrambled data coding should be used only on lines configured for 64 Kbps. Both ends of the link must use the same data coding.

network-type {dds | switched}
> Determines whether the line is configured for DDS (unswitched) or switched service. dds is the default for four-wire service; switched is the default for two-wire service.

remote-loopback
> By default, the service module accepts remote-loopback commands from the remote CSU/DSU. To disable remote loopback, use the no form.

switched-carrier {att | sprint | other}
> The switched-carrier setting must be appropriate for your 56k provider. att is the default on four-wire CSU/DSUs; sprint is the default on two-wire CSU/DSUs. This command can be used only if the network-type is set to switched.

service-module t1

```
service-module t1 parameters
no service-module t1 parameters
```

Configures   Internal T1 CSU/DSU

Default   Depends on the command

Description
The service-module commands are for routers that have T1 CSU/DSU modules built into them. These commands set various options on the internal CSU/DSU. The parameters that can be configured are:

clock source {internal | line}

By default, the clock source for a T1 CSU/DSU is the line, which is provided by the carrier. This command allows you to switch to the internal clock source on the module.

data-coding {inverted | normal}

By default, the data coding is set to normal. Setting the data coding to inverted instructs the module to convert all 1s to 0s and all 0s to 1s. If the data coding is inverted on one end of the line, the other end must also be inverted or the connection will fail.

framing {esf | sf}

This command sets the framing type for the T1 module, which can be esf (Extended Superframe) or sf (Superframe). The default framing type for a T1 module is ESF.

lbo {-15 db | -7.5 db | none}

This command sets the line build-out value. -15 db decreases the outgoing signal by 15 decibels; -7.5 db decreases it by 7.5 decibels. Your provider will know what the build-out should be for your link. The default is no build-out (none) on the outgoing signal.

linecode {ami | b8zs}

By default, the line encoding is set to b8zs. It can be changed to ami with this command. Your service carrier provides the T1 linecode type.

remote-alarm-enable

This command allows the generation and detection of remote alarms on the T1 line. All alarms are disabled by default.

remote-loopback {full | payload}

By default, the service module accepts full and payload remote-loopback commands from the remote CSU/DSU. The no form of this command allows you to disable this behavior.

timeslots {all | range} [speed 56|64]

This command defines the timeslots that make up a fractional T1 line. The keyword all includes all the timeslots; to specify a subset of the available timeslots (i.e., fractional T1), use a range of numbers between 1 and 24 (for example, 1–3,7 for timeslots 1, 2, 3, and 7). The optional speed parameter defines the timeslot speed, which can be 56 or 64. The default is all timeslots operating at 64 Kbps.

service-policy (interface)
interface

```
service-policy {input | output} policy-map-name
no service-policy {input | output} policy-map-name
```

Configures policymap

Default None

Description

This command attaches a policy map to an interface or Virtual Circuit (VC). Use the input or output keyword to apply the policy map to the input or output traffic on an interface.

Example

```
interface serial 1/1
  service-policy output policy1
```

---

service-policy (policy-map)   policy-map

policy-map-name
no service-policy *policy-map-name*

Configures   policy map

Default   None

Description   This command attaches a policy map directly to a class.

Example

```
policy-map classes-def
  class gold
    bandwidth percent 50
  class silver
    bandwidth percent 30
  class bronze
    bandwidth percent 10
!
policy-map map1
  class customer1
    shape average 38400
    service-policy classes-def
```

---

service timestamps   global

service timestamps {log | debug} [uptime]
service timestamps {log | debug} datetime [msec] [localtime] [show-timezone]
no service timestamps {log | debug}

Configures   Timestamps on log messages

Default   No timestamps

Description
This command forces timestamps on logging or debugging messages. uptime is the
default if no options are specified.

log
    Applies timestamps to logging messages.

debug
    Applies timestamps to debugging messages.

uptime
    Optional. The time is calculated since the router was started.

datetime
   Uses the actual clock time.
msec
   Optional. Displays the millisecond value in the timestamp.
localtime
   Optional. Timestamps are relative to the local time zone.
show-timezone
   Optional. Displays the time zone value in the timestamp.

session-limit line

```
session-limit number
no session-limit
```

Configures   Maximum sessions per line

Default
Depends on the hardware; show terminal shows you the default for your device

Description
This command sets the maximum number of terminal sessions per line.

session-timeout line

```
session-timeout minutes [output]
no session-timeout
```

Configures   Minutes before a session on the line times out

Default   0 (never times out)

Description
This command sets the interval that the router waits for traffic before closing the connection, i.e., the amount of time the line can be idle. The timeout period is specified in *minutes*. The output keyword tells the router to use both input and output traffic to reset the counters. If you omit this keyword, only the input traffic on the line causes a counter reset.

set as-path route-map

```
set as-path {tag | prepend as-path-string}
no set as-path {tag | prepend as-path-srting}
```

Configures   Properties of routes matching a route map

Default   None

Description

Route maps let you select routes based on certain criteria and modify the properties of those routes using one or more set commands. This command allows you to modify the autonomous system path for BGP routes that match the route map's criteria. (To define a route map, use the route-map command; to specify a route map's matching criteria, use the match command.) The set as-path command has the following arguments:

tag
> When redistributing routes into BGP, converts the tag of the route directly into an autonomous system (AS) path.

prepend *as-path-string*
> Adds the *as-path-string* to the beginning of any AS path.

Example

In this example, we create a route map called test-as-path. Inside the map, we match any AS path list with the number 1. We then use the set as-path command to prepend our local autonomous system (300) to all routes advertised to our neighbor (10.10.1.1).

```
route-map test-as-path
  match as-path 1
  set as-path prepend 300
!
ip as-path access-list 1 permit .*
!
router bgp 300
  neighbor 10.10.1.1 route-map test-as-path out
```

---

set atm-clp
policy-map

```
set atm-clp
no set atm-clp
```

Configures   QoS setting within a policy map class

Default   CLP is 0

Description

This command sets the cell loss priority (CLP) bit within a policy map class.

Example

```
class-map ip-precedence-is-zero
  match ip precedence 0
!
policy-map set-atm-clp
  class ip-precedence-is-zero
    set atm-clp
```

set automatic-tag

```
set automatic-tag
no set automatic-tag
```

Configures   Properties of routes matching a route map

Default   None

Description

This command causes automatic tag calculation for a learned route that is matched by a route map.

set community

```
set community {community-number [additive]} | none
no set community {community-number [additive]} | none
```

Configures   Properties of routes matching a route map

Default   None

Description

This command sets the BGP community for a route matched by the route map.

community-number
    The community number to use; its value can be a number from 1 to 4,294,967,200, or the predefined communities of no-export or no-advertise.

additive
    Optional. Causes the new community to be added to any communities that the route already belongs to.

none
    Optional. Removes all community attributes from the route.

set cos

```
set cos cos-value
no set cos cos-value
```

Configures   QoS setting within a policy map class

Default   None

Description

This command sets the layer-2 class of service (CoS) value of a packet within a policy map class.

cos-value
    The CoS value to use, from 0 to 7.

Example

```
policy-map map1
   class voice
     set cos 1
```

---

set default interface   route-map

```
set default interface interface [... interface]
no set default interface interface [... interface]
```

Configures   Properties of routes matching a route map

Default   None

Description

This command sets the output interface for destinations that match the criteria in the route map if there is no explicit route to the destination. In other words, if the route is matched by this route map and has no explicit destination, this command can tell it which interface to use as a default route. This allows you to have different default routes for different hosts or networks.

You may list any number of interfaces; if the first interface in the list is down, the next is tried, and so on. This command should be used in conjunction with the ip policy route-map command.

Example

The following commands establish a route map named policy-one for policy-based routing. This map takes all packets for the destinations matched by access list 1 (i.e., all destinations that match 10.1.0.0/16) and sends them out through interface serial0.

```
interface ethernet0
   ip policy route-map policy-one
   ip address 10.1.1.1 255.255.255.0
!
! this access-list is for the match ip command below
access-list 1 permit 10.1.0.0 0.0.255.255
!
route-map policy-one
   match ip address 1
   set default interface serial0
```

---

set discard-class   policy-map

```
set discard-class value
no set discard-class value
```

Configures   QoS setting within a policy map class

Default   0

Description

This command marks a packet with the specified discard value within a policy map class. The value can be a number from 0 to 7.

Example

```
policy-map map1
  class voice
    set discard-class 2
```

---

set dscp

```
set dscp value
no set dscp value
```

Configures   QoS setting within a policy map class

Default   None

Description

This command marks a packet with the DSCP (differentiated services code point) value within a policy map class. The value can be from 0 to 63.

Example

```
policy-map map1
  class class1
    set dscp 15
```

---

set fr-de

```
set fr-de
no set fr-de
```

Configures   QoS setting within a policy map class

Default   Bit is set to zero (0)

Description

This command sets the discard eligible (DE) bit for a frame relay packet within a policy map class.

Example

```
policy-map map1
  class class1
    set fr-de
```

set interface

```
set interface interface [ ... interface]
no set interface interface [ ... interface]
```

Configures   Properties of routes matching a route map

Default   None

Description
This command is similar to the set default interface command. It differs in that the interface specified in this command is always used regardless of any other routing information: it can't be overridden by an explicit route to the destination. This command should be used in conjunction with the ip policy route-map command.

set ip default next-hop

```
set ip default next-hop ip-address [ ... ip-address]
no set ip default next-hop ip-address [ ... ip-address]
```

Configures   Properties of routes matching a route map

Default   None

Description
This command sets the next-hop address for an incoming packet if there is no explicit route for the packet already. This command should be used in conjunction with the ip policy route-map command. The IP address does not have to be an address that is adjacent to the router.

set ip next-hop

```
set ip next-hop ip address [ ... ip address]
no set ip next-hop ip address [ ... ip address]
```

Configures   Properties of routes matching a route map

Default   None

Description
This command sets the next-hop address for an incoming packet regardless of any explicit route for the packet. It is similar to the set ip default next-hop command except that a next-hop address specified with this command cannot be overridden by an explicit route. This command should be used in conjunction with the ip policy route-map command. The IP address does not have to be an address that is adjacent to the router.

set ip precedence route-map

```
set ip precedence qos
no set ip precedence
```

Configures The precedence bits in the IP header

Default Disabled

Description

This command sets the Quality of Service bits in the IP header. The Quality of Service value, qos, can be specified either by number or by name. Table 17-20 lists the valid number and names that can be used.

Table 17-20. QoS numbers and names

QoS number	QoS name
0	routine
1	priority
2	immediate
3	flash
4	flash-override
5	critical
6	internet
7	network

set ip tos route-map

```
set ip tos [value]
no set ip tos
```

Configures Properties of routes matching a route map

Default Disabled

Description

This command sets the Type of Service (ToS) for a packet that matches the route map. The value is a number from 0 to 15.

set level route-map

```
set level {level-1 | level-2 | level-1-2 | stub-area | backbone}
no set level {level-1 | level-2 | level-1-2 | stub-area | backbone}
```

Configures Properties of routes matching a route map

Default backbone for OSPF; level-2 for IS-IS

Description

This command sets the level into which routes that match the route map are imported.

level-1
> Imports into level-1 area.

level-2
> Imports into level-2 subdomain.

level-1-2
> Imports into both level-1 and level-2.

stub-area
> Imports into the OSPF NSSA area.

backbone
> Imports into the OSPF backbone area.

---

set local-preference

route-map

```
set local-preference value
no set local-preference value
```

Configures   Properties of routes matching a route map

Default   100

Description

This command sets the preference value for routes that match the map. In BGP, the preference influences route selection.

---

set metric

route-map

```
set metric metric-value
no set metric metric-value
```

```
set metric bandwidth delay reliability loading mtu
no set metric bandwidth delay reliability loading mtu
```

Configures   Properties of routes matching a route map

Default   The default metric for the routing protocol

Description

This command sets the metric value for a matching route. The first form of the command (with a single metric-value parameter) is used for most routing protocols; the metric value must be appropriate for the protocol's routing metric. For IGRP and EIGRP, you must use the second form of the command with five parameters:

bandwidth
> The bandwidth of the route in kilobits per second. The value can be from 0 to 4,294,967,295.

delay
> The route delay in tens of microseconds. The value can be from 0 to 4,294,967,295.

reliability
> A value from 0 to 255. 0 indicates total unreliability; 255 indicates complete reliability.

loading
> A value from 0 to 255. 0 means no load; 255 means 100% loaded.

mtu
> The smallest MTU for any link in the route, in bytes. The value can be from 0 to 4,294,967,295.

---

set metric-type   route-map

```
set metric-type {internal | external | type-1 | type-2}
no set metric-type {internal | external | type-1 | type-2}
```

Configures   Properties of routes matching a route map

Default   Disabled

Description
This command sets the metric type used for routes that match the map. The metric type is used by the OSPF and IS-IS protocols.

internal
> IS-IS internal metric.

external
> IS-IS external metric.

type-1
> OSPF external type 1 metric.

type-2
> OSPF external type 2 metric.

---

set metric-type internal   route-map

```
set metric-type internal
no set metric-type internal
```

Configures   Properties of routes matching a route map

Default   Disabled

Description

This command is for BGP routing. It causes the MED value for all advertised routes that match the route map to be set to the corresponding interior routing protocol metric of the next hop.

set mpls-label

```
set mpls-label
no set mpls-label
```

Configures   Properties of a route map

Default   Disabled

Description

This command enables a route to be distributed with an MPLS label if it matches the conditions in the route map.

set origin

```
set origin {igp | egp as-system | incomplete}
no set origin {igp | egp as-system | incomplete}
```

Configures   Properties of routes matching a route map

Default   The default origin value

Description

This command sets the BGP origin code for the matched route. The possible origins are:

igp
     The route was learned from an interior routing protocol.

egp as-system
     The route was learned from an exterior routing protocol with the given autonomous system number.

incomplete
     The origin of the route is unknown.

set ospf router-id

```
set ospf router-id
no set ospf router-id
```

Configures   Properties of a route map

Default   Disabled

Description

This command allows the router to set a separate OSPF ID for each interface on a provider edge.

---

set-overload-bit

router, IS-IS

```
set-overload-bit
no set-overload-bit
```

Configures   The overload bit for IS-IS routing

Default   Disabled

Description

This command sets the overload bit, which tells other routers not to use it as the intermediate hop in the shortest path first (SPF) calculation.

---

set precedence

policy-map

```
set precedence value
no set precedence value
```

Configures   QoS setting within a policy map class

Default   Disabled

Description

This command sets the precedence value, from 0 to 7, of packets that match the policy map class.

Example

```
policy-map map1
  class class1
    set precedence 7
```

---

set qos-group

policy-map

```
set qos-group group-id
no set qos-group group-id
```

Configures   QoS setting within a policy map class

Default   None

Description

This command sets the quality of service group identifier of packets that match the policy map class. The *group-id* can be any number from 0 to 99.

Example

```
policy-map map1
  class class1
    set qos-group 1
```

set tag
route-map

set tag *value*

no set tag *value*

Configures   Properties of routes matching a route map

Default   The route's tag is passed directly into the new routing protocol

Description

This command sets the matched route's tag value. The value can be from 0 through 4,294,967,295.

setup
command

setup

Description

This command places the router in setup configuration mode. In this mode, the router asks a series of questions; the answers allow the router to build a basic configuration. You must be in enable mode to run this command.

Example

Here is the beginning of the system configuration dialog:

```
ROUTER#setup

          --- System Configuration Dialog ---

Continue with configuration dialog? [yes/no]: yes

At any point you may enter a question mark '?' for help.
Use ctrl-c to abort configuration dialog at any prompt.
Default settings are in square brackets '[]'.

First, would you like to see the current interface summary? [yes]: n

Configuring global parameters:

  Enter host name [ROUTER]: myrouter

  The enable secret is a password used to protect access to
  privileged EXEC and configuration modes. This password, after
  entered, becomes encrypted in the configuration.
  Enter enable secret:
```

set weight

```
set weight value
no set weight value
```

Configures   Properties of routes matching a route map

Default   The default weight value

Description

This command sets the BGP weight value for a matched route. The weight value can be 0 through 65,535.

---

shape

```
shape {average | peak} cir [burst-committed burst-excess]
no shape {average | peak} cir [burst-committed burst-excess]

shape {average | peak} percent percent-value [burst-committed burst-excess]
no shape {average | peak} percent percent-value [burst-committed burst-excess]
```

Configures   traffic shaping

Default   None

Description

This command allows you to configure traffic shaping for a policy-map class. You can specify either the committed information rate (CIR) in bits per second or you can specify a percentage of the available bandwidth.

average
    Specifies the average rate shaping.

peak
    Specifies the peak rate shaping.

cir
    Specifies the CIR in bits per second.

percent
    Specifies the percentage of bandwidth to use. The value can be from 1 to 100.

burst-committed
    Optional. Specifies the committed burst (bc) size in milliseconds. This value can be from 10 to 2,000.

burst-excess
    Optional. Specifies the exceeded burst (be) size in milliseconds. This value can be from 10 to 2,000.

Example

This example configures traffic shaping using an average of the available bandwidth. We set the average rate to have a CIR of 50 percent, a committed burst (bc) of 400 milliseconds, and an exceeded burst (be) of 600 milliseconds.

```
policy-map map1
  class class1
    shape average percent 50 400 600
```

show   command

show *parameters*

Description

The show commands are extremely helpful when configuring or debugging a router. Just about anything you want to know about the router's configuration or state can be found with a show command. Table 17-21 summarizes the common show commands.

Table 17-21. Common show commands

Command	Subcommand	Displays
show access-lists [*acl*]		All access lists. If you give an access list number, this command displays that particular list.
show accounting		All the accounting information on the system.
show adjacency		CEF adjacency table.
show aliases [*mode*]		All aliases that have been defined for commands. If you provide the name of a mode, this command only displays the aliases for that mode. Use ? to see the list of acceptable modes. Aliases are created with the alias command.
show arp		The router's ARP table.
show async	bootp	BOOTP parameters for an asynchronous interface.
	status	Status of the asynchronous interfaces.
show atm	accounting	ATM accounting information.
	addresses	Active ATM addresses.
	arp-server	ATM ARP server table.
	bundle	Attributes assigned to each bundle's virtual circuit.
	connection-traffic-table	ATM connection traffic parameters.
	filter-expr	ATM filter expressions.
	filter-set	ATM filter sets.
	ilmi-configuration	ILMI configuration information.
	ilmi-status	ILMI status information.
	interface	ATM information relative to an interface.
	map	ATM static maps to remote hosts.
	qos-defaults	Default ATM QoS configuration.

Table 17-21. Common show commands (continued)

Command	Subcommand	Displays
	resource	ATM global resource manager configuration.
	rmon	Status of the ATM RMON MIB.
	route	ATM routing table.
	signalling	ATM signaling information.
	snoop	ATM port snooping configuration.
	snoop-vc	ATM port snooping configuration per virtual connection.
	snoop-vp	ATM port snooping configuration per virtual path.
	status	Current ATM status for the router.
	traffic	ATM traffic layer information.
	vc	Information about ATM virtual connections.
	vp	Information about ATM virtual paths.
show auto secure		AutoSecure configuration.
show auto qos		Displays configurations created by AutoQoS.
show bridge		Entries in the bridge forwarding database.
	circuit-group	Status of the interfaces in a circuit group.
	group [verbose]	Status of all bridge groups.
	multicast	Transparent bridging multicast state information.
	vlan	Virtual LAN subinterfaces.
show bootflash:		Information about the router's bootflash.
show bootvar		Contents of the bootvar variable.
show buffers		Buffers and buffer statistics.
show calendar		Calendar hardware setting.
show caller		Incoming caller information on access servers.
show cef		Cisco Express Forwarding information.
	interface	CEF interface level statistics.
show cdp		Global CDP information.
	entry	Information about an entry in the CDP table.
	interface	Interfaces for which CDP is enabled.
	neighbors [detail]	Information about CDP neighbors.
	traffic	Traffic information from the CDP table.
show cef		Information about Cisco Express Forwarding.
show class-map		Class maps and their matching criteria.
show clock [detail]		Current clock information;
show compress		Compression statistics.
show configuration		Initial startup configuration. This command has been replaced with show startup-config.

Table 17-21. Common show commands (continued)

Command	Subcommand	Displays
show controllers [*controller*]		Information about the physical port. By default, you get all the controller information. Use the *controller* parameter to name a specific controller.
show cops servers		Policy server.,
show crypto cisco		Cisco encryption policies.
	algorithms	Supported cryptographic algorithms.
	connections	Pending and completed encrypted connections.
	key-timeout	Timeout values for the router's session keys.
	pregen-dh-pairs	Pregenerated pairs.
show crypto engine		Information about the cryptographic engine.
	configuration	The cryptographic engine's configuration.
	connections	Current connection information.
show crypto key		Public key information.
	mypubkey	The router's public keys.
	pubkey-chain	The peer's public keys.
show crypto map		All cryptographic maps.
	interface	All cryptographic maps for a specific interface.
	tag	Maps for a specific tag.
show debugging		Type of debugging that is enabled.
show dhcp	lease	DHCP information learned from a server.
	server	DHCP servers that the router knows about.
show diag		Power-on diagnostics for certain types of routers.
show dialer		All dialer configuration and state information.
	interface	Dialer information for a specific interface.
	maps	Dialer map information.
show environment		Current temperature and voltage information. Only available on some routers.
show file		Information for a class C filesystem. This command has been replaced by the more command.
	descriptors	Open file descriptors.
	information *url*	Information about a specific file.
	systems	All available filesystems.
show flash		The status and contents of flash memory.
show frame-relay	ip rtp header-compression	IP/RTP statistics.
	ip tcp header-compression	IP/TCP statistics.
	lapf	LAPF status.

Table 17-21. Common show commands (continued)

Command	Subcommand	Displays
	lmi	LMI statistics.
	map	Frame Relay map table.
	pvc	PVC statistics.
	qos-autosense	qos-autosense information.
	route	Frame Relay route.
	svc maplist	SVC information.
	traffic	Frame Relay protocol statistics.
show hardware		Hardware information like IOS image, memory, flash size, interface list, and config-register setting.
show history		The commands in the history buffer
show hosts		The host table, which lists hosts whose addresses are explicitly configured in the router.
show hub		Information about hub interfaces.
show interfaces		Statistics for all interfaces.
	interface	Statistics for a specific *interface*.
	interface accounting	Interface accounting.
	interface crb	Routing and bridging information.
	interface irb	Routing and bridging information.
	interface type	Virtual LAN types.
	fair-queue	Fair-queuing statistics for interface.
	ip-brief	A single-line IP status for each interface.
	random-detect	WRED information.
	rate-limit	CAR information.
	stats	Information about packets handled and switching paths for interfaces.
	switch	Details about switching paths for interfaces.
show ip access-lists [*list*]		All the current IP access lists. Optionally, you can provide the number of a specific list.
show ip accounting		Information about packets that passed access control and were routed successfully.
	access-violations	Information about packets that failed access control and were not routed.
	checkpoint	The checkpoint database.
	output-packets	Information about successfully routed packets.
show ip aliases		The IP addresses that have been mapped to ports for reverse telnet.
show ip arp		The ARP cache.
show ip bgp		Entries in the BGP routing table.
	cidr-only	Routes that have CIDR network masks.

Table 17-21. Common show commands (continued)

Command	Subcommand	Displays
	community *community*	Routes that belong to a specific BGP community.
	community-list	Routes permitted by a specific BGP community list .
	dampened-paths	Information about route dampening.
	filter-list list-number	Routes permitted by a specific BGP filter list.
	inconsistent-as	Routes with inconsistent originating AS numbers.
	neighbors	Statistics about BGP neighbors.
	paths	All BGP paths in the BGP database.
	peer-group	Statistics about BGP peer groups.
	regexp *expression*	All routes that match the given regular expression.
	summary	Status of all current BGP connections.
show ip cache		The routing table for fast-switched IP traffic.
	flow	The flow table for switching cache.
show ip cef		Global information about CEF.
show ip dvmrp route		Contents of DVMRP routing table.
show ip egp		All EGP connections and neighbors.
show ip eigrp	interfaces	Interface-specific EIGRP information.
	neighbors	Discovered EIGRP neighbors and their holdtime status.
	topology	The EIGRP topology table.
	traffic	The types of EIGRP packets that were sent and received.
show ip flow export		Information about flow export statistics.
show ip http server		Status of the HTTP configuration for the device.
show ip igmp	groups	Multicast groups learned via IGMP.
	interface [*interface*]	Multicast information about all interfaces. If you list a specific interface, this command displays multicast information about that interface.
show ip interface [brief]		Interfaces configured for IP. By default, you get all interfaces; you can specify a single interface. Use the brief command to get a summary.
show ip irdp		The status of the Router Discovery Protocol and which interfaces have it enabled.
show ip local policy		The route map used for local policy routing.
show ip local pool		The IP address pools.
show ip masks		The network masks that are currently used, which helps when doing variable-length subnet mask troubleshooting.

Table 17-21. Common show commands (continued)

Command	Subcommand	Displays
show ip mcache		Contents of the IP multicast fast switching cache.
show ip mpacket		Contents of the circular cache-header buffer.
show ip mroute		Contents of the IP multicast routing table.
show ip nat		
	statistics	NAT statistics (total translations, interfaces, hits, misses, and expired translations).
	translations	Active translations.
show ip nbar		Network-Based Application Recognition (NBAR).
	pdlm	Packet Description Language Module in use by NBAR.
	port-map	Port mappings in use by NBAR.
	protocol-discovery	Statistics gathered by NBAR.
show ip nhrp		The NHRP cache.
show ip ospf		General information and statistics about OSPF.
	border-routers	The routes to the ABR and ASBR in the internal routing table.
	database	The entire OSPF database for the device. Options to this command give you more specific information: asb-summary, router, network, external, summary, and database-summary.
	interface	Interface-specific OSPF information, or information about a given interface.
	neighbor	Information about OSPF neighbors on an interface basis.
	request-list	All LSA requests by a router.
	retransmission-list	All LSA requests waiting to be retransmitted.
	statistics	Statistics about shortest-path-first (SPF) algorithm.
	virtual-links	Information about configured OSPF virtual links.
show ip pim		Protocol Independent Multicast (PIM) information.
	interface	Information about interfaces that are configured for PIM.
	neighbor	All PIM neighbors that the router has discovered.
	rp	The rendezvous-point routers that are used with sparse-mode multicast.
show ip policy		Policy routing information.
show ip protocols		The currently configured IP routing protocols and their state information.

Reference R-S

Table 17-21. Common show commands (continued)

Command	Subcommand	Displays
show ip redirects		Default gateways and the IP addresses from which redirects have been received.
show ip route		The routing table.
	[*routing-protocol*]	Routes for the specified protocol.
	summary	Summary of the IP route table.
	supernets-only	Only the supernets in the routing table.
show ip rpf		Information about reverse path forwarding for multicast routing.
show ip sockets		IP sockets that are currently open.
show ip ssh		SSH version and configuration information.
show ip tcp header-compression		Statistics about TCP header compression.
show ip traffic		General statistics about IP traffic.
show isdn		Various ISDN statistics.
	active	All current calls.
	history	Historic ISDN information.
	memory	ISDN memory pool statistics.
	status	ISDN interface status; you can list a specific interface to get a status report for that interface.
	timers	Layer 2 and Layer 3 timer information.
show isis	database	The contents of the IS-IS database.
	spf-log	When and how often the router had to perform an IS-IS SPF calculation.
show key chain		All information about authentication key chains.
show lane		ATM LANE information for an interface or a complete summary.
	bus	ATM LANE information for the BUS.
	client	Information for LANE clients.
	config	Information for the LANE configuration server.
	database	The database of the LANE configuration server.
	default-atm-addresses	The automatically assigned ATM address for each LANE component.
	le-arp	The LANE ARP table.
	name	The LANE ARP server.
	server	Global information for the LANE server.
show line		Information about configured serial lines (AUX, TTY, and VTY). On TTY ports, a large number of overruns might signal a bad cable.
show logging		The logging that is enabled.
show memory		Information about the device's memory usage.

Table 17-21. Common show commands (continued)

Command	Subcommand	Displays
show microcode		The microcode image information for a line card.
show modem		Statistics for manageable modems. Used for access servers and for routers with managed (internal) modems.
	at-mode	Manageable modems that have current AT sessions.
	call-stats	Call statistics and disconnect reasons.
	configuration	Current modem configurations.
	connect-speeds	Connection speed statistics.
	cookie	Information about the modem cooki.
	csm	Information about the CSM.
	log	Modem event history.
	mapping	All the firmware versions for the modems.
	mica	Information about MICA modems.
	operational-status	Performance statistics for modems.
	summary	A summary report for all managed modems.
	test	The managed modems test log.
	version	Modems firmware information.
show modem-pool		Status and configuration for a modem-pool.
show network clocks		Information about network clock sources.
show ntp	associations	A table of NTP hosts and their status.
	status	The status of NTP on the device.
show policy-map		Configuration of all classes for a policy map.
	class	Specify a specific class within a policy map to display.
	interface	Display statistics for all policy map classes defined for an interface.
show ppp multilink		Information about PPP Multilink.
show privilege		All the privilege levels currently configured for the device.
show processes		All the processes that are currently running on the device.
	cpu	CPU utilization for each process.
	memory	Memory utilization for each process.
show protocols		Configured routing protocols and protocol information for each interface.
show queue interface		The queue status and queuing strategy for the specified interface.
show queueing		All configured queuing methods: custom, fair, priority, random-detect, vc.

Table 17-21. Common show commands (continued)

Command	Subcommand	Displays
show registry		Registry ATM information.
show reload		When the next reload is scheduled.
show rhosts		Which hosts are configured for remote shell usage.
show rmon		General RMON statistics.
	alarms	The RMON alarms table.
	events	The RMON events table.
show route-map		Information about all current route maps; if you provide the name of a route map as an argument, displays information about the specified route map.
show rsp		Current memory cache policies.
show ip rtp header-compression		RTP compression information.
show running-config		The configuration that is currently running.
show service-module		Performance information for an integrated CSU/DSU.
show sessions		Telnet or rlogin connections to the device.
show snapshot		Current snapshot routing information.
show snmp		Status of SNMP on the device.
	mib	The object IDs supported by the currently loaded MIBs .
show spanning-tree		Spanning tree information.
show spantree	vlan/port	Display spanning tree information for a virtual LAN or port.
show sscop		SSCOP details for ATM interfaces.
show ssh		Status of SSH connections.
show stacks		Stack utilization of internal processes.
show standby		Information about HSRP.
show startup-config		The stored configuration that will be used when the router boots.
show tacacs		Current TACACS+ statistics.
show tcp		Status of all TCP connections.
	brief	Summarizes the status of TCP connections.
show tech-support		Information to be used when calling for technical support.
show terminal		The terminal configuration parameters for the current connection.
show traffic-shape		Traffic shaping information.
	queue	Elements queued by traffic shaping at the interface level.
	statistics	Current traffic-shaping statistics.
show users [all]		For all users currently logged in, displays the line number, the username, the user's idle time, and the location of the user's terminal. Use the all keyword to show all lines, even if no one is connected to them.

Table 17-21. Common show commands (continued)

Command	Subcommand	Displays
show version		Boot image, memory, interfaces, and config-register settings.
show vc		Active virtual circuits.
show vlans		Displays VLAN subinterfaces.
	dot1q	Statistics for 802.1q VLAN interfaces.
show vlan-switch	{brief | id vlan | name *vlanname*}	Displays VLAN information.
show vpdn		Session and tunnel information for a virtual private dial-up network.
	session	Information about L2F or L2TP sessions in a virtual private dial-up network .
	tunnel	Information about L2F or L2TP tunnels in a virtual private dial-up network.
show vtp		Displays information about VLAN Trunk Protocol.
show whoami		Information about the current user.

shutdown
interface

```
shutdown
no shutdown
```

Description
This command shuts down the interface: no packets will be routed to it and all routing protocols will be notified that the interface is unavailable. It is a common mistake for new users to configure the interface and forget to do a no shutdown.

Example
Use the following sequence of commands to reset an interface:
```
Router(config)#interface serial0
Router(config)#shutdown
Router(config)#no shutdown
```

smt-queue-threshold
global

```
smt-queue-threshold number
no smt-queue-threshold number
```

Configures   FDDI queue size

Default   The number of FDDI interfaces on the router

Description
This command sets the queue size for unprocessed FDDI station management frames (SMT) to *number* frames.

snapshot

```
snapshot client active-time quiet-time [suppress-statechange-updates] [dialer]
no snapshot client active-time quiet-time [suppress-statechange-updates]
    [dialer]
snapshot server active-time [dialer]
no snapshot server active-time [dialer]
```

Configures   Snapshot routing

Default   Disabled

Description
Configures a client or a server router for snapshot routing. Snapshot routing is useful for dial-on-demand connections where you don't want routing updates to bring up the link but you still want to use a dynamic routing protocol (as opposed to static routes). When performing snapshot routing, the router alternates between active periods, when it contacts all the route servers and builds a snapshot route table, and quiet periods, when the snapshot route table is used and no route updates are performed.

active-time
> Time in minutes during which routing updates are exchanged between client and server. The value can be from 5 to 100.

quiet-time
> Time in minutes for which routing updates are suppressed after an active period.

suppress-statechange-updates
> Optional. Disables routing updates during interface state changes.

dialer
> Optional. Tells the router that it needs to dial the remote router.

Example
To configure a client for snapshot routing:

```
interface dialer 1
  snapshot client 2 100 suppress-statechange-updates dialer
```

To configure a server for snapshot routing:

```
interface dialer 1
  snapshot server 2
```

snmp-server

```
no snmp-server
```

Configures   Disables SNMP

Default   Enabled

Description
This command, which is not part of the router's configuration, disables the router's SNMP agent. It exists only in the negative form.

snmp-server chassis-id

global

```
snmp-server chassis-id string
no snmp-server chassis-id
```

Configures   A number to identify the device

Default

Certain high-end routers use their serial number as the default; otherwise, no default

Description

This command sets the value of the router's serial number to *string*. The chassis ID can be obtained via SNMP. This number is assigned by the user, and is not necessarily the serial number of the router.

Example

```
snmp-server chassis-id 123456789
```

---

snmp-server community

global

```
snmp-server community string [view view-name] {ro | rw} [access-list]
no snmp-server community string
```

Configures   SNMP community access strings

Default   Read-only access; community string public

Description

This command sets the community string for SNMPv1 protocol access.

string
　　The password for the SNMP access.

view *view-name*
　　Optional. *view-name* is the name of a view defined with the snmp-server view command. view defines which SNMP objects can be viewed with this SNMP community string.

ro
　　Defines the community string for read-only access.

rw
　　Defines the community string for read/write access.

access-list
　　Optional. The number of a standard access list. The community string defined with this command is usable only by hosts whose IP addresses match this access list.

Example

The following command defines the community string mystring, which allows read-only access from any IP address.

```
snmp-server community mystring RO
```

snmp-server contact

global

```
snmp-server contact text
no snmp-server contact
```

Configures   SNMP agent

Default   None

Description

This command sets the value of the SNMP contact string (system.sysContact). It has no effect on the router's behavior. You can provide any text, but by convention, you should include contact information for the person responsible for administering the router.

snmp-server enable traps

global

```
snmp-server enable traps [type] [option]
no snmp-server enable traps [type] [option]
```

Configures   SNMP agent; trap behavior

Default   Disabled; with no arguments, this command enables all traps

Description

This command enables SNMP traps. Traps are unsolicited messages from the router to the management stations. Usually, traps notify the management station of an event or error. At least one trap recipient must be defined (using the snmp-server host command) before any traps are generated.

type
> Optional. This command allows you to enable or disable a specific trap type. Valid trap types are shown in Table 17-22.

option
> Any options that are valid for the trap type. Most trap types do not have any options; the exceptions are atm pvc, envmon, isdn, and repeater.

Table 17-22, the list of trap types, is a puzzle. Cisco's documentation shows similar but different lists of trap types for this command and snmp-server host. Since the commands are used together, there's no reason why the two trap lists should be different. It would be easy to write this off as mistaken documentation, but a check on some routers reveals that the built-in help for these commands also shows different trap lists. Table 17-22 lists all the traps, regardless of which command accepts them as arguments; it indicates whether a trap is documented for snmp-server enable traps, snmp-server host, or both. Use it in good health. Fortunately, the traps for which there is disagreement correspond to fairly exotic features that aren't on all routers.

Table 17-22. Valid trap types

Trap type	Description	enable/host
atm pvc	ATM Permanent Virtual Circuit information. Options are interval *seconds* and fail-interval *seconds*.	enable
bgp	Border Gateway Protocol state change information	both
config	Configuration changes on the router	both
dspu	Downstream Physical Unit notifications	host
entity	Entity MIB modifications	both
envmon	Environment monitor traps (7000 series). Options are voltage, shutdown, fan, supply, temperature.	both
frame-relay	Frame Relay traps	both
hsrp	Hot Standby Routing modifications	both
isdn	ISDN traps. Options are call-information and isdn u-interface.	both
llc2	Logical Link Control, type 2 traps	host
repeater	Ethernet hub repeater traps. Options are health, reset.	both
rsrb	Remote Source Route Bridging traps	host
rsvp	Resource Reservation Protocol notifications	both
rtr	Response Time Reporter notifications	both
sdlc	SDLC traps	host
sdllc	SDLLC traps	host
snmp	SNMP specific traps	both
stun	Serial tunnel traps	host
syslog	Error message traps	both
tty	Cisco Enterprise-specific traps	host
x25	X25-specific traps	host

snmp-server engine-id global

```
snmp-server engine-id local string
no snmp-server engine-id
```

Configures   SNMP Version 3

Default   None

Description

This command sets the ID of the router's SNMP engine to *string*. The engine ID is used by SNMP Version 3 when it computes various cryptographic keys. This book doesn't cover SNMPv3 configuration, so there isn't a lot to say about the engine ID. However, if you have configured SNMPv3, it is important to know that changing the engine ID has many side effects, including invalidating the authentication information for all SNMP users.

The ID string is 24 characters long. If you do not specify the entire 24 characters, it will be padded with zeros on the right.

snmp-server group

```
snmp-server group [name access] [mode view] [access access-list]
no snmp-server group
```

Configures   SNMP

Default   No groups defined

Description

This command allows you to associate one or more views (defined by the snmp-server view command) in a group for the purpose of controlling access to the data objects included in the view.

name access

The *name* of the group, followed by the type of *access* allowed to the group. The *name* is any string; possible values for *access* are listed in Table 17-23.

Table 17-23. Types of SNMP access

Access type	Privileges granted
v1	Access allowed to SNMP Version 1 managers (insecure).
v2c	Access allowed to SNMP Version 2 managers (insecure).
v3 auth	Access allowed to SNMP Version 3 managers; cryptographic authentication required; the packets themselves are not encrypted.
v3 noauth	Access allowed to SNMP Version 3 managers; no authentication required (insecure).
v3 priv	Access allowed to SNMP Version 3 managers; cryptographic authentication required; the packets are encrypted.

mode view

The mode in which access is granted, followed by the name of the view to which the privileges apply. *mode* may be either read (read-only access), write (write-only access), or notify (access to traps and notifications). Cisco recommends against using the notify option; use the snmp-server host command to control trap destinations. In one command, you can specify a read view, a write view, and a notify view. If you don't specify any views, the router generates a group that contains a read-only view of the entire Internet (1.3.6.1) object tree.

access access-list

An access list that controls access to the group.

If you're using SNMPv3, you must also use the snmp-server user command to define users and their cryptographic keys.

snmp-server host

```
snmp-server host hostname [version {1 | 2c}] community [udp-port port] trap-
    type
no snmp-server host hostname
```

Configures   SNMP agent; trap behavior

Default   Disabled

Description

This command defines which host should receive SNMP traps.

hostname
> The hostname or IP address of the host that should receive traps.

version *n*
> The version of SNMP to use (1 or 2c).

community
> The SNMP community string to use when sending traps to this host.

udp-port *port*
> The UDP port to use. Default is 162.

trap-type
> Optional. Specifies which types of traps are sent to this host. If no trap type is specified, all traps are sent to this host. Possible values are listed in Table 17-22, under the command snmp-server enable traps.

Example

```
snmp-server enable traps
snmp-server host myhost.xyz.com public
```

---

snmp-server location   global

```
snmp-server location text
no snmp-server location
```

Configures   SNMP agent

Default   None

Description

This command sets the SNMP location string (system.sysLocation). It has no effect on the router's behavior. This can be any text, but it should represent the router's physical location.

---

snmp-server packetsize   global

```
snmp-server packetsize size
no snmp-server packetsize size
```

Configures   SNMP agent

Default   1,500 bytes

Description

This command controls the maximum packet size for SNMP. The *size* can be 484 to 8,192 bytes.

---

snmp-server queue-length

global

```
snmp-server queue-length length
no snmp-server queue-length length
```

Configures   SNMP message queue length

Default   10 traps

Description

This command specifies the number of SNMP trap packets that can be held for each trap destination before the queue is cleared.

---

snmp-server system-shutdown

global

```
snmp-server system-shutdown
no snmp-server system-shutdown
```

Configures   SNMP agent

Default   Disabled

Description

This command enables or disables the SNMP remote reload feature, which allows a remote host with the SNMP read/write community string to reboot the router. The no form of this command disables this feature.

---

snmp-server tftp-server-list

global

```
snmp-server tftp-server-list access-list
no snmp-server tftp-server-list
```

Configures   SNMP agent

Default   Disabled

Description

This command allows an access list to be applied to SNMP TFTP server tasks, which include loading and saving of configuration files.

---

snmp-server trap-source

global

```
snmp-server trap-source interface
no snmp-server trap-source
```

Configures   SNMP agent; trap behavior

Default   The router uses the closest interface to the destination

Description

This command specifies the interface (and consequently the IP address) that should be used to send SNMP traps. If you have a separate network for management tasks (a good idea), you can use this command to ensure that traps are sent only over the management network.

Example

The following command tells the router that all SNMP traps should be sent via the ethernet0 interface:

```
snmp-server trap-source ethernet0
```

snmp-server trap-timeout   global

snmp-server trap-timeout *seconds*

no snmp-server trap-timeout *seconds*

Configures   Time to keep an SNMP trap in the queue

Default   30 seconds

Description

If the device wants to send a trap to a host that is unavailable, the device puts the trap in a queue. This command states how long the packet will remain in the queue before timing out and being retransmitted.

snmp-server user   global

snmp-server user *name group version* [encrypted] [auth *hash auth-pwd*
   [priv des56 *priv-pwd*]] [access *access-list*]

no snmp-server user *name*

Configures   SNMP users

Default   None

Description

This command defines SNMP users, associates them with a group (which in turn defines the information they're allowed to view), and specifies encryption requirements together with the appropriate passwords.

name
> The name of the user you are defining.

group
> The SNMP group the user is associated with.

version
> The version of SNMP that is in use. Possible values are v1, v2c, and v3; v3 is the only version that supports encryption.

encrypted

If this keyword is present, the *auth-pwd* and *priv-pwd* passwords are present as an MD5 hash rather than in plain text.

auth *hash auth-pwd*

SNMPv3 only. Configures an authentication key for the user. *hash* is the name of the hashing algorithm used to create the key; possibilities are md5 and sha. *auth-pwd* is the actual password assigned to the user. The router stores this password in encrypted form.

priv des56 *priv-pwd*

SNMPv3 only. Configures an encryption key for the user, using the des56 algorithm. (Currently, des56 is the only algorithm supported.) *priv-pwd* is the actual password assigned to the user. The router stores this password in encrypted form.

access *access-list*

Optional. An access list that restricts the hosts from which the user can access the group.

The encryption of the password and the authentication key depend on the router's SNMP engine ID. This ID is set with the command snmp-server engineid. Changing the engine ID therefore invalidates all users that are currently defined.

---

snmp-server view   global

```
snmp-server view view-name oid-tree {excluded | included}
no snmp-server view
```

Configures   An SNMP view

Default   None

Description

This command defines an SNMP view that can be used in the snmp-server community command. A view is a list of SNMP object trees. By default, the entire SNMP object tree is available for access. A view restricts access to some subset of the entire tree. Different views can be made available to different SNMP communities.

view *view-name*

A unique name that identifies this SNMP view.

oid-tree

An SNMP object ID (in either numeric or human-readable form). All nodes underneath the given object belong to the tree. Asterisks can be used as wildcards when specifying the object ID.

excluded *or* included

Specifies whether the given *oid-tree* is included in or excluded from the view.

Example

Say that you want to give some group SNMP access to the ifEntry table for interface 2. (Perhaps this group is connected to the router through interface 2. Note that the interface number here is an index into the SNMP interface table, not an IOS interface name.)

To achieve this, define a view:

```
snmp-server view subset2 ifEntry.*.2 included
```

Then set the community string for this view:

```
snmp-server community sub2in view subset2 RO
```

Now users can use the community string sub2in to access the ifEntry table for interface 2, but aren't allowed to access other SNMP objects.

snmp trap link-status   interface

```
snmp trap link-status
no snmp trap link-status
```

Configures   SNMP agent; trap behavior

Default   Enabled

Description
This command allows you to enable or disable the sending of SNMP traps when an interface goes up and down. This command is useful on interfaces that you expect to change state frequently (for example, dial-on-demand interfaces). You may not want to send an SNMP trap to your network management stations whenever these interfaces change state.

source-address   interface (hub)

```
source-address mac-address
no source-address mac-address
```

Configures   Hub behavior

Default   All addresses are allowed

Description
The source-address command allows you to specify a MAC address that will be the only traffic source for a specific port. In other words, only network traffic from the specified *mac-address* will be allowed on the port. By default, traffic from all MAC addresses is accepted on all hub ports.

Example
The following commands restrict the traffic forwarded to port 0 of hub 4 to traffic with the source Ethernet address of 00:00:0c:ff:d0:04.

```
hub ethernet 0 4
    source-address 0000.0cff.d004
```

spanning-tree backbonefast

```
spanning-tree backbonefast
no spanning-tree backbonefast
```

Configures   BackboneFast feature

Default   Disabled

Description

The command enables the BackboneFast feature, which should be enabled on all routers that contain an Ethernet switch network module. BackboneFast provides quicker convergence on the network backbone after a spanning-tree topology change by enabling the switch to detect an indirect link failure and to start the spanning-tree calculation faster than the normal spanning-tree rules would allow.

spanning-tree cost
interface

```
spanning-tree cost value
no spanning-tree cost value
```

Configures   Path cost for the interface for spanning-tree calculations

Default   Depends on the bandwidth of the interface

Description

The command specifies a spanning tree path cost for an interface. Valid values are 1 to 200,000,000 for IOS releases 12.1(3a)E and later. For earlier releases, the valid values are 1 to 65,535. Defaults vary by the bandwidth of the interface: Ethernet, 100; FDDI, 10; ATM, 6; GigibitEthernet, 1; and HSSI, 647.

spanning-tree port-priority
interface

```
spanning-tree priority value
no spanning-tree priority value
```

Configures   The port priority value for spanning-tree calculations

Default   128

Description

The command specifies a spanning-tree path priority value for an interface, which is used when two bridges tie for position as the root-bridge. The priority value breaks the tie. Valid values are from 2 to 255, with a default of 128.

spanning-tree vlan

```
spanning-tree vlan vlan-id [forward-time seconds | hello-time seconds |
   max-age seconds | priority priority | protocol protocol | [root { primary |
   secondary} [ diameter diameter [hello-time seconds]]]]
no spanning-tree vlan vlan-id
```

Configures   The port priority value for spanning-tree calculations

Default   Varies by option (details below)

Description
The command configures Spanning-Tree Protocol (STP) settings for each VLAN.

vlan-id

> The ID of the VLAN, from 1 to 1,005.

forward-time

> Optional. Sets the STP forward delay time, which can be from 4 to 30 seconds. Default is 15 seconds.

hello-time

> Optional. Sets the interval between configuration messages from the root bridge; can be from 1 to 10 seconds. Default is 2 seconds.

max-age

> Optional. Sets the maximum number of seconds that a BDPU packet is valid, which can be from 6 to 40 seconds. Default is 20 seconds.

priority

> Optional. Sets the STP bridge priority, which can be from 0 to 65,535. Default is 128 (with the ieee protocol, default is 3,278).

protocol

> Optional. Sets the STP protocol. Valid choices are dec, ibm, ieee, and vlan-bridge. ieee is the default.

root primary

> Optional. Forces this device to be the root bridge.

root secondary

> Optional. Forces this device to act as a secondary switch, which means it becomes the root switch if the primary root fails.

diameter

> Optional. Set the maximum number of switches between any two end stations. Value can be from 2 to 7.

Example
```
! Enable spanning-tree on vlan 100
spanning-tree vlan 100
```

speed
line

```
speed bits-per-second
no speed
```

Configures   Transmit and receive speeds for a line

Default   9,600 bps

Description
This command sets the transmit and receive speeds for this line to *bits-per-second*. Use the no form of this command to remove the command from the configuration and return to the default setting.

squeeze
command

```
squeeze filesystem:
```

Description
This command cleans the filesystem by permanently deleting files that have been marked for deletion. It works only for Class-A filesystems; it is ignored on other filesystem types.

squelch
interface

```
squelch {normal | reduced}
no squelch {normal | reduced}
```

Configures
Allows certain interfaces to extend the 10baseT limit of 100 meter cables

Default   Normal

Description
This command allows a 10baseT segment to exceed the 100-meter cable length limitation. Currently, this option is available only on the Cisco 4000 series router.

normal
> The default setting for a 10baseT Ethernet segment.

reduced
> Allows 10baseT cables beyond the 100-meter length.

sscop cc-timer
interface

```
sscop cc-timer seconds
no sscop cc-timer
```

Configures   ATM

Default   10 seconds

Description

This command sets the SSCOP connection control timer value to *seconds*. This value determines the transmission times between SSCOP BGN, END, or RS PDUs.

---

sscop keepalive-timer interface

```
sscop keepalive-timer seconds
no sscop keepalive-timer
```

Configures   The ATM SSCOP keepalive timer

Default   30 seconds

Description

This command sets the keepalive timer to *seconds*. This value determines the number of seconds between polling PDUs when no other traffic is transmitted.

---

sscop max-cc interface

```
sscop max-cc retries
no sscop maxcc
```

Configures   Maximum number of transmits of control messages for SSCOP

Default   10 retries

Description

This command sets the maximum number of times that SSCOP sends control messages until an acknowledgment is received. The value of *retries* can range from 1 to 1,600.

---

sscop poll-timer interface

```
sscop poll-timer seconds
no sscop poll-timer
```

Configures   ATM SSCOP poll timer

Default   10 seconds

Description

This command sets the number of *seconds* between SSCOP poll PDUs.

sscop rcv-window

```
sscop rcv-window packets
no sscop rcv-window
```

Configures   ATM SSCOP receive window in packets

Default   7 packets

Description

This command sets the size of the receive window in *packets* . This value determines the number of packets the interface receives before sending an acknowledgment. The value of *packets* can range from 1 to 6,000.

sscop send-window

```
sscop send-window packets
no sscop send-window packets
```

Configures   ATM SSCOP send window in packets

Default   7 packets

Description

This command sets the size of the send window in *packets*. This value determines the number of packets the interface transmits before expecting an acknowledgment. The value of *packets* can range from 1 to 6,000.

standby authentication

```
standby [group] authentication string
no standby [group] authentication string
```

Configures   HSRP authentication string

Default   Group, 0; authentication string, "cisco"

Description

This command enables authentication for a hot standby group. *group* specifies the hot standby group number, and *string* sets the authentication string (essentially a password). All HSRP routers must use the same authentication string in order to communicate. *string* can be from 1 to 8 characters long.

Example

```
interface serial 0
  ip address 10.1.2.1 255.255.255.0
  standby 1 authentication letmein
```

standby ip

interface

```
standby [group] ip address [secondary]
no standby [group] ip address [secondary]
```

Configures   Hot Standby Routing Protocol (HSRP)

Default   None; *group* defaults to 0

Description
This command enables the specified IP *address* to be used as the HSRP address. The optional secondary keyword is useful if the interface has a secondary IP address applied to it. (See Chapter 5 for a discussion of secondary IP addresses.)

standby preempt

interface

```
standby [group] preempt
no standby [group] preempt
```

Configures   Hot Standby Routing Protocol (HSRP)

Default   Disabled; *group* defaults to 0

Description
This command instructs the interface to become the active HSRP interface if no other HSRP router within the given *group* has a higher priority. In other words, if this interface becomes active and has the standby preempt command, it interrupts any other HSRP interface and becomes the active HSRP interface. The default group number is 0.

standby priority

interface

```
standby [group] priority value
no standby [group] priority value
```

Configures   Hot Standby Routing Protocol (HSRP)

Default   Group, 0; priority value, 100

Description
This command defines the interface's HSRP priority within the given *group*. The priority *value* can be from 0 to 255.

standby timers

interface

```
standby [group] timers hello-seconds hold-seconds
no standby [group] timers hello-seconds hold-seconds
```

Configures   Hot Standby Routing Protocol (HSRP)

Default   Group, 0; hello seconds, 3; hold seconds, 10

Description

This command allows you to change the hello and hold intervals for HSRP. If this router doesn't hear from another router in this HSRP *group* for a period of *hello-seconds*, the other router is considered "down." Once a router is declared "down," it is considered down for a period of at least *hold-seconds*.

---

standby track   interface

```
standby [group] track interface [interface-priority]
no standby [group] track interface [interface-priority]
```

Configures   Hot Standby Routing Protocol (HSRP)

Default   Group, 0; interface priority, 10

Description

This command configures the HSRP interface to track another *interface*. If the other interface goes down, the HSRP interface's standby priority decreases by the value *interface-priority*. The rationale for this behavior is that if the tracked interface is down, this router is less desirable as a standby router. The standby track command must be used in combination with the preempt command.

Example

In this example, ethernet0 is the HSRP interface tracking interface serial0. If serial0 goes down, ethernet0's priority is decreased by 20. When serial0 comes back up, ethernet0's priority is increased by 20 (i.e., returned to its original value).

```
interface ethernet0
    standby 1 ip 10.10.1.1
    standby 1 preempt
    standby 1 track serial0 20
```

---

stopbits   line

```
stopbits {1 | 1.5 | 2}
no stopbits
```

Configures   The stop bits transmitted per byte

Default   2

Description

This command sets the stop bits transmitted per byte for the specified line. The settings are limited to 1, 1.5, or 2 stop bits.

---

summary-address

BGP:

```
summary-address address subnet-mask
no summary-address address subnet-mask
```

OSPF:

```
summary-address address subnet-mask [not-advertise] [tag tag-value]
no summary-address address subnet-mask
```

IS-IS:

```
summary-address address subnet-mask {level-1 | level-2 | level-1-2}
no summary-address address subnet-mask {level-1 | level-2 | level-1-2}
```

Configures   Route summarization

Default   Disabled

Description

This command allows you to create a single route that covers a set of smaller routes, thus reducing the number of routes in the routing table. Use the no form of the command to return to the default, where the router does not summarize routes.

address
   The destination address for the summarized route.

subnet-mask
   A subnet mask that indicates which addresses should be included in the summarized route.

level-1, level-2, level-1-2
   IS-IS only. The router summarizes only routes that are being redistributed into the given level.

not-advertise
   Optional. OSPF only. Routes are not advertised when translating a type 7 link state announcement from OSPF.

tag *tag-value*
   Optional. OSPF only. Used as a match value for route maps.

Example

Assume that we know routes for 10.10.1.0, 10.10.2.0, 10.10.3.0, and so on. Instead of advertising separate routes, we can summarize by combining these routes into a single route for 10.10.0.0:

```
summary-address 10.10.0.0 255.255.0.0
```

synchronization

```
synchronization
no synchronization
```

Configures   Synchronization between a BGP and an IGP protocol

Default   Enabled

Description

The no form of this command causes the router to advertise a network route without waiting for the other routing protocol. The rule of synchronization says that an IBGP router cannot advertise a route until the route is known via an IGP routing protocol. See Chapter 10 for more information about the synchronization command.

---

table-map   router, BGP

table-map *route-map*
no table-map *route-map*

Configures   Behavior of BGP routes

Default   None

Description

This command allows you to specify a route map that modifies metric and tag values when the routing table is updated with routes learned from BGP. The given *route-map* is called whenever the routing table is updated with BGP routes.

This command can also be used to filter routes from entering the routing table without preventing them from being maintained and propagated by BGP.

---

tacacs-server attempts   global

tacacs-server attempts *count*
no tacacs-server attempts *count*

Configures   Number of user login attempts

Default   3

Description

This command sets the maximum number of times the router allows a user to attempt to login (via TACACS) before closing the session. In other words, the user has this number of failed login attempts before the session is closed.

---

tacacs-server authenticate   global

tacacs-server authenticate connection [always]
tacacs-server authenticate enable
tacacs-server authenticate slip [always] [access-lists]
no tacacs-server authenticate

Configures   User authentication with TACACS and extended TACACS

Default   Disabled

Description

This command causes the router to contact the TACACS server and authenticate the user under the following conditions:

connection
> When the user makes a TCP connection.

enable
> When the user enters the enable command.

slip
> When the user starts a SLIP or PPP connection.

For authenticating TCP or SLIP connections, the always keyword indicates that the router should always perform authentication even if the user is not logged in. Note that it is possible for a SLIP or PPP user to be connected, but not yet logged in. For authenticating SLIP connections, the access-lists keyword tells the router to check with the TACACS server to see if an access list needs to be installed for the user.

If you are using TACACS+, use the aaa authorization command instead of the tacacs-server authenticate command.

---

tacacs-server directed-request
global

```
tacacs-server directed-request
no tacacs-server directed-request
```

Configures   Which TACACS server is contacted

Default   Enabled

Description

This command causes the router to split each username into two parts, separated by the @ symbol. The first part is the actual username used for authentication; the second part is the name of the TACACS server to send the request to. Disabling this feature causes the TACACS servers to be queried in order; the entire username string is used for authentication.

---

tacacs-server extended
global

```
tacacs-server extended
no tacacs-server extended
```

Configures   Extended TACACS

Default   Disabled

Description

If you have an extended TACACS server, this command enables the extended TACACS protocol.

tacacs-server host
global

```
tacacs-server host hostname [single-connection] [port number] [timeout seconds]
  [key string]
no tacacs-server host hostname
```

Configures   The hostname of a TACACS server

Default   None

Description

This command allows you to list the TACACS servers you have available. If you list more than one hostname, the router attempts to contact them in the order they are listed.

hostname
  The hostname of a TACACS, extended TACACS, or TACACS+ server.

`single-connection`
  Optional. This keyword specifies that the router maintains a single connection to the TACACS server. In other words, after making a request, the router waits on the same connection for the server to respond. This feature works only with the TACACS+ protocol and CiscoSecure.

`port` *number*
  Optional. Use this option to run your TACACS server on a different port than the default (port 49).

`timeout` *seconds*
  Optional. This option allows you to specify a timeout value for this server in *seconds*. It overrides the default or the global setting configured by the `tacacs-server timeout` command.

`key` *string*
  Optional. This option allows you to specify an encryption key for this server. It overrides the global setting configured by the `tacacs-server key` command.

tacacs-server key
global

```
tacacs-server key key-string
no tacacs-server key
```

Configures   TACACS encryption key

Default   None

Description   This command sets the encryption key for the TACACS server.

tacacs-server last-resort

```
tacacs-server last-resort {password | succeed}
no tacacs-server last-resort {password | succeed}
```

Configures   Behavior if the TACACS server doesn't respond

Default   The request is denied

Description
This command sets the router's behavior when the TACACS servers you have config-ured don't respond to a request. For security reasons, the default behavior is to deny the request. The password keyword challenges the user for the enable password before authorizing the action. The succeed keyword simply allows the action, and is discour-aged because it blindly allows the user to do what they want without authorization.

tacacs-server notify

```
tacacs-server notify {connection [always] | enable | logout [always] |
    slip [always]}
no tacacs-server notify
```

Configures   Sends messages to the TACACS server

Default   None

Description
This command tells the router to send messages to the TACACS server for accounting. It does not work with TACACS+; for that protocol, use the aaa accounting command. The following keywords specify when messages are sent:

connection
> When a connection is made by a user.

always
> Optional. A message is sent even if the user is not logged in. Note that it is possible for a SLIP or PPP user to be connected but not yet logged in.

enable
> When a user uses the enable command.

logout
> When a user logs out.

slip
> When a user starts a SLIP or PPP connection.

tacacs-server optional-passwords

```
tacacs-server optional-passwords
no tacacs-server optional-passwords
```

Configures   Password authentication

Default   Disabled

Description

This command makes the user's password optional, depending on the TACACS server's configuration. When this feature is enabled, the router tries to authenticate the user with the username only. If that fails, the router tries again with both the username and password.

This command is for TACACS and extended TACACS only; it does not work with TACACS+.

tacacs-server retransmit

```
tacacs-server retransmit number-of-times
no tacacs-server retransmit
```

Configures   Number of times to try a TACACS server before giving up

Default   2

Description

This command sets the number of times the router should try to contact a TACACS, extended TACACS, or TACACS+ server before giving up and moving on to the next server.

tacacs-server timeout

```
tacacs-server timeout seconds
no tacacs-server timeout
```

Configures   The amount of time to wait for a response from a TACACS server

Default   5 seconds

Description

This command sets the maximum amount of time that the router should wait to receive a response from a TACACS, extended TACACS, or TACACS+ server. If the router doesn't receive a response within this time, it retries the connection attempt. The number of retries is set by the `tacacs-server retransmit` command.

tag-switching

```
tag-switching
no tag-switching
```

Configures   MPLS

Default   None

Description

The `tag-switching` commands have been replaced with the newer `mpls` command. Table 17-24 shows a few examples.

Table 17-24. mpls commands that replace tag-switching commands

Old command	New command
tag-switching atm	mpls atm
tag-switching cos-map	mpls cos-map
tag-switching advertise-tags	mpls advertise-tags
tag-switching prefix-map	mpls prefix-map
show tag-switching	show mpls

terminal editing

```
terminal editing
terminal no editing
```

Configures   Advanced editing keys for the terminal session

Default   Enabled

Description

This command is enabled by default, allowing you to use control keys for advanced editing capabilities. These key sequences are listed in Chapter 1. Use the no form of the command to disable the advanced editing keys.

terminal escape-character

```
terminal escape-character ASCII-value
```

Configures   The escape character for the terminal line

Default   Ctrl-^ (Control+Shift-6)

Description

This command sets the value for the escape terminal character to *ASCII-value*, which is the ASCII value for the desired character. The escape character is used to escape certain processes in a router. For example, if you are pinging a device that isn't responding, you can cancel the ping by typing the escape character.

terminal history command

```
terminal history [size number]
terminal no history
```

Configures   Terminal history for the current session

Default   Enabled; 10 lines

Description

This command enables history logging for the current session; it can also be used to change the size of the history buffer for that session. To enable history logging, use the terminal history command, which takes the last-used size as the buffer size. To change the size of the current history buffer, use the size keyword followed by the *number* of lines you want to save in the buffer. The buffer's size can be from 1 to 256 lines.

Use Ctrl-P or the up arrow to go up in the history list; use Ctrl-N or the down arrow to return to more recent commands in the list. To see the entire list, use show history.

Example

This example changes the history size to 100:

```
router# terminal history size 100
```

terminal length command

```
terminal length number-of-lines
```

Configures   Window page size

Default   24 lines

Description

This command sets the size of the window for the current user session to *number-of-lines*. If output from any command exceeds your window size, the router suspends output and prompts you for a keystroke (--More--). This command is useful if you are using a terminal or terminal emulator with a viewing area that is not 24 lines long. Set *number-of-lines* to 0 to disable the --More-- prompt.

Warning: Setting the length to 0, which disables paging, can be useful, but it can present a problem on long output.

Example

To set the window size to 10:

```
Router#terminal length 10
```

To disable the --More-- prompt:

```
Router#terminal length 0
```

terminal monitor

command

```
terminal monitor
terminal no monitor
```

Configures   Debug and system error messages for the current terminal and session

Default   Disabled

Description

This command enables the display of debugging messages and system error messages for the current terminal (i.e., VTY or asynchronous line) session. It does not apply to the console itself; to disable console logging, use the command no logging console.

---

tftp-server

global

```
tftp-server flash [flash-partition-number:]filename [alias filename] [access-
    list]
tftp-server rom alias filename [access-list]
no tftp-server {flash | rom}
```

Configures   TFTP server

Default   Disabled

Description

The tftp-server flash command allows the router to act as a TFTP server that serves files from its flash filesystem. The *flash-partition-number* is the number of the specified partition number within the flash filesystem. If no partition is specified, the first partition is used. The *filename* is the name of the file that the TFTP service uses in answering read requests. The alias keyword allows you to provide an alternate name for the file.

The tftp-server rom command configures the router to serve the contents of its ROM using TFTP. The alias keyword, which is required for this form of the command, provides a name to be used to access the ROM contents.

Either form of the command allows you to specify an *access-list* that limits the hosts allowed to make incoming TFTP requests.

---

timers basic

router

```
timers basic update-value invalid-value holddown-value flush-value [sleeptime-
    value]
no timers basic
```

Configures   Routing protocol timers

Default   The default timer values are shown in Table 17-25.

Table 17-25. Default timer values

Timer	IGRP	RIP default
update	90 seconds	30 seconds
invalid	270 seconds	180 seconds
holddown	280 seconds	180 seconds
flush	630 seconds	240 seconds
sleeptime	0 milliseconds	N/A

Description

This command allows you to adjust the routing timers. All values expect for *sleeptime* are in seconds.

update-value
> The interval at which routing updates are sent.

invalid-value
> The interval after which a route is considered invalid if an update does not arrive.

holddown-value
> The time that the router waits after deciding that a route is invalid before accepting further information about it. For example, if a router decides that a certain route has become invalid, it waits for the hold-down period to pass before believing any other information stating that the route is valid. This procedure helps to maintain routing stability.

flush-value
> The interval after which invalid routes are purged from the routing table.

sleeptime-value
> Optional. This timer's value is the interval in milliseconds to wait after a flash update. This value should be less than the update value. Sleeptime is not applicable to RIP.

timers bgp   router, BGP

```
timers bgp keepalive holdtime
no timers bgp
```

Configures   BGP timers

Default   *keepalive*, 60 seconds; *holdtime*, 180 seconds

Description

This command allows you to configure the keepalive and holdtime timers for BGP. *keepalive* specifies the interval in seconds between the keepalive message that a router sends to its peer routers. *holdtime* is the time in seconds after which a peer is considered unreachable because a keepalive message wasn't received.

timers spf

```
timers spf delay-time hold-time
no timers spf delay-time hold-time
```

Configures   OSPF timers

Default   Delay time, 5 seconds; hold time, 10 seconds

Description
This command sets the two types of timers that are important to the OSPF protocol. *delay-time* is the interval in seconds between the arrival of a topology change and the time OSPF starts the shortest path first (SPF) calculation. *hold-time* is the minimum interval between two consecutive SPF calculations. Both timers must be in the range 0 to 65,535. Reducing these values may cause the router to switch to a different path more quickly, but this may be a detriment to performance; the SPF calculation is CPU-intensive.

---

trace, traceroute

```
trace [host]
traceroute [ host]
```

Description
This command allows you to determine the most likely path to a specified *host*. It is often useful in troubleshooting, and is similar to the traceroute command on Unix systems or the tracert command on Windows systems. If you omit the hostname, you'll be prompted for the necessary information. As with the ping command, the prompts differ depending on the mode you are in. The output from the trace command uses the special characters shown in Table 17-26.

Table 17-26. Special characters for trace output

Character	Meaning
xx msec	Round-trip time in milliseconds.
*	Packet timeout.
?	Unknown packet received.
A	Administratively unreachable; possibly means that an access list or equivalent function on another router is blocking the packets.
H	Host is unreachable.
N	Network is unreachable.
P	Protocol is unreachable.
Q	Source quench.
U	Port unreachable.

Reference
T-W

Example

This example shows what happens when you use the trace command without supplying a hostname. Note that you're prompted for many values that can't be specified on the command line. Omitting the hostname therefore gives you more control over the command's behavior than you would otherwise have.

```
Router#trace
    Protocol [ip]:                 Protocol
    Target IP address: 10.10.1.2   Can be hostname or network address
    Source address:                The IP address of the interface to use
    Numeric display [n]: y         Numeric display is not the default
    Timeout in seconds [3]:        Seconds to wait for each probe
    Probe count [3]:               Number of probes to execute at each TTL.
    Minimum Time to Live [1]:      The first TTL level to begin the trace
    Maximum Time to Live [30]:     The TTL level to stop the trace
    Port Number [33434]:           The UDP port number to probe
    Loose, Strict, Record, Timestamp, Verbose[none]:    Header Options

    Type escape sequence to abort.
    Tracing the route to 10.10.1.2
      1 10.10.1.2 0 msec 4 msec 0 msec
```

---

traffic-shape adaptive   interface

```
traffic-shape adaptive [bit-rate]
no traffic-shape adaptive
```

Configures   Traffic shaping on a Frame Relay subinterface

Default   Disabled

Description

This command enables traffic shaping on a Frame Relay subinterface. Traffic shaping means that the interface estimates the available bandwidth on the link when it receives BECNs (backwards explicit congestion notifications). The *bit-rate* parameter is optional and specifies the lowest bit rate (in Kbps) at which traffic is shaped.

---

traffic-shape fecn-adapt   interface

```
traffic-shape fecn-adapt
no traffic-shape fecn-adapt
```

Configures   Traffic shaping on a frame relay subinterface

Default   Disabled

Description

This command enables the interface to reflect FECN bits as BECN bits, which notifies the sending DTE that it is transmitting at a rate too fast to handle.

Example

This configuration sets up traffic shaping with an upper limit of 128 Kbps and a lower limit of 64 Kbps. With the `fecn-adapt` command, our router reflects FECN packets as BECN packets.

```
interface serial 1
   encapsulation frame-relay
interface serial 1.1
   traffic-shape rate 128000
   traffic-shape adaptive 64000
   traffic-shape fecn-adapt
```

---

traffic-shape group   interface

traffic-shape group *access-list bit-rate* [*burst-size* [*excess-burst-size*]]
no traffic-shape group *access-list*

Configures   Traffic shaping for general outbound traffic

Default   Disabled

Description

This command allows you to specify an access list that selects the packets to which traffic shaping applies.

access-list
　Traffic shaping is applied to packets that match this access list.

bit-rate
　The access bit rate in your service contract with your Frame Relay service provider.

burst-size
　Optional. The sustained number of bits that can be transmitted per interval, defined in your service contract with your Frame Relay service provider. Default is the *bit-rate* divided by 8.

excess-burst-size
　Optional. The maximum number of bits that can exceed the burst size during a congestion event. The default is the *burst-size*.

---

traffic-shape rate   interface

traffic-shape rate *bit-rate* [*burst-size* [*excess-burst-size*]]
no traffic-shape rate

Configures   Traffic shaping for all outbound traffic

Default   Disabled

Description

This command applies the traffic shaping to all outbound traffic. It is similar to traffic-shape group, but does not use an access list to select traffic.

bit-rate
> The access bit rate in your service contract with your Frame Relay service provider.

burst-size
> Optional. The sustained number of bits that can be transmitted per interval, as defined in your service contract with your Frame Relay service provider. Default is the *bit-rate* divided by 8.

excess-burst-size
> Optional. The maximum number of bits that can exceed the burst size during a congestion event. The default is the *burst-size*.

---

traffic-share   router, IGRP, EIGRP

```
traffic-share {balanced | min}
no traffic-share {balanced | min}
```

Configures

How traffic is distributed when multiple routes exist for the same destination

Default   balanced

Description

This command defines the way multiple routes are handled when they have different costs.

balanced
> Traffic is distributed based on the metric ratios.

min
> All traffic is sent using the route with the minimum cost.

---

transport   line

```
transport input protocol
transport output protocol
transport preferred protocol
```

Configures   The transport protocol

Default   Output and preferred, telnet; input, none

Description

This command specifies the transport protocol the router should use. input specifies the protocol to use for incoming connections on a line; output is for output connections on a line; and preferred is the transport protocol to use when the user does not specify one.

Using the command transport preferred none helps to prevent typos at the command line from causing a bogus DNS lookup. (With the default output setting, a mistyped command is frequently interpreted as a hostname for the telnet, initializing a DNS lookup.)

The *protocol* parameter specifies which protocol to use; possible values are given in Table 17-27.

Table 17-27. Transport protocols

Protocol	Meaning
lat	DEC LAT protocol, when connecting to DEC hosts
mop	Maintenance operation protocol
nasi	Netware asynchronous services interface protocol
none	No protocol selection is to be made on this line
rlogin	The Unix rlogin protocol
telnet	TCP/IP telnet protocol
ssh	SSH (Secure Shell)
all	All in the list
v120	ISDN asynchronous protocols

Example

Routers do not allow incoming network connections to a TTY by default, so you must use the transport input command to enable this feature:

```
line tty 2
  transport input all
```

tunnel checksum   interface

```
tunnel checksum
no tunnel checksum
```

Configures   The checksumming of packets on a tunnel interface

Default   Disabled

Description

This command enables packet checksumming on a tunnel interface. It applies to GRE tunnels only. When enabled, the router drops packets that fail the checksum test.

tunnel destination   interface

```
tunnel destination destination
no tunnel destination destination
```

Configures   The IP address or hostname of the tunnel's destination

Default   None

Description

This command specifies the tunnel's destination IP address or hostname.

Example

The following commands set up a tunnel interface called tunnel0. The source address for the tunnel is the address of the serial0 interface; the destination of the tunnel is 172.25.1.1. The tunnel uses the GRE protocol.

```
interface tunnel0
   tunnel source serial0
   tunnel destination 172.25.1.1
   tunnel mode gre ip
```

tunnel key   interface

tunnel key *key*
no tunnel key *key*

Configures   A key identifier for a tunnel

Default   None

Description

This command assigns a key to a tunnel. In this case, the *key* is just an integer that serves as a tunnel ID; it is not a cryptographic key. As such, it provides at best very weak security. The range for *key* is 0 to 4,294,967,295.

tunnel mode   interface

tunnel mode *type*
no tunnel mode *type*

Configures   The type of tunnel

Default   General Routing Encapsulation (GRE)

Description

This command sets the encapsulation mode for a tunnel. Values for *type* are given in Table 17-28. Both ends of the tunnel must use the same encapsulation type.

Table 17-28. Tunnel types

Tunnel type	Meaning
aurp	AppleTalk Update Routing Protocol
cayman	Cayman TunnelTalk with AppleTalk encapsulation
dvmrp	Distance Vector Multicast Routing Protocol
eon	EON-compatible CLNS tunnel
gre ip	General Route Encapsulation (GRE) protocol over IP
nos	KA9Q/NOS-compatible over IP
gre multipoint	Multipoint General Encapsulation (GRE) protocol

tunnel sequence-datagrams interface

```
tunnel sequence-datagrams
no tunnel sequence-datagrams
```

Configures   The tunnel interface

Default   Disabled

Description

This command tells the tunnel interface to drop any tunnel packets that arrive out of sequence.

tunnel source interface

```
tunnel source source
no tunnel source source
```

Configures   The source IP address of the tunnel

Default   None

Description   This command specifies the tunnel's source IP address.

Example

The following commands set up a tunnel that uses the address of the serial0 interface as its source address. The destination of the tunnel is 172.25.1.1.

```
interface tunnel0
  tunnel source serial0
  tunnel destination 172.25.1.1
  tunnel mode gre ip
```

txspeed line

```
txspeed bits-per-second
no txspeed
```

Configures   Transmit speed

Default   9600 baud

Description

This command sets the transmit speed. Use the no form to remove the command from the configuration.

Example

The following example sets the transmit speed on line 1 to 1,200:

```
line 1
  txspeed 1200
```

undebug

command

undebug {*debug-level* | all}

Description

This command turns off debugging at the selected *debug-level*. Use the all keyword to turn off all currently active debugging.

Example

If you enabled debug with:

    #debug ip eigrp

You can disable it with:

    #undebug ip eigrp
    or
    #undebug all

---

undelete

command

undelete *file-number* [*device*:]

Description

This command allows you to recover deleted files on Class A and B filesystems. The *file-number* is the index of the file in the directory. The *device* field is optional and specifies the flash device you wish to undelete from: bootflash, slot0, or slot1. This command cannot recover files after they have been purged by the squeeze command.

---

username

global

username *name* [nopassword | password *password*] [access-class *access-list-number*] [autocommand *command*] [callback-dialstring *phone-number*]
[callback-rotary *rotary-group-number*] [callback-line [tty] *line-number* [*ending-line-number*]] [nocallback-verify] [noescape] [nohangup]
[privilege *level*]

Configures   Username information for authentication

Default   None

Description

The username command provides authentication information for a user. It is used to build a username database on the router itself (as opposed to on an external server, like a RADIUS server). Many different types of information can be provided, using the following options:

nopassword

>   No password is required for the user; this option is useful when combined with autocommand.

password *password*

>   Specifies a password for the user.

access-class *access-list-number*
> Specifies an outgoing access list for the user, overriding the access list specified in the access-class command in the line configuration.

autocommand *command*
> Causes the specified command to be issued automatically when the user connects. This is commonly used to start PPP sessions.

callback-dialstring *phone-number*
> Specifies the phone number to pass to the modem for asynchronous callback.

callback-rotary *rotary-group-number*
> Specifies the rotary group to use for asynchronous callback.

callback-line tty *line-number ending-line-number*
> Specifies which lines can be used for asynchronous callback. The optional tty keyword restricts the callback to TTY lines.

nocallback-verify
> Callback not required for this user.

noescape
> Prevents the user from using an escape character.

nohangup
> Prevents the communication server from disconnecting. The user gets another login prompt when he attempts to disconnect.

privilege level
> Sets the privilege level for the user.

Example

The following commands create two users. An access list is applied to the user Bob for the duration of his sessions. The router automatically starts PPP when the user Jane logs in.

```
username bob password letmein access-class 10
username jane password thisisme autocommand ppp
```

---

vacant-message   line

vacant-message *delimiter message text delimiter*
no vacant-message

Configures   A message displayed to an idle line

Default   None

Description

This command sets the message that is displayed when a terminal is idle and waiting to begin a session. It is often used at terminals that are connected to routers or access servers for generic network access. The message is specific to a particular line; you must specify the message explicitly for every line. *delimiter* marks the beginning and end of the message; it can be any single character that is not used in the message itself. To disable this message, use the no form of this command.

Example

```
Router(config)#line 2
Router(config-line)#vacant-message # Welcome to the Network,
    Press return to begin! #
```

validate-update-source

```
validate-update-source
no validate-update-source
```

Configures   Validation of routing sources

Default   Enabled

Description

The validate-update-source command checks to make sure that the source IP address of incoming routing updates is on the same network as the interface receiving the update. This feature gives some protection against spoofing attacks.

Example

To disable this feature, use the no form of this command:

```
router rip
    network 10.10.0.0
    no validate-update-source
```

variance

```
variance multipler-value
no variance multipler-value
```

Configures   Multiplier value for load balancing

Default   1 (equal-cost load balancing)

Description

This command lets you specify a *multiplier-value* for use in load balancing with IGRP and EIGRP. The *multiplier-value* can be from 1 to 128. Routes within a factor of *multiplier-value* of the best routes are used to carry traffic. Normally, all traffic is sent over the route with the best metric; if two or more routes share the same metric, load balancing takes place between those routes.

Example

Assume that your router has three routes to the same destination. The routes have metrics of 10, 30, and 50. With the default variance of 1 (equal-cost load balancing), all traffic is sent using the route with the metric of 10. For load balancing to take place, another route with a metric of 10 must appear in the routing table.

To force the router to use multiple paths in this situation, you can change the variance (unequal-cost load balancing). If you increase the variance to 3, routes with a metric within a factor of 3 of the best route are used. In this situation, the routes with metrics of 10 and 30 will be used to carry traffic, and the route with a metric of 50 will not.

```
router eigrp 100
   variance 5
```

verify   command

```
verify {flash | bootflash}
```

Description
This command verifies the *flash* checksum value with the stored flash image.

Example
```
Router#verify flash

System flash directory:
File   Length    Name/status
  1    6070088   igs-j-1.110-3
[6070152 bytes used, 2318456 available, 8388608 total]

Name of file to verify? igs-j-1.110-3
Verifying checksum for 'igs-j-1.110-3' (file # 1)...  OK
```

version   router (RIP)

```
version {1 | 2}
no version
```

Configures   Version of RIP protocol to use

Default   Accepts both versions but transmits only Version 1

Description
This command specifies which version of the RIP protocol to use. The `ip rip` command can also be used to select the RIP protocol version.

Example
The following commands configure the router to communicate only with RIPv2.

```
router rip
   network 10.10.0.0
   version 2
```

vlan

vlan config mode

```
vlan vlan-id [are hops] [ backupcrf mode ] [ bridge type | number]
   [ media type ] [mtu mtu-size] [name vlan-name] [parent parent-vlan-id]
   [ring ring-number] [said sa-id-value] [state {suspend | active}]
   [stp type type] [tb-vlan1 id] [tb-vlan2 id]
no vlan vlan-id
```

Configures   A specific VLAN

Default   None

Description

This command configures a VLAN while in the VLAN configuration mode.

vlan-id

> The VLAN number, from 2 to 1,001.

are *hops*

> Optional. Specifies the maximum number of All Route Explorer hops for this VLAN, from 0 to 13. If not defined, 0 is the default.

backupcrf *mode*

> Optional. Enables or disables the backup concentrator relay function (CRF). Valid values are enable or disable.

bridge

> Optional. Sets the bridging characteristics of the VLAN. Valid values for the type are srb or srt. Valid values for the bridge-number are 0 to 15. No default.

media *type*

> Optional. Specifies the media type of the VLAN. Values can be ethernet, fd-net, fddi, trcrf, and trbrf. Default is ethernet.

mtu *mtu-size*

> Optional. Specifies the MTU (Maximum Transmission Unit) for the VLAN. Valid values are 576 to 18,190. Defaults are dependent on the VLAN type but it is usually 1,500.

name *vlan-name*

> Optional. Specifies a text string to identify the VLAN. The name can be from 1 to 32 characters in length. Default is vlan*XXXX* where *XXXX* represents the VLAN ID number.

parent *parent-vlan-id*

> Optional. Specifies the ID number for parent VLANs for FDDI or Token Ring networks. Can be a value from 2 to 1,001. No default.

ring *ring-number*

> Optional. Specifies the ring number of VLAN for FDDI or Token Ring networks. Can be a value from 2 to 1,001. No default.

said *sa-id-value*

> Optional. Specifies the security association identifier. Can be from 1 to 4,294,967,294. Default is 100,000 plus the VLAN ID number.

state

> Optional. Sets the state of the VLAN, which can be active or suspended. A suspended VLAN does not process packets. Default is active.

stp type

> Optional. Sets the Spanning Tree Protocol type, which can be ieee, ibm, or auto. No type is specified as default.

tb-vlan1

> Optional. Specifies the ID number of the first translational VLAN for this VLAN. Can be from 2 to 1,001, and zero is the default, which means none defined.

tb-vlan2

> Optional. Specifies the ID number of the second translational VLAN for this vlan. Can be from 2 to 1,001, and zero is the default, which means none defined.

vlan database

vlan database

Configures   Enters VLAN configuration mode.

Default   N/A

Description

This command enters the VLAN configuration mode. In this mode, you can use the following commands:

abort

> Exits the VLAN configuration mode without saving the changes you have made.

apply

> Saves and applies the current VLAN changes.

exit

> Saves and applies the current VLAN changes then exits the VLAN configuration mode.

reset

> Abandons any changes and reloads the saved VLAN information.

show

> Displays the current VLAN database information.

vlan

> Edit VLAN information. See the separate vlan command listing for more information.

vtp

> Edits VLAN trunking protocol (VTP) information. See the separate vtp command listing for more information.

Example

This example shows entering the VLAN database and creating VLAN 100.

```
Router# vlan database
Router(vlan)#vlan 100
Router(vlan)#exit
```

vtp client

```
vtp client
no vtp client
```

Configures   VLAN Trunking Protocol (VTP)

Default   Server mode

Description

This command places the device into VTP client mode. When a device is in VTP client mode, it changes its configuration to duplicate the configuration of the VTP server.

vtp domain

```
vtp domain name
no vtp domain name
```

Configures   VLAN Trunking Protocol (VTP)

Default   None

Description

This command configures the VTP administrative domain name for the device. This name is case-sensitive. A device will not transmit any VTP advertisements until a domain name is configured.

vtp password

```
vtp password string
no vtp password
```

Configures   VLAN Trunking Protocol (VTP)

Default   None

Description

This command configures a VTP domain password, which is an ASCII string from 1 to 32 characters.

vtp server

`vtp server`

Configures   VLAN Trunking Protocol (VTP)

Default   Server mode

Description

This command sets the device into VTP server mode, which is the default. You use the command if you have previously configured the device as a client. Also, this command is the equivalent of using no `vtp client`.

vtp transparent

`vtp transparent`
`no vtp transparent`

Configures   VLAN Trunking Protocol (VTP)

Default   Server mode

Description

This command places the device into VTP transparent mode, which disables VTP from the local device but does not remove the device from the VTP domain.

vtp v2-mode

`vtp v2-mode`
`no vtp v2-mode`

Configures   VLAN Trunking Protocol (VTP)

Default   Disabled

Description

This command places the device into VTP version 2 mode. All devices within a VTP domain must run the same version of VTP. You can simply configure this on one device (like the server VTP switch) and all devices will be reconfigured to version 2 via VTP, provided that all devices are v2-mode capable.

vty-async

`vty-async`
`no vty-async`

Configures   VTY line features

Default   Disabled

Description

This command configures all virtual terminal lines to support asynchronous protocol features.

---

vty-async dynamic-routing   global

```
vty-async dynamic-routing
no vty-async dynamic-routing
```

Configures   VTY line features

Default   Disabled

Description

This command enables dynamic routing on all VTY asynchronous lines.

---

vty-async header-compression   global

```
vty-async header-compression [passive]
no vty-async header-compression
```

Configures   VTY line features

Default   Disabled

Description

This command enables header compression on all VTY asynchronous lines. The passive keyword is optional. It tells the router to compress headers only if headers on the incoming packets on the same line are compressed as well.

---

vty-async keepalive   global

```
vty-async keepalive seconds
no vty-async keepalive seconds
```

Configures   VTY line features

Default   10 seconds

Description

This command specifies the keepalive frequency on VTY asynchronous lines. The value can be from 1 to 32,767.

vty-async mtu

vty-async mtu *bytes*
no vty-async mtu

Configures   VTY line features

Default   1,500 bytes

Description
This command specifies the MTU of IP packets sent over this line. The value can be from 64 to 1,000,000 bytes.

vty-async ppp authentication

vty-async ppp authentication {chap | pap}
no vty-async ppp authentication {chap | pap}

Configures   VTY line features

Default   Disabled

Description
This command enables PPP authentication on the VTY asynchronous lines.

vty-async ppp use-tacacs

vty-async ppp use-tacacs
no vty-async ppp use-tacacs

Configures   VTY line features

Default   Disabled

Description
This command tells PPP sessions using VTY lines to use TACACS for authentication.

width

width *characters*
no width

Configures   The terminal width for a line

Default   80 characters

Description

This command sets the width, in *characters*, of a terminal line. Setting this value correctly helps deal with lines that are too long to be displayed on your terminal window or screen.

---

write

command

```
write erase
write memory
write network
write terminal
```

Description

The write commands are used to work with the current configuration. They are obsolete and have been replaced by the copy, show, and erase commands. Table 17-29 shows the correspondence between the two sets of commands.

Table 17-29. Write commands and their equivalents

Write command	Equivalent
write erase	erase startup-config
write memory	copy running-config startup-config
write network	copy running-config tftp
write terminal	show running-config

Appendix: Network Basics

Throughout this book, I use IP address notation without much explanation. I take for granted that you understand the meaning of 192.168.0.1/24. And most likely, you probably do. However, I find that even the seasoned professional can sometimes forget the simplest information. This appendix serves as a useful reminder in those moments of brain fog when the network basics elude you. In addition to IP address notation and subnetting, this appendix reviews the OSI reference model and provides some details about IPv6.

IPv4 Subnetting

Back in the early days of the Internet, there were three major classes of addressing that were labeled A through C. Table A-1 shows how many hosts the Internet could support based on this system.

Table A-1. Original IPv4 class system

	Networks per class	Hosts per network	IP range
Class A	126	16,777,214	1.0.0.0–127.255.255.255
Class B	65,000	65,534	128.0.0.0–191.255.255.255
Class C	2,000,000	254	192.0.0.0–223.255.255.255

Note: Two other classes, D and E, were reserved for multicast and "future use," respectively.

With the growth of the Internet, these classes became obsolete for a few reasons, the biggest of which was address space depletion. In the early 1990s, we could see that we would run out of address space to give to new Internet users. Another problem was that the routing tables on the Internet backbone routers were growing out of control. Without the ability to summarize routing information, the routing tables were growing beyond the router's capacity to store them.

In order to solve these problems, a new system of subnetting the IP address space was developed: classless inter-domain routing.

Classless Inter-Domain Routing

Classless inter-domain routing (CIDR) was developed to address IP address depletion and growing routing tables. The two main features of CIDR are:

- Route table aggregation (which produces more efficient routing tables)
- Effective use of the existing IP address space

The adoption of CIDR and other technologies such as network address translation (NAT; see Chapter 13 for details) has minimized but not resolved the problems of IP address space depletion and burgeoning routing tables. The problems that still exist in IPv4, even with the use of CIDR and NAT, have been addressed with the development of IPv6, described later in this appendix.

CIDR notation

In CIDR notation, a network address is represented by a prefix, which is simply the network address followed by a slash and the number of bits in the subnet mask. For example, the network address of 192.168.1.0 with a subnet mask of 255.255.255.0 is represented as 192.168.1.0/24. As Table A-2 shows, there are 24 consecutive leftmost 1 bits in the binary representation, which gives us the /24 value. In other words, if you count the leftmost consecutive 1's in the binary representation of this prefix, you will count 24 bits.

If you are using the old class notation with CIDR, Class A would /8, Class B would be /16, and Class C is /24.

Table A-2 shows possible subnets of a /24 address space. In this table, the subnet binary representation illustrates the number of bits in the subnet. The usable hosts column is the number of addresses that can be used for host addresses, which is the actual number of addresses in the subnet minus the network and broadcast addresses. For example, the /27 prefix gives us actually 32 addresses. The first address is used for the network address and the last address is used for the broadcast address, which leaves use with 30 possible usable host addresses (32 − 2 = 30). See the "Subnet Math" section later in this appendix for more information on this calculation.

If you are considering taking a certification test in the future, committing Table A-2 to memory is a fairly good idea.

Table A-2. Subnets for the /24 address space

	Usable subnets	Hosts	Subnet mask	Subnet binary	Notes
/24	1	254	255.255.255.0	11111111.11111111.11111111.00000000	Entire class C notation
/25	2	126	255.255.255.128	11111111.11111111.11111111.10000000	CIDR and subnet-zero networks only
/26	4	62	255.255.255.192	11111111.11111111.11111111.11000000	
/27	8	30	255.255.255.224	11111111.11111111.11111111.11100000	
/28	16	14	255.255.255.240	11111111.11111111.11111111.11110000	
/29	32	6	255.255.255.248	11111111.11111111.11111111.11111000	
/30	64	2	255.255.255.252	11111111.11111111.11111111.11111100	
/31	0	0	255.255.255.254	11111111.11111111.11111111.11111110	Invalid because no bits are left for the host
/32	0	1	255.255.255.255	11111111.11111111.11111111.11111111	Single host subnet mask

All zero and all ones subnets are included in the Usable Subnets calculation.

In Table A-2, you see that /31 is marked invalid because there are no bits left for the host. However, in IOS version 12.2(4), Cisco allows that subnet to be used on IPv4 point-to-point links, which is a good thing because it effectively doubles the number of point-to-point links that can be obtained from a given IP address range.

Table A-3 shows the entire CIDR table with dotted decimal subnet masks and the number of classful networks for each prefix.

Table A-3. Entire CIDR table

	Subnet mask	Number of addresses
/1	128.0.0.0	2,048,000,000
/2	192.0.0.0	1,024,000,000
/3	224.0.0.0	512,000,000
/4	240.0.0.0	256,000,000
/5	248.0.0.0	128,000,000
/6	252.0.0.0	64,000,000
/7	254.0.0.0	32,000,000
/8	255.0.0.0	16,000,000
/9	255.128.0.0	8,000,000
/10	255.192.0.0	4,000,000
/11	255.224.0.0	2,000,000

Table A-3. Entire CIDR table (continued)

	Subnet mask	Number of addresses
/12	255.240.0.0	1,024,000
/13	255.248.0.0	512,000
/14	255.252.0.0	256,000
/15	255.254.0.0	128,000
/16	255.255.0.0	64,000
/17	255.255.128.0	32,000
/18	255.255.192.0	16,000
/19	255.255.224.0	8,000
/20	255.255.240.0	4,000
/21	255.255.248.0	2,000
/22	255.255.252.0	1,000
/23	255.255.254.0	512
/24	255.255.255.0	256
/25	255.255.255.128	128
/26	255.255.255.192	64
/27	255.255.255.224	32
/28	255.255.255.240	16
/29	255.255.255.248	8
/30	255.255.255.252	4
/31	255.255.255.254	2
/32	255.255.255.255	1

Subnet Math

When subnetting IP addresses, there are a few really important formulas. Most of these formulas entail basically converting the IP address to a binary number and then OR'ing or AND'ing it with the subnet mask or network number.

Subnet zero reminder

In the past, subnets with all ones and all zeros were not allowed. (Some legacy network hardware still follows this rule.) With Cisco devices, these subnets are allowed if the command ip subnet-zero is used. In all current versions of IOS, this command is enabled by default. It's important to keep this in mind as we describe the subnet calculations.

Calculating a network address from a host address

This subnet calculation is nothing more than a logical AND between the subnet mask and the host address. For example, if you had a host with an address of 192.168.1.161/27, you only need to perform the calculation in Table A-4 to find the network IP address.

Table A-4. Finding the network IP address for 192.168.1.161/27

Host address	192.168.1.161	11000000.10101000.00000001.10100001	
Subnet mask	255.255.255.224 (/27)	11111111.11111111.11111111.11100000	
Network address	192.168.1.160	11000000.10101000.00000001.10100000	(logical AND)

By AND'ing the subnet mask and the host address, we are left with a new binary address. This binary number translates to 192.168.1.160 in dotted decimal, which is the network address for this host address.

Calculating the broadcast address of a subnet

To calculate the broadcast address for any given subnet, it's a simple matter of logically OR'ing the inverted subnet mask with the network address. Shown in Table A-5 is the broadcast address calculation for the 192.168.1.160/27 network, which is same network as in the previous example.

Table A-5. Calculating the broadcast address for 192.168.1.160/27

Network address	192.168.1.160	11000000.10101000.00000001.10100000	
Inverted subnet mask	0.0.0.31	00000000.00000000.00000000.00011111	
Broadcast address	192.168.1.191	11000000.10101000.00000001.10111111	(logical OR)

In this example, the inverse of the subnet mask 255.255.255.224 is 0.0.0.31. If we take the binary representation of that number and OR it with the network address, we are left with the broadcast address binary. When translated back to dotted decimal, this address is 192.168.1.191, which is the correct broadcast address for 192.168.1.160/27 network.

Calculating available subnets

The following formula allows you to calculate the number of possible subnets in an address space, where N is the number of bits used in the subnet.

2^N = Number of subnets available if subnet-zero is allowed (the default)
$2^N - 2$ = Number of subnets available if subnet-zero is disabled

For example, what's the possible number of subnets of 192.168.1.0/27 if subnet-zero is enabled? If we look at Table A-2 for the /27 prefix, we see that there are 3 bits in the last octet of the subnet binary. So, 2^3 (2 to the power of 3) gives eight usable subnets. If we weren't allowed to use the subnet-zero command, we'd have to use the second formula, which is 2^3-2, which results in six usable subnets.

Calculating the number of hosts per subnet

Calculating the number of available hosts per subnet is a little easier because there is no confusion about subnet zero. With the host address space, the first and last addresses are reserved and cannot be used for a host, except in the case of the /31, which we described earlier. The first address is reserved for the network number and the last address is reserved for the broadcast address.

The following formula allows you to calculate the number of usable hosts per subnet. N is the number of bits used for the host.

$2^N - 2$ = Number of usable host addresses per subnet

If we use the same address as in the previous example, 192.168.1.0/27, we can find N by looking at Table A-2. If 3 bits are used in the last octet for the subnet mask, the host bit count is five. So, we plug 5 into our formula, which leaves us with 30 available host addresses ($2^5 - 2 = 30$).

More about Subnets

Our final section on IPv4 subnetting reviews the reserved private address space, how to change the way the router displays subnet information, and using VLSM.

Private address space

A certain amount of the original address space was reserved for private IP addresses. These address spaces are for private networks and are not routable on the Internet. Throughout this book, we use the private address space in all our examples so that we don't show any real addresses. Table A-6 shows the available private address space.

Table A-6. IPv4 private address space

Subnet	IP range
10.0.0.0/8	10.0.0.0 through 10.255.255.255
172.16.0.0/12	172.16.0.0 through 172.31.255.255
192.168.0.0/16	192.168.0.0 through 192.168.255.255

Changing the way the router displays subnet information

You can change the way the router displays subnet information. If you just want to change it for the current session, you can use the terminal ip netmask-format command, which is followed by the type decimal, bit-count, or hexadecimal. (Bit-count is the default.) The following example shows the output for all three versions of the command.

```
Router> terminal ip netmask-format bit-count
Router> show ip int
FastEthernet0/0 is up, line protocol is up
    Internet address is 192.168.1.161/27
...
Router> terminal ip netmask-format decimal
Router> show ip int
FastEthernet0/0 is up, line protocol is up
    Internet address is 192.168.1.161 255.255.255.224
...
Router> terminal ip netmask-format hexadecimal
Router> show ip int
FastEthernet0/0 is up, line protocol is up
    Internet address is 66.133.171.161 0xFFFFFFE0
```

To apply the format change to the entire router, use the ip netmask-format config-uration command, which takes the exact same parameters. The only difference is that the setting is stored in the router configuration and applies to all future sessions. However, this only changes the way the netmasks are displayed in the show and debug command output. When you enter an IP address in the router's configuration, you still need to use the 255.255.255.0 format.

Variable Length Subnet Masks (VLSM)

Variable Length Subnet Masks or VLSMs allow a single network to be configured with multiple different subnet masks. This allows the network administrator to divide a network up with finer granularity. Not all routing protocols support VLSM. For example, RIP-v1 and IGRP require classful networking in order to work. Modern network routing protocols such as EIGRP, RIP-v2, OSPF, and IS-IS all support VLSM. The older protocols (RIPv1 and IGRP) require all subnet masks within the network to be configured the same. Employing the same mask throughout a subnet is called Fixed Length Subnet Masking (FLSM). If you try to use VLSM in your network while running RIPv1 or IGRP, the routes with differing masks will not show up in the routing table.

To enable the router to support VLSM, configure the router with the ip classless command, which is enabled by default on current versions of IOS. This command changes the way the router behaves in terms of subnetting by removing an assumption. The assumption is as follows: if there is a connected subnet (for example,10.1.2.0/24), the router running a classful routing protocol assumes that it knows about every subnet in the network (in this example, subnet 10), which becomes a problem when there is a default route configured. If the router gets a packet for 10.200.1.0 and it does not appear in the routing table, the normal behavior is to assume that the route does not exist and drop the packet, even though the default route exists. When the ip classless command is enabled, this assumption is overridden and the packet is not dropped. Instead, the packet is sent along the default route.

In order to better understand the purpose of VLSM, consider the following example. We have the network address space of 192.168.10.0/24, which we would like to split up into nine separate networks with the following specifications:

- Four networks require six hosts per network.
- Three networks require thirty hosts per network.
- Two networks require sixty hosts per network.

Table A-7 shows how we could subnet our 192.168.10.0/24 network to support this configuration with VLSM. Remember that this solution is the not the only way to subnet to meet our needs. (You can subnet the network any way you like.)

Table A-7. VLSM example

	Hosts	Network	Host IPs	Broadcast
1	6	192.168.10.0/29	192.168.10.1–192.168.10.6	192.168.10.7
2	6	192.168.10.8/29	192.168.10.9–192.168.10.14	192.168.10.15

Table A-7. VLSM example (continued)

	Hosts	Network	Host IPs	Broadcast
3	6	192.168.10.16/29	192.168.10.17–192.168.10.22	192.168.10.23
4	6	192.168.10.24/29	192.168.10.25–192.168.10.30	192.168.10.31
5	30	192.168.10.32/27	192.168.10.33–192.168.10.62	192.168.10.63
6	30	192.168.10.64/27	192.168.10.65–192.168.10.94	192.168.10.95
7	30	192.168.10.96/27	192.168.10.97–192.168.10.126	192.168.10.127
8	62	192.168.10.128/26	192.168.10.129–192.168.10.190	192.168.10.191
9	62	192.168.10.192/26	192.168.10.192–192.168.10.254	192.168.10.255

OSI Reference Model

The OSI reference model is the foundation of all network communications. While a good understanding is certainly required at certification test time, it also has plenty of practical applications. For example, knowledge of the OSI layers greatly helps when troubleshooting a network problem.Table A-8 shows the entire OSI reference model.

Table A-8. OSI reference model

Layer	Name	Data encapsulation representation	Encapsulation with header information
7	Application	Protocol Data Unit	User Data
6	Presentation	Protocol Data Unit	User Data
5	Session	Protocol Data Unit	User Data
4	Transport	Segment	TCP Header + User Data
3	Network	Packets	IP Header + User Data
2	Data Link	Frames	LLC Header + User Data
			MAC Header + LLC Header + User Data
1	Physical	Bits	101010100000…

When data leaves a node to go out on the network, the data starts at layer 7 (the application layer) and travels all the way down until it finally exits at layer 1 (the physical layer). When data arrives at a node from the network, it arrives at the physical layer and works its way back up the stack until it reaches the application layer. As data travels up and down the OSI model, the network header information is added and removed from the user data, as shown in the last column of the table.

Layers 7 through 4 are considered the upper layers; layers 3 through 1 are the lower layers.

Application Layer

The application layer provides network services and protocols directly to end user applications. For example, an application might make an HTTP call to another computer. The HTTP interface is the network service that exists at this layer, not the application making the call. In other words, your browser doesn't operate at this layer, but the HTTP protocol does. Examples of other protocols that operate at this layer are SMTP, DNS, FTP, Telnet, and SNMP.

Presentation Layer

This layer is concerned with transforming application layer data, which ensures that the data is readable by the application layer of other computers on the network. Some encoding examples are ASCII, MP3, JPEG, and MPEG.

Session Layer

This layer creates, maintains, and terminates the session communication between computers by established rules regarding how the end devices will talk to each other. Methods for this communication include one-way (simplex), taking turns (half-duplex), or talking simultaneously (full-duplex).

Transport Layer

In TCP/IP, this is the layer at which TCP and UDP operate. By segmenting outgoing data and reassembling incoming data, this layer provides transmission of the data. Functions include sequencing, flow control, error detection, multiplexing, and the retransmission of bad or missing data.

Network Layer

By using logical addressing (IP or IPX addresses), this layer defines processes to route the data across network, which is assembled into packets and datagrams. Routers and Layer 3 switches operate at this layer. In other words, IP addressing and IP routing both occur at this layer.

Some show commands that help with debugging at this layer include:

- `show ip protocol` (addressing)
- `show interface` (addressing)
- `show ip interface brief` (addressing)
- `show ip route` (routing)
- `show ip eigrp/ospf/etc` (routing)

Data Link Layer

This layer defines how data is moved across a physical media such as Ethernet, FDDI, or Token Ring. Addressing of this layer is controlled through MAC addresses. Two sublayers divide this layer in two: MAC (Media Access Layer) and LLC (Logical Link Control). Of course, here is where layer 2 switches operate.

Some show commands for this layer are:

- `show interface`
- `show cdp neighbor`
- `show arp`

Physical Layer

This layer is the electrical specification for carrying bits over the media, such as signal voltages rates, maximum transmission distances, and other physical characteristics. Hubs and repeaters operate at this layer. For this layer, the show command that's most helpful is show controller.

IPv6

IPv6 is slated to replace the aging IPv4, which is the addressing scheme that is currently used on the Internet. Given the growth of the Internet, it's remarkable that IPv4 has lasted this long. (We have CIDR and NAT to thank for that.)

IPv6 seeks to solve the major problem of IPv4's limited address space by increasing the address size from 32 bits to 128 bits, which gives approximately 3.4×10^{38} possible addresses. By comparison, IPv4 has only 4.2×10^9 possible addresses.

Some of the benefits of IPv6 are:

- Much larger address space
- Authentication and encryption
- Inherits IPv4 characteristics
- Allows for coexistence with IPv4

IPv6 addresses are assigned to interfaces not hosts. So a certain host with more than one interface will have more than one IPv6 address. There are three types of IPv6 addresses: unicast, anycast, and multicast.

Unicast is an identifier for a single interface. A packet that sent to that identifier is for that interface only.

Anycast is an address for a set of interfaces that might belong to different nodes. A packet destined for an anycast address is delivered to the "nearest" interface.

Multicast is an address for a set interfaces that belong to different nodes. A packet that is destined for a multicast address is delivered to all nodes belonging to that address.

IPv6 has no broadcast addresses because their functionality is replaced by the multicast address.

IPv6 Notation

The 128 bits of an IPv6 address are represented as eight hexadecimal numbers separated by colons. For example, consider the following address:

    FEC0:0000:0000:0000:1101:0080:F5BF:0001

That is quite an address to type. Fortunately, there are some rules for writing IPv6 addresses in shorthand.

Shorthand rule one

The first rule is that leading 0s can be omitted in each field. For example, 001F can be written simply 1F. When we apply this rule to the above address, we are left with this:

FEC0:0:0:0:1101:80:F5BF:1

Shorthand rule two

The second rule is that any repeating sets of 0's can be represented with double colons (::), but only once per address. When we apply this rule to the above address, we get this:

FECO::1101:80:F5BF:1

Remember that the :: can only be used once. For example, the following address would be illegal:

FECO::1101::1

Here are two more examples of the :: notation:

FF01:0:0:0:0:0:0:1 → FF01::1
0:0:0:0:0:0:0:1 → ::1

 While the shorthand makes IPv6 addresses easier to type, they are still fairly long, which makes DNS even more important. To support IPv6 addresses, a new DNS record type called "AAAA" maps the hostname to an IPv6 address.

As far as subnetting notation, IPv6 follows the same prefix as CIDR in IPv4, which is the address followed by a slash and the subnet bits:

FEC0:0:0:0:1101:80:F5BF:1/60

Important IPv6 Addresses

Table A-9 serves as a guide for the most common IPv6 addresses that you may encounter.

Table A-9. Important IPv6 addresses

Description	Address	Notes
APNIC allocated space	2001:0200::/23 2001:0C00:/23	Asia Pacific Network Information Center (APNIC) for use in Asia
ARIN allocated space	2001:0400::/23	American Registry for Internet Numbers (ARIN) for use in the Americas
RIPENCC allocated space	2001:0600::/23 2001:0800::/23	Reseaux IP Europeans - Network Coordination Center (RIPE NCC) for use in Europe and the Middle East.
Global Unicast	2000::/3	Globally unique addresses
6to4 Tunnels	2002::/16	
Link Local Use	FE80::/10	For use with auto-configuration

Description	Address	Notes
Site Local Use	FEC0::/10	Equivalent to IPv4 private addresses
IPv4 Mapped	::FFFF:xxxx:xxxx	The x's are the IPv4 address. (192.168.30.1 is ::FFFF:C0A8:1E01)
Loopback	::1	Similar to 127.0.0.1 in IPv4
Multicast	FF00::/8	Full multicast space
Multicast	FF01::1	All nodes within the host
Multicast	FF02::1	All nodes on the local link
Multicast	FF01::2	All routers within the node-local scope
Multicast	FF02::2	All routers on the link-local scope
Multicast	FF05::2	All routers in the site-local scope

Enabling IPv6 on a Router

To enable IPv6 on a router, use the `ipv6 unicast-routing` command. For example:

```
ipv6 unicast-routing
!
interface ethernet0
  ipv6 FEC0:110:210:1::/64 eui-64
```

Using an IPv6 Address in a URL

Since the colon (:) is already used in URL definitions, you can't simply drop an IPv6 address into a URL. To use an IPv6 address in a URL, the address itself must be inside left and right brackets. For example:

http://[FEC0::AE14]:80/index.html

Although this is one method for making a URL call directly to an IPv6 address, it is still quite painful. Once again, this illustrates the importance of using DNS in the IPv6 address space.

Index

We'd like to hear your suggestions for improving our indexes. Send email to *index@oreilly.com*.

R

About the Author

James Boney has worked for the last eight years as a consultant specializing in a wide variety of subjects: network design, network management, Unix administration, and programming in Java, C/C++, and Perl.

For the last seven years, he has been working on the vLab project at Element K. vLab allows users to access routers and workstations over the Internet for training purposes. Jim currently lives in Severn, Maryland with his wife Peggy and his daughter Catherine.

Colophon

Our look is the result of reader comments, our own experimentation, and feedback from distribution channels. Distinctive covers complement our distinctive approach to technical topics, breathing personality and life into potentially dry subjects.

The animal on the cover of *Cisco IOS in a Nutshell*, Second Edition is a donkey, *Equus asinus*, also known as a domesticated ass. Today's donkeys are probably descendants of the African wild ass, and they were domesticated by the Egyptians around 4,000 B.C. They're about four feet tall, and they're known for long ears, a short mane that looks a bit like a push broom, and the braying noise they make. The big ears and braying enabled wild asses to keep in touch across the far distances that often separated them as they searched for sparse food sources in the African desert. Donkeys are relatives of the horse; although they are considerably smaller in stature than their cousins, they live longer, up to 25 or 30 years. They run as fast as 30 miles per hour.

Jamie Peppard was the production editor and proofreader for *Cisco IOS in a Nutshell*, Second Edition. Lydia Onofrei and Claire Cloutier provided quality control. Abby Fox provided production assistance. Ellen Troutman Zaig wrote the index.

Ellie Volckhausen designed the cover of this book, based on a series design by Edie Freedman. The cover image is a 19th-century engraving from the Dover Pictorial Archive. Karen Montgomery produced the cover layout with Adobe InDesign CS using Adobe's ITC Garamond font.

David Futato designed the interior layout. This book was converted by Keith Fahlgren from Word to FrameMaker 5.5.6. The text font is Linotype Birka; the heading font is Adobe Myriad Condensed; and the code font is LucasFont's TheSans Mono Condensed. The illustrations that appear in the book were produced by Robert Romano, Jessamyn Read, and Lesley Borash using Macromedia FreeHand MX and Adobe Photoshop CS. This colophon was written by Leanne Soylemez.

Better than e-books

Buy *Cisco IOS in a Nutshell,* 2nd Edition,
and access the digital edition FREE
on Safari for 45 days.

Go to www.oreilly.com/go/safarienabled
and type in coupon code YCDM-5XZD-IXR5-AFE8-BQ6W

Search
thousands of
top tech books

Download
whole chapters

Cut and Paste
code examples

Find
answers fast

Search Safari! The premier electronic reference
library for programmers and IT professionals.

Related Titles from O'Reilly

Keep in touch with O'Reilly

Download examples from our books

To find example files from a book, go to:
www.oreilly.com/catalog select the book,
and follow the "Examples" link.

Register your O'Reilly books

Register your book at *register.oreilly.com*
Why register your books? Once you've
registered your O'Reilly books you can:

- Win O'Reilly books, T-shirts or discount
  coupons in our monthly drawing.
- Get special offers available only to
  registered O'Reilly customers.
- Get catalogs announcing new books
  (US and UK only).
- Get email notification of new editions
  of the O'Reilly books you own.

Join our email lists

Sign up to get topic-specific email announcements of new books and conferences, special
offers, and O'Reilly Network technology
newsletters at:

elists.oreilly.com

It's easy to customize your free elists subscription so you'll get exactly the O'Reilly
news you want.

Get the latest news, tips, and tools

www.oreilly.com

- "Top 100 Sites on the Web"—PC Magazine
- CIO Magazine's Web Business 50 Awards

Our web site contains a library of comprehensive product information (including book
excerpts and tables of contents), download-
able software, background articles, interviews
with technology leaders, links to relevant
sites, book cover art, and more.

Work for O'Reilly

Check out our web site for current
employment opportunities:

jobs.oreilly.com

Contact us

O'Reilly Media, Inc.
1005 Gravenstein Hwy North
Sebastopol, CA 95472 USA
Tel: 707-827-7000 or 800-998-9938
    (6am to 5pm PST)
Fax: 707-829-0104

Contact us by email

For answers to problems regarding
your order or our products:
order@oreilly.com

To request a copy of our latest catalog:
catalog@oreilly.com

For book content technical questions
or corrections: **booktech@oreilly.com**

For educational, library, government,
and corporate sales: **corporate@oreilly.com**

To submit new book proposals to our
editors and product managers:
proposals@oreilly.com

For information about our international
distributors or translation queries:
international@oreilly.com

For information about academic
use of O'Reilly books:
adoption@oreilly.com
or visit:
academic.oreilly.com

For a list of our distributors outside
of North America check out:
international.oreilly.com/distributors.html

Order a book online

www.oreilly.com/order_new

Our books are available at most retail and online bookstores.
To order direct: 1-800-998-9938 • *order@oreilly.com* • *www.oreilly.com*
Online editions of most O'Reilly titles are available by subscription at *safari.oreilly.com*